Alexander Balmain Bruce

The Humiliation of Christ in it's Physical, Ethical, and Official Aspects

Alexander Balmain Bruce

The Humiliation of Christ in it's Physical, Ethical, and Official Aspects

ISBN/EAN: 9783337167363

Printed in Europe, USA, Canada, Australia, Japan

Cover: Foto ©Lupo / pixelio.de

More available books at **www.hansebooks.com**

IN ITS PHYSICAL, ETHICAL, AND OFFICIAL ASPECTS.

The Sixth Series of the Cunningham Lectures.

BY

ALEXANDER BALMAIN BRUCE, D.D.

PROFESSOR OF APOLOGETICS AND NEW TESTAMENT EXEGESIS,
FREE CHURCH COLLEGE, GLASGOW.

Author of "The Parabolic Teaching of Christ," "Miraculous Element in the Gospels," etc., etc.

SECOND EDITION REVISED AND ENLARGED.

New York:
A. C. ARMSTRONG & SON,
714 BROADWAY,
MDCCCLXXXIX.

PREFACE TO THE SECOND EDITION.

IN issuing a new edition of *The Humiliation of Christ*, I desire gratefully to acknowledge the appreciative spirit in which a very imperfect attempt to discuss a difficult subject of great importance was received by the theological public. In this edition scarcely any alteration has been made in the text of the Lectures which appeared in the first edition. But a new Lecture has been added, the Fifth in the present volume, on *Modern Humanistic Theories of Christ's Person*, which completes my original design. In this Lecture I have utilized the notes which appeared in the Appendix of the former edition on *the Ideal-Man Theory of Christ's Person*, and on *the title "Son of man,"* replacing them by new notes on other topics. I have also in the same Lecture embodied the substance of an article on *Naturalistic Views of Christ's Person*, which appeared in the *British and Foreign Evangelical Review* for January 1879. For the benefit of readers not familiar with the Greek and German languages I have given English translations of extracts from these tongues occurring in the Appendix, along with the original. I have not thought it necessary to follow the same course with extracts in notes at the foot of the page in the body of the work, because the drift of all such extracts is given in the text, so that the English reader loses nothing, except the power of verifying the accuracy of my representations. It was simply for the purpose of such verification that the extracts were given. I trust that these additions will have the effect of rendering the book more useful and acceptable. If I have not made more extensive alterations, it is not for want of a deep sense of the defects of my performance. If there are passages in the volume which do not satisfy the mind of the reader, they probably still less satisfy the mind of the writer. And yet I am not sure that if I were to try I could make them better. Let me express the hope that, in spite of defects, these studies may promote growth in the knowledge of our Lord and Saviour Jesus Christ, and by their very shortcomings stir up others to handle the high theme more worthily.

THE AUTHOR.

CONTENTS.

LECTURE I

CHRISTOLOGICAL AXIOMS.

The Purpose Explained,	1
The Doctrine of the States in Dogmatic Systems,	2
The Kenotic School,	4
The Advantages of the Method,	6
The Axioms difficult to fix,	8
The Previous Question,	10
Phil. ii. 5-9 explained,	15
The Axioms thence deduced,	22
Christ's Humiliation in Epistle to the Hebrews,	25
Doctrine of the *Homoüsia* there taught,	27
The Humiliation a Glorification,	30
Two additional Axioms,	36
Plan of the Course,	37

LECTURE II.

THE PATRISTIC CHRISTOLOGY.

Formula of Chalcedon,	39
Apollinarian Theory of Christ's Person,	40
Criticism of the Theory,	45
Nestorian Controversy,	48
Cyril on the Kenosis,	51
Theodoret on the Kenosis,	54
Cyril on Christ's Ignorance,	55
Eutychianism,	60
Leo's Letter to Flavian,	63
The Dreary Period of Christology,	69
John of Damascus,	71
Thomas Aquinas,	74
New Ideas in the *Summa*,	75
Christ both *Comprehensor* and *Viator*,	82

LECTURE III.

THE LUTHERAN AND REFORMED CHRISTOLOGIES.

Origin of the Controversy,	83
Stages of the Controversy,	84
The Christology of John Brentz,	86
The Christology of Martin Chemnitz,	96
The Formula of Concord,	105
Lutheran Christology criticised,	107
The Reformed Christology,	115
The Reformed Christology criticised,	121
By the Logos through His Spirit,	125
Double Consciousness or Double Life?	127
Realism of Reformed Christology,	130
Zanchius and Hulsius on Christ's Ignorance,	130
The *Homoñsia* in Reformed Christology,	133

LECTURE IV.

THE MODERN KENOTIC THEORIES.

Relation of these Theories to the Old Christologies,	134
Zinzendorf Father of Modern Kenosis,	137
Four Types distinguished,	139
The Theory of Thomasius,	139
Theory of Gess,	145
Theory of Ebrard,	153
Theory of Martensen,	160
Criticism of these Theories,	164

LECTURE V.

MODERN HUMANISTIC THEORIES OF CHRIST'S PERSON.

Classification of,	194
Thoroughgoing Naturalism,	196
Ideal-Man Theory—Schleiermacher,	207
Sentimental Naturalism—Keim,	209
Nondescript Eclectic Naturalism—Haweis,	218
Ideal-Man Theory—Beyschlag,	223
Conclusion of the Survey,	235

LECTURE VI.

CHRIST THE SUBJECT OF TEMPTATION AND MORAL DEVELOPMENT.

Physical Infirmities a Source of Temptation,	237
Hilary denied the Physical Infirmities,	238
Hilary's Apologists,	242
Cause of Hilary's Error,	247
Adoptianist View of Christ's Humanity,	250
Menken and Irving taught same Views,	251
Christ's relation to Disease and Death,	258
Temptation and Sinlessness,	264
Potuit non and *non potuit*,	269
Christ's Moral Development,	274
Christ perfected, how?	276
Christ's Priesthood, when begun?	280
Is a Sinless Development possible?	285

LECTURE VII.

THE HUMILIATION OF CHRIST IN ITS OFFICIAL ASPECT.

Christ a Servant,	291
Christ's Humiliation as an Apostle,	294
Socinian Theory of Salvation,	298
Christ's Humiliation as a Priest,	301
The Sanctifier one with the Sanctified,	301
Sympathy a Source of Suffering,	304
Sympathy Theory of Atonement,	305
Christ, as a Priest, a Representative; as Victim, a Substitute,	309
Theory of Redemption by Sample,	311
Mystic and Legal Aspects of Atonement compatible,	317
Were Christ's Sufferings penal,	318
M'Leod Campbell's Theory,	319
Bushnell's Latest Views,	322
Manifold Wisdom of God in Redemption,	326
Justice and Love both satisfied,	328
Ritschl and Arnold on the Leading Idea of the Bible,	332
Christ's Fellowship with His Father uninterrupted,	335
Under Divine Wrath during whole State of Humiliation,	337
Did Christ suffer Eternal Death?	341
Acceptilation Theory,	343
Elements of Value in the Atonement,	344
Scripture Representations of Christ's Sufferings,	347
Summary Formula,	348
Philippi's Equation,	349
Theories of Atonement classified,	352

APPENDIX.

LECT. I. NOTE A.—On Phil. ii. 6-8,		359
LECT. II. NOTE A.—Extracts from Cyril on Christ's Ignorance,		368
LECT. III. NOTE A.—Connection between Lutheran Christology and the Sacramentarian Controversy,		375
,, NOTE B.—Tübingen-Giessen Controversy concerning Krypsis and Kenosis,		376
,, NOTE C.—Schneckenburger on Connection between Lutheran Christology and Modern Speculative Christology,		380
,, NOTE D.—Schweitzer on Reformed Christology,		382
,, NOTE E.—Reformed Views of the Impersonality,		384
LECT. IV. NOTE A.—Kenotic Literature belonging to Thomasian Type,		388
,, NOTE B.—Kenotic Literature belonging to Gessian Type,		396
,, NOTE C.—Ebrard's Prefaces to his Works,		413
,, NOTE D.—Ebrard's Solutions of Speculative Christological Problems,		414
,, NOTE E.—Kenotic Literature belonging to Martensen Type,		419
,, NOTE F.—The Christology of Zinzendorf,		425
,, NOTE G.—Cyril on Metamorphic Kenosis,		429
LECT. VI. NOTE A.—On the Temperament of Christ,		430
,, NOTE B.—Views of Naturalistic Theologians on "the Flesh,"		431
,, NOTE C.—Socinus on the Priesthood of Christ,		437
LECT. VII. NOTE A.—The Pauline Doctrine of Atonement,		439
,, NOTE B.—Rupert of Duytz on Christ as a Penitent,		442
,, NOTE C.—Reformed and Lutheran Opinions on the Question, Did Christ suffer Spiritual and Eternal Death?		443
,, NOTE D.—St. Bernard on the Greatness of Christ's Sufferings, and its Cause,		447
,, NOTE E.—Jonathan Edwards on the Sense in which Christ endured Divine Wrath,		449

INDEX. 451

LECTURE I.

CHRISTOLOGICAL AXIOMS.

I PURPOSE in the following lectures to employ the teaching of Scripture, concerning the humiliation of the Son of God, as an aid in the formation of just views on some aspects of the doctrine of Christ's person, experience, and work, and as a guide in the criticism of various Christological and Soteriological theories. The task I enter on is arduous and delicate. It is arduous, because it demands at least a tolerable acquaintance, at first hand as far as possible, with an extensive literature of ancient, modern, and recent origin, the recent alone being sufficiently ample to occupy the leisure of a pastor for years. It is delicate, because the subject, while of vital interest in a religious point of view, is also theologically abstruse. The way of truth is narrow here, and through ignorance or inadvertence one may easily fall into error, while desiring to maintain, and even honestly believing that he is maintaining, the catholic faith. It has, indeed, sometimes been asserted that it is impossible to avoid error on the subject of the person of Christ, all known or conceivable theories oscillating between Ebionitism and Doketism.[1] This, it may be hoped, is the exaggeration of persons not themselves believers in the catholic doctrine of our Lord's divinity; yet it is an exaggeration in which there is so much truth, that it is difficult to enter on a discussion of questions relating to that great theme without conscious fear and trembling.

[1] I venture to print the words *docetism* and *docetic* with *k* instead of *c* (doketism, doketic), following the example of Mr. Grote, who in his *History of Greece* thus renders all Greek names in which k occurs into English, *e.g.* Sokrates instead of Socrates. One objection to the spelling docetism is, that to ill-informed minds it may suggest a derivation from *doceo* instead of from δοκέω. The terms doketism and doketic apply to that view of our Lord's person which makes His human nature and life a mere *appearance*.

Yet, on the other hand, no one can discuss to any purpose these questions in a timid spirit. Successful treatment demands not only reverence and caution, but audacity. Without boldness, both in faith and in thought, it is impossible to rise to the grandeur of the truth in Christ, as set forth in Scripture. Courage is required even for believing in the Incarnation; and still more for the scientific discussion thereof. What can one do, then, but proceed with firm step, trusting to the gracious guidance of God; expecting, in the words of St. Hilary,[1] that "He may incite the beginnings of this trembling undertaking, confirm them with advancing progress, and call the writer to fellowship with the spirit of prophets and apostles, that he may understand their sayings in the sense in which they spoke them, and follow up the right use of words with the same conceptions of things"?

The attempt I now propose to make is beset with additional difficulty, arising out of its comparative novelty. It has not been the practice of theological writers to assign to the category of the states of Christ, or of the state of humiliation in particular, the dominant position which it is to occupy in the present course of lectures. In most dogmatic systems, doubtless, there is a chapter devoted to the locus, *De Statu Christi;* but in some instances it forms a meagre appendix to the doctrines of Christ's person, or of His work, which might be dispensed with;[2] in other cases it is a mere framework, within which are included in summary form the leading facts of our Lord's history as recorded in the Gospels;[3] while in a third class of cases it serves the purpose of an apology or defence for a foregone Christological conclusion.[4] Exclusive study of the older

---

[1] *De Trin.* lib. i. 38. The style of this Father is so obscure that it is scarcely warrantable to quote from him without giving the original. His words are: "Expectamus ergo, ut trepide hujus coepti exordia incites, et profectu accrescente confirmes, et ad consortium vel prophetalis vel apostolici spiritus voces; ut dicta eorum non alio quam ipsi locuti sunt sensu apprehendamus, verborumque proprietates iisdem rerum significationibus exsequamur."

[2] In Turretine, the chapter "De Duplici Christi Statu" scarcely occupies two pages. Calvin and the older Reformed dogmatists make no use of the category at all. [3] So in Heidegger, *Corpus theologiae,* locus xviii.

[4] So with the Lutheran divines, concerning whom Strauss justly remarks (*Glaubenslehre,* vol. ii. 139), that they used the distinction of a twofold state, partly to

dogmatists would tend to discourage the idea of commencing a discussion on Christology with the doctrine of Exinanition as a mere conceit; or, to speak more correctly, it would probably prevent such a thought from ever arising in the mind. And yet the discriminating study of these very authors shows that the truths relating to the humiliation of Christ have exercised a more extensive influence on the doctrines of Christ's person and work than the bare contents of the locus *De Statu Christi* would lead one to suppose. This is especially manifest in the case of theologians belonging to the Reformed confession, whose whole views of Christ's person and work have been largely formed under the influence of the important principle of the likeness of Christ's humanity in nature and experience to that of other men.[1] Instances are even not wanting among the Reformed theologians of treatises on the Incarnation, commencing with a careful endeavour to fix the meaning of the *locus classicus* bearing on the subject of our Lord's humiliation, that, viz., in the Epistle to the Philippians.[2] Lutheran divines, on the other hand, constructed their Christology in utter defiance of the doctrine of humiliation, making the Incarnation, in its idea, consist in a deification of humanity rather than in a descent of God into humanity, and investing the human nature of Christ with all divine attributes, even with such metaphysical ones as are commonly regarded and described as incommunicable. But even in their case our category took revenge for the neglect it experienced at their hands, by compelling them, out of regard to facts and to the end of the Incarnation, to take down again their carefully constructed Christological edifice; the chapter on Exinanition being in effect an attempt to bring the fantastic humanity of Christ back to reality and nature, down from the clouds to the solid

complete, partly to cover, their dogma of the *communicatio idiomatum*. In Gerhard's *Loci*, cap. x.–xiii. of locus iv. (De Persona et Officio Christi) treat of the *communicatio idiomatum* in general, and in its particular forms; and cap. xiv. treats *De Statu exinanitionis et exaltationis*.

[1] Called in theological language the Homoüsia ($\dot{o}\mu oo\dot{v}\sigma\iota\alpha$).

[2] *E.g.* Zanchius, *De Incarnatione filii Dei.* Zanchius was a contemporary of the authors of the *Formula Concordiae*, and wrote a defence of the *Admonitio christiana*—the Reformed reply to that document.

earth; an attempt which, as we shall see, was far from being perfectly successful.

While the importance of keeping ever in view the doctrine of the states can only be inferred from the internal character of the old Christologies, in spite of the subordinate place assigned thereto in the formal structure of theological systems, it is, on the other hand, a matter of distinct consciousness with more recent writers on Christological themes. In passing from the system-builders of the seventeenth century to the theologians of the nineteenth, one is emboldened to trust the instinct which tells him that the category of the states is not merely entitled to have some sort of recognition in theology out of deference to the prominence given to it in Scripture, but is a point of view from which the whole doctrine concerning Christ's person and work may be advantageously surveyed. The method now contemplated has in effect been adopted by a whole school of modern theologians, who have made the idea of the *Kenosis* the basis of their Christological inquiries. The various Kenotic theories emanating from this school are, as we shall see, by no means criticism-proof; but their authors have at least done one good service to Christology, by insisting that no theory of Christ's Person can be regarded as satisfactory which is not able to assign some real meaning to their watchword, in relation to the divine side of that Person. The legitimacy and the importance of the proposed method of inquiry have also been recognised by a distinguished German theologian who was not an adherent of the Kenotic school, his sympathies being with the old Reformed Christology, and whose opinion on such a matter must command the respect of all. I allude to Schneckenburger, author of the instructive work entitled, *Comparative Exhibition of the Lutheran and the Reformed Doctrinal Systems*,[1] one of many valuable treatises on Christological and other

---

[1] *Vergleichende Darstellung des Lutherischen und Reformirten Lehrbegriffs.* This work was published after the author's death in 1855, the MSS. being prepared for publication by Güder, a pupil of Schneckenburger's, who has prefixed to the work an interesting discussion on the question as to the origin of the difference in the theological systems of the two confessions.

topics which owed their origin to the ecclesiastical movement towards the re-union of the two branches of the German Protestant Church, long unhappily separated by divergent views on the questions to whose discussion that copious literature is devoted. Besides the work just named, Schneckenburger wrote a special treatise on the two states of Christ,[1] designed as a contribution to ecclesiastical Christology, in which he endeavoured to show that the doctrines of the states taught respectively by the two contrasted confessions involved a corresponding modification of view not only on Christ's person, but also on the nature of His work on earth and in heaven, on the justification of believers, and even on the whole religious and ecclesiastical life of the two communions. It is true, indeed, that the proof of this position does not settle the question which was the determining factor, the doctrine of the states, or the other doctrines to which it stands related. It does, however, serve to show this at least, that the related doctrines of the states and of the person being, in mathematical language, functions of each other, it is in our option to begin with either, and use it as a help in the determination of the other. Nor has the distinguished writer to whom I have alluded left us in uncertainty as to which of the two courses he deemed preferable. Criticising the rectification of the Lutheran Christology proposed by Thomasius, the founder of the modern Kenotic school, he says: " The position that the doctrine of the person should not be explained by that of the states, but inversely, because the former is the foundation of the latter, is one which I must contradict, nay, which the author himself (Thomasius) virtually contradicts, inasmuch as he seeks to shape the doctrine of the person, or to improve it, by the idea of the states, especially by the doctrine of redemption, in so far as it falls within the state of humiliation."[2] I have no doubt this view is a just one. Indeed, it appears to me that the history of Lutheran Christology affords abundant evidence of the desirableness of commencing Christological

---

[1] *Zur Kirchlichen Christologie: Die orthodoxe Lehre vom doppelten Stande Christi nach Lutherischer und Reformirter Fassung.* This work was published before the other, in 1848. [2] *Vom doppelten Stande Christi*, p. 202.

inquiries with a careful endeavour to form a correct view of the doctrine of the states, and especially of the Scripture teaching concerning our Lord's humiliation. Had the Lutheran theologians followed this course, it is probable that their peculiar Christology would never have come into existence, and would therefore have stood in no need of rectification.

Theologically legitimate, the method I propose is recommended by practical considerations. Starting from the central idea, that the whole earthly history of our Saviour is the result and evolution of a sublime act of self-humiliation, the doctrine of His person becomes invested with a high *ethical* interest. An advantage this not to be overlooked in connection with any theological truth involving mysteries perplexing to reason. A mysterious doctrine, divested of moral interest, and allowed to assume the aspect of a mere metaphysical speculation, is a doctrine destined ere long to be discarded. Such, for example, must be the inevitable fate of the doctrine of an immanent Trinity when it becomes dissociated in men's minds from practical religious interests, and degenerates into an abstract tenet. The Trinity, to be secure, must be connected in thought with the Incarnation, even as at the first, when it obtained for itself gradually a place in the creed of the Church in connection with efforts to understand the nature and person of Christ;[1] even as the Incarnation itself, in turn, is secure only when it is regarded ethically as a revelation of divine grace. The effect of divorcing doctrinal from moral interests was fully seen in the last century, when the Trinity and kindred dogmas were quietly dropped out of the living belief of the Church, though retained in the written creed. Men then said to themselves, " What is practical, what is of moral utility, is alone of value; the doctrines of the Trinity and of the Deity of Christ are mere theological mysteries, therefore they may be ignored !" Thus, as Dorner, speaking of the period in question, remarks, " Many a point which forms a constitutive element of the Christian consciousness was treated as non-essential,

[1] *Vid.* Dorner, *History of the Doctrine of the Person of Christ*, div. ii. vol. i. p. 49 (Clark's translation).

on the ground of its being unpractical; and in particular, essential portions of Christology, and of that which is connected with it, were set aside."[1] The same spirit of narrow religious utilitarianism, of overweening value for the practical and the "verifiable," is abroad at the present time, working steadily towards the restoration of the state of things which prevailed in last century; and those who are concerned to counterwork the evil tendency, must apply their energies to the task of showing that discredited doctrines are not the dry, metaphysical dogmas they are taken for, but rather a refuge from dry metaphysics—truths which, however mysterious, are yet of vital ethical and religious moment; even the doctrine of the Trinity itself being the product of an ethical view of the divine nature, the embodiment of "the only complete ethical idea of God,"[2] not to be abandoned except at the risk of falling into either Pantheism or Atheism.

In this point of view it appears advisable to give great prominence to the self-humiliation of Christ in connection with Christological inquiries. This method of procedure procures for us the advantage of starting with an idea which is dear to the Christian heart, with which faith will not willingly part, and for the sake of which it will readily accept truths surpassing human comprehension. If the great thought, under whose guidance we advance, do not conduct us to new discoveries, it will at all events redeem the subjects of our study from the blighting influence of scholasticism.

In the New Testament, and more especially in the Epistle of Paul to the Philippians, and in the Epistle to the Hebrews, are to be found certain comprehensive statements concerning the meaning and purpose of our Lord's appearance on earth. These statements our method requires us

---

[1] *Vid.* Dorner, *History of the Doctrine of the Person of Christ*, div. ii. vol. iii. p. 28 (Clark's translation).

[2] This view is strongly maintained by Liebner in his *Christologie* (p. 66), a work of a very speculative character, and Kenotic in its Christology, but full of valuable and suggestive thoughts, and abounding in interesting expositions and criticisms of contemporary opinions. Liebner's work is especially valuable for the vigour with which it asserts the ethical conception of God over against the Pantheistic on the one hand, and the Deistic on the other.

in the first place to consider with the view of ascertaining what they imply, that we may use the inferences they seem to warrant as axioms in all our subsequent discussions. As the truths we are in quest of are to serve the purpose of axioms, they must, of course, be of an elementary character; but they are not on that account to be despised. The axiom, that things which are equal to the same thing are equal to one another, is a very elementary truth; but it is nevertheless one which you cannot neglect without serious consequences to your system of geometry. In theology, as in mathematics, much depends on the axioms; not a few theological errors have arisen from oversight of some simple commonplace truth.

Our object being merely to fix the axioms, it will not be necessary that we should enter into any elaborate, detailed, and exhaustive description of the doctrine of the states, or to attempt more than a general survey. And, further, as the main business of Christology is to form a true conception of the historical person Jesus Christ, we may confine our attention chiefly to the earlier of the two states which belongs to history and falls within our observation, concerning which alone we possess much information, and around which the human interest mainly revolves. Of the state of exaltation I shall speak only occasionally, when a fitting opportunity occurs.

In addressing ourselves, then, to the task of discovering Christological axioms, we are obliged to acknowledge that the fixation of these is unhappily no easy matter. Few of the axioms are axiomatic in the sense of being truths universally admitted. The diversity of opinion prevailing among interpreters in regard to the meaning of the principal passage bearing on the subject of Christ's humiliation —that, namely, in the second chapter of Paul's Epistle to the Philippians—is enough to fill the student with despair, and to afflict him with intellectual paralysis. In regard to the *kenosis* spoken of there, for example, the widest divergence of view prevails. Some make the kenosis scarcely more than a *skenosis*,—the dainty assumption by the unchangeable One of a humanity which is but a doketic husk, a semi-transparent tent, wherein Deity sojourns, and through which His glory, but slightly dimmed, shines with dazzling brightness. The Son of God, remaining in all respects what He was before His incarnation, became what He was not, and so emptied Himself. Others ascribe to the kenosis some sense relatively to the divine nature; holding that the incarnation involved even for that nature a change to some extent; that the Son of God did not remain in all respects as He was; that at least He underwent an occultation of His glory. A third class of expositors make the kenosis consist not merely in a veiling of the divine glory, but in a depotentiation of the divine nature, so that in the incarnate Logos remained only the bare essence of Deity stripped of its metaphysical attributes of omnipotence, omniscience, and omnipresence. According to a fourth school, the kenosis refers not to the divine nature, but to the human nature of Christ. He, being in the form of God, shown to be a divine man by His miracles and by His moral purity, emptied Himself of the divine attributes with which He, as a man, was endowed, so far as use at least was concerned, and in this self-denial set Himself forth as a pattern to all Christians, as well as fitted Himself for being the Redeemer from sin.

It is specially discouraging to the inquirer after first principles to find, as he soon does, that, as a rule, the interpretation of the passage in question depends on the interpreter's theological position. So much is this the case, that one can almost tell beforehand what views a particular expositor will take, provided his theological school be once ascertained. On the question, for example—a most important one—respecting the proper subject of the proposition beginning with the words, "Who, being in the form of God,"[1] expositors take sides according to their theological bias. The old orthodox Lutherans almost as a matter of course reply, "The subject concerning whom the affirmation is made is the *Logos* incarnate *(ensarkos)*, the *man* Christ Jesus; the meaning of the apostle being, that the man Christ Jesus, being in the form of God, and possessing as man divine attributes, did nevertheless, while on earth,

[1] Phil. ii. 6.

make little or no use of these attributes; but in effect emptied Himself of them, and assumed servile form, and was in fashion and habit as other men." The old Reformed theologians, on the other hand, after the example of the Church Fathers, with equal unanimity reply, "The subject of whom Paul speaks is the *Logos* before incarnation (*asarkos*), the Son of God personally pre-existent before He became man; and the sense is, that He, being in the form of God, subsisting as a divine being before the incarnation, emptied Himself, by being made in the likeness of man, and taking upon Him the form of a servant." Among modern theologians, the advocates of the kenosis, in the sense of a metaphysical self-exinanition of the Logos, whether belonging to the Lutheran or to the Reformed confession, side with the Fathers and with the old Reformed dogmatists. Those, on the other hand, who reject the doctrine of an immanent Trinity, and along with it the personal pre-existence of the Logos, naturally adopt the view of the Lutheran dogmatists, and understand the passage as referring exclusively to the historical person, the man Christ Jesus. They can do nothing else so long as they claim to have Biblical support for their theological and Christological systems. They come to this text with a firm conviction that it cannot possibly contain any reference to a free, conscious act of the pre-existent Logos. In arguing with expositors of this school there is therefore a previous question to be settled: Is the Church doctrine of the Trinity scriptural, or is it not?

This is, indeed, the previous question for all Christological theories. Every one who would form for himself a conception of the person of Christ must first determine his idea of God, and then bring that idea to his Christological task as one of its determining factors. Accordingly, in complete treatises on the person and work of Christ, like that of Thomasius,[1] we find the Christian idea of God and the doctrine of the Trinity discussed under the head of Christological presuppositions. In the present course of lectures, such a discussion would of course be altogether out of

[1] Thomasius, *Christi Person und Werk. Darstellung der Evangelisch-Lutherischen Dogmatik vom Mittelpunkte der Christologie aus.*

place; but I may here take occasion to express my conviction, that what I have called the previous question of Christology, is destined to become the question of the day in this country, as it has been for some time past in Germany. What is God? Is personality, involving self-consciousness and self-determination, predicable of the Divine Being; or is He, or rather it, merely the unknown and unknowable substratum of all phenomena,[1] the impersonal immanent spirit of nature, the unconscious moral order of the world in which the idea of the good somehow and to some extent realizes itself,[2] the absolute Idea become Another in physical nature, and returning to itself and attaining to personality in man; becoming incarnate not in an individual man, but in the human race at large?[3]—such, according to all present indications, are the momentous questions on which the thoughts of men are about to be concentrated. And if one may venture to predict the result of the great debate, it will probably be to show that between Pantheism, under one or other of its forms, materialistic or idealistic, and the Christian doctrine of God, in which the ethical predominates, there is no tenable position; in the words of a German theologian whom I have already had occasion to quote: " That the whole of speculative theology stands in suspense between the pure abstract One, general Being, ἓν καὶ πᾶν, in which God and world alike go down, and the ethical hypostatical Trinity, or between the boldest, emptiest, hardest Pantheism, and the completed ethical personalism of Christianity; all pantheistic and theistic modes, from Spinoza to the most developed forms of modern Theism, being only transition and oscillation which cannot abide."[4]

The influence of theological bias on the exegesis of the *locus classicus* in the Epistle to the Philippians being apparent in the case of so many theologians of highest

[1] *Vid.* Herbert Spencer, *Synthetic Philosophy*, *First Principles*, part i.

[2] *Vid.* Strauss, *Die christliche Glaubenslehre*, i. 392, and Mr. Matthew Arnold, *Literature and Dogma*. Arnold defines God as a Power that makes for righteousness; the power being impersonal, and, so to speak, neuter. Arnold's Power making for righteousness is the same with Fichte's moral order of the world, regarded simply as an ultimate fact, not as the result of a personal Providence

[3] So Hegel.   [4] Liebner, *Christologie*, pp. 266-7.

reputation, it would be intolerable conceit in any man to claim exemption therefrom. I, for my part, have no desire to put forth such a claim. On the contrary, I avow my wish to arrive at a particular conclusion with respect to the interpretation of the passage; one, viz., which should assign a reality to the idea of a Being in the form of God by a free act of gracious condescension becoming man. I am desirous to have ground for believing that the apostle speaks here not only of the exemplary humility of the man Jesus, but of the more wonderful, sublime self-humiliation of the pre-existent personal Son of God. For then I should have Scripture warrant for believing that *moral heroism* has a place within the sphere of the divine nature, and that love is a reality for God as well as for man. I do not wish, if I can help it, to worship an unknown or unknowable God called the Absolute, concerning whom or which all Bible representations are mere make-believe, mere anthropomorphism; statements expressive not of absolute truth, but simply of what it is well that we should think and feel concerning God. I am not disposed to subject my idea of God to the category of the Absolute, which, like Pharaoh's lean kine, devours all other attributes, even for the sake of the most tempting apologetic advantages which that category may seem to offer. A poor refuge truly from unbelief is the category of the Absolute! "We know not God in Himself," says the Christian apologist,[1] "therefore we can never know that what the Bible says of Him is false, and may rationally receive it as true." "We know not God," rejoins the agnostic man of science;[2] "and the more logical inference is, that all affirmations concerning Him in the Bible or elsewhere are incompetent; the Bible God is an *eidolon* whose worship is only excusable because it is wholesome in tendency." "God, strictly speaking, has no attributes, but is mere and simplest essence, which admits of no real difference, nor any composition either of things or of modes," declares the old orthodox dogmatist.[3] "So be it," replies a formidable modern opponent of orthodoxy, Dr. Baur of

---

[1] *Vid.* Mansel, *Limits of Religious Thought.*
[2] *Vid.* Herbert Spencer, *First Principles.*
[3] Quenstedt, quoted by Baur, *Lehre von der Dreieinigkeit*, vol. iii. p. 340.

Tübingen,[1] "I agree with you, but that proposition amounts to substantial Pantheism;" and the theological system of Schleiermacher shows that Baur is right. If, therefore, we wish to believe with our hearts in the Bible, we must hold fast by the ethical conception of God; and whatever disputes arise between us and others holding in common with us the same general idea of the Divine Being, we must settle on ethical grounds, not fleeing for refuge from perplexities to an idea of God which removes the very foundations of faith, and becoming in effect Pantheists or Atheists in order that we may not be Socinians. It is in vain to think of saving the catholic faith on the principles of theological nescience; foolish to seek escape from moral difficulties by means of sceptical metaphysics. As Maurice, in his reply to Mansel, well says: "Such an apology for the faith costs too much."[2] It saves such doctrines as those of the Trinity and the Incarnation and the Atonement at the cost of all the moral interest which properly belongs to them, and converts them into mere mysteries, which must be received because we are not able to refute them; but which, in spite of all the apologist's skill, will not be received, but will meet the fate of all mere mysteries devoid of moral interest,—that of being neglected, or even ridiculed, as they have been lately by the author of *Literature and Dogma;* ridiculed not in *mere* wantonness, though that is not wanting, but in the interest of a practical ethical use of the Bible as a book not intended to propound idle theological puzzles, but to lead men into the way of right conduct.

Holding such views, desirous to believe in a God absolutely full of moral contents, knowable on the ethical side of His nature *truly* though not *perfectly*, like man in that which most exalts human nature,—loving with a love like that of good men,—only incomparably grander, rising in point of magnanimity high above human love, as heaven is high above the earth,[3] passing knowledge in dimensions, but perfectly comprehensible in nature,[4] I am predisposed to

---

[1] Baur, *Lehre von der Dreieinigkeit*, vol. iii. pp. 339-352.
[2] Maurice, *What is Revelation?* p. 131.   [3] Isa. lv. 8, 9.
[4] Eph. iii. 18, 19. There is an unknowableness of God taught here, but it is a very different one from that asserted by the philosophy of the Absolute. It is the

agree with those who find in the famous text from the Epistle to the Philippians a clear reference to an act of condescension on the part of the pre-existent Son of God, in virtue of which He became man. Schleiermacher naively objects to the idea of humiliation as applied to the earthly state of Christ, because it implies a previous higher state from which the self-humbled One descended,—a view which he regards as at once destructive of the unity of Christ's person, and incompatible with the nature of God, the absolutely Highest and Eternal.[1] What Schleiermacher objects to in the idea of humiliation, appears to me its chief recommendation; and I agree with Martensen in thinking it a capital defect in Schleiermacher's Christology that it excludes the idea of the pre-existence of the Son, and along with it, the idea of a condescending revelation of love on the part of the eternal Logos.[2] I refuse to accept an idea of God which makes such condescension impossible or meaningless; nor am I able to regard that as the absolutely Highest which cannot stoop down from its altitude. The glory of God consists not simply in being high, but in that He, the highest and greatest, can humble Himself in love to be the lowest and least. The moral, not the metaphysical, is the highest, if not the distinctive, in the Divine Being.

While making this frank—it may even appear ostentatious—avowal of theological bias, and confessing that the Scriptures would contain for me no revelation of God, did they not teach a doctrine of divine grace capable of taking practical historical shape in an Incarnation, I do not admit that it is a far-fetched or strained interpretation which

---

unknowableness as to dimensions of a love believed to be most real, and in its nature comprehensible. It is the same kind of unknowableness which is spoken of in Job. xi. 7. It is not a question whether God can be known at all, but a question of finding out the Almighty unto perfection—of taking the measure of the Divine Being. The Scripture doctrine of divine unknowableness is the very opposite extreme to that of the philosophers. "Thy mercy, O Lord, is in the heavens, Thy truth reacheth unto the clouds: Thy righteousness is like the great mountains, Thy judgments are a great deep," say the Scriptures. "Mercy, truth, righteousness, judgment, are words which convey no absolutely true meaning with reference to the Divine Being," says the philosophy of the Absolute.

[1] *Glaubenslehre*, ii. p. 159.
[2] *Die Christliche Dogmatik*, p. 252.

brings such a doctrine out of Paul's words in his Epistle to the Philippians. That interpretation appears to me the one which would naturally occur to the mind of any person coming to the passage, bent solely on ascertaining its meaning, without reference to his own theological opinions. It may be regarded as a presumption in favour of this view when writers like Schleiermacher and Strauss, neither of them a believer in the doctrine of a personally pre-existent Logos, nevertheless admit that it is at least by implication taught in the passage. The former author, indeed, seeks to deprive the statements contained therein of all theological value, by representing them as of an "ascetic" and "rhetorical" character; the expressions not being intended to be "didactically fixed,"[1]—a convenient method of getting rid of unacceptable theological dogmas, which may be applied to any extent, and which, if applied to Paul's Epistles, would render it difficult to extract any theological inferences therefrom, inasmuch as nearly all the doctrinal statements they contain arise out of a practical occasion, and are intended to serve a hortatory purpose. Strauss, on the other hand, making no pretence of adhering to Scripture in his theological views, frankly acknowledges that, according to the doctrine of Paul in this place, Christ is One who, before His incarnation, lived in a divine glory, to which, after His freely assumed state of humiliation was over, He returned.[2]

It is now time that I should explain the sense in which I understand the passage referred to, which I shall do very briefly, relegating critical details to another place.[3] The subject spoken about is the historical person Jesus Christ, conceived of, however, as having previously existed before He entered into history, and as in His pre-existent state, supplying material fitted to serve the hortatory purpose the

---

[1] *Glaubenslehre*, ii. p. 161. Schleiermacher's admission is not hearty; for while the manner in which he explains away the apparent meaning of the passage implies such an admission as I have ascribed to him, he remarks that the way in which Paul here sets forth Christ as an example, is quite compatible with the idea that he has in view merely the appearance of lowliness in the life as well as in the death.

[2] *Die Christliche Glaubenslehre*, i. 420.

[3] See Appendix, Note A.

apostle has in view. Paul desires to set before the Church in Philippi the mind of Christ in opposition to the mind of self-seekers, and he includes the pre-existence in his representation, because the mind he means to illustrate was active therein, and could not be exhibited in all its sublimity if the view were restricted to the earthly career of the Great Exemplar of self-renunciation. It has been objected, that a reference to the pre-existence is beside the scope of the apostle, his aim being to induce proud, self-asserting Christians to imitate Christ in all respects in which it was possible for them to become like Him, while in respect of the Incarnation He is inimitable.[1] The objection is a very superficial one. It is true that the *act* by which the Son of God became man is inimitable; but the *mind* which moved Him to perform that act is not inimitable; and it is the mind or moral disposition of Christ, revealed both in imitable and inimitable acts, which is the subject of commendation. Therefore, though the great drama of self-humiliation enacted by our Saviour on this earth be the main theme of Christian contemplation, yet is a glimpse into the mind of the pre-existent Son of God a fitting prelude to that drama, tending to make it in its whole course more impressive, and to heighten desire in the spectators to have the same mind dwelling in themselves, leading them to perform on a humbler scale similar acts of self-denial. Another argument against the reference to a pre-existent state has been drawn from the historical name given to the subject of the proposition, *Jesus Christ*. But this argument is sufficiently met by the remark, that the same method of naming the subject is employed by Paul in other passages where a pre-existence

---

[1] Gerhard's *Loci Theologici*, locus iv. cap. xiv. "De Statu exinanitionis et exaltationis." Gerhard says: "Scopus apostoli est, quod velit Philippenses hortari ad humilitatem intuitu in Christi exemplum facto. Ergo praesentis, non futuri temporis, exemplum illis exhibet. Proponit eis imitandum Christi exemplum tanquam vitae regulam. Ergo considerat facta Christi quae in oculos incurrunt, in quorum numero non est incarnatio. In eo apostolus jubet Philippenses imitari Christum, in quo similes ipsi nondum erant, sed similes fieri poterant et debebant. Atqui erant illi jam ante veri homines, sed inflati ac superbi: Christum igitur eos imitari, et humilitati studere, jubet, incarnatione vero nemo Filio Dei similis fieri potest" (§ ccxciv.).

of some sort, real or ideal, personal or impersonal, is undeniably implied.[1]

Of Him whose mind is commended as worthy of imitation, the apostle predicates two acts through which that mind was revealed: First, an act of self-emptying, in virtue of which He became man; then a continuous act or habit of self-humiliation on the part of the incarnate One, which culminated in the endurance of death on the cross. Ἑαυτὸν ἐκένωσεν,—He emptied Himself,—that was the first great act by which the mind of the Son of God was revealed. Wherein did this κένωσις consist? what did it imply? The apostle gives a twofold answer; one having reference to the pre-existent state, the other to the sphere of Christ's human history. With reference to the former, the kenosis signified a firm determination not to hold fast and selfishly cling to equality of state with God. Thus I understand the words οὐκ ἁρπαγμὸν ἡγήσατο τὸ εἶναι ἴσα Θεῷ. The rendering in our English version ("thought it not robbery to be equal with God"), which follows patristic (Latin) exegetical tradition, is theologically true, but unsuited to the connection of thought, and to the grammatical construction of the sentence. The apostle's purpose is not formally to teach that Christ was truly God, so that it was not arrogance on His part to claim equality of nature with God; but rather to teach that He being God did not make a point of retaining the advantages connected with the divine state of being. Hence he merely mentions Christ's divinity participially by way of preface in the first clause of the sentence (ὃς ἐν μορφῇ Θεοῦ ὑπάρχων, who being, or subsisting, in the form of God), and then hastens on to speak of the mind that animated Him who was in the form of God, as a mind so different from that of those who esteem and desire to exalt themselves above others, that He was willing to part with equality in condition with God. This part of the sentence, beginning with οὐκ ἁρπαγμόν, cannot, as Alford justly remarks, "be a mere secondary one, conveying an

---

[1] 1 Cor. x. 4-9; Col. i. 14, 15. The use of the historical name in reference to the pre-existent Logos in these and other passages is admitted by Beyschlag (*Die Christologie des neuen Testaments*, p. 240), who does not admit a personal, but only an ideal pre-existence of the Logos.

additional detail of Christ's majesty in His pre-existent state, but must carry the whole weight of the negation of selfishness on His part;"[1] unless we can suppose the writer guilty of an irrelevancy tending to weaken the force of his appeal by introducing one idea when another is naturally expected. But further, the grammatical construction precludes such a rendering of this clause as is given in the English version. In the text, the idea expressed by ἁρπαγμὸν ἡγήσατο, etc., is opposed to the idea expressed by the words ἑαυτὸν ἐκένωσεν, the connecting particle being ἀλλά (but), so that in the former clause is stated negatively what in the latter is stated positively. He did not practise ἁρπαγμόν with reference to equality with God; but, on the contrary, emptied Himself. The patristic rendering, retained in the English version, requires the connecting particle to be a word signifying "nevertheless;" not ἀλλά, but a word equivalent to the Attic phrase οὐ μὴν ἀλλά.[2] Beyond all doubt, therefore, whatever τὸ εἶναι ἴσα Θεῷ may mean, it points to something which both the connection of thought and the grammatical structure of the sentence require us to regard the Son of God as willing to give up.

Looking now at the connection between the prefatory participial clause and the one we have just been considering, we must regard " to be equal with God " as exegetical of " being in the form of God." Those interpreters who take the whole passage as having exclusive reference to the earthly history of Christ, distinguish the two; regarding the *form of God* as something possessed by Christ even in the state of humiliation, and *equality with God* as a thing to be attained in the state of exaltation, a privilege for which the Lowly One was content patiently to wait, abstaining from prematurely clutching at it, by making an unseasonable parade of His divine dignity. But the subordinate position assigned to the phrase τὸ εἶναι ἴσα Θεῷ in the

---

[1] Alford in *loco*.

[2] This is frankly acknowledged by Zanchius: "illa vox ἀλλά," he says, "adversativa cum sit particula, et in praecedenti versu non ita liquido apparet cuinam verbo adversetur, reddit constructionem utcunque difficilem. Syriac. faciliorem facit cum habeat ella, id est nihilominus."—*De filii Dei Incarnatione,* lib. i. cap. ii. 7.

clause to which it belongs, it being placed at the end, while οὐκ ἁρπαγμὸν ἡγήσατο stands in the forefront to catch the reader's eye, as the principal matter, shows that it simply repeats the idea already expressed by the words ἐν μορφῇ Θεοῦ ὑπάρχων.

The two phrases being equivalent, it follows that no meaning can be assigned to either which would involve an inadmissible sense for the other. By this rule we are precluded from understanding by the form of God the divine essence or nature; for such an interpretation would oblige us to find in the second clause the idea that the Son of God in a spirit of self-renunciation parted with His divinity. We must decline here to follow in the footsteps of the Fathers, who, with the exception of Hilary,[1] invariably took *form* as synonymous with *nature;* possibly misled by a too absorbing desire to find in the passage a clear undeniable assertion of our Lord's proper divinity,—a desire which could have been gratified without having recourse to misinterpretation; inasmuch as the *implied* assertion of that truth which the words of the apostle, rightly interpreted, really do contain, is even more forcible than a formal didactic statement would have been. Μορφή does not mean the same thing as οὐσία or φύσις. Even the old Reformed theologian Zanchius, while following the patristic tradition in the interpretation of the word, acknowledges the distinguishableness of the terms, and quotes with approbation a passage from a contemporary, Danaeus, in which they are very clearly distinguished, οὐσία being defined as denoting the naked essence, φύσις as the οὐσία clothed with its essential properties, and μορφή as adding to the essential and natural properties of the essence, other accidents which follow the true nature of a thing, and by which, as features and colours, οὐσία and φύσις are shaped and depicted.[2] Thus understood, μορφή presupposes οὐσία and φύσις, and yet is separable

---

[1] Hilary varied in his interpretation, sometimes identifying, sometimes distinguishing, μορφή and φύσις. See Appendix, Note A.

[2] Zanchius, *De filii Incarnatione*, lib. i. cap. xi.: "Οὐσία proprie significat nudam essentiam . . . φύσις ipsi essentiae addit proprietates essentiales et naturales: μορφή addit essentiae et proprietatibus essentialibus et naturalibus alia etiam accidentia quae veram rei naturam sequuntur, et quibus, quasi lineamentis et coloribus οὐσία et φύσις conformantur atque depinguntur."

from them; it cannot exist without them, but they can exist without it. The Son of God, subsisting in the form of God, must have possessed divine οὐσία and divine φύσις; but it is conceivable that, retaining the οὐσία and the φύσις, He might part with the μορφή. And in point of fact such a parting for a season with the μορφή seems clearly taught in this place. The apostle conceives of the Incarnation as an exchange of divine form for the human form of existence. In what the thing parted with precisely consists, and what the dogmatic import of the exchange may be, are points open to debate. As to the former, we must be content, meantime, with the general statement that the thing renounced was not divine essence, or anything belonging essentially to the divine nature. The Logos remained what He was in these respects when He became what He was not; equal to God in nature (ἴσος Θεῷ), while ceasing for a season to be His equal in state (ἴσα Θεῷ). As to the latter, the exchange of forms may, as Martensen and others hold, be compatible with the theory of a *double life;* not an absolute exchange, but one relative to the incarnate life of the Logos. All that can be confidently affirmed is that the apostle does conceive the Incarnation under the aspect of an exchange of a divine form for a human form of being; so that, as expositors, we are not entitled to interpret the words, "being in the form of God," as meaning "continuing to subsist in divine form."

The *kenosis*, being first represented negatively, with reference to the pre-existent state, as a free determination not to hold fast equality with God, is next represented positively, with reference to the historical existence, as consisting in the assumption of the form of a servant, and in being made in the likeness of man. Μορφὴν δούλου λαβών, ἐν ὁμοιώματι ἀνθρώπων γενόμενος ("taking the form of a servant, being made in the likeness of men"). The ethical quality of Christ's human life is described in the former of these two clauses; the fact of His becoming man is referred to in the latter. The first clause declares the end of the Incarnation, the second sets forth the Incarnation itself as the means to that end. The Son of God took human nature that He might, as a man, live in the form of a servant.

The servant-form is thus not to be identified with the human nature, any more than the form of God is to be identified with the divine nature. The human nature was simply the condition under which it was possible to bear the form of a servant, even as the divine nature is the presupposition of existence in the form of God. The order in which the two clauses are arranged is rhetorical rather than logical. That is placed first which is of most importance to the writer's purpose, as the eulogist of the mind which was in Christ; the mere fact of the Incarnation is spoken of subordinately, and in the second place, simply to explain in what circumstances Christ took the form of a servant, viz. in human nature. In this connection it is not unworthy of remark that the participle in the first clause is active, while that in the second clause is passive. Christ was *made* man, but He *took* servile form. His end in becoming man was that He might be able to wear that form of existence which is at the greatest possible distance from, and presents the greatest possible contrast to, the form of God. He desired to live a human life, of which servitude should be the characteristic feature,—servitude in every conceivable sense, and in the extreme degree; so that the whole of His history might be summed up in His own words to His disciples: "I am among you as one who serveth." Such was Christ's mind in resolving to enter into this time world, as conceived of here by Paul. He would come to earth not to be ministered unto, but to minister. No view of our Lord's person and work can be satisfactory which does not do full justice to this great truth.

Having described the first great act in which the mind of Christ revealed itself,—the *kenosis*,—the apostle next proceeds to describe the second, the *humiliation* (ταπείνωσις), in these terms: "And being found in fashion, or guise, as a man, He humbled Himself and became obedient as far as death, even the death of the cross." Here, again, what is emphasized is not the humanity of Christ, but the servile, suffering character of His life as a man. The humanity is described in terms which, if meant to be emphatic, might suggest a doketic view of the Incarnation—"being found in guise as a man, a man to look at, and in outward appearance." But the apostle is bent, not on asserting dogmatically the reality of Christ's humanity, but on holding up to admiration the humility of the man Christ Jesus. Now actually become man, recognisable as a man by all His fellow-men, *He humbled Himself.* And how, according to the apostle, did Christ as man show His humility? By persevering in, and carrying out, the purpose for which He became man. Having become man that He might be a servant, He, being now a man, gave Himself up to service; became obedient—carried obedience to its extreme limit, submitting even to death, and to death in its most degrading form; so, for divine glory renounced, receiving in exchange the deepest ignominy to which even a slave can be subjected. Why obedience was carried this length is not explained; the reason is assumed to be known. The point emphasized is, that Christ humbled Himself to this extent, and so realized His aim in becoming man, and persevered in the same mind to the very last.

In view of the foregoing exposition, these inferences from the passage we have been considering seem warrantable:—

1. The account given of the mind of the Subject spoken about, presupposes the existence previous to the Incarnation of a divine Personality capable of a free resolve to perform the sublime act of self-exinanition which issued in the Incarnation.

2. This act of self-exinanition involved a change of state for the Divine Actor; an exchange, absolute or relative, of the form of God for the form of a servant.

3. Notwithstanding this change, the personality continued the same. Kenosis did not mean *self-extinction*, or metamorphosis of a Divine Being into a mere man. He who emptied Himself was the same with Him who humbled Himself; and the *kenosis* and the *tapeinosis* were two acts of the same mind dwelling in the same Subject.

4. The humiliation (tapeinosis) being a perseverance in the mind which led to the kenosis, implies not only identity of the subject, but continuity of self-consciousness in that subject. The man Christ Jesus knew that, being in the form of God, He had become man, was acquainted with the mind that animated Him before His Incarnation, and

made it His business in the incarnate state to carry out that mind.

5. Christ's life on earth was emphatically a life of service.

6. Throughout the whole drama of self-exinanition, as indeed the very word implies, Christ was a free agent. He did not merely experience kenosis and tapeinosis,—He emptied Himself, He humbled Himself. The kenosis must be ethically conceived, not as bringing the subject once for all into a state of physical inability to assert equality with God, but as leaving room for a voluntary perseverance in the mind not to assert that equality, on the part of One who could do otherwise. This voluntariness, however, is not to be conceived of as excluding a reign of natural law in Christ's humanity; such being necessary to the *reality* of that humanity, and involved, indeed, in the very idea of a human *nature*. To imagine that Christ hungered, and thirsted, and slept, and felt weariness by a special act of will,—making possible by a miracle what would otherwise have been impossible,—is unmitigated doketism. This form of doketism, as I shall have occasion hereafter to point out, is not unknown in the history of doctrine.

These inferences are all in harmony with the main scope of the passage, which is to eulogize the humility of Christ. The first gives to that humility unbounded scope to display itself, by introducing the self-renouncing mind even within the sphere of divinity; the second makes self-exinanition a *reality* even for God; the third secures that whatever in the earthly experience of the man Christ Jesus involved humiliation, shall be predicable of a divine person; the fourth gives infinite moral value to every act of self-humiliation performed by Christ on earth, by making the actor conscious of the contrast between His past and present states, performing every lowly service as One who knew "that He was from God;"[1] the fifth exhibits the contrast between the pre-incarnate and the post-incarnate states in the strongest possible light; and the sixth, by representing Christ as, in the whole course of His humiliation, a free agent, not merely the passive subject of an involuntary experience, makes Him in all a proper ex-

[1] John xiii. 3.

ample of humility, as well as a fit subject of reward by exaltation.

While full of instruction regarding the mind of the Divine Being known in this world's history by the name of *Jesus Christ*, the passage whose meaning we have now ascertained is vague and general in its statements concerning the *humanity* assumed by that Being in a spirit of self-exinanition. It does not tell us how the humanity was assumed, nor does it teach any definite doctrine on the more general question: how far the assuming agent was like other men. That there was a genesis of some sort, and a likeness to some extent, is all that is expressly indicated. The phrases in which the likeness is asserted[1] have even a superficial look of doketism about them, which, while not without its value as an incidental proof that the subject spoken of is something *more* than man, at the same time seems to imply that He is also something *less*. It would be altogether unwarrantable, however, to found a serious charge of doketism on the manner in which the apostle expresses himself.[2] For, while it may not be impossible to put a doketic construction on the letter of the passage, such a construction is utterly excluded by its spirit. The form of a servant ascribed to the incarnate One, implies likeness to men in their present condition in all possible respects; for how could one be in earnest with the servant's work whose humanity was in any sense doketic? Then, from the mind in which the Incarnation took its origin, the complete likeness of Christ's humanity to ours may be inferred with great confidence. He who was not minded to retain His equality with God, was not likely to assume a humanity that was a make-believe or a sham. It would be His desire to be in all things " like unto His brethren." [3]

[1] ἐν ὁμοιώματι ἀνθρώπων γενόμενος, σχήματι εὑρεθείς ὡς ἄνθρωπος.

[2] As Baur has done in his *Apostel Paulus*, Zweite Theil, p. 50 ff. (Zweite Auflage). The Gnostic style of thought supposed to characterize the passage, ii. 5–9, involved in the doctrine of the kenosis, and also in the doketic view of Christ's humanity, is Baur's chief argument against the genuineness of the Epistle to the Philippians.

[3] Van Mastricht finds even in the phrase καὶ σχήματι εὑρεθείς ὡς ἄνθρωπος a testimony to the reality of Christ's humanity. He says: " Notat habitum,

On these grounds the *homoüsia*[1] of Christ's humanity with ours may be regarded as a legitimate inference from the passage we have been considering. But that important doctrine does not rest on mere inference; it is expressly taught in other places of Scripture, especially in the Epistle to the Hebrews, where it is proclaimed with great clearness and emphasis. The writer of that Epistle, like the writer of the Epistle to the Philippians, treats of the subject of Christ's humiliation, but from a different point of view. Paul exhibits that humiliation as something voluntarily endured by Christ in a spirit of condescension and self-renunciation, which he exhorts his readers to admire and imitate. The writer of the Epistle to the Hebrews, on the other hand, regards the same humiliation as an experience to which Christ was subjected, and which, as apparently incongruous to His intrinsic dignity, demands explanation. The point of view is adapted by the writer to the spiritual condition of his readers. The Hebrew Christians to whom he writes can see in the earthly experience of Jesus nothing glorious or admirable, but only a dark, perplexing puzzle, a stumbling-block to faith, which makes it hard to believe that Jesus can be the Christ. Hence, for one who would establish them in the faith and keep them from apostasy, it becomes an imperative task to endeavour to set the earthly history of the object of faith in such a light that it should not only cease to be a stumbling-block, but even b converted into a source of strength and comfort. To this task the writer accordingly addresses himself with great boldness, skill, and eloquence. Disdaining the expedient for making the task easy of lowering the essential dignity of Christ, he commences his Epistle by setting forth that dignity in terms which, for fulness, clearness, and intensity,

---

gestum, speciem omneque externum, quod incurrit in sensus a quo quid agnoscitur, quo veritatem humanae suae naturae passim Christus demonstravit (Luc. xxiv. 39; John xx. 27). Non est idem ($\sigma\chi\tilde{\eta}\mu\alpha$) cum $\mu o \rho \varphi \tilde{\eta}$ $\delta \mu o \iota \omega \mu \alpha \tau \iota$, non inanis figura et species corporis, quasi Christus non esset verus homo, sed talis habitus qui demonstrat rei veritatem sicut $\tau \acute{v} \rho \alpha \nu \nu o \nu$ $\sigma \chi \tilde{\eta} \mu \alpha$ $\check{\epsilon} \chi \epsilon \iota \nu$ apud Sophoclem, est se tyrannum praestare, demonstrare. Hinc $\epsilon \acute{v} \rho \epsilon \theta \epsilon \acute{\iota} \varsigma$ dicitur, inventus, compertus, certissimis argumentis est, $\acute{\omega}\varsigma$ $\check{\alpha}\nu\theta\rho\omega\pi o\varsigma$, sicut homo, scil. verus, vulgaris, ut $\acute{\omega}\varsigma$ hic sit affirmantis, seu veritatis nota, non similitudinis."—*Theor. pract. Theologia*, lib. v. cap. ix. pars exeget.   [1] *Vid.* p. 3, note 1.

are not surpassed by any to be found in Scripture. Then having declared Christ to be the Son of God, the brightness of God's glory and the express image of His person, the Lord of angels, the Maker of worlds, the everlasting King, he approaches the subject of His humilation, and sets himself to show how it can be reconciled with His inherent majesty. The proof is given in the second chapter of the Epistle from the fifth verse to the end, and presents a train of reasoning characterized by profundity of thought, and by a rhetorical skill which knows how to make every thought bear upon the practical purpose in view,—that, viz., of strengthening weak faith and comforting desponding hearts. This argument it is not necessary for our present object to expound elaborately; it will suffice to indicate the leading idea. The grand thought, then, in this remarkable passage is this, that Christ to be a *Saviour* must be a *Brother*, and that, as things actually stand, that means that He must be humbled, must pass through a *curriculum* of temptation and suffering as a man, in order that He may be in all respects like unto His brethren. This great principle of brotherhood is formally enunciated in the eleventh verse in these terms: " Both He that sanctifieth and they who are (being) sanctified are all of one;" a proposition in the precise interpretation of which expositors are much divided, but whose general import plainly is, that the Sanctifier and those whom He is to sanctify, however different in character, stand in such a relation to one another, that the nearer they are in all other respects, the greater the power of the Sanctifier to perform His sanctifying work. Sanctifier and those to be sanctified must be all of one race, all one party, having one interest, one lot, a brotherhood to all intents and purposes; the Holy One descending first into the state of the unholy, that He may raise them in turn to His own proper level in privilege and in character.[1] Having enunciated this general

---

[1] In the interpretation of this important text I agree generally with Hofmann, whose views are to the following effect: The statement is to be understood as a general proposition, as is shown by the present tenses ($\dot{\alpha}\gamma\iota\dot{\alpha}\zeta\omega\nu$, $\dot{\alpha}\gamma\iota\alpha\zeta\dot{o}\mu\epsilon\nu\sigma\iota$), which express not a habitual activity on the part of the Saviour, but a thing done once for all in Christ's history. Only as a general proposition could the statement serve the purpose for which it was intended. Were it merely a historical fact, it

principle, as one which he hopes may commend itself as self-evident to the minds of his readers, the writer next proceeds to show that it is recognised, has its root, in Old Testament Scripture, and thereafter to supply some examples of its practical application. With the former view he makes three quotations from the Psalms and the prophets, the first of which indicates that Messiah stands before God, not without, but within a community, and in it as a community of persons whom He regards as brethren, and to whom He has been drawn closer in fellow-feeling by suffering; the second, that in the performance of His work, Messiah stands in the same relation to God, that of faith and dependence, as those whose good He has at heart; and the third, that Messiah has associated with Him in His work fellow-workers, to whom He is knit by the close bond of human kinsmanship, even as God gave to Isaiah his own children to be joint-prophets with him, "for signs and for wonders in Israel from the Lord of hosts."[1] These three quotations the writer follows up with three examples of the application of the principles which the quotations are intended to establish. The principle is applied, first, to the *Incarnation;* second, to the *death* of Christ; and thirdly, to His *whole experience of suffering and temptation* between the beginning and the end of His ministry. The

would need to be shown why the fact was so; whereas the object is to show how the vocation of Christ as a Saviour, as a matter of course, required Him to assume a suffering nature like ours. The idea of $ἁγιάζειν$ involves that the Actor and those for whom He acts are all of one origin. $Πάντες$ is not superfluous, nor is it = $ἀμφότεροι$; but it signifies that the difference between Sanctifier and sanctified does not affect descent, in reference to which they are rather $πάντες$ $ἐξ ἑνός$. What follows I give in Hofmann's own words: "Freilich muss man nicht gleiche Herkunft aus Gott verstehen, von der es heissen müsste dass sie von ihnen nicht minder, als von ihm gelte; nicht $πάντες$ sondern $ἀμφότεροι$ müsste es heissen; dann aber auch nicht $ἐξ ἑνός$, da der Nachdruck darauf läge, dass der Eine Gott es ist, von dem er und von dem sie herkommen, sondern $ἐκ τοῦ ἑνός$" (that is, descent from *God* is not meant, otherwise it would have been said *both*, not all are of one, both they as well as He, and it would further have been said not of one, but of the One). "Mit $πάντες ἐξ ἑνός$ ist nicht betont, von wannen sie sind, sondern dass sich die Allgemeinheit des gleichen Herkunft über den Gegensatz des $ἁγιάζων$ und der $ἁγιαζόμενοι$ erstreckt." (The object is not to emphasize from whom or whence the parties take their origin, but to point out that the community of origin covers the contrast between $ὁ ἁγιάζων$ and $οἱ ἁγιαζόμενοι$.)—*Schriftbeweis*, ii. 52–3.

[1] So substantially Hofmann, *Schriftbeweis*, ii. 54.

principle upon which the work of salvation proceeds being, that Sanctifier and sanctified are all of one, it follows first, that inasmuch as the subjects of Christ's work are partakers of flesh and blood, He also must in like manner become partaker of the same (the likeness of the manner extending even to the being born, so that He might be one of the *children*); second, that inasmuch as the subjects of Christ's work are liable to death and to the fear of it, He also must die that He may deliver His brethren from their bondage; third, that inasmuch as the subjects of Christ's work are exposed through life to manifold trials and temptations, therefore He must pass through a very complete curriculum of temptation, that He might be perfected in sympathy, and gain the confidence of His brethren as one who could not fail to be a merciful and trustworthy High Priest in things pertaining to God.

The doctrine of the *homoüsia*, taking the term as signifying likeness both in *nature* and in *experience*, thus shines forth in full lustre in this magnificent paragraph of the Epistle. It is enunciated as an axiomatic truth; it is established by Scripture proof; it is illustrated by outstanding facts in Christ's history, His birth, His death, His experience of temptation; it is re-asserted in the strongest terms it is possible to employ: "In all things it behoved Him to be made like unto His brethren." Nor does this exhaust the testimony to the doctrine contained in the Epistle. Indirect allusions to, and confirmations and enlargements of, the same truth are scattered over its pages like gems; the first hint occurring at the ninth verse of the second chapter, where the Lord of angels, and rightful object of angelic worship, is described as one made lower than the angels.[1] Why? Because He is the appointed Restorer of Paradise and of all that man possessed there, and, in particular, of lordship over all; and man being now no longer lord, but rather a degraded slave, the second Adam must take His place beside him, assuming the form and position of a servant, that He may lift man out of his degradation, and restore to him his forfeited inheritance. An eloquent reiteration of the doctrine occurs at the close of that part of

---

[1] Heb. ii. 9: Τὸν δὲ βραχύ τι παρ' ἀγγέλους ἠλαττωμένον.

the Epistle which treats of the eternal *Sabbatism*, another element of the paradisaical bliss lost by the fall, whereof Jesus is the appointed Restorer. In this place the great High Priest of humanity, and the Joshua of the Lord's host, Himself now entered into the heavenly rest, is represented as one who can be touched with a feeling of our infirmities, seeing He was tempted in all respects as we are, was once a weary wanderer like ourselves,—the statement being made only the more emphatic by the qualifying clause " without sin." " Tempted in all respects as we are," speaking deliberately, the sole difference being that He never yielded to temptation while in the wilderness, as we too often do. The chapter following contains a touching allusion to a special point in the similitude of our Lord's experience to ours, which brings Him very close to human sympathies. It is in the place where Jesus is represented as offering up, in the days of His flesh, prayers and supplications, with strong crying and tears, unto Him that was able to save Him from death.[1] Even thus far did the likeness extend. The Sanctifier shared with His brethren the fear of death, through which they are all their lifetime subject to bondage. Once more, the comprehensive view given in this Epistle, of the work of Christ as the Author of salvation, suggests by implication an equally comprehensive view of the likeness between Him and His brethren. The writer, in describing the work of redemption, keeps constantly before his mind the history of man in Paradise. He makes salvation consist in lordship of the world that is to be, in deliverance from the fear of death, in entrance into a rest often promised but yet remaining, an ideal unexhausted by all past partial realizations—the perfect Sabbatism of the people of God. These representations plainly point back to the dominion over the creatures conferred on man at his creation, and lost by sin; to the death which was the wages of sin, and which Satan brought on man by successfully tempting him to disobedience; and to God's rest after the work of creation was finished, in which unfallen man had part, and in which man restored is destined again to share. Salvation thus consists in the

[1] Heb. v. 7.

cancelling of all the effects of the fall, and in the restoration of all that man lost by his sin. But if this be the nature of salvation, what, on the principle that Sanctifier and sanctified are all of one, must the likeness of the Saviour to the sinful sons of Adam amount to? Evidently to *subjection to the curse in its whole extent, as far as that is possible for one who is Himself without sin.*

The view thus presented of our Lord's state of humiliation is admirably fitted to serve the purpose which the writer of the Epistle to the Hebrews had in mind (that of fortifying his readers against temptations to apostasy, whether arising out of the internal difficulties of the Christian faith, or out of eternal affliction suffered on account of the faith), giving as it does to our Lord's whole earthly experience a winsome aspect of sympathy with humanity in its present sorrowful condition. But we have not yet exhausted what the author of this Epistle has to say by way of reconciling the Hebrew Christians to what had hitherto been an offence unto them. He is not content with *apologising* for Christ's humiliation; he boldly represents that experience as in another aspect a *glorification* of its subject. He speaks of Jesus as crowned with glory and honour; not *because* He has tasted death for men, but in order that He, by the grace of God, might taste death for men.[1] It has been customary, indeed, to regard this passage as referring to the state of exaltation, in which Christ receives the reward of His voluntary endurance of the indignities connected with the state of humiliation; but I agree with Hofmann[2] in thinking that the reference is rather to an honour and glory which is not subsequent to, but contemporaneous with, the state of humiliation,—the bright side, in fact, of one and the same experience. It is the honour and glory of being appointed to the high office of Apostle and High Priest of the Christian profession, the Moses and the Aaron of the new dispensation. That office

---

[1] Heb. ii. 9.

[2] *Schriftbeweis*, ii. 46 ff., Zweite Auflage. Hofmann's exposition of the whole chapter is extremely good, and seems to me to bring out the connection of thought better on the whole than anything I have seen. His discussions on the Epistle to the Hebrews, generally, are most instructive, though not free from characteristic eccentricities.

doubtless involves humiliation, inasmuch as it imposes on Him who holds it the necessity of tasting death; but even in that respect His experience is not exclusively humiliating. For while it is a humiliation to *die*, it is glorious to taste death *for others;* and by dying, to abolish death, and bring life and immortality to light. To be appointed to an office which has such a purpose in view, is *ipso facto* to be crowned with glory and honour, and is a mark of signal grace or favour on the part of God. And this is precisely what the writer of the Epistle would have his readers understand. He would not have them see in the earthly career of Jesus *mere* humiliation,—degradation difficult to reconcile with His Messianic dignity; but rather the rough, yet not degrading experience, incidental to a high, honourable, holy vocation. "We see," he says in effect, "two things in Him by whom the prophecy in the eighth Psalm is destined to be fulfilled in the restoration of man to lordship in the world to come. On the one hand, we see Him made lower than angels by becoming partaker of mortal flesh and blood; a lowering made necessary by the fact that it was men, not angels, whose case He was undertaking,—men subject to the experience of death, whom, therefore, on account of that experience, He could help only by assuming a humanity capable of undergoing the same experience.[1] On the other hand, we see in this same Jesus, humbled by being made a mortal man, one crowned with glory and honour in being appointed to the office of Restorer of Paradise and all its privileges, including lordship over all; an office, indeed, whose end cannot be reached without the endurance of death, but whose end is at the same time so glorious that it confers dignity upon the means; so that it may be said in sober truth that the divine Father manifested signal grace towards His Son in giving Him the opportunity of tasting death for others; that is to say,

---

[1] With Hofmann, I connect $\delta\iota\grave{\alpha}$ $\tau\grave{o}$ $\pi\acute{\alpha}\theta\eta\mu\alpha$ $\tau o\tilde{v}$ $\theta\alpha\nu\acute{\alpha}\tau o v$ (ver. 9) with the foregoing clause, and understand it as referring not specially to Christ's own sufferings, but generally to the experience of death, to which man is subject. It points out that in man's condition, on account of which Christ had to be made lower than angels, so far as this implied becoming man. Those whose case Christ undertook were *men* subject to *death*, therefore He too must become man that it might be possible for Him to die.

of abolishing death as a curse, and making it quite another thing for them, by enduring it in His own person."

That such is the import of this notable text I have little doubt, although I am constrained to admit that the meaning now taken out of it has comparatively little support in the history of interpretation. Most commentators explain the passage as if, with the Hebrew Christians, they thought the humiliation of Christ stood very much in need of apology. Disregarding the grammatical construction, the scope of the argument, and the hint given in the expression " we see," which indicates that what is spoken of is something falling within the sphere of visible reality, they almost with one consent relegate the glory and honour to the state of exaltation, as if the mention of such things in connection with the state of humiliation were out of the question, and altogether unwarranted by Scripture usage; although the Apostle Peter speaks of Jesus as having received from God the Father " honour and glory" when there came such a voice to Him from the Excellent Glory: " This is my beloved Son, in whom I am well pleased;"[1] and although further, in this very Epistle, it is said of Jesus, as the *Apostle* of our profession, that He was counted worthy of more " glory" than Moses,[2] and, as the *High Priest* of our profession, that even as no man took upon himself the honour of the Jewish high-priesthood, " so also Christ glorified not Himself to be made an high priest, but He that said unto Him: 'Thou art my Son, to-day have I begotten Thee.'"[3] And as to taking the " grace of God" spoken of in the last clause of the sentence as manifested directly, not to those for whom Jesus died, but to Jesus Himself *privileged* to die for them, it is an interpretation which, though yielding a thought true in itself and relevant to the purpose in hand, does not seem even to have occurred to the minds of most expositors. This is all the more surprising, that the pointlessness of the expression in question, as ordinarily interpreted, has not escaped notice. Ebrard, for example, feels it so strongly that he falls back on the ancient reading χωρὶς Θεοῦ, adopted by Origen and the Nestorians, and used by the former as an argument in favour of his theory of uni-

---

[1] 2 Pet. i. 17. [2] Heb. iii. 3. [3] Heb. v. 4, 5.

versal restitution,[1] and by the latter as a proof text in support of their doctrine of a double personality in the one Christ. "The reading χάριτι,"[2] Ebrard remarks, "is certainly clear as water, extremely easy to understand, but also extremely empty of thought, and unsuitable;" herein echoing the tone as well as the thought of Theodore of Mopsuestia, who calls it ridiculous to substitute χάριτι Θεοῦ instead of χωρὶς Θεοῦ, and represents those who do so as adopting a reading which appears to them easy of comprehension, because they fail to see the sense of the true, more difficult reading; that sense being, in his view, that the man Jesus tasted death apart from God the Logos, to whom in life He had been joined, it being unseemly that the Logos should have any personal connection with death, though it was not unseemly that He should make the man Jesus, as the Captain of Salvation, perfect through suffering.[3] It is not surprising that the Master of the East should have preferred a reading which seemed to favour his peculiar Christological theory; but it does seem strange that a modern theologian, holding very different views on Christology, should feel himself forced to fall back on that read-

---

[1] *Comment. in Joann.* tom. i. c. 40: "μέγας ἐστὶν ἀρχιερεύς, οὐκ ὑπὲρ ἀνθρώπων μόνον, ἀλλὰ καὶ παντὸς λογικοῦ τὴν ἅπαξ θυσίαν προσενεχθεῖσαν ἑαυτὸν ἀνενεγκών. Χωρὶς γὰρ Θεοῦ ὑπὲρ παντὸς ἐγεύσατο θανάτου, ὅπερ ἔν τισι κεῖται τῆς πρὸς Ἑβραίους ἀντιγράφοις, χάριτι Θεοῦ. Εἴτε δὲ χωρὶς Θεοῦ ὑπὲρ παντὸς ἐγεύσατο θανάτου, οὐ μόνον ὑπὲρ ἀνθρώπων ἀπέθανεν, ἀλλὰ καὶ ὑπὲρ τῶν λοιπῶν λογικῶν." Origen includes within the scope of the παντός all existing beings except God, viewed as tainted with man's sin. "Καὶ γὰρ," he says, "ἄτοπον ὑπὲρ ἀνθρωπίνων μὲν αὐτὸν φάσκειν ἁμαρτημάτων γεγεῦσθαι θανάτου, οὐκ ἔτι δὲ ὑπὲρ ἄλλου τινὸς παρὰ τὸν ἄνθρωπον ἐν ἁμαρτήμασι γεγενημένου· οἷον ὑπὲρ ἄστρων, οὐ δὲ τῶν ἀστρων πάντως καθαρῶν ὄντων ἐνώπιον τοῦ Θεοῦ."

[2] *Der Brief an die Hebräer erklärt,* p. 90.

[3] Theo. Mops. *in Epistolam Pauli ad Hebraeos commentarii Fragmenta,* Migne, Patrologiae cursus, tom. lxvi. p. 955. Theodore's words are: "Γελοιότατον δή τι πάσχουσι ἐνταῦθα, τὸ χωρὶς Θεοῦ ἐναλλάττοντες καὶ ποιοῦντες χάριτι Θεοῦ οὐ προσέχοντες τῇ ἀκολουθίᾳ τῆς Γραφῆς, ἀλλ᾽ ἀπὸ τοῦ μὴ συνιέναι ὅτι ποτὲ ἔφη τὸ χωρὶς Θεοῦ ἀδιαφόρως ἐξαλείφοντες μὲν ἐκεῖνο, τιθέντες δὲ τὸ δοκοῦν αὐτοῖς εὔκολον εἶναι πρὸς κατανόησιν." He goes on to say that it was not Paul's custom, χάριτι Θεοῦ τιθέναι ἁπλῶς —using the expression as a pious commonplace—ἀλλὰ πάντως ἀπό τινος ἀκολουθίας λόγου; which is quite true of Paul and of all the New Testament writers, and favours the interpretation given above.

ing, from sheer inability to assign a suitable and worthy sense to the reading in the received text, while such an interpretation as I have ventured to suggest was open to him. Is it, then, really an inadmissible thought, that God showed favour to Christ in appointing Him to taste death for every man? is it out of keeping with the general strain of this Epistle? does it not fit in naturally to what goes before and to what comes after? Was it not worth while to point out to persons scandalized by the humiliation of Christ, that what to vulgar view might seem a mark of divine disfavour, was, in truth, a signal proof of divine grace; that even in appointing the Son of man to go through a curriculum of suffering, God had been mindful of Him, and had graciously visited Him, opening up to Him the high career of Captain of Salvation? And how are we to understand the assertion following, that it became Him who is the first cause and last end of all to perfect the Captain of Salvation by suffering, if not as a defence of the bold idea, contained, as it appears to me, in the preceding verse? The import of that assertion is simply this: The means and the end of salvation are both worthy of the Supreme, by whom and for whom all events in time happen; the end manifestly and admittedly—for who will question that it is worthy of God to lead many sons to glory?—the means not less than the end, though at first they may appear to compromise the dignity both of the Supreme Cause and of His commissioned Agent. It was honourable for the Captain of Salvation to taste of death in the prosecution of His great work; it was an honour conferred upon Him by God the Father to be appointed to die for such a purpose.

This, then, is another truth, besides the *homoüsia* of Christ's humanity with ours, which we learn from the Epistle to the Hebrews: *that Christ's humiliation is at the same time in an important sense His glorification;* that it is not merely *followed* by a state of exaltation, according to the doctrine of Paul in his Epistle to the Philippians, but carries a moral compensation within itself; so that we need not hesitate to emphasize the humiliation, inasmuch as the more real and thorough it is, the greater the glory and honour accruing to the humbled One. The glory is that of one " full of grace and truth," manifested not in spite of, but through His humiliation made visible by the Incarnation and the human life of the Son of God, as the Apostle John testifies when he says in the beginning of his Gospel: " The Word was made flesh and dwelt among us, and we beheld His glory." The evangelist explains, indeed, that the glory of which he speaks is the glory as of the Onlybegotten of the Father; but he does not mean by that the glory of metaphysical majesty visible through the veil of the flesh in consequence of its doketic transparency. He means the glory of divine love which the Only-begotten, who was in the bosom of the Father, came forth to reveal, and of which His state of humiliation on earth was the historical exegesis. It has, indeed, been confidently asserted by certain writers that John knows nothing of a state of humiliation,—that the Incarnation of the Word is for Him not an abasement, but a new means of revealing His glory, the representation of Christ's death in his Gospel as an exaltation or a glorification being adduced as conclusive proof of the fact; and Protestant scholastic theologians have been severely blamed for overlooking or ignoring the undeniable truth. It is a characteristic illustration of the haste and one-sidedness of modern criticism.[1] As if the two ideas of glorification and humiliation were absolutely incompatible; as if John, the apostle of love, was not a very likely person to comprehend their compatibility; as if the things alleged in proof of his ignorance of a state of humiliation did not rather prove his complete mastery of the truth now insisted on, viz. that the humiliations of Christ were on the moral side glorifications ! The glory of which John speaks is that of divine grace revealed in word, deed, and *suffering*, to the eye of faith. This glory the Only-begotten won by renouncing the comparatively barren glory of metaphysical majesty. Thus, in becoming poor, He at the same time enriched Himself. In the words of Martensen, " Because only in the state of humiliation could He fully reveal the depths of divine love, and because it was by this His poverty that He made all

[1] *Vide* Reuss, *Théologie Chrétienne*, ii. 455.

rich, it may be said that as the Son of man He first took full possession of His divine glory; for then only is love in full possession when it can fully communicate itself, and only then does it reveal its omnipotence, when it conquers hearts, and has the strong for a prey."[1]

The foregoing discussion of the passages in the Epistle to the Hebrews, bearing on the subject of the humiliation of Christ, thus yields us the following additions to the list of elementary truths:—

7. The service Christ came to render, His vocation as the Captain of Salvation, or the Sanctifier, was such as to involve likeness to men in all possible respects, both in nature and in experience; a likeness in nature as complete as if He were merely a human personality; a likeness in experience of temptation, and, in general, of subjection to the curse resting on man on account of sin, limited only by His personal sinlessness.

8. Christ's whole state of exinanition was not only worthy to be rewarded by a subsequent state of exaltation, but was in itself invested with moral sublimity and dignity; so that, having in view the honour of the Saviour, we have no interest in minimizing His experience of humiliation, but, on the contrary, are concerned to vindicate for that experience the utmost possible fulness, recognising no limit to the descent except that arising out of His sinlessness.

And now, having furnished ourselves with this series of axioms, our next business must be to use them as helps in forming a critical estimate of conflicting Christological and Soteriological theories. But before entering on this, the main part of our undertaking, it will be expedient here to indicate the plan on which our subsequent discussions will be conducted. It will not be necessary, for the purpose I have in view in these lectures, that I should treat with scholastic accuracy of the different stages or stations in the *status exinanitionis*. I do not know that for any purpose such a mode of treatment would be of much service. I question, indeed, whether exactitude in handling this theme be practicable; at all events, it is certain that anything approaching to exactitude is not to

[1] *Die Christliche Dogmatik*, p. 246.

be found in dogmatic systems. In the works of the leading dogmaticians the stages of our Lord's humiliation are very variously enumerated, though, of course, certain features are common to all the schemes. Occasionally confusion of thought is discernible,—acts being confounded with states, and generals treated as particulars. The Incarnation, *e.g.*, is sometimes reckoned to the state of exinanition, whereas it is in truth the efficient cause of the whole state, the original act of gracious condescension whereof the state of humiliation is the historical evolution and result. An instance of the other sort of confusion, that of turning a general into a particular, may perhaps be found in the answer given in the Shorter Catechism to the question referring to Christ's humiliation, where the "wrath of God" comes in, apparently as a particular experience, like "the cursed death of the cross" mentioned immediately after; while the expression, though peculiarly applicable to particular experiences, really admits of being applied to the whole state of humiliation as a designation thereof from a certain point of view, as in fact it is applied in the Heidelberg Catechism.[1]

Instead, therefore, of attempting an exact enumeration of the stations, I propose to consider the whole state of humiliation under these three leading aspects: the *physical*, the *ethical*, and the *soteriological*.

Under the first of these aspects we shall have to consider the bearing of the category of humiliation on Christ's person. The Son of God became man, the Word was made flesh, the Eternally-begotten was born in time of the Virgin; what is the dogmatic significance of these facts in reference to the person of the Incarnate One?

Under the second aspect, the ethical, we shall have an opportunity of contemplating the incarnate Son of God as the subject of a human experience involving moral trial, and supplying a stimulus to moral development. Christ was *tempted* in all points like as we are, and He was *perfected* by suffering; in what sense, and to what extent, can

---

[1] *Quaestio* 37. Quid credis, cum dicis, passus est? Eum toto quidem vitae suae tempore quo in terrâ egit, praecipue vero in ejus extremo, iram Dei adversus peccatum universi generis humani, corpore et anima sustinuisse.

temptation and perfecting be predicated of One who was without sin?

Under the third aspect we shall have to consider Christ as a *servant*, under law, and having a task appointed Him, involving humiliating experiences various in kind and degree.

To the physical aspect four lectures will be devoted. One will treat of the ancient Christology, the formula of Chalcedon being taken as the view-point for our historical survey; a second, of the Christologies of the old Lutheran and Reformed Confessions; a third, of the modern kenotic theories of Christ's person; a fourth, of modern humanistic views of Christ's person, which practically evacuate the idea of the Humiliation of all significance by regarding the Subject thereof merely as a man, whether as the Perfect Ideal Man, or, as in the case of the naturalistic school of theologians, not even so much as that.[1] The other two aspects of our Lord's humiliation will occupy each a single lecture.

[1] This lecture was not delivered, and appears in this edition for the first time.

LECTURE II.

THE PATRISTIC CHRISTOLOGY.

The Christology of the ancient Church took final shape at the Council of Chalcedon, A. D. 451, in the following formula:—"Following the holy Fathers, we all with one consent teach and confess one and the same Son, our Lord Jesus Christ, the same perfect in Deity, and the same perfect in humanity, truly God, and the same truly man, of reasonable soul and body, of the same substance with the Father as to His divinity, of the same substance with us as to His humanity; in all things like to us, except sin; before the ages begotten of the Father as to His Deity, but in the latter days for us, and for our redemption, begotten (the same) of the Virgin Mary, the mother of God, as to His humanity; one and the same Christ, Son, Lord, Only-begotten, manifested in two natures, without confusion, without conversion, indivisibly, inseparably. The distinction of natures being by no means abolished by the union, but rather the property of each preserved and combined into one person and one hypostasis; not one severed or divided into two persons, but one and the same Son and Only-begotten, viz. God, Logos, and the Lord Jesus Christ."[1]

[1] Ἕνα καὶ τὸν αὐτὸν ὁμολογεῖν υἱὸν τὸν κύριον ἡμῶν Ἰησοῦν Χριστὸν συμφώνως ἅπαντες ἐκδιδάσκομεν, τέλειον, τὸν αὐτὸν ἐν θεότητι, καὶ τέλειον, τὸν αὐτὸν ἐν ἀνθρωπότητι· ὁμοούσιον τῷ πατρὶ κατὰ τὴν θεότητα, καὶ ὁμοούσιον τὸν αὐτὸν ἡμῖν κατὰ τὴν ἀνθρωπότητα, κατὰ πάντα ὅμοιον ἡμῖν χωρὶς ἁμαρτίας . . . ἐκ Μαρίας τῆς παρθένου, τῆς θεοτόκου . . . ἕνα καὶ τὸν αὐτὸν Χριστὸν, ἐκ δυῶν φύσεων (al. ἐν δύο φύσεσιν) ἀσυγχύτως, ἀτρέπτως, ἀδιαι-

This famous creed, formulated by the Fourth General Council, was the fruit of two great controversies, the Apollinarian and the Nestorian; the one having reference to the integrity of our Lord's humanity, the other to the unity of His person. In these two controversies all parties may be said to have been animated by an orthodox interest, and to have been sincerely desirous to hold fast and establish the Catholic faith. All accepted cordially the Nicaean Creed, and sought to construct a Christology on a Trinitarian foundation. These remarks apply even to Apollinaris, who, however much he may have failed in his attempt at a construction of Christ's person, seems to have meant that attempt to be a defence of the Christian doctrine of the Incarnation against its assailants. He was a man held in high esteem by his contemporaries for his learning, piety, and eminent services to the cause of truth, till in his old age he promulgated his peculiar Christological theory. Epiphanius speaks of him as one who had always been beloved by himself, Athanasius, and all the orthodox; so that when he first got tidings of the new heresy, he could hardly believe that such a doctrine could emanate from such a man.[1] He had done excellent service as champion of the Nicaean symbol against the Arians, and had given a still more conclusive proof of his zeal in that cause by suffering exile on account of his opposition to the Arian heresy.[2]

The theory of Christ's person propounded by Apollinaris was this, that the humanity of Christ did not consist of a reasonable soul and body, as in other men, but of flesh and an animal soul without mind, the place of mind being supplied in His case by the Logos. Of the inner genesis of this theory in its author's mind we have no accounts, and we can only conjecture what were its hidden roots. Among these may probably be reckoned familiarity with,

μέτως ἀχωρίστως γνωριζόμενον· οὐδαμοῦ τῆς τῶν φυσέων διαφορᾶς ἀνηρημένης διὰ τὴν ἔνωσιν, σωζομένης δὲ μᾶλλον τῆς ἰδιότητος ἑκατέρας φύσεως, καὶ εἰς ἓν πρόσωπον καὶ μίαν ὑπόστασιν συντρεχούσης, οὐκ εἰς δύο πρόσωπα μεριζόμενον ἢ διαιρούμενον, ἀλλ' ἕνα καὶ τὸν αὐτὸν υἱόν, καὶ μονογενῆ Θεὸν λόγον Κύριον Ἰησοῦν Χριστόν

[1] *Adv. Haereses*, lib. iii. tom. ii.; *Dimocritae*, c. 2, see also c. 24.
[2] *Adv. Haereses*, lib. iii. tom. ii.; *Dimoeritae*, c. 24.

and partiality for, classic Greek literature, and more especially the works of Plato;[1] antagonism on other matters to Origen, the first among the early Fathers to give prominence to the doctrine that Christ's humanity was endowed with a rational soul, predisposing to a diverse way of thinking on that particular subject likewise; and above all, determined hostility to the opinions concerning the person of the Saviour, characteristic of the Arian heretics. So far as one can judge from contemporary representations, and from the fragments of the work on the Incarnation which have been preserved, the Apollinarian theory was attractive to the mind of its inventor chiefly on these accounts: as enabling him to combat successfully the Arian doctrine of the *fallibility* of Christ; as ensuring the unity of the *person* of Christ, with which the doctrine of the integrity of His humanity seemed incompatible; and as making the Incarnation a great reality for God, involving subjection of the divine nature to the experience of *suffering*. As to the first, the Arian doctrine of the person of Christ was, that in the historical person called Christ appeared in human flesh the very exalted, in a sense divine, *creature* named in Scripture the Logos,—the Logos taking the place of a human soul, and being liable to human infirmity, and even to sin, inasmuch as, however exalted, He was still a creature, therefore finite, therefore fallible, τρεπτός, capable of turning, in the abuse of freedom, from good to evil. Apollinaris accepted the Arian *method* of constructing the person, by the exclusion of a rational human soul, and used it as a means of obviating the Arian conclusion, which was revolting to his religious feelings. His reply to the Arian was in effect this: "Christ is, as you say, the Logos appearing in the flesh and performing the part of a human soul; but the Logos is not a creature, as you maintain; He is truly

---

[1] An interesting evidence of this is supplied in the fact, that when the Emperor Julian interdicted the reading of the classic poets and orators in the Christian schools, in the year 362, Apollinaris, along with his father, set himself to provide a kindred literature in the shape of versions of the Scriptures, the father taking up the Old Testament, and turning the Pentateuch into heroic verse, in imitation of Homer, and doing other portions into comedies, tragedies, and lyrics, in imitation of Menander, Euripides, and Pindar; while the son took up the New Testament, and turned the Gospels and Epistles into dialogues, in the style of Plato.

divine, eternally begotten, not made, and therefore morally infallible." In no other way did it seem to him possible to escape the Arian mutability (τρεπτόν), for he not only admitted the fallibility of all creatures, however exalted, but he believed that in human beings at least a rational soul, endowed with intelligence and freedom, not only may, but must inevitably fall into sin. Freedom, in fact, usually supposed to be a distinction of the human mind, exalting it in the scale of being above the lower animal creation, was in his view an evil to be got rid of,—and accordingly he sought to get rid of it, in the case of Christ, by denying that He had a human mind, and ascribing to Him only an immutable divine mind which, to quote his own words, "should not through defect of knowledge be subject to the flesh, but should without effort bring the flesh into harmony with itself"[1] (as its passive instrument).

As to the second advantage believed to be gained by the theory, that, viz., of securing the *unity* of Christ's person, Apollinaris contended that, on the supposition of the two natures being perfect, the unity could not be maintained. "If," said he, "to perfect man be joined perfect God, there are two, not one: one, the Son of God by nature; another, the Son of God by adoption."[2] On the other hand, he held that his theory gave one person, who was at once perfect man and perfect God, the two natures not being concrete separable things, but two aspects of the same person. Christ was true God, for He was the eternal Logos manifest in the flesh. He was also true man, for human nature consists of three component elements, body, animal soul, and spirit, and all these were combined, according to the

[1] Gregory of Nyssa, *Adv. Apollinarem*, c. 40. The words of Apollinaris are: Οὐκ ἄρα σώζεται τὸ ἀνθρώπινον γένος δι' ἀναλήψεως νοῦ, καὶ ὅλου ἀνθρώπου, ἀλλὰ διὰ προσλήψεως σαρκός, ᾗ φυσικὸν μὲν τὸ ἡγεμονεύεσθαι (whose nature it is to be ruled) ἐδεῖτο δὲ ἀτρέπτου νοῦ, μὴ ὑποπίπτοντος αὐτῇ διὰ ἐπιστημοσύνης ἀσθένειαν, ἀλλὰ συναρμόζοντος αὐτὴν ἀβιάστως ἑαυτῷ. All the accounts of the views of Apollinaris agree in ascribing to him the strange, almost Manichaean, doctrine, that freedom, the attribute of a rational soul, necessarily involved sin. Vid. Athanasius, *De Incarnatione Christi* (near the beginning): ὅπου γὰρ τέλειος ἄνθρωπος (complete man, metaphysically) ἐκεῖ καὶ ἁμαρτία; also *De Salutari Adventu Jesu Christi, sub init.* Epiphanius, *Adv. Haereses*, l. iii. t. ii.; *Dimoeritae*, c. 26.

[2] Greg. cc. 39, 42.

theory, in the person of Christ; while, on the common theory, there were four things combined in Him, whereby He became not a man, but a man-God,[1] a *monstrum*, resembling the fabulous animals of Greek mythology. True, it might be objected that the third element in the person of Christ, the *nous*, was not human but divine. But Apollinaris was ready with his reply. "The mind in Christ," he said in effect, "is at once divine and human; the Logos is at once the express image of God and the prototype of humanity." This appears to be what he meant when he asserted that the humanity of Christ was *eternal*,—a part of his system which was much misunderstood by his opponents, who supposed it to have reference to the *body* of Christ.[2] There is no reason to believe that Apollinaris meant to teach that our Lord's flesh was eternal, and that He brought it with Him from heaven, and therefore was not really born of the Virgin Mary; though some of his adherents may have held such opinions. His idea was, that Christ was the *celestial man; celestial*, because divine; *man*, not merely as God incarnate, but because the Divine Spirit is at the same time essentially human. In the combination whereby Christ's person was constituted there was thus nothing incongruous, though there was something unique; the divine being fitted in its own nature, and having, as it were, a yearning to become man. This was the speculative element in the Apollinarian theory misapprehended by contemporaries, better understood, and in some quarters more sympathized with, now.[3]

The third advantage accruing from his theory, that of making God in very deed the subject of a suffering human experience, Apollinaris reckoned of no less value than the other two. It seemed to him of fundamental importance,

[1] Greg. c. 49.

[2] So Gregory Nys., Athanasius, and Epiphanius: in the works referred to in previous note.

[3] See Dorner, *Person of Christ*, div. i. vol. ii. p. 372 (Clark's translation). Dorner's account of the Apollinarian theory is very full, able, and candid, and, as far as I can judge, satisfactory; though, as we have only fragments to judge from, there must always be uncertainty on some points. For passages out of the wo k of Apollinaris bearing on the subject of the affinity of the divine and the human natures, see cap. 48-55 in Greg. *Adv. Apoll.* Baur's account (*Die Lehre von der Dreieinigkeit*, vol. i.) is less reliable.

in a soteriological point of view, that the person of Christ should be so conceived of, that everything belonging to His earthly history, both the miracles and the sufferings, should be predicable directly and exclusively of the divine element in Him. On this account he was equally opposed to the Photinian and to the ordinary orthodox view of Christ's person: to the former, because it made Christ merely a divine man (ἄνθρωπος ἔνθεος),[1] the human, not the divine, being the personal element; to the latter, because it virtually divided Christ into two persons, a divine and a human, referring to the divine only the miracles of power and knowledge, and ascribing to the human everything of the nature of suffering. On either theory, it appeared to him, the end of the Incarnation remained unaccomplished; man was not redeemed, unless it could be said that God tasted death. A man liable to the common corruption cannot save the world; neither can we be saved, even by God, unless He mix with us. He must become an impeccable man, and die, and rise again, and so destroy the empire of death over all; He must die as God, for the death of a mere man does not destroy death, but only the death of one over whom death cannot prevail.[2] Such thoughts as these appeared to Apollinaris arguments in favour of his theory; for he maintained that on the common theory the divine had really no part in Christ's sufferings;[3] a statement not without some plausibility in reference to the orthodox Fathers, whose views regarding the impassibility of the divine nature were very rigid. To rectify this defect was a leading, we may say the leading, aim of the new Christology. Gregory of Nyssa, in his polemical treatise against Apollinaris, states that the whole scope of the work in which the latter promulgated his opinions was to make the deity of the only-begotten Son mortal, and to show that not the human in Christ endured suffering, but the impassi-

---

[1] Greg. c. 6: Τὸ ἄνθρωπον ἔνθεον τὸν Χριστὸν ὀνομάζειν, ἐναντίον εἶναι ταῖς ἀποστολικαῖς διδασκαλίαις· ἀλλότριον δὲ τῶν συνόδων· Παῦλον δέ (of Samosata) καὶ Φωτεινὸν καὶ Μάρκελλον τῆς τοιαύτης διαστροφῆς κατάρξαι (these men began this perverse way of speaking of Christ).

[2] Greg. cap. 51, 52.   [3] Greg. cap. 27.

ble and unchangeable nature in Him, converted to participation in suffering.[1]

It is easy to understand what a fascination a theory like the foregoing would have for a speculative mind; nor are we surprised to learn that, on its being promulgated, it was received with enthusiasm by many. It was a theory whose appearance in the course of doctrinal development was to be looked for, and in some respects even to be desired; and it could not have an author and advocate better qualified by his gifts and character to do it full justice, and secure for it the respectful and serious consideration of the Church, than it found in Apollinaris. Yet the defects of this theory are very glaring. One radical error is the assumption that to get rid of sin we must get rid of a human mind in Christ. Gregory of Nyssa, referring to the apostolic dictum, "tempted in all points like as we are, without sin," very pertinently remarks, parenthetically, "but mind is not sin."[2] If it *be* sin, then, to be consistent, the theory ought to take away mind not merely from Christ, but from human nature itself. Yet Apollinaris is so far from doing this, that he represents mind (νοῦς) as the leading element in human nature (τὸ κυριώτατον).[3] It is because νοῦς is τὸ κυριώτατον that its omission is necessary in order to secure the *unity* of Christ's person. If Christ consists of two perfect, that is, complete, unmutilated natures, then, according to Apollinaris, He is two persons, not one. It thus appears that to the *metaphysical* perfection of human nature νοῦς is indispensable, while for its *moral* perfection the removal of the same element is equally indispensable; a view which on the one hand involves a Manichaean attitude towards the first creation, and on the other hand makes a theory of sanctification impossible. The old man is inevitably bad because he is free; and the new man is to be made good, either by the mutilation of his nature, or by a magical overbearing of his nature by divine power.

Another manifest defect in the theory is, that it adopts

---

[1] Greg. cap. 5.
[2] Cap. 11: ὁ δὲ νοῦς ἁμαρτία οὐκ ἔστι.
[3] Greg. Nys. *Adv. Apoll.* c. 23: Christ was οὐκ ἄνθρωπος, ἀλλ' ὡς ἄνθρωπος διότι οὐκ ὁμοούσιος τῷ ἀνθρώπῳ κατὰ τὸ κυριώτατον.

means for excluding the possibility of sin in Christ, which defeat another of its own chief ends, that, viz., of making the Divine partaker of suffering. Place is found for the physical fact of death, but no place is found for the *moral* suffering connected with temptation. Christ is so carefully guarded from sin, that He is not even allowed to know what it is to be tempted to sin. The author of the theory is so frightened by that Arian scarecrow, the τρεπτόν, that he solves the problem of Christ's sinlessness by annihilating the conditions under which the problem has to be worked out. There is no human *nous*, no freedom, no struggle; the fragment of human nature assumed yields itself passively to the sweet control of the Divine Spirit, which dwells within it as its active principle;[1] the so-called temptations and struggles recorded in the Gospels are reduced to a show and a sham, and a cheap virtue results, devoid of all human interest, and scarcely deserving the name. It is true Apollinaris did what he could to prevent this consequence, and to make Deity enter fully and really into the conditions of human life, by regarding the Incarnation as involving for the Logos a self-division (διαίρεσις), by which He entered into an inequality with Himself, and was at once infinite and finite, impassible and capable of becoming partaker in human sufferings and conflicts; not, however, by a physical necessity, but by a free act of love.[2] But this device of a double aspect in the Logos falls short of the purpose. To arrive at the result aimed at—a real and full participation in suffering,—the theory must go further, and

---

[1] Greg. Nys. *Adv. Apoll.* c. 41: ἀβιάστως, φησί, τὴν σάρκα ἡ θεότης προσάγεται. Gregory takes αβιάστως as meaning freely: τὸ ἀβίαστον, δηλαδή, τὸ ἑκούσιον λέγει. But Apollinaris uses the word to express the pliancy of the flesh, resulting from its having no will of its own. The flesh was literally as clay in the hands of the Logos as the Potter.

[2] Such seems to be the meaning of the following obscure extracts from Apollinaris in Gregory's work, c. 29: Διαιρῶν μὲν τὴν ἐνέργειαν κατὰ σάρκα, ἰσῶν δὲ κατὰ πνεῦμα . . . Ὅπερ ἔχει τὴν ἐν δυνάμει πάλιν ἰσότητα καὶ τὴν κατὰ σάρκα τῆς ἐνεργείας διαίρεσιν· c. 58: Ὁ Σωτὴρ πέπονθε πεῖναν, καὶ δίψαν, καὶ κάματον, καὶ ἀγωνίαν, καὶ λύπην· . . . Καὶ πάσχει τὸ ἀπαράδεκτον πάθους, οὐκ ἀνάγκῃ φύσεως ἀβουλήτου, καθάπερ ἄνθρωπος, ἀλλὰ ἀκολουθίᾳ φύσεως. Gregory looks upon the words from οὐκ ἀνάγκῃ as unintelligible, and asks what is the difference between necessity of nature and consequence of nature.

convert the Logos into an ordinary human soul, having the advantage of starting on its career free from sinful bias, but exposed like other souls to temptation, and possessing only a power not to sin (*posse non peccare*), and this would bring it round to meet the opposite extreme, the hated Arian fallibility.

The argument against the Apollinarian theory was conducted by the Fathers chiefly from a soteriological point of view. Gregory Nazianzen put the matter in a nut-shell when he said: "That which is not assumed is not healed."¹ The patristic theory of redemption was, that Christ redeemed man, so to speak, by *sample*, presenting to God in His own person the first-fruits of a renewed humanity. Athanasius contrasts the Apollinarian and the orthodox theories of redemption thus: "Ye say that believers are saved by similitude and imitation, not by renovation, or by first-fruits."² Salvation being by first-fruits, of course the Saviour must be physically like His brethren in soul as well as in body, otherwise the sample would not be like the bulk. As Cyril put it: Christ must take flesh that He might deliver us from death; and He must take a human soul to deliver us from sin, destroying sin in humanity by living a human life free from all sin,—rendering the soul He assumed superior to sin by dyeing it, and tinging it with the moral firmness and immutability of His own divine nature.³ But while insisting on this view of salvation, the opponents of Apollinaris pointed out that even on his own soteriological theory it behoved Christ to assume a perfect humanity. How, asked Athanasius very pertinently, can there be imitation tending to perfection unless there be first a perfect exemplar?⁴

---

¹ *Epist.* I, *ad Cledonium*: τὸ γὰρ ἀπρόσληπτον ἀθεράπευτον.

² *De Salutari Adventu Jesu Christi* (about the middle): Ἀλλὰ λέγετε τῇ ὁμοιώσει καὶ τῇ μιμήσει σώζεσθαι τοὺς πιστεύοντας, καὶ οὐ τῇ ἀνακαινίσει, καὶ τῇ ἀπαρχῇ.

³ *De Incarnatione Unigeniti*, tom. viii. Opera, Migne, p. 1214.

⁴ *De Incarnatione Christi* (near the beginning): μίμησις δὲ πῶς ἂν γένοιτο πρὸς τελειότητα, μὴ προϋπαρξάσης τῆς ἀνενδεοῦς τελειότητος. On the Apollinarian theory of redemption, see Dorner, who, in opposition to Baur and Möhler, denies that it was a mere doctrine of imitation. Cyril seems to have looked on it in this light, for in the Dialogue on the Incarnation he makes one

The Nestorian controversy, which broke out about half a century after the death of Apollinaris,[1] may be regarded as the natural sequel of the controversy concerning the integrity of Christ's humanity, whereof a brief account has just been given. The Church, by the voice of Councils and of its representative men, having declared in favour of a complete unmutilated humanity, the next question calling for decision was, How do the two natures in Christ, the divine and the human, stand related to each other? On this momentous question the Antioch school of theologians took up a position diametrically opposed to that of Apollinaris. Whereas Apollinaris had sacrificed the integrity of Christ's humanity for the sake of the unity of His person, the Syrian theologians, represented by Theodore of Mopsuestia, and by his pupils, Nestorius, patriarch of Constantinople, and Theodoret, bishop of Cyrus, seemed disposed to sacrifice the unity of the person in favour of the integrity of the humanity. Their attitude was substantially this: they were determined at all hazards to hold by the reality of the two factors, and especially of the humanity, the latter being the thing assailed; and to admit only such a union as was compatible with such reality. Christ must be a man, at all events, whatever more; a man in all respects, save sin, like other men, having a true body, a reasonable soul, and a free will, liable to temptation, and capable of real, not merely apparent, growth, not only in stature, but in wisdom and virtue. Such was the Christ they found in the New Testament, such the Christ who could lay hold of human sympathies; in such a Christ, therefore, they were determined to believe, both as men devoted to exegetical studies, and as men of an ethical rather than a theological bent of mind.

With the resolute maintenance of the reality of Christ's manhood, the theologians of Antioch did not find it possible to accept of any union of the natures, except one of an

of the interlocutors ask: "What if they should say that our state needed only the sojourning of the Only-begotten among us? but as He wished to be seen of mortals, and to have intercourse with men, and to show to us the way of evangelic life, He put on (œconomically) flesh like ours, as the divine in its own nature cannot be seen."—Cy. Op., Migne, viii. p. 1212.

[1] Between 380 and 392 A. D.; exact date uncertain.

ethical character. They rejected a physical union (ἕνωσις καθ' οὐσίαν) because it seemed to them inevitably to involve a mixture of natures (κρᾶσις), and therefore to lead either to a dissipation of the humanity, or to a degradation of the unchangeable divine element, or to both. In his animadversions on the second of Cyril's twelve anathemas against Nestorius (which condemns those who deny a union by hypostasis, hypostasis being taken in the sense of substance), Theodoret says: "If by union (καθ' ὑπόστασιν) he means that a mixture of flesh and Deity has taken place, we confidently contradict him, and charge him with blasphemy. For of necessity confusion follows mixture; and confusion ensuing, destroys the properties of either nature. For things mixed do not remain what they were before. But if mixture took place, God did not remain God, nor could the temple (His humanity) be recognised as a temple; but God was temple, and temple was God."[1] From jealousy of this mixture, supposed to be taught by their opponents, the Antiochians disliked the term Θεοτόκος (mother of God) applied to the mother of our Lord, which was the occasion of the outbreak of the controversy, and became famous as the battle-cry of orthodoxy in the fierce war against Nestorian heretics. They did not absolutely deny the applicability of the epithet; but they looked on it with disfavour, as extremely liable to abuse, and fitted to create the erroneous impression that the Word literally became flesh; and they preferred to give Mary the title of Χριστοτόκος (mother of Christ), and to Christ Himself the title Θεοφόρος (God-bearer); their idea of the Incarnation being that Mary gave birth to a human being, to whom, from the first moment of His conception, the Logos joined Himself.[2] This union, formed at the earliest possible period, between the Logos and the man Jesus, those who followed the Nestorian tendency described

[1] Cyril. *Apologeticus contra Theodoretum*, pro. xii. capitibus, Anath. ii.

[2] Cyril quotes Nestorius, saying: If any simple person likes to call Mary Θεοτόκος, I don't object; only don't let him call the Virgin a goddess, μόνον μὴ ποιείτω τὴν παρθένον θεάν.—*Adv. Nestorium* (Cy. Op., Migne, t. ix. p. 57). Nestorius was jealous of the heathenish tendency of the name, mother of God, not without reason. Theodoret, in his animadversions on Anathema i., condemning those who deny to Mary the title Θεοτόκος, apologises for those who had been jealous of the word by saying, "We, following the Gospel statement, assert that God the Word was not naturally made flesh, or changed into flesh, but He as

by a variety of phrases, all proceeding on the idea of an ethical as opposed to a physical union. They called it an inhabitation;[1] and the general nature of the inhabitation, as distinct from that by which God dwells in all men, through His omnipresent essence and energy, they indicated by the phrase, " by good pleasure " (καθ' εὐδοκίαν); and this indwelling by good pleasure in Christ they further discriminated from God's indwelling in other good men, by representing it as attaining in Him the highest possible degree. This indwelling of the Logos in Christ was also said to be according to fore-knowledge,[2] the Logos choosing the man Jesus to be in a peculiar sense His temple, because He knew beforehand what manner of man He should be. Such was the way Theodore of Mopsuestia, in particular, viewed the union. Among other favourite phrases current in the same school were such as these: union by conjunction;[3] union by relation,[4] as in the case of husband and wife; union in worth, honour, authority;[5] union by consent of will;[6] union by community of name;[7] and so forth; for it were endless to enumerate the Nestorian tropes or modes of union.

It is manifest from these and the like phrases that the Nestorian manner of conceiving the person of Christ really involved a duality of persons. In Christ were united by physical juxtaposition and ethical affinity two persons: one, the Son of God by nature; the other, a Son of God by adoption. Yet Nestorius and his friends did not wish to teach a duality of persons or of sons, and would not allow their opponents to represent them as teaching such a doctrine. Their position as defined by themselves was: there are two hypostases, but only one person (πρόσωπον), one Son, one Christ.[8] Nestorius, as quoted by his great

---

sumed flesh, and tabernacled among us, according to the word of the evangelist, and the teaching of Paul, when he speaks of Christ *taking* the form of servant (μορφὴν δούλου λαβών)."—Cyril. *Apolog. contra Theodoret.* Anath. i. Op. Migne, ix. p. 392. [1] ἐνοίκησις.

[2] κατὰ πρόγνοιαν. [3] συνάφεια. [4] ἕνωσις σχετική.

[5] κατ' ἀξίαν, καθ' ὁμοτιμίαν, καθ' αὐθεντίαν.

[6] κατὰ ταυτοβουλίαν. [7] καθ' ὁμωνυμίαν.

[8] Cyril. *Apolog. contra Theodoret.* Anath. iii.: ἓν μὲν πρόσωπον καὶ ἕνα Υἱὸν καὶ Χριστὸν ὁμολογεῖν εὐσεβές· δύο δὲ τὰς ἐνώσεως ὑποστάσεις, εἴτουν φύσεις, λέγειν οὐκ ἄτοπον, ἀλλὰ κατ' αἰτίαν ἀκόλουθον.

opponent Cyril, said: "There is no division as to conjunction, dignity, Sonship, or as to participation in the name Christ; there is only a division of the Deity and the humanity. Christ as Christ is indivisible; for we have not two Christs, or two Sons: there is not with us a first and a second, nor one and another, nor one Son and another Son; but one and the same is double, not in dignity, but in nature."[1] Hence the question, Were Nestorius and those who thought with him *Nestorians* in the theological sense? may be answered both affirmatively and negatively: negatively, if you look to what they said they held and honestly *wished to hold;* affirmatively, if you look to the logical consistency of their system. They made Christ as much an independent, self-subsistent man as if He were altogether distinct from the Logos; they described the union between Him and the Logos by phrases implying only a very close moral affinity; so that the natural inference would seem to be, that the Logos was *personally* as distinct from Jesus as from any other good man, though more closely *related* to Him than to any other man. But they refused to draw the inference; they declared there were not in Christ one and another (ἄλλος καὶ ἄλλος), but only one who was double.

The great opponent of the Antiochian Christology, Cyril, archbishop of Alexandria, held its advocates responsible for the logical consequences of their theory; and the strong side of his polemic is the manner in which he brings great principles to bear against the doctrine of a divided personality. Specially noticeable is the use which he makes of the idea of *kenosis,* in arguing against that doctrine. Again and again the thought recurs in his various controversial writings, that if the Logos did not become man, but merely assumed a man, then what took place was not a kenosis of the Divine Subject, but, on the contrary, an exaltation of the human subject. Thus, in one place he says: "If, as our adversaries think, the only-begotten Word of God, taking a human being from the seed of David, procured that He should be formed in the holy Virgin, and joined Him to Himself, and caused Him to experience

[1] Cyril. *Contra Nestorium,* lib. ii. c. v.

death, and, raising Him from the dead, conveyed Him up to heaven, and seated Him on the right hand of God,—vainly, in that case, as it appears, is He said by the holy Fathers, and by us, and by all inspired Scripture, to have become man; for this and nothing else John means when he says, the Word became flesh (ὁ λόγος σὰρξ ἐγένετο). For on this theory the whole mystery of the economy in the flesh is turned to the contrary, and what we see is not the Logos, being God by nature and coming from God, letting Himself down to *kenosis*, taking the form of a servant, and humbling Himself; but, on the contrary, a man raised to the glory of Deity, and to pre-eminence over all, and taking the form of God, and becoming exalted to be an assessor on the throne with the Father."¹ In another place we find him arguing against the Nestorian doctrine of assumption in favour of his own doctrine of union by hypostasis, to the effect that the kenosis requires that the human attributes should be predicable of the Divine Subject. "Do you think," he asks his opponent Theodoret, "that St. Paul meant to deceive the saints when he wrote, 'that, being rich, He became poor on our account'? But who is the rich One, and how became He poor? If, as they make bold to think and say, a man was assumed by God, how can He who was assumed and adorned with preternatural honours be said to have become poor? He only can be said to have been impoverished who is rich as God. But how? we must consider that question. For, being confessedly unchangeable in nature, He was not converted into the nature of flesh, laying aside His own proper nature; but He remained what He was, that is, God. Where, then, shall we see the humility of impoverishment? Think you in this, that He took one like ourselves, as the creatures of Nestorius dare to say? And what sort of poverty and exinanition would that be which consisted in His wishing to honour some man like us? For God is not injured in any way by doing good. How, then, became He poor? Thus, that being God by nature, and Son of God the Father, He became man, and was born of the seed of David according to the flesh, and subjected Himself to the servile,

---

¹ *Quod unus sit Christus*, Opera, tom. viii., Migne, pp. 1279-83.

that is, to the human measure;[1] and having become man, He was not ashamed of the measure of humanity. For, not having refused to become like us, how should He refuse those things by which it would appear that He had really for our sakes been made like us? If, therefore, we separate Him from the humanities, whether things or words, we differ in no respect from those who all but rob Him of flesh, and wholly overturn the mystery of the Incarnation."[2] Supposing some one to object, that it was altogether unworthy of God to weep, to fear death, to refuse the cup, he goes on to say: "When the exinanition appears mean to thee, admire the more the charity of the Son. What you call little, He did voluntarily for thee. He wept humanly, that He might dry thy tears; He feared economically, permitting the flesh to suffer the things proper to it, that He might make us bold: He refused the cup, that the cross might convict the Jews of impiety; He is said to have been weak as to His humanity, that He might remove thy weakness; He offered prayers, that He might render the ears of the Father accessible to thee; He slept, that thou mightst learn not to sleep in temptation, but be watchful unto prayers."[3]

I have made these quotations at some length, because, while fully illustrating the style of Cyril's argumentation from the *kenosis* against the Nestorian theory, they at the same time set forth clearly his conception of the kenosis as resulting from a hypostatical union, in virtue of which all the humanities in Christ's earthly history were predicable of the Logos as the personal subject. Looking now at these passages and others of similar import from a controversial point of view, there can be no doubt that they have great argumentative force against the Nestorian view of Christ's person *as conceived by Cyril*. Yet the advocates of the controverted theory did not feel themselves mortally wounded by such arguments. On the contrary, they in turn argued from the *kenosis* against their antagonist. In his animadversions on Cyril's third anathema, which asserts

---

[1] δουλοπρεπὲς ὑπέδυ μέτρον, τουτέστι τὸ ἀνθρώπινον.
[2] *Apolog. contra Theodoret, pro XII. capitibus*, Anath. x. tom. ix. p. 440.
[3] *Apolog. contra Theodoret.* Anath. x. tom. ix. p. 441.

a physical as opposed to a merely moral union of the natures, Theodoret objects that such a union makes the kenosis a matter of physical necessity, instead of a voluntary act of condescension. " Nature," he says, " is a thing of a compulsory character and without will. For example, we hunger physically, not suffering this willingly, but by necessity; for certainly those living in poverty would cease begging if they had it in their power not to hunger. In like manner we thirst, sleep, breathe by nature; for these are all without will; and he who does not experience these things, of necessity dies. If, therefore, the union of the form of Son to the form of a servant was physical, then God the Logos was joined to the form of a servant as compelled by a certain necessity, not in the exercise of philanthropy, and the universal Lawgiver shall be found complying with compulsory laws, contrary to the teaching of Paul, who says: 'He humbled Himself, taking the form of a servant.' The words ἑαυτὸν ἐκένωσε point to a voluntary act."[1] To the same effect John of Antioch, criticizing the same anathema, speaking in the name of the whole Syrian church, asks: " If the union is physical, where is the grace, where the divine mystery? For natures once formed by God are subject to the reign of necessity."[2]

Now Cyril certainly did recognise a reign of physical law, both in the constitution of Christ's person and in the course of His incarnate history. He held that the person was not secure against dissolution unless it were based on physical laws, rather than on a gracious relation of the Logos to the man Jesus, such as the Nestorian party advocated.[3] And he considered that the Logos, in becoming man by a voluntary act, gave to physical laws a certain dominion over Himself: took humanity, on the understanding that its laws, conditions, or measures, were to be respected. In this very act of voluntary self-subjection to

[1] Cyril. *Ap. c. Theod.* Anath. iii. Anath. iii. runs: Εἴ τις ἐπὶ τοῦ ἑνὸς Χριστοῦ διαιρεῖ τὰς ὑποστάσεις μετὰ τὴν ἕνωσιν, μόνῃ συνάπτων αὐτὰς συναφείᾳ τῇ κατὰ τὴν ἀξίαν ἤγουν αὐθεντίαν ἢ δυναστείαν, καὶ οὐχὶ δὴ μᾶλλον σύνοδον τὴν καθ' ἕνωσιν φυσικήν.

[2] Cyril. *Apolog. pro XII. capitibus contra Orientales,* Anath. iii.

[3] *Quod unus sit Christus,* t. viii. p. 1296: οὐ γὰρ ἀνύποπτον εἰς ἀποβολήν, ὁ μὴ φυσικοῖς ἐρηρείσται νόμοις.

the laws of humanity did the kenosis consist. By this principle Cyril explained the facts of birth, growth in stature, and experience of sinless infirmities, such as hunger, thirst, sleep, weariness, etc., in the earthly history of the Saviour. "It was not impossible," he says in one place, "for the omnipotent Logos, having resolved for our sakes to become man, to have formed a body for Himself by his own power, refusing birth from a woman, even as Adam was formed; but because that might give occasion to unbelievers to calumniate the Incarnation, saying it was not real, therefore it was necessary that He should go through the ordinary laws of human nature."[1] With reference to physical growth, he says in another place: "It was not impossible that God, the Word begotten of the Father, should lift the body united to Him out of its very swaddling-clothes and raise it up to the measure of mature manhood. But this would have been a thaumaturgical proceeding, and incongruous to the laws of the economy; for the mystery was accomplished *noiselessly*. Therefore, in accordance with the economy, He permitted the measures of humanity to prevail over Himself."[2] In a third passage he applies the same principle of compliance with the laws of humanity to explain a group of infirmities, including the *appearance of ignorance* (a point of which I shall speak more particularly forthwith). "With humanity, the only-begotten Word bore all that pertains to humanity, save sin. But ignorance of the future agrees to the measures of humanity; therefore, while as God knowing all, as man He does not shake Himself clear of the appearance of ignorance as suitable to humanity. For as He, being the life of all, received bodily food, not despising the measure of the kenosis (He is also described as sleeping and being weary); so likewise, knowing all, He yet was not ashamed to ascribe to Himself the ignorance which is congruous to humanity. For all that is human became His, sin alone excepted."[3]

[1] *Adv. Nestor.* lib. i. cap. i. t. ix. p. 22: κεχώρηκεν ἀναγκαίως διὰ τῶν ἀνθρωπίνης φύσεως νόμων.

[2] *Quod unus Christus,* t. viii. p. 1332: Ἐτελεῖτο γὰρ ἀψοφητὶ τὸ μυστήριον (a fine expression!). Ἤφίει δὴ οὖν οἰκονομικῶς τοῖς τῆς ἀνθρωπότητος μέτροις ἐφ' ἑαυτῷ τὸ κρατεῖν.

[3] *Adv. Anthropomorphitas,* c. xiv.; vid. Appendix, Note A.

In advocating this reign of physical law, Cyril proclaimed an important truth, and committed no offence against the freedom of the Logos. His fault rather lay in restricting the reign of law to the material sphere, excluding it from the intellectual or moral. This in point of fact he did. He recognised no real growth in wisdom or in character in Christ. He felt, indeed, that the claims of the kenosis extended to the mind as well as to the body, and he made every possible effort to satisfy those claims; but he did not see his way to letting the intellectual and moral growth of Christ be anything more than an *appearance*. The union between the Logos and the humanity was so close and of such a nature, in his view, that the Logos *per se* could not be conceived as possessing knowledge of which the incarnate person was not also consciously possessed. If, as all admitted, ignorance could not be predicated of the former, neither could it be predicated of the latter. To ascribe to Christ real ignorance was in effect to dissolve the union, and to make Him a man connected with the Logos by an intimate ethical relation. Cyril was fully sensible of the critical importance of the problem, how the ascription to Christ in the gospel history, of growth in knowledge as a child, and of ignorance even in ripe manhood, was to be understood. He returns to it again and again; he discusses it in at least eight different places of his extant works, sometimes at considerable length; he exercises his ingenuity in inventing forms of language by which to express his idea: but he never gets beyond *appearance*. The kenosis is real in the physical region, it is doketic in the intellectual. Practically the position in which Christ is placed is this: the measures of the kenosis require Him to *seem* ignorant, as ignorance belongs to the state He has assumed—being an attribute of ordinary humanity; but the Logos is incapable of so adapting Himself to the human nature He has assumed, that the ignorance of the theanthropic person shall in any case be real, even the child's growth in knowledge being in reality only a gradual manifestation to others of a knowledge already inwardly complete. In every one of the passages in which Cyril discusses the question, this is the way the case is put. Now he represents Christ as *usefully pretending* not to know the day of judgment, now as not shunning the appearance of ignorance as *decent* in one who had assumed humanity, now as *economizing* or *schematizing* in *speaking* of Himself as ignorant. The growth of the boy in knowledge is resolved into a gradual revelation of Himself to the world, out of respect to the physical law by which in ordinary men bodily and mental growth progress together; this law in Christ's case being complied with by a real growth of the body, and by a studied appearance of growth in the mind. "We teach," says Cyril, in his second *oratio ad reginas*, putting the matter as precisely as possible,—"we teach that it was agreeable to the measures of the kenosis that Christ should receive bodily growth and gradual consolidation and strengthening of the bodily organs, and likewise that He should seem to be filled with wisdom; because it was most meet that the manifestation of His indwelling wisdom should keep pace with the increase in His bodily stature."[1]

At this point the views of Cyril stand in the sharpest possible contrast to those of the Oriental theologians, who took the Gospel statements in their plain, natural sense, and believed that Christ grew in knowledge as well as in stature, and made progress in virtue through real conflict with temptation. The difference in this respect between the two schools was the natural result of their respective points of view. The Alexandrians started from the divine side, and made the humanity as real as seemed compatible with its hypostatic union to the Logos; the Orientals started from the human side, and made the union between the man and the Logos as intimate as was compatible with the reality of the humanity. Both schools failed on different sides: the Orientals, on the side of the unity of the person; the Alexandrians, on the side of the reality of the human nature and experience. Both failed from one cause—overconfident dogmatism as to the conditions and possibilities

[1] The question concerning the knowledge of Christ being important, and the views of Cyril having been misunderstood by some, *e. g.* Forbes in his *Instructiones historico-theologicae*, I deem it advisable to give the passages in Cyril's work bearing on the topic in full. These accordingly, eight in all, of which Forbes quotes only three, the reader will find in Appendix, Note A, with an English translation in parallel columns.

of the Incarnation. Both started from the assumption that a union such as is implied in God becoming man, as distinct from that formed by God assuming a man, is not compatible with a completely real human experience. It would have been wiser in both to have accepted the facts, whether they could explain them or not. Had Cyril, in particular, taken this course, he would have escaped moral and intellectual doketism; he would not have felt it necessary to place Christ in the unworthy position of being obliged, out of regard to decency, to feign an ignorance which was not real; he would have conceived it possible that the Logos might be conscious of the child Jesus, while the child was unconscious of the Logos, or entirely without self-consciousness; he would not only have taught a gradual revelation of the Logos through Jesus to others, but, with his predecessor Athanasius, he would have admitted that the Logos revealed Himself to Himself in Jesus,[1] and grew in Himself; the Wisdom of God building in Jesus a house for Himself, and causing the house to make progress in wisdom and grace. How these things can be, it may be difficult, or even impossible, to explain—more ways of explaining them than one have been proposed; but we must not suspend acceptance of facts till we have found a theory which accounts for them; we must accept the facts first, and seek for our theory at leisure.

The manner in which Cyril disposed of the problem of mental growth may be regarded as an index of the general character of his Christology. That Christology has been characterized as *physical* rather than *ethical;*[2] and it may be further described as monophysitical in tendency, though, it must be admitted, not avowedly, for its author repudiated mixture and confusion of the natures, as earnestly as Nestorius repudiated the charge of teaching two Sons.[3] Cyril looked on the divine and the human natures as two

---

[1] Oratio iii., Con. Arianos, c. 52: Καὶ τοῦ λόγου φανεροῦντος ἑαυτὸν ἑαυτῷ. Then a little below in the same place: Εἰ χρὴ δὲ τὸ πιθανῶς μετὰ τοῦ ἀληθοῦς εἰπεῖν, αὐτὸς ἐν ἑαυτῷ προέκοπτε· ἡ σοφία γὰρ ᾠκοδόμησεν ἑαυτῇ οἶκον, καὶ ἐν αὐτῇ, τὸν οἶκον προκόπτειν ἐποίει.

[2] Dorner, *Doctrine of the Person of Christ*, div. ii. vol. i. p. 73.

[3] Vid. Quod unus sit Christus, p. 1260: γέγονεν ἄνθρωπος οὐκ εἰς σάρκα τραπείς, ἢ φυρμὸν ἢ κρᾶσιν, ἢ τι τῶν τοιούτων ἕτερον ὑπομείνας,

elements, or things, as he sometimes calls them,[1] so closely connected that they were as one. He closes his treatise on the unity of Christ's person, confessing one and the same Son, of two things appearing ineffably as one somewhat out of two;[2] and in another place he declares that the incarnate nature of the Logos must be regarded as one after the union, comparing the composite nature successively to that formed by the union of body and soul in an ordinary man, to a live coal, a pearl, and a lily; the Logos being the fire in the coal, the brightness in the pearl, and the sweet odour in the lily.[3] He betrays his monophysitic tendencies also by occasional representations of the relation between the two natures, somewhat akin to the Lutheran doctrine of the communication of properties *(communicatio idiomatum)*. He speaks of the humanity as deified;[4] of the Logos as collecting both natures into one, and mixing up together the properties of the two;[5] of John the Evangelist as, in the preface of his first Epistle, almost gathering into one the natures, and conducting the virtue of the properties of both, as confluent streams into one common watercourse;[6] of the *flesh* of Christ as endowed with life-giving power.[7] On the other hand, just as in the Lutheran doctrine of communication, while the divine nature communicates some of its properties to the human, the human in turn communicates nothing to the divine. The divine element remains impassible amid the sufferings of the humanity, as heat in a mass of heated iron remains untouched by a stroke through

καθεὶς δὲ μᾶλλον ἑαυτὸν εἰς κένωσιν, etc.; also p. 1292: Ἕτερον μέν τι καὶ ἕτερον θεότης καὶ ἀνθρωπότης ... ἀλλὰ ἦν ἐν Χριστῷ ξένως τε καὶ ὑπὲρ νοῦν εἰς ἑνότητα συνδεδραμηκότα συγχύσεως δίχα καὶ τροπῆς.

[1] πράγματα, in *Apolog. pro XII. cap. contra Orientales*, Anath. iv.; *Quod unus sit Christus*, p. 1254.

[2] *Quod unus sit Christus*, p. 1254.

[3] *Adv. Nestorium*, lib. ii. pp. 60–62: μία γὰρ ἤδη νοεῖται φύσις μετὰ τὴν ἕνωσιν ἡ αὐτοῦ τοῦ λόγου σεσαρκωμένη.

[4] *Thesaurus*, Assertio 28, p. 429: οὕτως ἐν σοφίᾳ προέκοπτεν ἡ ἀνθρωπότης θεοποιουμένη δι' αὐτῆς.

[5] *De Incarnatione Unigeniti*, p. 1244.

[6] *De Incarnatione Unigeniti*, p. 1249: μονονουχὶ καὶ συναγείρων τὰς φύσεις, καὶ εἰς μισγάγκειαν ἄγων τῶν ἑκατέρᾳ πρεπόντων ἰδιωμάτων τὴν δύναμιν.

[7] *Adv. Nest.* lib. iv. cap. v.: σάρκα ζωοποιὸν (ὁ λόγος) ἀπέφηνεν.

which the iron itself is injured.¹ The blending of the natures issues in the weaker being, so to speak, swallowed up by the stronger. The humanity is still there; but it is so exalted and, as it were, transformed by its connection with divinity, that one may hardly dare speak of it as consubstantial with that of ordinary men.²

Such being the character and general tendency of the Cyrillian type of Christology, it was a matter of course that the Nestorian controversy should pass into the *Eutychian Phase*, in which the question at issue was: Are there in the one person of Christ two distinct natures, or only one? Concerning the opinions of Eutyches we have little exact information; but we know enough to be able to say that he had not the honour of originating a new and peculiar heresy. Eutychianism, as expounded by the man from whom it takes its name, was simply Cyrillianism gone mad—monophysitic tendencies carried to extremes, with the characteristic extravagance of a monk who had brooded in his cell over his pet views till they assumed in his heated brain the form of fixed ideas. The party whom Eutyches represented, including the monks of Constantinople and Egypt, and the unscrupulous bishop of Alexandria, Dioscuros, like Cyril, laid a great, one-sided emphasis on the unity of the person, and insisted on regarding all Christ's human experiences as predicable of the Divine Subject who had become incarnate. God, said they, was born; God died. They did not mean by such statements to teach that God, in becoming man, had been changed into flesh, or that the divine nature was in itself passible. They do indeed seem to have indulged in a style of expression which, strictly

---

¹ *Quod unus sit Christus*, p. 1357. Cyril apologizes for this metaphor, in introducing it to illustrate how the divine nature remained impassible amid the sufferings of Christ. Well he might; for the metaphor fails to do justice either to the nature of God or to the nature of suffering. Of course the divine nature cannot suffer as the body suffers; but there is a moral suffering of which God is capable because He is love.

² In one place (*Quod unus sit Christus*, p. 1332) Cyril remarks that the Apostle Paul sometimes seems to shrink from calling Christ a man, instancing those words in the Epistle to the Galatians: " Paul, an apostle, not of men, nor by man, but by Jesus Christ," Gal. i. 1. It is significant that such an interpretation of Paul's words should have occurred to Cyril's mind. It is a straw showing the current of his thoughts.

interpreted, laid them open to the charge of teaching such opinions, if we may rely on the accuracy of the representation of their position given by Theodoret in the work entitled, *Eranistes, or Polymorphos*, and manifestly directed against Eutychian views, though Eutyches is nowhere named. The title of this book sufficiently indicates the opinion entertained by its author of the views it is intended to controvert,[1] suggesting the idea of a piebald system of heterogeneous tenets begged from sundry heresies. In explaining the name he had given his work, Theodoret illustrates his meaning by representing the parties whom he has in his eye as borrowing from Marcion the appropriation of the name Christ to God alone, from Valentine the birth of the Logos by mere transition through Mary, from Apollinaris the union of divinity and humanity into one *nature*, and from Arius and Eunomias the ascription of the passion to the divinity of Christ.[2] It is clear, however, that both in the selection and in the explanation of his title, Theodoret avails himself of a licence permissible in the dialogue form of composition, and draws his characters in bold outline for the sake of effect. His book is virtually a work of fiction, not containing a historical account of the exact opinions of certain individuals, but a free description of the affinities and tendencies of these opinions, intended to show their advocates the ultimate consequences to which they lead. Yet, notwithstanding the high colouring of the preface, the author allows it to appear clearly, in the course of the discussion between the two interlocutors, that the beggar is not so great a heretic as he at first seemed. The monk with the parti-coloured garment has no theory as to how the Logos became man. He simply says, "The Word became flesh; how, He Himself knows."[3] Sticking to the words of the evangelist, as Luther stuck to the words "this is my body" in his sacramentarian controversy with Zuingli, he maintains that Christ, though of two natures, had only one nature after the union; but when asked how the two became one, —whether by chemical union, as in the case of gold and silver combining to form *electron*,—he replied that the union

[1] Ἐρανιστής, beggar; πολύμορφος, many-shaped.
[2] *Vid.* πρόλογος.   [3] *Dialogue* i. p. 7 (Opera, Paris, 1642, vol. iv.).

is not of that kind, that it cannot be explained in words, that it surpasses all comprehension; and only after being further pressed for an answer does he venture to say, "the divinity remains, and the humanity is absorbed by it as a drop of honey is absorbed by the sea;"[1] but when the absorption took place, whether at the conception or after the resurrection, he hardly can tell. He asserts that God suffered; but he admits the divine impassibility, and represents God in Christ as suffering through the flesh, and voluntarily, in gracious love to men.[2]

It is plain from those representations that Eutyches had no distinct definite conception of the constitution of our Lord's person. He *felt* rather than *thought* on the subject of Christology. He did not pretend to comprehend the mystery of the Incarnation, but rather gloried in proclaiming its incomprehensibleness. He knew that God and flesh were altogether different things, and he believed that Christ's flesh was real; but the divinity bulked so large in his eye, that the humanity in comparison vanished into nothing. And if compelled by fact to admit that the humanity was still there, not drunk up like a drop of honey by the sea of the divinity, he refused, at all events, to regard it as on a level with ordinary humanity: reverence protested against calling Christ's divine body *consubstantial* with the bodies of common mortals. It would have been well had the course of events permitted such a man to pass his life in obscurity. But it was otherwise ordered. Eutyches became the representative of a theory which engaged the attention of three Synods; being condemned by the first,[3] approved by the second,[4] and re-condemned and finally disposed of as a heresy by the third, the famous Œcumenical Council of Chalcedon, whose decree is quoted at length at the commencement of the present lecture.

The policy of that Council was to steer a middle course between Nestorianism and Eutychianism; the former being conceived as teaching two persons in Christ, the latter as

---

[1] *Dialogue* ii. pp. 67, 77.   [2] *Dialogue* iii. p. 121.
[3] Held at Constantinople, A.D. 448.
[4] Held at Ephesus, A.D. 499; called the Robber Synod on account of the violent character of its proceedings.

teaching that there was not only but one person, but, moreover, only one nature; the one nature being predominantly divine, and, in so far as human, not like the nature of other men. Between the two extremes, so conceived, there was plenty of room for a middle course, and no very skilful pilotage was needed to keep the vessel within the limits of safe navigation. The pilot in this emergency, as is well known, was the Roman Bishop Leo, whose letter to Flavian, patriarch of Constantinople, concerning the errors of Eutyches, guided the deliberations and fixed the judgment of the Fathers assembled at Chalcedon, and thus became an epoch-making document in the history of Christology. The substance of that celebrated epistle is as follows:— The Son of God became man by birth from the Virgin Mary, and in the incarnate Word two natures were combined into one person, each nature retaining its distinct property. For the deliverance of men from sin, an inviolable nature was united to a passible nature, that one and the same Mediator between God and man, the man Christ Jesus, might be able to die in the one, and might be incapable of dying in the other. Thus, in the entire and perfect nature of a true man true God was born *totus in suis, totus in nostris*, the *nostra* including everything but sin. This assumption of servile form by the Son of God, while exalting the humanity of Christ, did not diminish His divinity; for the kenosis by which the Lord of all willed to become one of mortals was not a loss of power, but an act of condescending compassion,[1] which, so far from introducing an alteration into God, only demonstrated the unchangeableness of His will, which cannot be deprived of its benignity, and which refused to be baffled by the wiles of the devil aiming at the destruction of mankind. The Incarnation, being a fulfilment of divine love, involved at the same time for the Son of God no loss of divine glory. He descended from the celestial abode, not receding from the glory of His Father;[2] the immensity of His majesty was simply veiled by the assumption of a servile form. On the other hand, as God was not changed by compassion.

---

[1] Inclinatio fuit miserationis, non defectio potestatis.—*Epist.* c. 3.
[2] De coelesti sede descendens, et a Paternâ gloriâ non recedens.—*Epist.* c. 4.

so man was not consumed by dignity.[1] He who was true God was also true man—there was no lie in the union; the humility of the man and the altitude of Deity were co-existent in the same person. Each nature in Christ performed in communion with the other what was congruous to itself, the Word doing what suited the Word, and the flesh what suited the flesh; the former coruscating with miracles, the latter submitting to injuries; the Word not receding from equality in glory with His Father, the flesh not leaving the nature of our race. While the natures continue distinct in their properties, yet, in virtue of the unity of the person, things are sometimes predicated of the one which in strictness belong to the other. The Son of man is said to have descended from heaven, in allusion to the Incarnation; and the Son of God is said to have been crucified and buried, though He suffered these things not in His divinity, but in the infirmity of human nature.[2]

It is easy to recognise in this letter of Leo the source of the formula framed and adopted by the Council of Chalcedon. The letter and the formula are virtually one From the "*totus in suis, totus in nostris*" of the letter comes the "perfect in Deity and the same perfect in humanity" of the formula; and the ἀσυγχύτως, ἀτρέπτως, ἀδιαιρέτως, ἀχωρίστως[3] of the formula do but condense into four words the various phrases scattered up and down the letter, in which the writer sets forth the distinctness and integrity of the two natures on the one hand, and their intimate, inseparable union in one person on the other. If, now, we inquire how far the letter and the formula together were fitted to put an end to controversy, it must be admitted that they did at least indicate the cardinal points of a true Christology, in which all controversialists should agree. They laid down these two fundamental propositions: Christ must be regarded as one person, the common subject of all predicates, human and divine; and in Christ must be recognised

---

[1] Sicut enim Deus non mutatur miseratione: ita homo non consumitur dignitate.—*Epist.* c. 4.

[2] Propter hanc unitatem personae in utraque natura intelligendam, et Filius hominis legitur descendisse de coelo, et rursus Filius Dei crucifixus dicitur ac sepultus.—*Epist.* c. 5.

[3] Without confusion, unchangeably, indivisibly, inseparably.

two distinct natures, the divine and the human—the divine not converted into the human, the human not absorbed into the divine; the latter side of the second proposition, the integrity and reality of the humanity, viz., being chiefly emphasized, as the state of the controversy required. But they did little more than this. Leo and the Council told men what they should believe, but they gave little aid to faith by showing how the unity of the person and the distinctness of the natures were compatible with each other; aid which, if it could be had, was urgently needed, for the whole controversy may be said to have arisen from a felt inability to combine the unity and the duality,—those who emphasized the unity failing to do justice to the duality, and those who felt compelled to insist strongly on the integrity of Christ's humanity not knowing well how to reconcile therewith the unity of His person. Aid of this kind was not to be looked for, indeed, in the decree of a Council, but it might perhaps have been reasonably expected from an epistle which almost assumed the dimensions of a theological treatise. Leo, however, makes no attempt at a solution of the problem, but contents himself with stating its conditions. Certain points of critical importance he passes over in silence. For example, he says nothing on the question of Christ's knowledge, with which Cyril grappled so earnestly, though unsuccessfully. He does not say whether ignorance and growth in wisdom are or are not included under the phrase *totus in nostris;* and the omission is all the more noticeable that he does enter into some detail on the properties of Christ's humanity, reckoning among them birth, infancy, temptation, hunger, thirst, weariness, and sleep. It would have been instructive to know how the Roman bishop applied the formula *totus in suis, totus in nostris* to the category of knowledge; and in case he reckoned omniscience among the *sua*, and ignorance among the *nostra*, to know how he combined these two opposites in one person, and how in this case each nature performed that which was common to it in communion with the other. From the style in which Leo expresses himself concerning the divine in Christ, one rather fears that he had no light to give on that subject. His doctrine of divine immutability is very rigid. The Son of God in becoming man did not recede from the equality of paternal glory,[1]—a statement not in harmony either with the word or with the spirit of Scripture in speaking on the humiliation of Christ, and, indeed, as Dorner has observed,[2] not in keeping with a thought of Leo's own, occurring in an earlier part of his epistle, viz., that the Incarnation does not violate divine immutability, inasmuch as it is the deed of a will which loved man at his creation, and which does not allow itself to be deprived of its benign disposition towards man, either through his sin or through the devil's wiles. If God's unchangeableness be secured by the immutability of His loving will, why guard His majesty in a way that tends to make His love a hollow unreality? why not let love have free course, and be glorified, even though its glorification should involve a temporary forfeiture of glory of another kind? From our Christological point of view, that of the *exinanition*, this is a part of Leo's letter with which we cannot sympathize. The doctrine of exinanition demands the unity of the person and the distinctness of the natures, especially the reality and integrity of the human nature; but it does not require us to guard the Divine Majesty as the disciples guarded their Master from the intrusion of the mothers with their children. With reference to such zeal, the Son of God says: "Suffer me to humble myself." Even Cyril understood this better than Leo, for he spoke of the Son of God as somehow made less than Himself in becoming man.[3]

On another subject Leo is silent—the question of the personality of the human nature. He teaches the unity of the person, but he does not say to which of the natures the personality is to be appropriated, or whether it belongs to both, or is distinct from both. Whether the humanity of Christ was personal or impersonal, whether Christ was not

---

[1] Sicut verbum ab aequalitate Paternae Gloriae non recessit ita, etc.—*Epist.* c. 4.

[2] *Doctrine of the Person of Christ*, div. ii. vol. i. p. 88.

[3] Ὑπερέχοντα μὲν τῶν τῆς κτίσεως μέτρων ὡς Θεόν· ἑαυτοῦ δέ πως μονονουχὶ καὶ ἡττώμενον καθὸ πέφηνεν ἄνθρωπος.—*Ad reginas de verâ fide*, oratio altera, xvi. The manner in which Cyril here expresses himself is curiously guarded and embarrassed, πως μονονουχί, somehow almost!

merely man but a man, whether personality is to be reckoned among the *nostra* ascribed to Christ in their totality, —these are questions which either did not occur to his mind, or on which he did not feel able to throw light. The former supposition is probably the correct one; for the writers of the patristic period did not conceive a person as we do, as a self-conscious Ego, but simply as a centre of unity for the characteristics which distinguish one individual from another.¹ According to this view, Christ would be " the result of the conjunction of natures, the sum total of both, the collective *centre* of vital unity which is at once God and man." ²

The Council of Chalcedon proved utterly impotent to stay the progress of controversy; its only immediate effect being to produce a schism in the Church, whereby the Monophysite party became constituted into a sect. The great debate went on as if no ecclesiastical decision had been come to, prolonging its existence for upwards of three hundred years, and passing successively through three different stages, distinguished respectively as the Monophysite, the Monothelite, and the Adoptian controversies. The Chalcedonian formula left a sufficient number of unsettled questions to supply ample materials for further discussions. Are unity of the person and a duality of natures mutually compatible? what belongs to the category of the natures and what to the category of the person, and, in particular, to which of the two categories is *the will* to be reckoned? is personality essential to the completeness of each nature, in particular to the completeness of the human nature? These questions in turn became the successive subjects of dispute in the long Christological warfare which ensued; the first being the radical point at issue in the Monophysite phase, the second in the Monothelite, the third in the Adoptian; the great controversy thus returning in its final stage, at the close of the eighth century, pretty nearly to the point from which it started at the beginning of the fourth, Adoptianism being, if not, as some think, with some difference of form, virtually Nestorianism

---

¹ Dorner, *Person of Christ*, div. i. vol. ii. p. 320.
² *Ibid.* div. ii. vol. i. p. 87.

redivivus, at least the assertion of a double aspect in Christ's personality. Of the many contests which raged around these questions in the course of the next three centuries, I will not here attempt to give even the most cursory account. The subject is indeed by no means inviting. From the Council of Chalcedon to the Council of Frankfort may be called the dreary period of Christology, the sources of information being comparatively scanty, the points at issue minute or obscure, and even when both clear and important, as in the Monothelite controversy, involving subtle scholastic discussions distasteful to the religious spirit, and presenting to view an *anatomical figure* in place of the Christ of the Gospel history. The doctrine, I suppose, had to pass through all the phases referred to,—probably not one of the battles, great or small, could have been avoided; still one is thankful his lot is cast in better times than those in which they were fought out. Who would care to spend his life discussing such questions as those which occupied the minds of men in the sixth century, and in reference to which Monophysite was at war with Monophysite, as well as with his orthodox opponents? Was Christ's body corruptible or incorruptible—*naturally* liable to death, suffering, need, and weakness, or liable only because and when the Logos willed? was it created or uncreated? nay, could it be said after the union with the Logos to exist at all? Such were the questions on which men felt keenly in that unhappy age, and in connection with which they bestowed on each other nicknames offensive in meaning, unmusical in sound; the deniers of the corruptibility calling their antagonists Phthartolatrae, worshippers of the corruptible; the asserters of corruptibility retorting on their opponents with the countercharge of Aphthartodoketism;[1] the parties in the question whether the body of Christ after union with the Logos was to be regarded as created or as uncreated, calling each other in kindred spirit Aktistetes and Ktistolators; while those who completed the *reductio ad absurdum* of Monophysitism, by denying all distinctive reality to the humanity of Christ after the union, went by the name of Niobites, taken from the surname of the founder,

[1] See for further particulars in reference to this controversy, Lect. vi.

Stephen, an Alexandrian Sophist. Two other disputes embraced within the Monophysitic controversy were of a more dignified character; those, viz., relating to the participation of the Logos in Christ's sufferings, and to the knowledge possessed by Christ's human soul. But it is a curious indication of the confused nature of the strife going on in those years, to find parties in the latter of these two disputes changing sides,—the Monophysites maintaining the position which one would have expected the defenders of the Chalcedonian formula to take up. The Agnoetes, that is to say, those who asserted that the human soul of Christ was like ours, even in respect of ignorance, were a section of the Monophysite party; and their opponents embraced not merely the straiter sect of the Monophysites, but the Orthodox, who, as represented, *e.g.*, by Bede, taught that Christ from His conception was full of wisdom, and therefore did not really grow in knowledge as in stature. Amid the smoke of battle men had got bewildered, and, fighting at random, fired upon their own side.[1]

Passing, then, without any great effort of self-denial, from these obscure wranglings, and leaping over, also without much regret, the Monothelite controversies which followed in what may called the era of *anatomical* Christology, I shall close this lecture with brief notices of two representative men with whom we shall hereafter find it convenient to have some acquaintance: one of them showing the state of Christology after the close of the controversy concerning the two wills, and before the rise of the Adoptian controversy; the other exhibiting the prevailing Christology of the mediaeval period, when the process of reaction which set in after the Council of Frankfort, in the direction of a one-sided assertion of Christ's divinity, had attained its complete development. I refer to John of Damascus, who flourished about the middle of the eighth century, and Thomas Aquinas, one of the great lights of the thirteenth.

---

[1] See on this curious phenomenon, Dorner, *Person of Christ*, div. ii. vol. i. p. 142; and Baur, *die Lehre von der Dreieinigkeit*, vol. ii. pp. 87-92. Dorner and Baur agree in their view of the Agnostic controversy, and give the same representation as that in the text.

John of Damascus carried the distinctness of the natures to its utmost limit, short of the recognition of two hypostases in the one Christ. He advocated the doctrine of two wills, on the ground that the faculty of willing is an essential attribute of rational natures.[1] The controversy concerning the two wills had arisen *within* the Church, and between the adherents to the Chalcedonian formula, because it was not self-evident to which of the two categories, the natures or the person, the will should be referred. Doubt on this point was very excusable, inasmuch as a good deal could be said on both sides. John recognises the legitimacy of such perplexity by virtually treating the will as a matter pertaining both to the natures and to the person. "To will," he says, "in the abstract—the will faculty is *physical*, but to will thus and thus is *personal*."[2] There are two will faculties but only one willer, the one Christ who wills according to both natures using the will faculty of each.[3] On the principle of conceding to each nature all its natural properties, John ascribes to the human will the faculty of self-determination (τὸ αὐτεξούσιον); but this is very much a matter of form, for he represents the human soul of Christ as willing freely the things which the divine will wished it to will.[4] His doctrine, therefore, while dyothelitic in one respect, is monothelitic in another; the human will being in effect reduced to the position of a natural impulse of desire to do this, to shun that, to partake of food, to sleep, etc., and entering only as a *momentum* into the one determining will of the one Christ.[5]

Recognising in the above fashion two wills, the Damas-

---

[1] *De Duabus Voluntatibus*, c. 22.

[2] *De Duabus Voluntatibus*, c. 24: Θελητικὸν ζῷον ὁ ἄνθρωπος· τὸ δὲ θελητὸν οὐ φυσικὸν μόνον, ἀλλὰ καὶ γνωμικὸν, καὶ ὑποστατικόν. Ἀλλ' οὐ πᾶς ἄνθρωπος ὡσαύτως θέλει, οὐδὲ τὸ αὐτό· ὥστε τὸ τῶς θέλειν καλῶς ἢ κακῶς, ἢ τὸ τί θέλειν, τό δε, ἢ ἐκεῖνο, οὐ φυσικὸν ἀλλὰ γνωμικὸν, καὶ ὑποστατικόν.

[3] *De Fide Orthodoxâ*, lib. iii. cap. xiv.: ἐπειδὴ τοίνυν εἷς μὲν ὁ Χριστὸς καὶ μία αὐτοῦ ἡ ὑπόστασις, εἷς καὶ ὁ αὐτός ἐστιν ὁ θέλων θεϊκῶς τε καὶ ἀνθρωπίνως.

[4] *De Fide Orthodoxâ*, lib. iii. c. xviii.: ἤθελε μὲν αὐτεξουσίως κινουμένη ἡ τοῦ Κυρίου ψυχή, ἀλλ' ἐκεῖνα αὐτεξουσίως ἤθελε ἃ ἡ θεία αὐτοῦ θέλησις ἤθελε θέλειν αὐτήν.

[5] So Dorner, div. ii. vol. i. p. 210.

cene, carrying out the theory embodied in the phrase "of two and in two distinct natures," asserts a duality in respect to everything pertaining to the nature of God and of man in common. Christ has all the things which the Father hath, except the property of being unbegotten; He has all the things which the first Adam had, except sin alone. Therefore He has two physical wills, two physical energies, two physical faculties of self-determination ($αὐτεξούσια$), two wisdoms and knowledges.[1] John even goes the length of conceding to Christ's humanity *personality*, but not separate independent personality: It was without hypostasis in itself, never having had an independent subsistence; but it became enhypostatized through union with the Logos. No nature, he admits, can be without hypostasis, nature apart from individuality being a mere abstraction; but then he holds that the two natures united in Christ do not necessarily possess separate hypostases; they may meet in one hypostasis, so that they shall neither be without hypostasis nor possess each a peculiar hypostasis, but have both one and the same.[2] In this way Christ becomes a human individual, and the person of Christ is to be regarded as composite.[3]

Still, in spite of his efforts to make it formally complete, the humanity of Christ in the system of the Damascene remained a lifeless thing. The anatomical process to which the human nature was subjected left it an inanimate carcase with the form and features of a man, but without the inspiring soul. Already what Dorner happily calls the *transubstantiating* process has begun, which was to evacuate Christ's humanity of all its contents, and leave only the outward shell with a God within. In several most important respects, Christ, as exhibited in John's system,—the last important utterance of the Greek Church on the subject of Christology,—is not our brother, like us in all points save sin. At the very first stage of His incarnate history there is an ominous difference between Him and us. His body was not formed in the womb of the Virgin by gradual

---

[1] *De Fide Orthodoxâ*, lib. iii. cap. xiii.
[2] *De Fide Orthodoxâ*, lib. iii. c. ix.
[3] *De Fide Orthodoxâ*, lib. iii. c. iii.: εἰς μίαν ὑπόστασιν σύνθετον.

minute additions, but was perfected at once.[1] Then the soul of the holy child knew no growth in wisdom. Jesus is said to have increased in wisdom and stature; because He did indeed grow in stature, and because He made the *manifestation* of the indwelling wisdom keep pace with that growth:[2] just the old doctrine of Cyril, who at this distance appears a saint, and is quoted without hesitation as an orthodox Father. Doubtless the flesh of our Lord was *per se* ignorant; but then, in virtue of the identity of the hypostasis and the indissoluble union, His soul was enriched with the knowledge of future things;[3] and to assert that it really grew in wisdom and grace, as receiving increment of these, is to deny that the union was formed *ab initio*—is to deny the hypostatic union altogether. If the flesh was truly united to Deity from the first moment of conception, and possessed hypostatic identity therewith, how could it fail to be perfectly enriched with all wisdom and grace?[4] Of course temptation was not a very serious affair for such a Christ. He was tempted from without, apart from any internal suggestions, and He repelled and dissipated the assaults of the enemy *like smoke*.[5] In like manner Christ had no personal need for prayer; He prayed simply as sustaining our person and performing our part, asking what He did not need by way of example to us; teaching us to ask of God and to raise our souls to Him, and through His holy mind preparing a way for our ascent to the throne of grace.[6]

While carrying the formal doctrine of the distinction between the natures to its utmost limits, John considered it

[1] *De Fide Orthodoxâ*, lib. iii. c. ii.: οὐ ταῖς κατὰ μικρὸν προσθήκαις ἀπαρτιζομένου τοῦ σχήματος· ἀλλ' ὑφ' ἓν τελειωθέντος.

[2] *De Fide Orthodoxâ*, lib. iii. c. xxii.: τῇ μὲν ἡλικίᾳ αὔξων, διὰ δὲ τῆς αὐξήσεως τῆς ἡλικίας τὴν ἐνυπάρχουσαν αὐτῷ σοφίαν εἰς φανέρωσιν ἄγων.

[3] *De Fide Orthodoxâ*, lib. iii. c. xxi.: διὰ δὲ τὴν τῆς ὑποστάσεως ταυτότητα καὶ τὴν ἀδιάσπαστον ἕνωσιν πατεπλούτησεν ἡ τοῦ Κυρίου ψυχὴ τὴν τῶν μελλόντων γνῶσιν.

[4] *De Fide Orthodoxâ*, lib. iii. c. xxii.

[5] *De Fide Orthodoxâ*, lib. iii. c. xx.: ὡς καπνὸν διέλυσεν.

[6] *De Fide Orthodoxâ*, lib. iii. c. xxiv.: τὸ ἡμέτερον οἰκειούμενος πρόσωπον, καὶ τυπῶν ἐν ἑαυτῷ τὸ ἡμέτερον, καὶ ὑπογραμμὸς ἡμῖν γενόμενος, καὶ διδάσκων ἡμᾶς παρὰ Θεοῦ αἰτεῖν, καὶ πρὸς αὐτὸν ἀνατείνεσθαι, καὶ διὰ τοῦ ἁγίου αὐτοῦ νοῦ ὁδοποιῶν ἡμῖν τὴν πρὸς Θεὸν ἀνάβασιν.

his duty to do what he could towards the establishment of a communion between the natures as asserted in the formula of Chalcedon. For this purpose he lays stress on the hypostatic union, the permeation of the human by the divine,[1] and the mutual communication of names which takes place between the natures.[2] The last-mentioned means of communion amounts to nothing more than the verbal communication of attributes taught by the Reformed Christology; but the second, the permeation (περιχώρησις), involves something approaching at least to the real communication of the Lutherans. To this permeation, as well as to the hypostatic union, is due the perfection in knowledge *ab initio* of the human soul of Christ already spoken of. Hence also it comes that the flesh of Christ is life-giving, and that the human will of Christ is omnipotent, though in itself limited in power.[3] These are instances in which the divinity communicates to the humanity its own glorious properties, and by the communication in a manner deifies it.

As in the Cyrillian and the Lutheran Christologies, so in the system of John, the communication of attributes is all on one side. There is no kind of communication by which the divine nature becomes partaker of the humiliation of humanity, corresponding to that by which the human nature becomes partaker of the glories of divinity. The divinity communicates to the body its proper virtues, but it remains non-participant in the sufferings of the flesh.[4] The Logos is indeed spoken of as appropriating to itself the humanities; but that is meant simply in the sense that the flesh and all its properties are connected with it personally.[5] For the divine nature in Christ, the words humiliation, service, suffering, have no real sense. Christ, we are told, was

---

[1] περιχώρησις. [2] τρόπος τῆς ἀντιδόσεως, lib. iii. c. iii.

[3] *De Fide Orthodoxâ*, lib. iii. c. xviii. Contrasting the divine and human wills in Christ, John represents the former as without beginning, and omnipotent and apathetic; the latter, as having a beginning in time, subject to physical and sinless affections, and naturally not all-powerful, but having become truly and physically the property of God the Logos; it also is thereby rendered almighty. ὡς δὲ τοῦ Θεοῦ λόγου ἀληθῶς καὶ κατὰ φύσιν γενομένη, καὶ παντοδύναμος.

[4] *De Fide Orthodoxâ*, lib. iii. c. xv.: Τῶν μὲν οὖν οἰκείων αὐχημάτων ἡ θεότης τῷ σώματι μεταδίδωσιν· αὐτὴ δὲ τῶν τῆς σαρκὸς παθῶν διαμένει ἀμέτοχος.

[5] *De Fide Orthodoxâ*, lib. iii. c. iii.: οἰκειοῦται δὲ τὰ ἀνθρώπινα ὁ λόγος.

not a *servant*—to teach otherwise is to Nestorianize; all that we may say is, that the flesh of Christ *per se*, and conceived of as not united to the Word, was of servile nature.[1] The relation of the Logos to the passion is illustrated by the metaphor of a tree on which the sun shines being cut down with an axe. The axe fells the tree, but it does no harm to the sunbeams; and so in like manner the divinity of the Logos, though united hypostatically to the flesh, remains impassible while the flesh suffers.[2] What a loose, inadequate idea of the Incarnation is suggested by such a comparison! The Logos in the humanity like the sunlight among the branches of an oak! One is thrown back on the question whether, on such a conception of the Divine Being as is implied in the figure, an incarnation be possible; and our doubts are deepened when we observe how John speaks of the great mystery of godliness in the opening chapter of the book which treats of the divine economy of the Incarnation. "Bending the heavens, He descends; that is, humbling without humiliation His majesty, which cannot be humbled, He descends to the level of His servants, by a condescension inexpressible and inconceivable."[3] The practical import of this self-cancelling sentence is: the Scriptures teach that He who was in the form of God humbled Himself, and therefore we must teach likewise; but the thing taught is philosophically impossible.

Passing now from John of Damascus to Thomas Aquinas, separated from the former by an interval of five centuries, we find that the lapse of time has brought along with it a great change indeed, but a change more in the method of treatment than in the substance of the doctrine. Many thoughts with which we have become familiar, through the writings

---

[1] *De Fide Orthodoxa*, lib. iii. c. xxi.: δούλη ἐστίν ἡ σάρξ, εἰ μὴ ἥνωτο τῷ Θεῷ λόγῳ· ἅπαξ δὲ ἑνωθεῖσα καθ' ὑπόστασιν, πῶς ἔσται δούλη; εἰς γὰρ ὢν ὁ Χριστὸς οὐ δύναται δοῦλος ἑαυτοῦ εἶναι καὶ Κύριος.

[2] *De Fide Orthodoxa*, lib. iii. c. xxvi.: Εἰ γὰρ ἡλίου δένδρῳ ἐπιλάμποντος, ἡ ἀξίνη τέμνοι τὸ δένδρον, ἄτμητος καὶ ἀπαθὴς διαμένει ὁ ἥλιος, πολλῷ μᾶλλον, κ. τ. λ.

[3] *De Fide Orthodoxa*, lib. iii. c. i.: Κλίνας οὐρανοὺς κατέρχεται· τουτέστι τὸ ἀταπείνωτον αὐτοῦ ὕψος ἀταπεινώτως ταπεινώσας, συγκαταβαίνει τοῖς ἑαυτοῦ δούλοις συγκατάβασιν ἄφραστόν τε καὶ ἀκατάληπτον.

of John, reappear in the pages of Thomas, the Eastern monk being, in fact, the chief Christological authority of the great Western scholastic. Three ideas, however, present themselves to view in the *Summa*, which, if not entirely new in the history of the dogma, are developed in that work with a fulness which justifies us in connecting them with the name of its author. These ideas are: the conception of the Incarnation as an incarnation, not of the divine nature, but of a divine *person;* the conception of the human nature of Christ as a recipient of *grace;* and the conception of Christ in His humanity as the *Head* of the Church. With respect to the first of these topics, the view of the Church had not before Thomas' time assumed a fixed form, as we learn from the sentences of Peter the Lombard, in which the vacillating state of opinion is faithfully reflected. Peter proposes for discussion the question, Whether a person or a nature assumed humanity, and whether the nature of God was incarnated? and he answers the question by virtually allowing validity to both alternatives. "Desiring," he says, "to remove from the sacred pages every trace of falsehood and contradiction, we agree with orthodox Fathers and catholic doctors in saying both that the person of the Son assumed human nature, and that the divine nature was united to human nature in the Son, and united and assumed it to itself; on which account the divine nature is truly said to be incarnate."[1] Thomas, on the other hand, while allowing that the latter mode of putting the matter was not wholly inadmissible, pronounced in favor of the former alternative as the only appropriate way of stating the fact.[2] But what did he mean by taking up this position? The view that the union exhibited in the Word Incarnate was made not *in naturâ*, but *in personâ*, might be intended simply to serve the purpose of adjusting the doctrine of the Incarnation to the doctrine of the Trinity; the first and third persons of the Trinity being exempted from participating in the Incarnation, by the exclusion of

---

[1] *Sententiarum*, lib. iii. distinct. v.: Dicentes, et personam filii assumpsisse naturam humanam et naturam divinam humanae naturae in filio unitam, eamque sibi unisse vel assumpsisse, unde et vere incarnata dicitur.

[2] *Summa*, pars iii. qu. ii. artt. i. ii. The questions are put thus: Utrum unio verbi incarnati sit facta in naturâ. Utrum unio verbi incarnati sit facto in personâ.

the common divine nature from all direct participation therein. Or the thesis might be designed to guard against monophysite confusion, and to affirm with the greatest possible emphasis the distinctness of the two natures of Christ within the personal unity. Or, finally, it is conceivable that the position in question might be laid down by one who meant to teach that the distinctive attributes of the divine nature, omniscience, omnipotence, etc., while still possessed by the divine person who became man, did not enter into the incarnate state, and reveal themselves in the incarnate life of the God-man. Now there can be no doubt that Thomas, in formulating his doctrine of the Incarnation, had in view the former two of these three purposes;[1] but there does not appear to be any good ground for ascribing to him the idea of a *double life* of the Logos implied in the third hypothetical explanation of his meaning; though, of course, the question may be raised whether that idea be not a logical consequence of his theory. Dorner seems inclined to think otherwise. He represents the significance of the Incarnation, in Thomas' view, as being limited to the fact that the divine person of the Son, as distinct from His divine nature, was inserted into the human nature; the divine personality standing, of course, in intimate connection with its own nature, but not allowing any part of it to pass over into the human nature. This limitation, which he characterizes as remarkable, he represents as being made not merely for Trinitarian reasons, but also in order to render the problem of Incarnation an easier one, which in Dorner's judgment is equivalent to evading the problem in one essential particular, or even to letting it entirely fall.[2] Baur, on the other hand, recognises in Thomas' way of stating the Incarnation, simply the development of the

---

[1] Under quaestio iii. art. ii. he discusses the question, "Utrum divinae naturae conveniat assumere," stating as an objection that if it belonged to the nature to assume, it would follow that it belonged to the three persons, and thus the Father would have assumed human nature as well as the Son. This objection he meets by saying that the divine nature is the *principium assumptionis*, but not itself the *terminus assumptionis*. Esse terminum assumptionis non convenit naturae divinae secundum seipsum, sed ratione personae in qua consideratur. Et ideo primo quidem et propriissime persona dicitur assumere.

[2] *Doctrine of the Person of Christ*, div. ii. vol. i. pp. 331, 332.

ecclesiastical doctrine, that in Christ two natures, distinct in themselves, and remaining distinct after the union, were united in one person.[1] According to this view, the more correct one, as it appears to me, the new element in Aquinas' formula was not the promulgation of a new theory, but simply a greater measure of strictness in adapting the form of expression to the established theory. The sense in which Aquinas meant his thesis to be understood, may be gathered from the use to which he puts it in solving problems respecting the knowledge and the power possessed by Christ's human soul. Thus the question, Had Christ any knowledge besides the divine? is decided in the affirmative, because the union affected only the personal being, and knowledge belongs to the person only in virtue of its being an attribute of one or other of the natures. Duality of knowledge therefore follows from the duality of natures, unless we mutilate the human nature, and deprive it of an attribute which it possesses in all other men.[2] The question whether Christ's soul possessed the particular species of knowledge called the knowledge of the blessed, is answered affirmatively by the application of the same principle; the objection, that a knowledge which the saints have by participation in the divine light cannot be ascribed to a being who, as divine, had not His light by participation, but as an essential attribute of His indwelling divinity, being disposed of by the remark that divinity was united to the humanity of Christ as to the person, not as to the essence or nature, and that with the unity of the person the distinction of natures remains. The consequence is, that the soul of Christ, which is a part of the human nature, is, by a certain light borrowed from the divine nature, perfected unto the blessed knowledge whether God is seen as He is.[3] Once more the question, whether the soul of Christ

[1] *Die Christliche Lehre von der Dreieinigkeit und Menschwerdung Gottes*, Zweite Theil, p. 795.

[2] Pars tertia, quaest. ix. art. i.: Ex parte ipsius unionis non potest poni in Christo aliqua scientia. Nam unio illa ad esse personale, scientia autem non convenit personae nisi ratione alicujus naturae.

[3] Quaest. ix. art. ii. The question is: Utrum Christus habuerit scientiam quam habent beati vel comprehensores. In favour of the negative, Thomas conceives the following argument as being advanced: Scientia beatorum est per participati-

had absolute omnipotence, is decided in the negative; because in the mystery of the Incarnation the union is so made in the person that the distinction of natures remains, each nature retaining that which is proper to itself.[1] It is easy to see from these examples that Thomas' way of stating the doctrine of the Incarnation really amounted to little more than the formula, that in Christ two *distinct* natures were united in one person. In the next lecture we shall find the same mode of stating the doctrine reappearing in the Reformed Christology in the same interest, *i.e.* as a means of emphasizing and guarding the distinctness of the united natures.

Passing to the second of the three thoughts characteristic of the Christological system set forth in the *Summa*, the conception of Christ as the recipient of grace, Thomas divided the grace conferred into two parts,—the grace of *union*, that is, the honour bestowed upon the human nature of the Incarnate Son of God in being united to divinity, and *habitual* grace. He deemed it necessary to ascribe to Christ the latter sort of grace for three reasons. *First*, because His soul was united to the Logos, it being evident that the nearer anything of a receptive nature is to a source of influence, the more it must participate of its influence. *Second*, on account of the nobility of that soul whose activities behoved to come as near as possible to God in knowledge and love, for which end the human nature needed to be elevated by grace. *Third*, on account of Christ's relation as man to the human race, that viz. of Mediator, which required Him to have grace in Himself that it might overflow from Him to others.[2] But a previous question

onem divini luminis secundum illud, Ps. xxxvi. 10. *In lumine tuo videbimus lumen.* Sed Christus non habuit lumen divinum tanquam participatum, sed ipsam divinitatem in se habuit substantialiter manentem. To which he replies: Divinitas unita est humanitati Christi secundum personam non secundum essentiam vel naturam; sed cum unitate personae remanet distinctio naturarum. Et ideo anima Christi, quae est pars humanae naturae, per aliquod lumen participatum a natura divina perfecta est ad scientiam beatam quâ Deus per essentiam videtur.

[1] Quaest. xiii. art. i.: In mysterio incarnationis ita facta est unio in personâ, quod tamen remansit distinctio naturarum utrâque scilicet natura retinente id quod sibi est proprium . . . Cum igitur anima Christi sit pars humanae naturae, impossibile est quod omnipotentiam habeat.

[2] Pars iii. quaest. vii. (De Gratia Christi, prout est quidam singularis homo) art. i.

naturally arises, viz., Was not the communication of habitual grace rendered superfluous by the *fact of union?* and a little consideration suffices to satisfy us that the idea of such a communication has for its presupposition a very emphatic assertion of the distinctness of the natures within the union. Accordingly, we find that Thomas disposes of this very objection by falling back on the distinction. Having stated as an argument against ascribing to Christ habitual grace, that He is God, not participatively, but according to truth, he disposes of it by saying that Christ is true God as to His person and His divine nature; but inasmuch as with the unity of the person the distinction of natures remains, the soul of Christ is not by its essence divine, and therefore it can become divine only as believers do, viz. by participation, which is according to grace.[1] The communication of *grace*, that is to say, is to be regarded in the light of a corollary from that view of Christ's person which emphasizes the distinctness of the natures; just as the communication of *properties* is a corollary from that view of Christ's person which allows the distinction to be eclipsed by the unity. This remark will prepare us to understand how it came to pass that the Reformed Christologists espoused the former of these ideas, as taught by Thomas; while the Lutheran Christologists, on the other hand, patronized the latter, and the kindred notion of physical pervasion as taught by John of Damascus.

Aquinas represented Christ as being a recipient of grace in a double capacity; as a singular man, and as the Head of the Church; the grace being in both cases the same as to essence, differing solely as to the ground and reason of communication.[2] This conception of Christ as the head of the Church is the third prominent idea in the Christology

[1] Pars iii. quaest. vii. art. i. The objection is: Gratia est quaedam participatio divinitatis in creaturâ rationali secundum illud, 2 Petri i. 3. Per quem maxima et pretiosa promissa nobis donavit ut divinae simus consortes naturae. And the reply: Christus est verus Deus sec. personam et naturam divinam. Sed quia cum unitate personae remanet distinctio naturarum anima Christi non est per suam essentiam divina, Unde oportet quod fiat divina per participationem quae est sec. gratiam.

[2] Quaestio viii. (De Gratia Christi, prout est caput Ecclesiae) art. v.: Eadem est sec. essentiam gratia personalis qua anima Christi est justificata, et gratia ejus, sec. quam est caput ecclesiae justificans alios; differt tamen sec. rationem.

of the great schoolman, well characterized by Baur as one of those in which he rises above the dry formalism of the scholastic theology.[1] The Christological value of this idea, as of the one preceding, lies in the implied assertion of the likeness of Christ in all essential respects to His brethren. While as the Head, exalted above all, He is still the representative of a mystical body, to whom He stands in the relation of *Primus inter pares*. This is not indeed the aspect of the truth emphasized by Aquinas; for what he insists on is rather the superiority than the similitude. Christ is head, according to the analogy of the human head, in respect of order, perfection, and virtue. As the head of a human body is the first part of man beginning from above, so Christ as to the grace of nearness to God is first and highest; as to the head of the human body belongs the perfection of containing within itself all the senses external and internal, while in the other members is the sense of touch alone, so Christ is perfect as possessing the plenitude of all graces; and as the powers, motion, and government of all the members of the body are centred in the head, so Christ has the power to pour grace into all the members of the Church; and on all these accounts He is properly called the Head of the Church.[2] Still, it must be observed, all this superiority is ascribed to Christ as *man*. To an objection based on a sentence from Augustine which seems to teach a contrary opinion, Thomas replies, that while to give grace or the Holy Spirit belongs to Christ as God authoritatively, it also belongs to Him as man instrumentally, inasmuch as His humanity was the instrument of His divinity.[3] Another objection taken to the applicability of the figure, from the fact that the head is a particular member receiving influence from the heart, while Christ is the universal principle of the whole Church, he disposes of thus: The head has a manifest eminence compared with the other members; but the heart has a certain secret influence. Therefore the Holy Spirit, who invisibly vivifies and unites the Church, is compared to the heart; but Christ is compared to the head, as to His visible

[1] *Dreieinigkeit*, ii. p. 802.
[2] Quaestio viii. art. i. (Utrum Christum sit caput Ecclesiae). [3] Quaestio viii. art. i.

nature, as a man is set over other men.[1] As a man over other men, therefore, is Christ Head of the Church; so that while His Headship implies supremacy, it no less clearly implies fraternity.

From the foregoing exposition it will have appeared that the three ideas characteristic of the Christological system set forth in the *Summa* all point in one direction, that, namely, of the emphatic assertion of the *homoüsia* taught in our seventh axiom: Christ in all possible respects, both in His human nature and in His human experience, like unto His brethren. But on looking into other parts of that system, we find that what is given with one hand is taken back again by the other. The Christ of Aquinas is after all not our brother, not a *man*, but only a ghastly *simulacrum*. In many most important respects He is not like the members of His mystical body. Not to speak of His material part, which, according to the author of the *Summa*, was perfectly formed from the first moment of conception, and born without pain;[2] the soul of Christ differed from ours to an extent which makes us feel that between Him and us there is little in common. Recipient of grace in all its plenitude, the soul of Jesus was without the two cardinal graces of faith and hope; because, forsooth, the possession of these, while in one respect a merit, is in another a defect.[3] The gifts of knowledge, on the other hand, imparted to Christ as a man, made the gulf between Him and us, already too wide, wider still. His soul possessed at once the knowledge of the blessed, the knowledge which comes through innate ideas, and the knowledge which comes through the senses; the first consisting in the perfect vision of God and

[1] Quaestio viii. art. i.: Capiti autem comparatur ipse Christus sec. visibilem naturam, sec. quam homo hominibus praefertur.

[2] Quaestio xxxiii. (De modo et ordine conceptionis Christi) art. i. (Utrum corpus Christi fuerit formatum in primo instanti conceptionis?) The answer is: In primo instanti quo materia adunata pervenit ad locumlgenerationis fuit perfecte formatum corpus Christi, et assumptum. The painless birth is taught under quaestio xxxv. (De nativitate Christi) art. vi.: Christus est egressus ex clauso utero matris, et propter hoc in illo partu nullus fuit dolor sicut nec aliqua corruptio; sed fuit ibi maxima jucunditas. To the arguments in favour of the contrary position, that it behoved Christ's life to begin as it ended, with pain, and that the pain of birth was a part of the curse, Aquinas replies that the pain was the mother's, not the child's, and that Christ took on Him death voluntarily, not as under necessary subjection to the curse.

[3] Quaestio vii. (De gratia Christi) art. iii. and iv.

of all things in the mirror of the Logos, infinite in the sense of embracing all reality though not all possibility, and complete from the moment of conception, admitting of no growth, and rendering the knowledge gradually acquired through the senses, one would say, superfluous, as the moon is superfluous in presence of the sun, and causing the very faculty for acquiring experimental knowledge to degenerate into a mere rudimentary organ dwarfed by disuse.[1] This picture of a humanity which is inhuman, or at all events unearthly, receives the finishing touch in the doctrine that Christ, even in the days of His humiliation, was a *comprehensor* as well as a *viator*[2]—one, that is, who had already reached the goal, as well as one hastening on toward it, and as such could not increase in grace or in knowledge, being perfect from the first; nor in felicity, save by deliverance from the passibility to which His body and the lower part of His soul were subject previous to the resurrection; and could not know at all by experience what it is to walk by faith, and to be supported under trial by hope. How can such a Christ as this succour us when are tempted? How can one so little acquainted with suffering be a perfect Captain of salvation? The author of the *Summa* indeed pleads on behalf of his theory, that the goal to which men are to be conducted being the beatific vision, and the medium through which they are conducted being the humanity of Christ, it was meet that the Captain should possess what the army led are destined to attain, seeing that the cause should always be more powerful than the object on which it exerts its force.[3] But the argument overlooks the fact that Christ's present power is derived in great measure from His earthly weakness, and that whilst it did certainly behove Him to enter into glory in order to become the Author of salvation, it not less certainly behoved Him to be perfected by an experience as like as possible to our present condition. It was reserved for another age and for other theological teachers to give the due prominence to this great truth.

[1] Quaestio ix. (De scientia Christi in communi) art. i.–iv., quaestion. x.–xii.

[2] Quaestio xv. (De defectibus animae a Christo assumptis) art. x. The term *comprehensor* is derived from the two texts, 1 Cor. ix. 24, sic currite ut comprehendatis, and Phil. iii. 12, sequor autem, si quo modo comprehendam.

[3] Pars tertia, quaestio ix. art. ii.: Semper causam oportet esse potiorem causato.

LECTURE III.

THE LUTHERAN AND REFORMED CHRISTOLOGIES.

IN the sixteenth century, memorable on so many other accounts in the annals of the Church, Christology passed into a new phase. Only a few years after the commencement of the Reformation, there arose a dispute on the subject of Christ's person, which continued without intermission for a century, producing in its course a separation of the German Protestants into two rival communions, distinguished by the names Lutheran and Reformed, and even giving rise to bitter internal contentions between the members of that section of the German Church which claimed Luther for its founder and father. The long, obstinate, and in its results unhappy controversy, originated in what to us may appear a very small matter—a difference of opinion between Luther and Zuingli as to the nature of Christ's presence in the sacrament of the Supper. Zuingli maintained that the Redeemer was present spiritually only, and solely for those who believe,—the bread and wine being simply emblems of His broken body and shed blood, aids to faith, and stimulants to grateful remembrance. Luther vehemently asserted that the body of the Saviour was present in the Supper, in, with, and under the bread, and was eaten both by believers and by unbelievers; by the former to their benefit, by the latter to their hurt. It is easy to see what questions must arise out of such a diversity of view. If Christ's body be present in the Supper, then it must be *ubiquitous;* but is this attribute compatible with the nature of body, with the ascension of the risen Lord into heaven, with His session at the right hand of God, with the promise of His second coming? and how did the body of Christ come by this marvellous attribute? was it an acquisition made subsequently to the exaltation, a characteristic feature in the state of heavenly glory conferred on Christ as the reward of His voluntary humiliation on earth? or did the humanity of the Incarnate One possess the quality of omnipresence before the ascension or the resurrection, nay, even from the first, from the moment of conception, the necessary result, perhaps, of the union of the divine and human natures in one person, involving the communication to the inferior nature not merely of ubiquity, but of all the august attributes of the superior nature? Supposing this last position to be taken up, then the further question arises: How is such a humanity, invested with all that belongs to divine majesty, to be reconciled with the facts of Christ's earthly history, with His birth and growth in wisdom; with His localization in different places at different times; with His weakness, temptations, and death? Such, in fact, were the questions discussed with more or less clearness and fulness by the combatants in all the stages of the great controversy; with this difference, that in the first stage, that in which Luther himself and his opponents Zuingli, Œcolampadius, and Carlstadt were the disputants, the contention was mainly confined to the doctrine of the Supper itself, and the single attribute of ubiquity; while in the second stage, from Brentz to the Formula of Concord, the debate widened into a discussion of the person of Christ, and the consequences of the union of the two natures in that person, with a view to a firm Christological basis for the doctrine of the Supper; and in the third and last stage, that of the Giessen-Tübingen controversy (internal to the Lutheran Church), the leading subject was the earthly humiliation of Christ, the aim being to adjust Lutheran Christological theories to historical facts. The final result of the whole controversy on the Lutheran side was the formation of a doctrine concerning the person of Christ so artificial, unnatural, and incredible, that any difficulty one may at first experience in understanding the Lutheran position, arises not from want of clearness in the writers, but from the slowness of a mind not familiar with the system to take in the idea that men could seriously believe and deliberately teach what their words seem plainly enough to say. The Christology of the Lutheran Church to an outsider wears the aspect of a vast pyramid resting in a state of most unstable equilibrium on its apex, Christ's bodily presence in the Supper; which again rests upon a water-worn pebble,—the word of institution, "This is my body," easily susceptible of another simple and edifying meaning,—the pyramid being upheld solely by the strong arms of theological giants, and tumbling into irretrievable ruin so soon as the race of the Titans died out.[1]

In making these general observations, I regard the Lutheran Christology as one great whole, distinguished by certain broadly marked characteristics from the rival Christology of the Reformed Confession. On closer inspection, however, we find that the former of the two Christologies resolves itself into two distinct types, which made their appearance at a very early period, and reproduced themselves throughout the whole course of the century during which the dogma was a subject of active controversy. The two types may be designated, from the names of their first expositors, as the *Brentian* and the *Chemnitzian;* the former being the more extreme, bold, and logical form of the theory; the latter, the more moderate, timid, and rational. Both started from the principle that the personal union of the two natures necessarily involved the communication to the human nature of divine attributes; but they differed in their use of the common premiss. Brentz and his followers reasoned out the principle to its last results, regardless of consequences. The Chemnitzian school, on the other hand, having some fear of facts before their eyes, applied the common assumption in a half-hearted manner, the result being a system less consistent but also less absurd; illogical, but just on that account nearer the truth. We shall form to ourselves the clearest idea of the Lutheran Christology as a whole, and put ourselves in a position for understanding the doctrine of the Formula of Concord, by making ourselves acquainted with the distinctive peculiar-

[1] On the connection between the Lutheran Christology and the Sacramentarian controversy, see Appendix, Note A.

ities of these two schools; and therefore I propose here to give a brief account of the views of their founders—John Brentz, the friend of Luther and reformer of Würtemberg, and Martin Chemnitz of Brunswick, a disciple of Melanchthon, best known by his work on the Council of Trent.

The Christological views of Brentz are contained in a series of treatises collected together in the eighth volume of his works, published at Tübingen in 1590. His fundamental position in reference to the person of Christ is this: Although the natures or substances are altogether diverse, and have each their own peculiar idioms or properties, nevertheless these same substances are conjoined in such a union that they become one inseparable hypostasis, *suppositum* or person, and their respective properties are mutually communicated so familiarly, that whatever is a property of either nature is appropriated by the other to itself.[1] The two natures, that is to say, are not merely united *in* one person, the Ego tying together two altogether dissimilar substances still continuing dissimilar; they are united *into* one person, their union constituting the person, and involving *ipso facto* a communication of their respective properties. The Reformed idea, as consisting in a mere sustentation of the humanity by the Logos, Brentz repudiated as not a personal union at all, but merely a common union such as God may form with any man. The difference between Christ and Peter, he held, arose not from the sustentation or inhabitation of the man Jesus by the Son of God, but from the communication to Him of the divine properties of the latter. The Son of God, though He fills Peter with His essence, as He fills the man Christ, does not communicate to Peter all His properties, but only some. He vivifies Peter, keeps him in life, gives him the power of casting out devils, yea, of raising the dead; but He does not make him omnipotent, omniscient, omnipresent. The Son of man, assumed from the Virgin, on the contrary, He adorns not with some only, but with all His gifts, and communicates to Him all His properties. The qualification "as far as He is capable" cannot be allowed; Christ was made capable of all divine

[1] *De Personali unione duarum naturarum in Christo.* Opera, vol. viii. p. 841.

properties, without any exception; if He had not such capacity, there would be no difference between Him and other men, nor could the Word become incarnate.[1]

At first Brentz showed a disposition, following the example of Luther, to apply his fundamental thesis impartially to both sides of the composite person, and to make the divine nature appropriate human properties, as well as the human nature divine properties.[2] And there was no reason *à priori* why this should not be done, for it is surely just as possible for the Infinite to become partaker of the finite and its properties, as for the finite to become partaker of the Infinite. But Brentz apparently soon found out that to apply his principle both ways would be either to reduce the communication of properties, on which so much stress was laid, to the alloiosis of Zuingli, which drove Luther mad with rage, or, in case the communication was held to be real, to make either nature swallow up the other in turn; therefore in his later works he quietly ignored one side and worked out his theory solely on the other side, that, viz., of the appropriation by the human nature of the properties characteristic of the divine nature.

In the working out of his theory Brentz exhibits at once great boldness and no small amount of dialectical skill; shrinking from no legitimate inference, and at the same time doing his utmost to answer or obviate objections, though sometimes with very indifferent success. He is careful to explain that in the person of Christ neither nature is changed into the other, but both remain inviolate

---

[1] *De Majestate Domini Nostri Jesu Christi ad Dextram Dei Patris, et De Vera Praesentia corporis et sanguinis ejus in Coena,* pp. 898-9. This work was a reply to Peter Martyr and Henry Bullinger, *Cingliani dogmatis de Coena Dominica propugnatoribus,* and it is sadly disfigured by the asperities too common in theological controversy.

[2] *De Personali unione,* p. 839: Nos autem intelligimus in hac materia per idiomata, non tantum vocabularum, sed etiam rerum proprietates: ut cum per communicationem idiomatum de Christo dicimus, Deum esse passum et mortuum, non sit sententia, quod Deus verbum dicatur tantum sermone vocabuli pati et mori, res autem ipsa nihil prorsus ad Deum pertineat, sed quod Deus, etsi natura sua nec patitur, nec moritur, tamen passionem et mortem Christi ita sibi communem faciat, ut propter hypostaticam unionem passioni, et morti personaliter adsit, et non aliter, ut sic dicam, afficiatur quam si ipse pateretur et moreretur.

and in possession of their essential properties.[1] There is no exaequation of the humanity to the divinity. The former is indeed declared to be omnipotent, omnipresent, etc., but it is not declared to be omnipotence itself. Of God alone is this affirmed; the humanity possesses only a communicated divinity, and is made equal to God not in being (οὐσίᾳ), but in authority (ἐξουσίᾳ).[2] But if each nature retains its essential properties, the question at once arises, in reference to the humanity, what *are* its essential properties? Is to be in a particular place, *e.g.*, one of them? and if so, how is the retention of that property to be reconciled with omnipresence? At first Brentz seems to have been doubtful what position to take up on this point; for, in a passage near the commencement of his earliest treatise, that on the personal union, he remarks: "If you say that to be in place is so proper to body that it cannot be separated from it, let us suppose meantime that this is in its own way true, yet it cannot be denied that what is impossible to nature is not only possible but easy to divine power."[3] It was not absolutely necessary that he should call in question the position of his opponents in reference to the nature of body, for it was open to him to follow the course adopted by Luther, and to maintain the possibility of body existing in two different ways at the same time; locally, here or there in space; and illocally, everywhere. This course, in point of fact, he did follow, as we shall see;

[1] *De Personali unione*, p. 837.
[2] *De Incarnatione Christi*, p. 1001: Non igitur exaequamus humanitatem Christi divinitati οὐσίᾳ sed tantum ἐξουσίᾳ
[3] *De Personali unione*, p. 837. It must be stated, however, that in the immediately preceding sentence Brentz says: "In loco esse non sit corporis substantia, sed tantum proprietas substantiae accidentaria." In the paragraph preceding that in which these words occur, he quotes the sentence of Augustine: "Tolle spatia locorum corporibus, nusquam erunt, et quia nusquam erunt, non erunt," and remarks that he is aware that the things which are said concerning the majesty of Christ seem very absurd to human reason, and plainly impossible; but the hypostatic union of most diverse natures is taught in Scripture, and therefore, though the absurdity of absurdities, must be believed; and this greatest absurdity being once accepted, many other things which appear absurd to human intellect follow of course. This defiant attitude towards reason and philosophy pervades Brentz' writings. In one place, however, he claims philosophy as on his side, on the question whether to be *in loco* be essential to body. See *De Div. Majestate*, p. 934.

but he did not rely solely on that line of argument, but, moreover, boldly took up the position from which, as it appears, he at first shrunk, that to be *in loco* is after all not an essential attribute, but only an accident of body. This view underlies all his representations of the invisible world. Brentz ridicules the Zuinglian conception of heaven as a certain place not on this earth, but distant and far removed from it, distinct also from the visible lower heavens, not everywhere, but situated above the clouds, and above this corruptible world, yea, above all heavens, *in excelsis*, the house of the Father, the abode and seat of Christ and His elect, an abode happy, divine, eternal, immense, splendid, spiritual, corporeal, having spaces, and these most spacious, in which they walk, sit, stand, and, " for aught I know, recline, for this is not expressly stated."[1] Heaven is, in his view, simply a state separated from hell, not by space, but by disposition and condition; heaven being where God is known in the majesty of His grace, and hell where He is known in the majesty of His severity.[2] Going to heaven means going to the Father, who is the Locus of His people, their all in all, the all-including locality; their heaven, earth, place, food, drink, as well as their justice, wisdom, virtue, gladness, joy, and beatitude.[3] The mansions spoken of by Christ to His disciples[4] are purely spiritual.[5] It is not, indeed, absolutely to be denied that there is a certain place of beatitude in which Christ dwells with His saints, but the question is whether the place be *such* a place as Zuinglians contend for,—*superficies corporis continentis—Locus circumscriptus*,—in other words (ours, not Brentz'), whether it be, properly speaking, a place at all.[6] For, in truth, both space and time, as un-

---

[1] *De Divina Majestate Christi*, p. 947: ... Locus certus ... in quibus localiter itur, sedetur, statur, et ambulatur; atque haud scio, num etiam ibi jaceatur, hoc enim non invenio additum.   [2] *De Ascensu Christi in Coelum*, pp. 1040-47.

[3] *Ibid.* p. 1067: Cum igitur Deus erit in nobis OMNIA, certe erit nostrum coelum, nostra terra, noster *locus*, etc.   *Vid.* also *De Div. Maj.* p. 959.

[4] John xiv. 2; on which Bullinger wrote a treatise, the aim of which was to show that heaven was a definite locality, the abode of Christ and His people.

[5] *De Ascensu Christi in Coelum*, p. 1046.

[6] *De Sessione Christi ad dextram Dei*, p. 1076. Brentz shows manifest signs of distress here: De hoc controvertitur; num beatitudinis locus sit talis, TALIS

derstood in this world, are to be destroyed in heaven, burnt up in the great conflagration which shall usher in the new heavens and the new earth, wherein shall be not space and time, but righteousness.[1] The right hand of God means the omnipotence and majesty of God. The session of Christ at the right hand of God signifies His being crowned with glory and honour, having all things subject to Him, possessing all power in heaven and on earth.[2] It has no relation to place; on the contrary, space is one of the things put under Christ's feet; for place has a name and body has a name, and it is written that He is to be placed above everything that has a name in this world.[3] Christ's glorified body has no form, if by form be meant external figure or appearance; it has only the power of assuming such a form at will by way of economy, as when Christ appeared to Stephen and Paul, and as He shall appear at His second coming. The body of the exalted Lord is not in heaven with wound-prints in the hands (*cicatricibus in manibus*), it retains only the essence of body (whatever that may be); its form is incomprehensible, inconceivable, intolerable to mortal men.[4] And the same thing holds true of the bodies of the saints. They shall have no more to do with space and time than the angels to whom, the Lord taught, the glorified shall be equal. They shall still be true bodies as to essence; but for the rest they shall be altogether spiritual, without visible figure. Such an account of the spiritual body excites curiosity to know what the essence of body as distinct from spirit may be; and one naturally inquires what becomes of the resurrection on these terms. Our author assures us that it still remains,—not without indignation at those who ventured to insinuate that his theory left no place for it; but his assurance does not dispel our doubts.[5] Once more, in view of this sublimating process, intended to make room for the doctrine of ubiquity, one not unnaturally inquires, Are all spiritual bodies then

inquam, qualem, etc. The *talis* in large capitals betrays the irritation of a disputant at his wits' end.

[1] *De Ascensu Christi in Coelum*, p. 1048.
[2] *De Divina Majestate*, p. 920, and in many other places.
[3] *Ibid.* pp. 913, 914.   [4] *Ibid.* pp. 930, 1047, 1081, 1091.
[5] *De Sessione*, p. 1092.

ubiquitous, those of the saints as well as that of Christ? Brentz himself asks the question; but his reply is far from satisfactory: "Let us," he says, "not be solicitous at present, and in this life, concerning the state of the saints in the world to come; but give Christ His own peculiar majesty, more excellent than all that can be named, and join His saints to Him."[1]

The foregoing views of the invisible world, and of the conditions of existence there, might be available, as they were actually used by Brentz, to meet objections to the doctrine of ubiquity drawn from the hypothesis of a localized heaven to which the glorified body of Christ is confined;[2] but they are manifestly inadequate to the task of reconciling the attribute of ubiquity, supposed to be communicated to Christ's humanity by the personal union, with the conditions of existence on earth. Whatever be the nature of our Lord's glorified body, it is certain at all events that His earthly body had a local existence. How then did Brentz seek to secure, as his theory required, even for the earthly body the attribute of ubiquity? As Luther had done before him,[3]

---

[1] *De Divina Majestate Christi*, p. 959.

[2] Thomasius (*Person und Werk*, ii. 358) animadverts on a statement made by Heppe (*Geschichte des Deutschen Protestantismus*), that Brentz did not derive the doctrine of ubiquity from the union of the natures, but from the full entrance of the exalted man Christ into the glory of God, and from the session of the Son of God at the right hand of the Father, as one which the slightest acquaintance with Brentz' writings shows to be the direct contrary of the actual fact. Heppe is certainly grossly in error; but his error lies not in what he affirms, but in what he denies. The truth is, Brentz based his doctrines of ubiquity both on the personal union, and on the nature of Christ's glorified body, and of spiritual bodies in general.

[3] Luther, after the Scholastics, distinguished three ways in which a thing could be in place: localiter or circumscriptivé, definitivé, and repletivé. Localiter, as when place and bodies correspond; as wine in a vessel takes no more space, and the vessel gives no more space, than the quantity of wine requires. Definitivé, when a thing is in a particular place, but cannot be measured by the space of the place, taking more or less room at will, as in the case of angels, who can be either in a house or a nutshell. Repletivé, when a thing is at the same time wholly in all places, filling all places, and yet is measured and contained by no place. This third way belongs to God alone. All three ways of being were, according to Luther, possible for Christ's body. The first it had on earth when it took and gave space according to its dimensions; the second when it rose out of the grave through the stone at the mouth of the sepulchre and passed through closed doors; the third it had and has in virtue of personal union with the omnipresent God. Bekenntniss vom Abendmahl Christi, *Luther's Sämmtliche Werke*, 30er Band, Erlangen ed. pp. 207-217.

viz., by conceiving of the *ubiquity* as ILLOCAL, and maintaining the co-existence simultaneously in Christ of two ways of being—a local existence here or there in space, and an illocal, omnipresent being in the Logos to which the humanity was united. He admitted frankly that local ubiquity could not be predicated of Christ's humanity either on earth or in heaven. "I am not ignorant," he says, "that certain of the ancients disapproved of this saying: the humanity of Christ is everywhere. I myself would disapprove of it if by this word *(ubique)* locality were signified. Let us therefore *docendi gratiâ* posit a threefold ubiquity—viz. a local, a repletive, and a personal. Now there is nothing whatever, either spiritual or corporeal, which is everywhere by a local ubiquity; but God alone by His nature is everywhere by a repletive ubiquity. And after the Son of God united to Himself humanity, it necessarily follows that that humanity, assumed into the unity of one person by the Son of God, is everywhere by a *personal* ubiquity."[1] This distinction between a local and a personal ubiquity—or, as it was afterwards epigrammatically expressed, between a ubiquity *in loco* and a ubiquity *in Logo*[2]—being allowed, the combination of an omnipresent manner of existence with the limitations of earthly life becomes easy. It can be said at once, as Brentz does say, that Christ was confined within the Virgin's womb, and filled the whole world;[3] that when He was in Bethany about to ride on an ass into Jerusalem, He was at the same moment in the Holy City and the Praetorium;[4] that at the institution of the Holy Supper He sat circumscriptively in one certain place at the table, and at the same time gave to His disciples His own true body in the bread to be eaten, and His own true blood in the wine to be drunk.[5]

It will readily be seen that a theory which, to maintain its consistency, did not shrink from such positions as these, was not likely to find any insuperable difficulty in ascribing

---

[1] *De Personali unione*, p. 842.
[2] See Thomasius, ii. 418, on Aegidius Hunnius.
[3] *De Divina Majestate Christi*, p. 928.
[4] Eodem loco.
[5] *De Sessione Christi ad dext. Dei*, p. 1073; see also *De Incarnatione*, 1021.

to the humanity of Christ even on earth not only ubiquity, the principal matter in dispute, but all other divine attributes. This accordingly Brentz does. He invests the humanity of Christ with all divine qualities, or, to use his favourite phrase, comprehensive of everything, with DIVINE MAJESTY, from the moment of Incarnation. He does not hesitate to say that the ascension and the session at the right hand of God took place not after the resurrection, but from the very beginning, from the moment when the hypostatical union of the two natures took place.[1] Incarnation and exaltation are in his view identical.[2] He does not indeed deny the historical reality of the ascension from the Mount of Olives; he distinguishes it as the *visible* ascent, from the invisible one which took place at the moment of Incarnation, and explains it to have been a spectacle economically prepared by Christ, partly to fulfil Scripture, partly to make the disciples understand that they were to be favoured no longer with such apparitions as they had enjoyed during the forty days following the resurrection; the time of such general and familiar appearances being now at an end.[3]

It thus appears that, in the system of Brentz, the two states of exaltation and humiliation are not successive, as we have been accustomed to regard them, but rather simultaneous and co-existent. The only difference between the earthly and the heavenly states is, that in the former Christ was at once humbled and exalted in the same sense, while in the latter He enjoys His exaltation unalloyed by

---

[1] *De Personali unione*, p. 847: Quid autem opus est, de tempore tantum resurrectionis et ascensionis Christi dicere, cum jam inde ab initio, in momento incarnationis suae ascenderit invisibiliter in coelum, et ad dextram Dei patris sui sederit?

[2] *De Div. Maj.* p. 923: Deinde non est sentiendum, quod humanitas Christi tum primum exaltata est in summam sublimitatem, et acceperit omnem potestatem in coelo et in terra, cum ascendit visibiliter ex monte Oliveti in coelum, sed cum verbum caro factum est, et cum in utero virginis Deus assumpsit hominem in eandem personam.

[3] *De Ascensu Christi in Coelum*, p. 1038; Voluit Christus hoc spectaculo finem facere generalium suarum apparitionum, quibus hactenus per quadraginta dies veritatem resurrectionis suae testificatus est. Etsi enim postea visus est etiam Paulo: tamen non apparuit amplius generaliter eo modo, quo per quadraginta dies apparuit, ut una cum discipulis familiariter colloqueretur, ambularet, et convivaretur. Hoc igitur externum spectaculum, ascensus Christi ex monte Oliveti, est clausula eorum apparitionum, quibus se hactenus a resurrectione discipulis gratifecerat.

any accompanying humiliation. The earthly Christ combined in Himself, so to speak, two humanities, a humbled one, and an exalted one; this being omnipresent, omniscient, omnipotent, etc., that localized, visible, tangible, limited in knowledge and power. One is naturally sceptical of the possibility of such a combination, and curious to know by what means Brentz secures their mutual compatibility. But on careful examination, one finds that our author does not greatly trouble himself about the solution of this difficult problem, but places majesty and exinanition side by side, and leaves them to adjust themselves to one another as best they can. He divides the things which can happen to the person of Christ into *three* grades. The first grade is that of divine majesty, in which the man Christ was from the beginning; the second grade is that of exinanition or humiliation, in which He existed in the days of His flesh till the resurrection; the third grade is that of economy or dispensation, terms applicable to Christ's whole life on earth, but which may be conveniently restricted to those acts or events in which Christ after the resurrection, and even after His ascension into heaven, appeared in one particular place, and shall appear in the last day.[1] This third grade Brentz explains after the following fashion. It is economy when Christ does anything, or appears not according to His majesty, but in accommodation to our power of comprehension, or for our benefit. When He had risen from the dead, and was being sought by the women in the sepulchre, the angel said: "He is risen, He is not here." It was truly said, but not *juxta majestatem*, but *juxta economiam*. He was not in the sepulchre dead, as the women sought to find Him. He was not in the sepulchre according to the external aspect. But He was nevertheless not in the sepulchre only, but even in heaven and earth, according to the majesty of His divinity—the divinity communicated to His humanity.[2] The same epithet *economical* is applied to the appearances of the risen Christ, to His eating, to the prints of the nails which He showed to Thomas. These things did not form a part of Christ's *humiliation*, for that was past; but neither did they belong to His

---

[1] *De Divina Majestate Christi*, p. 928.   [2] *Ibid.* p. 929.

exaltation, for the glorified body of the Saviour is neither visible, nor disfigured by wounds, nor liable to hunger; they were simply an accommodation or condescension to the weakness of the disciples.

Passing over this third grade, and returning to the question concerning the compatibility of the other two, we find, as already stated, that Brentz does little more than assert their actual co-existence. Christ the man, being born, was bound in swaddling-clothes and laid in a manger; and if you regard His exinanition, He was not then in any other place; but if you consider His majesty, He could not be confined to the manger, but filled the whole universe. He lay in the sepulchre dead, *exinanitione;* He governed heaven and earth alive, *majestate.* With reference to the attribute of omniscience, indeed, the author expresses himself with less decision. Alluding to certain passages in Luther's writings, quoted by opponents, in which Christ is spoken of as like other men, not thinking of all things at once, or seeing, hearing, and feeling all things at the same time, he explains that these statements are to be understood with reference to the exinanition; so that while, if you look at the majesty of the man Christ, He was from the beginning of the Incarnation *in formâ Dei*, and could think, hear, see, and feel all things at one time, nevertheless He humbled Himself, and was made in the likeness of men, so that He now eat, now drank, now preached, now slept, and did not always think or see all things.[1] This *could*, this *potuit*, is not thoroughgoing; it is the only hesitating word to be found in Brentz. To be consistent, he ought rather to have affirmed that Christ saw, and yet did not seem to see, all things at once. The logic of his theory required him to affirm a dissembled omniscience and omnipotence, as well as an invisible omnipresence. And when he is speaking in general terms of the majesty, he shows that he is fully aware of what his system demands. He expressly says that Christ dissembled His majesty in the time of exinanition;[2] meaning that it was there in all its fulness, but

[1] *De Incarnatione*, p. 1001.
[2] *Ibid.* p. 1027: Personalis unio duarum naturarum in Christo non ita est intelligenda, quod divinitas mutetur in humanitatem, aut quod humanitas fuerit ab

only concealed from view by the servile form assumed in humility, and because the work of salvation made such assumption necessary; not always or perfectly concealed, however; for although in the time of His humility He did not exhibit the supreme majesty which He had, nevertheless He did not altogether so dissemble it (our author assures us) that it did not sometimes appear, as in the forty days' fast, the walking on the waters, the occasional assumption of invisibility, and the transfiguration.[1]

In passing from John Brentz to Martin Chemnitz we enter into a very different intellectual and moral climate, the author of the work on the two natures of Christ (*De duabus naturis in Christo*) being a scholar thoroughly acquainted with the literature of his subject, and able to enrich his pages with a multitude of apt quotations, patristic and scholastic, and at the same time a man of a calm, dignified, peace-loving temper. Of this excellent book, in which it is easy to recognise the sobering and modifying influence of extensive knowledge, and of cordial sympathy with men representing diverse theological tendencies, well becoming one who had been a disciple both of Luther and of Melanchthon,[2] it would be a pleasant task to give a full analysis, but I must content myself here with a brief indication of the points in which the Christological system contained therein differs from that of the Würtemberg reformer.[3]

aeterno, aut quod humanitas transfuderit suas imbecillitates in divinitatem, sed quod salva utriusque substantia divinitas ornavit in incarnatione humanitatem omni sua majestate, *quam tamen majestatem humanitas, tempore exinanitionis, suo modo dissimulavit*, donec eam resurrectione, et missione Spiritus Sancti, Ecclesiae, quantum quidem in hoc seculo ad salutem cognitu necessarium est, patefecit. This sentence is a brief statement of Brentz' whole theory at the close of his treatise on the Incarnation. [1] *De Personali unione*, p. 848.

[2] Melanchthon, as is well known, took the Reformed view of the person of Christ and of Christ's presence in the Supper.

[3] For a more detailed account of both the Brentian and the Chemnitzian Christology, readers are referred to Dorner, *Person of Christ*, div. ii. vol. ii., and still better to Thomasius, *Christi Person und Werk*, vol. ii. pp. 342-404. Those who desire to peruse a clear exposition of the Lutheran Christology in all the stages of its history, will find what they want in the valuable work of the last-named author, who devotes upwards of two hundred pages to the subject (vol. ii. 307-526), and traces the course of the controversy from Luther to the period of the Saxon Decisi- at the close of the Tübingen-Geissen dispute, in a very lucid and interesting manner.

In common with Brentz and all advocates of the Lutheran Christology, Chemnitz held that the personal union of the two natures involved a real communication of the properties of the divine nature to the human, limited only by the principle that each nature must preserve its essential properties, earnestly repudiating the Reformed conception of the union as a sustentation of the human by the divine, or as a mere gluing together of two separate and entirely heterogeneous natures.[1] He differed from Brentz in the application of the limiting principle, in the view he took of the mode and the effect of the communication, and in the adjustment of the same to the state of exinanition. As to the first point, Chemnitz held visibility, tangibility, existence *in loco*, to be essential properties of matter; and by the accidential properties of Christ's humanity he understood the infirmities to which human nature is liable on account of sin, and which Christ in the state of exinanition voluntarily assumed that He might suffer for us.[2] In accordance with this view, he consistently held that even the post-resurrection, glorified body of Christ possessed, and will for ever possess, figure, and a localized manner of being. Jesus rose from the dead with that very substance of human nature which He received from the Virgin Mary, having hands, feet, sides, flesh, bones; in that body He ascended to heaven, and He will return to judgment as He was seen to ascend, so that men shall see that very body which they pierced with nails in the passion.[3] The ascension was not a mere economic spectacle, but the actual progress through space of a real body rising gradually from earth up to a locally defined heaven.[4] And as Christ while on earth was *in loco* as to His body, just like other men; so now, according to natural law, He occupies with His glorified body a certain space, just as saints after the resurrection will do, whose bodies, though *spiritual*, will still be material, not angelic in nature.[5] Even the glorified

---

[1] *De duab. nat.* caput v. pp. 24, 25.

[2] *Ibid.* p. 4: Naturale ratione sit (hum. nat.) visibilis, palpabilis, physica locatione uno loco circumscripta. Accidentalia idiomata vocantur infirmitates propter peccatum humanae naturae impositae.

[3] *Ibid.* p. 17.   [4] *Ibid.* p. 185.   [5] *Ibid.* p. 186.

body of the Redeemer is by itself and of itself bounded by the property of its nature, and after the manner of glorified bodies is somewhere; and the *where* is not on earth. Ordinarily, Christ is now no longer present in His Church, either after the mode of His earthly body or after the mode of His glorified body.[1]

On the subject of the *communicatio idiomatum*, Chemnitz, while asserting the Lutheran position against the Reformed, was particularly careful to guard against anything like exaequation of the natures. While Brentz boldly set aside the axiom *finitum non capax infiniti* as virtually rendering the Incarnation impossible, Chemnitz allowed its validity, and admitted that no divine property could become habitually or formally a property of humanity. He therefore conceived of the communication in question, not as an endowment of the human nature of Christ with a second-hand divinity, which after the endowment has once taken place it can claim as its own, but rather as a *pervasion* of the human nature by the divine, using it as its organ, and exerting its energy in, through, and with it.[2] His watchword, borrowed from John of Damascus, is περιχώρησις; and his favourite, oft-repeated, elaborately-expounded, illustrative figure, the patristic *mass of heated iron*. He carefully prepares his way for the assertion and proof of this pervasion of the human organ by the divine actor, by a systematic classification of all the different modes in which communication of the natures can take place, scrupulously pointing out

[1] *De duab. nat.* pp. 186, 187: De modo igitur praesentiae juxta rationem et conditionem hujus seculi, visibili, sensibili, locali ac circumscripto dicta illa loquuntur—secundum quem modum praesentiae Christus jam ordinarie ecclesiae suae interris non amplius est. . . . Et hac etiam forma visibili seu conditione corporum glorificatorum Christus corpore suo, nobis in hac vita in ecclesia in terris militante non est praesens, sed in coelis, unde ad judicium redibit.

[2] *De duab. nat.* p. 126: Quod scilicet div. nat. τοῦ λόγου non transfuderit extra se in assumptam naturam majestatem, virtutem, potentiam, et operationem eandem cum divina, vel aequalem divinae majestati, virtuti, potentiae, et operationi quae a divinitate separata, proprie, peculiariter et distinctim, formaliter, habitualiter aut subjective, humanitati, et secundum se inhaerunt sed quod tota plenitudo divinitatis in assumpta natura personaliter ita habitet, ut div. majestas tota sua plenitudine in nat. assumpta luceat; utque div. virtus, et potentia, majestatis et omnipotentiae suae opera *in* assumpta natura *cum* illa, et *per* illam exerceat et perficiat. These prepositions, *in*, *cum*, *per*, constitute a standing formula for Chemnitz.

how far the Reformed go along with him, and showing manifest anxiety to go as far with them as he can. Then at length he takes his stand on this point of difference; but even here he does not wholly differ from his opponents, for he includes under his third and highest grade not only the divine properties communicated to the humanity after the manner in which the power of burning is conveyed to heated iron, but those hyperphysical extraordinary gifts and graces with which the Reformed themselves declared the human nature of Christ to have been endowed in order that it might become a fit organ of Deity.[1] Indeed, it is questionable whether there was any serious difference of a theoretical kind between the Reformed and him. For granted, on the one hand, as Chemnitz does grant, that the divine attributes are the divine essence, and therefore inseparable from it, and on the other, that whatever habitually or formally belongs to human nature must be finite, there does not seem much harm in the doctrine of perichoresis, according to which the Logos pervaded the humanity as fire pervades heated iron, or the human soul pervades the body. The point of divergence lay not so much in the theory as in the use made of it in connection with the sacramentarian controversy.[2]

The position taken up by Chemnitz on the subject of

---

[1] *De duab. nat.* caput xii. Chemnitz was the first to make such a classification, though Damascenus had made such distinctions as might easily suggest the scheme to his mind. He distributed idiomatic propositions into three classes: the first, in which the subject is the whole person *in concreto*, the predicate a property of either nature; the second, in which the subject is either nature, the predicate an activity pertaining to the work of redemption in which both natures concur; the third, in which divine properties are ascribed *realiter* to the human nature. These kinds of propositions in the dialect of the Lutheran scholastics were distinguished respectively as the *genus idiomaticum*, the *genus apotelismaticum*, and the *genus majestaticum* or *auchematicum*. Strauss (*Glaubenslehre*, ii. 134) remarks that to be complete a fourth genus should have been added, viz. *genus ταπεινωτικόν*; including those propositions in which human properties, such as suffering, death, etc., are ascribed to the divine nature. The dispute between the Lutherans and the Reformed had reference to the third genus. Thomasius is of opinion that by this classification Chemnitz did no real service to Christology, but only tended to foster a scholastic way of teaching the subject (vol. ii. 387).

[2] Dorner (*Person of Christ*, div. ii. vol. ii. p. 204) remarks that Danaeus objected mainly to the second part of Chemnitz' treatise, that which treats of the presence of the whole person of Christ in the Church.

Christ's bodily presence in the Supper, and in the Church generally, was different both from that of the Reformed and from that of Brentz. His characteristic doctrine is not that Christ in His whole person *is* everywhere present, but that He is *able* to be present *when*, *where*, and *how* He pleases, even in invisible form.[1] He teaches not a necessary omnipresence, but a hypothetical or optional multipresence. He acknowledges that such multipresence is not only above, but contrary to, the nature of body; and he frankly admits that had there been no express word or special promise in Scripture concerning Christ's presence, even in His human nature, in the Church, he would neither have dared nor wished to teach anything on the subject. He dogmatizes only because Christ said, "This is my body." And he thinks it right to limit dogmatism to the cases specified in Scripture. He declines to say whether the body of Christ be in stones, trees, etc., as Luther affirmed, because there is no evidence that Christ wishes His body to be there, and the discussion of such questions yields no edification; and for the rest, all such mysteries are relegated to the Eternal School, to which our author often piously refers, and where he humbly hopes to learn many things he does not understand now, and among them the incomprehensible riddles arising out of the Incarnation. At the same time, while grounding his doctrine of potential omnipresence on the words of Scripture, Chemnitz holds it to be a legitimate deduction from the union of natures. For him, as for all adherents of the Lutheran Christology, it is a sacred canon: after the union the Logos is not outside the flesh, nor the flesh outside the Logos (*Logos non extra carnem, et caro non extra λόγον*). To deny that canon, as the Reformed did, is to deny the Incarnation.[2]

From this canon it follows that the humanity is always

---

[1] *De duab. nat.* p. 188: Christum, licet naturalem modum praesentiae corporis sui, ordinarie terris abstulerit . . . tamen suo corpore, etiam post ascensionem, et ante judicium praesentem adesse, aut praesentiam corporis sui exhibere posse in terris, quandocunque, ubicunque et quomodocunque vult, etiam invisibili forma.

[2] *De duab. nat.* p. 20: Quae unio adeo arcta, individua, inseparabilis, et indissolubilis est, ut div. nat. τοῦ λόγου nec velit, nec possit, nec debeat extra hanc cum carne unionem, sed in arctissima illa unione cogitari, quaeri, aut apprehendi; caro etiam assumpta, non extra, sed intra intimum τοῦ λόγου assumentis com-

intimately, inseparably, and *indistanter* present to the Logos;[1] and from this presence to the Logos follows in turn the possibility of the humanity being present at will to any part of the creation. Why only the *possibility* is inferred, is a question which naturally arises. One would suppose that if the humanity be always present to the Logos in virtue of the union, it must also be present in some manner, local or illocal, to the universe. But it is not our business to justify, but merely to expound, the theory now under consideration. This limitation of the effect of the union and communion of the natures to a merely potential omnipresence or multipresence was the peculiarity of Chemnitz and his school, and one of the outstanding points of difference between him and Brentz. It was a point greatly debated in after days in the controversy between the Giessen and the Tübingen theologians; the Giessen men contending for the distinction between the two kinds of presence, that to the Logos and that to the world, which had come to be named respectively *praesentia intima* and *praesentia extima*, and holding that the former involved only the possibility of the latter; the Tübingen men holding that the distinction in question was imaginary, and that a potential omnipresence was an absurdity. The course of the debate ran into very subtle discussions, which it would be unprofitable and tedious to speak of here. Suffice it to say, that much use was made on the Giessen side of the Chemnitzian conception of the divine majesty communicated to Christ's humanity as ENERGY: the Logos,

plexum cogitanda, quarenda, et apprehenda est. Again, p. 194: Ratione hypostaticae unionis jam post Incarnationem, persona τοῦ λόγου extra unionem cum assumpta natura, et sine ea seorsim aut separatim, nec cogitari nec credi pie et recte vel potest vel debet; nec vicissim assumpta natura extra λόγον, et sine eo.

[1] *De duab. nat.* p. 195: Ita ergo toti plenitudini Deitatis filii personaliter unita est assumpta nat. ut λόγος intra arcanum, arctissimum, intimum, profundissimum et praesentissimum complexum totius div. suae naturae, quae supra et extra omnem locum est, secum, intra se, apud se, et penes se, personaliter unitam atque praesentissimam semper habeat, et in illa plenitudine unitae Deitatis assumpta natura suam ἀδιαίρετον καὶ ἀδιάστατον, juxta Damascenum, individuam seu inseparabilem, et indistantem, seu locorum intervallo indisjunctam habeat immanentiam. Haec vero praesentia non constat ratione aliqua aut conditione hujus seculi, quae ratione nostra comprehendi possit, sed est magnum, incomprehensibile et inennarrabile illud mysterium hypostaticae unionis.

according to Chemnitz, communicated His energy to the human nature, as heat communicates its virtue to iron. By this way of conceiving the matter he tried to meet the objection, that if any divine attributes were communicated to Christ's human nature, all must have been, for example, eternity and immensity. These attributes, he said, are quiescent; they remain within the divine essence; they have no operation *ad extra;* therefore they are not directly communicated, but only indirectly through their connection in the divine nature with the operative attributes.[1] The Giessen theologians applied this distinction between operative and inoperative attributes to the question of ubiquity. They said, by omnipresence is meant not immensity, which is an incommunicable attribute of Deity, but presence in the world as an actor,—operative omnipresence. But God is free in action, therefore He is free to be present to the world or not as He pleases. The use of presence is a matter of free will.[2] This sample of controversial subtlety may suffice as an illustration of the thorny paths into which the dialectics of the Lutheran Christology led its adherents. Let us return to Chemnitz, that we may, in the last place, make ourselves acquainted with his view of the exinanition.

On this subject, as on that of ubiquity, the position taken up by Chemnitz is difficult to understand, for the simple reason that it is not self-consistent, being an eclectic attempt to combine opposite points of view. Generally speaking, however, his doctrine may be discriminated from that taught by Brentz as follows. The Brentian state of exinanition *(status exinanitionis)* consisted in possession, with habitual furtive use of majesty; the Chemnitzian, in possession, with occasional use and prevailing non-use. According to Brentz, Christ in His state of humiliation not only *could* use, but *did* use, and *could not help* using, His majesty as a communicated attribute of His human nature; only in that state the use was dissembled, hidden; while in the state of exaltation it is open. According to Chemnitz, Christ in the state of humiliation *could* use majesty in, through, and with His humanity, and *sometimes did* use it

---

[1] *De duab. nat.* p. 127.
[2] Usurpatio praesentiae est liberrimae voluntatis; see Thomasius, vol. ii. p. 431.

to show the fact of possession; but generally He did not *wish* to use it. In the state of exaltation, on the other hand, He entered into the full and manifest use of His divine majesty in and by His assumed human nature.[1] Sometimes Chemnitz seems inclined to ascribe not only partial use, but even partial defective possession, to the *status humilis*. He adopts from Ambrose the idea of a retraction on the part of the Logos, as explaining the exinanition. The power, he says, and operation of the Logos was not idle *per se* in the time of exinanition, but administered all things everywhere with the Father and the Spirit; but in the human nature during that time He concealed His glory, power, and operation under the infirmities of the flesh, and, as Ambrose speaks, withdrew it from activity,[2] so that natural properties and infirmities alone seemed to abide and predominate in the assumed nature not merely in the face of men, but even before God; while, nevertheless, that fulness of divinity in the Logos elsewhere performed most powerfully all things with the Father and the Holy Ghost.[3] This passage not only teaches by implication partial non-possession of majesty by the humanity in the state of humiliation, but involves a contradiction of the Lutheran axiom, *Logos non extra carnem*, representing the Logos as, in the state of humiliation, operative where the

---

[1] Chemnitz' usual phrase to describe the exaltation is the plenary and manifest use and exhibition of majesty. Thus, cap. xxxiii. p. 215: Per sessionem vero ad dexteram Dei ingressus est in plenariam et manifestam usurpationem et ostensionem ejus potentiae, virtutis, et gloriae Deitatis, quae tota plenitudine personaliter in assumpta natura ab initio unionis habitavit. Thomasius (ii. 401) represents Chemnitz as applying the terms *plenaria* and *manifesta* to *possessio* as well as *usurpatio*, in describing the state of exaltation, and quotes in proof the following: Deposita servi forma, assumpta natura humana ad plenariam et manifestam ejus majestatis possessionem et usurpationem, per sessionem ad dextram Dei, collocata et exaltata est. These words have escaped my observation in reading Chemnitz' treatise, but it is quite possible they do occur; for the author's doctrine is not self-consistent, the *retractio* of which he speaks really implying partial non-possession, defective περιχώρησις, imperfect communication of heat to the iron; and, moreover, a similar mode of expression occurs in the *Formula of Concord* which Chemnitz helped to compose; see part ii. cap. viii. § 26: Ad plenam possessionem, et div. majestatis usurpationem evectus est.

[2] *Ab opere retraxit*, p. 217.

[3] Cum tamen interea plenitudo illa divinitatis λόγου alibi omnia fortissime cum Patre et Spiritu Sancto operaretur.—P. 217.

humanity was not. Yet Chemnitz can hardly have meant to teach the Calvinistic *extra*, as it was called by the Tübingen theologians of a later generation in their warfare with their opponents of Giessen, whom they charged with entertaining that notion so abhorrent to all thoroughgoing Lutherans; for he speaks of Christ, even in the state of humiliation, as showing when He wished that the fulness of divinity dwelt in His flesh, and as manifesting its use as far as He wished through the assumed nature.[1] On the whole, his idea of the exinanition seems to have been full possession, the necessary consequence of the personal union, but prevalent abstinence from use, so as to present the aspect of non-possession,—the mass of iron being heated through and through, yet remaining black to sight and cold to feeling. The illustration is the author's own, and it serves well not only to explain his idea, but to show the difficulty of his theory of a possession unaccompanied by use. Exinanition in this view is a perpetual miracle, well characterized by the author himself as incomprehensible and indescribable.[2] When the theory is applied to omniscience, the exinanition appears not only a miracle, but, as the school of Tübingen maintained against the school of Giessen, an impossibility. For what can we understand by abstinence from the use of omniscience? Chemnitz himself seems to have found it hard to tell, for his statement on this point looks like the utterance of a man at his wits' end. "Christ, as to His divine nature, had omniscience; as to His human nature, He had infused habits of knowledge in which He grew. But even when He grew in wisdom He was full of wisdom, because the plenitude, as of Deity, so of wisdom and divine knowledge, dwelt *personally* in the

---

[1] Christus, ipso tempore exinanitionis, quando voluit ostendit plenitudinem illam in sua carne habitare, et usum ejus quando voluit, et quantum voluit, per assumptam naturam, ipso exinanitionis tempore exercuit, manifestavit, exeruit.

[2] Haec est incomprehensibilis et inennarrabilis exinanitio. Infinitis enim modis plus est, quam si ignis in ferro prorsus ignito, nec speciem, nec vim, nec operationem suam exereret.—P. 217. Again, p. 218: Si in ferro undiquaque perfecte ignito Deus manifestationem et operationem virtutis lucendi et urendi ad tempus supersedeat, ut frigidum, nigrum, et obscurum videntibus et contrectantibus appareret. That represents the state of humiliation. The state of exaltation is when the iron is not only heated, but shows its heat—vim suum lucendi et urendi

assumed nature, in which and through which, as far as the exinanition would allow, it manifested itself more and more. Whence in the time of exinanition Christ's human nature *could* be ignorant and grow in wisdom; but in the state of exaltation it is omniscient indeed."[1]

Such were the two forms which the Lutheran Christology assumed in the hands of Brentz and Chemnitz. It is manifest that they present sufficient points of difference to make any attempt at reconciliation somewhat difficult. An attempt, however, was made by representatives of the Swabian and Lower Saxon schools,—Chemnitz himself taking a leading part in the work of reconciliation,—and the *Formula of Concord* was the result. The method of reconciliation adopted in the composition of this ecclesiastical symbol was that of giving and taking; opposite points of view being placed side by side, and troublesome questions being passed over *sub silentio*. It was declared, *e.g.*, that in the personal union each nature retains its essential properties; but while the essential properties of the divine nature are carefully enumerated, the essential properties of the human nature are not distinguished from the accidental. To be bounded and circumscribed, and to be moved from place to place, are mixed up with properties which are certainly accidental, such as to suffer and die; and we are not told whether the former are essential or not. The whole list are simply called properties. It is further declared that the human nature of Christ was exalted to the possession of divine properties over and above its own spiritual and natural ones; and that this exaltation to divine majesty took place first *through the personal union*, even from the moment of conception, and afterward through glorification after the resurrection; and in proof of the possession of majesty from the first, is adduced birth from the Virgin *inviolata ipsius virginitate*.[2] This majesty of the human nature, however, we are told, was for the most part concealed in the state of exinanition, and as it were dissembled,—secret use being implied.[3] Yet in another place possession without use, kenosis as to use in opposition to

[1] P. 139.   [2] *Formula of Concord*, part ii. c. viii. 8.
[3] *Formula of Concord*, part ii. c. viii. 12, 13.

krypsis, is asserted.[1] Christ always was in possession of the majesty in virtue of the personal union, but He emptied Himself in the state of humiliation; and hence it came that He grew in age, wisdom, and grace, and only after His resurrection entered into a plenary use, as a man, of omniscience, omnipotence, and omnipresence; or, as it is put in another place, into a full *possession* and use of divine majesty.[2] On the subject of ubiquity, both a hypothetical and a general or necessary omnipresence were taught. The Chemnitzian phrase, Christ can be with His body wherever He wishes, is used, and at the same time quotations from Luther are made, which assert in the strongest possible manner an absolute omnipresence, rendering of course the assertion of a power to be present anywhere at pleasure quite superfluous. Of the distinction suggested by Chemnitz between presence to the Logos and presence to the world, no notice is taken.

A document constructed on such a principle of compromise, and so open to a double interpretation, was not likely to put an end to controversy; and certainly the *Formula of Concord* utterly failed to produce that effect. It only supplied material for fresh disputes to another generation, in which the combatants ranged themselves respectively on the Brentian and the Chemnitzian sides; each party being able to find something in the formula in support of its particular views. On one most important subject the symbol was specially vague and unsatisfactory, that, viz., of the relation of the majesty communicated to the human nature of Christ, by the personal union, to His earthly state of humiliation. It seemed to teach at once full possession and secret use; full possession and prevalent abstinence from use; and not only partial use, but even partial and defective possession. Here was a question around which fierce strife was sure to be waged. Possession with hidden use, or possession without use, involving in some sense even defective possession; on which side did the truth lie?

---

[1] *Formula of Concord*, part ii. c. viii. 66.
[2] *Ibid.* part i. c. viii. 16. In part ii. cap. viii. 22, a partial and occasionally manifest use of majesty by Christ, *pro liberrima voluntate* in the *statu exinanitionis* is taught.

Around these points skirmishing went on incessantly for a generation, until at length the great final war between Tübingen and Giessen broke out, in which the combatants went into battle to the respective war-cries of krypsis and kenosis, and fought with indomitable prowess and deadly bitterness for the space of some twenty years, till its noise was drowned in the louder din of a still more protracted war, carried on for another cause, with more substantial but not more carnal weapons.[1]

1. Proceeding now to offer a few critical observations on the Lutheran Christology, I begin by repeating a remark already made, that the principle on which the system is based is therein arbitrarily applied. That principle is, that the union of natures in one person involves communication of attributes; and there seems to be no reason *à priori* why the communication should not be reciprocal.[2] But we are given to understand that the communication is all on one side; divine attributes are communicated to the human nature, but not *vice versâ*. The axioms *finitum non capax infiniti* is set aside, while the correlative proposition *infinitum non capax finiti* is assumed to be axiomatically certain. In the classification of the various kinds of communications, one, by which the human nature becomes partaker of the majesty of Deity, is recognised; but for one by which the divine nature becomes partaker of the weakness, and subject to the measures of human nature, no place is found.[3] God is not at liberty to descend; He can only

---

[1] See Appendix, Note B.

[2] Gerhard says on this point: In hoc communicationis genere reciprocatio non habet locum. Ratio haec est, quia div. nat. est simpliciter ἀναλλοίωπος καὶ ἀμετάβλητος, ideo per unionem nec perfici, nec minui, nec evehi, nec deprimi potuit; hum. autem nat. quia humilis est et ἐνδεής ideo per unionem potuit exaltari, evehi ac perfici. Nec est, quod regeras, unionem esse reciprocam, proinde etiam communicationem. Quamvis autem unio respectu sui ipsius considerata sit aequalis et reciproca, tamen ratione unitarum naturarum considerata exhibet nobis hanc differentiam, quod in unione ὁ λόγος sit assumens, caro autem sit assumpta: ὁ λόγος assumpsit carnem, caro autem non assumpsit λόγον, jam vero assumpti provectio est, non assumentis, ut dicunt pii veteres.—Loci iv. c. xii. § cci.

[3] Thomasius, ii. p. 459, points out that the Tübingen theologians in their controversy with the Giessen school taught a *genus tapeinoticon*, and says that in this they returned to Luther, and enriched the Lutheran Christology. This genus, however, called ἰδιοποίησις or οἰκείωσις, was not analogous to the *genus*

make man ascend: Incarnation means not God becoming man, but man becoming God. Now this one-sided application of the distinctive principle might be politic and prudent, but it is not logical; nor can it boast of any moral recommendations to compensate for its want of logic. It is not a doctrine worthy of all acceptation, that Incarnation cannot possibly mean the humiliation of God, but must signify the exaltation or deification of man. It is a doctrine contrary to the spirit of Scripture,[1] and to right ideas of the glory of God. This constant talk about the *majesty* communicated to the humanity of Christ in virtue of the personal union, savours of moral vulgarity, inasmuch as it implies that God's glory lies not in His grace, but chiefly in being infinite, omnipotent, omnipresent, and so forth. If obliged to make a choice, I would rather take up with the *genus tapeinoticum* than with the *genus auchematicum*, to speak in the language of the schools; in plain terms, a God letting Himself down to man's level seems a grander thing than a God raising man to His level, especially when the latter is not an act of grace, but of necessity, a condition *sine quâ non* of Incarnation.

2. The Lutheran Christology, to say the least, threatens with extinction the reality of Christ's human nature. Doubtless its advocates are careful to say that each nature after the union retains its essential properties, and to protest against their doctrine being held to imply confusion, equalization, or abolition of the natures; and, of course, we believe that they did not mean to teach such errors. But if the question be, What are the logical consequences of their theory? it is difficult to see how such conclusions can be avoided. It does not suffice to save the reality of the humanity to say, with Brentz, that the Deity possessed

---

auchematicum. Neither the Tübingen theologians nor Luther ascribed to the divine nature human qualities as they ascribed human qualities to the human nature; but only in the sense in which the Reformed understood the doctrine of the *communicatio idiomatum.*

[1] Lutheran theologians admitted that the ancients identified *exinanitio* with *incarnatio,* but claimed to have Scripture on their side when they taught that *exinanitio* proper was subsequent in idea to the Incarnation. Hence they called *exinanitio* in the former sense *ecclesiastica,* and *exinanitio* in their own sense *Biblica.* So Gerhard, loci iv. cap. xiv. § xciii.

by that nature is a communicated one; for the whole question is, whether such communication be compatible with the nature of that humanity. As to the attribute of ubiquity, indeed, it must be admitted that the ingenious distinction between local and illocal presence evades the argument drawn by the Reformed from the reality of Christ's body against the ascription of that attribute to the human nature. If any one choose to ascribe to Christ's body an illocal ubiquity, he cannot be refuted, any more than he could be refuted were he to ascribe a similar ubiquity to the body of any ordinary man. The only question is, whether this illocal ubiquity be itself a reality, or only a mere ghost, with which no man can fight,—an invention to save a theory, and by which, while saved in appearance, the theory is substantially sacrificed. The authors of the Reformed reply to the *Formula of Concord* characterized the Lutheran distinctions between various kinds of presences as impudent and wicked sophisms, cunningly and fraudulently devised to defend a false position.[1] This may be rather strong language, but the statement is substantially correct; and one cannot but feel that when once refuge was taken in the epithet "illocal," the controversy concerning the communication of omnipresence to the humanity of Christ degenerated, as Le Blanc hints, into a mere logomachy.[2] The distinction between the two kinds of presence is virtually a giving up of the theory. The same remark may be made with reference to the Chemnitzian mode of

---

[1] *Admonitio Neostadtiensis*, c. viii., falsa hypothesis iv. Hae strophae et Sphingis aenigmata nihil sunt nisi impudentissima et nequissima sophismata ad illudendum Deo, et decipiendos homines, versute et fraudulenter excogitata, etc. The *Admonitio* is contained among the works of Zachary Ursinus, the author and expositor of the Heidelberg Catechism.

[2] *Theses Theologicae: De unione duarum in Christo naturarum et inde consequente idiomatum communicatione.* Le Blanc says: Quâ in controversia forte plus est logomachiae atque pertinaciae, quam realis discriminis, nam aliquo sensu concedere possumus, realem communicationem proprietatum naturae divinae naturae Christi humanae factum esse, quatenus ut dictum est, in na ura illa humana realiter et personaliter inhabitat, et est divinitas cum omnibus suis proprietatibus, quemadmodum realiter ignis est in ferro ignito, sed quemadmodum ex illa ignis cum ferro unione recte quidem dicere possumus, ferrum hoc urit, ferrum hoc candit, non tamen recte dicitur, ferreitas urit, ferreitas lucet, quia ignis in ferro, non ipsa tamen ferri natura, ita agit.

conceiving the communication of divine attributes in general to the human nature as analogous to the pervasion of iron by heat. There can be no doubt that this manner of representing the matter effectually guards against equalizing of the natures. But it does this by failing to teach the Lutheran doctrine of communication. For what the heat communicates to the iron is not anything contrary to, or even above, the nature of the latter; for it is the nature of iron to receive heat, and by it to be made hot and luminous. This illustration, therefore, of heated iron, to which Chemnitz was so partial, does not suffice to justify a communication of all divine attributes to the human nature, but only such a communication as the Reformed Christology allowed,—a communication, viz., of all the gifts and graces which human nature is capable of receiving.[1]

3. This theory, consistently worked out, leaves no room for such an exinanition in the earthly life of Christ as shall satisfy the requirements of historical truth and the aim of the Incarnation. The humiliation which is admitted to be soteriologically necessary is Christologically impossible. The act of Incarnation endows the human nature of Christ with attributes, of which no doctrine of exinanition, however ingeniously constructed, can deprive it, without destroying the Christological basis on which the whole superstructure rests. The distinction between possession and use is entirely inadequate to the task of reducing the humanity, supposed to be already endowed with divine majesty, to the sober measures of the kenosis. This is specially manifest in reference to the attributes of omniscience and omnipresence, to which the distinction cannot even be intelligibly applied. No doubt attempts were made by the Lutheran theologians to apply the distinction to these at-

[1] The Reformed theologians were not slow to point this out. Sadeel, *e.g.*, remarks that the ancients used the simile of the burning sword principally with reference to the soul of Christ, to show how it gained from union with the Logos, *e.g.* in being sinless. He also remarks that though fire gives to iron heat and light, it does not give it its own property of ascending, and in like manner " ὁ λόγος non ea tribuit hum. nat. quorum hum. ipsa nat. capax esse non potest, cujusmodi est infinitum esse et ubique esse, sed eam illustrat suo fulgore, et exornat dotibus incomprehensibilibus, quatenus ipsius naturae conditio fieri potest."—*De Veritate Humanae Naturae Christi*, pp. 184, 185. To the same effect the *Admon. Neost.*

tributes by the invention of other still more subtle distinctions; but these attempts bear failure stamped on their front. Gerhard, for example, following Chemnitz, disposes of the omniscience of Christ in the state of exinanition in the following fashion: "We teach that the soul of Jesus in the very first moment of the Incarnation was *personally* enriched, as with other divine excellences, so also with the proper omniscience of the Logos, through and in virtue of the real, most intimate, and indissoluble union and communion with the Logos. But as He did not always use His other gifts truly and really communicated to Him in the state of exinanition, so also the omniscience personally communicated to Him as man He did not always exercise *actu secundo*, and hence the soul of Christ truly made progress according to *natural* and *habitual* knowledge,—the omniscient Logos not always exercising through the assumed humanity His energy, which is *actu* to know all things, but in the state of exaltation the full use of omniscience at length ensued."[1] The distinction taken in this passage between the omniscience which the soul of Christ possesses *personaliter*, and the limited knowledge which it possessed *naturaliter*, means, if it means anything, that the attribute of omniscience was not really communicated to the human nature, but was merely possessed by the divine person to whom that nature was united. That is to say, the positing of the distinction is the giving up of the Lutheran theory, and a virtual return to the Reformed point of view. As for the other distinction between being omnis-

[1] Loci iv. c. xii. § cclxxix.: Docemus animam Christi in primo status incarnationis momento, ut aliis divinis ἐξοχαῖς, ita quoque omniscientia τοῦ λόγου propria *personaliter* esse ditatam per et propter realem, arctissimam et indissolubilem cum λογῷ omniscio unionem et κοινωνίαν. Sed ut aliis donis, vere ac realiter sibi communicatis in statu exinanitionis, non semper est usus, ita quoque omniscientiam personaliter sibi ut humini communicatam non semper actu secundo exeruit, ac proinde anima Christi juxta *naturalem* et *habitualem* scientiam vere profuit; λογῷ omniscio ἐνέργειαν suam, quae est actu omnia scire et cognoscere, per assumptam humanitatem non semper excrente, sed in statu exaltationis plena demum omniscientiae usurpatio fuit insequuta. Readers will observe in this passage a confusion of the person of Christ with His human nature. This use of the concrete in place of the abstract, the man instead of the humanity, is characteristic of the Lutherans, and was a frequent source of complaint on the part of the Reformed.

cient *actu primo*, and exercising omniscience *actu secundo*, it is simply one of the many subtleties which abound in the Lutheran Christology, and tend to create suspicion as to the soundness of a theory which stands in need of them.

The same thing may be said of the Chemnitzian distinction between *praesentia intima* or *praesentia extima*, intended to apply the principle of possession without use to the attribute of omnipresence. The Tübingen theologians correctly characterized it as an ingenious invention for the purpose of concealing the weak point in the system of their opponents.[1] It is, in truth, simply a disguised retreat from the Lutheran position, *Logos non extra carnem*, which cannot be maintained unless one be prepared to assert with the school of Tübingen, that wherever the Son of God is, there is the Son of man; and inasmuch as the Son of God, even in the time of the humiliation, was not only present to His flesh, but by a substantial propinquity to all creatures, therefore also the human nature assumed into the unity of the person was not only present to the Word, but also by a substantial propinquity to all creatures.[2]

Speaking generally, it may be said that the Chemnitzian school of Christologists saved the historical Christ, by in effect sacrificing the communication of properties in the Lutheran sense, in reference to the state of humiliation. On the other hand, the Brentian school saved the Lutheran theory at the expense of historical truth. The occult use of divine majesty yields no real state of humiliation. The later representatives of this school, sensible of this, sought to remedy the defect of the Brentian doctrine of exinanition, by the usual method of introducing some new subtle distinctions. They distinguished between *direct* and *reflex* use of majesty,[3] and asserted abstinence from the latter in the state of humiliation; but only a partial abstinence, in connection, namely, with the priestly office. Christ as a high priest made no personal use of His majesty, while at the same time He used it occultly as a king. Thus the later Tübingen theory, in brief, was: exinanition in the sacerdotal office by occultation and abstinence; in the kingly office,

---

[1] Thomasius ii. 450.   [2] *Ibid*. ii. 450.
[3] *Ibid*. ii. 469.

by occultation alone.[1] An utterly untenable theory, involving the ascription to Christ at the same time, and with reference to the same nature, of two series of contrary states. As a king He was omnipresent, as a priest He walked on earth in local circumscription; as a king He reigned, when as a priest He suffered on the cross; as a priest He truly died and rose again, as a king He continued alive in an occult manner, and afterwards manifested Himself alive to men. Well might the Giessen theologians ask, in reference to this theory: Who can exhaust the sea of absurdities into which it leads?[2] Good right had they to charge the advocates of such a theory with making the earthly life of the Saviour a spectacle of simulated servitude *(spectaculum simulatae servitutis);* as good a right, indeed, as their opponents had to charge *them* with betraying the cause of Lutheran Christology. Each party made good its accusation against its rival; and the result of the Tübingen-Geissen controversy was, to substantiate the statement that the Lutheran theory, consistently worked out, leaves no room for a state of humiliation.

4. In the Lutheran theory, the state of exinanition, admitted to be a fact, is an effect without a cause. The Gospels tell how Christ was conceived in the womb of the Virgin, was born, grew gradually up to manhood, was in all respects found in fashion as a man, subject to all sinless human infirmities, and to the ordinary conditions of human existence on earth. All these things the theory under consideration recognises as historical realities, and reckons to the state of exinanition; but it is unable to give any satisfactory account of them. The Incarnation does not account for them; for incarnation in the Lutheran Christology signifies simply the union of the Logos to a humanity endowed with divine attributes: omnipotent, omniscient, omnipresent, and as omnipresent possessing no locally cir-

---

[1] Exinanitio in officio sacerdotali, per occultationem et *retractionem*, in officio regio per solam occultationem facta est. Luc. Osiander in Thomasius, ii. 469.

[2] Thomasius, ii. 482: Ne plura dicenda sint, num Christus ut sacerdos vere mortuus est et vere revixit, ut rex autem vivus permansit occulte et latenter, et postea sese vivum hominibus manifestavit. Quis tandem exhauriat tantum mare absurditatum?

cumscribed existence. Incarnation and exinanition are entirely distinct; the former in idea precedes the latter, and it does not necessarily involve the latter. How, then, is the state of exinanition to be explained? Must we conceive of the Incarnation as not merely in idea but in reality preceding; and of the state of exinanition, including the conception, as the result of a voluntary act of self-humiliation on the part of the already pre-existent God-man? There is no other alternative open, if the historical humanity of Christ is not to be left standing as an inexplicable riddle. The Lutheran theologians did not fairly face this great difficulty besetting their theory. They shrank from asserting the real existence of a humanity of Christ, prior to the humanity which commenced with the conception; but, in so doing, they simply deprived themselves of the only possible means of accounting for the existence of the latter.[1]

5. Once more, the Lutheran Christology, in its zeal for the deification of Christ's humanity, really robs us of the Incarnation. If, as Lutheran theologians taught, the personal union necessarily involves the communication of divine attributes to the humanity, then, in so far as Christ's humanity was like ours, it was uninformed with Diety. Christ, *quâ real* man, was *mere* man. The incarnate God was not to be seen in Jesus of Nazareth; He was an airy, ghostly personage, as invisible as God Himself, omnipresent after an illocal manner, intangible, superior to all human needs and infirmities, immortal, omniscient, omnipotent. No wonder that speculative theologians of modern times should be found asserting that the Lutheran Christ is an

---

[1] Both Dorner and Schneckenburger agree in holding that a real God-manhood, pre-existent, and the cause of the humanity whose existence began with the conception, was the logical consequence of the Lutheran theory. Dorner, however, finds fault with Schneckenburger for not recognising that, in point of fact, the Lutheran theologians did not teach such a pre-existent humanity. "The actual doctrine," he says, "of the old dogmatics is one thing, the conclusion which may be drawn from it another. In this respect we have also conceded that the most strictly logical form of Lutheran Christology must be driven to the assumption of a pre-existent majesty." I do not suppose Schneckenburger meant to say anything more than this. See Dorner, *Person of Christ*, II. ii. 292–297, and 431–435. And Schneckenburger, *zur Kirchlichen Christologie*, pp. 20, 21; also *Vergleichende Darstellung*, ii. 208.

ideal, not a historical person,[1] and imagining themselves the children of Luther, and the true representatives of his Christological tendency, when they teach a Pantheistic doctrine in which Incarnation means the eternal identity of the divine and the human realizing itself, not in Christ in particular, but in humanity at large; the *krypsis* being the condition of the finite spirit, which in its earthly mode of existence is no longer conscious of what it has itself produced, as the absolute organizing reason of the world. The old Lutherans were not Pantheists, nor did they look on the historical Christ as an ordinary man; but their Christology was undoubtedly of such a character, as to make it possible for modern Pantheistic Christologies to lay claims to orthodoxy with a show of plausibility.[2]

PART II.—THE REFORMED CHRISTOLOGY.

IN passing from the Lutheran to the Reformed Christology, we encounter a markedly different manner of regarding the person of Christ. The two Christologies are distinguished by certain broad features, recognisable at a glance. While the Christology of the Lutheran Church emphasizes the *majesty* of Christ's humanity, that of the Reformed confession insists on its *reality*. The very titles of the treatises which emanated from the two schools reveal their respective tendencies. The Lutheran wrote, *con amore*, books treating of the divine majesty of Christ;[3] the Reformed chose for his congenial theme, the verity of the human nature of Christ.[4] The whole subject in dispute was looked at by the adherents of the two confessions from different points of view. The Lutheran formed his idea

---

[1] *Vid.* Weisse, *Die Christologie Luther's, und die Christologische Aufgabe der Evangelischen Theologie*, p. 79 ff., also p. 219.

[2] On the inner relations between the old Lutheran Christology and modern speculative Christology, some striking observations are made by Schneckenburger in his *Vergleichende Darstellung*. See Appendix, Note C.

[3] *De Divina Majestate Christi.* Brentz and Thummius wrote treatises with this title.

[4] *De Veritate humanae naturae Christi.* This is a title of a work by Sadeel.

of Christ from the state of exaltation, as the abiding form of His existence; regarding the state of humiliation as something transient, accidental, economical, not in accordance with the idea, and requiring to be reconciled with it in the best way possible. The Reformed, on the other hand, formed his idea of Christ from the state of humiliation, as that concerning which most is known, and which it most concerns us to know, and which, being known, prepares us for understanding the subsequent state of exaltation. For him the state of exinanition was not, as for the Lutheran, a strange perplexing thing, as unaccountable as it was undeniable; but rather a thing of course, the natural result of an Incarnation which was itself an act of divine condescension. In the Reformed view, Incarnation and exinanition were practically one. It was not denied, indeed, that the two things are distinguishable in idea, even that the Incarnation might conceivably have taken place in a manner which should have ushered in at once a state of exaltation;[1] but it was held that the idea of Incarnation did not demand an immediate or necessary exaltation; that it was compatible with either state; that it settled nothing as to the mode; that God could be as truly incarnate in a state of humiliation as in a state of exaltation; and that the end of the Incarnation being kept in view, the way of humility was the only one open. From these points of differ-

---

[1] Heidegger, c. g., says: In nativitate qua coepit esse in similitudine hominis, imo et conceptione ipsa, licet exinanitus Christus fuerit, non tamen exinanitio proprie in ἐνσαρκώσει, ἐνανθρωπήσει, incarnatione ejus consistit. Nam simpliciter hominem fieri, in similitudine hominis esse, non est exinaniri, humiliari. Qui exinaniri debuit, homo esse debuit; sed non quisquis homo est, exinaniri debet. Nam etiam in statu exaltationis mansit homo; neque tamen vel exinanitus vel humiliatus amplius. Et exinanitus, minoratus est מעט, βραχύ τι, paulisper. ad breve tempus. Sed homo fuit non paulisper, nec ad breve tempus; sed inde a nativitate semper fuit, est, et erit. Potuit igitur esse homo, et non exinaniri, sed esse ἴσα Θεῷ. instar Dei. Ideo S. Paulus, Phil. ii. 7, eas phrases γενέσθαι ἐν ὁμοιώματι ἀνθρώπων, esse in similitudine hominum, et μορφὴν δούλου λαβεῖν, σχήματι εὑρίσκεσθαι ὡς ἄνθρωπον, servi formam accipere, habitu inveniri ut hominem, diligenter distinguit, innuens non prius, sed duo haec posteriora exinanitionem dicere ... In eo ergo exinanitio Christi hominis consistit, quod non simpliciter homofactus; sed ejusmodi homofactus est, ut μορφὴν δούλου habuerit, et σχήματι ut homo repertus fuerit. Corpus Theologiae, locus xviii. cc. iv. v. See on the Reformed doctrine on this point, Ebrard, Dogmatik, ii. 208.

ence it followed, of course, that the two Christologies should be discriminated in two other respects, viz., that while the Lutheran was speculative in tendency, and theological in its general character, the Reformed, on the other hand, was under the influence of the historical spirit, and of an anthropological bias. The advocates of the Lutheran theory believed many things about Christ which were not verifiable or historically attested truths, but simply *à priori* deductions from a preconceived idea of Christ's person, as constituted by the union of the divine and human natures. The Reformed doctors, on the contrary, adhered rigidly to the facts of the gospel history, and refused to draw any speculative inferences from the doctrine of Incarnation. And their hearts were at home in these sober, humble facts. It was not an offence to them that in Christ the man was more apparent than the God, that behind the veil of flesh Deity hid itself. They accepted the occultation as an undeniable truth; nay, they gloried in it. For, while profoundly convinced that in Christ God became man, they were, if possible, more intensely interested in what God had *become*, than in what the Incarnate One *continued to be*. They made much of Christ's consubstantiality with men: " In all things like His brethren, sin excepted," was their watchword; the man Christ Jesus, true God, yet emphatically man, was their hope and consolation.

Among the Reformed theologians no such wide diversity of opinion existed, on the subject of Christ's person, as are found to prevail among the Lutherans. The Reformed Christology is a self-consistent scheme, taught with much uniformity by all the theologians of the Calvinistic confession; the only difference perceptible consisting in the more or less complete working out of common principles. We might therefore take any well-known divine as our guide in the exposition of this theory. It will be best, however, to select, as the type and standard of Reformed opinion, a work written at the period when the antagonistic theory took definite shape in an ecclesiastical symbol, and designed to be a formal reply to that theory, as embodied in symbolic documents. I refer to a treatise I have already had occasion to quote, the *Admonitio Christiana*, usually designated from the place where it was first published in 1581, *Admonitio Neostadtiensis*, in which the views of the Reformed on the disputed subjects of the person of Christ and the presence in the Supper are stated and defended, in opposition to those set forth in the *Formula of Concord*, in a full, lucid, learned, and dignified manner.[1]

In this important work the Reformed doctrine concerning the person of Christ is briefly repeated to the following effect.[2] The eternal counsel of God for man's salvation demanded that the eternal Son of God should become Mediator and victim, reconciling us to the Father, and regenerating us into sons of God by the Holy Spirit. Therefore He assumed into the unity of His person a nature truly human, consisting of a rational soul and a human body, formed and sanctified by the power of His own Spirit in the womb of the Virgin, of the substance of His mother, joining and coupling it to Himself not only inseparably, but also by a secret and inscrutable *vinculum* in a most intimate and ineffable manner, so that the eternal Logos or Son of God, and this mass of the nature assumed, are at the same time the substance of the one person of Christ, who, one and the same, is true Son of God and true Son of man, true God and true man, born from eternity of the Father, and in time of the Virgin. In virtue of this union, divinity is not in Christ as in all creatures for their conservation and government; nor does it dwell in Him as in saints, making them conformable to Himself by grace and His own Spirit, but the Logos so inhabits and bears, moves and vivifies this His own flesh, that with it, once for all assumed into the unity of one person with Himself, He remains the hypostasis of one and the same person of Christ, as soul and body are so united by a secret inexplicable *nexus* that they are substantial parts of one man, and the body would perish unless it were so borne by the soul; indeed, the Logos co-

[1] The full title of this book is, *De Libro Concordiae quem vocant, a quibusdam Theologis, nomine quorundam Ordinum Augustanae Confessionis edito, Admonitio Christiana, scripta et approbata a Theologis et ministris ecclesiarum in ditione illustrissimi Principis Iohannis Casimiri Palatini ad Rhenum Bavariae Ducis, etc.* Zachary Ursinus was the principal author of this book, and it is included in his works published at Heidelberg in three vols. in 1612.

[2] Caput i. De persona Christi, verae doctrinae repetitio.

heres with His flesh more closely than the soul with the body, so that even when His soul was separated from His body by death, He was not separated from either. On the other hand, while thus closely united, the natures are not changed or mixed or confused, but remain distinct while united, and retain their respective essential properties. Hence in the one person there is a twofold substance, essence, or nature; one divine, uncreated, creating, sustaining, and vivifying the other, spiritual, uncircumscribed, and always existing everywhere the same and whole; the other human, created, sustained, and vivified by the former, finite, corporeal, circumscribed by quantity and definite figure, having part beyond part, and existing only in one place at one time. Also a twofold mind or intellect; one divine and increate, knowing all things past, present, future, possible, impossible, from eternity to eternity, by itself, in one unchangeable act or intuition, and the fountain of all creaturely intelligence; the other human, created, knowing and contemplating all things which it wishes to know, and when it wishes, through the divine mind united to it; able to perceive all sensible things by diverse, distinct acts of sensation and perception. Also a twofold will and operation; the one divine and increate, performing whatever it wishes, *volens et nolens*, from eternity, immutably and in His own time, exciting the other and governing it at pleasure, as a part acting on another part of the one entire perfect Christ, the first cause of all His actions; the other human and created, ever agreeing with the divine, depending on it, willing and doing by its guidance whatever is its proper function. Also a twofold wisdom, strength, and virtue, one divine, increate, being the unique, total, most simple, infinite, and immutable essence of Deity; the other, human and created by the divine, itself neither the essence of Deity nor of humanity, nor even a thing subsisting by itself, but a quality and property produced in the human nature by the Logos through His own Spirit, and inhering therein as in its own subject, which grew in Christ humbled with His age, and in Christ glorified arrived at perfection; yet, while surpassing the gifts, comprehension, and intelligence of all men and angels, is nevertheless finite in the divine view, and can never be equal to the essential wisdom, power, and virtue of God; the finite to the infinite, the creature to the creator.

In virtue of this union, whatever is said of Christ is said truly and really of His whole undivided person, sometimes in respect of both natures, sometimes in respect of one or other. The former, when the predicate has reference to Christ's office; He being Mediator, Redeemer, Intercessor, King, Priest, Prophet, in respect both to His Deity and to His humanity, and each nature performing its proper part in all official acts; the latter, when the predicate has reference to a peculiar property or operation of one of the natures. Thus it can be said that God was born, died, rose, ascended, but only in respect to the human nature of Christ; and again, that the man Christ Jesus is omnipotent, omniscient, omnipresent, in virtue, not of His humanity, but of His divinity. Yet in both cases the predication is not merely verbal, but real, in consequence of the union. It is the union which makes it proper to say, in the case of Christ, God suffered, the man Jesus is omniscient; while it would be improper to say, in the case of the Baptist, God suffered because he suffered, or the Baptist was omnipresent because God dwelt within him as well as without him.

As to the distinction between the two states of humiliation and exaltation, it has a bearing on the properties of both natures, but in very different ways. With reference to the properties of the divine nature, it is a distinction simply between partial concealment and open manifestation. Christ in the state of humiliation had these properties not less than He has them now in glory; for they are His eternal and immutable divinity itself. He was then as omniscient, omnipotent, and omnipresent, as to His divinity, as now. *But He did not manifest these properties then as now.* He concealed His divinity in the state of exinanition, and revealed it only in a modified manner, and so far as was needful for the office of that time. With reference to the properties of the human nature, on the other hand, the distinction between the states is more radical, implying for the state of exaltation the loss of some accidental properties possessed in the state of humiliation, the perfected development of others, and the retention of the essential properties. The accidental properties left behind by Christ, when He entered into glory, are the physical and mental infirmities which He assumed with humanity—liability to hunger, thirst, fatigue, grief, suffering, death, and ignorance. The properties in which He was perfected, also accidental, that is, not inseparable from the idea of human nature, are those of glory and majesty, as strength, agility, incorruptibility, brightness, wisdom, gladness, virtue. These Christ had in the state of humiliation, as far as was needful for His perfect purity and sanctity, and for the discharge of His office on earth; but in the state of exaltation He received such increase thereof, that, in the number and degree of His gifts, He far excels not only the highest excellence of angels and men, but even His own attainments in the days of His flesh.

1. In the foregoing condensed statement, the leading peculiarities of the Reformed Christology, as opposed to the Lutheran, are clearly though briefly indicated. The first outstanding point calling for remark is the *idea of the union*. The Lutherans were accustomed to say that, according to the Reformed conception of the union, the two natures were simply glued together like two boards, without any real communion. It must be confessed that, at first sight, the Reformed theory of the person of Christ does give this impression. The two natures stand out so distinctly, as to seem two altogether separate things, tied together by the slender thread of the divine Ego. From the nature of the case, the tendency on the side of those who opposed the Lutheran doctrine of communication was, to carry the assertion of the distinctness of natures as far as was compatible with recognition of the unity of the person. This tendency is apparent in the strong, bold assertion by the author of the *Admonitio* of a *gemina substantia, gemina mens, gemina sapientia robur et virtus;* its influence is traceable also in the language they employ to describe the act of union, the Son of God being represented as joining and coupling the human nature to Himself by a secret and inscrutable *vinculum*. This outwardness in the Reformed mode of conceiving the union became still more marked as

time went on. Van Mastricht, for example, explains the nature of the hypostatic union in these terms: "It is nothing else than a certain ineffable relation of the divine person (in Christ) to the human nature, by which this human nature is peculiarly the human nature of the second person of the Deity."[1] In this rather vague and unsatisfactory explanation, which in truth explains nothing, there comes out, by the way, another characteristic of the Reformed style of thought, due to the same tendency to keep as far apart as possible the two natures in Christ. Van Mastricht speaks of a certain ineffable relation of the divine *person* to the human nature; herein following the example of Aquinas, who, as we have seen,[2] taught that in the Incarnation, not the divine *nature*, but the *person* only of the Logos became man. The preference of this mode of conceiving the Incarnation, though common among the Reformed theologians, is not clearly marked in the *Admonitio*.

2. The authors of that historical document were, indeed, very far from wishing to make the union of the natures a merely nominal and formal thing. They earnestly believed in a communion of the natures, and did what they could to make that communion a reality. The means they adopted for that end are the second point which invites our attention. These were, on the one hand, the ascription to the Son of God, in virtue of the personal union, of participation in the sufferings of His humanity; and, on the other hand, the doctrine adopted from Aquinas, of the communication of *charisms* to the human nature, fitting it to be the companion, so to speak, and organ of Deity. Both of these *media* of communion are briefly hinted at in the *Repetitio*, and enlarged on in subsequent parts of the *Admonitio*. God, it is stated, is truly said to suffer, because the suffering humanity is the proper humanity of God. More light is thrown on the point further on in the book, where, in reply to the Lutheran charge of teaching that in the passion of Christ the Son of God had no concern, reference is made

---

[1] *Theologia theoretico-practica*, lib. v. cap. iv. sec. vii.: Ineffabilis quaedam relatio divinae personae ad humanam naturam, per quam haec humana natura peculiariter est humana natura secundae personae Deitatis.

[2] *Vid.* Lecture ii. p. 73.

to the exclamation of the exalted Saviour, "Saul, Saul, why persecutest thou me!" and an argument *à fortiori* is drawn from the suffering by sympathy implied in the words, to a still more real participation in His own suffering.[1] The part performed by the divine nature in the passion is more exactly defined elsewhere thus: "The human nature suffers and dies innocently, and becomes a victim for sin, willing this obedience; the divine nature also wills this obedience, and conceals its power and glory, not repelling from the human nature death and ignominy, yet sustains that nature in torment, seriously desires that the eternal Father may receive us into His favour on account of this victim, and adds such dignity to the victim which He offers to the Father, that it is a sufficient ransom and price for the sins of the whole world."[2] These determinations go a certain length in helping us to understand the mystery of divine suffering, but perhaps the hint at suffering by sympathy is of more value than them all. It reminds us of a truth we are apt to lose sight of in our abstruse discussions, viz. that the divine and human natures, though metaphysically wide apart, are *morally of kin*, and that therefore, though the Divine Spirit cannot, as indeed the human spirit also cannot, suffer *physical* pain, it can suffer all that holy love is capable of enduring. The infinite mind can suffer in the same way as the sinless finite mind; it can have sorrow in common with the latter, as well as wisdom, knowledge, and virtue; and if there be any difference between divine and human sorrow, it is a difference of the same kind as that which obtains with reference to the last-named attributes. The authors of the *Admonitio* recognise the truth that in some attributes Deity and humanity stand related as archetype and image, wisdom and virtue being included among the number; and with reference to those attributes, it makes the distinction of natures one mainly of degree, divine wisdom and virtue being infinite, while human wisdom and virtue, however great, are limited. Is it a heresy to include among the common attributes of Deity

---

[1] *Admonitio*, caput iii. (Dilutio accusationis falsae) sec. vi.
[2] *Ibid.* sec. v.

and humanity a capacity of sorrow on account of sin, and to say that Deity differs from humanity only in possessing an infinitely greater capacity? If so, then what does Scripture mean when it speaks of the Divine Spirit being vexed and grieved? what are we to understand by Paul's rapturous language about the height and depth, and length and breadth of divine love?

On the communication of *charisms* to the humanity of Christ, the Reformed theologians laid great stress; it was their equivalent or substitute for the Lutheran communication of divine properties, and they carried it as far as the axiom *finitum non capax infiniti* would permit. The authors of the *Admonitio* had this doctrine in view, when in their repetition they spoke of the wisdom and virtue of the humanity of Christ, as qualities wrought in that nature by the Logos through His Spirit. In answering the Lutheran charge of degrading the hypostatic union into a mere *conglutination*, they return to the topic and enter a little more into detail. "Divinity," they say, "communicated to the humanity this highest dignity, that it is the flesh of the Son of God; He conferred on it all celestial gifts which can be bestowed on human nature in the highest degree; He communicated to it fellowship in the office of Mediator, Head of the Church, Governor and Judge of the whole world. He communicated to it fellowship in one honour and adoration with the Logos."[1]

It is easy to see what attractions, beyond the merely controversial advantage of enabling them to defend themselves against the invidious accusations of their opponents, this doctrine must have had for theologians of the Reformed tendency. One leading recommendation of it was, that in representing the man Jesus as the recipient of communicated gifts and graces, it helped to extend and establish the highly valued doctrine of the *homoüsia*, the practically precious truth that Christ was in all respects like unto His brethren; the Head of the Church like the members. Like them in the constituent elements of His human nature, in subjection to sinless infirmities, in exposure to temptation, He was like them further even in this, that He was fitted

[1] Caput iii. sec. ii.

for the duties of His office by the influences of the Holy Spirit; unlike only in the degree in which these influences were vouchsafed, the Spirit being poured out on Him alone without measure. Looked at from this point of view, the communication of charisms is undoubtedly a doctrine of real importance; and by giving it prominence in their Christological scheme, the Reformed theologians did good service to the Church. But, while of undoubted *religious* value, this doctrine is somewhat embarrassing theoretically, inasmuch as it seems difficult to adjust its relations to the personal union. The questions occur: Why should not the graces with which the soul of Jesus was enriched be the direct result of the union of the Logos to the humanity; why this roundabout way of communicating spiritual gifts through the Holy Ghost; does not this form of representation tend to make the union of the natures still more external—in fact, to make the divine factor in the union superfluous, and so land us in a purely human personality? In connection with these questions it is important to notice the way in which the *Admonitio* puts the matter. It speaks of the wisdom and virtue of the man Jesus as a quality wrought in His human nature *by the Logos through His own spirit*. This phrase, "by the Logos through His own spirit," unites two points of view which were often disjoined by Reformed theologians, some preferring the one, some the other; and suggests a method of dovetailing the doctrine of the communication of charisms into the doctrine of the personal union. The spirit, whose gracious influences were poured into the soul of Christ, was the spirit proceeding from the Logos, His own spirit communicated freely by Himself; and the doctrine that the Logos worked on the humanity of Christ through His spirit, may be taken to mean that the influence of the Logos on the human nature was not physical but moral, not the immediate and necessary effect of the union of natures, but the free, ethically mediated action of the one on the other.[1] This is a

---

[1] So Schneckenburger, *Vergleichende Darstellung*, ii. 239, 240: So wenig war die unio personalis und der darin gesetzte Einfluss des Logos auf die menschliche Seele eine die natürliche sündlose Schwäche aufhebende Gewalt wider deren Entwickelung und Lebensverlauf als einen wahrhaft menschlichen (that, according to

principle of great importance in its bearing both on the nature of the union and on the course of Christ's human life on earth.

3. A third prominent feature in the Reformed Christology is its doctrine of exinanition. Unlike the Lutherans, the Reformed theologians applied the category of exinanition to the divine nature of Christ. It was the Son of God who emptied Himself, and He did this in becoming man. The Incarnation itself, in the actual form in which it took place, was a kenosis for Him who was in the form of God before He took the form of a servant. But the kenosis or *exinanitio* was only *quasi*, an emptying as to use and manifestation, not as to possession, a hiding of divine glory and of divine attributes, not a *self-denudation* with respect to these. The standing phrase for the kenosis was *occultatio*, and the favourite illustration the obscuration of the sun by a dense cloud. Zanchius, for example, says: "Under the form of a servant the form of God was so hid that it scarcely appeared any longer to exist, as is also the light of the sun when it is covered by a very dense cloud; for who would not then say that the sun had laid aside all his light, and denuded himself of his splendour?"[1] But the question here suggests itself, How is this *occultation* to be understood? Does it signify merely that the manifestation of the divine attributes of the Logos was hid from the view of the world, or does it mean that there was also a suspension of their exercise for Christ Himself; in such a way, for example, that the omniscience of the Logos was practically non-existent for the man, not intruding itself into His human consciousness? On this topic the Reformed theologians were very reserved, insomuch that Schneckenburger, who was well acquainted with the literature of the subject, expresses himself doubtfully as to the import of the *gemina mens*.

Calvin and Hulsius, Christ could even forget in a moment of mental anxiety what He previously knew). Schneckenburger continues: Die influentia war nicht physica, sondern moralis, quae a voluntate pendet. Die voluntas des Logos war aber die, der rein menschlichen Lebensentwickelung und Lebensbethätigung Raum zu geben. (The influence was not physical but moral, depending on the will; but the will of the Logos was to give room for a purely human development and activity.)

[1] *De Incarnatione*, lib. i. p. 34.

As I shall have occasion to refer to the views of this scholar in the next lecture, in enumerating the various attempts which have been made in recent times to reconcile the divinity of Christ with the reality of His human life as unfolded in the gospel history, I may here quote what he says on the point. "It is very questionable," he remarks, "whether according to the logic of the (Reformed) theory the time-conditioned consciousness of the God-man and the eternal self-consciousness of the second person of the Trinity are required to meet in the divine-human subject, developing Himself in time. The matter probably stands thus: That instead of the Lutheran division of the human nature into its illocal and local subsistence, a distinction is to be made in the life of the *divine*, according to which the *mens duplex* is to be distributed between the Logos, as a person of the Trinity, and the concrete God-man in so far as that person reveals and develops Himself in Jesus after a human fashion, that is, as a human individual. The Logos *totus extra Jesum* is the second person of the Trinity as such, with the *scientia personalis;* the Logos *totus in Jesu* is the same all-pervading and animating divine hypostasis, as the life principle of this individual, the God-man, whose individual consciousness is not absolutely all-embracing." [1] According to this view the Logos had a *double life*, one unaffected by the Incarnation, another in the man Christ Jesus, in which His action is so self-controlled as to leave room for a natural human development involving growth in stature, wisdom, and grace. Traces of such a view may be found in Reformed authors, in reference to divine power. Zanchius speaks of the kenosis as involving not merely an

---

[1] *Vom doppelten Stande Christi.* To the same effect in *Vergleichende Darstellung*, ii. p. 198, in disposing of three objections brought against Reformed Christology by modern writers: that it allows the dualism of the two natures to remain unresolved, that it posits a *double series of parallel states of consciousness* in the God-man, and that its doctrinal point of view is purely traditional. To the last Schneckenburger replies by pointing to the communication of charisms, and the action of the Holy Ghost as the bond of union as fresh contributions to the doctrine; to the first, by admitting the charge as inevitable; to the second, by repeating the view given in the above extract, assigning the *scientia personalis* to the Logos *per se*, and the *scientia habitualis* to the Logos incarnate, or to Jesus in whom the Logos became incarnate.

occultation of divine glory, but a withholding of divine omnipotence in Christ, supporting his view by a reference to the Ambrosian doctrine of *retractio*;[1] and Heidegger and Mastricht combine the idea of restraining or withdrawing with that of concealing, in their representation of the effect of the Incarnation on Christ's glory.[2] That no such statements occur in reference to omniscience, may be due to the felt difficulty of conceiving the application of the idea expressed by *retentio* to that attribute. Silence must not therefore be construed into a denial of its applicability. Rather ought regard to be had to other elements in the Reformed theory which seem to demand exclusion of omniscience from the consciousness of the man Christ Jesus. Such an element is the ignorance which the leading Reformed authorities do not hesitate to ascribe to Christ on earth. That ignorance they regard as real, not, like Cyril, apparent only or feigned. But how can it be real if the *gemina mens* means two series of parallel states of consciousness ? It is as hard to conceive of two such series keeping apart and having no communication with each other, as to conceive of two rivers flowing in the same channel without mixing their waters. Yet keep apart they must, if the ignorance is to be real, and, it may be added, if the Reformed theory is to be consistent with itself in opposing the communication of attributes taught by the Lutherans. For if the divine consciousness is to run into the human, so that the supposed ignorance of Christ shall simply mean that the knowledge He possessed in a particular case did not come to Him *through* His human nature, what is this but the Lutheran communication—omniscience communicated to the soul of Christ in virtue of its personal

---

[1] *De Incarnatione,* lib. i. p. 35: Ergo retentio suae virtutis et omnipotentiae in illa carne κένωσις et exinanitio appellatur, et ideo ait Ambrosius quod λόγος in carne potentiam suam et majestatem ab opere retraxit. The *retentio*, however, was not absolute. Deitas in illa carne non statim, non semper, non in omnibus, non abunde sese exeruit, sed quasi otiosa mansit. This *otiositas* was the κένωσις. —P. 36.

[2] Heidegger, *Corpus Theologiae Christianae,* loc. xviii., De Statu Jesu Christi: "gloriam suam ... ad tempus occultavit, et *cohibuit.*" Mastricht associates the word *subducere* with the verb *occultare. Theol. Theoret. Tract.* lib. v. cap. ix. Pars exeget.

union with the Logos. On the whole, then, having regard to the ascription by the Reformed to Christ of real ignorance in childhood and even in manhood, to their conception of the union as mediated through the Holy Spirit, to their determined antagonism to the Lutheran communication, and to their well-known formula: "The whole Logos beyond Jesus, the whole Logos in Jesus,"—there does seem reason to think that the distinguished modern theologian just quoted has correctly interpreted the bearing of the Reformed theory on the point in question.[1] The conception of a *double life* of the Logos is certainly a difficult one; to some it may even seem absurd or impossible. Yet the idea has commended itself to men distinguished both for their ability and for their theological independence, including a well-known and highly esteemed English essayist, who, in grappling with the problem of the reconciliation of Christ's divinity with the reality of His humanity, says: "If there be an indestructible moral individuality which constitutes self, which is the same when wielding the largest powers and when it sits alone at the dark centre,—*which for anything I know may even live under a double set of conditions at the same time*,—I can see no metaphysical contradiction in the Incarnation."[2]

4. The last outstanding feature of the Reformed Christology remaining to be noticed, is the emphasis with which it asserts the likeness of Christ's humanity in all respects, sin excepted, to that of other men. Zeal for this truth, Schneckenburger justly remarks, is the distinctively Reformed interest in Christology.[3] Not merely on theoretical but on religious grounds, the upholders of the Reformed theory of Christ's person were determined that the Saviour should be a true Son of man, our Brother and Head; and hence "a decided antidoketic realism" pervades their whole method of treating Christological subjects.[4] The influence

---

[1] Schweitzer (*Die Glaubenslehre des Evangelischen Reformirten Kirche Dargestellt und aus der Quellen belegt*) takes the same view as Schneckenburger; *vid.* Appendix, Note D.

[2] *Essays Theological and Literary*, by R. H. Hutton, vol. i. p. 260.

[3] *Vergleichende Darstellung*, ii. p. 229.

[4] *Vergleichende Darstellung*, ii. p. 229: Der entschiedenste antidoketische Realismus beseelt die reformirte Betrachtungsweise.

of this motive is apparent in all the features of their system of thought already referred to, as well as in other peculiarities not yet mentioned; as, *e.g.*, the representation of Christ, as man, as the subject of predestination, and as personally bound to obedience, and the analogy drawn between the Incarnation and regeneration, the union of the natures in Christ, and the mystical union of the believer to Christ, both being accomplished by the agency of the Holy Ghost. It may be observed, however, that the doctrine of the *homoüsia* was not by any means so fully worked out in the early period as it came to be afterwards in the course of the 17th century. Some of the Reformed divines who lived near the time of the Reformation seem to have been half unconscious of the genius and tendency of their own theory, their views being by no means self-consistent or homogeneous. This remark applies very specially to Zanchius, who while teaching the Reformed doctrine concerning Christ's person in opposition to the Lutheran, nevertheless adopted almost in their entirety the views of Aquinas concerning the knowledge of Christ's soul and other topics; so making Christ's humanity every whit as unreal as it was in the Brentian system. The soul of Jesus, we are told, possessed in perfection from the first the vision of all things in God. Possessing this, it did not and could not possess faith as the evidence of things not seen, nor hope which rests on faith; for what a man sees he doth not hope for. That is to say, the man Christ Jesus, while represented as the recipient of all manner of gifts and graces, is yet declared to have been rendered by the hypostatic union incapable of exercising two of the cardinal graces—incapable of brotherhood with us in the faith which says: " I will put my trust in Him," and in the hope which cheers the soul under present tribulation,—being a *comprehensor* even while a *viator*, and therefore a pilgrim and a stranger on the earth only in outward guise![1] How widely different from

---

[1] *De Incarnatione*, lib. ii. quaestiones viii. xi. Le Blanc (*Posthuma opuscula*, cap. iii. p. 191) adverts to the different opinions among the Reformed *de Scientia Animae Christi*, and gives an account of those held by Zanchius in particular as peculiar to him and a few others. He underestimates the importance of the question when he calls it merely scholastic: " Quaestiones sunt mere scholasticae."

these views those taught a century later by Hulsius, who represented Christ as like us in all respects save sin, and therefore in imperfection of knowledge which is not necessarily sinful; declared the happiness of Christ on earth to have been imperfect not less than His knowledge—being the felicity of one who was only a wayfarer to the blessed country (*viator*), not that of one who has arrived at the end of his journey, and at last attained possession of the object of his hope (*comprehensor*); nay, not even the felicity of Adam in paradise, such felicity being incompatible with His mediatorial office, which required Him to bear the guilt and to taste the misery of sinners. This Dutch divine, according to the account given of his views by Schneckenburger, held that Christ's work as Saviour demanded that both His ignorance and His unhappiness should be most real, and he protested against any inferences being drawn from the hypostatic union prejudicial to their reality. The union must be so conceived of as to allow full validity to the "form of a servant." The prayer, "let this cup pass," and the natural fear out of which it sprang, must not be rendered a theatrical display by the overpowering physical influence of the divine nature upon the human. Rather than admit the agony and the fear in the garden to have been unreal, one may dare to say that, under the influence of extreme perturbation of mind, Christ for the moment forgot the divine decree under which He was appointed, by death to become the Saviour of sinners. Such forgetfulness, according to Hulsius, was not impossible. The knowledge of a decree as to habit is one thing, the actual conscious recollection of that knowledge is another thing; the latter, the vehemence of anxiety could take away, though not the former. A bold assertion this, of the important *rôle* played by *Infirmity* in the experience of Christ, which seems to justify the commentary of Schneckenburger: "Therefore even the heavenly decree, consequently His personal vocation, consequently His personal being, His *esse divinum*, His *unio personalis*, could the God-man in such moments forget; the act of cognition could cease, though not the habit (that is, the act could not so cease that it could not be forthwith restored). So little was the personal union, and the thence resulting influence of the Logos upon the human soul, a power annulling natural, sinless weakness, and antagonistic to a truly human development and life course. The influence was not physical, but moral, depending on the will of the Logos, which was minded to leave room for such a development."[1] But whether we be successful or not in *reconciling* the thorough reality of Christ's human nature and human experience with the doctrine that that nature and that experience belonged in very truth to the Son of God, there can be no doubt at all that we are bound by Scripture teaching to assert both in the most unqualified manner, the reality of the humanity not less, though of course not more, than the reality of the divinity. As indicated in our seventh axiom, the humanity must be allowed to be as real as if Christ had been a purely human

[1] The work of Hulsius (*Systema Controversiarum Theologicarum*, Lugd. Bat. 1677) I have failed to get a perusal of. It seems to be scarce even in Germany, for Ritschl in his *Lehre von der Rechtfertigung und Versöhnung* quotes him at second hand,—a fact to which Professor R. Smith of Aberdeen directed my attention. The above account of Hulsius' views is taken from Schneckenburger (*Vergleichende Darstellung*), who makes large use of this author in his chapter on the Reformed doctrine of the Redeemer's *homoüsia* with us. Ritschl doubts the accuracy of Schneckenburger's representation of the views of Hulsius on Justification, and a certain amount of dubiety must attach to all statements which one has not the means of verifying. As, however, Schneckenburger gives a number of extracts, there can be little doubt that his representation of the opinions taught by Hulsius is substantially correct. These opinions seem to have been set forth in a controversial writing against the Catholic theory on the "Scientia et beatitudo comprehensorum." Among the extracts given by Schneckenburger are these (vol. ii. pp. 237-240): Fuit nobis per omnia similis excepto peccato, ergo et quoad imperfectionem scientiae nobis similis . . . Id enim (beatitudo comprehensorum) adversatur officio mediatorio, quo sponsoris persona in se pro peccatore suscipere debuit reatum et poenam peccati, adeoque miseriam, cui peccatum obnoxium reddit peccatorem . . . To exclude inferences in favour of the Catholic theory, from the Unio, it is said: Ab influentia physica ad moralem quae a voluntate pendet non valet consequentia. Habuisse humanitatem Christi praerogativas magnas ex unione hypostatica, sed inde inferri istam summam beatitudinem non admittebat forma servi . . . With reference to the agony: Per anxietatis vehementiam praesentem memoriam illius decreti fuisse oblatam (oblitam?). Aliud ergo est decreti cognitio quoad habitum, aliud istius cognitionis actualis recordatio; hanc potuit tollere anxietatis vehementia, quoad momentum, illam non item. Schneckenburger represents Hulsius as inferring ignorance of the exact bearing of the decree of election on individuals from Christ's tears shed over Jerusalem's impenitence. Had Christ known for certain that the inhabitants were doomed to perdition, He could not have earnestly wished to save them, or have wept because they would would not be saved.

personality; and on that account it is permissible to speak of Him, as is freely done in the Gospels, as a human person, while not forgetting that He is at the same time a divine person.[1] If we find the reconciliation of the two aspects of the personality a hard task, we must not think of simplifying it by sacrificing some of the cardinal facts, least of all those pertaining to the human side, which give to the life of the Saviour all its poetry, and pathos, and moral power. We must hold fast these facts, even if we should have to regard the person of Christ as an inscrutable mystery— scientifically an insoluble problem.[2] Till the era of the Reformation an opposite course was pursued. Believing in Christ's divinity, theologians thought it necessary, in the interest of faith, to reduce His humanity to a mere metaphysical shell emptied of all moral significance. The Council of Chalcedon had indeed said a word in behalf of the humanity; but its formula remained for the most part a dead letter. To the Reformed branch of the Protestant Church belongs the honour of having asserted with due emphasis the long neglected claims of the much-wronged human nature. Sincerely confessing the Saviour's divinity, they did not suffer their eyes to be so dazzled thereby that they could not look the facts of the gospel plainly in the face. To their mental views the sun was so obscured by the dense cloud of the state of humiliation, that they could regard the Incarnate One as He regarded Himself—as the Son of man, the man of sorrows and acquainted with grief. In Him they found rest for their souls as theologians, and still more as sinners.

[1] On the views of the Reformed on the subject of the human aspect of Christ's personality, see Appendix, Note E.
[2] So Ritschl, *Die Christliche Lehre von der Rechtfertigung und Versöhnung*, iii. p. 394.

LECTURE IV.

MODERN KENOTIC THEORIES.

During the last fifty years the minds of the learned in Germany have been extensively and intensely exercised upon theological problems. All the dogmas in the Christian creed have been in turn made the subject of searching critical inquiry; sometimes in a sceptical spirit and with destructive intent, but much more frequently with a view to the conservation of the faith, and the reconstruction of the doctrinal system. The doctrine of our Lord's person has received its full share of attention in this great movement of modern religious thought; it has indeed been the subject of a quite extraordinary interest due in part to its intrinsic importance and attractiveness, but arising also in no small measure out of the ecclesiastical movement which had for its object the reunion of the two great branches of the German Protestant Church. This union enterprise, which commenced as early as the year 1817, naturally led to a consideration of the ground of separation, either in a spirit of antiquarian curiosity, or with the more serious purpose of determining the practical question: what was the intrinsic importance of the points of difference—were they of such a nature that they might rightly be treated as matters of forbearance, and therefore no barrier to church fellowship, by men not occupying the position of theological indifferentism? And so it came to pass, that the scheme for bringing into closer relations the adherents of the two confessions, while only partially successful in attaining its avowed object, became the occasion of a most fruitful activity of mind, on the subjects involved in the great controversy between the Lutheran and Reformed churches. The tree of union flourished into a copious Christological literature, many-sided in its aspects, genial in tone, animated by a scientific truth-loving spirit, and of value far surpassing that of the ephemeral controversial writings, which similar movements in other lands have called into existence.

Of this Christological literature the theories of the modern kenotic school, of which some account is to be given in the present lecture, form no insignificant part. The Christology of kenosis in its origin and aim had a close connection with the union movement: it offered itself to the world, in fact, as a union Christology. Its advocates said in effect, some of them said expressly:[1] We have studied the Lutheran and the Reformed Christologies; we have made ourselves thoroughly familiar with their respective positions, and with the arguments by which these were defended; we find both in their old forms untenable; but in this new, yet most ancient scriptural doctrine of kenosis, we bring something different from either of the old Christologies, yet having affinities with both, which therefore we hope will be accepted by the members of the two communions as the common doctrine of a reconstructed church. This claim to a two-sided affinity, made in behalf of the kenotic theory, has *primâ facie* support in the fact that the theory numbers among its adherents distinguished theologians belonging to both confessions; and it does not altogether break down on closer investigation. There are at least footpaths, if not highways, along which one may advance to the kenosis, both from Lutheran and from Reformed ground. You may

[1] Gaupp, *e. g.*, who in his work, or pamphlet rather, entitled *Die Union*, Breslau 1847, expounds the kenotic theory under the title of a *Vermittelungsversuch*, after having previously subjected both the Lutheran and the Reformed doctrines to a critical review in which their weak points are exposed. This little work contains some interesting historical particulars concerning the union movement from the year 1817 down to 1846, when the General Synod was held, at which a formula of ordination was framed containing a summary of the fundamental doctrines of the sister churches. Gaupp charges this *Ordinations-formular* with intentional ambiguity designed to meet the case of persons who were in doubt even about fundamentals, instancing the case of a comma after *Gott dem Vater*, making it possible for opponents of the Church doctrine of the Trinity to apply the word "Gott" to the Father alone!—P. 169.

reach the kenotic position from the Lutheran territory along the path of the *communicatio idiomatum*, simply by the inverse application of the principle; teaching with reference to the earthly state of Christ a communication of human properties to God, instead of a communication of divine properties to man. You may reach the same position from the Reformed territory along the path of the *exinanitio*, to which the Logos became subject in becoming man, by assigning thereto a positive meaning, and converting the Reformed *occultatio* or *quasi-exinanitio* into a real self-emptying of divine glory and divine attributes. These hints may suffice to indicate in a general way the relation of the modern theory to the older forms of the doctrine current in the sixteenth and seventeenth centuries. The precise respects in which the new and the old modes of thought agree or differ will become apparent as we proceed.

An exposition of the various kenotic theories of Christ's person may be fitly introduced by the remark, that it is a feature common to modern Christologists of all schools, to insist with peculiar emphasis on the reality of our Lord's humanity. It is admitted on all hands that every Christological theory must be reckoned a failure, which does not faithfully reflect the historical image of Jesus as depicted in the Gospels, and allow Him to be as He appears there, a *veritable*, though not a mere man. In this respect modern Christology, under all its phases, follows the Reformed rather than the Lutheran tendency. But this cordial and earnest recognition of Christ's true and proper humanity gives increased urgency to the question, How is the humanity to be reconciled with the divinity? Some have answered the question by denying the Incarnation in the sense of the creeds, and the doctrine of the Trinity on which it rests, and representing Jesus as divine, simply inasmuch as He was a perfect man, divinity and humanity being regarded as essentially one. Of the views of this school I will give some account in the next Lecture, though they are not very closely connected with our whole inquiry, the very idea on which it is based being rejected by its members. Our business at present is with those only who build their Christology on the old foundations, and who set themselves the task of constructing a theory of Christ's person according to which He shall be at once true God and true man; or, to speak more exactly, with one section of what may be called the modern orthodox party. For those who have addressed themselves to the common problem in a conservative spirit have not all followed the same method in solving it. Three different solutions have been suggested; one by Schneckenburger, consisting in a restatement, with explanations or modifications, of the old Reformed theory; another by Dorner, who, in his great work on the history of the doctrine, propounds or rather hints the theory of a *gradual* Incarnation, leaving ample room for a true normal human development, for which he claims the valuable support of Luther's earlier Christological views; the third solution being the kenotic theory, which seeks to make the manhood of Christ real, by representing the Logos as contracting Himself within human dimensions and literally becoming man. It is this third solution which is now to engage our attention.

The idea of kenosis in the modern sense, to be carefully distinguished from the meaning attached to the term in the old Giessen-Tübingen controversy,[1] seems to have been first broached by Zinzendorf, the founder of the Moravian Brotherhood. The grain of thought cast by him into the ground lay dormant for a hundred years; then in the fourth decade of the present century, it began to germinate, and ever since it has gone on multiplying abundantly, till now the kenotic school has attained considerable dimensions, and can number its adherents among theologians by scores. The forms which the new theory assumes in the hands of its expounders are scarcely less numerous than the expounders themselves. It would probably be difficult to find two writers who state the common doctrine in precisely the same way. Happily, however, it is possible to reduce the many diverse shapes of this Protean Christology to a few leading types, which, though they may not comprehend all the subordinate phases of opinion, do at least fairly and sufficiently represent the outstanding characteristics of the school as a whole.

[1] See Appendix, Note B, Lect. iii.

The dominant idea of the kenotic Christology is, that in becoming incarnate, and in order to make the Incarnation in its actual historical form possible, the eternal pre-existent Logos reduced Himself to the rank and measures of humanity. But when this general idea has been announced, three questions may be asked regarding it. First, is the depotentiation *relative* or *absolute*? that is to say, does it take place simply so far as the Incarnation is concerned, leaving the Logos *per se* still in possession of His divine attributes; or does it take place without restriction or qualification, so that, *pro tempore* at least, from the moment of birth till the moment of exaltation, the second person of the Trinity is denuded of everything pertaining to Deity, but its bare, naked, indestructible essence? Second, in what relation does the depotentiated Logos stand to the man Jesus? Is He the soul of the man, or is there a human soul in the man over and above? Is the Logos metamorphosed into a human soul, or is He simply self-reduced to the dimensions of a human soul, in order that, when placed side by side with a human soul, He may not by His majesty consume the latter, and render all its functions impossible? Third, how far does the depotentiation or metamorphosis, as the case may be, go, within the person of the Incarnate One? is it partial, or is it complete? does it make Christ to all intents and purposes a mere man, or does it leave Him half man, half God,—in some respects human, in other respects superhuman? All these questions have been variously answered by different writers. Some teach a relative kenosis only, some an absolute; some take a dualistic view of the constitution of Christ's person, as formed by the union of the depotentiated Logos, with a human nature consisting of a true body and a reasonable soul; others regard the person of Christ from a metamorphic point of view, making the self-emptied Logos take the place of a human soul. Finally, there are differences among the kenotic Christologists as to the extent to which they carry the kenosis,—some being Apollinaristic in tendency, though careful to clear themselves from suspicion on that score; others inclining to the humanistic extreme. Had each of the possible combinations of these three sets of alternatives its representative among the writers of this school, the task before us would be formidable indeed. Fortunately, however, we are not required by the history of opinion to be mathematically complete in our exposition, but may content ourselves with giving some account of *four* distinct kenotic types, which may for the present be intelligibly, if not felicitously, discriminated as, (1) the *absolute dualistic type*, (2) the *absolute metamorphic*, (3) the *absolute semi-metamorphic*, and (4) the *real* but *relative*. Of the first, *Thomasius* may conveniently be taken as the representative; of the second, *Gess;* of the third, *Ebrard;* and of fourth, *Martensen*.

(1) *Thomasius*,[1] the earliest advocate of the kenosis in the present century, in setting forth his views, exhibits great solicitude to clear himself of the charge of doctrinal innovation. He claims to have the ecclesiastical consensus on his side, and professes to be in sympathy both with the patristic and with the old Lutheran Christology. He recognises the Chalcedon Formula as fixing the limits within which theories laying claim to orthodoxy must confine themselves;[2] and he regards his own theory as the legitimate outcome of the fundamental principles on which the Lutheran doctrine of Christ's person is based. He admits, of course, that the old Lutherans did not teach the kenotic theory; but he holds that "the dialectic of the dogma" inevitably leads thereto. The Lutheran conception of the union of the natures demands one of two things: either that the infinite should come down to the finite, or that the finite should be raised to the infinite.[3]

[1] The statement of the views held by this author is based exclusively on the work, *Christi Person und Werk*, Erlangen 1856. Thomasius propounded his theory in an earlier publication, entitled *Beiträge zur Kirchlichen Christologie*, 1845, being a reprint of articles which had previously appeared in the *Zeitschrift für Protestantismus und Kirche*. The *Beiträge* is simply a brief rudimentary sketch of the scheme elaborated in the larger and later work.

[2] *Christi Person und Werk*, vol. ii. pp. 112-115.

[3] The author quotes a passage from the writings of the Tübingen theologians who took part in the old kenotic controversy, to show that they had the two alternatives present to their minds: Ex necessitate consequitur, aut infinitam $\tau o\hat{v} \lambda \acute{o} \gamma o v$ $\dot{v}\pi \acute{o}\sigma\tau a\sigma\iota v$ ad finitam carnis praesentiam (ad fines humanae naturae) esse detractam, aut humanam naturam assumptam ad infinitam $\dot{v}\pi \acute{o}\sigma\tau a\sigma\iota v$ (ad majestatem infinitatis et omnipraesentiae) evectam esse. *Person und Werk*, ii. pp. 483, 484.

The old Lutherans took the latter way, and found that it let them into insuperable difficulties; therefore modern Lutherans, who would be faithful to the first principles of Christology taught by their fathers, must forsake the ancient path of the *majestas*, and strike into the new path of the *kenosis*.

Our guide into the new way leads us along the following line of thought. The life image of the Redeemer, as it lies open to view in the Gospel, is that of a genuinely human personality. Jesus is a man, the Son of man, and it seems as if the proper subject of this person were the human Ego.[1] But, on the other hand, in these same Gospels Jesus appears as more than man; He speaks of Himself as standing in a peculiar relation to God; He is spoken of as having existed personally before He appeared in the world, as the Logos who was in the beginning, and was with God, and was God; and in view of these facts it seems as if the Divine should be regarded as the proper subject of this person.[2] Yet there are not two Egos in Christ, but only one, who is conscious at once of His premundane being in God, and of His intramundane human existence, as both appertaining to Himself. It is the same Ego who says of Himself, " Before Abraham was, I am," and, "I came forth from the Father, and am come into the world;" the same Ego of whom it is written, that He is the absolute Truth, and that He called on God with strong crying and tears.[3] Christ having pre-existed as the Son of God before He became man, the Ego of the Son of God is to be regarded as the proper person-forming principle of the Incarnation. The Incarnation itself is to be regarded in two lights,—as the *assumption* by the Son of God of human nature in its integrity,[4] and as the *self-limitation* of the Son of God in the act of assuming human nature.[5] The latter is necessary in order to the former. Were there no self-limitation,—did the Son of God, in the human nature assumed by Him, continue in His divine mode of being and working, in His supramundane status, and in the infinitude

---

[1] *Person und Werk*, ii. pp. 14, 16.   [2] *Ibid.* ii. p. 22.
[3] *Ibid.* ii. p. 24.   [4] *Ibid.* ii. p. 126.
[5] *Ibid.* ii. p. 141.

of His world-ruling, world-embracing government, the mutual relation of the two united natures would involve a certain duality. The divine would in that case embrace the human, as a wider circle a narrower; with its knowledge, life, and activity, the former would far outreach the latter; the extra-historical, the temporal; the in-itself-complete, that which is in process of becoming; the all filling, all determining, that which is conditioned and bound down to the limits and laws of earthly existence. The consciousness of the Logos *per se* would not coincide with that of the historical Christ, but would, as it were, hover over it; the universal activity, which the former continues to exercise, would not be covered by the theanthropic action of the Incarnate One in the state of humiliation. That is to say, there would be no true Incarnation.[1] Therefore the theanthropic person can be constituted only by God really taking part in a human mode of existence, as to life and consciousness; and the Incarnation must consist in this, that the Son of God enters into the form of human finitude, into an existence subject to the limits of space and time, and to the conditions of a human development.[2] That is,

---

[1] *Person und Werk*, ii. p. 141: Bleibt nämlich Er, der ewige Sohn Gottes, in der endlichen von ihm assumirten, menschlichen Natur in seiner göttlichen Seins- und Wirkungsweise, beharrt er in seiner überweltlichen Weltstellung, in der Unbeschränktheit seines weltbeherrschenden und weltumfassenden Waltens, so bleibt auch das gegenseitige Verhältniss beider immer noch mit einer gewissen Duplicität behaftet. Das Göttliche überragt dann gleichsam das Menschliche wie ein weiter Kreis den engern, es geht mit seinem Wissen, Leben, und Wirken unendlich weit darüber hinaus, als das Aussergeschichtliche über das Zeitliche, als das in sich Vollendete über das Werdende, als das Allerfüllende und Allesbestimmende über das Bedingte, an die Grentzen und Gesetze des irdischen Daseins Gebundene. Das Bewusstsein, das der Sohn von sich und von seinem universalen Walten hat, fällt mit dem des historischen Christus nicht in eins zusammen,—es schwebt gleichsam über ihm; die universale Wirksamkeit, welche jener fortwährend übt, deckt sich nicht mit seinem gottmenschlichen Thun im Stande der Erniedrigung,—es liegt darüber oder dahinter; "während der Logos in allerfüllender Gegenwart die Schöpfung durchwaltet, ist der Christus auf das Gebiet der Erlösung, zeitweilig wenigstens auf einem bestimmten Raum eingeschränkt." Es ist also da eine zwiefache Seinsweise, ein doppeltes Leben, ein gedoppeltes Bewusstsein, der Logos ist oder hat noch immer etwas, was nicht in seiner geschichtlichen Erscheinung aufgeht, was nicht auch des Menschen Jesus ist—und das scheint die Einheit der Person, die Identität des Ich zu zerstören; es kommt so zu keiner lebendigen und vollständigen Durchdringung beider Seiten, zu keinem eigentlichen Menschsein Gottes. [2] *Ibid.* ii. p. 143.

Incarnation is for the Son of God, necessarily, self-limitation, self-emptying, not indeed of that which is essential to Deity in order to be God, but of the divine manner of existence, and of the divine glory which He had from the beginning with the Father, and which He manifested or exercised in governing the world.[1] Such is the view given by the apostle in the Epistle to the Philippians,[2] such the view demanded by the evangelic history; for on no other view is it possible to conceive how, for example, Christ could sleep in the storm on the Sea of Galilee. What real sleep could there be for Him, who as God not only was awake, but, on the anti-kenotic hypothesis, as ruler of the world, *brought on*, as well as *stilled*, the storm?[3]

This doctrine, according to its author, while scriptural, satisfies at the same time all theological requirements. For one thing, it complies with the Lutheran axiom: "The Word not outside the flesh, nor the flesh outside the Word" (*nec verbum extra carnem, nec caro extra verbum*).[4] Then the personality of Christ becomes what it ought to be, a divine-human personality. The Son of God continues to be Himself, yet, having undergone kenosis in the manner aforesaid, He is at the same time a human Ego.[5] Christ is the personal unity of divine essence and humankind, the man who is God.[6] Furthermore, on this theory the two natures are preserved entire and distinct. On the one hand, God is not destroyed by self-limitation, for self-limitation is an act of will, therefore not negation but rather affirmation of existence. The essence of God is not stiff, dead substance, but out and out will, life, action, self-asserting, self-willing, self-controlling self.[7] Self-limitation, therefore, does not contradict the essence of the absolute. The absolute were impotence if it could not determine itself as it wills. Then it must be remembered that God is love; and if limits are to be placed to God's power of self-exinanition,

---

[1] *Person und Werk*, ii. p. 143. [2] *Ibid.* ii. p. 148.
[3] *Ibid.* ii. p. 156. [4] *Ibid.* ii. p. 201.
[5] *Ibid.* ii. p. 200.
[6] *Ibid.* ii. p. 203: Christus ist die persönliche Einheit göttlichen Wesens und menschlicher Art: der Mensch, welcher Gott ist.
[7] *Ibid.* ii. p. 203: Es ist sich selber setzendes, wollendes, seiner schlechthin mächtiges Selbst.

they must be wide enough to give ample room for His love to display itself. God may descend as far as love requires. Love was the motive of the Incarnation, and love is the sole measure of its depth; otherwise God is not the absolutely free, His power is not servant to His will, but a tyrant over it.[1] On the other hand, the humanity too remains intact. For, according to our author, it is assumed entire, with a reasonable soul as well as a body; the doctrine of metamorphosis being repudiated as destructive at once of humanity and of divinity.[2] Then, on this theory, the human nature is not only entire as to its constituent parts, but it possesses personality, and is no mere selfless medium.[3] Christ is conscious of being a man, not less than of being the Son of God. The Son of God, entering into the existence form of creaturely personality, made Himself the Ego of a human individual; and hence His consciousness was specifically human,—the consciousness of a man limited in nature, and possessing both a body and a soul, having the same contents and the same conditions as ours. The only difference between Christ and us is this, that the Ego in Him was not originally born out of the human nature, but was rather born into it, in order to work itself out of it, and through it, into a complete divine-human person.[4] Yet again, this theory, according to its author, does not disturb the immanent Trinity, for it makes the Son of God, in becoming man, part with no essential attributes of Deity It strips Him, indeed, of omnipotence, omniscience, and omnipresence, the Redeemer being, during His earthly state, neither almighty, nor omniscient, nor omnipresent. But these are not *essential* attributes of God, they are only attributes expressive of His free relation to the world which He has made; attributes, therefore, not of the immanent, but only of the economical Trinity, with which God can part and yet be God, retaining all essential attri-

---

[1] *Person und Werk*, ii. p. 204.

[2] The author makes such repudiation in connection with the views of Hahn and Gess, who represent the Logos as taking the place of a human soul or spirit in Christ. *Vid*. ii. p. 196.

[3] *Ibid*. ii. pp. 201-207.

[4] *Ibid*. ii. pp. 206-208. The author's view is stated briefly in the text. Those who possess the work referred to are recommended to read the whole passage.

butes of Diety,—absolute power, absolute truth, absolute holiness and love.[1] These last the Son of God did retain when He parted with the other relative attributes; far from losing them in becoming incarnate, He rather entered into a state in which He had an opportunity of revealing them. For the humiliation of Christ was not all kenosis; it was revelation as well as exinanition. It meant exinanition so far as the relative attributes of Deity were concerned,—self-emptying of omnipotence, omniscience, and omnipresence.[2] But it meant also, and partly on that very account, revelation, manifestation of the absolute essential attributes,—of absolute might as free self-determination, of absolute truth as knowledge of His own being and of His Father's mind, of absolute holiness and love.[3] Finally, the kenosis, while complete so far as the relative attributes of Deity are concerned, is nevertheless not a state of helpless passivity. Even when the passivity is at its maximum, —in the conception, in death,—the kenosis is free, and reaches its highest points of activity. In these moments the Son of God makes the highest display of His obedience towards God; they are the *magna opera* of His redeeming love, thought, willed, done by Himself. *How*, we may not be able to explain, but the fact is so. A right conception of what is meant by *potence* helps, at least, to understand

---

[1] This distinction between the relative and essential attributes of God is the speculative foundation of the Thomasian Christology. For a detailed exposition of the author's doctrine of the attributes and of the Trinity, the reader is referred to *Christi Person und Werk*, vol. i. pp. 47-136.

[2] *Person und Werk*, ii. p. 238. The miracles of Christ our author does not regard as evidence of omnipotence; they were wrought through the Holy Spirit, and proved not Christ's divine nature, but only His divine mission. *Vid.* p. 250.

[3] *Ibid.* ii. pp. 236, 237: Es ist Offenbarung der immanenten göttlichen Eigenschaften, der absoluten Macht, Wahrheit, Heiligkeit und Liebe. . . . Und diess gilt nicht blos von den beiden zuletzt genannten, auch die beiden ersten eignen ihm in dem früher (I. Th. § 11 u. 16) bezeichneten Sinne: die absolute Macht als die Freiheit der Selbstbestimmung, als der sein selbst vollkommen mächtige Wille, die absolute Wahrheit als das klare Wissen des Göttlichen um sich selbst, näher, als das Wissen des Menschgewordenen um sein eigenes Wesen und um den Willen des Vaters. Nicht gelernt hat er diesen in irgend einer menschlichen Schule; innerlich, vermöge seiner Einheit mit dem Vater, schaut er dessen ewige Gedanken. The author goes on to say, that though this knowledge was only gradually developed through the Holy Ghost, it was but a development of what lay in the depths of Christ's being.

the mystery. Potence, as the word implies, does not signify something impotent or empty, but being contracted to its innermost ground, fulness concentrated in itself from the circumference of appearance and activity, having therefore power over itself. Such power was latent in the Logos, even after He had been reduced, through Incarnation, to the state of a mere potency.[1]

(2) In constructing a theory of Christ's person to correspond with the historical facts, as inductively ascertained, *Gess*[2] lays stress on three scriptural representations of the Incarnation, in which that event is exhibited, (1) as an *outgoing from the Father*, (2) as a *descent from heaven*, and (3) as *becoming flesh*. By the first of these representations, the author understands an exit, on the part of the pre-existent Logos, out of the intimacy of His communion with the Father,[3] having for its result, not a dissolution of the mutual indwelling of the Father, Son, and Spirit, but a suspension of the influx of the eternal life of the Father who hath life in Himself into the Son, in virtue of which the Son *pro tempore* ceased to have life in Himself. The Son, in becoming man, lost the consciousness, and with the consciousness the activity, and with the activity the capacity to receive into Himself the influx of the Father's life, and to cause that instreaming life to flow forth from Himself again.[4] By the descent from heaven is signified the humili-

[1] *Person und Werk*, ii. p. 243: Beides lässt sich in den Begriff der Potenz zusammenschliessen, von welcher wir sagten, dass sich der Logos, menschwerdend, auf sie zurückgezogen habe. Denn die Potenz ist, wie schon der Ausdruck andeutet, nicht etwas Ohnmächtiges oder Leeres, sondern das in seinem innersten Grunde zusammengefasste Wesen, die aus der Peripherie der Erscheinung und Actuosität in sich concentrirte unendliche Fülle, welche ebendeshalb die Macht ihrer selbst ist. Und diese Macht trägt auch das göttliche Selbstbewusstsein, zwar nicht als reflectirtes, gegenständliches, doch aber als latitirendes, mithin als wirklich vorhandenes in sich. Es ist mit einbegriffen in der freien Willensthat, kraft deren der Gottmensch sich selbst dahingibt. *Vid.* Appendix, Note A, for an account of the kenotic literature coming under the *Thomasian* type.

[2] The following statement of Gess' theory is based on his work, *Die Lehre von der Person Christi entwickelt aus dem Selbstbewusstsein Christi und aus dem Zeugnisse der Apostel*, Basel 1856. The author has published a new larger work on the same theme, entitled *Christi Person und Werk*, of which the first volume has for its subject the self-witness of Christ. No material change of view appears in this volume.

[3] *Die Lehre von der Person Christi*, p. 294. [4] *Ibid.* ii. p. 307.

ation or kenosis whereof the apostle speaks; which, according to the most natural interpretation of the words, imports a transition, on the part of the Logos incarnate, from a state of equality with God into a state of dependence and need, a laying aside of His pretemporal glory: that is, not merely of the blessed life in light, but of the life which is independent and self-sufficient, and of which omniscience and omnipotence are attributes.[1] These attributes, therefore, the Logos parted with in His descent from heaven; nay, not only with these so-called relative attributes, but also with those which Thomasius by way of distinction names the immanent attributes of Deity. Incarnation involved the loss not only of the perfect knowledge of the world, called omniscience, but of the perfect vision of God, denominated in the Thomasian theory absolute knowledge.[2] For the Logos, in becoming man, suffered the extinction of His eternal self-consciousness, to regain it again after many months, as a human, gradually developing, variable consciousness, sometimes, as in childhood, in sleep, in death, possessing no self-consciousness at all.[3] All this is inevitably involved in *becoming flesh*, for this third scriptural representation of the Incarnation signifies, that the flesh with which the Logos was united became for Him a determining power, even as, apart from sin, it is a determining power for the ordinary human soul. According to the creative decree of God, the life development of the soul depends upon the development of the body; it requires a certain maturity of the physical organization for the soul to waken up to self-conscious voluntary life, in order that thereafter, as personal soul, it may gradually subject its bodily organ to the laws inscribed on itself by the hand of divine holiness. Christ's life was subject to the same decree. It was first a natural life, in which the Logos was subject to the power of the flesh; then it became a personal life, in which the Logos became self-conscious, and made

---

[1] *Die Lehre von der Person Christi*, ii. p. 296.

[2] *Ibid.* p. ii. 311. Gess disallows the Thomasian distinction between relative and immanent attributes, and remarks, that if the doctrine of kenosis is to be built on such an insecure foundation, it is in a bad way. P. 312.

[3] *Ibid.* ii. p. 312.

the flesh subject to Himself, until, at the close of His human development, the body of His flesh became transformed into a glorious body, that is, a body fitted to be the perfect organ of the Logos, once more restored to the fulness of divine life.[1] In virtue of this subjection to the determining power of the flesh, it came to pass that, when the Logos in the child Jesus began to be self-conscious, He knew nothing of His Logos-nature, and did not waken up forthwith to the Logos-work of world-quickening, illumination, and government, but only to the work of calling "my Father, my mother,"[2] and of distinguishing between good and evil. Doubtless the potence, the abstract capacity for these works, was there from the first, for the Logos-essence remained unchangeable; the attributes of omniscience, omnipotence, and omnipresence may be said to have simply entered into a state of rest; but it was a rest out of which they could not return into a state of activity, so long as the moving power, the eternal self-consciousness, on which they all depend, was itself not there.[3] How and when, then, did the Logos, plunged by Incarnation into the oblivion-causing waters of Lethe, at length attain to self-consciousness? Was it by recollection of His pre-existent state? Not principally, for a clear and constant recollection would be incompatible with a life of faith.[4] Or was it by reflection and inference exercised on Old Testament Scriptures? This was undoubtedly one means towards self-knowledge. The birth of Christ in the midst of the Jewish race made it possible for Him to attain to a knowledge of who He was, by the *way of a truly human development*. Had He been born a Greek, that would have

---

[1] *Die Lehre v. d. Person Christi*, ii. pp. 308, 309. [2] *Ibid.* ii. p. 306.
[3] Die Ablegung der Allwissenheit und ewigen Heiligkeit kann als ein unmöglicher Gedanke erscheinen, aber die Sache wird klar, wenn man zurückgeht auf die Wurzel des Selbstbewusstsein. Mit dem allwissenden Ueberschauen der Welt war aber zugleich auch das allvermögende Regieren derselben aufgegeben, und mit diesem das Allem Gegenwärtig sein. Nicht als wären diese Vermögen schlechtweg dahingewesen: die Logoswesenheit war ja auf Erden dieselbe, wie zuvor im Himmel, man kann also sagen, diese Vermögen waren nur in den Stand der Ruhe getreten, aber in eine Ruhe, aus welcher sie nicht in die Aktivität zurückkehren konnten, so lange die sie bewegende Kraft, nehmlich das ewige Selbstbewusstsein selbst, nicht als solches da gewesen ist.—*Die Lehre v. d. Person Christi*, ii. p. 317.
[4] *Ibid.* ii. p. 355.

been impossible.¹ At the same time, it is not to be supposed that self-consciousness was reached merely by reflection and inference. There must have been latent in the incarnate Logos a certain *instinct*, as men call that mysterious gift whose true name is an inspiration of God.² As the children of God know themselves to be such by the witness of the Spirit; as the prophets knew that God had called them, and had made a revelation to them, by an inward assurance based on an intercourse between the divine Spirit and the human soul, whose laws elude our comprehension, but whose reality is indubitable; so the knowledge possessed by Jesus of the secret of His person was based upon the peculiarly intimate fellowship which subsisted between His Father and Himself.³ And for the rest, who will deny that the recollection of the pre-existence might occasionally flash through into the human consciousness of the Incarnate One?⁴ As for the time at which the Logos incarnate attained to a clear self-consciousness, it cannot be precisely determined. The morning twilight of His self-knowledge appeared when He was a boy of twelve years; the perfect day had arrived by the time He went forth to commence His ministry. Between twelve and thirty the great mystery of godliness, God manifest in the flesh, had become fully revealed to the Incarnate mystery Himself.⁵ Probably the revelation took place long before He had reached the latter period of life; for Jesus had to learn to wait as none other ever had. In all likelihood, it was a part of His discipline, that He had to wait for the appointed time for commencing His life-work long after He had become aware what the work was to which He was called.⁶

[1] *Die Lehre v. d. Person Christi*, ii. pp. 357–8: Unter den Griechen geboren, hätte Jesus sich nicht auf dem Wege wahrhaft menschlicher Entwicklung als den Sohn Gottes zu erkennen vermocht.

[2] *Ibid.* ii. p. 358: Jenes Geheimnissvolle, das man etwa den geistigen Instinct nennt, dessen eigentliches Wesen aber ein Anhauch Gottes ist.

[3] *Ibid.* ii. p. 358.

[4] *Ibid.* ii. p. 358: Und wer wollte schlechthin leugnen, dass in einzelnen Momenten die Erinnerung der Präexistenz den Fleischgewordenen durchblitzen mochte? Nur dass sie zur bleibenden Leuchte seines Inneren geworden sei, dürfen wir um des oben angeführten Grundes willen nicht annehmen.

[5] *Ibid.* ii. p. 359.   [6] *Ibid.* ii. p. 361.

Here, then, we have a tolerably complete metamorphosis of the Logos, manifestly standing in great need of adjustment to correlated doctrines. What, *e.g.*, on this theory, is to be said of the *integrity* of Christ's assumed humanity? The Logos, to all intents and purposes, is transformed into a human soul; does He then assume another human soul over and above? Gess replies in the negative. The Church, he says, quite properly affirmed, in opposition to Apollinaris, that Christ had a true human soul; but it did not see, what however is the truth, that the Logos Himself *was* that soul. He did not assume, He *became* a human soul, and thereby the presence of another soul was rendered entirely superfluous.[1] The only possible objection to calling the incarnate Logos a human soul is, that His soul was not derived from Mary; but this objection has force only for those who hold the traducian theory concerning the origin of souls, which however is untenable according to our author, all souls coming directly from God. The only difference between the Logos and a human soul was, that he became human by voluntary kenosis, while an ordinary human soul derives its existence from a creative act.[2] And how, again, are we to think on this theory of Christ's *moral* integrity, His sinlessness? Was that sinlessness, admitted as a fact, due to an inability to sin (*non posse peccare*), as in the Apollinarian system, which made the Logos take the place of a human spirit in Jesus, in order to get rid of the bare possibility of sin? Not so, according to our author. A capability of sinning (*posse peccare*) must be ascribed to Christ, otherwise the reality of His humanity is denied. To represent the Saviour as from the first in possession of a will unalterably decided for God, is to revive in a new form the error of Apollinaris, who made an unchangeable being take the place of the changeable human soul.[3] The loss of eternal holiness was

---

[1] *Die Lehre v. d. Person Christi*, ii. p. 321: Dass eine wahrhaft menschliche Seele in Jesu war, versteht sich für und von selbst: er war ja sonst kein wirklicher Mensch. Aber die Frage ist, ob der in's Werden eingegangene Logos selbst diese menschliche Seele, oder ob neben dem in's Werden eingegangenen Logos noch eine besondere menschliche Seele in Jesu war? P. 324: Wozu diese Doppelheit und wer kann sie verstehen?

[2] *Ibid.* ii. p. 325 ff. [3] *Ibid.* ii. p. 349.

one of the accompaniments of Incarnation. Not that there is any need for asking in alarm, what would have happened, had the possibility been converted into an actual fact, for the Incarnation proceeded upon a divine foreknowledge that the Incarnate Logos *would* not fall into sin; a foreknowledge which at the same time in no way interfered with Christ's freedom, or imposed upon Him an eternal necessity of not sinning.[1] That Christ was simply an ordinary man, who in virtue partly of His peculiar birth happened not to sin, is not asserted. Our author is not willing to admit that his doctrine amounts to a metamorphosis of the Logos into a man; he is anxious to make it appear that there was a superadamitic element in Jesus.[2] But he contends that that element did not consist in a *non posse peccare*, but only in an extraordinary devotion, on the part of the Incarnate Logos, to His Father's will, which was accompanied by an equally extraordinary measure of the Spirit's indwelling and influence, and of knowledge concerning divine things.[3]

The theory in question stands in need of adjustment also to the received doctrine of the divine unchangeableness and to the doctrine of the Trinity. How is it possible, one may well ask, that a Divine Being can thus all but extinguish Himself? The ready reply is: It is possible just because He is God, and not a creature. The dependence of an ordinary man appears, not merely in his inability to raise himself to a higher scale of being than he was designed for, but also in his inability to make his life cease, or to reduce it into a state of unconsciousness. The Logos, on the contrary, has life in Himself; His voluntary reception of the life streaming into Him out of the Father is the ground

---

[1] *Die Lehre von der Person Christi*, ii. p. 318.

[2] *Ibid.* ii. p. 350: In dieser Erkenntniss dass der irdische Entwicklungsgang des Sohnes die Möglichkeit des Sündigens in sich schloss, und dass eben diess zur Aufgabe Jesu gehörte, den Naturzug seines ewigen Geistes zu Gott zum geheiligten Charakter zu erheben, darf uns auch die Frage nicht irre machen, was doch geworden wäre, wenn der, welcher sündigen konnte, wirklich gesündigt hätte. Die Antwort, welche auf diese Frage gegeben werden kann, ist nur die, dass Gott sein sündloses bestehen aller Versuchungen vorausgesehen hat.

[3] *Ibid.* p. 331, note in reply to Liebner.

of His life, His self-consciousness is His own deed.[1] Hence
He can extinguish His self-consciousness; He would not be
almighty if He had not power over Himself. The power
of God indeed is not limitless, nor is His freedom arbitrary.
But the only limit of divine power is holiness or love. If,
therefore, the holy love of God desires to help us, and if
for that end Incarnation is necessary, and if Incarnation
involves in its very nature transient extinction of the divine
self-consciousness, and the resumption of the same as
human, and subject to growth, then such an experience
must be possible.[2]

How, finally, is this metamorphic theory of the Incarnation to be reconciled with the doctrine of the Trinity?
The author admits that his theory involves these four consequences for the internal life of the triune God: (1) the
eternal forth-streaming of the divine life of the Son out of
the Father is brought to a stand during the time of the
kenosis; (2) for that reason, during the same time, the Son
cannot be the life-source out of which the Holy Ghost
flows; (3) during that time the subsistence of the world in
the Son, its upholding and government through the Son,
is suspended; (4) as the glorified Son remains man, from
the time of His exaltation a man is taken up into the trinitarian life of God. He remarks that the three first consequences could easily be got rid of by adopting the theory
of *a double life* of the Logos, and holding that while the
Son of God, as the man Jesus, emptied Himself utterly of
divine glory, and lived, our like, with purely human consciousness and will, nevertheless His divine trinitarian being and
rule underwent no interruption. He declines, however, to
adopt this view, and prefers to escape difficulties by adjusting the doctrine of the Trinity to his own theory. This he
does by introducing into the Trinity a certain inequality
between the persons. The Father alone possesses the
property of being from Himself (aseity). The Son, indeed,
also hath life in Himself; but it is as a gift of the Father's

---

[1] *Vid.* Zweiter Abschnitt, cap. 3, p. 222, "Die göttliche Herrlichkeit Jesu auf Erden."
[2] *Ibid.* p. 319.

eternal love.[1] If the relation between the persons were one, according to which they were all mutually conditioning and conditioned, then the kenosis would either be impossible, or it would imperil the Godhead of the Father. But as the Father alone possesses aseity, and as it is His free love which begets the Son, it is possible for the Father, during the period of exinanition, to substitute, for the overflow of His life into the Son, that gentle influx of life into Jesus, wave by wave, which corresponds to the Son's position as a man subject to gradual development in time,[2] reserving to Himself, the while, the government of the world and the administration of the Spirit. Nor does this change affect the eternity of divine life, or of the generation of the Son (though that process during the exinanition comes to a temporary pause [3]), or of the procession of the Holy Ghost from the Son. Eternity does not consist in the exclusion of change. The eternity of the Father lies in His aseity; the eternity of the Son and Spirit in the freedom of their life, which streams forth from the Father, and is essentially equal to the life of the Father. By entering into time, and

---

[1] *Die Lehre von der Person Christi*, p. 396 ff. In proof that the Father alone possesses aseity, Gess refers to the text: "The Father hath given the Son to have life in Himself," and to the fact that in Scripture the Father is called *Der Gott*, while the Son is called only *Gott*, and that He is also called the God of Christ (pp. 402, 403).

[2] Wäre das Gottsein des Vaters durch die ewige, ewig gegenwärtige Zeugung des Sohnes bedingt, so liesse sich nicht verstehen, wie der Sohn sich seiner Gottesherrlichkeit entäussern, wie die ewige Zeugung des Sohnes durch den Vater, das ewige Ausströmen des Gotteslebens vom Vater in den Sohn sich stille stellen kann: die Gottheit des Vaters selbst würde dadurch gefährdet scheinen. Noch weniger wäre die Selbstentäusserung des Sohnes möglich, wenn auch diesem ein Antheil zukäme an Gottes Aseität, an Gottes Selbstbegründung, so dass nur in der dreipersönlichen Selbstbegürndung Gottes, wie jede der drei Personen, so die Totalität derselben ihr Leben hätte. Aber es ist die freie Liebe des Vaters, welche den Sohn zeugt, darum kann der Vater, für die Zeit der Selbstentäusserung des Sohnes, an die Stelle der vollen Ueberströmung des Gotteslebens vom Vater in den Sohn jenes sanfte Einfliessen einer Lebenswelle um die andere in Jesum eintreten lassen, welches dem Eingegangensein des Sohnes in die Verhältnisse eines allmählig sich entwickelnden, überhaupt der Zeitlichkeit unterworfenen Menschen entspricht.—*Die Lehre von der Person Christi*, p. 403.

[3] *Ibid.* ii. p. 405. The glorification of Christ after the time of exinanition was past, consisted in the recommencement of the process of eternal generation which took place immediately after, so that the Son of God had power to raise His own body.—*Vid.* also pp. 380–382.

undergoing kenosis for thirty years, the Son did not become subject to time, but rather revealed the eternal as the King of time. To master time, so that it shall not stand over against the supra-temporal as an unapproachable Other, but be a form of existence at His command, is God's highest revelation of His eternity.[1] [2]

(3) The kenotic theory as expounded by *Ebrard* possesses interest not only as a distinct type of the doctrine, but as a contribution to the literature of the subject, by a prominent modern representative of the Reformed communion, professing cordial, though not slavish, attachment to the doctrinal tendency of his church. Ebrard first promulgated his view of the person of Christ in a work on the dogma of the Holy Supper, published in 1845-46, and designed to promote the cause of union; and subsequently at greater length in a work on Christian dogmatics, published in 1851-52.[3] This able, learned, but somewhat whimsical and unreliable writer, agrees with Gess in making the incarnate Logos take the place of a human soul. The ancient Church was of course right in maintaining, against Apollinaris, that Christ had a true human soul; for, in truth, the Logos, in undergoing Incarnation, became a human soul. According to the representation in Scripture, Jesus did not consist of a body in which, in place of a human soul, dwelt the eternal Logos—a monstrous conception—the eternal Logos dwelling in a space-bounded body! but the eternal Son of God in becoming man gave up the form of eternity, and in full self-limitation assumed the existence-form of a human life-centre, of a human soul; had, as it were, reduced Himself to a human soul.[4] This self-

---

[1] *Die Lehre von der Person Christi*, pp. 405, 406: Dieses freie Hineintreten in die Zeitlichkeit, um wieder zurückzukehren in die Ewigkeit, ist also gerade ein Triumphiren der Ewigkeit über die Zeitlichkeit, eine Erweisung des Ewigen als des Königes der Zeit welche ihm dienen muss, indem er sich in ihren Dienst begiebt und welche ihn nicht festhalten kann, nachdem er sein Werk vollbracht. Königlich die Zeit zu bemeistern, dass sie dem Ueberzeitlichen nicht als ein unnahbares Anderes gegenübersteht, sondern als eine Form seines Daseins zu Gebote steht, das ist Gottes höchste Offenbarung seiner Ueberzeitlichkeit.

[2] See Appendix, Note B, on literature belonging to the Gessian type.

[3] See Appendix, Note C.

[4] *Christliche Dogmatik*, ii. p. 40: Der ewige Sohn Gottes hatte die Form der Ewigkeit aufgegeben und in freier Selbstbeschränkung die Existenzform eines

reduction, however, does not in the scheme now under review, as in that of Gess, amount to a depotentiation of the incarnate Logos. The Son of God in becoming man underwent not a loss, but rather a *disguise* of His divinity; not, however, in the old Reformed sense of occultation, but in the sense that the divine properties, while retained, were possessed by the Theanthropos only in the time-form appropriate to a human mode of existence. The Logos, in assuming flesh, exchanged the form óf God, that is, the eternal manner of being, for the form of a man, that is, the temporal manner of being. Herein consisted the kenosis.[1] The kenosis does not mean that Christ laid aside His omnipotence, omnipresence, and omniscience; but that He retained these in such a way that they could be expressed or manifested, not in reference to the collective universe, but only in reference to particular objects presenting themselves to His notice in time and space. Omnipotence remained, but in an *applied form*, as an unlimited power to work miracles; omniscience remained in an applied form, as an unlimited power to see through all objects which He *wished* to see through; omnipresence remained in an applied form, as an unlimited power to transport Himself whither He would.[2] The incarnate Son of God stood over against nature as the absolute Lord ruling over it in a free creative manner; not, indeed, in the form of world-governing omnipotence, but in the form of omnipotence applied to particular cases, in particular times and places. Though He no longer possessed eternal omniscience, yet He possessed, in reference to particular objects which came in His way, a knowledge which, compared with the knowledge of sin-

menschlichen Lebenscentrums, einer menschlichen Seele, angenommen, hatte sich gleichsam bis zu einer Menschenseele reducirt. See also vol. ii. p. 7, note on the miraculous conception, where we read: jene δύναμις Gottes hatte nicht das Geschäft, eine Seele (ein Lebenscentrum) zu erzeugen, sondern sie hatte nur das weibliche *ovulum* so zu verändern, dass der Sohn Gottes welcher, in die Form der unbewussten Seele eingehend, als solche zugleich in's *ovulum* eingehen wollte, im *ovulum* allen zur Bildung einer embryonischen Leiblichkeit nöthigen Stoff vorfand.

[1] *Christliche Dogmatik*, ii. p. 34: Die μορφη Θεοῦ gab er auf, d. h. das ἴσα Θεῷ, das "auf gleiche Art wie Gott sein," also die Ewigkeitsform, und nahm dafür die Form der Menschheit (σχῆμα ἀνθρώπου). Similarly, *Das Dogma von II. A.*, i. p. 191.

[2] *Das Dogma von heil. Abendmahl*, ii. p. 790.

ful man, is altogether supernatural. In walking on the sea, He exhibited a wonder of applied omnipresence.[1] In the use of these powers He was subject to His Father's will; but, nevertheless, they were inherent in His person; He had free control over them; it is conceivable that He might have made a wrong use of them, and herein lay the point of the temptation in the wilderness.[2]

Ebrard accepts the Chalcedonian formula—two natures in one person; but he puts his own meaning on the word "natures." By the two natures he understands not two parts or pieces, two subsistent essences united to each other, but two *abstracta* predicated of the one Christ; two aspects of the one divine human person. In particular, the human nature was not an existing thing, but only a manner or form of being, a complex of properties. The thesis, the Son of God assumed human nature, is equivalent to this: that the Son of God, giving up the form of eternity and entering into time-form, and beginning to exist as a human life-centre, formed for Himself out of this life-centre a humanity in the concrete sense, that is, a human body, soul and spirit, or all momenta and essences which the human life-centre needed for its concrete being and life. Hence the divine nature and the human nature stand related to each other as essence and form: Divine nature as an *abstractum* is predicated of Christ, because He is the eternal Son of God entered into a time-form of existence, possessing the ethical and metaphysical attributes of God (that is, God's essence) in a finite form of appearance. Human nature is predicated of Christ, because He has assumed the existence form of humanity, and exists as centre of a human individuality with human soul, spirit, body, development. Christ is therefore not partly man, partly God, but wholly man; but if the question be asked, who is this, the answer must be: He is the Son of God, who has by a free act denuded Him-

---

[1] *Dogmatik*, ii. pp. 20, 29.

[2] *Ibid.* ii. pp. 30, 31. The view stated above, Ebrard defends against Lange, who maintains (*Leben Jesu*) that Jesus was conditioned by the will of the Father, not merely in the voluntary use of His miraculous power, but in the possession of the power itself, just like any of the prophets. This position Ebrard holds to be contrary to Scripture.

self of His world-governing, eternal form of being, and entered into the human form of being. It is a divine person who has made Himself a human person.[1] Ebrard reckons it as the fault of Nestorius, and after him of the old Lutherans (whom he charges with Nestorianism, resulting in the state of exaltation, in the opposite extreme of Eutychianism), that the two natures of Christ were treated as concretes. On the other hand, he claims for the old Reformed Christologists a clear understanding of the true state of the case. They meant just what he teaches when they said, that in the Incarnation a divine person was not united with a human person, or a divine nature with a human nature; but a divine person assumed a human nature.[2] In one respect only did they come short, viz. in reference to the question how the concrete consciousness and life of the person Christ are to be conceived. On this point, according to our author, the Reformed Church has never attained to a clear understanding; the reason, in his judgment, being, that the Christology of that Church has failed to grasp the distinction between the eternity-form (*Ewigkeitsform*) and the time-form (*Zeitlichkeitsform*) of the divine essence. The Reformed theologians, notwithstanding their controversy with the Lutherans, came at last to think of the incarnate Logos as world-governing, and possessing omnipotence, omniscience, and omnipresence in reference to the universe at large,—a view which came practically to the same thing as the Lutheran one. All the difference was this: the

[1] *Dogmatik*, ii. pp. 41, 42: Die nat. div. und die nat. hum. sind also nicht zwei Subsistenzen oder Theile in Christo, sondern zwei *abstracta*, die von dem Einen Christus prädicirt werden. Göttliche Natur wird von ihm prädicirt, sofern er der in die Zeitform eingegangne ewige Sohn Gottes ist, und die ethischen und metaphysischen Eigenschaften Gottes, d. h. das Wesen Gottes, wiewohl in endlicher Erscheinungsform, besitzt. Menschliche Natur wird von ihm ausgesagt, wiefern er die Existenzform der Menschheit angenommen hat, und als Centrum einer menschlichen Individualität mit menschlicher Seele, Geist, Leib, Entwicklung existirt. (Göttliche Natur: menschliche Natur=Wesen: Existenzialform.) Er ist also nicht theilweise Mensch und theilweise Gott, sondern er ist ganz Mensch; aber auf die Frage: Wer ist dieser? (nicht, was?) heisst der Antwort: der, der dieser Mensch ist, ist der Sohn Gottes, der sich in freiem Akte seiner weltregierenden Ewigkeitsform begeben, und in die menschliche Seynsform versetzt hat. Er ist also Eine Person, die *persona divina*, welche sich zu einer *persona humana* gemacht hat.

[2] *Ibid.* ii. p. 41.

Lutheran taught that the human nature in the *status exinanitionis* either renounced or did not exercise omniscience, etc., while the Logos at the same time retained and used it, so that the latter knew all, while the former did not; the Reformed, on the other hand, taught that the Logos incarnate was omniscient, and in the world-governing sense, while the human nature was not. Both positions alike were virtually Nestorian.[1] The true view is, that the powers of the eternal Godhead revealed themselves in Christ, not alongside of the powers of His humanity, not as superhuman, but *in* the powers of His humanity; even herein, that His human powers were supernatural, that is, exceeded the capacities of nature as depraved by sin, and He was absolutely superior to this depraved nature, so that when and where He wished to work it formed no limit to His power.[2]

By this view our author believes the problem is solved: how the divine and the human attributes which constitute the two natures can co-exist in the same person without cancelling each other. The divine attributes remain in an applied form, and in that form they are truly human. Applied omnipotence is simply the dominion of the spirit over nature, which belongs to the idea of man. Applied omniscience is the dominion of the spirit over the objects of knowledge, to which man was originally destined. Applied omnipresence, the power to be where one wills, is simply the dominion of the spirit over the material body, which man was designed to attain; the body in its ultimate idea not being a foreign burden subject to elementary influences, but a free projection of the soul in space, released from all subjection to the elements, to death, or to the law of gravity.[3] Whether this be a successful solution of the problem in hand or not, it will be apparent that it is at all events a very different view of the historical Christ from that which we had last under consideration. Gess' view of Christ is thoroughly humanistic; Ebrard's, on the other hand, has far more of the divine element in it, and wears a much more

---

[1] *Abendmahl*, ii. p. 792. Ebrard gives Zuingli and Olevian credit for having clearer views than most of the Reformed on the subject of the divine attributes.
[2] *Dogmatik*, ii. p. 143.
[3] *Abendmahl*, i. pp. 192, 193. *Dogmatik*, ii. pp. 28, 29.

decided appearance of Apollinarism. As if to compensate for the Apollinarian tendency on the *metaphysical* side, our author is most decidedly anti-Apollinarian in the view he takes of the *ethical* aspect of Christ's humanity, ascribing to the incarnate Logos a *posse peccare*, representing Him as gaining confirmation in obedience by the practice of it under trying circumstances, reaching the higher freedom through the right use of freedom of choice, and gaining heavenly glory strictly as a reward of His filial virtue—all this being demanded by the time-form of existence.[1]

We now understand in what sense the kenotic theory as taught by Ebrard can be described as metamorphic. The metamorphosis consists simply in an exchange of the eternal for the time-form of existence; an exchange which, once made, is perpetual.[2] It remains to be added that this change of form is not relative merely, but absolute; involving the absolute and perpetual renunciation of the eternal form of being, not simply the renunciation of it with reference to the incarnate life of the Logos. Our author is indeed at this point extremely difficult to understand, and I am doubtful whether the words just used correctly describe his position, or even whether his position be a self-consistent one. For, on the one hand, he says in one place that there is nothing in Scripture to countenance the idea that the Logos retained the form of eternity on entering into the time-form, and while He was in Christ, governed the world over and above.[3] But, on the other hand, he recognises it as a part of the Christological problem to be solved: how can the Logos, conscious of Himself as the eternal, be also conscious of the man Jesus existing in time as Himself? and, on the other hand, how can the man Jesus, existing in time, be conscious of the eternal Logos

---

[1] *Dogmatik*, ii. p. 22.

[2] *Ibid.* ii. p. 37: Form der Menschheit und Form der Ewigkeit (im Sinn von Ueberzeitlichkeit) schliessen sich schlechthin aus; Christus hat die letztre für immer aufgegeben, die erstre für immer angenommen, und der Uebergang aus der unter dem Tod geknechteten Menschheit in die vom Tode befreite, verklärte, hat im Verhältniss seiner göttlichen Natur zu seiner menschlichen nichts geändert.

[3] *Dogmatik*, ii. p. 35: Die h. Schrift weiss nichts davon, dass der λόγος die Form der Ewigkeit beibehalten habe, und während er in Christo war, nebenbei auch noch die Welt regiert habe, sondern er WARD Mensch.

as Himself? in other words, is a unity of consciousness between the eternal and the incarnate Logos conceivable?[1] The same problem is also put in this form: How is a personal unity between the world-governing Son of God in the Trinity and the incarnate Son of God, who has given up the form of eternity, possible, the one being world-governing, omniscient, etc., while the other is not?[2] It is true the problem is regarded as a psychological one, and may be said to have for its aim to demonstrate the possibility of conscious personal identity surviving the change from the eternal to the time-form of existence. But the very terms in which the problem is stated seem to show that the eternity-form is not thought of as having ceased to exist. Indeed, it is expressly admitted that such language is meaningless with reference to the Eternal. Speaking strictly, we ought not to say the Son of God *has given up* the *Ewigkeitsform*, for in eternity there is no " has " and no " given up." Words implying tense are inapplicable to eternity, whose relation to time is not such that one can say eternity is before time, or after it, or during it.[3] Then, further, supposing the psychological problem to be satisfactorily solved for the period of Christ's mature manhood, that is, granting that then the man Jesus could be conscious of His identity with the eternal, world-governing Logos, which is all that is claimed as made out,[4] what of the period of immaturity, of childhood? With reference to this period, the author remarks that identity of person is not to be confounded with unity or continuity of consciousness.[5] Perfectly true; but the question is not as to identity of the person, but as to the combination in the same person of

[1] *Abendmahl*, i. p. 186: Ob sich der seiner als eines ewigen, bewusste Logos, des zeitlich existirenden Menschen als seiner selbst bewusst seyn könne, und ob der zeitlich existirende Mensch Jesus sich des ewigen Logos als seiner selbst bewusst seyn könne; ob also eine Einheit des Bewusstseins zwischen dem ewigen und dem menschgewordenen Logos denkbar sei.

[2] *Dogmatik*, ii. p. 144: Wie ist zwischen dem weltregierenden Sohn Gottes in der Trinität und dem menschgewordenen Sohn Gottes, der die Ewigkeitsform aufgegeben hat, eine persönliche Einheit denkbar? Jener ist weltregierend allwissend, dieser nicht.

[3] *Ibid.* ii. p. 146.   [4] *Ibid.* ii. p. 145.

[5] See Appendix, Note D, for an account of Ebrard's method of solving the problem.

two modes of existence; a question which must surely be answered in the affirmative, if it be admitted that the Logos was self-conscious even when the child Jesus was utterly unconscious. This position Ebrard, so far as appears, does not call in question, and therefore it might be legitimate to represent his theory as one which teaches only a relative metamorphosis of the Logos,—a change in the form of existence which is after all not so much an exchange, as the adding of one form of existence to another. Such is the sense in which the theory has been understood by some of its author's own countrymen,[1] and the correctness of the interpretation might with some confidence be inferred from the fact that a double existence is expressly taught by other writers whose Christological views come nearest to the Ebrardian type. Nevertheless it is not advisable to force on any author a doctrine which he seems disinclined to hold, and therefore we must reckon it as the characteristic of the present type of kenosis, that it teaches an absolute and perpetual exchange of the Eternal for the time-form of existence, as necessarily involved in the idea of Incarnation.

(4) *Martensen*,[2] on the other hand, is beyond all doubt an advocate of a *real yet only relative kenosis*. This distinguished Danish theologian, in whose writings are finely blended philosophic insight and poetic grace, distinguishes between the *Logos revelation* and the *Christ revelation*. The revelation of the Son of God in the fulness of time implies

---

[1] By Gess, at least, who, having quoted a passage from Schöberlein (*Grundlehren des Heils*), to the effect that the Logos incarnate has a double existence, and that we must recognise at once a real kenosis and a possession, yea, a use without concealment of the divine glory, adds in a note: "Aehnlich Ebrard in der Dogmatik." *Die Lehre von der Person Christi*, p. 390. On the other hand, Hofmann, *Schriftbeweis*, ii. p. 24, seems to understand the exchange of eternity-form with the time-form taught by Ebrard as an absolute one. With reference, and in opposition, to Ebrard's view he remarks: Aber auch so ist es nicht, dass er die Ewigkeitsform mit der Zeitlichkeitsform vertauscht hat, sondern aus seinem geschichtlichen Stande der Ueberweltlichkeit, des weltbeherrschenden Könnens und Wollens und Gegenwartigseins ist er, der hier und dort gleich Ewige, in die Innerweltlichkeit, in die menschliche Umschranktheit des Daseyns und Wissens und Könnens eingegangen, die eine geschichtliche Bethätigung seines ewigen Wesens mit der andern vertauschend.

[2] *Die Christliche Dogmatik, Deutsche Ausgabe*, Berlin 1856, pp. 221-272.

a pre-existence, which does not signify merely an original being in the Father, but also an original being in the world. As the Mediator between the Father and the world, it belongs to the essence of the Son to live not only in the Father, but also in the world. As "the heart of God the Father," He is at the same time the eternal heart of the world, through which the divine life flows into the creation. As the Logos of the Father, He is at the same time the eternal world-Logos, through whom the divine light rays forth into the creation. He is ground and source of all reason in the creation, whether in man or in angel, in Greek or in Jew. He is the principle of law and promise in the Old Testament, the eternal light which shines in the darkness of heathendom; all holy germs of truth to be found in the heathen world have been sown in the souls of men by Him. He is the eternal principle of providence, amid the confusion of the world's life; all forces of nature, all ideas and angels, being ministering instruments of His all-ordering, all-guiding will. But, in His pre-existence, He is only the essential, not the real Mediator between God and the creature; the contrast between Creator and created is cancelled in essence only, not in existence; the variance between God and the sinful world is done away with only in idea, not in life. Therefore it was needful that the pre-existent Logos should become man, and supplement the Logos-revelation by a Christ-revelation.[1] The novel element in the latter is such a union of the divine and human natures that a man appears on the earth as the self-revelation of the divine Logos, as the *God-man.*[2] The eternal omnipresent Word became flesh, was born into time. That, however, does not mean that, with the Incarnation, the eternal Logos ceased to exist in His general world-revelation, or that the Logos, as self-conscious personal Being, was inclosed in His mother's womb, was born as an infant, grew in knowledge; for such a representation is incompatible with the idea of birth. Temporal birth necessarily implies a progress from the unconscious to the conscious, from possibility to reality, from germ to mature organization; and any other mode of conceiving

---

[1] *Dogmatik*, pp. 221, 222. [2] *Ibid.* p. 224.

the birth of the God-man must be characterized as doketic. The birth of the Logos means that He enters into the bosom of humanity as possibility, as a holy seed, that He may arise within the human race as a mediating, redeeming, human revelation; that the divine fulness individualizes itself in a single human life, so that the entire sum of holy powers is herein involved. That the Son of God was in His mother's womb not as a self-conscious divine Ego, but as an immature unborn child, is indicated by the words of the angel to Mary: "That holy thing which shall be born of thee shall be called the Son of God."[1] But as that holy thing, in the course of growth, became conscious of Himself as a human Ego, in the same measure He became conscious of His Godhead, and knew Himself as a divine human Ego, because the fulness of Godhead was the life-ground of His human life; knew Himself as not only having part in the divine Logos, but as the divine-human continuation of the everlasting life of Godhead. Hence, while Christ said, "I and the Father are one,"—an affirmation of unity implying a personal distinction,—He never said, "I and the Logos are one," because He *was* the Logos revealing Himself in human form.[1]

In view of these statements, it is easy to see in what sense the *kenosis* is to be understood. It means that the Logos, *qua* incarnate, possesses His Godhead in the limited forms of human consciousness. He is true God; but, in the Christ revelation, the true Godhead is never outside the true humanity. It is not the naked God we see in Christ, but the fulness of Godhead within the compass of humanity; not the properties of the divine nature in their unlimited world-infinitude, but these properties transformed into properties of human nature; the omnipresence becoming the blessed presence of Him who said: "Whoso seeth me seeth the Father;" the omniscience becoming the divine-human wisdom which reveals to the simple the mysteries of the kingdom; the omnipotence becoming the world-conquering and

---

[1] Luke i. 35: τὸ γεννώμενον ἅγιον (neuter).

[2] *Dogmatik*, pp. 244, 245: Obgleich daher Christus zeugt: "Ich und der Vater sind Eins," sagt er doch niemals: Ich und der Logos sind Eins. Denn er ist die menschliche *Selbst*offenbarung des göttlichen Logos.

completing might of holiness and love of Him, to whom was given all power in heaven and on earth. Christ, in possession of these transformed attributes, is not less God than the Logos in His universal world-revelation; for the Deity of the Son is the Deity of the Mediator God, or of God as the revealer of God; and in no form is the Son in a truer sense the Mediator and the Revealer of God, than in the form of the Son of man.¹ And while the kenosis is perfectly compatible with essential Deity even in the Son of man, it does not exclude the continued existence of the Logos as the Mediator and Revealer for the world at large. As the omnipresent Logos, the Son of God continues to shine through the whole creation.² He lives a *double life:* as the pure divine Logos, He works throughout the kingdom of nature, preparing the conditions for the revelation of His all-completing love; as Christ, He works through the kingdom of grace and redemption, and indicates His consciousness of personal identity in the two spheres, by referring to His pre-existence, which to His human consciousness takes the form of a *recollection.*³

On two points Martensen does not fully explain himself: the human soul of Christ; and the question, How is the duality in the *life* of the Logos to be reconciled with the unity of His personality? As to the former, though it is nowhere said, it seems to be tacitly implied, that the incarnate Logos took in Christ the place of a human soul. The latter topic also the author passes over in discreet silence, thinking it better, possibly, to attempt no solution, than to offer his readers such an abstruse speculation as that by which Ebrard endeavours to explain how the Eternal and

---

¹ *Dogmatik*, pp. 247, 248.

² *Ibid.* p. 246: Als der allgegenwärtige Logos die ganze Schöpfung durchleuchtet.

³ *Ibid.* p. 247: Wohl aber müssen wir sagen dass der Sohn Gottes in der Oekonomie des Vaters ein doppeltes Dasein führt, dass er ein Doppelleben lebt in weltschöpferischer und weltvollendender Thätigkeit. Als der reine Gottheit-logos durchwirkt er in Alles erfüllender Gegenwart das Reich der Natur, wirkt die Voraussetzungen und Bedingungen für die Offenbarung seiner Alles vollendenden Liebe. Als Christus durchwirkt er das Reich der Gnade, der Erlösung, und Vollendung, und weist zurück auf seiner Präexistenz. See also p. 250, where Christ is spoken of as recollecting His pre-existence: Erinnert er sich seiner ewigen Präexistenz und seines Ausgangs vom Vater.

the Incarnate Logos can have an identical consciousness.¹ He animadverts on the dualism, not to speak of the monstrosity, introduced into the person of Christ by the old orthodox Christology, according to which Christ, as a child in the cradle, secretly carried on the government of the world with the omniscience that work required; while, at the same time, in His human nature He grew in knowledge and wisdom. By such a grotesque representation, he contends, the unity of the person is annulled, two parallel series of conscious states which never unite are introduced, and the result is in effect a Christ with two heads.² But the friends of antiquated orthodoxy might turn round and ask: What better are we on your theory? You say we teach a Christ with two non-communicating or non-coincident consciousnesses, or with two heads; you teach a Logos with a double life: one in the world at large, another in the man Jesus; infinite in the former, limited, self-emptied, in the latter; a mere unconscious possibility to begin with, and never exceeding the measures of humanity: show us the possibility of such a double life, and its compatibility with a single personality. This demand some believers in a real but relative kenosis treat as legitimate, and attempt to satisfy. Martensen seems to have preferred to regard the problem as a mystery, deeming the *kenosis* in the sense explained an indubitable Scripture doctrine and historical fact, and the continued activity of the world-sustaining Logos an obvious corollary from His distinctive function as the Mediator and Revealer in relation to the universe, and not holding himself bound to reconcile the two, any more than to clear up in a perfectly satisfactory manner any other mystery of the Christian faith.³

Such are the leading forms which the modern kenotic theory has assumed in the hands of its advocates. In proceeding now to a critical estimate of this theory, certain

---

¹ See Appendix, Note D.

² *Dogmatik*, p. 249: Die Einheit der Person wird aufgehoben, und wir bekommen in Christo zwei verschiedene Bewusstseinsreihen, die niemals zusammen gehen werden. Wir bekommen gleichsam einen Christus mit zwei Köpfen, ein Bild, welches nicht nur den Eindruck des Uebermenschlichen sondern des Monströsen macht, und dem die *ethische* Wirkung fehlt.

³ *Vid.* Appendix, Note E, for literature belonging to the Martensen type.

general considerations suggest themselves, which may here be submitted by way of preface.

1. The theory in question, whether tenable or not, is at all events animated by a genuinely orthodox interest; as, indeed, might be inferred from a rapid glance at the roll of its supporters, which includes, in addition to those already mentioned, the names of such men as Delitzsch and Hofmann, whose orthodoxy, in the catholic sense, is above suspicion. Kenosis, in all its forms presupposes the Church doctrines of the Trinity and the pre-existence of the Logos. The very aim of the theory is to show how the eternally pre-existent Son of God, second person of the Trinity, by a free self-conscious act of self-exinanition, made Himself capable of Incarnation after the manner recorded in the Gospels. It is true, indeed, that some advocates of the kenotic Christology have deemed it necessary to lay a foundation for the self-emptying of the Logos in a conception of the Trinity, or of the Trinitarian Process, as it is called, which involves a Subordinatian view of the relation of the Son to the Father.[1] But the abler or more cautious members of the school avoid this opinion in their statement of the doctrine;[2] and there does not appear to be any necessary connection between the kenosis implied in the Incarnation, and an eternal inequality of the persons within the immanent Trinity. In every Christological theory it is a problem why the Son and not the Father became incarnate; and all theories alike are liable to err in the solution of the problem, if they attempt it and do not prefer to let it alone.[3]

2. This theory further proposes to itself most legitimate and even praiseworthy ends. It may be said to have two ends in view, one religious, the other scientific—to do full justice to the divine Love as manifested in the Incarnation,

---

[1] *E. g.* Gess, Liebner.   [2] *E. g.* Hofmann, Delitzsch.
[3] Schneckenburger thinks that the kenotic theory, if logically carried out to its ultimate consequences, involves the dissolution of the Trinity. *Vom doppelten Stande Christi, Beilage,* p. 196 ff., being a review of Thomasius' *Beiträge.* He says, p. 201: Kurz ich sehe nicht ein, wie das Trinitätsdogma bestehen kann mit der vorgeschlagenen Korrektur (*i. e.* the rectification of the old Lutheran Christology by the Thomasian doctrine of kenosis). But the opinion is not supported by argument.

and to give such a view of the person of Christ as shall allow His humanity to remain in all its historical truth. The former aim is very apparent in the Christological utterances of the father of modern kenosis, Zinzendorf.[1] The celebrated founder of the Moravian brotherhood went great lengths in the assertion of Christ's likeness to His brethren. Living in a time when men were ashamed of the humiliation of Christ, and gave prominence only to what was rational and intelligible, and in a worldly sense respectable, in Christianity, he deemed it his vocation to glory in Christ's passion, and to assert with all possible emphasis the Incarnation as a lowering of Himself in love, on the part of God the Son, to the level of humanity. This self-lowering he represented as taking place to such an extent, that Bengel, with every desire to give an impartial account of his doctrinal system, spoke of him as a new Unitarian, who, while differing widely from other Unitarians, in assigning to the Son not only a place in the Trinity, but a monopoly of divine functions, creation, redemption, and sanctification, came by so much the nearer to them on the other side, as one who journeys towards the east, going as far as he can, at length comes round to the west.[2] Jesus, according to Zinzendorf, while never ceasing to be God, was in all matters to be considered as a simple man; and all our comfort is to be derived from His humanity, viewed not only as like us in its weakness, but as characterized by a maximum of weakness, so that the most miserable creature can think of Christ as weaker than himself. The Son of God incarnate thought of Himself as a man; if the thought, "I am God," entered into His mind, it was only *in transitu*, as a man of thirty years may remember, in a dream, something he had said or done when a child of two or three years.[3] Thus far did He carry the business of self-emptying; and in carrying it so far, He but glorified His love. For the greatest thing in the Saviour was not His Godhead, or His majesty, or His miracles, but His becoming freely *so little*.[4] Thus thought the Saviour Himself before

---

[1] See Appendix, Note G.

[2] *Abriss der so genannten Brüdergemeine*, pp. 28-41.

[3] Plitt, *Zinzendorf's Theologie Dargestellt*, Zweiter Band, p. 171.

[4] *Ibid.* p. 161, where he quotes from Zinzendorf a passage respecting the sur

He came in the flesh. He esteemed it a favour conferred on Him by His Father to be permitted to become man, that He might die for a sinful world. Yea, He reckoned it an additional favour, that, in order to become man, it was necessary that He should go out of the Godhead, and at least for an hour, for a moment, know what it is to be God-forsaken.[1] In more recent writers we miss both the eloquence and the extravagance characteristic of Zinzendorf, in proclaiming the most thoroughgoing kenosis as the glorification of divine love. Modern kenosists are influenced much more by the scientific than by the religious interest, which in the case of Zinzendorf was the supreme, if not the exclusive, object of consideration. Nevertheless, even with regard to the former, there is truth in the remark of Dorner, that the Christology of which Zinzendorf may be regarded as the forerunner, represents a religious trait, viz. the desire to conceive the divine Love as having become as like to, as intimately united with, men as possible.[2] And in this respect the Christology in question, under any of its forms, commends itself to our sympathy. It is impossible not to have a kindly feeling towards a Christological theory which is earnestly bent on making the exinanition of the Son of God a great sublime moral reality. An error is readily pardoned in a theory animated by such an evangelic aim. Even when the resulting view of Christ's person wears a suspicious resemblance to that given in the Socinian theory, we are conscious of a sympathy with the one which we cannot have for the other. We remember that the kenotic Christ, however like the Socinian in other respects, is the result of an act of free grace, on the part of a Divine Being emptying Himself of His divinity as far as possible, in order that He might become flesh and dwell

---

prise of contemporaries, at seeing a people (the brethren) to whom the greatest thing in Christ was, that He became so little (das ihnen das Grösste ist, dass der Heiland so klein gewesen ist).

[1] Plitt, i. p. 272: Die Concession, die Willigkeit des Vaters, dass der Sohn hat können Mensch werden, dass er hat können sein Leben lassen, das ist das Präsent das ihm der Vater gethan hat. Er sieht es als eine neue Gnade an, dass er hat dürfen, um Mensch zu werden, aus der Gottheit herausgehen und zum wenigsten eine Stunde, einen Augenblick erfahren, was das heisset, von Gott verlassen sein.

[2] Dorner, *Doctrine of the Person of Christ,* div. ii. vol. iii. p. 258.

among men full of grace and truth. The historical phenomenon may be to a large extent the same in either system, but the moral and theological significance of the phenomenon is *toto coelo* different. The Christ of the kenosis is God self-humbled to man's level; the Socinian Christ is man exalted to the highest human level. The conceptions of the Deity cherished by the two systems are equally diverse. The God of the one system is self-sacrificing love; the God of the other system is a Being who cannot descend from the altitude of His metaphysical majesty.[1]

The scientific aim of this theory is equally entitled to respect, its declared purpose being to reconcile the doctrine of Christ's person with the facts of the gospel history; or more definitely, so to conceive the Incarnation, as to leave room for a real progressive human development, intellectually and morally, not less than physically. This purpose all Christological theories profess to keep in view, and all have tried in one way or another to satisfy its requirements. The attempts have been varied in their nature, but all have involved a more or less distinct recognition of the need of a kenosis of some kind on the part of the Logos, in order that the truth of Christ's humanity may remain unimpaired. Irenaeus taught a rest or quiescence of the Logos in connection with the temptations, crucifixion, and death of Christ;[2] Ambrose spoke of the Logos withdrawing Himself from activity, that He might be subject to infirmity.[3] Hilary conceived of the Logos incarnate as having exchanged the form of God for the form of a servant, and in the assumed form tempering Himself to conformity with the human habit, lest the infirmity of the assumed nature should be unable to bear the power and infinitude of the divine nature.[4] Even Cyril, while rejecting a meta-

---

[1] Ritschl characterizes the kenotic theory as *verschämter Socinianismus*.

[2] Ὅσπερ γὰρ ἦν ἄνθρωπος, ἵνα πειρασθῇ, οὕτω καὶ λόγος, ἵνα δοξασθῇ· ἡσυχάζοντος μὲν τοῦ λόγου ἐν τῷ πειράζεσθαι ... καὶ σταυροῦσθαι, καὶ ἀποθνῄσκειν. Contra Haereses, lib. iii. cap. xix. 3.

[3] Exinanivit se, hoc est, potestatem suam ab opere retraxit, ut humiliatus otiosa virtute infirmari videretur.—*Comment. in Epistolam ad Philipp.*

[4] In formâ Dei, manens formam servi assumpsit, non demutatus sed se ipsum exinaniens, et intra se latens, et intra suam ipse vacuefactus potestatem; dum se usque ad formam temperat habitus humani, ne potentem immensamque naturam

morphic Incarnation, kenosis in that sense being, in his view, excluded by the σκήνωσις ascribed by the evangelist to the incarnate Logos, in the same text in which he represents Him as becoming flesh,[1] nevertheless did homage to the demands of the kenosis, by admitting that the superhuman endowments of the man Jesus must at all events be carefully concealed, that He might at least seem to be what in truth He was not, and wear to spectators the guise and fashion of a child, a boy, and a man, while His inward habit was that of a God.[2] The Lutherans yielded reluctant obedience to the requirements of history, by ascribing to the man Christ Jesus a possession without use of divine attributes; while the Reformed, on the other hand, made room for growth and experience in the life of the Saviour, by so conceiving of the union of natures, that the human nature should not be overlaid or swallowed up by the divine.[3] In recent times the pressure of the problem has been felt more heavily than ever; and men of all schools, believing in the doctrine of the Trinity, have been of one mind as to the necessity of such a construction of Christ's person as, while recognising His Godhead, shall nowise infringe on the integrity and full reality of His humanity. All, as already remarked,[4] have not followed the same method in the work of reconstruction. Some are content with the old Reformed theory carefully re-stated in the light of modern requirements, teaching a duality, not in the *consciousness* of the God-man, but in the life of the Logos; distributing the *mens duplex* between the Logos as a person in the Trinity and the concrete God-man, so far as that divine person exhibits and develops Himself in Jesus in a human manner, or as a human individual, being the life principle of this man, sustaining Him, conditioning His existence and personality, dwelling in Him by the

---

assumptae humilitatis non ferret infirmitas, sed in tantum se virtute incircumscripta moderaretur, in quantum oporteret eam usque ad patientiam connexi sibi corporis obedire. *De Trinitate*, lib. xi. 48. The *exchange* of forms, though not taught here, is asserted in other passages; see Appendix, Note A, Lect. i.; also Thomasius, ii. p. 172 sqq. Thomasius, without good ground, claims Hilary as a supporter of kenosis in his own sense.

[1] See Appendix, Note G.   [2] See Lecture ii.
[3] See Lecture iii.   [4] See p. 136.

Holy Spirit.[1] Others teach what may be called a gradual Incarnation, conceiving of the union as at first comparatively outward and dissoluble, gradually becoming more intimate as the human development of Jesus progressed, till at length, after the resurrection, the Logos and the man became absolutely one,[2]—a view in some respects having close affinity to the one previously described; the

---

[1] So Schneckenburger, *Vom doppelten Stande Christi*, p. 218: Anstatt jener Lutherischen Spaltung der menschlichen Natur in ihre illokale und lokale Subsistenz, vielmehr in die Lebensäusserung der göttlichen eine Distinktion fällt, wonach die *mens duplex* sich eigentlich vertheilt an den Logos, sofern er Person der Trinität ist, und den conkreten Gottmenschen, sofern sich in Jesus jene Person menschlich, d. h. als menschliches Individuum darstellt und entwickelt. Der Logos *totus extra Jesum* ist die *secunda persona trinitatis* als solche, mit der *scientia personalis*, der Logos *totus in Jesu* ist dieselbe alles durchdringende und belebende göttliche Hypostase, sofern sie Lebensprincip dieses Individuums ist, des Gottmenschen, dessen individuelles Bewusstsein nicht schlechthin Alles umfasst. Lebensprincip dieses Individuum ist der Logos, weil er *hominem Jesum sustentat*, sein Dasein und Personsein absolut bedingt, ihm *gratiose* inwohnt durch den heiligen Geist. Schneckenburger speaks of the Reformed theory, so stated, as satisfying pretty much the Dornerian desiderata, and says that the Reformed theanthropic life-development is the normal human development of Him who, on account of His unique intimate relation to the Logos (who is the ground of all rational being), is the God-man.

[2] So Dorner, *Doctrine of the Person of Christ*, div. ii. vol. iii. p. 250, where he states his own view in opposition to the kenotic theory: "On the only other possible view (other than the kenotic), we can merely speak of a limitation of the self-communication of the Logos to humanity, not of a lessening or reduction of the Logos Himself. The being and actuality of the Logos remained unchanged; but Jesus possessed the being and actuality of the Logos in virtue of the *unio*, merely so far as was compatible with the truth of the human growth. For this reason the eternal *personality* of the Logos did not immediately, and ere there was a human consciousness, become divine-*human*." "On this view the object of the volition of the Logos is, in the first instance, solely the production of a divine-human *nature*, not a divine-human person." The union is "*not completely accomplished* until the personality of the Logos also became divine-*human*, through the coming into existence of a human consciousness able to be appropriated and able also itself to appropriate." Further on, Dorner refers to Origen's doctrine of an *eternal* generation of the Son, as analogous to this doctrine of a gradual Incarnation, one "constantly growing and reproducing itself on the basis of the being." He then adds, by way of explaining this idea: "At the centre of His being, it is true, this man is from the beginning divine-human essence: but many things are yet lacking to this person; other things in it are still dissolubly united —for example, the body is still mortal; other things are still mutable, without detriment to its identity. The divine-human articulation, the bodily and the spiritual organism of the divine-human person, needs first to be developed " (p. 258). The idea is, that the physical *unio* is a momentary act, but its effects, physical and moral, are only gradually worked out.

main difference being, that in the Reformed theory the Logos consciousness never becomes absolutely coincident with the human consciousness of Christ, the distinction between the *Logos totus extra Jesum* and the *Logos totus in Jesu* being eternally valid, while in the other theory the ultimatum or goal is an absolute identity, in the old Lutheran sense, between the divine and the human—the divine become wholly human, and the human wholly divine; and the Lutheran axiom, *Logos non extra carnem*, being realized in the eternal, as it could not be in the earthly state. The advocates of kenosis, in the sense of depotentiation, total or partial, are not satisfied with either of those schemes, and therefore they bring forward their own. And they are quite entitled to do so, and it is our duty to listen to them, not refusing to hear on the ground that the speculation is idle, that there is no problem to solve, no need for any new attempt to answer the question, How can Christ be God without at the same time ceasing to be man? We may indeed enter on the study of this new theory with a suspicion that it will turn out a failure, yea, with a rooted conviction that all theories whatsoever will break down; only believing firmly that Christ is both God and man, and determined that no theory, orthodox or heterodox, old or new, shall rob us of our faith in either of the factors which constitute our Lord's mysterious person, and using our critical faculties mainly to protect ourselves against such a result. In that case, we shall come to the task of examining the latest Christological speculation in the orthodox interest, with very moderate expectation of new light. But our examination need not on this account be careless, prejudiced, or contemptuous, as if the interests of science, as distinct from those of faith, had already been fully satisfied, and all further theorizing, or theological inquiry on the matter, were a simple impertinence.

3. One other general observation remains to be made with reference to the kenotic theory, viz., that it does not seem advisable to dispose of it in a summary manner, by *à priori* reasoning from the divine unchangeableness. This attribute, doubtless, offers a very tempting short road to the refutation of a theory which we have previously made

up our minds not to believe. It is very easy for one, taking his stand at that point, to ask imposing and formidable questions. Is this so-called kenosis metaphysically possible? can the almighty God depotentiate Himself? can the infinite One limit Himself? can the omniscient One reduce Himself to the state of a mere human germ, without knowledge, or even so much as self-consciousness? For my part, I do not care to ask such questions; I am not inclined to dogmatize on what is possible or impossible for God: I think it best to keep the mind clear of too decided prepossessions on such matters. It appears to me not very safe to indulge in *à priori* reasonings from divine attributes, and especially from divine unchangeableness. It is wiser in those who believe in revelation to be ready to believe that God can do anything that is not incompatible with His moral nature, to refuse to allow metaphysical difficulties to stand as insuperable obstacles in the way of His gracious purposes, and so far to agree with the advocates of the kenosis as to hold that He can descend and empty Himself to the extent love requires. For *à priori* reasoning from divine attributes, besides being liable to a charge of presumption, is apt to be dangerous. We may put weapons into the hands of foes to be wielded with fatal effect against doctrines dear to our hearts. What if the attribute of unchangeableness should be brought to bear against the Incarnation itself! What if men should begin to ask such questions as these: "If God be unchangeable, how can He become flesh? If God be essentially unlimited, how can He so subject Himself to the limitations of the humanity of Christ, as in Him to be really with us?"[1] How is Strauss to be answered when he argues: "A God who performs single acts is certainly a person, but not the Absolute. Turning Himself from one act to another, or now exercising a certain kind of activity—the extraordinary—anon allowing it to rest, He does and is in one moment, what He neither does nor is in another, and so falls altogether under the category of the changeable, the temporal, the finite"? Here are creation, providence, incarnation,

---

[1] Dorner, *Doctrine of the Person of Christ*, div. ii. vol. i. p. 65, with reference to the views taught by Cyril concerning the divine immutability.

miracles, demolished by a single stroke of resistless *à priori* logic, reasoning with unhesitating assurance from the attribute of immutability. They that take the sword shall perish with the sword; therefore let believers in these and kindred revealed truths put up again the two-edged sword of *à priori* reasoning into his place, and be content to try current theories by humbler and more patient methods, mindful what obstacles every Christian truth has encountered in its way to a place in the established creed of the Church, arising out of speculative presuppositions and prepossessions.

In this spirit, then, I proceed now to make some critical observations upon the theory in question, some of these being but repetitions or expansions of objections stated by German theologians, who have not seen their way to give the kenotic hypothesis their unqualified approval.

1. First of all, there is a great initial difficulty to be got over. According to the *Thomasian* theory the Incarnation involves at once an act of assumption and an act of self-limitation; the two acts, distinct in thought, being coincident in time, and simply different aspects of one and the same act. Now the difficulty is, that these two phases show the same act in what seem contradictory lights, at once as an *assertion* and a *deposition* of divine power. The Incarnation, as assumption of human nature on the part of the Logos, is an exercise of omnipotence; as self-limitation, on the other hand, it is the loss of omnipotence. One act of will has contrary effects; one effect being the creation of the human nature; the other, the entire waste or dissipation of force in the act of creation. Are such contrary effects of one act of will compatible?[1] And why should this particular act of creation be followed with the extinction or absorption of creative force, any more than that by which the Logos brought into being the world at large, or the first man? Is the difference due to the fact that the

---

[1] Schneckenburger, *Vom doppelten Stande Christi*, p. 214: Eine und dieselbe Willensthat, deren Effekt eine göttliche übernatürliche Machtäusserung, *assumptio*, und zugleich eine übernatürliche Machtentleerung wäre, ist der vollendete Widerspruch, der sich nur halten kann, wenn die Entleerung zu einer *quasi-exinanitio* gemacht wird.

product in this case is personally united to the producer? Then we are landed in a heathenish view of the Incarnation, according to which matter is accredited with power to reduce even Deity united to it to a state of impotence; and the kenosis ceases to be a voluntary act of self-depotentiation, except in the sense that the Logos freely resolves to bring Himself into contact with a creature which, He knows beforehand, will of necessity absorb all His divine energy.[1] It might, indeed, seem a very easy way out of these difficulties to make the kenosis and the assumption two really and temporally separate acts, either of the same actor or of different actors. The Incarnation might be conceived of in one or other of two ways. Either thus: the Logos fully depotentiated Himself; then the Holy Spirit did what the depotentiated Logos was no longer able to do—created a human nature, consisting of a body and a soul, and united this creation to the depotentiated Logos. On this hypothesis there is no assumption, but only a union between the Logos become incapable of such an act, and a human nature, effected by the Holy Ghost; and the thing united to the Logos is not merely a human nature, but a complete human being.[2] Or thus: the Logos first partially depotentiated Himself, leaving Himself enough power to create and assume human nature, and then the process of depotentiation was consummated when the union had been effected.[3] On this hypothesis, however, there arises, for a moment at least, that very dualism which the kenotic theory is intended to get rid of—a self-conscious

[1] Schneckenburger, *l. c.*, adduces against the ascription of the absorbtive power to the nature of the ἐναμενον (the human nature), the fact that, in the union with the assumed nature, the Logos ultimately becomes active and potent again, when the kenosis is at an end. He compares the depotentiation of the Logos, which, according to Thomasius, takes place in connection with the Incarnation, to the loss of consciousness sustained by God, according to Lenau's expression, "in the rush of creation." Etwa so wie, nach Lenau's Ausdruck, Gott im Schöpfungsrausch das Bewusstsein verloren haben soll, würde des Logos in Assumtionsakt seine Gottheit bis zum *minimum*, jedenfalls bis zur Bewusstlosigkeit erschöpft und eingebüsst haben.

[2] Schneckenburger, *Vom doppelten Stande*, pp. 212, 213. Of this hypothesis Schneckenburger remarks: "und so haben wir einerseits die reformirte Lehre, andrerseits noch ein Häretisches zu der reformirten Lehre hinzu, nämlich das ἐκ δύο φύσεων, die *assumptio hominis*, nicht *naturae humanae*."

[3] *Ibid.* p. 212.

and potent, if not omnipotent, Logos united to a human foetus, and freely resolving to depotentiate Himself still further, even completely, in order that His state may be perfectly congruous to that of the nature He has assumed.

2. Assuming the initial difficulty to have been surmounted, other difficulties confront us in connection with the incarnate state. One is, that the kenosis reduces the Logos to a state of helpless passivity or impotence. Thomasius, indeed, endeavours to meet this objection by the remark that "Potenz" does not signify something impotent or empty, but fulness concentrated in itself, withdrawn from the circumference of manifestation indeed, yet present in the centre, and having power over itself.[1] But the question is: has this "Potenz" power at will to radiate forth to the circumference of manifestation in action, or is it under a necessity of remaining at the centre confined to a mere mathematical point? If the former alternative be adopted, as it is by Ebrard,[2] then there is really no depotentiation, as Ebrard consistently holds, but only a change in the *mode* of manifesting and exercising power. If the latter alternative be adopted, as it is in the frankest manner by Gess,[3] then "Potenz," in spite of the protest of Thomasius, is practically equivalent to impotence. And Thomasius virtually admits this, by representing the development of Christ as taking place under the guidance of the Holy Ghost. He quotes with approval an observation of Kahnis, that the miracles of Christ proved, not His divine nature, but His divine mission; and while not denying them to be expressions of an indwelling power, yet he speaks of them as wrought at the bidding and with the assistance of the Father, and through the medium of the Holy Ghost.[4] In like manner does he account for Christ's knowledge of the divine. That knowledge, we are told, Christ got in no human school; in virtue of His union with the Father, He saw His eternal thoughts, not as one who received them by revelation, but through His own immediate intuition. But at the same time it is admitted that these divine thoughts came gradually to Christ's consciousness through the mediation

[1] See p. 143.   [2] See p. 152.   [3] See p. 146.
[4] *Christi Person und Werk*, ii. p. 250.

of the Holy Spirit; though an effort is made to lessen the importance of the admission by the further statement, that this growth in knowledge, under the education of the Spirit, was but the development of what lay hid in the depths of His own being.[1] Now what is the consequence of this passivity of the Logos, reluctantly admitted by Thomasius, more frankly conceded by Gess? It is this, that in the Thomasian theory the depotentiated Logos associated with a human soul seems superfluous; it would make little difference though He were not there;[2] and that in the Gessian theory, the Logos, become a human soul, is allowed no benefit from His antecedents, the divine elements fall into abeyance so completely, that His sinlessness and His consciousness of personal identity are rendered all but unaccountable; insomuch that if Jesus had happened to be a Greek instead of a Jew, without the benefit of the Hebrew Scriptures, He could not have known who He was by the way of a truly human development—in other words, without a miraculous revelation.

3. But this passivity of the depotentiated Logos involves another consequence, which constitutes a third difficulty in the way of accepting the kenotic theory, at least in its Thomasian and Gessian forms. By one act of self-depotentiation, the Logos is reduced to such a state of impotence, that His kenosis becomes a matter of physical necessity, not of loving free-will. The love which moved the Son of God to become man consumed itself at one stroke. There is a breach of continuity in the mind which gave rise to the Incarnation. A mighty impulse of free self-conscious love constrained the eternal Son to descend into humanity, and in the descent that love lost itself for years; till at length the man Jesus found out the secret of His birth, and the sublime spirit of self-sacrifice to which it owed its origin,

[1] *Christi Person und Werk*, ii. p. 237.
[2] See Dorner, div. ii. vol. iii. p. 254: "Nay more, on such a supposition the Incarnation of the Logos is of no advantage whatever to the humanity. It does not allow the Logos to communicate Himself in ever-increasing measure, and so as to direct the development of the man assumed. . . . Consequently, the hypothesis of a self-depotentiation of the Logos . . . renders it necessary to look out for another principle than the Logos, to wit, the Holy Ghost, to conduct the growth of the God-man" (so, for example, with Thomasius and Hofmann).

and made that spirit His own, said Amen to the mind which took shape in the kenosis,[1] and resolved thenceforth to act on it, and so reunited the broken thread of personal identity. On this view, the Logos had no acquaintance with some of the most interesting stages in the experience of Christ. He knew what it was to be conceived in the Virgin's womb, or rather to resolve that He should be; for by the time the fact was accomplished, He was no longer conscious; and He knew what it was to be tempted in the wilderness, and to endure the contradiction of sinners during His ministry, and to die; for by the time these experiences came to Jesus, He had ascertained who He was. But the Logos knew not what it was to be an infant in the cradle, or on His mother's breast; what it was to be a boy subject to His parents; what to grow in wisdom as in stature; what to be an apprentice carpenter: for in those years He was asleep—unconscious. Therefore with infants, children, and youths He has not learned to sympathize; only with full-grown tempted men has His experience fitted Him to have a fellow-feeling.[2] On this account, one desiderates a way of making the Logos accommodate Himself to the human development otherwise than by depotentiation, that His love may not appear exhausted by a single act, and that the initial act of sympathy may not disqualify Him for entering sympathetically into all the experiences of human life—those of the first thirty, not less than those of the last three years of Christ's

[1] Schneckenburger, *Vom doppelten Stande*, p. 204, represents Reinhard as teaching a *nachträgliche Genehmigung* on the part of the man Jesus, of the *exinanitio* to which, according to the old Lutheran theory, He was a party from the moment of conception. The humanity of Christ unconsciously divested itself of divine properties at the conception, and consciously consented to the act on reaching maturity, somewhat as a Christian homologates the vows to which he was unconsciously a party at his baptism. In the same way the modern kenosists are shut up by their theory to an *ex post facto* homologation by the man Jesus of the original act of kenosis which resulted in the Incarnation.

[2] Dorner, div. ii. vol. iii. p. 253: "The truth of the kenosis of the Logos is the love which stirred in Him in eternity, in virtue of which He condescends to the creatures who stand in need and are susceptible of Him, that He may know what is theirs and communicate what is His. But the kenosis of self-depotentiation fails to perform that at which it aims. For if the Logos has given up His eternal self-conscious Being, where is His love during that time? Love without self-consciousness is an impossibility." Dorner further questions the necessity of this "unethical sacrifice of Himself."

earthly history. Is this impossible? In the words of Dorner, " Is it impossible for the Logos to acquire power over the central susceptibility of humanity which He finds in Jesus, and to belong to it in a unique manner, save by ceasing to stand in any actual relation to others? or save by reducing Himself to a level of equality with this man?"[1]

4. The Thomasian form of the kenotic theory is open to objection with reference to the personal unity. It teaches the presence in Christ of two life centres, the depotentiated Logos and the human soul. Now this doctrine is in danger of being impaled on one or other of the horns of the following dilemma. Either these two life centres are " homogeneous magnitudes" or they are not. If they are not, then a dualism ensues in the consciousness of the God-man, and the depotentiation of the Logos has taken place in vain; for the very object of that depotentiation was to exclude dualism. Such a dualism can be escaped only by a perfect equality of the two life centres in spiritual endowment. The two yoke-fellows must draw equally and keep pace, else the course of the human development will be other than smooth and harmonious. If, on the other hand, the two life centres be homogeneous, then the unity of self-consciousness may indeed be secured; but only with the effect of raising the question: To what purpose this duality in the life basis? Why two human souls to do the work of one? for, *ex hypothesi*, the depotentiated Logos is to all intents and purposes a human soul. Instead of this roundabout process, according to which the Logos first reduces Himself to the dimensions of a human soul, and then associates with Himself another human soul, why not say at once the Logos became a human soul? On the Thomasian theory, the depotentiated Logos, or, if you will, the human soul of Christ, is degraded from the position of a necessary constituent of the personality to that of a dispensable ornament. The two life centres, the self-reduced Logos and the human soul, are like the two eyes or the two ears of a man. As the sensations of both organs coalesce in one mental act of perception, the duality of the organs does not produce

[1] Dorner, div. ii. vol. iii. p. 254.

any duality of consciousness, while it adds to the symmetry and grace of the person; but on the other hand, it is not necessary to the act of perception, one eye or ear being able to do the work of the two.[1]

This being the state of the case as regards the Thomasian form of the kenotic hypothesis, it is not surprising that the preponderance of opinion, among theologians of the same Christological school, should be decidedly in favour of the metamorphic form of the theory, which gets rid of the duality of life centres by representing the Logos as undergoing conversion into, or as taking the place and performing the function of, a human soul. This form of the theory now invites our attention.

5. The metamorphic theory of Christ's person, as expounded by Gess, is liable to two grave objections. One of these has reference to the power which this theory gives to the flesh of the incarnate Logos to determine His condition. The text, "the Word became flesh," means, that the flesh and blood which he assumed became in this union a determining power for the Logos. The Incarnation signifies the subjection of Deity to the dominion of matter. Contact with flesh is fatal to the free, conscious life of God; it is a plunge into a Lethe stream, which involves loss of self-consciousness, and therewith of the divine attributes of omniscience, omnipotence, omnipresence, and even of eternal holiness. It is true these attributes are in the metamorphosed Logos in a state of rest; but it is a rest out of which they cannot return until the Logos wakens up to self-consciousness, and that wakening does not take place fully till death has delivered the imprisoned Deity from the bondage of His mortal corruptible body. "Not in entire forgetfulness," indeed, did the Son of God pass His life on earth previous to His passion.

---

[1] On this objection to the Thomasian theory, see Dorner, div. ii. voi. iii. pp. 255, 256. Dorner says: "It does not even help the question of the unity of the divine and human, unless we should say that the depotentiation was in itself Incarnation, that is, conversion into a human existence. . . . If, however, no conversion be supposed to have taken place, and yet the kenosis be assumed for the purpose of the *unio* . . . we should have nothing but two homogeneous magnitudes in or alongside of each other, . . . and the result arrived at resembles a duplication of one and the same, through which the one or the other is rendered useless."

By instinct, by perusal of the Scriptures, by close communion with His Father, Jesus had found out who He was by the time He began His public ministry; and the conclusion at which He had arrived by these means was, or at least may possibly have been, confirmed by flashes of recollection lighting up the darkness of the incarnate state, and for a moment revealing the heavens whence He had come. But not till He tasted death did He perfectly recover possession of Himself. Then the bound powers of Godhead were immediately, and we may say *ipso facto*, released from the enslavement of matter. For though our author speaks of Jesus after His death as made alive in the spirit by the Father,[1] this is only a convenient use of Scripture language to express the idea that death itself gave Him back His life in all its native energy. Death, so to speak, disengaged the divine power of the Logos, which had been reduced to a latent state by entrance into connection with matter, somewhat as heat applied to water disengages the latent force of steam. Depotentiated at His conception in the Virgin's womb, the incarnate Logos became repotentiated at His death, so that He was able to raise His own body from the grave, and transform it into a fit organ for the manifestation of His recovered life in all its fulness—transform it at once, *per saltum*, not gradually; for a body retaining any particle of gross materiality could not be a fit companion for the Logos returned to Himself, but would only bring Him again, partially at least, into a state of most unseasonable bondage.[2]

The other grave difficulty besetting the Gessian theory is, that it ensures the reality of Christ's human experience

---

[1] *Die Lehre von der Person Christi*, p. 379: Nach der Tödtung am Fleisch ward Jesus von dem Vater lebendig gemacht am Geist, und nachdem er im Geiste den Geistern im Gefängniss geprediget hatte, ward sein im Grabe liegender Leib von ihm selbst wieder aufgerichtet, sein im Tode hingegebenes Leben von ihm selbst wieder hingenommen.

[2] *Die Lehre von der Person Christi*, p. 379. In the above remarks I have given not Gess' own words, but what I regard as the legitimate outcome of his theory. He teaches an immediate transformation of the risen body, and I suggest a reason naturally arising out of his theory for holding that doctrine. With regard to the Ascension, Gess remarks: Die Himmelfahrt ist für die Leiblichkeit Jesu nicht der Eintritt einer neuen Epoche, sie ist nur das letzte um der Jünger willen in feierlicher Auffahrt geschehende Scheiden des Auferstandenen. P. 380.

in a way which imperils the end of the Incarnation, viz., the redemption of sinners, for which it is indispensable that the Redeemer Himself should be free from sin. This theory is so thoroughly in earnest with the conversion of the Logos into a human soul, that it quite consistently treats sin as a real possibility for Jesus. And while, of course, all who advocate this theory agree in believing that, as a matter of fact, the possibility did not become actual, I do not think they succeed in giving any good reason for the fact. The risk of moral evil appearing in the life of Jesus is not duly provided against. All that Gess has to say is, that God foreknew that the man Jesus would not fall into sin, and therefore was willing that the risk should be run.[1] That is, the chances might be ten, a hundred, a million to one, against the preservation of sinlessness, but God foresaw that the barely possible would happen, therefore He decreed that the Incarnation should take place. This is simply giving up the problem as insoluble; a remark applicable also to the Schleiermacherian method of securing the sinlessness of Christ, viz., by a determinism which excludes real moral freedom, *i.e.* by physical force. Other supporters of the kenotic theory, seeing the unsatisfactoriness of leaving the vital matter of the Saviour's moral perfection to the chapter of accidents, or, what comes to the same thing, to the power of an unethical necessity, have sought a solution of the problem in the remanent divinity of the Logos incarnate. Liebner, for example, while apparently agreeing with Gess in making the Son of God, entered into "Werden," take the place of a human soul, insists on ascribing to the incarnate Son a large superhuman, superadamitic element.[2] He will not have Christ be regarded as a human being put, by His immaculate conception, in the same position as Adam before the fall, capable of being either good or evil, and having used His freedom well, exhibiting in His person as an individual saint the character of a normally developed Adam.[3] He will have us understand

[1] See p. 149. [2] See Appendix, Note B.
[3] *Christologie*, p. 318: Es giebt einen gewissen höheren Ebionismus, dem es nur auf einen einzelnen Heiligen ankommt, und dem daher Christus nur wieder

that, being the Logos incarnate, Christ could not but live a holy life; for this among other reasons, because His existence in this world was preceded by an ethical being in the eternal world, of which He had the benefit in His earthly career. Now this may be true as a matter of fact, but in proportion as it is true, is, if not the reality of Christ's moral experience as a man, at least its similarity to that of other men, compromised. And in general it may be remarked in reference to kenotic theories of the Gessian type, that they seemed doomed to oscillate between Apollinarism and Ebionitism. Either they make the Logos, *qua* human soul, not human enough or too human. Either they retain for the Logos a little of His divinity to carry Him safely through His curriculum of temptation, or, compelling Him to part with all but His metaphysical essence, they reduce Him strictly to Adam's level, and expose Him to Adam's risks.[1]

6. In the form given to it by *Ebrard*, the kenotic theory certainly does not err by making Christ too much of a man. The Christ presented to us under this type, as has been remarked by a recent German writer, wears the aspect of a middle Being[2]—neither God nor man, but more the former than the latter. He retains all His divine attributes, only not in the absolute form suited to the eternal mode of existence, but in the applied form suited to existence in time; and, retaining these attributes in applied form, He assumes flesh, and is found in fashion as a man. One's first thought is that such a Being is a man only in appearance; but

---

der normal entwickelte Adam ist. Aber Christus muss sowohl auf der persönlichen, als auf der Naturseite zugleich von Adam unterschieden werden. Es bedarf mehr als nur des normal entwickelten Adam, es bedarf eines Allbefreiers, eines universalen und centralen Hauptes.

[1] Hodge, *Systematic Theology*, vol. ii. p. 431, while disapproving of the kenotic theory, indicates a certain favour for Gess. Referring to Gess' claim to have arrived at his conclusion by the study of the Scriptures, he remarks: "There is ground for this self-congratulation of the author, for his book is far more scriptural in its treatment of the subject than any other book of the same class with which we are acquainted. It calls for a thorough review and candid criticism." Hodge's acquaintance with the kenotic literature seems to have been superficial and fragmentary.

[2] Nösgen, *Christus der Menschen- und Gottessohn*, Gotha, 1869, p. 235: "Ebrard's Auffassung macht Christum zu einem menschlich-göttlichen Mittelwesen."

Ebrard stoutly denies that his theory lays him open to a charge of doketism. The Logos, retaining His divine properties in their altered form, does not exceed the dimensions of humanity. His endowments, indeed, far exceed those of man in his present degenerate state, but they are nothing more than the realization of the ideal of humanity. Christ is simply the sinless, pleromatic, wonder-working man, exercising dominion over the laws of nature as depraved by sin. Through the Incarnation of the Son of God was given a man who, as to His will, was in the state of integrity, like Adam before the fall; who, as to His natural gifts, bore within Him all the powers of humanity, which lay as undeveloped germs in the first federal head of the race, like a sun gathering these up into Himself as concentrated radii of a complete all-sided development; and who, as to His power, stood exalted as Lord over the laws of the depraved order of nature.[1] This man was neither more nor less than the ideal man, the head of the human race, in whom the organism of humanity found its unity. If it be objected that, according to this doctrine, man and God are practically one, our author replies: Even so, that is the eternal truth of the matter. He holds that it was the eternal purpose of God, altogether irrespective of the entrance of sin into the world, that on the one hand God should enter into time by becoming man, and that on the other hand man should rise to the full realization of his ideal in becoming God, and attaining to dominion over the laws of nature, over the objects of knowledge, and over space, such as we see exemplified in the applied omnipotence, omniscience, and omnipresence of Christ.[2] Therefore Christ, even in His miracles, in His penetration into the secrets of the future, in His power to transport Himself

---

[1] *Dogmatik*, ii. 32: Durch die Menschwerdung des Sohnes Gottes war also gegeben ein Mensch der (*a*) was sein WOLLEN betraf, im stat. integr. stand, d. h. sich, wie Adam vor dem Fall, frei entscheiden konnte für gut oder bös; (*b*) was sein NATÜRLICHE BEGABUNG betraf, alle Kräfte der Menschheit, die in dem ersten Stammvater Adam, unentwickelt, keimartig, lagen, als zusammengehende Radien des vollendeten, allseitigen Entwickelung sonnenhaft in sich trug; (*c*) was sein KÖNNEN betraf, schlechthin erhaben und herrschend über den Gesetzen der depravirten Naturordnung stand.

[2] *Vid*. Appendix, Note D.

at will from one place to another, was not superhuman, but only ideally human. In these acts of applied omnipotence, omniscience, and omnipresence, He was at once God and man; combining in His person the two natures, not indeed as separate parts, but as two aspects of one and the same being—even the Son of God become man, man sinless, pleromatic, wonder-working, still man—not possessing the eternal world-governing form of the metaphysical attributes of God, not even the eternal form of the ethical attributes, such being incompatible with the idea of man.[1]

On the ambitious speculations concerning an Incarnation independent of sin, as the realization of the great end of creation, the union of God, the Creator, with man, the highest of His creatures, interwoven by Ebrard into his Christology, I offer no remark, all the more that they conduct to giddy heights, on which one accustomed to humbler levels of thought is apt to experience vertigo. I simply observe, that the Christological theory of this author seems to be more in harmony with the pretentious philosophy with which it is associated, than with the facts of gospel history, or with the catholic faith concerning our Lord's person. Ebrard, indeed, is very confident that his theory is at once scriptural and ecclesiastically orthodox; but this circumstance need not influence us much, as overweening confidence is one of his most marked intellectual characteristics. As to Scripture, it may be admitted that it does appear as if Christ possessed the inherent power to work miracles at will, His virtue in the temptation and at other times consisting in absolutely abstaining from making any use of His power for His own personal behoof. But how is the doctrine that Christ, as man, possessed applied omniscience, to be reconciled with His profession of ignorance? That profession Ebrard himself regards as *bonâ fide*, and he looks on the ignorance sincerely acknowl-

---

[1] *Dogmatik*, ii. p. 35: Die göttliche und menschliche Natur sind nicht zwei Stücke, oder Theile, aus denen die Person Christi zusammengeleimt ist, sondern der Sohn Gottes *ward* Mensch, so dass er nun eben Mensch war, zwar, sündloser, pleromatischer wunderthätiger Mensch, aber eben Mensch, nicht besitzend die mit dem Begriff des Menschen streitende ewige weltregierende Form der metaphysischen Eigenschaften Gottes, selbst nicht die ewige Form der ethischen.

edged, as an evidence that Christ did not possess omniscience in the eternal form.[1] But the question is, did He possess *applied* omniscience. the power of knowing this and that secret at will; and if He did, how is that attribute to be reconciled with real ignorance? Is it not an abuse of words to ascribe applied omniscience to one of whom ignorance can be predicated?[2] How, again, is the doctrine that Christ possessed divine attributes in an applied form, to be reconciled with the state of childhood? Did Christ as a child possess omnipotence and omniscience applicable at will? Ebrard could hardly reply in the affirmative, for he admits that Jesus really grew in wisdom as in stature.[3] He might indeed say that the child possessed these attributes unconsciously, as a sleeping man possesses knowledge: therefore in an inapplicable form. But this, again, is only playing with words. Unconscious, unavailable power is a euphemism for impotence; and unconscious, unavailable knowledge a euphemism for ignorance. Once more, where in Scripture are we taught that man is destined to attain to such divine powers as Ebrard ascribes to Christ, even to unlimited dominion of the spirit over nature, to unlimited power to penetrate all objects of knowledge, and to unlimited dominion over space? And if, indeed, this be man's ultimate destiny, to be attained in the state of glory, in what sense does Christ differ from all in whom this ideal of humanity is realized? Does not this doctrine lead to as many Incarnations as there shall be glorified

---

[1] *Dogmatik*, ii. p. 21: Was die Allwissenheit betrifft, so weiss er nicht die Zeit des Weltgerichts; selbst die Art seines Leidens sieht er mit näherer Bestimmtheit erst gegen Ende seines Lebens voraus.

[2] *Dogmatik*, ii. p. 20: Von dem Augenblick an, wo er in die Existenzform des menschlichen Embryo eingegangen war, entwickelte er sich als ächtes menschliches Individuum, ward geboren, lag als Kind in der Krippe, wuchs, und wuchs nicht etwa nur lieblich, so dass seine geistige Entwicklung so gleich von Anfang an vollendet und fertig, oder er gar etwa, während er in der Wiege lag, allwissend gewesen wäre, sondern es heisst von ihm, Luk. ii. 52, er nahm zu an Alter und Weisheit.

[3] See *Dogmatik*, ii. p. 145, where, with reference to the personal identity of the Incarnate with the pre-existent Logos, Ebrard emphasizes the truth that unity of person is not the same thing as unity of consciousness, and remarks that as every man is more than he knows, so it is conceivable that the incarnate Logos bore within Him the fulness of His eternal essential properties without being conscious of them.

saints? It is no bar to this conclusion to say that Christ possesses absolutely, what we shall possess relatively.[1] If "relatively" mean imperfectly, then after all it is not man's destiny to possess the unlimited power promised to him. If, on the other hand, "relatively" does not involve limitation, then how does it differ from "absolutely"?

The question of our author's orthodoxy, in the ecclesiastical sense, is one of secondary importance; but his self-complacency on this score provokes the remark, that his attempt to bring the Patristic and the Reformed Christologies into conformity with his views can hardly appear, to a dispassionate reader, in any other light than as a characteristic display of perverse ingenuity. It *may* be the case that the two natures in Christ are in truth only two aspects, two abstract properties belonging to the Son of God entered into the form of humanity: the divine nature signifying the properties which belong to Him as the incarnate SON OF GOD (uncreated, eternally-begotten, etc.); the human nature signifying those which belong to Him as the Son of God INCARNATE (conceived, born, dead, possessing a rational soul and a human body); but this is not the way in which the early fathers, or the Reformed theologians, conceived of the matter.[2] The two natures were not in their view two *persons*, but they *were* two subsistences, two things. John of Damascus may be taken as a more reliable expositor of the Church doctrine than the erratic modern divine. Having distinguished three senses in which the word nature may be viewed, according as it is considered either *sola cogitatione*, or *in specie*, or *in individuo*, John applies the distinction to the Incarnation as follows: God the Word, assuming flesh, neither took a nature, which is an object of mere mental contemplation (for this would not have been an Incarnation, but an imposture), nor that which

---

[1] *Abendmahl*, ii. 791: Der aber wer ohne Sünde und der Eingeborene vom Vater war, der besass absolut, was wir dereinst relativ zu besitzen bestimmt sind.

[2] Ebrard, *Dogmatik*, ii. p. 61, gives the above as the import of the doctrine formulated at the Council of Chalcedon: Die beiden φύσεις sind also nach chalcedonischer Lehre weder zwei Personen (der Logos und ein Mensch) noch auch zwei Subsistenzen in dem Einen menschgewordenen Logos (Naturen in concretem Sinn) sondern zwei abstracte, nur durch Abstraction denkbare Proprietäten, die dem in die Form der Menschheit eingetretenen Sohne Gottes zukommen, etc.

is considered *in specie*, but that only which is *in individuo*; not, indeed, as having subsisted by itself as an independent individual before its assumption, but as having its subsistence in the person of the Word.[1] The Reformed theologians concurred in this view. It is true, indeed, that in their controversy with the Lutherans they were accustomed to speak of the two natures as *abstracta*, with reference to the person, it being the habit of their opponents to overlook the distinction between person and nature, and ascribe to the human nature of Christ, *per se*, whatever might be ascribed to the man Christ. But this is a very different thing from regarding the human nature as simply an aspect of the incarnate Logos, as if, for example, the human soul of Christ were simply the Logos under the time-form of existence, subject to the law of succession in His thought, and applying His omnipotence not in all directions simultaneously, but now in this direction, now in that. In the Reformed Christology, Christ's soul was a numerically distinct entity from the Logos. Hence Ebrard finds it rather difficult to make citations from the Reformed writers, which even seem to support his views, and is under the necessity of correcting their inaccurate (?) expressions, in order to bring them up to the Ebrardian standard of orthodoxy. Thus, *e.g.*, one old expounder of the Reformed Christology says: " The human nature of Christ is a creature, visible, tangible, finite in essence, duration, and power, composed of body and soul; His divine nature is God invisible, impalpable, infinite as to essence, duration, and power, void of all composition, impassible, immortal." Our modern representative of the Reformed school of theology treats his predecessor as a blundering schoolboy, and after the words, " the human nature of Christ," writes within brackets ("better, Christ in His human nature").[2]

---

[1] *De Fide Orthodoxâ*, lib. iii. cap. xi.

[2] *Dogmatik*, ii. p. 114, quoting Wendeline: Ita humana Christi natura est [besser, Christus humanâ naturâ est] creatura, visibilis, palpabilis, finita[us] quoad essentiam, durationem, et potentiam, composita[us] ex corpore et anima; divina natura est Deus, invisibilis, impalpabilis, infinita[us] quoad essentiam durationem, potentiam, omnis compositionis expers, impatibilis, immortalis. Ebrard admits that in some writings of the Reformed school the two natures are spoken of as "two parts." On the other hand, he claims Zanchius as one who most clearly

7. The kenotic theory, in the form given to it by Martensen, escapes at least some of the objections to which, under the forms already considered, it is liable. The initial difficulty pointed out in connection with the Thomasian scheme does not meet us here, where the kenosis while real is only relative; inasmuch as, on this hypothesis, the Incarnation does not signify the assumption of human nature by an already absolutely depotentiated Logos, or by an act of power on the part of the Logos, which is at the same time an act of self-depotentiation; but consists in a voluntary act, by which the Logos becomes a human life centre, without His power becoming exhausted in the act. The passivity of the depotentiated Logos, and helpless subjection to the flesh, in the incarnate state also disappear; for to whatever extent the laws of physical nature have power over the Logos, in that state they have it by His own consent. For the same reason, this new form of the theory is not open to the charge of making the Logos, by one act of self-depotentiation, incapable of displaying His gracious love in connection with a large part of his human experience. While the Logos as man passes through the unconscious life of childhood, He is conscious of this stage of His incarnate being, and shows His love by

and consciously held the opposite view. The doctrine of Zanchius, however, is simply a repetition of that taught by Damascenus. (*Vid. Dogmatik*, ii. p. 104, in a long and very scholastic note on the various senses of the words "subsistence" and "substance," and on the use of them by the Reformed in connection with the Incarnation). In connection with Zanchius, another instance may be mentioned of Ebrard's habit of perverting the meaning of citations, occurring in the same place. He represents Zanchius as teaching that, in the Incarnation, the Logos became a limited Being. The ground of this representation is the following citation: "Christus in ea assumpta forma servi sese evacuavit omni sua divina gloria, omnipotentia, omnipresentia, omniscientia. Factus est ex ditissimo pauperimus, ex omnipotente infirmus, ex omnisciente ignarus, ex immenso finitus." These words, taken by themselves, might naturally suggest an absolute surrender of the divine attributes named, at least in the eternal form. But the following words of Zanchius, not quoted by Ebrard, show that the former author had no intention of teaching any such doctrine: "non quod," Zanchius continues, "reipsa desierit esse, quod erat $ἐν\ μορφῇ\ Θεοῦ$, sed quod in hac forma servi sicut factus est ex Deo homo, sic ex Domino servus, ex ditissimo pauperimus, ex omnipotente infirmus, ex omnisciente ignarus, ex immortali mortalis, ex immenso finitus, ex ubique praesenti, certis locis circumscriptus, denique ex aequali cum Patre, valde minor Patre; ac proinde quod secundum hanc naturam et formam servi, non potuit dici omnipotens, omniscius, ubique praesens." Zanchius, *De Filii Dei Incarnatione*, c. ii.

consenting to pass through it. While escaping these difficulties besetting the theory of an absolute metaphysical kenosis, Martensen's doctrine seems to satisfy the demands of the *ethical* kenosis taught in Scripture. The self-emptying ascribed to the Logos by the apostle does not necessarily require absolute physical depotentiation, but only that the Logos shall limit Himself so far as the incarnate state is concerned, and shall be able to predicate of Himself subjection to the limits of that state. Nor does it appear very difficult to reconcile this view with the exchange of form which, according to the most correct exegesis, seems to be taught in the passage in the Epistle to the Philippians. Granting that the kenosis involved a giving up of divine form, and a taking upon Him on the part of the Logos, in its stead, of the form of a servant in the likeness of man, it does not follow that the Logos ceased *absolutely* to be what He was; all that necessarily follows is, that the two forms were not combined in the incarnate life of the Logos. Notwithstanding what is said there, it may be that the Logos has a double life—one in the man Christ Jesus; one as the world-governing, world-illuminating Logos. Such a double life is certainly not taught in the passage, but neither is it formally excluded; nor can it be held to be excluded by implication, unless it can be shown that the doctrine of a double life is incompatible with the condescension of the Son of God implied in the Incarnation, and evacuates His self-humiliation of all real ethical significance. If the contrary of this be true, then the apostle had simply no occasion to pronounce on the question whether the kenosis was absolute or relative only; it was enough for his purpose to emphasize its *reality* with reference to the incarnate state; so that, for example, Jesus should not be a child merely in outward seeming, but in very truth, speaking as a child, thinking as a child, understanding as a child. Whatever the form of God may mean, three positions may be taken up as to what the apostle meant to teach concerning it in connection with the Incarnation. It may be held that he meant to teach, *either* that the Logos retained the form of God in becoming man, *or* that He absolutely renounced the divine form in becom-

ing man, or that in becoming man the Logos entered into
a form of existence which involved a real renunciation of
the divine form, whether absolute or otherwise not being
said, or possibly not even thought of. The first position is
that taken up by the Fathers: the second is the view which
naturally commends itself to advocates of a metamorphic
or semi-metamorphic kenosis, like Gess and Ebrard; the
third is the position which best fits in to the hypothesis
of a double life taught by Martensen. It is a perfectly
feasible position. Of course, even if allowed, this view of
the apostle's meaning does not prove the hypothesis in
question; it simply leaves room for it. But that is all
that is wanted to legitimate it as a hypothesis intended to
cover and account for all the facts of our Lord's history,
without creating more or greater difficulties than it solves.
That this hypothesis has no difficulties of its own to meet,
cannot indeed be pretended. The idea of a "double life"
of the Logos raises speculative questions which Martensen
has not attempted to answer, and which have not been
satisfactorily cleared up by those who have made the attempt. It is frankly admitted by some that the double life
has the appearance of positing a double personality, a double
ego; but it is explained that this appearance vanishes as
soon as we more closely consider the relation of time and
eternity as not temporal but causal. That being duly
weighed, we shall see our way to holding at once a real
kenosis, and the possession, yea, the use, without conceal-
ment, of the divine glory ($\delta\acute{o}\xi a$) on the part of the incarnate
Son of God.[1] But even after we have thought sufficiently
long and intensely on the relation referred to, trying to
conceive it as directed till the brain grows weary, we may
still find such a combination hard to conceive, and ask ourselves, how can the same mind be conscious and unconscious,
finite and infinite, ignorant and omniscient, at the same
moment?[2] It is indeed a hard problem, but in justice it

---

[1] So Schöberlein; see Appendix, Note E.

[2] Hodge, *Systematic Theology*, vol. ii. p. 435, states, as a conclusive objection
to Ebrard's theory, which he understands as teaching a double life of the Logos,
that "it assumes that the same individual mind can be conscious and unconscious,
finite and infinite, ignorant and omniscient, at the same time."

must be borne in mind that it is, in one form or another, a problem which presents itself to all who believe in the real Incarnation of an undepotentiated Logos. For Martensen and those who think with him, the problem is, how can one and the same *mind* (that of the Logos) be at once conscious and unconscious, omniscient and ignorant? for Schneckenburger and Dorner, and such as agree with them, the problem is, how can one and the same *person* be at once conscious and unconscious, omniscient and ignorant —the former in the Logos *per se*, the latter in the human soul of the child or the man Jesus?

On the whole, with every desire to give the kenotic theory a fair and candid hearing, one cannot but feel that there are difficulties connected with it which "puzzle" the mind and give the judgment "pause," and dispose to acquiescence in the cautious opinion of a German theologian, more than half inclined to support a hypothesis in favour with many of his countrymen: "The relations of eternity and time, of the ethical and physical, of the Incarnation to the primitive man, of the historical God-man to the previous activity of the Logos; the true and the untrue in Apollinarism, and the bearing of this hypothesis on the ἀσύγχυτον, must be made clearer and more comprehensible than heretofore, before the full scientific and practical fruit of recent Christological speculation can be reaped,"[1] or even, it may be added, rightly judged of as to its quality. One may well be excused, indeed, for assuming this attitude of suspended judgment, not merely in reference to the kenotic theories, but towards all the speculative schemes we have had occasion to notice in this lecture. The hypothesis of a *double life*, of a *gradual Incarnation*, and of a *depotentiated Logos*, are all legitimate enough as tentative solutions of a hard problem; and those who require their aid may use any one of them as a prop around which faith may twine. But it is not necessary to adopt any one of them; we are not obliged to choose between them; we may stand aloof from them all; and it may

---

[1] Nitzsch, *System der Christlichen Lehre*, sechste Auflage, p. 262, in a note on Liebner's *Christologie*, which he characterizes as "der bedeutendste Fortschritt der speculativen Lehre vom gottmenschlichen Leben und Bewusstsein zur Berichtigung der kirchlichen und der beiden confessioneller Lehrarten und Formeln."

be best when faith can afford to dispense with their services. For it is not good that the certainties of faith should lean too heavily upon uncertain and questionable theories. Wisdom dictates that we should clearly and broadly distinguish between the great truths revealed to us in Scripture, and the hypotheses which deep thinkers have invented, for the purpose of bringing these truths more fully within the grasp of their understandings. My esteemed predecessor in this lectureship, Principal Rainy, has said: "If there are sifting times before us, the effect will probably be to compel us with more stringency, with more discriminating regard to all considerations bearing on each point, to determine how much we can really say we know, how far we can say Scripture designed to guide our thought to this result, to this alternative, to this resting-place." Applying this most needful discipline to the great subject of our present studies, we shall probably find, after the most painstaking inquiry, that what we know reduces itself as nearly as possible to the axioms enumerated in our first lecture, and that the effect, though not the design, of theories of Christ's person, has been to a large extent to obscure some of these elementary truths,—the unity of the person, or the reality of the humanity, or the divinity dwelling within the man, or the voluntariness and ethical value of the state of humiliation. That is, certainties have been sacrificed for uncertainties, facts for hypotheses, faith for speculation. If this be the testimony of history, then the lesson is plain: Be content to walk by faith, and take care that no ambitious attempt to walk by sight rob you of any cardinal truth relating to Him in whom dwelleth all the fulness of the Godhead bodily.

LECTURE V.

MODERN HUMANISTIC THEORIES OF CHRIST'S PERSON.

THE discussions contained in the three preceding lectures leave on the mind the impression that the person of Christ is a great mystery. The catholic believer, who sees in Christ God manifest in the flesh, frankly confesses the mystery. For, while he accepts with unfeigned truth the doctrine of the Incarnation, and finds in that truth, on its ethical side, rest to his spirit, he feels and owns the speculative or scientific construction of Christ's person, as God incarnate, to be a hard if not an insoluble problem. The more he studies the history of past attempts at its solution, and observes how opinion has oscillated between Nestorian duality and Monophysite unity, and how open to criticism are the recent essays of the Kenotic school to construct a Christology not liable to these objections, the less he will be inclined for himself to undertake the task; while still clinging with unabated earnestness to a dogma which gives him a God who can condescend and perform morally heroic acts, and earn for Himself men's devoted love by a sublime career of self-humiliation and self-sacrifice.

It cannot be doubted that the mystery which envelops the doctrine of Christ's person, as set forth in the creed, presents a strong temptation to desert the catholic foundation, and to refuse to see in the Incarnation "the pillar and ground of the truth." Many in recent years have yielded to the temptation, and have adopted purely humanistic views of the subject. At the root of this departure from the catholic faith, in the case of many, is a naturalistic philosophy, which refuses to recognise the miraculous in the constitution of Christ's person as in every other sphere. In the case of some, however, dissent is professedly based not on philosophy, but on exegesis. Even in the case of those whose belief is determined by philosophic bias, the attitude assumed is not always precisely the same. There are shades and degrees of naturalism, and in giving an account of the naturalistic views of Christ's person it will conduce to accuracy to attend to these distinctions.

Those who advocate a purely humanistic view of our Lord's person, on whatever ground, may be divided into five classes. First, there are those who take their stand on absolute, thoroughgoing naturalism, refusing to recognise miracle in any sphere, physical or moral, and therefore declining to accept even the old Unitarian view of Christ, according to which, while only a man, He was yet a *perfect* man. Next, there are others who, while naturalistic in their philosophic proclivities, shrink from the thoroughgoing application of the principles with which they secretly sympathize, and though readily consenting to banish the supernatural from the physical sphere, at the expense of philosophic consistency retain it in the ethical, and with the Catholic Church confess the *sinlessness* of Jesus. A third party, though really at one with the former of these two schools in *opinion*, side with the latter in *feeling*, and, while in no instance and in no sphere recognising the veritably miraculous, nevertheless endeavour in their whole delineation of Christ's life and character to embrace in the picture as much as possible of the *extraordinary* and wonderful. To these three phases of modern naturalistic opinion concerning the Founder of our faith may be added a fourth, that, viz., characteristic of those who, while imbued with the scientific spirit of our time, and paying great deference to the incredulous attitude of science towards the miraculous, can scarcely be regarded as occupying any definite philosophic position. Men belonging to this school are quite willing to accept the account Jesus gave of Himself, as far as they can gather it from the evangelic records. Turning away from the multifarious theological controversies concerning the person of Christ, as matters which they cannot understand, and with which they have no sympathy, they go back to the fountainhead, and try to put themselves in the position of those who were eye and ear witnesses of the Word, and to form for themselves an impression of Him at first hand. And the impression they do form is very much the same as that expressed by Peter at Cæsarea-Philippi when he said, "Thou art the Christ, the Son of the living God." When asked what they mean by such words, they reply in effect, We cannot tell. "The power of Christ is to be felt, not explained." You may, if you like, manufacture theological dogmas out of them; it is quite possible that they can "by the kind of ingenuity common among professional theologians be brought within the proper lines of accepted opinion." But it is not worth while to do so; it is "a pitiful waste of time."[1] Finally, the fifth class embraces all those who, while agreeing with naturalistic theologians in rejecting the catholic doctrine, do so not on speculative grounds, but on the ground of positive exegesis.

To all these schools of opinion the person of Christ is a mystery not less than to those who cordially accept as their own belief the creeds of the Church Catholic. To whom shall we go to escape mystery? The personality of his beloved Master was a great mystery to the disciple Peter. But was it less of a mystery to the multitude which was broken up into parties in reference to the question, Who is this Son of Man?—some saying He is John the Baptist, others He is Elias, and others He is Jeremias, or one of the prophets? In like manner, it is vain for one who is perplexed by the mystery of the Catholic doctrine concerning Christ to go in hope of relief to any one of the parties we have discriminated as existing in our day. One and all of them, whether confessedly or not, believe in a Christ who is a mystery; insomuch that the element of mysteriousness must be set aside altogether as a test of truth or falsehood, and our faith be made to rest on entirely different grounds. It may be worth while to enter into some detail in proof of this assertion; for it is a great help to faith to realize distinctly and clearly the alternatives. Simon Peter having asked himself the question, To whom shall we go if we leave Jesus? and having clearly per-

[1] *Vid.* Haweis, *Current Coin*, pp. 312, 313.

ceived that he could not better his position, remained where he was, contenting himself with the Master he had hitherto followed in spite of all drawbacks. So we, when tempted to abandon the conception of Christ which the Church has taught us, because of its acknowledged difficulties, do well to ask ourselves, Shall we escape difficulty by exchanging that conception for any other offered us by current opinions? and to take pains to arrive at a well-considered answer.

1. The first of the five above specified forms of current opinion concerning Christ, that of thoroughgoing naturalism, does not homologate the sentiment of the apostle, "confessedly great is the mystery of godliness," as presented in the history and character of Jesus of Nazareth. It flatters itself that by the consistent unflinching application of its fundamental principle, the miraculous impossible, to the evangelic biography, it gets rid of all mystery. It finds there, indeed, a *marvel* of piety, but no miracle; a singularly good and wise man worthy of all love and admiration, but no sinless perfect being; a perfect man being a breach in the continuity of human history, a contradiction of the law that all which is real is relative, a moral miracle, and therefore an impossibility not less than the raising of a dead man to life would be. But do the advocates of this view really get rid of all mysterious elements in the life of Jesus, or do they accomplish more than to satisfy themselves that on their principles there ought to be none? Let us see. In the first place, if Jesus be a man chargeable with sin, as He is bound to be on their principles, how comes it to pass that it is so hard, even for those who apply themselves to the task with every good-will, to accuse Him of sin on the basis of the Gospel record? We know that many attempts have been made by men of this school to establish a charge of moral culpability against Jesus, and we also know how very much the reverse of signal successes these have been. In absence of more important material for such an accusation, the blasphemers of the Son of Man have been obliged to content themselves with such paltry things as these: that harsh word to His mother at Cana; the perversely mystic style of the sermon on the

bread of life in the synagogue of Capernaum, "bristling with statements fitted to irritate and disgust hearers," the sentence in the intercessory prayer, "I pray not for the world, but for them whom Thou hast given me;" the direction given to the disciples to let an offender who refuses to confess his fault be unto them as an heathen man and a publican; the harsh treatment of the Syro-Phœnician woman; the heartless reply to the disciple who would bury his father, "Let the dead bury their dead."[1] Contemptible arguments surely to bring against the doctrine of Christ's sinlessness, which it were a mistake in an apologist to honour with a serious reply, but which well deserve the indignant rebuke of a distinguished American divine: "These and such like specks of fault are discovered, as they think, in the life of Jesus. So graceless in our conceit have we of this age grown, that we can think it a point of scholarly dignity and reason to spot the only perfect beauty that has ever graced our world with such discovered blemishes as these! As if sin could ever need to be made out against a real sinner in this small way of special pleading; or as if it were ever the way of sin to err in single particles or homœopathic quantities of wrong. A more just sensibility would denounce this malignant style of criticism as a heartless and really low-minded pleasure in letting down the honours of goodness."[2] I sympathize with Bushnell's scorn and indignation, but at the same time I feel that the small captious critics of Jesus are to be pitied as well as denounced. Their philosophy requires them to speak evil words against the Son of Man; and if the materials for cursing are very scanty, what course is left for the Balaams of modern unbelief than to make the most of such as are available? In no other way can we account for the fact of such a grave and serious writer as Keim condescending to notice the incidents already referred to, and others of similar nature, as blemishes in the character of Jesus.[3]

Some writers of this school are fair enough to admit that the faults chargeable on our Lord are few and small, and

---

[1] See Pécaut, *Le Christ et la Conscience*, p. 250.
[2] Bushnell, *Nature and the Supernatural*, chap. x.
[3] *Vid. Geschichte Jesu von Nazara*, vol. iii. p. 641.

find themselves under the necessity of accounting for the fact, in harmony with the assumption of naturalistic philosophy, that He must have been, like all other men, in serious respects morally defective. One thing very specially insisted on in this connection is the fragmentary nature of our sources of information. "Suppose," says Pécaut, "no reliable indication of imperfection should be found in the history of Jesus, what inference could be drawn therefrom? We possess only fragments of His biography, and fragments relative to His public life; that is, to that which is best in the history of a man devoted to the good of others. Do you not know that the discourses and the public acts of every one of us are better than our internal state? Is that hypocrisy? God forbid: only the best of men speak and act as they wish to be in the bottom of their hearts. But what information have we as to the infancy of Jesus, His private and family history, and finally, as to His inner life?"[1] We might reply, We have the testimony of those who knew Him intimately during the period of His public ministry, and had access to information concerning the antecedent period, who even in His lifetime spoke of Jesus as the Holy One, and after His death spoke of Him as such absolutely and without qualification. But we are told that the testimony of the disciples and apostles, while justly making a favourable impression on the whole, does not go beyond the similar testimony borne by Xenophon to Socrates, who nevertheless, by his own confession, was not a sinless man.[2] We are thus thrown back on what is, after all, the most convincing evidence of the sinlessness of Jesus, viz., the utter absence of all trace of any consciousness of sin on His part. It is surely a very striking thing to find one whose moral perceptions were so delicate; who knew so well what was in man; who could see beneath a fair exterior rottenness and dead men's bones; who discerned fleshly sin even in licentious thoughts and looks; who had such abhorrence of vanity, pride, ostentation, and other sins of the spirit universally committed in the world, and commonly treated as no sins at all, bearing Himself

[1] *Le Christ et la Conscience*, p. 240.
[2] Keim, *Jesu von Nazara*, vol. iii. p. 641.

throughout as one who had no part in these sins of the flesh and spirit, though not exempted from experience of temptation. It is doubtless a ready suggestion that admiring attached disciples were not likely to record words or facts indicative of a sense of moral shortcoming. But it deserves to be noticed that the evangelists have not been afraid to record facts which might easily be mistaken for, and have in fact been mistaken for, proofs of moral infirmity, as, *e.g.*, the clearing of the temple, and very specially the great philippic against the religious heads of the people, which Renan and others have regarded as an evidence that Jesus had lost His self-possession, and grown intemperate and fanatical in feeling; a fact, if it were a fact, certainly revealing great moral weakness. Then it is further to be observed, that the question is not one of mere suppression of inconvenient facts which might reflect on the character of one's hero. The real state of the case is, that Jesus throughout bears Himself as no one could who had the consciousness of moral shortcoming. By artless narration, as opposed to artistic invention, the evangelists have set before us a man who seems constantly surrounded by the sunlight of a good conscience, void of offence towards God and towards men, entirely exempt from the dark moods of men who have passed through moral tragedies, having no occasion to exclaim with a Paul, " Oh, wretched man that I am ! " or to confess that the good He would, that He did not; and the evil He would not, that He did. Utterly remote from Pelagian views of human character and conduct, He walks about on this earth as one who enjoys perfect unbroken fellowship with His Father in heaven, and whose relations to men are regulated wholly by the love of righteousness and the spirit of mercy. He is the one man in human history who seems to have no consciousness of sin, His only relation to the sin of the world, to all appearance, being that of one who bears it in His heart as a burden by sympathy, and who, in some mysterious way, hopes to bear it away and destroy it; not a sinner, but a saviour from sin, come to save the morally lost by His love in life and in death.

This absence of all consciousness of moral shortcoming in one characterized by such exceptional depth and strength of moral conviction, is a second element of mystery in the person of Christ, which must greatly puzzle those who refuse to see in Him one " who knew no sin." Granting that the paucity of censurable materials in His recorded public life may be plausibly explained, this phenomenon cannot easily be accounted for. Had Jesus been a Greek, it might have been less unintelligible; for the spirit of the Greeks was much more sensitive to beauty than to sin, and it was possible for one belonging to the Hellenic race to walk about with serene, smiling countenance and light heart, though he had committed moral offences, his past misdeeds possibly present to his consciousness as occurrences, but no burden to his conscience as transgressions. But Jesus belonged to a race which had been trained by a stern legal discipline to regard sin as a terrible reality. By the law had come to Him, as to other Jews, if not the knowledge of sin, at least a highly educated conscience, a trained faculty of discernment between right and wrong, and an acute sense of the importance of moral distinctions. And the wonder and the mystery is, that with the Jewish conscience did not come to this man, as to others, the ordinary consciousness of sin. In saying this, I do not forget that there were other Jews in whom something superficially resembling this strange combination presented itself, self-satisfaction associated with the habit of moral discernment. There were men who could see and severely condemn sin in others, and yet see little or no sin in themselves: who beheld the mote that was in their brother's eye, and considered not the beam that was in their own; who could stand in the temple and thank God that they were not as other men, and with much unction recite their own virtues, while drawing out a catalogue of other men's vices. There were Pharisees, with consciences like a policeman's lantern, with its light side turned outward towards the breaker of the laws, and its dark side towards their guardian. But we cannot account for the mystery connected with the moral consciousness of Jesus by likening Him to this class of men; and so far as we are aware, it has not occurred to any one to suggest such a solution. Jesus was no Pharisee; He was the scourge of Pharisees, the unsparing exposer and denouncer of their moral obliquity, hypocrisy, and pride; the moral antipodes of the class in spirit and in judgment, loving those whom they despised, exalting to the place of supreme importance duties and virtues which they neglected, and regarding as trivialities practices which seemed to them of vital moment. And yet He agreed with the Pharisees in this, that He had not the consciousness of sin; He did not, He could not say, "God be merciful to me the sinner;" He felt not the need of repentance. Would not the Son of Man be almost tempted to regard this resemblance as a misfortune? He who so intensely loved the publicans and sinners, and whose spirit shrank back with such revulsion and loathing from Pharisaic self-righteousness, would rather have taken His place with the poor publican who stood afar off with downcast eyes, and smiting on his breast exclaimed, "God be merciful to me the sinner," than with the self-satisfied Pharisee who said, "God, I thank Thee that I am not as other men are." He certainly would have done it if He could, and He did that which came as near to it as possible. Since He could not repent, He felt for those who needed repentance; since He could not bear the burden of personal demerit, by an unspeakably deep and tender sympathy He took on His spirit the burden of those who were heavy laden with guilt; since He could not know sin, He made Himself a sinner by identifying Himself so closely with the sinful as to earn the honourable nickname of the Sinner's Friend.

But this beautiful unearthly compassion for the sinful which has earned for Jesus the blessings of so many that were ready to perish, reminds us of yet another direction in which an explanation may be sought for the mystery of His moral self-consciousness. It may be supposed that His serenity arose out of His own faith in the gospel which He preached to the sinful, the gospel of God's infinite pardoning mercy. He was happy in spite of shortcomings, just as any of us may be, just as every healthy-minded Christian is who believes that God has forgiven his sin, and stands in the same relation to him as if sin had never existed. His sky was cloudless, and His soul full of sunlight, because the mists engendered by an evil conscience had disappeared before the warm beams of a heavenly Father's boundless charity. If a Paul or a David could attain to a joy unmarred by the memory of past transgression, through faith in the loving-kindness and multitudinous tender mercies of God, why not a Jesus? If it was possible for a weeping penitent to go into peace on hearing the soothing words: "Thy faith hath saved thee," why may not the speaker Himself have entered into peace by the same door? May not His confidence in the power of faith to conduct to peace have been based on His own experience? It is painful to one who believes in the Sinless One to ask such questions, but we cannot deny that from the point of view of those who do not share our belief they are not irrelevant. What, then, shall we say in reply? We must remind unbelievers of another well-ascertained fact in the history of Jesus, viz., that He claimed to be the *Judge* of men, a claim which could not reasonably be made except by one who stood on a different moral level from other men. The fact of the claim and its moral significance are admitted by theologians of eminence belonging to the naturalistic school, as, *e.g.*, by Dr. Baur of Tübingen. This able writer, it need hardly be said, has no faith in a future judgment of the world, as popularly conceived. In his hands the judicial function of Christ resolves itself into the critical power of the truth. "If," he says, "we regard the doctrine and activity of Jesus from the ethical point of view, under which it is to be placed according to the Sermon on the Mount and the parables, it belongs thereto essentially that that doctrine and activity must be the absolute standard for the judgment of the moral worth and the actions and conduct of men. According to the diverse attitude of men towards the doctrine of Jesus, as the ground law of the kingdom of heaven, they are divided into two essentially different classes, whose moral worth, brought to its absolute expression, is expressed by the contrast of everlasting blessedness and everlasting damnation. But what holds in the first place of the doctrine of Jesus, holds also in the next place of His person, so far as He is the originator and promulgator of the same. With His doctrine His person is inseparably connected. He is the concrete embodiment of the eternal significance of the absolute truth of His doctrine. Is it His doctrine according to which the moral worth of men is to be judged for all eternity? then He it is who speaks the sentence as the future judge of men."[1] Now, even taking Baur's account of Christ's judicial function, what a high claim it involves! It implies that Jesus regarded Himself as the moral idea realized. For His claim is absolute, not relative. His doctrine concerning the judgment is not, I am the Judge in so far as I am in my own person a realization of the ethical ideal, so that the attitude men assume towards me (knowing what they do) determines their attitude towards that ideal, and the same may be said of every good man in proportion as he realizes in his character the ideal—not that, but, "I am the Judge," without any qualifying "in so far." It is true that the disciples are promised seats beside the King, as co-judges with Him of the tribes of Israel, even as it is said by Paul that the saints shall judge the world. But there is a wide interval between the judicial power of the saint or apostle and that of the Lord Jesus. Jesus is the Judge Absolute, all others—saints, apostles—are judges *longo intervallo*, and only in so far as they approximate the ideal which He alone realizes. That He claimed to be *the* Judge absolutely appears from the simple fact of His representing Himself ordinarily as the Judge exclusively, without any mention of assessors, or with such reference to other beings of high rank as puts them in the position of mere attendants; as in the account of the judgment in Matt. xxv., which opens with the words, "When the Son of Man shall come in His glory, and all the holy angels with Him, then shall He sit on the throne of His glory."

In view of the claim to be the Judge, it is impossible to regard the unburdened condition of Christ's conscience as the simple result of strong faith in divine forgiveness. That claim is rather a proof that He who advances it does not feel the need of forgiveness; and if the state of mind indicated by the claim be regarded as a hallucination, then the claim itself must be reckoned as a third element of mystery in the moral aspect of Christ's person, which can-

[1] *Neue Testamentliche Theologie*, p. 110.

not but perplex those who refuse to see in Him anything out of the common course. Here is one who is *ex hypothesi* a sinner, and, judging from the analogy of other men of outstanding force and magnitude of character, probably a great sinner, arrogating to Himself the position of Judge of the sinful, entitled, in discharge of His official functions, to say to the impenitent, " Depart from me, ye cursed, into the eternal fire." Is this a part we should expect such an one to aspire to? Is the claim to exercise such tremendous functions a psychologically probable one in the mouth of one who is himself a transgressor? We could imagine one who had sinned even grievously, and repented of his sin, *preaching* the doctrine of a judgment to come with great emphasis, seeking to persuade men as one who himself knew the terror of the Lord. So preached judgment Paul, the penitent and pardoned persecutor. But to preach judgment is a different thing from proclaiming oneself the Judge. Or we could imagine one who had been characterized by great moral frailty, and who was in the habit of looking on his own shortcomings and those of other men in a genial, indulgent way, as the effect of temperament, circumstances, and so forth, after the fashion of a Rousseau or a Burns, denying a judgment to come; representing Death as the great redeemer, setting the soul free from its base corporeal companion to rise to its native element of goodness, and to the society of blessed spirits who delight in virtue. But not only to be a preacher of judgment, but to proclaim oneself the Judge, becomes none save one who is at once holy, harmless, undefiled, and in character separate from sinners, and yet able, through His power of sympathy and His experience of temptation, to give due weight to all extenuating considerations. Such an one the Scriptures represent Jesus to have been—sinless, therefore entitled to be the Judge; tempted in all points as we are, therefore able to temper judgment with mercy.

In the foregoing observations I have confined myself to the personal character, as distinct from the public career, of Jesus, and have simply sought to emphasize these three questions: If Jesus was the sinful erring man naturalism requires Him to be, whence comes it that it is so difficult, from the record of His life, to convince Him of sin; that in His whole demeanour no trace of a consciousness of moral shortcoming can be discerned; that He claims to Himself the right to be the Judge of all men? When we pass from this restricted region of inquiry to the wider sphere of the public ministry, materials for a proof that to naturalism the character of Jesus must be a hopeless puzzle greatly multiply on our hands. Here, indeed, the naturalistic critic would find no difficulty in convicting the subject of his criticism of sin and folly. The difficulty rather is that sin and folly are so apparent and glaring on naturalistic principles, that it becomes hard to understand how they could be united with so much wisdom and goodness, as all must confess to have been manifested in the career of the Prophet of Nazareth. The central points of interest in this department are the claims of Jesus to be the Messiah, and the necessity laid upon Him by that claim of playing the part of a thaumaturge. That Jesus did make such a claim, and that the claim carried along with it an obligation to be, or at least to seem, a miracle-worker, are positions generally admitted. But from the naturalistic point of view, the Messiah idea was a hallucination, and miracles are impossible. Consequently Jesus, in giving Himself out for the Messiah, if not a deliberate deceiver, must have been Himself the victim of a national delusion, and in undertaking to work miracles must have degraded Himself to the level of a conjurer. But how to reconcile such imposture, self-delusion, and quackery with the wisdom and the moral simplicity so conspicuous in Jesus? Naturalism is here obliged to make patronizing apologies for its hero, in order, if possible, to mitigate the moral contradictions in His character. Baur tells us that Jesus could not do otherwise than claim to be the Messiah, if He wished to gain for His religion a starting-point from which it could go forth to conquer the world Christianity, as Jesus conceived it, had indeed nothing narrow or Judaistic about it: its essential characteristics were spirituality and universality; it was a purely moral religion, and therefore a religion for all mankind. But then Jesus Himself was a Jew, and therefore the universal religion must find its cradle among the Jewish people. But

no religious movement had any chance of taking a hold on
the Jewish mind unless it consented to take its form from
the Messianic idea. In other words, Jesus, in order to gain
influence in His own country, and so to make a beginning
in the conquest of the world, must call Himself the Christ,
and offer Himself to His fellow-countrymen as the fulfilment of the Messianic hope, knowing full well that the
hope, as cherished by them, and as expressed in Old Testament prophecy, was a dream that could never be realized;
accommodating Himself to a delusion for their good, and
for the ultimate good of the world. Similar apologies are
made by Renan for the thaumaturgic element in Christ's
career. He cannot deny that actions which would now be
considered signs of folly held a prominent place in the life
of Jesus. His historic conscience will not allow him to
listen too much to nineteenth century repugnances, and to
attempt to rescue the character of Jesus by suppressing
facts which in the judgment of contemporaries were of the
first importance. But he does not feel that these facts
give any occasion for concern about the character of Jesus.
The thaumaturgic aspect of His public career is after all
but a spot on the sun. Who would think of sacrificing to
that unwelcome side the sublime side of such a life? It is
enough to say that the miracles of Jesus were a violence
done to Him by His age, a concession extorted from Him
by a temporary necessity. The exorcist and the thaumaturge have passed away, but the religious reformer will live
for ever.[1] Plausible apologies both, but how inconsistent
with the well-ascertained spirit of Him who said, "My
kingdom is not of this world"! The Jesus of Baur and
Renan says in effect: I must mix a certain amount of the
alloy of falsehood with the pure gold of truth in order that
it may gain currency in the world. The Jesus of the
Gospels says: I decline to act on the principle of worldly
prudence, and am content with what success is compatible
with perfect truthfulness; and because He resolutely adhered
to this programme the world found Him an intolerable
nuisance, and nailed Him to a cross.

2. But I must leave this topic, and go on to notice very

[1] *Vie de Jésus*, p. 268.

briefly the second of the five forms of current opinion concerning the Author of our faith above enumerated, that, viz., which sees in Him no sin, and devoutly reveres Him as the Ideal Perfect Man. This view is familiar to all as that held by Unitarians such as Martineau and Channing, but we may connect it here with the name of Schleiermacher, as having in his system a peculiar philosophic significance. Schleiermacher's doctrine concerning Christ is this: As the original source of Christian life, He must, while a historical individual, at the same time be an Ideal Person, in whom the ideal of humanity is fully realized. As the Ideal Man, while like all men, in virtue of the identity of His human nature, He differs from all through the constant vigour of His God-consciousness, which was a proper being of God in Him, implying absolute freedom from moral taint, and from intellectual error in all things pertaining to His mission as a religious teacher. In Christ the ideal of humanity was for the first time realized; man as at first created fell short of the ideal, so that Christ is the completion and crown of the creation. It will be seen at a glance that this Christology, though coming short of orthodoxy, rises above the plane of naturalism into the region of the miraculous. Christ is, if not physically, at least ethically, a miracle; He alone of all men exhibiting in perfect and unvarying strength the God-consciousness, and maintaining with God a fellowship undisturbed by sin. Now, the philosophic significance of this Christology as taught by Schleiermacher is, that in his theology it is a departure from the general tendency of his system. It is a supernatural element in a creed which is predominantly influenced by a naturalistic, Pantheistic spirit. This inconsistency is characteristic of Schleiermacher. He is neither a Pantheist nor a Theist in his philosophy and theology, but a mixture of both. This fact explains the difficulty which every reader of the *Christliche Glaube* feels in clearly apprehending the author's meaning. Schleiermacher, unlike most Germans, writes a good pure style, and yet somehow you feel that there is a haze upon the page which prevents you from seeing distinctly the thoughts presented. You read the passage again with increased attention, like one straining his eyes to see some object in moonlight, and still you fail to see the idea clearly. The reason is that it *is* moonlight through which you are looking—the moonlight of Christian faith reflected from the Christian consciousness of the writer upon the dark planet of a Pantheistic philosophy. Strauss, with his usual sagacity, hit the truth about Schleiermacher when he said, that he had pounded Christianity and Pantheism to powder, and had so mixed them that no man could tell where Pantheism ended and where Christianity began. We cannot go wrong, however, in assuming that it was Christianity and not Pantheism that led Schleiermacher to acknowledge in clear unambiguous terms the sinlessness of Jesus. His Pantheism prevented him from recognising in Christ an incarnation of God in the sense of the creeds, and made him willing to abandon much of the miraculous in Christ's history, to treat as doubtful the miraculous conception, and to resolve the resurrection into a revival to consciousness from a state of suspended animation. But he was too much a Christian to be capable of following Pantheism as his leader in the ethical region. Pantheistic philosophy teaches that it is not the way of the ideal to realize itself in an individual, but only in the species; therefore Jesus as an individual historical person must have been more or less morally defective like all other men. To this doctrine Schleiermacher, with Moravian blood in his veins, and full of reverence and love towards the Redeemer, at whatever cost of inconsistency, could only give one answer: "Get thee behind me, Satan." Let us honour him for his inconsistency, and see in it an involuntary testimony to the force of truth, a witness to the impression of an unearthly purity which the image of Jesus makes on every ingenuous mind.

It is evident that the doctrine taught in the *Glaubenslehre* of Schleiermacher concerning the person of Christ cannot pretend to be clear of all mystery. That gifted author did his best to reduce the mystery and the miracle to a minimum, that he might commend his Christology to scientific and philosophic tastes. He taught that Christ, though the ideal man, and therefore a product of the creative energy of God out of the common course, was nevertheless but the completion of the creation, that to which the rudimentary man of the first creation was destined to reach, and towards which the human race in its onward course had been steadily approximating. While therefore there was certainly manifested in Christ a divine initiative, it was an initiative which did no violence to the law of evolution; though there was a miracle, it was a small one. But it is vain to attempt by such representations to conciliate unbelief. A little miracle is as objectionable to Pantheistic naturalism as a great one; the creation of a *moneron*, the rudest embodiment of the principle of life, as much an offence as the creation of a perfect man. If, therefore, the Christology of Schleiermacher has nothing more to say for itself than that it is an endeavour to present the faith of the church concerning its Founder in a form which, while retaining something distinctively Christian, shall be as inoffensive as possible on the score of mysteriousness, it must be pronounced an utter failure. It is useless for apologetic purposes, and must rest its claims to acceptance on other grounds.[1]

3. We come now to the views of the third party referred to at the commencement of this lecture, whom I described as with the naturalistic school in philosophy, but with the supernaturalists in feeling, and as endeavouring in their whole delineation of Christ's life and character to embrace in the picture as much as possible of the extraordinary, while recognising in no sphere the strictly miraculous. This party may be designated the mediation school, or perhaps better still, the school of *Sentimental Naturalism;* and it commands our respect by its sober, reverent manner of handling the Gospel history, and by the array of distinguished writers of which it can boast, including Ewald, Keim, and Weizsäcker. In perusing the works on the life

---

[1] Views similar to those of Schleiermacher have been propounded recently by Dr. Abbott, author of *Through Nature up to Christ*, and other works. Dr. Abbott is an eclectic in philosophy, naturalistic on the physical side, supernaturalistic on the ethical. He represents Christ as perhaps as incapable of working miracles such as those recorded in the Gospels as of *sinning*. The naivete of this is charming. Dr. Abbott does not seem to be aware that a *sinless* Christ is as great a miracle as a Christ who can walk on the water. *Vid.* Preface to *Oxford Sermons.*

of our Lord emanating from this school, one is struck with
the extent to which they recognise the historical character
of the Gospel, in comparison with the two lives of Jesus
by Strauss, as also with the marked contrast in the whole
tone and spirit of the performances. They recognise so
much as historically true, that you feel they would recognise all, if only their philosophy would allow them. The
person of Christ, if not essentially divine and absolutely
sinless, is yet in all respects unique, a veritable *wunder;*
if some of the miracles be impossible, and therefore the
narratives which record them mythical, others were actual
occurrences, especially the healing miracles, which, though
very extraordinary, were yet not contrary to or outside
the course of nature, being explicable on the principles of
"Moral Therapeutics." Even the resurrection of Jesus
was, in some respects, a reality. The appearances of the
"risen" one were not merely subjective visions, the hallu-
cinations of a heated brain; there was an objective basis
for the faith of the disciples. Not that the dead body of
Jesus came to life again, that of course was impossible; but
the spirit of Jesus, which survived His death, caused the
disciples to see these visions, sent these manifestations
from heaven as *telegrams*, so to speak, to assure them that
all was well, and so revive their hopes. All this is, doubtless, very gratifying and very reassuring to the believing
student of the evangelic narrative, tending to confirm him
in faith, and to make him confident that he is not following
cunningly-devised fables when he accepts the whole as
simple truth, without even such abatements as an Ewald
or a Keim would make. But while accepting thankfully
the concessions of this school, we must bear in mind that
these are apt to lead us to form a more favourable judgment concerning the position it occupies in contrast to
that of Strauss and other extremely negative critics than
it deserves. It may be that writers of this school go farther
than on their principles they are entitled to go, and that
Strauss, with all his brutal irreverent plainness of speech,
is the most reliable and consistent exponent of the naturalistic philosophy in its bearing on religious problems.
Strauss himself has no doubt on the point. In reviewing,

In the introduction to his *New Life of Jesus*, the works on the same theme which had appeared after the publication of his earlier *Life*, Strauss notices the views of Keim as expressed in an academical address on the human development of Jesus Christ, comparing them with those of Renan. While admitting Keim's superiority to Renan in some respects, *e. g.* in his appreciation of the respective merits of the Synoptics and of John, he thinks him inferior to the Frenchman in this, that, while holding Jesus to be a purely human person, he is nevertheless not willing that He should be one of many, but insists on His being a unique individual on whose mediation all humanity depends. This idea of Christ he characterizes as *sentimental*, and he expresses the conviction that the error of supposing it possible to reconcile the claim of a full and complete humanity in Jesus with that of a unique being elevated above humanity would much more clearly appear if Keim would undertake to write a detailed life of Jesus.[1] What Strauss desired, Keim has done, and in the *Geschichte Jesu von Nazara* we have the means of judging how far naturalism can go in recognising the exceptional in the person and history of the Saviour. Now my verdict is that Strauss was right when he affirmed, that on the principles of naturalism you cannot make Christ an exceptional unique person, but must be content to regard Him, as Renan has done, as a very remarkable man, and to recognise Him as the originator of spiritual religion, just as you recognise Socrates as the originator of philosophy, and Aristotle of science, that is, on the understanding that many attempts preceded these masters, and that since their time important improvements have been made, and may yet be made, but still without impeaching the eminent position generally conceded to these great original founders. While highly appreciating much that is excellent in the work, and greatly valuing its positive and reverent spirit, I must nevertheless say that what I find in Keim's *History of Jesus of Nazareth* is this: Naturalism by inflated exaggerated language striving hard to do justice to the *extraordinary* in its subject without recognising anything supernatural. It is a case of the frog trying to blow itself

[1] *New Life of Jesus*, i. 45.

out into the dimensions of the ox. The very style of the work reveals the impossibility of the attempted task; a remark applicable to Ewald also, who belongs to the same school of sentimental naturalism. Always, when writers of this school come to deal with a hard problem, such as the miracles of Jesus, or His assertion of a peculiar relation to God, or His resurrection, they lose themselves in long involved sentences charged with mystic poetic phraseology, from which it is impossible to extract any distinct idea. Strauss remarks, in reference to Ewald's treatment of the resurrection of Jesus, that his long, inflated rhetoric contains literally no fragment of an idea beyond what had been said by himself in his first *Leben* much more clearly, "though assuredly with far less unction." This remark is perfectly just. I remember the feeling of perplexity created in my mind on reading Ewald's remarks on the resurrection in his work on the history of Christ.[1] I supposed at the time that the obscurity was simply an idiosyncrasy of the writer, or, it might be, the effect of ignorance in the reader; till by and by it dawned upon me that Ewald's obscurity, like Schleiermacher's, was the result of his attempting to serve two masters. The drift of the whole discussion is: the resurrection did not, could not, take place, but the beautiful dream must be dealt with tenderly, and its reality denied with as much sentiment as if you meant to affirm it. The same observation applies to Keim's manner of dealing with similar topics. He is a sentimental anti-supernaturalist, who tries hard to affirm, while denying the supernatural element. The charge of sentimentalism he would not indeed resent, for he not only admits, but claims as a merit, a "pectoral" colouring in his delineation of the great biography.

As it is very important to be convinced of the illegitimacy of this attempt to reconcile faith and scepticism, and to understand that we must either go further than Keim or Ewald in belief, or not so far, I may briefly explain Keim's mode of dealing with the miraculous in Christ's history before considering the view held by him and others of the same school concerning the person of Christ and His po-

[1] The fifth volume of his *History of Israel*.

sition in the universe. As already remarked, Keim, in common with all writers of the same school, recognises to a far greater extent than Strauss the historical character of even the more remarkable passages in Christ's life as related in the Gospels. After all necessary deductions, he admits that the Gospels make on every sound mind the impression that in their narratives they do not rest simply on late legends and recent inventions, and that beyond doubt they contain many genuine historical facts, and possibly still more most genuine words of Jesus, and that it is not credible that the great deeds interwoven with the story are fictions. At the same time, being naturalistic in his philosophic view-point, he cannot afford to accept all the Gospel "miracles" as historical; he can admit only those which, however wonderful, can be conceived to have had a natural cause. To this class belong the *miracles of healing*. Our author thinks that though Jesus came not to do mighty works, but to preach, yet He could not avoid becoming a healer of disease. Events carried him on into this new path, not to be called "a false path," seeing that through it Jesus entered on a truly divine career. The trust of men and their misery pressed around the new teacher and desired His help, though in Galilee and Capernaum there might be no want of physicians, male and female. The synoptic Gospels indicate by their manner of narration that this was the way the healing miracles began; they ascribe not at the beginning, or even at all, the initiative to Jesus, but to those who came seeking help. The sick came to Him, He intensely sympathized with them; the question arose: Do this need of the people, and their appeal for help on the one hand, and my sympathy on the other, not indicate a new department of labour, and constitute a call to add to my work as a spiritual physician that of one who heals the diseases of the body? The heart of Jesus answered *Yes* to this question; and so He set Himself to heal the sick, which He did simply by a word, a word of faith acting on faith in the recipient of benefit. And, strange to say, by the two combined, the faith of Jesus revealing itself in confident words, and the faith of the sick exhibited in no less confident expectations, remarkable cures were wrought: diseases of body and mind yielded to the united faith-storm (Glaubensturm) of healer and healed! How were these cures brought about? Keim discusses all the various hypotheses that have been suggested, such as that the cures were strictly medical, effected by the professional knowledge of Jesus, or that they were produced by magic arts or by magnetism, or that they were answers to prayer. Rejecting all these hypotheses, he maintains that the cures must be held to spring in the first place from the spiritual life of Jesus, associated with His human will-force, and with His religious confidence, and also with that trait of deep sympathy, of inwardness, of devotion, which He brought to the victims of the world's woe; and in the second place, from the receptivity of the healed, for as spirit works primarily on spirit, the co-operation of the patient is indispensable, and, as a matter of fact, we see that stress was laid on it by Jesus. He did mighty works only where there was faith. Regarded by the simple folks of Galilee as the great man, as the prophet, as the deliverer, He by His love awakened love, by His faith called forth faith sufficient to alter the physical life course.

Marvellous results of the Glaubensturm and the moral therapeutics so eloquently described. Pity only that the Glaubensturm could not be more frequently raised, and that moral therapeutics, which Matthew Arnold assures us have not been sufficiently studied,[1] were not more generally understood! Speaking seriously, what are we to think of this new theory of moral therapeutics, by which men like Keim seek to reconcile their acceptance of the healing "miracles" with their philosophic naturalism? It looks very like a device to hide from themselves their true position, which is that of men drawn in two different directions, towards faith by the general impression of historical truth made on their minds by the Gospel narratives, towards unbelief by their philosophy. Moral therapeutics is a convenient phrase for a dark mysterious region into which those can take refuge who halt between two opinions. If it be true, as Matthew Arnold says, that moral therapeutics have not been sufficiently studied, it is per-

[1] In *Literature and Dogma*.

haps well for him and the like of him; for it is the darkness of the subject that makes it serve their turn. If ever moral therapeutics should be thoroughly studied, and the conclusion come to that there is not much in them, then men like Keim and Arnold will be forced to do violence to their historical sense, and to treat all the miraculous narratives together as alike legendary. Meantime they can talk in high-flown sentimental style about the *Glaubensturm* and the marvels it can work, without risk of immediate scientific contradiction not to be gainsaid.

It is easy to show that Keim's manner of dealing with the resurrection of Jesus is equally unsatisfactory. His view amounts to this: The resurrection did not happen, yet something happened, something corresponding to the phenomena of modern spiritualism, that something was not a miracle in the strict sense, but it was a " *wunder;*" " a wunder," says Weizsäcker, whose opinion on this topic is substantially the same as Keim's, " as truly as was the whole history or the person of Jesus."[1] It is not surprising that Strauss in his new *Leben Jesu* expressed himself as curious to see what Keim would make of the resurrection. " Having renounced," he remarks, " the visions spoken of by Renan, and generally excluded the supernatural from his treatment of the subject, there seems no other hypothesis open to him but that of suspended animation. If so, he comes at last to the signal fiasco of falling into the wake of Schleiermacher, whose views it was his ambition to surpass in point of historical accuracy." Keim has not fallen into that fiasco certainly, but he has come to a conclusion which is neither one thing nor another, and which Strauss apparently, with all his mental resources, was unable even to imagine. The old theft hypothesis adopted by Reimarus and kindred spirits he knew; the swoon hypothesis, according to which Jesus did not die on the cross, held by Schleiermacher and others, he was also acquainted with; the hypothesis of subjective visions, creatures of a heated brain, he himself strenuously advocated;[2] but as for this

---

[1] *Untersuchungen über die Evangelische Geschichte*, p. 573.

[2] Dr. Abbott in *Philochristus* seems to adopt this hypothesis. He speaks of the visions as continuing for little less than a year, " insomuch that if any one should

new spiritualistic hypothesis of Keim's, which resolves the appearances of the risen Christ into objective though immaterial manifestations, telegraphic messages from the departed Master to His disciples, he neither had seen it in books, nor had it entered into his mind to conceive it.

Let me now illustrate the peculiar characteristics of this school of theologians by the manner in which they conceive and represent the person of Christ. As I remarked on a former page, Keim does not recognise the sinlessness of Jesus; and a similar remark applies to Weizsäcker, who speaks of Christ's "sinlessness" as consisting in single-hearted devotion, and of His perfection as similar to that of Paul or any other devoted man. Nevertheless, while refusing to acknowlege the doctrine of the Church on this point, theologians of this school assign to Christ a unique place in His relation to God and the world. The views of Keim on this topic are specially emphatic. Nowhere are they expressed in a more characteristic manner than in the author's discussion of the remarkable text in Matt. xi. 27; which he calls Christ's great confession of sonship. After discussing the various readings of the text, and expressing his preference for the ancient[1] as against the canonical reading, he goes on to say:—

"Whichever form of the text we adopt we find therein the glory of Christ, and a great testimony and personal testimony in reference to His whole position. All is given to Him by His Father, that is, the God whom He here for the first time distinctly calls His Father, in contrast to all other men. The all things given are primarily those babes, the kernel of the people, to whom the Father has shown the

---

adventure to set forth all the manifestations of Jesus, and the time and place and manner of each, I suppose that the world itself could not contain the books that should be written," pp. 413, 414. Such long continuance Keim holds to be necessary to the vision hypothesis, and the fact that there is no evidence of anything of the kind, he holds to be conclusive against it. Having referred to *Philochristus*, I may remark that it may fairly be classed with the literature of sentimental Naturalism. In this interesting book the story of Christ is told in the name of one of His disciples, and a strange and incongruous combination of first century faith and reverence with nineteenth century scepticism is the result.

[1] "No man knew the Father save the Son, nor the Son save the Father," the clauses in our canonical Gospel being inverted and the tense changed. The Gnostics preferred this form because it supported their doctrine that the God of the Old Testament was not the God of the New, as it made Christ claim to be the first teacher of the Fatherhood of God.

Son; but likewise all Messianic rights among men, which the faith of the people legitimizes, and the unbelief of the wise avails not to frustrate. But what precisely are those mysterious intangible Messianic rights? He tells us plainly in the sequel. No one knew the Father except the Son, and the Son except the Father, and he to whom He reveals. His rights, His privilege, His singularity lies, above all, in the through Him for the first time completed knowledge of the Father, and in His becoming known to the humanity whom the Father gives Him, whilst He gives it the knowledge of the Son. It is, in short, the representation of the highest spiritual truths, as the exclusive mediator of which He, at once revealer and revealed, is appointed for a believing obedient world of men. In this great thesis lie three mighty utterances. He is the first and only one who through Him and through God has reached the knowledge of God the Father. In the second place, as He knows God, so God has known Him. He has known God as Father, as Father of men, and yet more as His own Father. God has known Him as Son, as Son among many, and yet more as the One among many, and exclusively related to each other. Each to the other a holy, worthy to be known, searched, discovered secret, they (Father and Son) incline towards each other with love, to discover each other, to enjoy each other, with self-satisfying delight, resting on equality of spiritual activity, of being, of nature. It the third place, this self-contained world of Father and Son opens itself to the lower world, to men, only by a free act, because they are pleased to open themselves up and to admit whom they choose to fellowship, and because the Father is still greater than the Son, even when the Son upon earth speaks to the ears of men; so it is finally not the Son but the Father who is the decisive revealer, interpreting to the spirits and hearts of men the Son, and in the Son Himself admitting the babes, excluding the wise and understanding."

More briefly he says again:—

"This place is, as no other, the interpreter of the Messiah-thought of Jesus. If we desire to reduce it to its simplest expression, it may be said that Jesus sought His Messiahship in His world historical spiritual achievement, that He mediated for humanity the highest knowledge of God, and the most complete blessed life in God." [1]

The bare reading of this passage suffices to convince one that the writer is wading beyond his depth. How perplexing the second of the three thoughts he finds in the text, on the assumption that the speaker is no more than man, and is distinguished from other men only by His more intimate knowledge of and fellowship with God, a knowledge and fellowship even in His case not absolutely perfect! The fellowship of Father and Son rests, we are told, on equality of spiritual activity, of being, of nature, and yet all that Christ here claims has for its fact-basis, according to our author, only this, that He was the Inbringer of a higher,

[1] *Geschichte Jesu von Nazara*, ii. 384.

more satisfying religion, the religion of Christians, the worship of the Father in spirit and in truth. If this were true, it would be better, with Strauss, to deny the genuineness of the saying reported by the evangelist in the text cited, on the ground of its mystic, pretentious, superhuman character, than, with Keim, to retain it as the unnatural extravagant utterance of one who was neither more nor less than the first teacher of a new and comparatively excellent religion. The words are natural and sober only in the mouth of one who is something more and higher than this; even one who occupies the position towards God, and performs the functions towards the world of the Johannine Logos, who was with God before He became man, and who is the light of every man that cometh into the world. The saying takes us out of the historical incarnate life of the speaker into the sphere of the eternal and divine. The claim to be the exclusive revealer of God the Father of itself justifies this assertion. For it does not mean that men who through want of opportunity know not Him, the historical Christ, must on that account be without such knowledge of God as is necessary unto salvation. It means that He is the light of every man in any land or in any age who has light, and that through Him every one is saved that is saved in any place or time; and that is a claim which could rationally be advanced only by one concerning whom the affirmations contained in the opening sentence of John's Gospel could be made: "In the beginning was the Word, and the Word was with God, and the Word was God."

4. I might here conclude this survey of the literature of naturalistic Christology, but as I have undertaken to give some account of current opinions respecting the Author of our holy faith, I could not well avoid saying something on a phase of thought which can scarcely be said to have any philosophic basis, and of which the chief interest is its crudity, which is neither orthodox nor heterodox, simply because it stops short of the point at which orthodoxy and heterodoxy diverge. Probably the best representative of this nondescript school in England is the Rev. H. R. Haweis, one of the pulpit celebrities of London in connection with

the Established Church, and author of several well-known books in which opinions on all manner of present-day topics are very freely expressed; whose popularity as a preacher and as a writer may be accepted as an indication that his way of thinking hits the taste of many. Mr. Haweis is emphatically a child of the *Zeitgeist*, and yields himself with unhesitating submission to the inspiration of the spirit of the age. He does not believe in miracles in the sense of events which have no natural causes. "As far as I can see," he says, "there are no divine *fiats* in the sense of things happening without adequate causes. From a close observation of the world about us, one and another event supposed to be by divine *fiat* is now seen to be due to natural causes."[1] This, however, does not prevent him from accepting most of the miracles recorded in the Bible—miracles of all sorts, miracles of healing, miracles of prophetic foresight, miraculous answers to prayer; because he thinks that for all such miracles a natural cause can be assigned. He finds the key that unlocks all mysteries in *animal magnetism*. Priests and prophets were men endowed with magnetic and spiritual gifts; hence their power to do things which seem miraculous, to see the future, to pass through fire unharmed, like Shadrach, Meshach, and Abednego; to tame wild beasts, like Daniel in the lions' den. In Christ and His apostles the magnetic and spiritual forces culminated. "God, who chose to speak to man through the man Christ Jesus, who thus revealed the divine nature under the limitation of humanity, also chose that Jesus Christ should take in the highest degree all the natural powers which were bestowed on humanity, both as regards magnetic force and spiritual receptiveness."[2] Hence the healing miracles; hence also the frequent *modus operandi* by the use of magnetised substances, "as when he made clay and anointed the blind man's eyes, and sighed or breathed hard upon him, another practice well known to magnetic doctors now." Magnetism also explains answers to prayer, whether recorded in the Bible or occurring in Christian experience now; for the magnetic element is the one thing common to those in the flesh and out of the flesh. And by prayer we put ourselves *en rapport* with

[1] *Speech in Season*, p. 243.   [2] *Ibid.* p. 49.

disembodied magnetisers, and receive through their magnetic influence the desired blessing, *e.g.*, restored health. No one will be surprised to find one who propounds so grotesque a theory of the miraculous giving utterance to somewhat eccentric ideas on such subjects as the Trinity and the divinity of Christ. Mr. Haweis' opinions on these topics are certainly eccentric enough. In his way he is a believer in a trinity, nay, he holds that every man who thinks persistently about God must think of Him as trinity in unity. For what, he asks, is our first idea of God? It is that of a vast, co-ordinating, perhaps impersonal force, which brought into form what we call the universe. This is our first rough notion of God—God in the widest sense, the Father. But this notion does not suffice; it leaves God too far off, and we need a God that is nigh. And so we next think of God as like ourselves, a magnified man. To us intellectually, sympathetically, God is perfect man. This second human aspect of God is so necessary to us, that even if we had no historical Christ at all, " we should be obliged to make a Christ, because our mind incarnates God in the form of Christ irresistibly and inevitably whenever we bring definite thought to bear upon the question of a divine being in relation to man. And such a Christ, whether ideal or historical, will be God the Son." But my Christ, where is He? Is He only an idea or a past historical character? That will not suffice. I must have a present God with whom I can commune, by whose influence I can be refreshed, a God who touches me and dwells within me. God so conceived is the Holy Ghost. And thus we have our trinity complete, the first of the three modes of Deity being God conceived of as creative force; the second, God conceived of as a man; the third, God conceived of as immanent—" God tangential." It is only a Sabellian trinity of course, as Mr Haweis himself acknowledges, and he has no objection to avoid the charge by identifying Manifestation with Personality, only he thinks the Church of the future is not likely to quibble over phrases with a view of evading the heresy of Sabellianism. From the foregoing doctrine of the Trinity we can ourselves determine what must be our author's doctrine concerning Christ. Christ is the second conception of God realized as a historical fact, an expression of God under the limitations of humanity. But it will be best to give his view in his own words: "When I am asked to define what I mean by Christ, I use such expressions as these. There was something in the nature of the great boundless source of being called God which was capable of sympathy with man. That something found outward expression, and became God expressed under the essential limitations of humanity, in Jesus. That such a revelation was specially necessary to the moral and spiritual development of the human race I believe; that such revelation of God was actually made to the world I believe. More than this I cannot pledge myself to."[1]

According to this view, Christ is the incarnation not of God, but of something in the nature of God which has affinity to man. God Himself, in the totality of His being, according to our author, cannot be incarnated. "There must," he says, "be infinite ranges in the Divine Being's relations to our world, aspects, and energies of Him that can never be comprehended under the limitations of humanity. But there is in Him a human aspect, like the bright side of a planet; that side is turned towards man, expressed outwardly to man in man, and fully expressed in the man Jesus Christ."[2] I am at a loss how to classify this Christological speculation. In some respects it reminds one of the kenotic theories of the Incarnation, according to which the Son of God in becoming man denuded Himself of the attributes of omnipotence, omniscience, and omnipresence, in order that He might be capable of living the life of a veritable man within the limits of humanity. But in other respects it has no affinity with the views of kenotic Christologists, or indeed with any views that can be characterized as Christian. The incarnation taught by Mr. Haweis has more resemblance to that believed in by the worshippers of Brahma, than to that embodied in the creeds of the Christian Church. Christ is simply an emanation from the one universal substance in which are elements of all sorts, the raw material out of which are manufactured all the individual beings which

[1] *Thoughts for the Times*, p. 82.
[2] *Current Coin*, p. 310.

together constitute the universe. He is the embodiment of the human element in the eternal Substance, as the stars are the embodiment of some other element. We should rather say He is *an* embodiment, for why Christ should be singled out as the solitary expression of the something in God that had affinity with men does not appear. All individual men, according to the Pantheistic theory of the universe, are incarnations of the human element in God, and all that can be affirmed of Christ is what Spinoza said of Him, viz., that He is, so far as known, the wisest and best of men. That is what Mr. Haweis would have said had he occupied any deliberately-chosen consistent philosophical standpoint; but being merely an eclectic and a child of the *Zeitgeist*, under its English form, he utters opinions on the subject of Christ's person which defy classification.

That such crude, undigested, and mondescript views should permanently satisfy many earnest minds is not to be expected. The only use they can serve is to be a temporary halting-place to those who, utterly out of sympathy with the formulated doctrines of the Creed, are yet unable to break away from Christianity and its Author. In this respect they are full of interest. It is certainly a striking phenomenon which is presented to our view in this nineteenth century in the person of such a man as Mr. Haweis, a man regarding creeds and dogmatic systems with morbid disgust, and yet compelled by the evangelic records to recognise in Jesus the Son of God in a sense in which the title can be applied to no other man. To some the phenomenon may appear a thing of evil omen, portending the disintegration of the Christian faith, and the ultimate dissolution of the Christian Church. But it has a bright, hopeful side, as well as a dark, discouraging one. It is Christianity renewing its youth, making a new beginning. It is Christ, the same yesterday, to-day, and for ever, presenting Himself to men whose minds have become theologically a *tabula rasa*, and making on them, through His words of wisdom and deeds of holy love, an impression very similar to that which He made on the minds of His first disciples, and to which the most appropriate expression was given in the confession of Peter, " Thou art the Christ, the Son of the living God." It is very much to be desired that an impression of this kind should be made at first hand on many minds in our day; for better far is even a crude elementary faith, right so far as it goes, which has been communicated direct to the soul by the Father in heaven, than a more developed orthodox creed held as a tradition received from flesh and blood. Such a faith is vital, and, like all things living, it will grow, and as the result of growth it may ultimately receive as truth dogmas from which at first it recoiled in incredulity, and so attain to the only orthodoxy which is of any value, that which is right in the spirit as well as in the letter, an orthodoxy of moral conviction, not of mechanical imitation.

5. It remains now to consider the views of those who, while advocating a theory of Christ's person similar to that of Schleiermacher, according to which Christ is the ideal, perfect man—and nothing more—do so, not on philosophic grounds, but solely because they believe they can prove that such is the view presented in Scripture. Substantially the theory held by this school is the same as that of the old Socinians, the main difference being, that while the Socinians emphasized the distinction between God and man, the modern advocates of the *Ideal Man theory* emphasize the essential identity of the divine and the human, and hence feel able to appropriate phrases and to adopt modes of expression from which the old Socinians would have shrunk. Thus Rothe speaks of God as *incarnate* in Christ; quarrelling with orthodoxy only because it believes in an Incarnation limited to Christ, instead of teaching, as he does, that God is incarnate in redeemed humanity at large, and that in the Incarnation of Christ we have only the beginning of a process.[1]

The place of representative man in connection with this theory may justly be assigned to *Beyschlag*, who, in his work on the Christology of the New Testament,[2] has made a most elaborate and ingenious attempt to show that it is in accordance with the teaching both of our Lord and of the apostles. Beyschlag's thesis is that Jesus Christ was

---

[1] *Dogmatik*, Zweiter Theil, erste Abtheilung, p. 153.
[2] *Die Christologie des Neuen Testaments*, Berlin 1866.

the divine idea of humanity for the first time realized in history, the perfect man, and just because the perfect man the Son of God, the natures of God and of man being essentially identical. This he holds to be the doctrine taught not only in the synoptical Gospels, but even in the fourth Gospel, here joining issue with the great founder of the Tübingen school of criticism, Dr. Baur. As is well known to those familiar with his writings, Baur discovers in the New Testament three distinct types of Christology, the first and lowest being that of the synoptical Gospels, the second and intermediate the Pauline, and the third and highest that of the fourth Gospel. The first is Ebionitic in its character, the Christ of the first three Gospels being a mere man endowed by the Holy Ghost with gifts and graces fitting for His Messianic office. In the second, Pauline type of Christology, Christ is still only a man, but He is a man deified— a man placed in a central position towards the universe corresponding to the universalistic views of Christianity advocated by the apostle of the Gentiles, the first-born of every creature, the head and lord of creation, worthy to receive divine honour and worship of all. In the third type of Christology—that set forth in the fourth Gospel—Christ ceases to be veritable man, and becomes a God who has assumed a human *body* that He may become manifest to the world. Beyschlag, on the other hand, contends that the Christology of the fourth Gospel is essentially the same as that of the first three, the proof offered of this proposition forming part of an attempt to establish the Johannine authorship of that Gospel. Beyschlag says in effect, there is no need to stand in doubt as to Johannine authorship so far as the Christology of the fourth Gospel is concerned. For the Christology of that Gospel is just the Christology of Matthew, Mark, and Luke. In all four Gospels one and the same Christ is found—a Christ who, when He calls Himself the Son of Man, means to assert that He is the man *par excellence*, the ideal man in whom all humanity's possibilities are realized, and who, when He calls Himself the Son of God, means to assert no metaphysical identity of nature, but only to claim for Himself a sonship based on ethical affinity, and manifesting itself by intimate fellowship of spirit, and therefore a sonship which, while in degree peculiar to Himself, is in kind common to Him with all good men. That Christ in the fourth Gospel much more frequently calls Himself by the latter name than in the other three, is simply due to the fact of his being placed in circumstances which make that natural in the Johannine representation. But what of the *pre-existence?* Is that not a peculiar feature in the Johannine Christology? Yes, Beyschlag replies, there is very notably a doctrine of pre-existence taught in the Gospel of John. But then the pre-existence is not such as the creeds of the Church mistakenly represented it. It is the pre-existence not of a real person, member of an eternally-existing essential trinity, but of a divine idea, an idea which is at once the Ebenbild of God —a mirror in which God sees His own image reflected— and the Urbild of man, the archetypal thought according to which God made man, destined in the course of the ages to be realized as it never had been before, in all its pleromatic fulness, in Jesus Christ. And when Christ asserts His pre-existence, it is not as a recollection of a previous conscious life in the bosom of God, but simply as an inference from His own consciousness of unity in spirit with God. In proportion as it becomes clear to Him that He is in perfect harmony with God, and therefore realizes the ideal of a humanity made in God's image, it also becomes clear to Him that He must have pre-existed as an idea in the divine mind, and in the language of poetry or imagination may be said to have been in the bosom of the Father, holding delightful converse with Him throughout the ages before He was born into the world.

I cannot here attempt a detailed examination of the proof offered by Beyschlag in support of these views, but must content myself with presenting a few samples of his exegesis, which may enable readers to form a clearer idea of the Christological scheme and to estimate its merits, while they will give me an opportunity of saying a few words on the important and interesting subject of Christ's self-witness, or the doctrine which He taught concerning His own person.

A prominent place in all Christological discussion is

due to the question, What is the precise import of the name which our Lord ordinarily and by preference employed to designate Himself, *the Son of Man?* On this question much diversity of opinion has prevailed, some regarding the name as a title of dignity, others as expressive of indignity, while a third class of interpreters think that, as used by Christ, it combines both the senses. Beyschlag is very decidedly of opinion that it is a title of dignity—is, in fact, a synonym for Messiah. He thinks the source of this name for Messiah is the text in Daniel concerning *one like unto the Son of Man;* herein differing from Schleiermacher, who regarded this opinion as a baseless fancy; and he finds no difficulty in determining from the prophetic text the precise import of the title. "His appearance in heaven seems to point at a not human, but a divine essence, while yet the name Son of Man presupposes not a divine, but a human essence." The solution of the difficulty thus presented is found in the consideration that in the idea of the Son of Man the human is not thought of in opposition to the divine, but as in affinity with it, so that the Messiah of Daniel is the *heavenly man.* He is man, not God; for He is conceived of as distinct from and dependent on God, but He is higher than any prophet; He is in heaven before He comes to earth to assume His kingdom, at home, so to speak, among the clouds of heaven, a companion of God, of celestial descent and heavenly essence. Hence it follows that He pre-existed before His appearance on the earth; but whether the pre-existence be real or ideal only, a pre-existence in the council and will of God cannot be decided from the passage: the question was not present to the mind of the prophet. Combining this result with the Bible doctrine of the creation of man in God's image, the writer finally arrives at this formula: the in-heaven-pre-existing Son of Man was the archetype of humanity, the image of God, of whom mention is made in the creation-history. Furnished with this idea, he comes to the New Testament and endeavours to show that it is the key to the true meaning of the many texts in the Gospel, some fifty in all, in which the title Son of Man occurs. This Messianic title in the mouth of Jesus, we are told, signifies that He is not a man as other men, but *the* man, the absolute, human-divine man; and three passages are singled out in which the meaning is said to be specially apparent These are Mark ii. 10 (Matt. ix. 6; Luke v. 24); Mark ii. 27, 28 (Matt. xii. 8; Luke vi. 5); and Matt. xii. 32 (Luke xii. 10). In the first it is said of the Son of Man that He hath power *on the earth* ($\dot{\epsilon}\pi i\ \tau\tilde{\eta}s\ \gamma\tilde{\eta}s$) to forgive sin. The expression italicized is assumed to be set over against an unexpressed $\dot{\epsilon}v\ \tau\tilde{\omega}\ o\dot{v}\rho\alpha v\tilde{\omega}$, and the following train of thought is extracted from the text: In heaven above God Himself, of course, forgives sin, but that His grace may be available to men He must have an organ upon earth, a Son of Man among the children of men, who knows the whole will of God in heaven, who as man can speak and act as one in complete unity with God, that is, the Messiah, as the man who is absolutely one with God, and the very image of God. In the second passage Christ claims for Himself, as Son of Man, lordship over the Sabbath day. Beyschlag thinks the Messianic import of the title in this place very clear, "since only as the Messiah can Jesus have the power to set aside a Mosaic, yea divine ordinance, like that of the Sabbath." He lays stress on the relation between the two assertions: the Sabbath was made for *man*, and the *Son of Man* is lord of the Sabbath, and thinks that the idea intended is this, that the Son of Man is archetype, prince, head of men, in whom the superiority to the Sabbath, in principle belonging to humanity, becomes an actual authority to break through its prohibitions. The third text is the well-known one concerning blasphemy against the Son of Man. Our author's comments thereon are as follows: "Let us consider the relation here indicated between the Son of Man and the Holy Ghost. It is a relation of distinction, and yet of close connection. The distinction is, that in the Son of Man the revelation of God to men is made in mediated, and, so far, veiled form, therefore may be misunderstood, so that the blasphemer can always have the benefit of the prayer, "Forgive them, they know not what they do;" but in the Holy Ghost the revelation is made immediately, inwardly, therefore unmistakably; therefore there is no excuse for the blasphemer.

At the same time, the Holy Ghost is not thought of as above the Son of Man, but in Him. The Son of Man is the man who has the spirit of God in His entire fulness, whose inmost though unrecognised essence is the Holy Spirit, the man whose human appearance is the medium of the absolute revelation of God. To this corresponds the fact, obvious in the text, that the blasphemy of the Son of Man is represented as the most heinous of pardonable sins."[1] These are very questionable interpretations of familiar sayings of Christ. Regarding the last of the three, in particular, I am very sure that it misses the point. "Offences against the Son of Man are pardonable, but that is all; such sins form the extreme limit of the forgivable," so gives the sense Beyschlag, very erroneously in my judgment. Jesus did not mean to represent sins against Himself as barely forgivable; but rather, with characteristic magnanimity, as easily forgivable, because not more heinous than sins against any other good man, and due to the same general causes. He looked upon it as a thing of course that He should be exposed to misunderstanding, calumny, criticism, contradiction, and that just because He was the Son of Man; and He warned the Pharisees of their danger, not because they were sinning against Him, the ideal Man, but because they were *not* sinning against *Him* through ignorance, misapprehension, and prejudice, but against the Holy Ghost; being convinced in their hearts that Beelzebub could not do the things they saw Him do, yet pretending to believe that he could and did. The second passage—that relating to the lordship of the Son of Man—does not, any more than the one just referred to, require for its interpretation that we understand the name Son of Man as a title of dignity. Christ claimed power to exercise lordship over the Sabbath in the interest of humanity, on the ground of His sympathy with mankind—a far more reliable interpreter of the divine purpose in the institution than the merciless rigour of the Pharisees. The Sabbath, He contended, was made for man; it is a gift of God to weary, burdened sons of Adam. Charity was the motive of the institution, and I, just because I am the Son of Man, heart

[1] *Christologie*, p. 24.

and soul in sympathy with humanity, and bearing its burden on my spirit, am Lord of the Sabbath day, fitted and entitled to say how it may best be observed. The first of the three texts is more obscure, though one can have no hesitation in pronouncing Beyschlag's interpretation forced and artificial, as even he himself seems to feel, from the apologetic manner in which he introduces it, asking: " Do we draw too much from the words when we find in them the following train of thought ?" To my view, our Lord meant to meet with a redoubled, intensified negative the Pharisaic notions in respect to the forgiveness of sin. They viewed God's relation to sin altogether from the side of His majesty and holiness. The pardon of sin was an affair of state, performed with a grudge, and with awe-inspiring ceremony, and competent only to the divine king. Christ regarded God's relation to sin from the side of His grace and charity. In effect, He says to His sanctimonious hearers: God is not such an one as ye imagine Him. He is not severe and implacable, and slow to pardon offences, and jealous of His prerogative in the rare grudging exercise of mercy. He is good and ready to forgive, and He has no desire to monopolize the privilege of forgiving. He is willing that it should be exercised by all in whom dwells His own spirit of love, that men on earth should imitate the Father in Heaven, and say to a penitent: Thy sins be forgiven. My right to forgive rests on this, that I am the Son of Man, the sympathetic friend of the sinful, full of the grace and charity of heaven; but as this is a reason which ye seem unable to appreciate, let me show you in another way that I have the authority ye call in question by healing the pardoned one's physical malady.

In these texts, as I understand them, the title Son of Man signifies the *sympathetic* man, *qui nihil humani alienum putat*. In other texts the title seems rather to signify the *unprivileged* man *par excellence*. To this class belongs the familiar pathetic saying: " The foxes have holes, and the birds of the air have nests, but the Son of Man hath not where to lay His head." Beyschlag, indeed, claims this text also as a support to his theory, paraphrasing it, *though* Son of Man, yet such is my lot. But surely it is far more natural to find in the name the reason of the fact stated, and to read, Such is my lot *because* I am the Son of Man, and nothing else is to be looked for in my company. This construction is further recommended by the consideration that it removes from the saying a tone of querulousness which, on the other view, seems to characterize it, but which was utterly foreign to Christ's temper. Christ spoke of His lot as a homeless one, not as a very hard, unworthy lot for *Him*, the Ideal Man, but as a matter of course for the unprivileged Son of Man, in the same way as He regarded blasphemy against Himself as a commonplace occurrence, not as a specially heinous offence; for why should not He, the Son of Man, be evil spoken of as well as any other son of man ? So, in the parable of the tares, the lesson of patience with evil in the kingdom is tacitly enforced by the consideration that the Son of Man has to endure the counterworking of the evil one, and takes it patiently. I, the Son of Man, have to see my labour in sowing the seed of the kingdom marred; it is a part of the curriculum of trial through which I must pass. I meekly accept my lot as the Son of Man; see that ye bear kindred experiences in the same spirit.

These two attributes, then, at least, are denoted by the title under consideration. The Son of Man is the *unprivileged* man and the *sympathetic* man. But He is more. For there are texts in which the Son of Man, now humbled and unprivileged, is spoken of as the expectant of a kingdom, texts in which a conscious reference to the passage in Daniel is apparent, showing that it is at least one of the Old Testament sources of the title.[1] These texts show that if Jesus was emphatically the unprivileged man, He was so not by constraint, but voluntarily and from philanthropic motives, and that His position as the Man of Sorrows involved an incongruity between lot and intrinsic dignity. The Son of Man is more than He seems; there is a mystery about Him; the name assumed, while revealing much conceals something; revealing His heart, it conceals His dignity, it is an incognito congenial to the humour of

---

[1] Among other sources which have been suggested are the eighth psalm and the Protevangelium. Keim favours the former, Hofmann the latter.

a loving lowly nature. I agree, therefore, with such writers as Keim, who recognise in this title, Son of Man, the expression of a double consciousness, that of one whose present state and mind are lowly, and that of one who knows that a high destiny awaits Him; the former phase of consciousness being the one mainly turned outwards towards the world; the latter, the one kept in the background or in the shade—the side turned inwards, away from the light. And with special reference to Beyschlag's theory, I must maintain that the title Son of Man, as ordinarily used by Christ, denotes rather the reality of His humanity than its ideality, though the latter as a fact I do not deny. The reality is the thing emphasized, with what motive may be a question. Dorner and others say, to bring out the truth that humanity is not the native element of the speaker, and just on that account is the thing which needs to be asserted. Jesus calls Himself the Son of Man, because He is conscious of being more than man. It is doubtful if we are entitled to go so far, though certainly, while it is not possible to demonstrate to the satisfaction of opponents that a divine consciousness forms the background of the human consciousness directly expressed by the title, the view of Dorner fits well into the doctrine of Christ's divinity, assumed to be established by other evidence. I prefer to find the secret of the emphasis with which Jesus asserted the reality of His humanity in the spirit of humility and love which regulated His whole conduct. He called Himself Son of Man as the bearer of the *grace* of the divine kingdom, even as He called Himself *Christ* as the *head* of the kingdom, to whom all its citizens owed allegiance, and *Son of God* as the proper object not only of obedience but of *worship*.

Into the elaborate discussion of the last-mentioned title contained in Beyschlag's treatise I cannot enter. Suffice it to say that in the theory now under review the two titles, Son of Man and Son of God, are practically equivalent. From an analysis of texts the author determines the following as the characteristics of Christ's divine sonship: dependence on His heavenly Father, likeness to His Father, and heavenly descent, implying negatively sinlessness, and positively that Christ is not an ordinary man, but *the* man, the heavenly man. The chief interest of his discussion of the Johannine account of our Lord's teaching concerning His person turns on the manner in which he deals with the doctrine of pre-existence. That he resolves into an ideal pre-existence in the divine mind. As a sample of his way of making texts conform to his theory, we may take his remarks on the words, "Before Abraham was, I am."[1] He admits that the text is susceptible of the traditional interpretation, but contends that it is equally susceptible of his, which is to the following effect: "Jesus beyond question speaks of Himself as the Messiah. Abraham had rejoiced to see in vision the day of Messiah's appearing. What more natural than the thought: Before Abraham could be upon the earth must the Messiah have been already in heaven; before God could choose Abraham to be the father of the people of the promise, the content of the promise, Christ, must have existed for God and in God." The pre-existence asserted is thus a mere logical inference, and it is a mere pre-existence in idea or in purpose. This may be a very simple thought, as Beyschlag calls it, but it does not seem a very likely thought to be introduced with a "Verily, verily, I say unto you." Such a solemn formula was fitted to prevent hearers from seeing the real nature of the assertion as a mere truism. If Jesus had meant nothing more than that God's promise of a Messiah presupposed the existence in God's mind of the Messianic idea, He would naturally have uttered the word as a matter of course, not with the solemn preface of a "Verily, verily." Beyschlag thinks the use of the present tense εἰμί, *I am*, instead of ἤμην, is in favour of his interpretation. Before Abraham was, I was, would have expressed real existence; "Before Abraham was I am," expresses merely ideal existence. But by the same reasoning we might make out the existence of God Himself to be merely ideal, which yet Beyschlag does not believe it to be. For is it not written in the ninetieth psalm, "Before the mountains were brought forth, ere ever Thou hadst formed the earth and the world, from everlasting to everlasting, Thou (art), O God." I am is

[1] John viii. 58.

the proper expression to denote eternal existence; I was would have conveyed the idea of a temporal existence, though earlier than that of Abraham; in other words, the phrase would have suggested an Arian idea of the pre-existent state.

Not to go over all the texts discussed, I give just one more sample of Beyschlag's style of interpretation. In John xiii. 3 he finds the culmination of the process by which Jesus gradually came to know who He was,—viz. the Ideal Man, *Ebenbild* of God, *Urbild* of man,—and what therefore *must have been* His history before He came into the world. The evangelist, we are told, expressly signalizes that the peculiar consciousness of Jesus first reached the acme of clearness on the threshold of death. When, in the introduction of the history of the passion, he writes: *Jesus, knowing that the Father had given all things into His hands, and that He was come from God, and went to God,* this observation were wholly idle and unintelligible, if thereby he did not mean to say that Jesus then became more distinctly and clearly conscious than ever before of His relation to God, His origin from Him, and His return to Him. In this instance Beyschlag's ingenious but artificial exegesis seems to me to reach the acme of unsatisfactoriness. In the words quoted, the evangelist expresses in the first place his own sense of the magnitude of the condescension of his Lord, by contrasting the intrinsic dignity of Christ with the lowly act He performed in the supper chamber. He to whom all things were given, who came forth from God, and who was about to go to God, did thus and thus. He alludes to Christ's consciousness of all this ($\epsilon i\delta\grave{\omega}\varsigma\ \acute{o}\ \text{'}I\eta\sigma o\tilde{v}\varsigma$), that the act recorded may appear not merely outwardly an act of condescension, but an act expressive of a wonderful *spirit* of condescension. He who did this had not forgot who He was and what was His high destiny. All the truth about Himself was present to His mind, as at other times, so also then. The intention of the narrator is not to assert a heightening of the self-consciousness of Christ, but simply to remark for the sake of contrast that it was *there*. The main question of course is, what were the contents of that self-consciousness. Into that subject I do not here go at length; only I may remark, that Beyschlag's theory seems to me to make Christ's consciousness a very artificial one. He ascribes to Himself a great many high-sounding titles, and makes concerning Himself a great many extraordinary affirmations, which have hitherto led the whole catholic Church to believe that nothing could do justice to them short of the doctrine of a personal pre-existence before the Incarnation, but which we are given to understand are nothing more than inferences (or intuitions) from a certain opinion Jesus entertained of Himself as the Ideal Man. Starting with a purely human consciousness of His relation to God, as His sinless, holy child, He comes by and by to think of Himself as "the Son of Man" prophesied of in Daniel, the thought dawning on Him at the Jordan when He was baptized; and this idea once conceived gives birth to all the mystic utterances recorded in the Gospels; utterances rising ever higher and higher, and revealing an ever increasing clearness of consciousness—one notable stage in the development being signalized by the saying recorded in Matt. xi. 27, and the climax being reached on the occasion of the feet-washing, when Jesus at length knew, as He never knew before, that all things were delivered to Him, that He came forth from God, and was about to return to God. Could a consciousness having such a genesis be properly called knowledge? Every one of the mystic affirmations made by Jesus concerning Himself is simply an inference from a theory. Christ speaks not as one conscious of certain things as matters of fact concerning Himself, but as a Platonic philosopher, out of the depths of His inner consciousness constructing a theory concerning His person. He infers His pre-existence from the notion of His being the Ideal Man, just as Plato inferred, from his way of conceiving the universe, the eternal existence of the ideas of all things in the divine mind. And the pre-existence is of the same sort. It is merely a notional existence. The author indeed is not willing to allow this. He maintains that the pre-existence is real as well as ideal. The pre-existence, he tells us, is in the highest sense real, and even personal in a sense, for how can the eternal image (*Ebenbild*) of the personal God, in which God reflects Himself, be otherwise than personal? yet over against the existence of the historic personality it is ideal. It is real not only because all that God thinks and wills here is in Him already reality, but because there can be nothing more real than the divine essence as God represents it to Himself, and distinguishes it from Himself in order to reveal it outwardly; ideal, because in comparison with the historical person it is not identical therewith, but is the *Urbild*, the eternal idea, the inter-divine principle of this historical person.

It will be evident to every one who endeavours to form to himself a distinct conception of the pre-existence of Christ as represented by Beyschlag, that the theory advocated by this author with much ingenuity does not, any more than the theories previously examined, escape from the charge of mystery. For myself, I confess my inability to form any clear idea of what the pre-existent state of the Logos is in this theory. It is neither one thing nor another; it hovers between idea and reality; it is impersonal, yet shares in the personality, thought, and will of God. And while speculatively indefinite, the theory has no practical compensations to commend it. It is liable to the grave objection that it includes the possibility of seeing in the Incarnation a manifestation of gracious, free condescension. Christ did not come into the world, freely, to save sinners. He was sent, as we are all sent, without knowledge, consciousness, or choice; sent in the sense of being born into an existence which dates from birth. All beyond, the so-called pre-existence, is simply a *nimbus* engendered by a poetic imagination.

In closing this review of modern humanistic theories of Christ's person, are we not justified in repeating the question: To whom shall we go to escape mystery? We cannot go to Baur, for there we meet with a Christ whom theory requires to be sinful, while all the facts testify to sinlessness. Neither can we go to Schleiermacher, for there we meet with a Christ who is a moral miracle, while in the interest of naturalistic philosophy He is not allowed to be miraculous in other respects. We cannot go to Keim, for there we meet with a Christ who is a natural-supernatural being, a mere man, yet something altogether exceptional and outside the sphere of ordinary humanity. Still less can we go to Haweis and other popular apostles of theological liberalism, for there we meet with a Christ who is a congeries of crudities, not to say absurdities. We cannot even find rest to our souls in the Christ offered to our faith by Beyschlag; for while we gladly accept Him as the ideal of humanity realized, we cannot understand the relation in which He stands to God, and are at a loss to know whether what is presented to our view be the eternal Son of the catholic theory, or something else of which we can form no distinct idea. We therefore decide to remain with the Christ of the creeds, feeling that if there be in Him that which perplexes and confounds our intellect, there is also that which gives unspeakable satisfaction to the heart; a Christ who came from glory to save the lost, who humbled Himself to become man and die on the cross; a Christ in whom God manifests Himself as a self-sacrificing being, and exhibits to our view the maximum of Gracious Possibility.

LECTURE VI.

CHRIST THE SUBJECT OF TEMPTATION AND MORAL DEVELOPMENT

WE are now to consider the humiliation of Christ on its *ethical* side; that is, we are to regard Christ on earth as subject to an experience of temptation, and undergoing a process of moral development.

1. With reference to the former of these topics, the teaching of Scripture is that Christ was tempted in all respects as we are, without sin. The task prescribed is, to present such a view of our Lord's curriculum of temptation, as shall hold the balance impartially between the two clauses of the statement just quoted; allowing the subject tempted, on the one hand, to be in all respects possible like unto His Brethren; and on the other, preserving the sinlessness of His nature and of His conduct inviolable. That the task is no easy one, is shown by the history of opinion, which presents variations ranging from the denial of everything in Christ's human nature that could be even the innocent occasion of temptation, to the opposite extreme of an ascription to that nature of such inherent *vitium* as, without external provocatives, directly involved temptations to sin of the most violent kind.

If we ask ourselves the question, What was there in Christ, on the supposition of His perfect sinlessness, which helped to make temptation, in some respects at least, if not in all, possible? it readily occurs to refer to the physical infirmities of His human nature. Every being who is capable of hunger and thirst, pleasure and pain, hope and fear, joy and sorrow, is liable to be tempted; for he may be placed in circumstances in which he is obliged to choose between doing wrong and denying himself the gratification of an appetite, a desire, or an affection in itself innocent. If we assume that, in becoming man, Christ took unto Himself a nature subject to such infirmities as are common to men, then we impose on ourselves the necessity of admitting that He entered into a state involving at least some experience of temptation. This assumption the Church catholic has in all ages made. Damascenus but expresses the common faith of Christians when he says: "We confess that Christ assumed all the physical and sinless affections of man. For He took the whole man, and all that belongs to man save sin. These physical sinless affections are the things which are not in our power, and which have entered into human life through the curse pronounced upon transgression—such as hunger, thirst, weariness, toil, tears, corruption, dread of death, fear, the agony, whence sweat and drops of blood."[1] Even this obvious and elementary truth, however, has not escaped contradiction. As is well known to students of Church history, the doctrine that Christ had experience in His body of the infirmities above enumerated was denied by one of the most eminent of the early Fathers, viz. Hilary of Poitiers, who may be regarded as the representative of one extreme in opinion on the present subject. This Father taught in the most explicit terms (for however obscure his style, there can here be no reasonable doubt as to his meaning), that Christ's body was not subject to pain, nor His soul to fear. In the crucifixion Christ sustained in His flesh the onset, but not the pain, of what we call the passion. When the nails were driven into His hands, and the spear was thrust into His side, it was as when a dart pierces water, or punctures fire, or wounds the air; the dart retains its power of piercing and puncturing and wounding, but does not exercise it on these objects; because it is not in the nature of water to be pierced, or of fire to be punctured, or of air to be wounded. The Lord Jesus Christ did indeed suffer when He was smitten, suspended, crucified, and when He died; but the passion rushing on His body, though a real passion, did not exert the

---

[1] *De Fide Orthodoxâ*, lib. iii. cap. xx. The Greek expression for sinless physical infirmities, as employed by Damas., is, $\tau\grave{\alpha}\ \varphi\upsilon\sigma\iota\kappa\grave{\alpha}\ \kappa\alpha\grave{\iota}\ \dot{\alpha}\delta\iota\acute{\alpha}\beta\lambda\eta\tau\alpha\ \pi\acute{\alpha}\theta\eta$.

nature of passion; the virtue of His body, without sense of pain or penalty, receiving the violence of the penalty raging against itself.[1] All the other physical infirmities were equally unreal, the outward phenomena being admitted as matters of fact but not allowed to retain the physiological or psychological meaning which they have for ordinary men. Christ hungered, thirsted, and wept; but these phenomena were simply an assumption of the custom or habit of the human body, in order to demonstrate the truth of His body. There is no evidence that Christ always ate or drank or grieved, when He hungered or thirsted or shed tears; but even when He did actually take food and drink, He was not satisfying the need of His body, but simply accommodating Himself to custom.[2] The mental affections ascribed to Christ in the gospel record, in connection with the passion, are explained away in similar fashion. His fear of death is absolutely denied.[3] His soul-sorrow in the garden was simply solicitude for the disciples, lest the coming trial should prove too much for their faith; His prayer that the cup might pass, if possible, was simply a prayer that God would spare these disciples a trial above what they could bear;[4] when He said, "My soul is exceeding sorrowful *even unto death*," He did not mean, by the expression "even unto death," to indicate that death was

[1] *De Trinitate*, lib. x. c. 23: In quo, quamvis aut ictus incideret aut vulnus descenderet, aut nodi concurrerent, aut suspensio elevaret, afferrent quidem haec impetum passionis, non tamen dolorem passionis inferrent: ut telum aliquod aut aquam perforans, aut ignem compungens, aut aera vulnerans, omnes quidem has passiones naturae suae infert, ut foret, ut compungat, ut vulneret: sed naturam suam in haec passio illata non retinet, dum in natura non est vel aquam forari, vel pungi ignem, vel acrem vulnerari, quamvis naturae teli sit et vulnerare, et compungere, et forare. Passus quidem est Dominus Jesus Christus, dum caeditur, dum suspenditur, dum crucifigitur, dum moritur: sed in corpus Domini irruens passio, nec non fuit passio, nec tamen naturam passionis exseruit; dum et poenali ministerio desaevit, et Virtus corporis sine sensu poenae vim poenae in se desaevientis excepit.

[2] *Ibid.* x. c. 24: Neque enim tum cum sitivit aut esurivit aut flevit, bibisse Dominus aut manducasse aut doluisse monstratus est; sed ad demonstrandam corporis veritatem, corporis consuetudo suscepta est, ita ut naturae nostrae consuetudine consuetudini sit corporis satisfactum. Vel cum potum et cibum accepit, non se necessitati corporis, sed consuetudini tribuit.

[3] *Ibid.* x. c. 27.

[4] *Ibid.* x. c. 37: Non ergo sibi tristis est, neque sibi orat; sed illis quos monet orare pervigiles, ne in eos calix passionis incumbat; quem a se transire orat, ne in his scilicet maneat.

the cause of His sorrow, but the end or limit of it; as only in the things which were to happen to Him before His death,—in the nocturnal apprehension, the scourging, the spitting, the crown of thorns,—was there any cause for solicitude lest the faith of His followers should fail; all that happened afterwards, such as the miracles accompanying the crucifixion and the resurrection, being rather fitted to confirm their weak faith.[1] As for the bloody sweat and the ministry of angels in the garden, it being impossible to find anything in the case of the disciples which could account for these, they are got rid of by the remark, that in very many Latin and Greek codices no mention is made of them;[2] and for those whom this summary course might not satisfy, it is added, that if Christ was sad for us, He must also have been comforted for us, and that the bloody sweat was no sign of infirmity, because it is contrary to nature to sweat blood, and therefore the phenomenon must be regarded as a display of power, rather than as an effect of weakness.[3]

The grounds on which Hilary based this strange doketic view of our Lord's human nature were these: Counter facts and words recorded in the Gospels indicative of power and triumph rather than of weakness and fear; the miraculous birth; and the sinlessness of Christ. As to the first: how could that body have the nature of our pain, which, unlike our bodies, could walk without sinking on the water? how could He burn with thirst, who is able to give drink to the thirsty; or endure the pangs of hunger, who could curse the tree that refused its fruits to Him? Again, how can He have feared death, who voluntarily delivered Himself to the armed band; or felt sadness in view of death, who, in reference to that very death, said: "*Now is the Son of Man*

---

[1] *De Trinitate*, x. cc. 36, 39.

[2] *Ibid.* x. c. 41: Nec sane ignorandum a nobis est, et in Graecis et in Latinis codicibus complurimis, vel de adveniente angelo, vel de sudore sanguinis nil scriptum reperiri.

[3] *Ibid.* x. c. 41: Si nobis tristis est, necesse est ut propter nos sit comfortatus; quia qui de nobis tristis est, et de nobis comfortatus est, ea comfortatus est conditione qua tristis est. Sudorem vero nemo infirmitati audebit deputare; quia et contra naturam est sudare sanguinem. Nec infirmitas est, quod potestas, non se cundum naturae consuetudinem, gessit.

glorified;" or experienced real desertion when He uttered the cry: "My God, my God, why hast Thou forsaken me?" who shortly before had said to His judges: "Henceforth shall ye see the Son of Man sitting on the right hand of power"?[1] As to the second ground of the theory, Hilary held that, in consequence of the miraculous conception, the body of Christ necessarily differed in its properties from the bodies of ordinary men. Inasmuch as it was born of the Virgin, it was a real body; but because it was conceived by the power of the Holy Ghost, it was a body free from all infirmity.[2] Not formed of terrestrial elements, although deriving its origin from the mystery of conception, the body of the Son of Man was exempt from the evils of a merely terrestrial body; the power of the Highest communicating to it His own virtue, while forming it in the Virgin's womb.[3] Finally, as to the third ground of his peculiar theory, Hilary held himself entitled or bound to exclude Christ's humanity from all participation in infirmity, because of its sinlessness, which he regarded as the result of the miraculous birth. He made no distinction between vice in the moral sense and infirmity in the physical sense, and from the absence of the former from the humanity of Christ he inferred the absence of the latter. In Christ, he held, was the truth of the human body, but not its vices, the similitude of sinful flesh, but not the flesh of sin itself. The Saviour's humanity, having a peculiar origin, was free from the sins and the vices of humanity coming into being by ordinary generation.[4]

[1] *De Trinitate,* x. cc. 23, 24, 27, 29, 31.

[2] *Ibid.* x. c. 35: Genuit etenim ex se corpus, sed quod conceptum esset ex Spiritu; habens quidem in se sui corporis veritatem, sed non habens naturae infirmitatem: dum et corpus illud corporis veritas est quod generatur ex virgine: et extra corporis nostri infirmitatem est, quod spiritalis conceptionis sumpsit exordium.

[3] *Ibid.* x. c. 44: Extra terreni est corporis mala, non terrenis inchoatum corpus elementis, etsi originem filii hominis sanctus Spiritus per sacramentum conceptionis invexit. Nempe et Altissimi virtus virtutem corporis, quod ex conceptione Spiritus Virgo gignebat, admiscuit.

[4] *Ibid.* x. c. 25: Habuit enim corpus, sed originis suae proprium; neque ex vitiis humanae conceptionis existens, sed in formam corporis nostri virtutis suae potestate subsistens: gerens quidem nos per formam servi, sed a peccatis et a vitiis humani corporis liber. So also c. 35: in natura ejus corporis infirmitatem naturae corporeae non fuisse. . . . et passionem illam licet illata corpori sit, non tamen

It is not surprising that men should be unwilling, or almost unable, to believe that a theologian of such eminence as Hilary could invent or countenance a theory so open to the charge of Doketism as the one of which an outline has just been given; and, accordingly, many attempts have been made to apologise for his views, and to bring them into tolerable accord with Catholic orthodoxy. So far as I can judge, these attempts are by no means successful. The best thing that could be said in Hilary's behalf, were it well grounded, is the statement made by Chemnitz, on the authority of Bonaventura, that William of Paris had seen a writing of the same Father, in which the doctrine taught in the treatise on the Trinity concerning Christ's human nature was retracted.[1] The apology, however, most in favour with theologians, both Catholic and Protestant, is, that Hilary's intention was to deny, not the reality, but the *necessity* of our Lord's experience of infirmity; in the words of Dorner, "to avoid representing the weakness of Christ as a physical determination and necessity; and, on the contrary, to view all His sufferings as deeds, that is, as ethical."[2] But this representation is doubly inaccurate. In the first place, Hilary does distinctly deny the reality of the pain supposed to be endured by Christ. What our Lord suffered on the cross was the impetus of the passion, not the pain of it. He was, so to speak, as one whose body is under chloroform, and while unconscious through its influence, undergoes surgical operations which in ordinary circumstances would produce pain. What Christ willed, therefore, was not to endure real pain, which was foreign to His miraculously conceived body, but simply to sustain assaults which would have caused pain to any other man. Hilary, in short, made Christ's whole experience of infirmity as doketic as Cyril made His growth in knowledge; it was

naturam dolendi corpori intulisse: quia quamvis forma corporis nostri esset in Domino, non tamen in vitiosae infirmitatis nostrae esset corpore qui non esset in origine, quod ex conceptu Spiritus sancti Virgo progenuit: quod licet sexus sui officio genuerit, tamen non terrenae conceptionis suscepit elementis.

[1] *De duabus naturis*, c. 3, p. 16.
[2] *Person of Christ*, div. i. vol. ii. p. 413. To the same effect Thomasius, *Christi Person und Werk*, ii. p. 183. Aquinas, *Summa*, pars iii. q. 15, says: Non veritatem doloris, sed necessitatem excludere intendit.

simply an economic accommodation to the fashion of that humanity which He had assumed. The painless One freely subjected Himself to experiences which ordinarily cause pain, just as, according to Cyril, the omniscient One, out of respect for the demands of the kenosis, consented to seem ignorant, and accommodate the manifestation of a knowledge perfect in itself from the first, to the stages of His physical growth. But if this comparison be disallowed, then we cannot do better than fall back on one employed by Hilary himself to explain his view, viz. between the way in which Christ bore griefs and pains, and the way in which He bore sins. We are accustomed to think of Christ as bearing sin, in the sense of bearing real griefs and pains as their penalty. But Hilary's doctrine is, that Christ bore grief *as* He bore sin. Quoting the prophetic passage beginning with the words, "surely He hath borne our griefs," he proceeds to say: "Therefore the opinion of human judgment is deceived, thinking that this man feels pain because He suffers. For, while bearing our sins, as having assumed the body of our sin, He Himself nevertheless sins not. For He was sent in the similitude of sinful flesh; bearing, indeed, sins in the flesh, but ours. So likewise He endures pain for us; not, however, as experiencing the sense of our pain, because He was found in fashion as a man, having in Himself the body of pain, but not having the nature which can feel pain; because though His habit is that of man, His origin is not of man, being due to a miraculous conception by the power of the Holy Ghost. Hence He was esteemed to be stricken with pain, smitten, and afflicted. For He took the form of a servant, and the fact of His being a man born of the Virgin gave rise to the opinion, that in His passion He endured the pain which is natural to us."[1]

[1] *De Trinitate*, x. c. 47: *Hic peccata nostra portat, et pro nobis dolet: et nos existimavimus eum in doloribus esse, et in plaga, et in vexatione. Ipse autem vulneratus est propter iniquitates nostras, et infirmitatus est propter peccata nostra. Fallitur ergo humanae aestimationis opinio, putans hunc (hinc ?) dolere quod patitur. Portans enim peccata nostra, peccati nostri scilicet corpus assumens, tamen ipse non peccat. Missus namque est in peccati carnis similitudine; portans quidem in carne peccata, sed nostra. Et pro nobis dolet, non et doloris nostri dolet sensu: quia et habitu ut homo repertus, habens in se doloris corpus, sed non*

Conceding, however, the point as to the *reality* of Christ's experience of pain, I remark in the second place, with respect to the apology for Hilary now under consideration, that it does not suffice to clear that Father from the charge of doketism to say, that he merely wished to make the Saviour's endurance of suffering a matter, not of necessity, but of free will. For there are two senses in which voluntariness may be predicated of Christ's sufferings and experiences of infirmity; one which is perfectly compatible with the ascription to His human nature of the same liability to sinless infirmity as that under which ordinary men lie; another, which excludes that liability, and makes all Christ's pains the miraculous effects of the forthputting at His pleasure of His divine power. To make this distinction plain, let me quote and comment on a statement of opinion, on the point in hand, by an orthodox doctor of a later age, who held what Hilary is supposed to have intended to teach, and who brought his views to bear against the prevalent errors of the Adoptianists. Alcuin, in his treatise against Felix of Urgellis, refuting the opinion that Christ was by natural condition a servant, says: "The Catholic verity confesses that Christ had all the infirmities of the flesh which He assumed, voluntarily, when He wished: a voluntary and true hunger when He came hungering to the fig-tree; a voluntary and true weariness when He sat down, fatigued with His journey, by the well; a voluntary and true wound, when He was pierced in the side by the soldier's spear; a voluntary and true death, when with bowed head He gave up the ghost upon the cross; a voluntary and true burial, when Joseph and Nicodemus placed Him, taken down from the cross, in the sepulchre. All these infirmities of the flesh, voluntary indeed, yet true, Christ had, because He took the nature of human flesh, not in phantasy, but in truth."[1] Take now one of these infirmities, say the

habens naturam dolendi, dum et ut hominis habitus est, et origo non hominis est, nato eo de conceptione Spiritus sancti. Hinc itaque aestimatus est et in doloribus, et in plaga et in vexatione esse. Formam enim servi accepit: et natus ex virgine homo opinionem nobis naturalis sibi in passione doloris invexit.

[1] Alcuini *Opera, Adv. Felicem*, lib. vi. cap. iv.: Catholica veritas confitetur secundum veram substantiam carnis, omnes ejusdem carnis, quas suscepit, infirmitates voluntarias habere Christum, cum voluisset. Voluntariam namque et veram

weariness by the well, that we may see the two different senses in which voluntariness may be predicated of it. We may say that Christ was voluntarily weary, meaning that He permitted—that is, abstained from using divine power to prevent—the heat of the sun and the long journey on foot to have their natural effect on a physical frame, as liable to be acted on by these causes as that of any other man. Voluntariness, thus understood, is perfectly compatible with the doctrine that Christ's humanity in physical constitution was exactly the same as ours. It is a voluntariness of this kind, not opposed to, but in harmony with, a reign of physical law, that Cyril teaches when he says, with reference to the death of Christ: "Therefore He appeared in our nature, and made His own body subject to corruption, according to the reasons inherent in nature, in order that He, being Himself the Life, might implant therein the good which belonged to Him—that is, life."[1] John of Damascus means the same thing when he says that "our infirmities were in Christ, both according to nature and above nature. According to nature, because He allowed His flesh to suffer what was proper to it; above nature, because in the Lord the physical states did not outrun His will. For in Him nothing compulsory is seen, but all is voluntary. Voluntarily he hungered, voluntarily He thirsted, voluntarily He feared, voluntarily He died."[2] This, then, is the one sense in which voluntariness may be

famem, cum esuriens ad ficulneam veniret; voluntariam et veram lassitudinem, cum fatigatus ab itinere super puteum sederet; voluntarium et verum vulnus, cum militis lancea percuteretur in latere; voluntariam et veram mortem, cum inclinato capite spiritum emisisset in cruce; voluntariam et veram sepulturam, cum eum depositum de ligno Joseph et Nicodemus ponerent in sepulchro. Has enim carnis omnes infirmitates voluntarias quidem, sed veras Christus habuit, quia carnis humanae naturam, non in phantasia, sed in veritate suscepit.

[1] *Quod unus sit Christus*, p. 1352: Ἀλλ' ἦν οὐχ ἑτέρως τὸ ἀπειδές τοῦ θανάτου καταδεῖσθαι κράτος, πλὴν ὅτι διὰ μόνης τῆς ἐνανθρωπήσεως τοῦ Μονογενοῦς· ταύτῃτοι πέφηνε καθ' ἡμᾶς, καὶ ἴδιον ἐποιήσατο σῶμα τὸ ὑπὸ φθοράν, κατά γε τοὺς ἐνόντας τῇ φύσει λόγους, ἵν' ἐπείπερ ἐστὶν αὐτὸς ἡ ζωὴ (γεγέννηται γὰρ ἐκ ζωῆς τοῦ Πατρὸς) ἐμφυτεύοῃ τὸ ἴδιον ἀγαθὸν αὐτῷ, τουτέστι τὴν ζωήν.

[2] *De Fide Orthodoxâ*, lib. iii. c. xx.: Ἀμέλει τὰ φυσικὰ ἡμῶν πάθη κατὰ φύσιν, καὶ ὑπὲρ φύσιν ἦσαν ἐν τῷ Χριστῷ. Κατὰ φύσιν μὲν γὰρ ἐκινεῖτο ἐν αὐτῷ, ὅτε παρεχώρει τῇ σαρκὶ παθεῖν τὰ ἴδια· ὑπὲρ φύσιν δέ, ὅτι οὐ προηγεῖτο ἐν τῷ Κυρίῳ τῆς θελήσεως τὰ φυσικά·

predicated of Christ's infirmities. But we may attach another idea to the word. Reverting to the infirmity of weariness by the well, we may say that Jesus was voluntarily weary, meaning that He brought on a feeling or state of weariness, which could not otherwise have been produced, by a deliberate act of will, having some particular end in view, such as, that He might have an excuse for entering into conversation with the woman of Samaria, by asking her for a drink of water. A voluntariness of this sort another opponent of Adoptianism, Paulinus of Aquileia, seems to have believed in, when, with reference to our Lord's soul-trouble recorded in the twelfth chapter of John's Gospel, he represented Christ as troubling Himself, so taking on Himself the affection of human infirmity, by a display of power which excluded the disgrace of real fear; the design of this act of self-troubling, and of the prayer which accompanied it, being to elicit a voice from heaven which might make an impression on the surrounding crowd.[1] Now it is manifest that voluntariness, taken in this sense, is not compatible with a reign of law in Christ's body, or with the reality of His human nature. To represent Christ as making Himself hungry, or thirsty, or weary, or sorrowful, is to give His whole life on earth a doketic aspect, and to degrade it into a theatric spectacle got up for effect—for the sake of example, or of doctrine, or to beget faith in the mystery of the Incarnation, or for all these together; a view, indeed, which the author last named does not hesitate plainly to avow.[2] And the question with respect to Hilary is, in which of the two senses are we to understand him as ascribing to Christ the experience of real, indeed, yet always voluntary infirmity? No one who considers

οὐδὲν γὰρ ἠναγκασμένον ἐπ' αὐτοῦ θεωρεῖται, ἀλλὰ πάντα ἑκούσια. Θέλων γὰρ ἐπείνησε, θέλων ἐδίψησε, θέλων ἐδειλίασε, θέλων ἀπέθανεν.

[1] Paulini *Opera, Contra Felicem Urgellitanum*, lib. i. cap. xxix.: Proximus igitur passioni, suscipiens in se humanae infirmitatis affectum turbavit semetipsum potestatis utique insignibus, non timoris, ut haeretici garriunt, dedecore.

[2] *Contra Felicem*, lib. i. cap. xxix.: Orabat quasi verus homo pro hominibus, sed potestatis insigni, non necessitatis dehonestae. Omne enim quod incarnata Dei Patris sapientia virtusque mirabiliter in locutione, in actione, in situ, in motu, in sessione, et resurrectione, ac deambulatione egit, aut exemplum, aut doctrina, aut mysterium fuit, aut utrumque et hoc et haec, et illud.

the stress which He lays on the miraculous birth as giving to our Lord's humanity a peculiar physical constitution, can hesitate as to the answer. In the view of this Father, our Lord's infirmities, if real at all, which is more than doubtful, were necessarily miraculous: they were not produced by reasons inherent in His human nature, but by His divine will. Whereas, on the true theory, the miracle would have lain in Christ's *not* feeling weary as He sat by the well, after His long journey under a hot sun; on Hilary's theory, the miracle was that Christ *did* feel weary, the sun and the journey being impotent to exhaust His frame, born of the Virgin, yet divine in origin.

Against the charge of doketism, then, this distinguished Father of the Western Church cannot be successfully defended; and instead of indulging in desperate attempts at apologising for his errors, we shall be more profitably occupied in endeavouring to discover how such a man could be led to take up so false a position on so vital a subject. The explanation is indeed not far to seek, being to be found in a law of controversy whose powerful influence is abundantly illustrated in the history of theological warfare,—that, viz., according to which every controversialist tends to take up a position as far as possible removed from that of his opponent, not unfrequently abandoning to the enemy the open fields of common truth, and shutting himself up within the narrow citadel of orthodoxy. Hilary was the defender of the Nicene faith against its formidable foes, the Arians. Now one way by which the Arians assailed the divinity of Christ was, by pointing to His experience of infirmity. That man Jesus, they argued, however exalted, cannot be divine, for God is impassible; but behold, that man suffered fear, sorrow, and pain. To which Hilary replied in effect: " I grant that God is impassible—that fear, sorrow, and pain cannot touch Him. But what of that ? Neither did Christ suffer any of these things; the statements in the Gospels which seem to ascribe infirmity to Him can all be satisfactorily explained." And so he saved Christ's divinity at the expense of His humanity, and in giving us a God *totus in suis*, robbed us of a Brother *totus in nostris*.

The foregoing discussion of the eccentric views entertained by an ancient Church Father finds its chief use, and best apology, in being a help towards realizing the importance of the commonplace category, "the sinless infirmities," in connection with Christ's experience of temptation. For every one sees at a glance what a different complexion is given to that experience, if it still deserve the name, on the assumption that Hilary's theory is true. No real fear of death, giving rise to earnest desire to escape it, if possible, only an acted fear for our sakes, to teach us not to fear in a similar situation; no impassioned prayer, with strong crying and tears, for His own deliverance, but only a compliance with the rule of prayer, for an example to Christians placed in straits; no real intense mental struggle or agony, as of one obliged to choose between two dread alternatives, but only the appearance of one, assumed and exhibited for the benefit of spectators; no veritable exhaustion, calling for angelic succour, but only a permitting of Himself to be comforted on the part of a strong One, who had no need of celestial help, that martyrs and confessors might be nerved to endurance by the assurance of seasonable aid; the bloody sweat, if real, no result of mortal weakness, but miraculously produced for the sake of such as should be called to suffer martyrdom, whether by consecrating the earth, on which it dropped, to be their burying-place, or by inspiring them with the hope of a better resurrection.[1] On such a theory there is no life-

---

[1] The above may seem overdrawn, but it is in truth little more than a free paraphrase of what Paulinus says in his work, *Contra Felicem*, lib. iii. c. v., in defence of the voluntariness (in the illegitimate sense) of Christ's passion. "Quod autem," he remarks, "tristatur, moeret, pavet, et taedet, et humanae apertius demonstratur veritas carnis, et nostrae per id praestatur infirmitatis quantocius fortitudo. Non enim infirmari coacte potuit inviolabilis virtus, nisi in quantum praestabilius voluntaria potestate illi pro nobis placuit infirmari." Then in reference to prayer this doctrine is applied thus: "Nam et orationis regulam tempore passionis ideo taliter informare voluit ut membra sua . . . inter angustias positi, et in oratione strenui, et in Dei Voluntate per subjectionem concordes, et fortes robore in agone certaminis permanerent." Concerning the celestial succour it is said: "Hinc est quod idem Redemptor noster, qui nullo modo alieno indigebat auxilio, in ipso, ut ita loquar, traditionis momento factus in agonia dum prolixius oraret, angeios se pro nostra consolatione permisit confortare, nulla prorsus exigente causa necessitatis, sed ut hoc exemplo," etc. etc. On the subject of the bloody sweat, Paulinus in

experience of temptation, but only a dramatic spectacle,—a God wearing a mask, and playing the part of a tempted man. On the other hand, grant the reality of infirmity, and all the events pass from the region of fictitious representation into the region of genuine human experience; Christ becomes the tempted man, tempted in some respects at least as we are, tempted both positively and negatively, positively, by the attractions of that which is agreeable to sense, as when the tempter in the wilderness set before Him the pleasant way of a worldly Messiahship; negatively, by the repulsions of pain impending or in course of being endured, as when Peter thoughtlessly performed Satan's part, and said, "Save Thyself;" or when the near prospect of the passion awoke in His own soul the wish, "Would that this cup might pass!"

"Tempted in some respects at least," I have said. But the Scripture says, "tempted in all respects as we are, without sin." The question therefore arises: Does the category of sinless infirmities afford a basis for a *catholic* experience of temptation; and if not, is there some other condition of the possibility of temptation to be taken into account, which has hitherto been overlooked? Now there have not been wanting men, at various periods in the Church's history, who have answered the former part of this question in the negative, and have deemed it necessary, in order to give fulness to Christ's experience as the tempted, to ascribe to Him not merely sinless physical or psychical infirmity, but participation in a morally vitiated human nature, without prejudice to His actual sinlessness. This view seems to have been first distinctly enunciated at the close of the eighth century by the Adoptianists, and particularly by Felix of Urgellis. It is not difficult to see how the advocates of the Adoptian theory of Christ's person might be led into such a line of thought. Their great

dulges in vapid rhetoric to which I am unable to attach any distinct meaning. His words are: "Unde et pro sudoris rore de corpore unici ejusdemque nostri consolatoris guttas sanguinis, quod certum est humanae omnino non esse naturae sudare, non frustratorie ab evangelista refertur in terram usque distillasse: quatenus per terram, in quam defluxerat, terrena beatorum martyrum depromeret membra, et purpureae guttulae punicum distillantis rorem roseo Christi sanguine eadem sanctorum martyrum purpurata depingeret membra."

concern was to vindicate the reality and completeness of our Lord's humanity, which appeared to them to be overlooked or thrown into the background, in the prevalent form of Christological doctrine; an impression certainly not without foundation, if their orthodox opponents, Alcuin and Paulinus, may be taken as fair samples of contemporary opinion on such subjects. Felix and others like-minded said: Jesus Christ is a man, our Brother. As a man, He is the Son of God by adoption, even as we Christians are; and He is God by name (nuncupative), in virtue of His connection with the second person of the Trinity, who in Him became incarnate. Having taken up this fundamental position, they of course laid hold of everything in the Scripture bearing on the *homoüsia* of Christ's humanity with ours as an argument in favour of their theory. They emphasized the facts that Christ was the subject of predestination and election, and the recipient of grace; they took in earnest all that is said of Christ employing the presence of infirmity or sinless imperfection, His ignorance, His refusal of the title "good" in the absolute sense, His tears, His agony, His prayers, not merely for others, but *bonâ fide* for Himself. They did this; and they did more: after the fashion of controversialists, they exaggerated some Scripture statements and misinterpreted others, in their eagerness to fortify their position; and so with much that was true and that needed to be said, they mingled not a little that was false and fitted to create a wholesale prejudice against everything advanced by them in support of their cause. They held that Christ was not only a servant, but a servant by natural condition and necessity, born into a servile state of a servile mother;[1] that He was baptized because He needed baptism, and in His baptism underwent regeneration;[2] that by His birth He was partaker of the

---

[1] Servus conditionalis, ex ancillâ natus. *Vid.* Alcuin, *Adv. Felicem*, lib. iii. c. iii., lib. iv. c. ix. Alcuin quotes Felix, asking: Quid potuit de ancilla nasci, nisi servus? *Vid.* lib. vi. c. ii.

[2] Alcuin, *Adv. Felicem*, lib. ii. c. xvi.: Has geminas generationes: primam videlicet quae secundum carnem est; secundam vero spiritalem, quae per adoptionem fit; idem Redemptor noster secundum hominem complexus in semetipso continet: primam videlicet, quam suscepit ex Virgine nascendo: secundam vero quam initiavit in lavacro a mortuis resurgendo. Felix draws a parallel between Christ and

old man,[1] belonged to the mass of perdition, was subject to the law of sin, and therefore to the curse of sin—death. Joshua, clothed with filthy garments, having Satan at his right hand to resist him, and plucked by Jehovah as a brand from the burning, was Jesus sordid with the sinful flesh He had assumed, clad in the tattered and torn garments of the human race, until the shuttle of the cross wove for Him a tunic of innocence, wearing a body half-burned by the transgression of His first parents and by the flame of their crimes, which, however, He was able by His virtue to rescue from being utterly consumed in the fire of hell.[2]

Views similar to these have been propounded in the present century both in Germany and in England; in the former country by Gottfried Menken of Bremen, in the latter by the better known Edward Irving. Menken seems to have been influenced both by theological bias, and by a practical religious interest in the doctrine of our Lord's humanity. In a homily on the text: "Who by the eternal Spirit offered Himself without spot to God,"[3] wherein he states his views on the question at issue, he makes the prefatory observation that theologians had been so much occupied in defending Christ's divinity against assailants, that Christians had not sufficiently contemplated Him as the Son of Man; and hence the testimonies of the Scriptures

Christians, and makes Him like them partake of two generations, one natural, the other spiritual begun in His baptism, completed in His resurrection.

[1] Alcuin, *Adv. Elipandum*, lib. i. c. xvi. Alcuin sums up the doctrine of Elipandus thus: Asserens Christum et veterem hominem esse, et nuncupativum Deum, et adoptivum filium, et secunda indiguisse regeneratione et alia plurima ecclesiasticae doctrinae inconvenientia.

[2] Alcuin, *Adv. Felicem*, lib. vii. c. viii.: Et Jesus erat indutus vestimentis sordidis, utique ex transgressione de carne peccati sordidus, quam induere dignatus est: unde et pannis involutus, et scissuras humani generis, dum in se illa suscepit, inspicitur; donec radio crucis, innocentiae tunica texeretur. Nonne inquit, hic titio extractus ab igne est? Titio extractus ab igne semiustulatus, non percombustus esse ostenditur. Corpus enim illud humani generis, quod ex protoplastorum transgressione et criminum flamma fuerat adustum, hoc induit Dominus, et quasi titionem semiustulatum a gehennae incendio liberavit. Alcuin represents Felix as fathering this interpretation on Jerome; but he calls in question the accuracy of the statement.

[3] *Homilien über das neunte und zehnte Capitel des Briefes an die Hebräer nebst einem Anhang etlicher Homilien über Stellen des zwölften Capitels*, Bremen, 1831. The homily referred to in the text is the sixth.

to the true and full humanity of the Son of God had not been duly considered, and were among the things least known and understood. By way of doing justice to the neglected doctrine, he maintains that Christ, when He came into the world, took not human nature as it came from the hand of God before the fall, before it became sinful and mortal in Adam through his disobedience. He took a mortal body, a body of flesh which might be called a body of sin: a body, at least, in which sin, suffering, and death were possible, and whose natural inevitable doom it was to die. Had He not assumed such a body, He would not have been a real member of the human race, a true Adamite. For sinfulness of nature and mortality belong, of necessity, to the essence of natural earthly humanity. A being free from the taint of original sin, and immortal, does not belong to that humanity, is no true full son of Adam and son of man; and of him can never be said that he was made in all things like his brethren the Adamites, the sinful mortal sons of Adam.[1] Therefore it is explicitly asserted by this author, that Christ, the sinless One, in His humanity partook not merely of the mortality, but of the sinfulness of human nature. Those who are familiar with the concatenations of thought characteristic of this school, will know beforehand what sort of doctrine to expect from such a quarter, on the subject of Christ's redeeming work. Christ's vocation as Redeemer was to make the whole lump of fallen humanity holy, by sanctifying the portion thereof He had assumed into connection with Himself,

---

[1] Sündlichkeit und Sterblichkeit gehören nothwendig zu dem Wesen der natürlichen irdischen Menschheit, zu dem Eigenthümlichen der Adamsfamilie. Ein Unsündlicher, und ein Unsterblicher gehört der natürlichen irdischen Menschheit nicht an; ein Unsündlicher und Unsterblicher ist kein natürlicher und wahrer Adamide, kein wahrhaftiger und völliger Adams- und Menschensohn. Von einem Unsündlichen und Unsterblichen kann auch nimmer mit Wahrheit gesagt werden, er sei den Adamiden, den sündlichen und sterblichen Adamskindern als seinem Brüdern IN ALLEM GLEICH GEWORDEN, theilhaftig ihres Fleisches und Blutes.— *Ibid.* p. 103. *Unsündlichkeit* in this extract evidently signifies freedom from corruption of nature or original sin, which, according to Ullmann, *Die Sündlosigkeit Jesu*, p. 25, is the strict meaning of the word, as distinct from *Sündlosigkeit*, which signifies freedom from actual sins. Menken ascribes to Christ *Sündlosigkeit*, but not *Unsündlichkeit*. He says, *ibid.* p. 105: Er hat die Sündlichkeit der menschlichen Natur, und das ist noch keine wirkliche Sünde.

which He did partly by living in His fallen flesh a perfectly holy life, partly by dying on the cross, as a sin-offering, offering up Himself without spot to God, and just on that account being a sin-offering; for His spotlessness meant that sin had been destroyed, and it was the peculiarity of the sin-offering, that in it the victim was totally consumed. Only by this theory, it is held, is justice done to Scripture statements, such as, " He hath made Him to be sin for us;" and, " God sent His Son in the likeness of sinful flesh, as a sin-offering, and destroyed sin in the flesh." Something more is meant by such expressions than the shallow, pitiful idea that Christ died for men; an idea hardly worth the trouble of understanding it: unworthy of the long preparation which had been made for Christ's coming, dishonouring to mankind, as if, forsooth, Jesus of Nazareth were the only one sufficiently inspired by the heroism of love to be willing to lay down His life for His brethren; not to say dishonouring to God, by placing the acceptable element of Christ's sacrifice in the mere fact of death. No, something far deeper, far more thorough, is signified by these Scripture oracles; even that Christ was made sin by taking sinful flesh; that He offered Himself without spot, by fighting a successful battle with sin; that He became the atoning sin-offering of the world, because in His own person He offered up and annihilated the sinfulness of human nature, made this nature in His person sinless, exhibited it in His person sinless, to God, angels, and devils, even as, when He re-entered heaven, He exhibited it immortal.[1]

These opinions, promulgated from a German pulpit some fifty years ago, so closely resemble those uttered about the same time in the ears of a London audience by an eloquent

---

[1] Er ist also zur Sünde gemacht, da er den schmählichen Leib des Fleisches anzog, da er die verachtetste aller Geistergestalten, die Gestalt des sündlichen Fleisches, annahm. Er hat sich selbst geopfert, da er durch fortgesetzte Ueberwindung und Aufopferung diese Gestalt in sich vernichtete. Er ist das versöhnende Sündopfer der Welt geworden, da er in seiner Person die Sündlichkeit der Menschennatur aufopferte und vernichtete, diese Natur in seiner Person unsündlich machte, die sündliche Menschennatur in seiner Person Gott und Engeln und Teufeln unsündlich dastellte, wie er sie hernach, als er in die Himmel einging, auch unsterblich dargestellet hat.—*Ibid.* p. 105.

but erratic Scotch preacher, that further exposition of the theory held in common by both is quite unnecessary. Irving differs from Menken only by greater elaboration and fuller detail, by the rhetorical extravagance of many of his statements, and by the confident assertion of his orthodoxy, in utter ignorance of the historical affinities of his system, which the better informed German theologian knew to be a comparative, though, as he deemed, justifiable novelty. The British divine seems to have been influenced, not less than the Continental one, by theological bias. Besides intense and most praiseworthy zeal in behalf of the reality of our Lord's humanity, there was at work in Irving's mind, as his treatise on the Incarnation plainly shows, a feeling of deep dissatisfaction with the current doctrine of atonement, which he bitterly and contemptuously nicknamed the "bargain and barter hypothesis."[1] Accordingly he too, like Menken, adopted, and with far more vehemence advocated, what may be called the theory of REDEMPTION BY SAMPLE;[2] that is to say, that Christ took sinful human nature into connection with His own person; battled heroically through life with the temptations springing out of that "fragment of the perilous stuff" He had assumed, that flesh of His wherein "all infirmities, sin, and guilt of all flesh was gathered into one"—in which all "sins, infirmities, and diseases" "nestled;" suffered death on the cross as the doom due to Him as in His human nature a "fallen," though personally a sinless man; yea, suffered the extremity of that divine wrath to which sinful flesh and blood is obnoxious; and after death descended in His soul into hell, there to endure a most fearful conflict; and so having maintained His personal sinlessness, and endured to the uttermost the penalty due to His sinful human nature, accomplished the reconciliation or atonement of

[1] *The Doctrine of the Incarnation Opened*, vol. v. of Collected Writings, p. 146.
[2] This theory, or hints of it, can be found in the writings of the early Fathers; *vid*. Lecture ii. of this course. But the theory in the hands of the Fathers did not mean that Christ took a portion of *sinful* humanity and made it holy, and through it sanctified the whole lump; but only that He took a portion of humanity in a sinless state, and kept it sinless through a life of temptation, and presented it to His Father as the first-fruits of a renewed humanity. *Vid*. for a fuller exposition of this theory, next Lecture.

God and man in His own person; what was done in one portion, in the sample, being "virtually accomplished in the whole."

Addressing ourselves now to the question, what is the worth of this theory of our Lord's humanity, held by the Adoptianists in the eighth century, and revived by Menken and Irving in the nineteenth, one remark occurs at the outset, viz., that the theory wears on its face as much the look of an extreme, as the very different one propounded by Hilary. *Primâ facie*, one is disposed to pronounce, that if Hilary made too much of the miraculous conception, the present theory errs as far in the opposite direction, of making too little of it. One is at a loss to see why, under this theory, Jesus should not have descended from Adam by ordinary generation, as He could not have been made more of a partaker in the sinfulness of the human nature by that method of birth than He actually was: not to mention that even if the opposite were true, that ought not, in the theory, to be an objection to, but rather a recommendation of, the method of ordinary generation, inasmuch as the very *raison d'être* of the theory is to make Christ in His humanity in all things like His brethren. It is true, indeed, that Irving speaks of the manner of Christ's conception as having the effect of taking away original sin.[1] But this is simply a quibble; for he explains his meaning by remarking that Christ was not a human *person*, never had personal subsistence as a mere man. Beyond a doubt, the theory requires that original sin should be ascribed to Christ; for original sin is a vice of fallen human *nature;* and the doctrine that our Lord's human nature was fallen, means, if it means anything, that it was tainted with original sin. And in this taint not merely the body but the soul of Jesus must be held to have participated; for whatever theory may be held as to the origin of souls, whether the traducian or the creatian, it is certain that the soul, in becoming wedded to the body, shares its mortal state. That Irving was aware of what the consequence of his theory required at this point, is manifest from his using the following argument against the opinion that Christ's soul was pre-existent: " Moreover,

[1] *Incarnation Opened,* p. 159.

then, creation hath not fallen wholly, for this pre-existent soul hath never found a fall; and, being united with the body of Christ, is still the creature in the unfallen state; and so the better half of the man Christ is unfallen, and and the other half of Him is fallen. Strange conjunction, and heterogeneous mixture!"[1] So that the influence of the Holy Ghost did not avail to keep even the soul of Jesus untainted by the fall, not to speak of His body!

Another thing very forcibly strikes the mind of one who has perused the literature of this theory, viz., the rhetorical inexactitude, and absence of carefully discriminated thought, characteristic of its advocates.[2] This feature is particularly noticeable in Irving. For example, he asserts, over and over again, that Christ's flesh was mortal and corruptible, without ever asking or deliberately considering whether these terms might not bear more than one meaning, but habitually using them as an equivalent for "fallen." And yet he himself uses at least one of the two words in two distinct senses. In many places he employs the word "mortal" in accordance with the requirement of his theory, as meaning, doomed of necessity to endure death, the curse of sin. Yet in one place he speaks of death, in relation to Christ, as a thing "which He was capable of as being in the fallen state, though not obliged to it as perfectly holy."[3] Mortal, *i. e.*, signifies capable of dying, and this is held to be a distinctive attribute of the fallen state! Another example of inexact thinking may be found in the manner in which Irving slumps together sin, guilt, disease, infirmity.[4] Like Hilary, he makes no distinction between sinless infirmities and *vitia;* extremes meeting here, only to opposite intents, the ancient Father denying to Christ all share in infirmity to save Him from *vitium*, the modern orator ascribing to Him a share in the vice of our nature,

---

[1] *Incarnation Opened*, p. 121.

[2] Ullmann, *Die Sündlosigkeit Jesu*, p. 119, characterizes the advocates of this theory as *meist schwärmerische Leute* (enthusiasts). He refers to several authors whose works I have not seen, viz., Dippel, Eschrich, Fend, and Peter Poiret. Of Menken he does not speak, but the name of Irving is alluded to.

[3] *Incarnation Opened*, p. 188.

[4] *Ibid.* pp. 174, 320: "All infirmity, sin, and guilt gathered into one." "All sins, infirmities, and diseases nestled in it."

because He unquestionably partook of our infirmities. Yet another instance of rhetorical inaccuracy, where carefully discriminated thought was specially called for, is afforded in the loose way in which Irving handles the subject of temptation. He makes no attempt to ascertain the conditions under which, and the extent to which, temptation is possible to a holy being living a human life in this world in a sentient but sinless nature; but seems to assume that temptation can be a reality only when it proceeds, as it often does in us, from evil lusts originating in a vice of disposition. Thus he says in one place: "I believe it to be necessary unto salvation that a man should believe that Christ's soul was so held in possession by the Holy Ghost, and so supported by the divine nature, as that it never assented unto an evil suggestion, and never originated an evil suggestion; while, upon the other hand, His flesh was of that mortal and corruptible kind which is liable to all forms of evil suggestion and temptation, through its participation in a fallen nature and a fallen world; and that thus, though at all points assailable through His flesh, He was in all respects holy; seeing wickedness consisteth not in being tempted, but in yielding to the temptation. This, I say, I consider to be an article of faith necessary to salvation; and the opposite of it, which holdeth that His flesh was unfallen, and not liable to all temptation by sin, nor conscious to it, I hold to be a virtual denial of His humanity."[1] The assumption here is, that unfallen flesh is not liable to temptation; yet such liability is held to be essential to the truth of humanity, whence it follows that Adam was either not a veritable man before the fall, or that, unfallen though he was, he was nevertheless liable to all temptation by sin. In another place our author triumphantly asks: "Doth any one doubt that there was in the flesh of Christ a repugnancy to suffer, a liability to be tempted in all things as we are tempted, and which was only prevented from falling before temptation by the faith of His Father's promises, and by the upholding of the Holy Spirit? Then I ask that man, What is Christ?—a man? No; for even unfallen manhood was disposed to fall into

[1] *Incarnation Opened*, p. 126.

sin. A fallen man? No; for fallen manhood doth nothing but sin. A creature? No; for defectibility is the very thing which distinguisheth creature from Creator."[1] Here we observe the confusion, before noticed, of sinless infirmity with a morally vitiated condition, a repugnancy to suffer being cited as evidence that Christ's human nature was fallen; and the consequent neglect to inquire how far sinless infirmity goes in accounting for "the liability to be tempted in all things as we are," which it is coolly assumed all opponents of the theory advocated must in consistency deny.

From the foregoing remarks it is manifest that there are certain questions bearing on the relation of our Lord's humanity to the fall, which require much more careful handling than they have received from the parties just adverted to, in order to an intelligent and sound decision of the important issue which their speculations raised. These questions may be stated in this way. Assuming that the human nature of Christ was unfallen, untainted by the corruption which is commonly called original sin, how does it stand related to the things which we are accustomed to regard as the effects and penalty of sin, such as disease and death? and further, on the same assumption, what limitations result, in Christ's experience of temptation?—the topic in which we are at present specially interested.

As to the former of these two questions, it is by no means an easy one to answer properly, as the history of its treatment shows. It formed one of the subjects of controversy between the different sects of the Monophysites in the sixth century; one party, the followers of Severus, Monophysite Bishop of Antioch, named Theodosians, and on account of their tenets nicknamed by their opponents *Phthartolatrists*, maintaining that Christ's body before the resurrection was mortal and corruptible; another party, the followers of Julian, Bishop of Halicarnassus, named Gajanites, and by their opponents nicknamed *Apthartodoketists*, maintaining, on the contrary, that Christ's body before, as after the resurrection, was in itself incorruptible and immortal, enduring hunger, pain, death, only by an act of will and by way

[1] *Incarnation Opened*, p. 170.

of economy, all sufferings and wants being foreign to His human nature, as indeed they were to man before the fall. The Emperor Justinian espoused the cause of the latter party, and endeavoured to get their view recognised by the Church as orthodox; but in this he failed, and the disputed question was allowed to remain undecided, the feeling probably being, that there was something to be said for both sides. Coming down to our own times, we find that something is said on both sides, by different men at one in regard to our fundamental assumption, and even by the same men. Thus, for example, an orthodox German commentator on the Epistle to the Hebrews, Riehm, in reference to the statement that Christ took flesh and blood in the same manner as we possess it, remarks: "It would be quite contrary to the sense of the writer to say that Christ took human nature as it was before the fall, in its original power and completeness. The children are such as need to be sanctified, and their flesh and blood, in which Christ took part likewise, is the human corporeal nature as weakened through the curse of sin, receptive to all outward impressions tending to tempt or to cause pain, and liable to death."[1] Yet this same writer, expounding the doctrine laid down in the fourth chapter of the Epistle, concerning Christ's experience of temptation, with express reference to Menken's views, recognises in the qualifying clause, χωρὶς ἁμαρτίας, a double limit to that experience, and understands it as not only excluding a sinful issue in connection with all temptations whatsoever, but as exempting from a certain class of temptations, those, viz., whose source is ἰδία ἐπιθυμία, there being in Christ no inborn sinful desire, no natural inclination to sin; His human nature, on the contrary, being perfectly free from sinful bias and evil lust.[2] Another better known German theologian, Ebrard, on the other hand, teaches that the *status humilis*, assumed by Christ in becoming man, consisted in a return to the condition of Adam before the fall; and yet with this doctrine in full view, he also maintains that Christ assumed humanity as it

---

[1] *Der Lehrbegriff des Hebräerbriefes dargestellt, und mit verwandten Lehrbegriffen verglichen*, 1868; vid. p. 314.
[2] *Ibid.* p. 322.

stood under the consequences of sin, that being, in his opinion, the very import of the phrase, in the Epistle to the Philippians, μορφὴν δούλου λαβών.[1] Here we have not only two doctors agreed on the main point differing from each other, but one of them, in appearance at least, contradicting himself.

This perplexing diversity, or seeming oscillation of opinion, is accounted for partly by the fact that the fallen and the unfallen states, physically considered, are not in all respects diverse, and partly by variation of the point of view from which the Incarnation and its design are regarded. As to the former, the state of Adam unfallen was one intermediate between inevitable subjection to death and absolute immunity from death. His body was mortal, in the sense in which every material organism must be mortal, that is not yet glorified or spiritualized, but dependent on outward nature, and standing in need of food, drink, sleep, and breath. Had he stood in his integrity, there is reason to believe that he would have passed from a corruptible to an incorruptible state, without tasting of death. On the other hand, when he fell, what had before been but a possibility was converted into a doom: he was left to the operation of natural laws which would not fail in due time to bring about decay and dissolution, if disease did not intervene to produce the result sooner. Mortal before, in the sense of possessing a body *de facto* capable of dying, and physically liable to the chance of death; he was mortal now, in the sense that he was, for his sin, deprived of the privilege of being raised above that capacity or liability, and doomed to remain on the level at which his trial found him, till the actual experience of death overtook him. The liability was common to the two states; the doom to remain under it, instead of rising above it, was a part of the penalty of transgression. Now the Son of God, in becoming man, certainly took what was common to both states. He took a body, mortal in the sense of being physically capable of and liable to death; a body which could be de-

---

[1] *Christliche Dogmatik*, ii. p. 220: compare ii. p. 34, where the μορφῂ δούλου is defined as "die der unter den Folgen der Sünde stehenden Menschheit." For the reconciliation of these two propositions, see ii. pp. 215-224.

prived of vitality by hunger, thirst, exposure to cold, by a fall from a precipice or by the thrust of a spear, and which, however sound in constitution and all vital organs, was not proof against evil influences in its environment, such as those of an unwholesome atmosphere tainted and poisoned by disease, putrefaction, malaria. *Emisit animam, non amisit*, said one of the ancient Fathers; and a modern writer, quoting the remark, says of Christ, that " He could, by an exercise of divine power, die without doing and without knowing sin."[1] Such language would convey a false impression were it understood to mean, that it was necessary that Christ should put forth divine power in order to bring about miraculously a state of death, which, otherwise, the pain of the cross and the spear-wound had been impotent to produce. Christ did doubtless die freely, not by necessity; but His freedom showed itself in His allowing Himself to fall into the hands of His enemies, and in permitting the physical causes of death to work their natural effect. It was not a miracle that the crucified and pierced One died; the miracle would have been had He lived in spite of nails and spear. Thus understood, mortality may properly be reckoned as belonging to the truth of Christ's humanity, as it is by the Reformed theologian Sadeel, when he says, " The Word assumed human nature, mortal, patible, and sin excepted, like us."[2]

These observations prepare us for understanding the peculiar position taken up by Ebrard, in reference to the *status humilis* in which Christ placed Himself by becoming man. On the one hand, he holds that that state, inasmuch as it involved merely the possibility of death, was a return to the state of Adam before the fall. The unfallen state he describes as consisting in these particulars: Moral integrity, or the power of not sinning, the *posse non peccare;* dominion over the creation; perfect physical health in a body not bearing the seeds of death in itself; yet a body for which, by reason of its constitution, death was a possibility convertible into a certainty in case of sin. The state

[1] Dods, *On the Incarnation of the Eternal Word*, pp. 99, 165.
[2] *De veritate humanae naturae Christi*, distinctio vi.: Ergo verbum assumpsit humanam naturam mortalem, patibilem, et nobis, excepto peccato, consimilem.

assumed by Christ he holds to have been exactly similar to this, embracing moral integrity, that is, not the impossibility of sinning, but the power not to sin: dominion over the creation manifested in His miracles; a physical organism free from the seeds of death, perfectly healthy, and so harmonizing with the morally healthy soul, yet capable of being injured by unwholesome natural influences, and of undergoing death by mechanical violence, not to say by disease in case of abnormal moral development. But, on the other hand, He holds that the *status humilis*, just because it involved even the *possibility* of death, in reality was the state of human nature as under the consequences of sin. For had there been no fall, had man stood his moral trial, the physical condition suited to a state of probation, that, viz., which involved the possibility of death, would have given place to a state involving absolute immunity from death; and the Incarnation (for even in that case there would have been an Incarnation, according to our author) would have consisted in the assumption of humanity in a glorified form, a *status humilis* being wholly excluded.[1]

That this ingenious theory does go a certain length in the solution of a difficult problem cannot be denied; but it is open to question whether it goes far enough in the direction of placing our Lord's humanity under the physical consequences of the curse. Ebrard's judgment is liable to suspicion, because his eye is not single, his aim being to construct a theory of the Incarnation, which, while not

---

[1] *Christliche Dogmatik*, ii. p. 221. On the two senses in which the term "mortal" may be used, see p. 222, note 2; and on the respects in which Christ's body was and was not liable to disease, see note 3. p. 223. Ebrard alludes to the medical distinction between health *dem Breitengrade nach*, and health *dem Höhengrade nach*, and says that one is healthy, in the former sense, who bears in himself no disposition to disease; and in the latter sense, whose organs, whatever their disposition to disease may be, are *de facto* for the time in a healthy working condition. Of one healthy in the former sense, he remarks that it is possible for him to be unhealthy in the second sense (the inverse case being equally true). Though perfectly sound in constitution, he may be injured in his vitals by cold, wounding, or poison, or even in the course of physical development. The former sort of health he ascribes to Christ, that is, perfect soundness of constitution, but still not such as to exclude diseases arising from various causes, such as diseases of development in childhood.

losing sight of the reason assigned in Scripture for that event, the redemption of sinners, shall at the same time satisfy the requirements of a wider plan, that, viz., of providing a crown for creation and a centre for humanity in a Pleromatic Man, endowed with all human gifts, and possessing divine attributes in the form adapted to the human mode of existence.[1] Is there any reason to believe that Jesus of Nazareth was the Pleromatic Man speculative theologians make Him out to be? In physical respects, for example; having a body the perfect model of human form, absolutely sound in constitution, happily blending together all temperaments,[2] so that to the second Adam may be applied the language in which poetry has described the first:

> "In native worth and honour clad,
> With beauty, courage, strength adorned,
> Erect, with front serene,
> He stands a man, the Lord, and King of nature all."

Do we not lose in reality what we gain in ideality by this theory? Is not the particular interest of fallen humanity somewhat sacrificed thereby to the supposed universal interest of creation? For what sorrow-laden men need is not an Apollo, the aesthetically perfect embodiment of manly beauty, but a Christ in whom they can confidently recognise a veritable Brother; and for this purpose a body like a broken earthen vessel, and a vision marred more than any man, may be better qualifications than the most classic beauty of face and form that ever Greek sculptor hewed out of marble. The wisest man of Greece represented Eros, son of Poros and Penia, as far from being tender, sleek, and beautiful as many supposed; but lean, ill-favoured, shoeless, and houseless, a poor penniless wanderer sleeping on the bare ground in the street, or on the wayside.[3] The striking picture was an unconscious prophecy of incarnate Love, a remarkable divination of what

---

[1] See Appendix, Note D, Lecture iv.   [2] See Appendix, Note A.
[3] Plato: ΣΥΜΠΟΣΙΟΝ Η ΠΕΡΙ ΕΡΩΤΟΣ (Sokrates loquitur) ἅτε οὖν Πόρου καὶ Πενίας υἱὸς ὢν ὁ Ἔρως, ἐν τοιαύτῃ τύχῃ καθέστηκε· πρῶτον μὲν πένης ἀεί ἐστι, καὶ πολλοῦ δεῖ ἁπαλός τε καὶ καλός, οἷον οἱ

it became such Love to be and look like, even a man of sorrow, in all things like unto His brethren, a participant in, that He might be a succourer to them under, all their infirmities. And even such was Jesus Christ. That He actually experienced disease is nowhere said; that He could not experience it we have no right to affirm.[1] The just view seems to be that expressed by Henry Alting, who ascribes to Christ the infirmities and defects, not of this or that individual, such as leprosy or blindness, but those of man's whole nature springing from the corruption of the same through sin.[2]

Passing now to the other question, viz., how far does the assumption that our Lord's human nature was entirely free from sinful bias limit His experience of temptation? it must certainly be admitted, as Riehm has pointed out, that one source of temptation is thereby cut off,—that, viz., indicated by the expression ὑπὸ τῆς ἰδίας ἐπιθυμίας, occurring in the Epistle of James. Christ was not and could not be tempted, in the sense of being "drawn away of His own lust, and enticed." His temptations were χωρὶς ἁμαρτίας, "without sin," not only in their *result*, but in their origin. But from this fact it cannot justly be inferred that Christ's experience of temptation must have been both narrow in range and slight in degree. For, in the first place, the same temptations may arise from various causes, and therefore the absence of a particular cause in any given case does not necessarily imply exemption from the temptation. Both the coward and the brave man may be tempted to shrink from the fight; the one, by effeminacy of spirit and an ignoble love of life; the other, by an involuntary sensitiveness of nature, or by a generous concern for his family. One man may be tempted by angry passion or by greed to take a neighbour's

---

πολλοί οἴονται, ἀλλὰ σκληρὸς, καὶ αὐχμηρὸς, καὶ ἀνυπόδητος, κτὶ ἄοικος· χαμαιπετὴς ἀεὶ ὤν, καὶ ἄστρωτος ἐπὶ θύραις, καὶ ἐν ὁδοῖς ὑπαιθρίοις κοιμώμενος.

[1] See note, p. 262, for Ebrard's view on this point.

[2] Loci communes, pars i. p. 145: Infirmitates et defectus, non hujus vel illius individui, ut lepra (Matt. viii. 2), caecitas (John ix. 1) sed *totius naturae*, ex ejusdem per peccatum corruptione suscepti. As examples of infirmity, Alting mentions *tristitia, dolor, timor, ira*, in the mind; in the body, *lassitudo ex itinere, sudor, lachrymae*.

life; another man may be tempted by the very intensity of his love to slay his own son, believing it to be his duty in this way to show that he loves God more than any created good. To ascertain this very thing was the object of Abraham's temptation, if we may infer the design from the declared result, which is stated in these terms: "Now I know that thou fearest God, seeing thou hast not withheld thy son, thine only son, from me." Without calling in question the reality of an objective command, it is not difficult to conceive that the command addressed itself to, and found a fulcrum in, an intense desire in Abraham's own heart to be himself satisfied on the same point. Of two possible careers, men may be tempted to choose that one which is not their true vocation, from very opposite motives. One man may be misled by vanity or ambition, eager to attain social distinction; another may be sorely tempted to forsake the better way, by a clear perception that the road along which gifts and conscience bid him travel will be rough, thorny, steep, and in all respects most repulsive to flesh and blood. So was Jesus tempted to choose the path of a worldly Messiahship. In His pure, holy soul the passions of vanity and pride had no place; but His temptation in the wilderness was not on that account a mere shamfight. Two ways were set before His mental view,—how, whether by objective Satanic suggestion, or by a vision in which God's thoughts and the world's concerning Messiah's career were placed in contrast side by side, it is immaterial to our present purpose to inquire;—but, in point of fact, the two ways were set before His mind, the way of popularity on the one hand, and the way of the cross on the other; and though the hosannas of the mob, and the insincere homage of the higher classes of society, might have small attractions for His lowly spirit, the wholesale desertion of spurious disciples, the incapacity of even genuine disciples to give Him the comfort of sympathetic companionship as He walked through the valley of the shadow of death, the hatred of sanctimonious religionists and of selfish unscrupulous politicians, the treason of a false friend, the infuriated crowd crying, "Away with him, away with him," the horrors of crucifixion,—these all passing as dark possibilities in panoramic view before His eye, were surely enough to make those "forty days and forty nights Christ was fasting in the wild," days and nights of most real temptation, of soul-trouble and agony, whereof forgetfulness of physical wants was but the natural result, as it was the fitting accompaniment! For we must now observe, in the second place, that not only may the same kind of temptation proceed from morally opposite causes, but the temptation which proceeds from a holy source may be in degree fiercer than that which has its origin in sinful lust. A familiar illustration will make this plain. Suppose the case of two men engaged in trade: one, a conscientious man, whose maxim is: "First righteous, then as prosperous as possible;" the other, a man not troubled with a passionate love of righteousness, vulgar in moral tone, and bent above all things on getting on in the world. Both are needy, and are also placed in circumstances which bring gain within their reach, provided they do not stick at a little fraud. Look now into the breasts of these men, and see what takes place there. The one says to himself, "I am embarrassed for want of money. I am not able to meet my obligations; my wife's anxious face, and my children's pinched features, make me wretched when I return home, and haunt me continually in the market-place. Here is an opportunity of obtaining relief from my difficulties by an act of dishonesty not seldom committed by men of good commercial standing. But, no; get thee behind me, Satan —away with the hateful thought! I dare not lie, I will rather starve and beg than directly or circuitously tell an untruth." The other says: "Ha! here at last is a chance for me. I have been miserably kept down hitherto. I shall get my head above water now; I see my way clear to making a very considerable profit by this transaction. No doubt I shall have to indulge in a little sharp practice. But what of that? Everybody does it; it is but a common trick of trade, and quite respectable; and whether it is respectable or not, it is necessary, and I must do it." Which, now, of these two men has the keener experience of temptation? Surely the virtuous, conscientious man. He passes through a kind of Gethsemane, an agony of bloody sweat, a mortal struggle between love for wife and children and desire to escape the disgrace of insolvency on the one hand, and a moral revulsion from iniquity on the other. The other man has no agony—he has not virtue enough for that; there is nothing in him to stop the current of evil suggestion and make it rage. He is not so much a tempted one, as one who has been drawn away of his own lust and enticed.

It thus appears that sinful dispositions, though certainly making men more liable to *fall* before temptation, do not increase the painful sense of being tempted, but rather diminish it. As a matter of psychological experience, it is the good man, not the bad, that is tempted. Temptation presupposes an attitude of antagonism to evil, and springs out of the difficulties encountered by all who make an earnest attempt to maintain this attitude. It is in this way that temptation is regarded by the author of the Epistle to the Hebrews, in connection with his doctrine concerning the sympathy of Christ with the tempted. The purpose he has in view is, to comfort Christians under the difficulties connected with the maintenance of their Christian profession, which were in effect so many temptations to apostasy; and the comfort he offers is: Jesus can sympathize with you, for He was in all respects tempted as you are, without sin. And from what has been said, it appears that, notwithstanding the qualifying clause, Jesus was the companion of tempted Christians in these two respects at least: He shared with them the attitude of resistance to evil, and He maintained that attitude against real, immense, and manifold difficulties. His difficulties were not, indeed, in all respects the same as those of His followers. A Christian, for example, may have to do battle even unto blood with a lust or appetite, or old habit that wars against his soul. Christ had no such battle to fight. He endured the contradiction of sinners, not that of inclinations to sin. But does that fact cut the regenerated drunkard off from the sympathy of his Redeemer? No; for in all *essential* respects his temptation was experienced by Him who knew no sin. The experience of the disciple consists in a conflict between the will of the spirit and the desire of the flesh; the experience of the Lord was essentially the same when He said, "Let this cup pass," with the *accidental*, though most momentous difference, that the desire of His sentient nature was in itself innocent. The disciple, in obedience to the will of God, has to put away the cup his flesh craves; the Master, in obedience to the same will, had to drink the cup from which His flesh shrunk. And while the temptations of both are *essentially* the same, it is well for the disciple that the accident of sinfulness was not present in the desires of his Lord's human nature. For had it been otherwise, what had been gained? Only companionship in moral weakness: an attribute which may qualify for receiving succour from the strong, but certainly not for being a succourer to the weak.

The conclusion, then, to which the foregoing discussion leads us is, that we need have no hesitation in understanding the qualifying clause "without sin" as involving the exclusion from Christ's human nature of all sinful proclivity, lest, by so interpreting it, we imperil the reality or the thoroughness of His experience of temptation, and rob ourselves of the consolations arising out of His experimentally acquired sympathy with the tempted.[1] But now another question arises in connection with this same qualifying clause, of which some notice must be taken before the present subject can be regarded as discussed on all its sides. "Without sin," by universal consent, signifies, at least, "tempted, but never with sinful result." The question readily suggests itself: How was this invariably happy issue of all temptation secured or guaranteed? It is a question much more easy to ask than to answer, for the mind of an inquirer is distracted by opposite interests, whose reconciliation is a hard speculative problem. On the one hand, there is a most legitimate jealousy of any method of guaranteeing a sinless issue which tends to undermine the reality of Christ's temptations; on the other, there is the not less strong feeling, that any other than a sinless result in His case cannot be seriously contemplated as a real possibility. Under the influence of the former motive,

[1] *Vid.* Appendix, Note B, for some remarks on the views of naturalistic theologians on the subject of "the Flesh."

one is inclined to describe Christ's moral state by the phrase *potuit non peccare*, thereby ascribing to Him a power of choosing and doing the right, which, however, implies the opposite alternative as a possibility. But when we allow our minds to dwell on the dignity of Christ's person, and on the soteriological importance of His sinlessness, we are impelled to alter our mode of expression, and for the phrase, *potuit non peccare*, to substitute the stronger one, *non potuit peccare*, and maintain an impossibility of sinning. Which of the two phrases is the more appropriate, or are they both neccessary to express the whole truth; and if so, how can they be reconciled, so that the one shall not virtually cancel the other? On these questions, as we might have expected, opinions differ widely; some preferring the weaker phrase, as the true description of Christ's moral condition during His life on earth; others insisting on the stronger, as alone doing justice to the moral perfection of the incarnate Son of God; while a third class see realized in Christ the unity of moral integrity and moral perfection, at once the power not to sin and that which made sin impossible. Whether this third position can be speculatively justified or not, there can be no doubt, at all events, that the combination of the two formulas most accurately and satisfactorily represents the facts. The *potuit non* signifies that Christ's experience of temptation was real; that in His temptations He was conscious of a force tending to draw Him to evil. The *non potuit*, on the other hand, signifies that there was in Christ a counter force stronger than the force of temptation, which certainly, though not without effort, ensures in every case a sinless result. In this view of our Lord's experience of temptation, which makes it consist in a constant conflict of two unequal opposing forces, it becomes very important to provide that a due proportion between the conflicting powers shall be maintained. If the truth represented by the *potuit non*—viz., that the force of temptation was strong enough to create the consciousness of a struggle—be overlooked, then the whole curriculum of moral trial through which Jesus passed on earth degenerates at once into a mere stage performance. This one-sided tendency characterized the ancient Church, and finds apt expression in the saying of John Damascenus, already quoted, that Christ " repelled and dissipated the assaults of the enemy like smoke."[1] In modern times this doketic view finds no acceptance; theologians of all schools being agreed that the forces of evil, with which the Son of Man fought so noble a fight, were not shadows, but substantial and formidable foes. Even those who, with the Catholic Church of all ages, believe in the essential divinity of Christ, energetically protest against the divine element being brought in as an overwhelming force on the side of good, so as to make the force at work on the side of evil relatively zero. The divinity, while regarded as potentially infinite, is conceived of as, in its applied form, only a finite power barely sufficient to counterbalance another operating in Christ's person in an opposite direction. In the eloquent words of a Scottish theologian, the work of the divine nature is "not to raise Christ's suffering nature to such a height of glorious power as would render all trial slight and contemptible; but to confer upon it such strength as would be infallibly sufficient, but not more than sufficient, just to bear Him through the fearful strife that awaited Him, without His being broken or destroyed,—so that He might thoroughly experience, in all the faculties of His soul and body, the innumerable sensations of overpowering difficulty, and exhausting toil, and fainting weakness, and tormenting anguish, though by the Holy Ghost preserved from sin,— and might touch the very brink of danger, though not be swept away by it; and feel all the horror of the precipice, but without falling over."[2]

This passage may be accepted as a satisfactory statement

---

[1] Lecture ii. p. 72.

[2] Sermon on the sympathy of Christ, by the late Professor M'Lagan, published in the work of Mr. Dods, *On the Incarnation of the Eternal Word;* see pp. 299, 300 of that work. This admirable discourse contains some well-selected examples illustrative of the truth, that temptations arising out of sinless infirmities may be far fiercer than those which arise out of sinful appetites. The author compares the cravings of the intemperate palate for wine, with the natural thirst of the parched traveller in the desert; the pampered appetite of the epicure, with the ravenous hunger of the famishing man, whose fearful power is exhibited in the story of the siege of Samaria, when mothers bargained to slay in succession their own children.

of the view of Christ's temptations held in common by Christologists of the Reformed tendency, who have ever been anxious so to conceive of our Lord's person, as to leave to the forces to temptation ample room wherein to display themselves. And as a clear exposition of what is required, in order that Christ's experience of temptation may possess the maximum degree of reality or intensity, without prejudice to His sinlessness, this statement leaves nothing to be desired. It is manifest, however, that the sentences quoted contain rather the statement than the *solution* of a problem. The necessity for an adjustment of the conflicting powers, so that they shall bear some finite proportion to each other, is distinctly recognised; but how the adjustment is brought about, how the potentially infinite force becomes finite in effect, is not explained. The question obviously carries us back to the already discussed problem of the kenosis. Moreover, even after that question has been disposed of, another comes up for consideration— viz., in what way is the divine force, become finite, made available as an aid to the successful resistance of temptation? The only hint at an answer to this question in the foregoing extract is contained in the words, "though by the Holy Ghost preserved from sin." The hint, brief though it be, condenses the substance of what the orthodox Reformed Christology has said on the subject to which it refers. That Christology, as we know, lays great stress on the influence of the Holy Spirit as the source or cause of Christ's holiness, representing the human wisdom and virtue of our Lord as qualities produced in His human nature by the Logos *through His own Spirit*.[1] This view may be construed to mean that the divine power, as an aid to holiness against temptation to sin, acted not directly as a physical force, but as a moral force taking the form of ethical motive. Thus construed, the representation in question is one of great importance; for undoubtedly the victory of Christ over temptation, to have ethical value, must be ethically brought about. It must not be the matter-of-course result of the physical ground of His being, but the effect brought about by the operations of the Holy

---

[1] *Vid.* Lecture iii. p. 125.

Spirit dwelling in Him in plenary measure, helping Him to exercise strong faith and to cherish lively hope, and inspiring Him with a love to His Father and to men, and with a consuming zeal for righteousness, which should be more than a match for all the temptations that might be directed against Him by Satan and an evil world, acting on and through a pure but tremulously sensitive human nature. So regarded, Christ's strife with sin is a fair fight, and His conquest a moral achievement, and the physical divine ground is simply the guarantee that gracious influences shall be supplied to the adequate extent. Doubtless the mystery remains how the guarantee comes into play, so as to ensure the desired result, through the operation of such influences. But the burden of that mystery presses equally on all who, whatever their theory of Christ's person, agree in maintaining His sinlessness; and no advocate of any modern theory has succeeded in saying anything better fitted to remove the load, than what was wont to be said by the expounders of the old Reformed Christology. Schleiermacher ensures Christ's sinlessness by a doctrine of determinism which excludes moral freedom, and which is able to dispense with the miracle of the Virgin-birth by making Christ's whole sinless life a physical miracle.[1] Rothe seeks his guarantee partly in the supernatural origin of Jesus, involving freedom from original sin; partly in His comparatively perfect upbringing in a circle which, through the Hebrew Scriptures, was in possession of the means of knowing fully the difference between good and evil, so that there was no risk of the holy child falling into sin through ignorance; partly in the moral energy acquired in the course of thirty years spent in virtuous retirement, which Jesus, in ripe manhood, brought to the hard task of His public career,[2]—all which, taken together, rendered sinlessness possible, or even, we may admit, probable, but not certain. The adherents of the modern kenotic theory have not been much more successful than these advocates of a purely humanitarian view of our Lord's person. One says, that Jesus would, in fact, maintain His innocence was foreseen,

---

[1] *Der christliche Glaube*, Band ii. p. 67 (§ 97).
[2] *Theologische Ethik*, Band ii. pp. 280, 281.

and therefore the risk involved in the Incarnation was run.'¹ Another ascribes to Jesus a *non posse peccare* from the outset, as a distinction necessarily belonging to a theanthropic uncreated personality, whose becoming in time was preceded by an ethical being, the benefit of which He reaped on entering into the incarnate state.² A third contents himself with saying that the incarnate Son of God could not deny Himself; the man Jesus, therefore, could not sin, His human historical will could not enter into contradiction with the eternal divine will dwelling within it, and the eternal God became man just because this was the way to certain victory over sin.³ A fourth, while admitting that a *posse peccare* was a possibility involved in freedom, represents it as only an abstract possibility which could not in Christ's case be realized.⁴ A fifth lays stress on the predominant *passion* of Christ's will preventing the slightest trembling in the balance, while the free will of all other men is intrinsically indifferent;⁵ which was certainly a characteristic of our Lord as a matter of fact; but the question forces itself on us, Whence this difference between Christ and all other men? The fact is the very thing to be accounted for. Yet another, to mention just one more, teaches that the *potuit non peccare* and the *non potuit peccare*, so far from excluding, rather imply each other; that the sinlessness of Christ is accounted for, neither by His free ethical fight with temptation alone, nor by His holy natural development alone, but by the union of both; and that the guarantee that the possibility of evil should never become a reality lay, not in Christ's virtue or innocence, the relation of merely negative goodness to temptation being always doubtful, not in the divine nature viewed apart from the human, any more than in the human nature viewed apart from the divine, but in the indissoluble bond between the two natures; a bond which could be strained to the uttermost by the power of temptation, but which

---

¹ Gess. See Lecture iv. p. 150.
² Liebner. See Appendix, Note B, Lecture iv.
³ Hofmann. See Appendix, Note C, Lecture iv.
⁴ Thomasius, *Christi Person und Werk*, ii. p. 126.
⁵ Mr. Hutton, *Essays, Theological and Literary*, p. 261. See Appendix, Note F, Lecture iv.

could never be broken asunder. Of all the utterances of the kenotic school this is the most satisfactory, and it emanates from one whose Christological theory comes nearest to the Reformed type.[1]

II. In the same book of the New Testament in which Christ is represented as passing through an experience of temptation, He is also spoken of as the subject of *moral development*. The tempted one is conceived of as in course of being *perfected*, and when the curriculum of temptation is ended He is regarded as *perfect*. The notion of perfecting, τελείωσις, is applied to Christ four times in the Epistle to the Hebrews. It is first introduced in the second chapter, where the Captain of salvation is represented as being perfected through sufferings;[2] it reappears in the fifth chapter, where it is said of the Son of God that, being made perfect, He became the Author of eternal salvation;[3] it occurs for the third time in the seventh chapter, where the Son, in the state of exaltation after His state of humiliation is past, is described as perfected for evermore;[4] and finally, it may be recognised in that place of the twelfth chapter where Jesus is called the leader and perfecter of faith; the idea being, that faith was one of the things in which Jesus Himself was perfected, and in which, therefore, He is a model to all Christians.[5]

That these two doctrines—viz. that Christ on earth was tempted, and that during the same period He was the sub-

---

[1] Martensen, *Die christliche Dogmatik*, pp. 263, 264: Die Möglichkeit des Bösen regt sich auch in dem zweiten Adam; dass aber diese Möglichkeit niemals Wirklichkeit wird, wie in dem ersten Adam, sondern nur als der dunkle Grund für die Offenbarung der Heiligkeit dienen muss, dafür bürgt nicht die Tugend oder die Unschuld, denn deren Verhältniss zur Versuchung ist immer gar ungewiss und zweifelhaft, nicht die göttliche Natur in ihrer Trennung von der menschlichen, auch nicht die menschliche Natur in ihrer Trennung von der göttlichen, sondern das unauflösliche BAND zwischen der göttlichen und menschlichen Natur, ein Band das zwar bis zum äussersten Gegensatz und zur äussersten Spannung zwischen den Naturen gebogen und bewegt werden, niemals aber zerreissen kann (p. 264).

[2] Heb. ii. 10: διὰ παθημάτων τελειῶσαι.

[3] Heb. v. 9: καὶ τελειωθεὶς ἐγένετο τοῖς ὑπακούουσιν αὐτῷ πᾶσι αἴτιος σωτηρίας αἰωνίου.

[4] Heb. vii. 28: υἱὸν εἰς τὸν αἰῶνα τετελειωμένον.

[5] Heb. xii. 2: τὸν τῆς πίστεως ἀρχηγὸν καὶ τελειωτὴν Ἰησοῦν.

ject of a perfecting process—should be taught by the same inspired writer, so far from being surprising, is rather a matter of course. For the two doctrines imply each other, and are complementary of each other. Wherever there is temptation, there is something to be learned, something that is actually learned; if not the habit of watchfulness against some moral infirmity whose presence has been revealed by temptation at least the virtues of patience and sympathy, and the need and use of faith and prayer. On the other hand, wherever there is room for a process of perfecting, there is room also for temptation. For as the perfect state is a state temptation-proof, so a state short of perfection is a state of liability to be tried and proved by temptation, and capable of being advanced, by this very trial and proof, to the higher perfect state in which temptation can have no place, because neither in the subject nor in His environment do the necessary conditions any longer exist.

In these observations I proceed, it will be observed, on the assumption that the notion expressed by the term τελείωσις has an *ethical* import, as applied to Christ in the Epistle to the Hebrews. This has been disputed, and the statements referred to have been explained to signify that Christ, by His earthly experience, was qualified for His office as High Priest; that on His ascension into glory He was, so to speak, consecrated or solemnly installed as a Priest whose sacerdotal office should last for ever, a Priest after the order of Melchizedek; and that at the same time He entered into a state of perfect personal felicity, exempt now and for ever from the infirmities and miseries of the days of His flesh. But the truth is, the term in question covers all these ideas, and that of moral development over and above. The perfecting process has reference at once to Christ's *office*, to His *condition*, and to His *character*. These three aspects, far from being mutually exclusive or incompatible, rather imply each other. For example, suppose we understand the passage in the second chapter as signifying that, by suffering, the Captain of salvation was perfected, fully fitted for His office of Saviour, the question at once arises, In what does the outfit of a Captain of salvation consist? What if that outfit should be found to include very specially a bond of sympathy between Leader and led, based on a common experience of hardship, and inspiring in those who are to be conducted to glory unbounded confidence in their Conductor? Why, then, it would follow that an ethical ingredient enters into the process of official perfecting. The Captain becomes perfectly fit for His office by this means, among others, that through comradeship in suffering He learns that intense sympathy with His followers which gains their hearts, and so gives Him unlimited moral power over them. Or, again, suppose we take perfected as signifying *beatified*—introduced into a state of perfect felicity. Whenever we begin to consider what such a state involves, we perceive that an ethical element enters into it. Part of Christ's felicity in the state of exaltation consists in His being delivered from those infirmities to which He was subject in the state of humiliation, and by which He was exposed to powerful temptations. That is to say, Christ's entrance into heavenly bliss signifies this among other things, that He thereby passed from a state in which He could be tempted into a state in which He cannot be tempted,—a transition implying an ethical progress from the incomplete to the perfect.

It thus appears that, whether we start from the official or from the beatific point of view, we end at last in an ethical conception of the τελείωσις predicated of Christ. And there can be no doubt that the writer of the Epistle, in which the deep thought expressed by that word is found, gives to the ethical side marked prominence. When he speaks of Christ as perfected for His office, he adduces the proof of His perfection thus: "In that He Himself hath suffered, being tempted, He is able to succour them that are tempted."[1] Nor is this faculty of help connected with personal experience of temptation in a merely casual way, as if it would have made little difference though the experience had been dispensed with. On the contrary, a curriculum of temptation is represented as indispensable, by way of training for office. "Wherefore in all things it behoved Him to be made like unto His brethren, that He

[1] Heb. ii. 18.

might be a merciful and trustworthy High Priest in things pertaining to God, to make reconciliation for the sins of the people."¹ In the second passage, in which the idea of perfectification occurs, it might be very fairly contended that the ethical side was the one directly and immediately presented to view, inasmuch as the thought is introduced in connection with the statement that Christ, though a Son, yet learned *obedience* by the things which He suffered. It seems a very legitimate inference, that "being made perfect" means, perfected in the virtue of obedience. But granting that we ought rather to interpret the phrase as signifying perfected for office, still it is impossible to deny that in the writer's view the process of perfecting has an ethical aspect. Christ's obedience to His Father is regarded as a quality which fits Him for receiving in turn the obedience of others, and for being the Author of eternal salvation to all them that do obey Him. And this obedience of His is spoken of as something *learned;* and, reading backwards, we find that the learning was by no means easy, but very irksome indeed, to flesh and blood. Thus we get the thought that, in order to perfect fitness for the office of Saviour as a Royal Priest, Jesus, in the days of His flesh, in the school-days of His earthly life, underwent a process of moral training whose end was to perfect Him in the virtue of obedience, and which was adapted to that end by the tremendous severity of the tasks prescribed, and the trials proposed. The official perfecting thus embraces within it a process of moral perfecting, which leaves the subject thereof in a higher moral state at the end than it found Him at the beginning. And this idea of a moral growth is by no means slurred over by the writer; on the contrary, he employs all his powers of eloquence to give it the greatest possible breadth and vividness. Starting from the general principle that no right-minded man taketh to himself offices of honour and high responsibility, above all, such an office as that of the priesthood, but only in obedience to a divine call,² he ap-

¹ Heb. ii. 17.
² Heb. v. 4: καὶ οὐχ ἑαυτῷ τίς λαμβάνει τὴν τιμήν.

plies it to the case of Christ by the remark: "So also Christ glorified not Himself to be made an high priest."[1] Then, to show how utterly remote such a thought was from the Saviour's mind, how utterly innocent He was of the spirit of self-glorification, in connection with the office to which He was called by the voice of God in Scripture, the writer goes on to describe the agony in Gethsemane endured by the Great Priest, just before He passed through the rent veil of His flesh, to make an offering for the sin of the world.[2] It is as if he had said: "Jesus took the honour of the priesthood on Himself? Ah, no! there was no temptation to that, in connection with an office in which the Priest had to be at the same time *victim*. Let the agony in the garden bear witness that Jesus was not in the mood to arrogate to Himself the sacerdotal dignity. That agony was an awfully earnest, utterly sincere, while perfectly sinless, NOLO PONTIFEX FIERI on the part of One who realized the tremendous responsibilities of the post to which He was summoned, and who was unable for the moment to find any comfort in the thought of its honours and prospective joys." It almost seems as if the writer had it in mind to suggest a parallel between Christ passing through the struggle in the garden, and the high priest of Israel presenting an offering first for himself before officiating in behalf of the people,—a parallel to the extent that in both cases there was a confession of weakness. Such a parallel is suggested by the sacrificial expression "offered up," used in reference to Christ's prayers with strong crying and tears; and also by the statement that He was heard for His piety, which seems to hint that His offering was accepted, even as that of the high priest was wont to be. The high priest's sacrifice for himself was accepted because it was a sincere confession of sin; Christ's prayer for Himself was accepted because it was an unreserved confession of weakness, unaccompanied by sin, inasmuch as its last word was, "Not as I will, but as Thou wilt." The high priest was accepted for the piety of sincere penitence; Jesus was accepted for

[1] Heb. v. 5: οὕτως καὶ ὁ Χριστὸς οὐχ ἑαυτὸν ἐδόξασε γενηθῆναι ἀρχιερέα.
[2] Heb. v. 7.

the piety of filial submission, triumphing over the sinless, though extreme, weakness of sentient human nature.[1]

It thus appears that the writer of this Epistle, far from glossing over the contrast between the imperfect and the perfect states of Christ, rather makes it as glaring as possible. His manifest design is, to represent our Lord's weakness as going to the utmost limits short of actual disobedience and sin. He has a double purpose in view, one being to magnify the merit of an obedience loyally rendered under so trying circumstances—to show, in fact, that one who passed through such an *experimentum crucis* was indeed morally perfect. The other purpose is to make evident how thoroughly fitted Jesus is to sympathize with the weak, He Himself having been compassed about with so great infirmity. He portrays the agony in lurid colours, for the same reason that it is so carefully recorded in the Gospels, and, may we not add, for the same reason that Jesus Himself allowed His inward trouble to appear so plainly in the presence of three witnesses, by whom it might be reported to all the world. Had He thought of Himself only, He might, like many a sufferer, have played the stoic. But He thought of the weak of all ages; therefore He hid not His own weakness, but gave it full vent in prayers and tears, and loud cries and prostrations, falling forward all His length on the ground, now praying in articulate language, now uttering inarticulate groans, anon subsiding into silent weeping; His soul resembling the sea in a storm, when the great billows rise up at a distance from the shore, roll on majestically nearer and nearer, then break on the sands with a mighty noise audible to men even in their slumbers.

In the third place, where the notion now under discussion occurs in the Epistle, the ethical aspect is not less conspicuous than in the two preceding. The Son, constituted a Priest after the order of Melchizedek, not by the Leviti-

---

[1] So Hofmann, *Schriftbeweis*, ii. 399, to whom I am indebted for the thought in the text. Hofmann says: Jesu Flehen um Abwendung des Todesleidens ist gleicher Massen wie des Hohepriesters Opfer für sich selbst eine fromme Aeusserung der Schwachheit, nur mit dem Unterschiede, welcher zwischen der Schwachheit des sündigen Hohepriesters und der des sündlosen Heilands besteht.

cal law, but by the word of the oath, is described as "perfected for evermore," in contrast with the Old Testament high priests, who are described as "men having infirmity." The infirmity alluded to is such as lays men open to temptations, through which they often fall into sin; such, therefore, as, in the case of the high priests, was indirectly the cause why they had to offer a sacrifice for themselves before offering one for the people. The perfecting of the Son, consequently, must be held to consist in deliverance from infirmity of the same kind; infirmity, that is, through which, in the days of His flesh, He became liable to temptation, and sin became a possibility, though nothing more than a bare possibility for Him. To be liable to temptation is regarded as a morally incomplete state, and the perfect state is conceived of as a state of exaltation above the region of temptation, where there is no infirmity to be used as a fulcrum by the tempter, and no tempter to take advantage of an opportunity.

The τελείωσις of Christ, then, according to the representation of it given in the Epistle to the Hebrews, includes a process of moral perfecting. This process does not exhaust the idea; for the perfection ascribed to Christ after His departure from the world is a comprehensive name for His state of exaltation in all its aspects, whether regarded as the state in which He exercises His Melchizedek priesthood, or as that in which He is free from the miseries of this mortal life, and enjoys the felicity of the life unending; or as that in which He is for ever exempt from temptation, and raised above the position of one undergoing moral probation. All that is here insisted on is, that this last item forms an essential and important part of the idea. The exalted Christ is regarded by the writer of the Epistle as one now morally perfected; the earthly state of humiliation is regarded as a school of virtue, in which Christ had to learn, and did thoroughly learn, certain moral lessons; the experience of temptation is viewed in the light of a curriculum of ethical discipline, designed to make the tempted One master of certain high heroic arts, the arts to be mastered being those of *Patience, Obedience,* and *Sympathy.*

The fact having been thus ascertained, that the notion of

moral development as applied to Christ has a foundation in Scripture, it remains to advert briefly to two questions which have been much discussed in connection with the present topic. One of these questions naturally arises out of that view of our Lord's earthly experience according to which it was a training for His office as the Saviour. The question is this: When, then, did Christ enter on His priestly duties? was it on earth when He suffered on the cross, or was it not till He had ascended into glory? The question was first formally propounded and discussed by Faustus Socinus; but theological controversy may be said to have stumbled on its threshold as early as the days of Nestorius and Cyril. The Antiochian school, true to its ethical tendency, insisted strenuously on the reality of a moral growth in Christ, and regarded His experience of temptation as an ethical discipline, by which He was prepared for the office of the priesthood. Conceiving that office as an *honour*, they spoke of Christ as advancing gradually to the dignity of high priest.[1] Cyril, on the other hand, admitted neither the growth nor the conception of the priestly office as an honour. He affirmed that Christ grew in virtue as in wisdom—that is, only in the sense of graduated manifestation; and the notion of a gradual advance to the priesthood as an honour, he combated by asking his opponents the question, If the priestly office was an honour to which Christ advanced, what becomes of the kenosis?[2] Thus, on the one side, the sacerdotal functions of Christ were referred to the category of *exaltation*, while on the other they were thought of as belonging to the state of *humiliation*. In justice, however, to the theologians of Antioch, it must be borne in mind that their position does not necessarily signify, that Christ's priesthood was wholly

---

[1] Cyril, *Adv. Nestorium*, lib. iii. cap. 3. Cyril quotes Nestorius speaking of Christ as οὗτος ὁ κατὰ μικρὸν εἰς ἀρχιερέως προκόψας ἀξίωμα (*Op.* vol. ix. p. 148). *Vid.* also *Apologeticus pro XII. capitibus*, Anath. x.; and *Apol. contra Theodoretum*, Anath. x.

[2] Cyril, *Adv. Nest.* lib. iii. c. 4: Κεκένωκε δὴ οὖν, καὶ τεταπείνωκεν ἑαυτὸν καθεὶς ἐν μείοσι· Πῶς οὖν ἔτι προέκοψεν εἰς ἀξίωμα γεγονὼς ἱερεύς (p. 152). Similarly in the other places referred to in preceding note. Εἰ δὲ προέκοψε, κατὰ τίνα κεκένωται τρόπον: Εἰ προέκοψε, πῶς κεκένωται, καὶ ἐπτώχευσεν.

relegated to a *state* of exaltation subsequent in time to the state of humiliation, and commencing after the latter was at an end. It might mean only that the office, which in one respect was a humiliation, was in another respect, and at the same time, an honour for which Jesus was gradually prepared by His course of obedience. In that case it is quite conceivable, that at least some of the duties pertaining to the high and honourable office might be performed on earth, and so fall within what we are accustomed to call the state of humiliation. In point of fact, Nestorius and his brethren of the same school did regard Christ's death as a priestly sacrifice, while apparently regarding it also as the last step in the process by which Christ was prepared for His Melchizedek priesthood, and became absolutely a *pontifex consummatus*.[1] In this double way of contemplating our Lord's passion—as on one side a humiliation, on another an exaltation; and again, as in one respect the final stage of a preparatory discipline, intended to qualify the sufferer for an eternal priesthood, and in another the offering of Himself a sacrifice for the sins of the world—the Syrian theologians were much superior to Cyril, who deemed dignity and suffering incompatible notions, failed to see that it was an honour to Christ to be appointed to an office which permitted and required Him to taste death for every man, and was therefore virtually compelled to regard the priestly office solely as an indignity to which the Son of God was subjected in the state of exinanition.

If the views of the Antioch school of Christologists were such as now represented, then the credit belongs to it of anticipating the true answer to the question raised in modern times by the founder of the Socinian sect.[2] For here, as in so many other cases, truth lies on both sides of the controversy. A candid and unbiassed examination of all the relative passages shows that two distinct, though not contradictory, ways of regarding the priesthood of Christ are to be found in the Epistle to the Hebrews. The Priest of the New Dispensation is the Antitype at once of Aaron and

---

[1] Cyril. *Apol. contra Theodor.* Anath. x.: ὃς πάσης ἁμαρτίας ὑπάρχων ἐλεύθερος, ἀρχιερεὺς ἡμῶν, καὶ ἱερεῖον ἐγένετο· αὐτὸς ἑαυτὸν ὑπὲρ ἡμῶν τῷ Θεῷ προσενεγκών (vol. ix. p. 437).

[2] See Appendix, Note C.

of Melchizedek. Regarded in the latter capacity, He is undoubtedly conceived of as entering upon His priesthood on His ascension into heaven, and this in entire harmony with the nature of the priesthood after the order of Melchizedek. For that order or species is the ideal of priesthood realized, and as such possesses the attributes of *eternity*, *perfect personal righteousness* as the qualification for office, *regal dignity*, and a *corresponding state of felicity*. In this light the Melchizedek priesthood is regarded by the writer of our Epistle. Introduced first apologetically, as a welcome means of showing that the Scriptures knew of another kind of priesthood besides the Levitical, and that therefore it was possible for Christ to be a priest though destitute of the *legal* qualifications, the idea, if we may say so, grows on the writer's mind till the more ancient institution, which on first view might appear a rude, irregular, and every way inferior species of priesthood, quite eclipses that which took its origin under the law, and, in accordance with the prophetic oracle in the 110th Psalm, becomes not only a *High* priesthood, but the highest possible priesthood; the ideally perfect order, whose specific characteristics are carefully ascertained by laying stress on the minutest particulars recorded concerning Melchizedek; nay, by emphasizing not only the *utterances*, but even the *silences*, of holy writ respecting that mysterious character. The name of that ancient priest means, king of righteousness; therefore perfect holiness must be one of the marks of the ideal species of priesthood. His place of abode was Salem, which means *peace;* therefore the appropriate seat of the ideal priest is the region of celestial bliss, where he is raised far above the sin and misery and strife which molest the vale of Sodom and Gomorrah, here below. Melchizedek was a king as well as a priest, king of Salem while priest of the Most High God; therefore the ideal priest must be a priest sitting on a throne in regal dignity and glory. Finally, the history makes no mention of Melchizedek's parentage, birth, or death; therefore the ideal priesthood is one which, unlike the Levitical, has no dependence on descent, and which in its nature and its effects is *eternal*.[1]

[1] Heb. vii. 1–3.

These being the notes of that species of priesthood whereof there can be but one sample, it is manifest that Christ, as the Melchizedek priest, properly enters on His office when He has gone successfully through His curriculum of temptation in the earthly school of virtue;[1] when He is raised higher than the heavens, thoroughly proved to be a holy, harmless, undefiled Man, separate in character from sinners;[2] when He takes His place as a king on the right hand of God, in the *country of peace*, the heavenly Salem;[3] when He has passed out of the time-world into the eternal, where there is no distinction between yesterday and to-day, and where priestly functions have absolute eternal validity.[4]

Such, accordingly, is the representation given in the Epistle of the priesthood of Christ, viewed as the Antitype of Melchizedek. But is quite otherwise when the point of view changes, from the primitive institution in ancient Salem, to the legal priesthood in Israel. Jesus as the GREAT High Priest exercises His office only in heaven: as the High Priest, as a Priest after the fashion of Aaron, He exercised His office on earth, and continued to exercise it when He ascended into heaven. As a Priest after the order of Aaron, He offered Himself a sacrifice on the cross, even as Aaron offered the victim on the altar on the great day of atonement; as a Priest after the same order, He presented Himself in His humanity before His Father in heaven, even as Aaron carried the blood of the slain victim within the veil, into the presence of Jehovah. Then and there the one species of priesthood became merged or transformed into the other higher, highest ideal species: the priesthood

---

[1] Heb. v. 10: Προσαγορευθεὶς ὑπὸ τοῦ Θεοῦ ἀρχιερεὺς κατὰ τὴν τάξιν Μελχισεδέκ—as it were, saluted by that name on entering heaven.

[2] Heb. vii. 26: Ὅσιος, ἄκακος, ἀμίαντος, κεχωρισμένος ἀπὸ τῶν ἁμαρτωλῶν, καὶ ὑψηλότερος τῶν οὐρανῶν γενόμενος.

[3] Heb. x. 12: Οὗτος δέ, μίαν ὑπὲρ ἁμαρτιῶν προσενέγκας θυσίαν εἰς τὸ διηνεκές, ἐκάθισεν ἐν δεξιᾷ τοῦ Θεοῦ—*sat down* a king-priest, in contrast to the legal priests, who *stand daily* ministering and offering *oftentimes* the *same* sacrifices, which can *never* take away sins. What a pathetic picture of the sacerdotal drudge labouring as in a treadmill at the bootless work of offering his tale of victims,—*ever* offering, *never* doing any real effectual service,—till death came to relieve the melancholy official, and make his place vacant for a successor!

[4] Heb. vii. 16: Ὃς οὐ κατὰ νόμον ἐντολῆς σαρκίνης γέγονεν, ἀλλὰ κατὰ δύναμιν ζωῆς ἀκαταλύτου.

exercised in humiliation, into the priesthood associated with regal dignity and glory: the priesthood whose functions were performed by one compassed with and unreservedly confessing infirmity, into the priesthood of one who, Himself abiding in the City of peace, yet hath an undying sympathy with the tempted and war-worn, and is ever ready to come to their succour with bread and wine; the priesthood whose one great achievement was the love-offering on Calvary, into the priesthood of an endless life, which gives to that historic work absolute perennial value.[1]

The other question naturally arising out of foregoing discussions has reference to the reconcilability of the doctrine, that Christ underwent a process of perfecting, with His sinlessness, or, in other words, to the possibility of a *sinless development*. *Primâ facie*, the two ideas of sinlessness and moral growth seem mutually incompatible, and one is disposed to assume it as axiomatically certain, that the imperfect or the incomplete has necessarily the nature of evil. As an axiom, accordingly, this position was advanced by Cyril against the Nestorian doctrine, that Jesus was gradually perfected for His office, as taught by his Nestorian opponents. Can any one doubt, he triumphantly asked, that whatever comes short of the perfection of virtue is blameworthy, and therefore sinful?[2] It was a position easy to take up, extremely plausible, and fitted to ensure for the party whose cause it supported an immediate controversial advantage. And yet even Cyril might have dogmatized less confidently on this point, had he asked himself the question, What would have been the moral history of a holy child of Adam in case there had been no fall?—a case which he would not have refused to regard as

[1] *Vid.* on the history of this controversy, Riehm, *Der Lehrbegriff des Hebräerbriefes*, p. 466, where also will be found a good statement of the solution of the difficulty, in substantial agreement with that given above. *Vid.* also Hofmann, *Schriftbeweis*, vol. ii.

[2] *Adv. Nestorium*, p. 153: Πῶς ἂν ἢ πόθεν ἐνδοιάσειέ τις, ὅτι τὸ ἡμαρτηκὸς τοῦ τελείως ἔχοντος κατὰ ἀρετὴν, ὑπὸ μῶμον ἔσται, καὶ οὐκ εἰς ἅπαν τεθαυμασμένον, μᾶλλον δὲ τάχα που καὶ ὑπὸ γραφὴν ἁμαρτίας. Also *contra Theodoret.* Anath. x. p. 444: Εἰ τελεῖται καθ' ἀρετήν, ἐξ ἀτελοῦς δηλονότι, καὶ ἐν χρόνῳ γέγονε τέλειος· τὸ δὲ ἀτελὲς ἅπαν εἰς ἀρετὴν, ὑπὸ μώμου γραφήν· τὸ δὲ ὑπὸ μῶμον, ὑφ' ἁμαρτίαν. Πῶς οὖν γέγραπται περὶ αὐτοῦ ὅτι 'Ἁμαρτίαν οὐκ ἐποίησε;

a possibility. Such a child would certainly have undergone a process of real growth in wisdom and goodness, keeping pace with his growth in physical stature. If so, then the sinlessness of His human nature was no reason why Jesus should not experience a similar process of growth. If the growth predicated of Him in the gospel history was, as Cyril strenuously maintained, not real but doketic, exhibitive merely, the reason lay not in the absence of sin, but in the presence of the divine nature—*i.e.* it was *metaphysical*, not *ethical*. Even if that reason were valid, its effect would not be to settle the question as to the possibility of a sinless moral development, but simply to make the case of Christ *exceptional*. The ethical problem would still remain, and might be discussed without reference to the peculiar case of incarnate Deity, in reference to the hypothetical case of an unfallen child of Adam, yea, even in reference to the real case of unfallen Adam himself. Adam before his fall was sinless; but was he perfect? If he was, how did he fall so easily before what appears a slight temptation? If a state so insecure was perfection, how shall we characterize that state of stable moral equilibrium, in which the subject is temptation-proof? Manifestly, whether we be able speculatively to justify it or not, we must at least recognise as *real*, the distinction between moral integrity and moral perfection: the former expression denoting the initial state of a being free from sinful inclination and habits, but liable to temptation and to the possibility of falling; the latter signifying the final state of the same being after he has successfully passed through his curriculum of temptation, and has become morally infallible.

An aid to faith in, if not to a speculative comprehension of, this distinction, may be found in the analogy of physical nature. In the physical world, growth by stages is the law. There is first the blade, then the green ear, then the ripe corn in the ear, in the production of grain; first the blossom, then the crude fruit, then the ripe fruit, in the production of the apple and other products of like kind. Christ Himself has taught us, in one of His parables, that the same law obtains in the spiritual world, the kingdom of God. There, too, both in the commonwealth at large and in individual citizens, there is "first the blade, then the ear, after that the full corn in the ear."[1] It is true, indeed, that this law of growth ordinarily applies to subjects whose development is abnormal, proceeding from a state of sin by a very chequered, wayward course, to a state of Christian sanctity. But the parallel drawn in the parable between the natural and the spiritual might of itself teach us, that the *abnormality* of the development is not the *cause* why the law of gradual growth obtains in the spiritual sphere. In nature, abnormality is not the cause of growth, but simply an accident to which it is liable, owing to some vice in the seed or tree, or to the unkindliness of the seasons bringing about imperfect or retarded development. There is no reason to think that the fact is otherwise in the moral sphere. Growth there also is normal; the abnormal is *stunted retarded* growth, due partly to vice of nature, partly to the influence of an evil world, producing fruit inferior in its kind, or which never attains to ripeness. Even in unfallen humanity there would have been first the blossom, then the green fruit, then the ripe fruit: the blossom being the state of integrity, the green fruit the period of probation, and the ripe fruit the ultimate condition of perfection contemplated from the first, and at length arriving "in its season."[2] In the two stages preceding the last, man would have been *imperfect*, yet *sinless*. *Imperfect*, because what his Maker looked for, and what the law or *ideal* of his being demanded,—the end to which all preceding stages were means,—was the ripe fruit of a character perfected in wisdom and goodness, by adequate trials of patience; yet *sinless*, because God and the law of His being demanded not ripe fruit *immediately*, but only in *its season*. To be sinless, it is enough to be as you ought at each season—to be a perfect blade at the blossoming period, a perfect green ear at the earing period, and a perfect stalk of ripe grain at the season of harvest. It is not sin to come short of the requirements of the law as the *ideal:* sin consists in coming short of the requirements of the *duty* incumbent on me in given circumstances, and at any particular stage in my

[1] Matt. iv. 26–29.
[2] Ps. i. 3.

development.[1] It is not sin in childhood, the blossoming time of human life, to think and speak as a child, and to be incapable of the wisdom and moral sense of manhood: it is enough to think and speak as a holy, innocent child. It is not sin in young-manhood, the time of the green ear, to be assailed by temptations to evil conduct, and to experience profound embarrassment in connection with the question, "What is truth?" It is enough that the tempted and perplexed youth choose aright his way of life, preferring the ways of holiness and of faith to the ways of pleasure and of pyrrhonism.

How far the *metaphysical* consideration, that Christ was a divine person, is a valid reason for denying the applicability to Him of the category of moral development, need not here be discussed. The point now insisted on is, that no *ethical* objection to the application arises out of the fact that He was sinless. It was possible for the holy One to grow in grace, advancing gradually from the fair spring blossom of early boyhood to the ripe fruit of perfect manhood. The wisdom of the boy of twelve years was such as could not be excelled at that time of life: yet it was but a boy's wisdom, and left ample room for expansion in all directions. The child who made the doctors wonder by His quick intelligence, and by His shrewd questions and answers, could not then have preached the Sermon on the Mount. The piety which found expression in the words, "Wist ye not that I must be about my Father's business?" was a presage of that devotion which in later years took for its motto, "My meat is to do the will of Him that sent me, and to finish His work;" yet the former was but a blossom of instinctive, half-conscious filial love, while the latter was that blossom slowly ripened into a deliberate and passionate self-consecration to a divinely-appointed task, whose requirements were fully understood. Nor was Christ's moral growth completed when He had reached mature manhood. There was room for further progress, even after

---

[1] See Müller, *Christian Doctrine of Sin*, vol. i. pp. 58-69, where the problem of a sinless development is solved by the distinction between law and duty, the latter being defined as "the determinate moral requirement made upon a given individual at a given moment of time."

He left the home of His childhood, and went forth to enter upon His public ministry. His baptism in the Jordan formed a crisis not merely in His outward life, but in His inward spiritual history. At that point He entered on a new phase of being, in which He was to learn, through contact with the world, moral lessons which could not be got by heart in the seclusion of private life. Then He went to school to become experimentally acquainted both with human wickedness and with human misery, and to learn to suffer from the one and to sympathize with the other. The new discipline in wisdom and virtue being high and abstruse, the Disciple needed a heavenly baptism to make Him an apt scholar; and hence, according to the gospel record, the Spirit of God descended upon Him, as a Spirit of truth, a Spirit of self-sacrifice, in the interest of righteousness, and above all, as a Spirit of gracious compassion towards suffering humanity. We must beware, indeed, of exaggerating the amount of learning acquired by Jesus after His entrance on His public career, following the example of those negative critics, according to whom the Son of Mary went forth from His retirement in Galilee with the vaguest possible notions of what He was going to do, or of the destiny awaiting Him—ignorant that He was the Messiah, ignorant that the world was bad enough to crucify one who should bear witness against its evil; conscious only of great powers stirring within Him, and unable any longer to bear the inactivity and dulness of life in Nazareth. Those who take this view have not sufficiently considered what self-knowledge and spiritual insight must have been reached, by such a one as even sceptical critics admit Jesus to have been, during the long period of privacy which the Gospels pass over in reverential silence. In an important sense, we may regard the life of unbroken stillness between twelve and thirty as the time of the green fruit, between the blossom and the ripe fruit; and the whole period of the public ministry, on the other hand, as the season of harvest, in which Christ appeared before the world mature in all essential respects—in the knowledge of Himself and of men, in purpose as the Founder of the divine kingdom, in plans for the execution of His purpose, in zeal for righteousness, in pity for the sinful and the miserable, in perception of moral and spiritual truth. Sermons on the Mount, philanthropic deeds, withering exposures of false religious profession, apologies for receiving sinners full of poetry and pathos, the doctrine of the cross as the means of the world's redemption, and as the stern law of life for Master and disciple,—such was the rich and varied fruitage of the brief harvest season for which the preceding lengthened period of silent thought and hidden communion with the Father in heaven was the preparation. By the time Christ entered on His public career His education was complete, so far as theoretic knowledge was concerned. But it is one thing to know by contemplation; it is quite another to know by experience. Fully equipped for His ministry of righteousness and love at the outset, Jesus yet learned Himself while He taught others; learned decision by temptation, zeal by the contradiction of sinners, sympathy by contact with the miserable, obedience by suffering.

LECTURE VII.

THE HUMILIATION OF CHRIST IN ITS OFFICIAL ASPECT.

It remains now to consider the humiliation of Christ on its *soteriological* or *official* side.

The apostle represents the Son of God, in His Incarnation, as taking upon Him the *form of a servant*. Our Lord, on a memorable occasion, said of Himself, "I am among you as the serving man."[1] These representations cover the whole state of humiliation. The assumption of servant-form is practically synonymous with becoming man; and the word spoken by Jesus to His disciples at the supper table might be taken as the motto of His whole life on earth. From first to last He was among men as He that serveth. Whose servant was He? God's or man's? Both.[2] The Servant of the Lord is one of Messiah's titles in the prophetic Scriptures; and Jesus said of Himself, "The Son of man came not to be ministered unto, but to minister," the recipients of the service being those from whom He might have claimed ministry. Jesus on earth served His Father's will in filial loyalty, and man's need in lowly love. What was the service? It has many names in Scripture. We might say that Christ's task was to found the kingdom of God, or we might prefer to say He came to save sinners; or we might combine both in one view, following the example of a recent writer, who regards

---
[1] Luke xxii. 27, ὡς ὁ διακονῶν.
[2] In the passage in Philippians, the Godward reference of Christ's service seems to be mainly in view. There is a contrast intended between the position of *equality* with God renounced, and the position of *a servant* assumed: He who was God's equal became God's servant.

Christianity not as a circle with one centre, but rather as an ellipse with two foci, the idea of the kingdom being one, and the idea of redemption being the other.[1] For the purpose of a preliminary definition, it will suffice to adopt the poetic title given to the incarnate Son of God by the writer of the Epistle to the Hebrews, and to call Christ, with reference to His work, "the Captain of salvation."

As the Captain, Leader, Author of salvation, commissioned by the First Cause and Last End of all to conduct many sons to glory, our Lord Jesus Christ has a variety of duties or offices to perform. He is at once a Prophet, a Priest, and a King. The former two of these three offices come most prominently into view in His state of humiliation. When our object is to see how Christ humbled Himself as the servant of God and of men, we have to consider Him specially as the Apostle and the High Priest of our confession—that is, on the one hand, as One sent forth from God to speak His final, full, and perfect word to men; and, on the other, as One acting for men in things pertaining to God. In both these functions Christ acted on earth, under appointment of the great First Cause and Last End, and in connection with both He experienced humiliation. Not that the offices of prophethood and of priesthood in themselves involve humiliation, for Christ exercises them both still, in His state of exaltation. Nor did the reason of the humiliation lie in this, that in the state of exinanition these offices were severed from the kingly function, by union with which they are now redeemed from indignity, and become a royal prophethood and a royal priesthood. Christ exercised both offices, even when on earth, as a King, as the Founder and Sovereign of the kingdom of God. To the question of Pilate, "Art thou a king then?" the Prophet of Nazareth replied, "I am a King; to this end was I born, that I should bear witness unto the truth; every one that is of the truth heareth my voice;"[2] and in His gracious invitation to the weary, the meek and lowly One asked them not only to learn of Him, but to take His yoke upon them. In like manner Christ, in sacrificing Himself as a Priest,

---

[1] Ritschl, *Die christliche Lehre von der Rechtfertigung und Versöhnung*, vol. iii. p. 6.   [2] John xviii. 17.

acted as a King. It is true, indeed, that He spoke beforehand of this very act of self-sacrifice, as the crowning evidence that He came not to be ministered unto. But this was only half the truth. He did come to be ministered unto, and He exercised His ministry of love as a means to that end. That was the way He took to get a kingdom, as opposed to the way by which the princes of the world attain sovereignty. He humbled Himself that He might be exalted. The greatest made Himself servant with an eye to lordship. Not in the offices themselves, then, nor in their severance from the regal office, did the cause of humiliation lie. It lay in this, that as the Apostle of our confession, come forth from God to reveal Him in the fulness of His grace and truth unto men, Jesus had to exercise His personal ministry *among* sinners; and that as the High Priest of our confession He had to exercise His earthly ministry before God, not only among sinners, but *for* sinners, His office requiring Him to act as their representative, to be in all things like His constituents, and to offer, in their name and behalf, gifts and sacrifices for sins. In the state of exaltation, the offices in question have no humiliating accompaniments, because the prophetic office is exercised by deputy, and the priestly office consists in a sympathetic intercession which amounts to a perpetual presentation of the one offering, by which the Sanctifier perfected for ever them that are sanctified. It may be instructive to follow out separately the two lines of thought just indicated, and to regard our Lord's humiliation, first, as incurred in connection with His prophetic office; and secondly, as incurred in connection with His priestly office. By pursuing this method, we may hope not only to obtain a somewhat full view of the indignities to which our blessed Lord was subjected, and which He freely underwent as the Captain of our salvation, but also to find legitimate opportunities for noticing, in at least a cursory way, the various theoretic view-points from which the work of redemption has been regarded. The method now proposed, let it be further observed, will not involve the partition of the Saviour's ministry into two distinct portions, following each other in historical succession. It will rather mean, looking at the same ministry under two different aspects, involving to a considerable extent the subsumption of the same facts under different categories, and the explanation of the same effects by different causes.

1. First, then, let us consider Christ as the Apostle of our confession, that we may see what indignities He endured in that capacity.

Christ's duty as the Apostle was to be by word, deed, and character, the revealer, interpreter, or exegete of the Father from whose bosom He came. Into that duty the Captain of salvation threw Himself with ardour, as the gospel history amply proves, and as is specially testified by the fourth evangelist, when he writes, "The Word was made flesh, and dwelt among us, full of grace and truth." The divine Apostle by whom God spoke His last word to men was faithful to Him that appointed Him; the Prophet like unto Moses, as combining the offices of prophecy and government, said, eloquently and exhaustively, those things whereof all that Moses said was but a testimony. The law was faithfully given by Moses to Israel, as God gave it to him on the Mount; but grace and truth *became*, came into being through, were incarnated in, Jesus Christ.[1] Christ's fidelity, as the minister of grace and truth, was absolute. Of His zeal as the minister of truth we have a typical example in the cleansing of the temple, which recalled to the remembrance of the disciples the word: "The zeal of Thine house hath eaten me up;"[2] and of His devotion as the minister of grace we have a not less striking example, in the interview with the woman of Samaria, at the close of which He said to His disciples who bade Him eat: "My meat is to do the will of Him that sent me, and to finish His work."[3] Through His fidelity, in both directions, Jesus brought upon Himself manifold humiliations. As the minister of grace,

---

[1] John i. 17. On the antithesis between ἐδόθη and ἐγένετο Godet remarks: Le régime légal était divin par son origine; le régime nouveau l'est par son origine et par son essence. Cette supériorité intrinsèque de l'évangile explique bien l'antithèse de ἐδόθη et ἐγένετο. En effet, si l'expression *a été donnée* rappelait l'institution extérieure et positive de la loi, le terme *sont venues* désigne avec force l'effusion réelle et spontanée de la source divine elle-même, jaillissant à flots sur la terre.—*Commentaire sur L'Evangile de Saint Jean*, i. p. 212.

[2] John ii. 17.
[3] John iv. 34.

He made it His special business to preach the gospel to the poor, the outcast, the morally bad, the socially disreputable; and enthusiasm in such evangelistic work brought the penalty of misunderstanding and reproach. Even well-affected persons, like the Baptist, stood in doubt concerning the validity of claims to be the Messiah, made by One who occupied Himself mainly in going about doing good; for John expected the Christ to come full, not of grace, but of the fury of the Lord, with axe or fan in hand; and when the event disappointed his expectation, he sent a doubting message of inquiry which put Jesus on His defence, and compelled Him to criticise His own forerunner that men might know what value to put on his present attitude, and might not be offended in Himself.[1] In the same love for the vile, the ill-affected found ample materials for scandalous misconstruction. They called Jesus, with a sneer, "the friend of publicans and sinners;" they asked, in a tone of sinister insinuation, "Why eateth He with such?"—they answered their own question by a reckless charge of gluttony and drunkenness. The nickname, the uncharitable query, the dishonourable imputation of the evil-minded, once more put the Apostle of divine mercy on His defence, and subjected Him to the humbling necessity of making an apology for this strange unheard-of love to the sinful; the apology itself being not less surprising than the conduct apologized for, expressing in a few choice sentences the quintessence of the gospel, and breathing in every word the spirit of One who was verily not ashamed to call the vilest of mankind His brethren.[2] It might have been expected that the miracles wrought by the divine Evangelist would have protected His character from assault, and saved Him the trouble of explaining His aims and motives. Instead of doing this, however, they only stimulated the wits of the unbelieving, to invent a theory which should deliver them from the necessity of accepting an unwelcome conclusion, and drove them on from the pardonable sin of speaking evil and uncharitable words against the Son of man, to the very brink of the unpardonable wickedness of blaspheming the Holy Ghost, by ascribing

---

[1] Matt. xi. 1-11. [2] Matt. ix. 10-13; Luke vii. 36-50; Luke xv.

to Satanic agency, works wherein no ingenuous mind could fail to recognise the power of the Spirit of God.[1]

While ever intent on His ministry of grace, Jesus did not forget the other part of His commission, that, viz., of bearing witness unto the truth. The two duties were in fact interwoven, each with the other. In seeking the lost, and bringing nigh to them the grace of God, the Saviour was bearing witness in action to a very important truth, viz., that true holiness does not separate itself from the unholy, and that any holiness which takes the form of exclusiveness is a heartless, hypocritical counterfeit. It was this well-understood didactic meaning, embodied in His conduct, that was the real source of offence. The Pharisees, who were essentially men of the coterie in their religion, saw at a glance that, in the manner of life followed by Jesus, a new type of holiness totally diverse from their own was revealing itself, and their instincts of self-preservation and self-complacency forthwith took alarm. Hence arose in their minds, at a very early period, an intense dislike of the Prophet of Galilee. The men of that generation were indeed to be pitied. God in His bounty had sent them two prophets, neither of whom was at all to their taste; not John, because he separated himself in disgust from those who thanked God they were not as other men, and with blunt sincerity tore off the mask with which they hid their true character; not Jesus, because He was so genial and sunny, so full of the gladness of One who felt Himself anointed to preach the acceptable year of the Lord, and, in the exuberance of His love, so utterly disregardful of the conventional barriers which separated the good from the bad, the holy from the profane. Though He had done no more than simply allow it to appear that He was full of grace, such an one as Jesus would have borne a witness to the truth emphatic enough, to give, without fail, decided offence to men full only of spiritual pride and conceit.

But Jesus did much more than this. While scrupulously careful not to give unnecessary offence, He did not conceal God's righteousness, in fear lest prejudiced or evil-minded men should take offence when none was intended. He used

[1] Matt. xii. 22-32.

to the utmost the wide liberty of the prophet, and, as occasion offered, applied the plummet of truth to the whole life of His time: pronouncing current religious profession to be worthless and even pernicious, as amounting in effect to the making void of God's law by the traditions of men; solemnly declaring, in set discourse, that the righteousness of the Scribes was not a passport into the kingdom of heaven; and placing the qualifications of citizenship in attributes totally diverse from those exhibited in the Pharisaic character—in humility, godly sorrow, soul hunger for righteousness still unattained, purity of heart, meekness, charity, and fidelity to God and duty, at all hazards. From such speech offences were sure to arise, and they did arise. He who, by His devotion as the minister of grace, had brought on Himself the "indignities of the world," in the form of nicknames, calumnies, irreverent, disrespectful criticism, which compelled Him to defend Himself at the bar of public opinion like any ordinary son of man, did also, by His fearless zeal as the minister of truth, provoke against Himself the bitter, determined "contradiction of sinners." Therefore He had to give His back to the smiters, and His cheeks to them that plucked off the hair, and His face to shame and spitting.[1] He heard the defaming of many, fear on every side; His speeches were reported by spies; His neighbours watched for His halting, saying, "Peradventure He will be enticed, and we shall prevail against Him, and we shall take our revenge on Him."[2] His death was the natural climax and crowning instance of the contradiction provoked by His inextinguishable zeal for righteousness. To such a length did the contradiction go; even to the infliction of the cross, with all its pain and shame. We need not hesitate, out of regard to the higher meanings of our Lord's death, to acknowledge this as an historical fact. Whatever more that death meant, it meant this at least: the witness for truth suffering for His fidelity in that capacity. He had borne witness for three short years; men could endure Him no longer, and that was the way they took to get rid of Him. He had told them what true righteousness

---

[1] Isa. l. 6.
[2] Jer. xx. 10.

was; He had opposed morality to ritualism, charity to pride, the fear of God to the traditions of men, the reality of spiritual worship to the shadows of ceremonialism, humility to ostentation; He had proclaimed the advent of a divine kingdom based on these contrasts as its foundations: He had announced Himself as the King, not only God's servant, but God's Son, the Hope of those who waited for the consolation of Israel; and the cross was the world's reply. In this light our Lord Himself presented His approaching death to His disciples, when first He began to speak to them unreservedly concerning it. What He said to them in effect was this: "I am destined to be a martyr to the truth; I must suffer for righteousness' sake. The elders, chief priests, and scribes hate me, and ere long they will kill me. I cannot escape this doom, except by *unfaithfulness*—by resolving henceforth from prudential considerations to speak no more in God's name; which I cannot do, for His word is like a fire in my bones, and I cannot refrain."[1]

Such is a hasty sketch of the humiliation endured by Christ in connection with His prophetic office. Now some are content with this as a full account of the matter, and see no need for any other way of explaining our Lord's sufferings on earth, than to regard these as the natural inevitable results of the faithful discharge of His duty as the Apostle of our confession. To such Christ is the Captain of salvation simply as the revealer of God, of His grace, of His truth, of the perfect ideal of human character, of the way of life that is God-pleasing; as the example of faith, patience, fidelity, fortitude; as the companion of those who imitate His example in the tribulations which inevitably come on all the good in this evil world; as their fellow-combatant in the warfare of life, their military comrade, so to speak; as the leader of faithful souls, and guide of all that travel to the sky, teaching them to despise and triumph over all the troubles of life, making them willing to bear a cross which has been borne before by their Master, and inspiring them with invincible courage by the sure and certain hope of everlasting life, begotten in their hearts by

[1] Matt. xvi. 21-28; Jer. xx. 9.

the well-authenticated fact of His own resurrection from the dead. On this view, the death of Christ is simply an incident in His career, a mortal yet not mortal wound received in battle; not the real ground of forgiveness or admission to heaven, but simply the antecedent to an event of still more importance, the resurrection, which moves men to live good lives, and so to commend themselves to a God who, as a matter of course, forgives all who repent and indulgently accepts an imperfectly yet substantially good life, as if it were perfect. Not that the sufferings of Christ are to be treated as of no moment. By no means: it was worthy of God to make His appointed Captain of salvation perfect through suffering. It was a signal proof both of His love and of His wisdom. Of His love, because in Christ, now exalted to heavenly glory, and having the keys of the kingdom of heaven in His hands, but once a suffering man like ourselves, He hath given us a Saviour who, having fully experienced all the evils to which we are liable, is able to sympathize with us and willing to succour us. Of His wisdom, because the curriculum of suffering through which He appointed the Saviour to pass was congruous to the vocation of the latter. It is fit that a captain should have full experience of military hardships: no one can be a good captain on any other terms. How can He lead an army to victory and glory, who shirks the risks of battle and the privations of the campaign? He who would be a Joshua to the Lord's host must lead the way in every peril. This, accordingly, our Joshua did. He drank of the brook by the way, thirsty and weary through the toil of the conflict. Therefore He is a good captain, well fitted to lead the Lord's host to glory. Having descended personally into the scene of strife, and become Himself a combatant, and stood in the very forefront of the battle, He draws us on to glory, honour, and immortality by the inspiration of His example. With a light heart we endure hardships, and confront trials, which our heroic Leader has encountered before us. Looking unto Jesus, the author and the perfecter of faith, who for the joy that was set before Him endured the cross, despising the shame, and is set down at the right hand of the throne of

God, we resist unto blood, striving against sin, and so gain admittance into the eternal kingdom.[1]

While readily acknowledging that important elements of truth are contained even in this scheme of thought, we cannot possibly regard as complete any theory of the Saviour's work which considers Him simply as the Apostle, and not also as the High Priest, of our confession. That the Socinian theory, just sketched, as good as ignores Christ's priestly office, is manifest. It is true, indeed, that that theory does ascribe to the Saviour a priestly function in His state of exaltation. But what does that function amount to? Simply to this, that the man Jesus, exalted to God's right hand, and constituted a semi-Deity, has a fellow-feeling for us, His brethren, which moves Him to use the power conferred upon Him for our advantage. We have in heaven an influential friend in the shape of a man, wearing our nature, who once passed through a curriculum of temptation and suffering similar to that appointed to other men; who therefore is always disposed to take our part and to succour our weakness, to view our conduct indulgently, and notwithstanding many defects, to admit us into His eternal kingdom. The priestly office is, in fact, substantially identical with the kingly office conferred by God on the man Jesus, that we erring sinful men might have, in Him, one qualified by His own experience to be a lenient judge and a sympathetic patron. That such a representation comes short of the scriptural view of Christ's priesthood hardly needs to be proved. To do justice to

---

[1] The above train of thought embodies the substance of the following passage from the *De Servatore* of Socinus: Neque enim parum refert, nos, qui Christo fidem habemus, et ejus praeceptis obedimus, scire, eum ipsum, qui vindicem et assertorum nostrum se constituit, potestatem habere ea bona omnia nobis largiendi quae sibi obedientibus ita constanter promisit. Praesertim cum eam viam ipse prior ingressus, quam nos tenere jussit, omnia mala expertus sit quae nobis, dum per eam gradimur, et illum sequimur, aut eveniunt, aut certe evenire possunt; adeo ut tanquam nostri mali non ignarus misereri nostrûm vere possit, et nobis miseris succurrere didicerit. . . . O admirabilem Dei bonitatem atque sapientiam! Non satis illi fuit nos hostes suos, ac desertores, scelerum nostrorum gratuita venia, et vitae aeternae amplissimo promisso ad se iterum recipere, atque convertere; nisi etiam ipsius vitae aeternae nobis largiendae potestatem fratri nostro, et tantae salutis duci ac principi a se constituto, quem per afflictiones perfectum reddidit, plenissimam concederet.—Pars prima, cap. **vi.**

that aspect of His work as the Captain of salvation, we must consider Him as the High Priest of our confession, not merely in His state of exaltation, but also in His state of humiliation; not only in the vague sentimental sense of being our sympathetic Brother on high, who presents His earthly experience as a plea why He should be allowed to exercise a partial and indulgent sway over such as consent to be His subjects, but in the strict, definite, substantial sense of being our representative before God, and offering gifts and sacrifices for our sins.

2. Proceeding then to consider Christ as the High Priest of our confession, that we may see what humiliation He had to endure in that capacity, I remark, that we place ourselves in the best position for understanding this part of our subject, by starting from the principle enunciated by the writer of the Epistle to the Hebrews in these words: "Both He that sanctifieth and they who are sanctified are all of one." The Captain of salvation is here call the Sanctifier, with special if not exclusive reference to His priestly office. It is not necessary to deny that the title might legitimately enough be applied to Christ, as Grotius held it to be, in fact, applied here, with reference to His moral power over men through His teaching and example. Nor can we deny that, when the title is understood in that sense, the principle laid down contains an obvious and important truth. One who is to be a sanctifier in the ethical sense— that is, who is to make the unholy personally holy—must be one in some respects with those whom he is to sanctify. The very separateness in character, between the parties, makes it necessary that in some sense they should be one. There must be a point of contact somewhere, else the one cannot act on the other; and it is evident that the more points of contact the better. The liker the sanctifier is to those whom he is to sanctify, and who are morally his unlike, the greater his influence for good upon them. He who is in all possible respects like unto his brethren, will manifestly have more power over them than one who is like them in only one or two points. The one acts like a mighty force brought to bear directly on an inert mass, so as to set it in motion; the other glides past, just grazing the mass

and leaving it where it was. Hence, in order to be a sanctifier even in a moral sense, it behoved Jesus, the holy One, to be in all possible respects like His unholy brethren; for in this sense the sanctifying power of Jesus lies in His example, His character, His history as a man. He makes us holy by reproducing in His own life the lost ideal of human character, and bringing that ideal to bear on our minds and hearts. But the ideal can be brought to bear with full effect only when it is realized amid circumstances as like as possible to those in which they are situated whom it is designed to influence. The Ideal must be an ideal *man*, bone of our bone, flesh of our flesh, the Son of man; He must be in His humanity *mere* man, stripped of all social advantages, down on the level of the common mass, and presenting there the ideal of excellence amid the meanest surroundings; He must be a *tempted* man, His virtue not a thing of course, but a real battle with sin, a triumph after a bloody struggle over all the forces of moral evil.

While all this may be true, however, it is not the line of thought which the writer of the Epistle means to suggest, when he enunciates the principle, that the Sanctifier and the sanctified are all of one. He calls Christ the Sanctifier, with reference to His office as the High Priest; and the work he ascribes to Him, is that of sanctifying the unholy representatively, so that on account of what He does they are esteemed holy in God's sight. He explains his own meaning further on, when he speaks of Christians as sanctified through the offering of the body of Jesus Christ once for all, and calls the blood of Christ the blood of the covenant wherewith we are sanctified, and represents Jesus as suffering without the gate, that He might sanctify the people with His own blood.[1] In the immediately following context, indeed, he indicates with sufficient clearness the nature of the service rendered by the Sanctifier, by the significant expression, "to make reconciliation for (to expiate) the sins of the people." But here, it is worthy of notice, the author applies his principle not only to the work of the Sanctifier, but to His qualifications for the work. "Wherefore," he writes, "in all things it behoved Him to

---

[1] Heb. x. 10, 29, xiii. 12.

be made like unto His brethren, that He might be *a merciful and trustworthy* High Priest in things pertaining to God, to make reconciliation for the sins of the people."[1] He means to say, on the one hand, that the nature of the work to be done by the High Priest in itself involves a unity between Him and those for whom He acts; and on the other, that the closer the union between the High Priest and His constituents, the better fitted is He for His office.

There are thus suggested two points of view from which we may regard the humiliation of Christ, in connection with His priestly office,—viz. either as a discipline by which He was qualified for office, or as suffering endured in the performance of priestly duty. The latter aspect is by far the most important; but before treating of it, it may be well to contemplate the subject for a moment under the former aspect.

One who is to act for men in things pertaining to God—in so supremely important a matter as that of making atonement for sin—must possess the confidence of his constituents. If he is not trusted, it is in vain that he transacts. Hence the writer of the Epistle to the Hebrews is careful to point out the qualities by which a high priest is enabled to gain the confidence of those he represents in holy things. The model high priest is photographed, in a single expressive phrase, as one able $\mu\epsilon\tau\rho\iota o\pi a\theta\epsilon\hat{\iota}\nu$[2]—to have compassion on the ignorant and erring, able to restrain the tendency to impatience and severity towards the morally weak. This faculty He is represented as acquiring through His own experience and consciousness of infirmity, which makes it necessary that, in offering for the people, He should at the same time offer for Himself. The purpose of the representation is to explain to the Hebrew Christians the *rationale* of Christ's humiliations, of the temptations and the sinless infirmities He experienced in the days of His flesh. He says to them in effect: "View Christ as a High Priest, and you will at once perceive the congruity of His experience to His office, and cease to find in the former a stumbling-block. You know what sort of a man every well-qualified high priest is. Taken from among men, to act for them in

[1] Heb. ii. 17.   [2] Heb. v. 2.

holy things, he feels himself one of the people; accounts even the erring and the ignorant, for whom atonement has to be made, as his brethren; is patient and sympathetic towards them, and checks all tendencies to impatience by the habitual recollection of his own weakness, which his very priestly duties do not suffer him to forget. Such an High Priest it behoved Jesus to be as far as was possible, without sin. Therefore He was made in all things like His brethren: first of all, like them in possessing their humanity, for He could not be a High Priest for men unless He were taken *from* men; then, like them, further, in possessing the sinless infirmities of humanity, and in being through these subject to temptations, which made Him ofttimes feel and confess His weakness. Why stumble at all this? why wonder that the Son of God should become man; that He should be a humble-born man, one of the people; that He should be a tempted man; that He should be conscious of weakness, and constrained to acknowledge it, as when He prayed, "If it be possible, let this cup pass from me"? All this was needful for one destined to a priestly vocation; all this was but a discipline fitting the Captain of salvation for being a merciful and trusty High Priest, in whose fidelity all can put implicit confidence."

It thus appears that we have scriptural sanction for treating the *sympathy* of Christ as *one* point of view from which to contemplate His humiliation. It is legitimate to say that Christ's experience on earth was due, in part at least, to this, that it behoved one who had His work to do to undergo a training in sympathy, or to have a history which afforded opportunities for the manifestation of sympathy already existing. The High Priest of humanity must learn to sympathize; or if He do not need to learn, He must *reveal* His latent sympathy in action and suffering. In this way we may satisfactorily enough explain to ourselves some outstanding facts in our Saviour's life—as, for example, His preference for, and habitual use of, the designation *Son of man*, and His *ministry of healing*. Many an explanation of the name Jesus was wont to give Himself has been suggested; but it seems as good as any to say that He called Himself by preference the Son of man, to announce to the world His consciousness of brotherhood with men, the humble, homely title rising to His lips as the spontaneous utterance of the human sympathy that filled His heart.[1] Then, if we ask ourselves why it was that Jesus, who came to save His people from their sins, spent so much of His time in healing the bodies of the sick, how natural the suggestion that the miracles of healing were partly the artless expression by kind deeds of unutterable compassion, and partly a method of action deliberately resolved on with intent to gain men's confidence for higher ends! Is not the former part of the suggestion, at least, borne out by those words of the evangelist, in which the miraculous cures wrought by Jesus are represented as a fulfilment of the prophetic oracle: "Himself took our infirmities, and bare our sicknesses"?—the thought intended to be conveyed obviously being: He bore man's sicknesses on His mind by compassion, and so He healed them by His divine power.

Thus far we may safely go in treating sympathy as one factor in the process whereby the Lord Jesus was made a man of sorrow, acquainted with grief. But some, not content with the recognition of sympathy as one factor, make it all in all. The one fact, according to such, necessary to account for Christ's whole earthly experience is, that He loved the sinful and the miserable with a love sympathetic, burden-bearing, *vicarious* in character, as it is the nature of all true love to be. This sympathy of the Son of God with man is the cardinal unity which binds together Sanctifier and sanctified,—a unity fruitful of many others, and sufficiently accounting for all. Because the holy One was one with the unholy, in the first place, through a sympathetic love whose nature it is to identify itself in all respects with the object loved, therefore He was not only willing, but eager—nay, under a kind of necessity—to come into their *lot*. Sympathetic love brought Him down from heaven to earth; and given proximity of situation, fellowship in suffering followed as a matter of course. The holy One incarnate became, of course, in lot like the unholy, in all respects possible to a holy being. There is no mystery

[1] For the sense of this title, see Lect. v. p. 226.

in the matter: "Understand that love is itself an essentially vicarious principle, and the solution is no longer difficult."[1] Who wonders that a mother suffers with and for her sick child? or a patriot with and for his unhappy country? Who wonders that Nehemiah, being a patriot, left the court of Persia and came to Jerusalem when its walls were lying in ruins? and that, once at the scene of desolation and misery, he became partaker in the afflictions of the people, their fellow-labourer in rebuilding the ruined walls —watching when they watched, fighting when they fought, tempted by treacherous foes when they were tempted, paying their debts and redeeming them from bondage, when they were burdened with debt and sold into slavery? The explanation of the whole is, that Nehemiah loved his country with a love which was essentially vicarious, just because it was genuine. In like manner, why wonder that the Son of God visited this dark, sinful, wretched world by becoming man, and that, once arrived here, He experienced all the sinless infirmities of human nature, the privations and indignities of a mean outward condition, temptation, bad usage, the fear of death, and death itself, "even the death of the cross"? The cardinal unity of sympathy explains all these resultant unities of lot. And as for the cardinal unity itself, it needs no explanation. What need to explain the fact of the holy One loving the unholy with a sympathetic love, which makes Him and them as one? Such love is the law of the moral universe—for God, for angels, for good men. The unity subsisting between Sanctifier and sanctified, therefore, depends not on any positive divine institution, or on any office to which the former is appointed. Christ's unity with the sinful is antecedent to, independent of, constitutions and offices, and is due simply to His being what He is—One whose inmost nature is holy love. For, to quote the words of the most eloquent modern expounder of the theory: "Such is love, that it must insert itself into the conditions, burden itself with the wants and woes and losses, and even wrongs, of others. It waits for no atoning office, or any other kind of office. It undertakes because it is love, not because a pro-

[1] Bushnell, *The Vicarious Sacrifice*, p. 11.

ject is raised or an office appointed. It goes into suffering and labour and painful sympathy, because its own everlasting instinct runs that way. There can be no greater mistake, in this view, than to imagine that Christ has the matter of vicarious sacrifice wholly to Himself, because He suffers officially, or as having undertaken it for His office to supply so much suffering. He suffered simply what was incidental to His love, and the works to which love prompted, just as any missionary suffers what belongs to the work of love he is in."[1]

To one holding such views it would not be an effective reply to point out, that the sympathetic love ascribed to Christ does not of itself constitute priestly action in the strict sense of the word, but simply amounts to a personal qualification for the office; because the offices of Christ are ostentatiously held in light esteem, and in particular the priestly office is regarded as a mere figure of speech. The advocates of the theory which accounts for Christ's whole state of humiliation by sympathy, explain the prominence given to the priestly aspect of His work in the Epistle to the Hebrews, as an accommodation to Jewish modes of thinking adopted for apologetic purposes. The writer believed that he could commend Christianity to his readers, by presenting the object of faith to their view under a priestly aspect; and therefore he ran a parallel between Christ and the Aaronic high priests, straining the similitude to an extent justified by the paraenetic aim, but which it would be a stupid mistake in us to take too much in earnest. The argument is rhetoric rather than theology; and Christ is called a priest by poetic licence rather than in plain prose. In point of fact, He does nothing in the way of making atonement for men before God; His action is all manward, and its sole design and effect is to gain moral power over the sinful through the manifestation of divine love in self-sacrifice; so, as it is put by the author already quoted, "at the expense of great suffering, and even of death itself, to bring us out of our sins themselves, and so out of their penalties."[2] To one whose mind has slowly

[1] Bushnell, *The Vicarious Sacrifice*, pp. 67, 68 (English Edition, 1871).
[2] *The Vicarious Sacrifice*, chap. i. p. 7.

passed through various phases of opinion on the present weighty subject, and who certainly has not been insensible to the fascinations of the sympathy-theory of redemption advocated by Bushnell, it may be permitted to remark, that such a summary and unceremonious method of handling the important category of our Lord's priesthood, does not commend itself to a sober and reverent judgment. Unless we are to treat the Epistle to the Hebrews as a portion of Scripture possessing no permanent value to the Church, as a source of instruction in Christian truth,—as being, indeed, nothing more than an ingenious piece of reasoning, serving admirably the temporary purpose of carrying Hebrew Christians safely through a crisis in their spiritual history,—we must regard Christ's priesthood as a great reality, as *the* reality, whereof the legal priesthood was but a rude shadow, not even an exact image. If so, then this Man must have something to offer to God for us; and His offering must possess all the properties needful to efficacy—must be the absolutely perfect, and therefore eternally valid sacrifice for sin, perfecting the worshipper as to conscience—that is, delivering him completely from the painful sense of guilt, making him in God's sight holy, and establishing between him and God a relation of peace and fellowship upon which sin exercises no disturbing influence. And because Christ as a priest offers an ideally perfect sacrifice, valid for and having effect upon God in His relation to men, therefore His priesthood must be a matter of divine appointment. Were it a mere affair of gaining moral power over men by a career of self-sacrificing love, then nothing more would be needed to constitute sanctifier and sanctified one, than sympathetic feeling, and every one might take up the vocation of a saviour who had a mind. But if the sanctifier is to act not only on men but for men, and to prevail with God to certain intents and purposes, then sympathy alone will not suffice to form a nexus between him and the unholy. There must be a divine appointment to the priestly office. No man taketh *this* honour to himself but he that is called of God. Sympathy may be a very important *qualification* for office. It is so indeed. No one could do Christ's work who was merely an "official" performing all his duties in a perfunctory spirit; and this is a truth which, by way of antidote to the chilling effect of a scholastic method of discussing the Saviour's offices, may very properly and profitably be insisted on by such as have been led to feel strongly about it. The very antipodes of officialism did the Christ behove to be, even one possessed with a very passion for saving the sinful, and in the intensity of His love ready to descend to the lowest depths, to put His shoulder beneath the heaviest burdens, and to feel the keenest pangs in His vocation as Saviour, *yea, feeling such pangs just because He loved*. This was needful as a qualification for office, not only with a view to gain the confidence of men, but, as will appear, equally with a view to satisfy Him from whom the appointment to office emanated. Still it was nothing more than a qualification. It neither superseded the necessity of an appointment, nor did it amount to a full discharge of official duty.

Passing, then, from the qualifications for the priestly office to the office itself, I remark that the principle of identity, in this connection, means, not that the sanctifier and the sanctified are, or are required to be, one in all circumstances conditioning moral power, or one in all particulars of lot as the result of spontaneous sympathy; but that the two parties are so one in God's sight and by His appointment, that what the Sanctifier does in His official capacity, He does representatively in the name of those He represents, and for their behoof, so that in Him, and in virtue of His transactions, they are in the divine view sanctified, holy. In such a relation the high priest of Israel stood to the people. On the great day of atonement he offered sacrifice, in the name and as the representative of the people; and the result of his representative action was, that Israel was cleansed from all sin, and was in God's sight holy. In the same relation Christ stands to the spiritual Israel. He is the representative of the people, and in Him God regards as sanctified those who are in themselves unholy. But this is not the whole truth. The High Priest of our confession is not only a Priest, but a victim. He put away sin by the sacrifice of *Himself*. Hence, while as a Priest He is our representative, as a sacrifice He is our substitute. For as, in the law, the sins of the people were laid on the head of the victim, and expiated by the shedding of its blood; so Christ bore our sins in His own body, and died on the cross, the just for the unjust, that He might bring us to God.

It was chiefly in the capacity of a victim that Christ encountered humiliation, in the exercise of the office of a Priest. In itself the priestly office involved no humiliation; on the contrary, to be the sacerdotal representative of the people was a great honour, so great that no man might take it unto himself, but he that was called of God, as was Aaron. It is true, indeed, that the nature of the office, as having to do with sin, and all its duties, as in one way or another calling sin to remembrance, required the sacerdotal representative of the congregation to be a man humbling himself habitually before the Lord for the sins of his brethren, not to speak of his own. But while the priest who offered sacrifices for sin, and the victim sacrificed, remained distinct, the lowest depth of humiliation could not be reached. It was reserved for Him in whom the ideals of priesthood and of sacrifice were both united and perfectly realized, to prove by experience the humiliating power of sin in the superlative degree. As the sacrifice for sin, Christ endured the humiliation of becoming a sinner in legal standing, made sin for us that we might be made the righteousness of God; made like unto the unholy in respects in which it was barely possible for a holy Being to be assimilated to such, even in subjection to the curse, to the wrath of God, to death as the penalty of sin, that we might be delivered from these evils.

This statement, however, is not homologated by all who agree in holding the principle, that the Sanctifier and those who are sanctified are one, in the sense that the former represents the latter before God. Many, while admitting Christ to be the representative of sinners, deny that He is their substitute. The denial implies, for one thing, that no independent substantive value is attached to Christ's death, it being regarded simply as the crowning act of obedience and devotion to the divine will. It further implies that the priestly action of Christ always includes Himself as an object. The Sanctifier sanctifies Himself as well as the community; sanctifies the community by sanctifying Himself. This is the idea underlying that view of Christ's redeeming work, which has been more than once referred to in these lectures, as the theory of *redemption by sample*, but which is more commonly known as the mystical theory, the title adopted by Schleiermacher to distinguish his own view of the doctrine from the orthodox, which he called the "magical," on the one hand, and from the Socinian, termed the "empirical," on the other.[1] Common to all forms of this so-called mystical theory is the position, that what Christ did for men He did also for Himself, and that He did it for us by doing it for Himself, acting as the Head and representative of humanity before God. The High Priest of humanity sanctified Himself for the sake of humanity, and in so doing presented the whole lump holy to the Lord. The point on which the advocates of this theory are not agreed is the question, Wherein did Christ's self-sanctification consist? The ancient Fathers, many of whom held this theory, in addition to their grotesque fancy, that the death of Christ was a price paid to the devil, for the ransom of men's souls from his dominion, sometimes identified the sanctification of humanity in Christ's person with the Incarnation. Thus Hilary: "For the sake of the human race the Son of God was born of the Virgin, and by the Holy Ghost, that being made man He might receive the nature of the flesh unto Himself, and that, by the admixture, the body of the whole human race might be sanctified in Him; so that as all were included in Him through His will to be corporeal, He might in turn enter into all through His invisible part."[2] Stress was sometimes, however, laid on the holy life of Christ in human nature; as in a passage quoted from Cyril in a previous lecture, where Christ is spoken of as destroying sin in humanity, by living a human life free

[1] *Der christliche Glaube*, ii. 99-101.

[2] *De Trinitate*, l. ii. c. 24: Humani generis causa Dei filius natus ex virgine est et Spirito sancto ... ut homo factus ex virgine naturam in se carnis acciperet, perque hujus admixtionis societatem sanctificatum in eo universi generis humani corpus exsisteret: ut quemadmodum omnes in se per id quod corporeum se esse voluit conderentur, ita rursum in omnes ipse per id quod ejus est invisibile referretur.

from all sin, rendering the soul He assumed superior to sin, by dyeing it with the moral strength and unchangeableness of His own divine nature.[1] In the theory of Menken and Irving, in principle the same with that taught by the Fathers, the Sanctifier makes the lump of humanity holy, by taking a portion of the corrupt mass tainted with the vice of original sin and subject to sinful bias, and by a desperate life-long struggle sanctifying it, subduing all temptations to sin arising out of its evil proclivities, and at last consuming the body of death as a sin-offering on the cross. In the patristic form of the theory the sample was of better quality than the lump; in the Menken-Irving theory the sample was, morally as well as metaphysically, just a fair sample of the lump, and was only made better by a painful process of self-mortification. In the hands of Maurice, the mystical theory assumes a kindred but somewhat modified form. Christ, as the root and archetype of humanity, in His own person offers up man as an acceptable sacrifice to God, in the sense of exhibiting in His life and death the entire surrender of the whole spirit and body to God, and the complete renunciation of that self-will which is the cause of all men's crimes and of all their misery. Such self-sacrifice was what was really meant by all the legal sacrifices: for the victims died, not as substitutes for the offerer, but as symbols of his devotion. What these legal sacrifices but dimly foreshadowed, Christ perfectly realized. In His life and death He offered up the one complete sacrifice ever offered, the perfect example of self-surrender and devotion to the divine will; and God accepted the sacrifice, as made not by an individual, but by the race as represented by its archetypal man.[2]

It is impossible within the compass of a single lecture, and indeed it is quite unnecessary, to follow out into further detail the exposition of this type of doctrine. It must suffice to say, that since the time of Schleiermacher, what he called the "mystical" theory in contradistinction to the "magical," but what, imitating his epigrammatic style, I prefer to call the theory of redemption by sample, as op-

[1] *Vid.* Lecture ii. p. 47.
[2] Vid. *The Doctrine of Sacrifice*, and *Theological Essays*.

posed to redemption by substitute, has been much in favour among German theologians.[1] And by way of criticism of this in some respects most attractive theory, I offer only two observations. The first is, that advocates of the doctrine of substitution, and of the correlate doctrine of imputation, are nowise concerned to meet with unqualified denial the underlying postulate of the theory—viz., that whatever Christ did for us He did for Himself, or that His priestly action was inclusive, not exclusive, of Himself. To a certain extent this is quite true. The Sanctifier was holy for Himself as well as for us; and in so far as His death was necessary to the maintenance in unbroken continuity and closest intimacy, at all hazards, of His fellowship with His Father, we may even concede to Ritschl that He died for Himself as well as for us.[2] For the same reason I admit that Jesus prayed for Himself as well as for us; a fact which the author just named thinks has been entirely overlooked by the upholders of the orthodox theory.[3] Ritschl describes the priestly activity of Christ for us as consisting in bringing us nigh to God; that idea, in his opinion, covering the whole design and effect of the ancient sacrifices.[4] Christ's priestly action for Himself, on the other hand, consisted in maintaining His originally existing nighness to God, in presence of circumstances tending to produce separation and alienation; His death was His last crowning effort for that purpose. On this view it was as necessary that Christ should die in His own interest, in His capacity as a Priest, as it was that He should die in His capacity as a Prophet. In the latter case, He died that He might be faithful to Him that appointed Him, in His vocation as an Apostle. In the former, He died that He might be faithful to us as our High Priest. Dying as a Prophet, He maintained to the end His solidarity with God; dying as a Priest, He maintained to the end His solidarity with men.[5] All this I am ready to accept; but in doing so, I observe that

---

[1] On the recent German literature bearing on the subject, *vid.* Philippi, *Kirchliche Glaubenslehre*, vol. iv. zweite Hälfte, pp. 156-204. Also Ritschl, *Die christliche Lehre von der Rechtfertigung und Versöhnung dargestellt*, vol. i. pp. 465-520.
[2] *Die christliche Lehre von der Rechtfertigung und Versöhnung*, vol. iii. p. 414.
[3] *Ibid.* iii. p. 412.   [4] *Ibid.* ii. p. 210.   [5] *Ibid.* iii. p. 490.

Christ did not die for Himself, or, to put it more generally, maintain His fellowship with God, even unto death, for Himself, in the same sense as for us. As a Priest, acting in His own interest, He simply ensured that He should continue what He *was—holy*. As a Priest, acting for us, He ensured, by His holiness in life and death, that we, the unholy, should be holy in God's sight—" accepted in the Beloved." What is this but to sanctify, or, to use the more correct expression in this connection, to justify the unholy by imputation ? It is true, indeed, that Ritschl rejects the doctrine of justification by imputation of Christ's *righteousness*, and in its place substitutes justification by imputation of *fellowship* with Christ, proposing as the appropriate formula the following: " God imputes to the members of the community of Christ, their fellowship with Christ, as the condition under which He admits them to fellowship with Himself."[1] This formula certainly seems to convey the idea that, after all, it is not the perfect righteousness of the Sanctifier which forms the ground why God accepts as righteous the unholy, but rather the incipient righteousness of those who are justified, manifested in their voluntary fellowship with Christ. But in that case what becomes of the author's doctrine, that justification is a " synthetic judgment," that is, a gracious act of the divine will affirming of the subject that which is not contained in the idea of it; as thus, " The sinner is to God righteous; he is adopted by God; he is brought nigh to God " ?[2] This doctrine, taken along with the above formula, would seem to imply that God justifies the sinner, pardoning his sin and accepting him as righteous in His sight, not for any incipient goodness in himself, but for the righteousness of Christ, imputed to him and received by faith. But it must be confessed that this inference, however legitimate, does not seem to be accepted by Ritschl. In explaining, with a view to illustrate his doctrine of justification, those passages

---

[1] *Die christliche Lehre von der Rechtfertigung und Versöhnung*, iii. p. 482: Gott den Gliedern der Gemeinde Christi ihre Gemeinschaft mit Christus als die Bedingung anrechnet, unter der er sie zur Gemeinschaft mit sich selbst zulässt.

[2] *Ibid*. iii. 466: Der Sünder ist Gott recht, er ist Gott angeeignet, er ist in die Nähe Gottes versetzt.

of Scripture in which God is represented as forgiving sin, out of regard to the intercession or the righteousness of good men like Moses or David, he gives the matter this turn: "In the recognition of an intercession as a ground of forgiveness, no judgment contrary to truth is pronounced; but a resolution of confidence is formed out of regard to the probability that one who is deemed worthy of the fellowship of an honourable man, is worthy also to be received again into the fellowship of the party injured. In like manner is the righteousness of David represented as a motive of divine forgiveness; because the Israelites, in spite of their disobedience, have the honour to possess in David a representative whose fellowship with them awakens the conjecture that they are not incapacitated for obeying God."[1] Far-fetched, forced explanations, indeed, indicating a very decided reluctance to recognise the goodness of one man, as the real ground of gracious judgments and actions, on God's part, towards others.

These remarks lead us naturally to the second observation which I have to offer, by way of criticism, on the mystical theory of redemption. It is chargeable with the vice of ambiguity, inasmuch as it does not clearly indicate in what way Christ's action avails for us. Does the sample really sanctify the whole lump in God's sight? or does it merely exhibit a result which has to be reached in every individual member of the race, which it somehow helps us to reach, and which, when realized, or foreseen as realized, is the ground of God's judgment in accepting us as holy? The theory stated in general terms leaves these points indeterminate; it is compatible with either alternative; and according as it inclines to the one side or the other, it goes

[1] *Die christliche Lehre von der Rechtfertigung und Versöhnung*, iii. P. 58: In der Anerkennung einer Fürbitte zum Zwecke der Verzeihung wird also kein wahrheitswidriges Urtheil gefällt, sondern ein Entschluss des Vertrauens ausgeübt durch Vermittelung eines Urtheils der Wahrscheinlichkeit, dass derjenige, welcher von einem ehrenhaften Manne der Gemeinschaft gewürdigt wird, werth ist, auch von dem Beleidigten zur Gemeinschaft wieder angenommen zu werden. Demgemäss wird auch die Gerechtigkeit Davids als Motiv der göttlichen Verzeihung vorgestellt, weil die Israeliten trotz ihres Ungehorsams die Ehre haben, an David einen Repräsentanten zu besitzen, dessen Gemeinschaft mit ihnen die Vermuthung erweckt, dass sie zum Gehorsam gegen Gott befähigt sind.

over either to the side of orthodoxy or to the side of Socinianism. The mystical scheme is distinct from other forms of doctrine, only so long as it deals in general imposing phrases, and refuses to be explicit. Whenever it condescends to explain itself, it is seen to be identical either with what Schleiermacher was pleased to call the magical view, or what the same author stigmatized as the empirical view. In point of fact, the tendency of the mystical school has been for the most part towards the latter; that is to say, their doctrine of atonement turns out to be simply a form of the moral influence theory. This is particularly true in reference to Schleiermacher. When we find him saying that, "as of the whole Jewish people the high priest alone appeared before God, and God, as it were, saw the whole people in him; so Christ is on this account our High Priest, because God sees us not every one for himself, but only in Him,"[1]—we are ready to come to the conclusion, that here we have God accepting the unholy, on account of the righteousness of Christ imputed to them. But, reading on, we find that the doctrine, that Christ's obedience is our righteousness, or that His righteousness is imputed to us, means, for Schleiermacher, that "Christ as our High Priest represents us perfectly before God in virtue of His own complete fulfilment of the divine will, to which, through His life in us, the impulse is active in us also; so that, in this connection with Him, we too are objects of the divine complacency."[2] That is, Christ *in* us, not Christ *for* us, is the ground of justification. Christ, the founder of the divine kingdom, has introduced a new principle of life into the community called by His name. This principle, or, in other words, the life image of Christ, works like a leaven in the mass, gradually assimilating the members to the great Exemplar and Head. Because of this process of assimilation going on in those who are connected with Christ by a fellowship of life, God is well pleased with them, notwithstanding existing imperfection. Redemption is thus purely subjective; fellowship of life with Christ in His holiness and in His blessedness is the whole outcome

[1] *Der christliche Glaube*, ii. p. 133.
[2] *Ibid.* ii. p. 133.

of His work;[1] and as in Schleiermacher's system this fellowship is not immediate, but only through the medium of the Church, direct personal fellowship with the Saviour being branded as magical, the redemptive influence emanating from the founder of the Christian religion reduces itself to the influence of a society, in which more or less clear ideas prevail, of that founder's teaching, spirit, and history. That is to say, as Baur has pointed out,[2] Schleiermacher's mystic conception of redemption and reconciliation passes over into that which he named the empirical, which wholly excludes the supernatural, and makes men's salvation simply the natural result of doctrine and example acting on their minds, by way of moral influence. The same thing, however, it is cordially admitted, cannot be said of all who, more or less, share the Schleiermacherian point of view. Theologians like Nitzsch[3] not only recognise a direct personal fellowship with Christ, but teach a Christ for us as well as a Christ in us, and acknowledge that the work of redemption has an objective, Godward side, as well as a subjective. And when this is done, there need be no jealousy of the mystic theory. For redemption by sample can be combined with redemption by substitute. The doctrine of a Christ in us and that of a Christ for us are not only compatible, but complementary of each other; either is but a half truth without the other. The two points of view, the mystic and the legal, are both recognised in Scripture; they are found meeting together amicably within a few verses of each other in a well-known chapter of one of Paul's Epistles. When, speaking in the name of Christians, the apostle says, "We thus judge: if one died for all, then all died," he presents to view the mystic aspect of the truth, the death of Christ being here regarded as a sample of what has to be realized in each individual believer, and is realized in him, in proportion as he lives not to himself,

---

[1] Schleiermacher divides the work of Christ into two parts, distinguished respectively as the redeeming and the atoning activity. The redeeming activity consists in taking sinners into fellowship in His holiness; the atoning, in taking them into fellowship in His blessedness. Vid. *christliche Glaube*, ii. pp. 94, 102.

[2] *Die christliche Lehre von der Versöhnung*, p. 619.

[3] *System der christlichen Lehre*, pp. 279-283, 6te Auflage.

but to Him that died and rose again. He presents the same subject on the legal side, when, at the close of the same chapter, addressing men whom he urges to be reconciled to God, he writes, "For He hath made Him to be sin for us, who knew no sin, that we might be made the righteousness of God in Him;" the death of Christ being viewed here as an event which takes place in order that we might not die, but be justified in God's sight,[1]—in other words, as the penalty of our sin inflicted on Christ as our substitute or vicar.[2]

But can such a transference of legal responsibility as seems to be taught in this text really have taken place? Is such a transference possible? Is it worthy of the great Sovereign of the universe, the First Cause and Last End of all? Is it in accordance with the facts of Christ's history? These are the questions to which we must now turn. Now, as to the first, it scarcely needs to be remarked, that what is affirmed by the Catholic doctrine is not transference of guilt or moral turpitude, but simply of legal liability. Christ was made sin for us, simply to the extent and effect of bearing penalty for our sin. Some prominent defenders of the Catholic doctrine have indeed hesitated to go even so far as this. Archbishop Magee, *e. g.*, in his well-known work on the atonement, maintains that the idea of punishment in the strict sense cannot be abstracted from that of guilt; and, while admitting that Christ's sufferings were judicially inflicted, he holds that they can be called the punishment of our sins, only in the sense that they were the sufferings due to us the offenders, and which, if inflicted on the actual offenders, would then take properly the name of punishment.[3] A more recent writer, the Donellan lecturer for the year 1857, in a work on the atonement, which has for its praiseworthy aim to exhibit the Catholic doctrine cleared of such careless expressions and imperfect definitions as tend to awaken hostility or furnish a handle for scepticism, endorses the distinguished prelate's view, and says, "that we must, when we speak of the penal suf-

---

[1] 2 Cor. v. 15, 21. [2] See Appendix, Note A.
[3] *Discourses and Dissertations on the Scriptural Doctrines of Atonement and Sacrifice*, Dissert. No. 42, p. 457 (4th ed.).

ferings of Christ, admit that we use the word 'penal' in a peculiar sense, as expressing the relation of those sufferings not to Him who bore them, but to our demerits, in which they originated."[1] Such scruples are entitled to respect, yet there is truth in the remark of another theologian, that, in conceding the *judicial* character of Christ's sufferings, these writers admit all that is intended to be taught when the epithet "penal" is applied to them.[2] The vital question is, Can these sufferings be rightly regarded as judicial in their nature? Now, looking at this question from our peculiar point of view, that of Christ's voluntary humiliation, I remark, that if descent into the legal standing of a sinner were at all possible, Christ would gladly make the descent. It was His mind, His bent, His mood, if I may so speak, to go down till He had reached the utmost limits of possibility. So minded, He would be predisposed to find the imputation of men's sin to Himself, to the intent of His bearing their penalty *within* these limits. By an antecedent act of subjective self-imputation, He would, so to say, prejudge the question in favour of the possibility of an objective imputation. What the moral government of God is supposed to forbid, the sympathy of the Son of man would be prone to ordain as a law for itself. The truth of this observation is tacitly acknowledged by the peculiar theory of atonement taught by the late Dr. M'Leod Campbell; the sole value of that theory, indeed, lies in the fact that it involves such an acknowledgment. That writer, repudiating the orthodox doctrine of imputation as a theological figment, and improving a hint thrown out by President Edwards respecting an alternative method of satisfying for sin, namely, by an adequate confession of sin,—a hint which he might have got from a schoolman of the twelfth

---

[1] MacDonnel, *The Doctrine of the Atonement deduced from Scripture*, Lect. vi. p. 198. It is well known that Anselm, who first formulated the theory of satisfaction, did not regard Christ's death as penal. Satisfaction in his system did not consist in paying the penalty, but was rather one of two alternatives, the other being the paying of the penalty. Thus he says, in *Cur Deus Homo*, i. c. 15: " Necesse est, ut omne peccatum satisfactio aut poena sequatur." See Baur, *Versöhnungslehre*, p. 183. If the disuse of a word would reconcile thoughtful men to the truth intended to be conveyed, one might easily forego it.

[2] Professor Crawford, *On the Atonement*, p. 184.

century,[1]—propounds the doctrine that Christ, bearing us and our sins on His heart before the Father, made a perfect confession of human sin: a confession which "was a perfect Amen in humanity to the judgment of God on the sin of man;" "a confession due in the truth of things, due on our behalf though we could not render it, due from Him as in our nature and our true Brother, what He must needs feel in Himself because of the holiness and love which were in Him, what He must needs utter to the Father in expiation of our sins when He would make intercession for us;" a confession which had in it "all the elements of a perfect contrition and repentance, excepting the personal consciousness of sin."[2] The theory has been treated by critics of all schools as the eccentricity of a devout author, who, dissatisfied with the traditional theory, has substituted in its place another, involving not only greater difficulty, but even something very like absurdity. The idea of a confession made by a perfectly holy being, involving *all* the elements of a perfect repentance, *except* the personal consciousness of sin, is certainly absurd enough. It is either the play of Hamlet without the part of Hamlet; or, if the repentance have any real contents, then the remark of a Transatlantic critic is most pertinent: "After having implied that Christ repented of the sins of the race, we do not see why Mr. Campbell should object to the theory that He was punished for these sins."[3] Repentance is certainly the more difficult, and more obviously "impossible" task of the two, for a holy being to perform. But, as already hinted, this eccentric theory has at least this much value, that it bears testimony to the truth that, from whatever quarter objections to the imputation of our sin to Christ were to come, they were not likely to emanate from Christ Himself. The Saviour, according to this theory, through His holy, loving sympathy, imputes the sins of humanity to Himself, as sins for which a confession was due from Him as in our nature, our true Brother. The statement even implies an objective imputation, to the extent of

---

[1] Rupert of Duytz.
[2] J. M‘Leod Campbell, *On the Nature of the Atonement*, p. 138.
[3] Professor Park, quoted in Bushnell's *Forgiveness and Law*, p. 31.

demanding such a confession. For if the confession was due to God in the very truth of things, surely God could claim His due; and to claim His due from Christ means to make Him responsible for the debt. In principle, the theory differs little from the orthodox; its peculiarity lies simply in this, that it makes the debt payable not by *suffering* merely, but by *confession*. But not to insist on this, and regarding the theory in question as denying objective imputation of sin to Christ, we may still say of it that it asserts, with even extravagant emphasis, the subjective self-imputation of sin to Himself by Christ, as a thing inevitable to one minded as He was. And here at least it speaks the truth, though it may be in an exaggerated form; for, without a doubt, it was the instinctive impulse of the Redeemer to impute to Himself the world's sin, and in the light of such imputation, to regard the evils of His earthly lot as a personal participation in the curse pronounced on man for sin. It was a satisfaction to His heart to feel that, in being born into a family whose royal lineage and mean condition, combined, bore expressive witness to the misery that had overtaken Israel for her sins, in being subjected to the necessity of earning His bread by the sweat of His brow, in being exposed to the assaults of Satan, in having to endure the contradiction of sinners, in being nailed to the cross, He was indeed made partaker of our curse—in this respect, too, our Brother, and like unto His brethren. From the same subjective point of view we may, with Rupert of Duytz, regard Jesus, as He went from Nazareth to the Jordan to be baptized by John, as going forth to do penance for the sin of the world, clothed in the very habit of a penitent, Himself the Holy of Holies, yet alone fit to render penitence for the sins of the elect, and, as the sinbearer, receiving the baptism of repentance among the penitent multitude.[1] Every one who, like the Abbot of Duytz, takes a strong hold of the great truth of Christ's self-humiliating love, must sympathize with such a view.

We can cite, in favour of this self-imputation of sin on the part of the Saviour, yet another witness, not a mediaeval, but a modern one—viz. Bushnell, author of the work

---

[1] See Appendix, Note B.

already quoted in this lecture, on *The Vicarious Sacrifice*. This ingenious author, having ceased to be entirely satisfied with the views set forth in the latter portions of that work, published a new treatise, entitled *Forgiveness and Law*, recalling these sections of the older publication, and substituting in their place certain new views, which had come into his mind, he tells us, almost like a revelation.[1] The new views are promulgated with as much confidence as the old ones, as the unquestionable solution of the great problem. The overweening confidence of the writer is indeed the gravest fault of the book. That a man should be slow of heart to understand the full meaning of Christ's death is no reproach; at least it is one which it would not become every Christian disciple to bring against a brother. That one who has made the great theme of redemption his study of many years should have something to learn and to unlearn still, is not to be wondered at; for therein is revealed the many-sided wisdom of God,[2] and who has yet seen all the sides? nay, who has not, by the very intensity of his gaze at this or the other side, rendered himself as good as blind to the other sides, perhaps equally important? But one who claims to have got new light, and by the very claim confesses previous partial error, ought to avoid the oracular style, and to speak with the modesty of one who feels he may have to confess to yet further changes of view. Certainly, if the Catholic doctrine be true, Bushnell had still a good deal to learn; for he denounces that doctrine, as he understands it, with all the old vehemence. Still in the new work he makes an approach to the denounced theory in two important directions. He here admits an objective real propitiation of God, as opposed to a purely subjective one, as previously asserted, in which the disciple merely objectivizes his own feelings, conceiving that God Himself is representatively mitigated or become

---

[1] Since these lectures were delivered, Horace Bushnell has passed to his rest; and I cannot refrain from expressing my admiration of the man, and the great enjoyment, intense stimulus, and frequent help I have gained from the perusal of his writings, in which, whatever debateable opinions they may contain, sanctified genius shines out on every page. Readers of his biography will learn thence how well he deserves to be called an earnest seeker after truth.

[2] Eph. iii. 10.

propitious, because he is himself inwardly reconciled to God.' Instead of this, the author here asserts a real propitiation of God, "finding it in evidence from the propitiation we instinctively make ourselves when we heartily forgive,"[2] —having observed, that is, that men who want to forgive thoroughly have first to overcome their own moral disgust, by doing acts for the offender which cost them effort and sacrifice.[3] The other approximation consists in asserting that Christ was "incarnated into the curse," as a necessary condition of His being able to raise men out of the curse into the sphere of Christian liberty. The author represents Christ as "consciously" suffering "the curse or penal shame and disaster of our transgression," in all the leading crises of His life—in the temptation, in the scene upon Mount Olivet when He wept over Jerusalem, in the agony of Gethsemane, and in the crucifixion. His Incarnation, we are told, put Him in the compass of all that belongs to the solidarity of the curse, except that He is touched by none of its contaminations.[4] "Under the curse He feels as if the condemnations of God were upon Him—as they are in all the solidarities of the race into which He is come."[5] "He suffers all the suffering of mankind; not as we do, in mere sympathy with the suffering itself, but as beholding it in its guilty causes,—a suffering in which the displeasures of God and His compassions are united, by a conjunction that is itself the utmost possibility of suffering."[6] Here is a sufficiently distinct recognition of the subjective imputation of sin to Himself by Christ, who, according to the theory, looks on Himself throughout life as under the curse, the penal shame and disaster of transgression, the condemnations and displeasures of God. The author seems inclined to go even further than this, and to admit that Christ's sufferings in these penal aspects were appointed by God, and in some sense a divine infliction. When the prophet says, "He was wounded for our transgressions, and bruised for our iniquities," it is not to be doubted that he conceives

---

[1] *Forgiveness and Law*, p. 12.   [2] *Ibid.* p. 12.
[3] For illustrations, see pp. 40-48 of the work.
[4] *Forgiveness and Law*, p. 151.   [5] *Ibid.* p. 155.
[6] *Ibid.* p. 155.

some kind of penal infliction in the suffering endured.[1] The only thing doubted is, whether "it is the penalty of our state of discipline, or of justice itself." Bushnell strenuously maintains the former alternative. Conceding that Christ's sufferings were penal, not only to His feelings, but by God's will, he contends that they were not judicial, but merely penal-sanction sufferings—just the inverse of the position taken up by Archbishop Magee. He holds that there is no such thing as judicial suffering in this world, strict justice being reserved for the world to come. Here men are under a scheme of "probatory discipline," and all the sufferings they undergo are of a disciplinary character. The curse of the law is not the justice of God, but simply the penal-sanction discipline we are under.[2] And what is true of us is true of Christ. His suffering may legitimately enough, perhaps, be regarded as a divine infliction, but it does not follow that the infliction is judicial penalty; for it can as well be penal-sanction suffering, as we certainly know that all other suffering in this world is.[3] "The retributive liability He is in, is indeed severe enough to bear even a look of justice. We only happen to know that no suffering of our own under the curse is justice, and that He is suffering with us in our lot as it is. If we call it penal, as I have called the disciplinary sanction arranged for, it is not the penalty of justice."[4]

From this account of the latest speculations of this very able and earnest American theologian two inferences may fairly be drawn. One is, that what I have named the subjective imputation of sin to Himself by Christ, will ever appear, on due consideration, to be an essential element of His self-humiliation. The other is, that it will be found difficult to hold a *subjective* imputation, without admitting a corresponding *objective* imputation. Once reckon it as necessary to the completeness of our Lord's humiliation that He should become like unto His brethren, even to the extent of reckoning Himself a partaker in the penal consequences of sin, not merely as evil, but as penalty, and you are forced to ask yourself: Does this subjective con-

---

[1] *Forgiveness and Law*, p. 170. [2] *Ibid.* p. 166.
[3] *Ibid.* p. 172. [4] *Ibid.* p. 167.

sciousness of the Saviour answer to any objective law or principle of divine government? or is it merely an exaggerated, though amiable, assertion of His solidarity with the race, on the part of one who burns with the enthusiasm of humanity? The latter alternative is not likely to commend itself to a considerate mind. For Christ in His humiliation was not wilful. He was not a "*voluntary*" in His humility. He humbled Himself in the spirit of obedience, doing, doubtless *con amore*, what was required of Him, but not more than was required of Him. If so, then it was the Father's will that His Son should be on earth as a sinner, suffering penalty for sin. In this light He regarded His Son Himself; in this way He would have His Son view His own position; in this way He would have all men regard Him. He sent Him into the world, as it were, saying, "Behold the Lamb of God, who beareth the sin of the world."

But, all this conceded, there still remains the great question, In what sense is Christ the bearer of sin by divine appointment? is it in the sense of suffering for sin under a judicial infliction, or is it merely in the sense of suffering under the penal sanctions of this present state of probationary discipline? The question here has reference not to *what* Christ suffered, but to the *design* for which He suffered. On either alternative the material of Christ's sufferings may be the same; but the design varies, according as we adopt the one or the other mode of conceiving them. If we conceive those sufferings as a judicial infliction, then we regard them as a ground on which God, with a due regard to the claims of justice, grants remission of sin, involving exemption from all penal consequences, and especially from the wrath to come. If we conceive the sufferings as simply amounting to participation in the penal sanctions of a disciplinary state, then their design may be simply to enhance the moral power of the sufferer to bring us out of our sins, and so, as a matter of course, out of their penal retributions, temporal and eternal. Christ comes down to our level in order that He may lift us to His. Finding us under the law, under the curse, under a system of penal sanctions expressive of divine displeasure against sin, yet remedial in their aim, He Himself comes under the law, the curse, the penal sanctions; that He may, by the moral power thus gained, raise us out of law into liberty, out of the curse into the blessedness of holiness, out of penal sanctions into the privileges of sonship. This latter design is thought to be eminently worthy of God, while the former is denounced as utterly unworthy of the First Cause and Last End of all.

Does the case indeed stand so? Must we, as an increasing number of voices declare, give up the celebrated doctrine of satisfaction as indefensible, and, in particular, as derogatory to the divine wisdom? This is a question which cannot be adequately discussed here; but a few general observations may be submitted, with special reference to the bearing of the subject upon the character of the supreme Ruler of the universe. That it became Him for whom are all things, and by whom are all things, *for one reason or another*, to subject the Captain of salvation to a curriculum of suffering, is generally admitted. The point in dispute is, whether it became Him to subject the Saviour of men to suffering in the form of legal penalty for sin. Now here it greatly behoves us to recall to mind that expression of the Apostle Paul's, already casually referred to, wherein he speaks of the work of redemption through Christ, as containing a revelation or exhibition of the manifold, many-sided, or, many-coloured wisdom of God—$\dot{\eta}$ πολυποίκιλος σοφία τοῦ Θεοῦ. The precise connection of thought in which the expression occurs it is not necessary to point out; it bears the stamp of a phrase coined by the apostle, to embody the feeling produced in his mind, by deep and protracted reflection on the gracious purpose of God in Jesus Christ. After long, rapt meditation on the sublime theme, Paul feels that the divine idea of redemption has many aspects. The pure light of divine wisdom revealed in the gospel is resolvable into many coloured rays, which together constitute a glorious spectrum presented to the admiring view of principalities and powers in heavenly places, and of all men on earth whose eyes have been opened to see it. Entering into the apostle's mind on this great theme, we too should come to the study of our Lord's sufferings, prepared to find therein a many-sided revelation of divine wisdom: not merely the righteous One suffering for righteousness' sake at the hands of the unrighteous; or the Holy one suffering sympathetically with the unholy, that He may win their confidence; or a revelation of divine love in self-sacrifice, meant to overcome the distrust with which human beings regard the Deity, and assure them of His good will; or the Son of God stooping to conquer, voluntarily humbling Himself, because that is the way to gain sovereignty over human hearts, and to obtain the highest of all dominion—that, viz., which wields sway through moral influence, not through mere physical force; or a contrivance for securing that the pardon of sin shall not be prejudicial to the interests of government and good morals; or, "a sacrifice to satisfy divine justice:" but all these together. Why not look on the cross as a prism which analyzes the light of divine wisdom into all these coloured rays, and possibly into others whose presence we may have hitherto failed to detect; so, in place of insisting that Christ's earthly sufferings could serve only one end, acting as if we believed that the greater the number of ends served in mutual harmony, the more these sufferings became Him who, as the First Cause and Last End of all, appointed them as means to accomplish His own wise purposes? Unity amid variety is doubtless to be desired; and if we can get one theoretic principle from which we can deduce all particulars as corollaries, it is well; but meantime it is most important to take heed that we exclude none of the facts, and that our induction of particulars be complete. If we be at a loss as to which aspect of the subject should be placed first, as the most important, let us at least be careful to omit none of the aspects. Perhaps in past times theologians have been more anxious to have their cut and dry theory, than to make a full collection of the facts; and it is gratifying, therefore, to find recent inquirers on this as on other theological subjects, preferring the inductive to the deductive method, according to which, in the words of Professor Crawford, who has himself adopted this method, " we first of all address ourselves to the actual statements of Holy Scripture upon the subject,—deferring in the meanwhile all theories and assumptions,—and endeavour, by a fair examination and a careful comparison and classification of these statements, to arrive at such conclusions as are deducible from them."[1]

Now it would certainly be very surprising if it should turn out, as the result of such an induction, that the sufferings of Christ stood in no relation to the attributes of divine holiness and justice. One would expect to find the satisfactory manifestation of these attributes taking its place among the ends for the accomplishment of which it became the Supreme to make the Captain of salvation a sufferer, alongside the manifestation of divine compassion in sympathizing with man's misery, and of divine mercy in forgiving man's sin, and of divine condescension in stooping to man's low level, and of divine love in bearing man's woe. Why should the cross reveal all these last-named attributes, and not also God's holy hatred of sin, and His justice in punishing sin? In revealing these not less than those, does it not only the more completely display the divine wisdom, by exhibiting that attribute as one which can accomplish many different ends by one and the same means? If Christ crucified be the wisdom of God as satisfying His love through self-sacrifice, is He not still more the wisdom of God in satisfying at once *both* His *love* and His *justice*—His love, by suffering in sympathy with the sinner's misery; His justice, by suffering penalty for sin in the sinner's stead?[2]

To this it may be replied: Yes, were the two ends com-

[1] *The Atonement*, p. 3.

[2] Some may prefer to make the reference to justice spring out of the idea of love. In this way is the subject regarded in a recent American publication which I have read with very great pleasure: *Old Faiths in New Light*, by Newman Smith (Scribner, New York). Mr. Smith says: "In thinking of the ways of God which meet in the Incarnation, our all-illumining conception must be derived from the purest human experience of love. . . . Now human love has in it three essential elements; there are three primary colours in love's perfect light; and these three are, the giving of self, or benevolence; the putting self in another's place, sympathy, or the vicariousness of love; and the assertion of the worth of the gift, of the self which is given—self-respect, or the righteousness of love. Under the conception of vicariousness, and the assertion of its own worth involved in perfect love, the Christian doctrines of Atonement and Redemption need to be regarded; and when considered from any lower point of view, as that of law or government, the sacrificial work of Christ is hardly lifted out of difficulties and shadows into a pure moral light."—P. 277.

patible; but they are not. The dogma of satisfaction, in the ecclesiastical sense, makes God a merchant of Venice, who stands for justice, and demands the pound of flesh from one quarter or another—just, but utterly ungenerous; nay, not even just, for the dogma involves the perpetration of the injustice of inflicting upon the innocent penalty due to the guilty—an injustice miserably cloaked by the theologic fiction of imputation. Now, certainly any theory which were justly chargeable with degrading the Most High into a Merchant of Venice, would be worthy only of reprobation. But before condemnation is pronounced, care must be taken to ascertain that it is not a case of extremes meeting. What if the two characters compared meet in the one point of standing for justice, and be in all other respects the moral antipodes of each other? The fact is even so. What God demands is, as we shall see, not the exact pound of flesh, neither more nor less; and what He does demand, He takes not from *any* quarter, even from an *enemy*, but from the heart of His own beloved Son. A similar observation may be made in reply to Ritschl's objection, that the orthodox doctrine makes God a Pharisee, who will have dealings only with perfectly righteous men.[1] Here again we have a case of extremes meeting. It is quite true in one sense that God has dealings only with the morally perfect; for, as Schleiermacher has said, Only the complete can stand before Him.[2] But herein God differs *toto coelo* from the Pharisee, that He has taken pains to establish a mediated fellowship with the imperfect through the perfect One. We are "accepted in the Beloved." God hath dealings with the sinful in such a way that His zeal for holiness is above suspicion. While holding loving intercourse with the morally defective, He keeps the realized Ideal of moral excellence ever in His eye, and requires us to do the same, that we may know our standing to be, not on our merit, or on divine laxity, but on divine grace. How different from the Pharisee is God in all this! Pharisaic righteousness is exclusive; God's righteousness is self-

[1] *Lehre von der Rechtfertigung und Versöhnung*, vol. ii. p. 312, iii. p. 96.
[2] *Der christliche Glaube*, ii. p. 135: Nur das Vollkommne vor Gott vorstehen kann.

communicative. The Pharisee knows of no way to show his love for righteousness, other than by holding aloof from the unrighteous. God, in His beloved Son, makes such a manifestation of His righteousness, that He appears at once as a just God and as a Saviour; righteous, and making righteous him that believeth on Jesus, accepting the unrighteous for the sake of His righteous One.

But the main stress of the objection to the Catholic doctrine is not directed against the idea of God being well pleased with the imperfect out of regard to the perfect One; for what else but this is meant by Ritschl's own doctrine, that God imputes to sinners their fellowship with Christ as a ground for a fellowship between them and Himself? The offence lies in the idea of the innocent suffering in the place of the guilty, as if their unrighteousness were imputed to Him, and made a ground of penal procedure against Him. But are not the two imputations one in principle? does not the one imply the other? Ritschl, indeed, as we have seen,[1] will not hear of an imputation of Christ's righteousness to us, but only of an imputation of our fellowship with Him. Be it so; the question then takes this shape: If our fellowship with Christ may be imputed to us as a ground of favour before God, may not Christ's fellowship with us be imputed to Him as a ground why He should become in a judicial sense the bearer of our iniquities? Of the reality of the fellowship there can be no doubt. The innocent One who suffers for the guilty is no stranger who has fortunately been discovered somewhere in the universe, and found willing to become the sacrificial victim. He is a kinsman of the guilty, one with them not only in sympathy, but also by divine appointment, as truly as the members of one family are brethren. This fact helps at least to explain the strange phenomenon of innocence suffering for guilt. It were too much to say that the covenant oneness between Christ and sinners makes everything axiomatically plain; for, as Professor Crawford has pointed out, by connecting our Lord's sufferings with a covenant, we shift the difficulty rather than solve it.[2] The question may be raised regarding such a covenant, Was it not a *pactum il-*

---

[1] *Vid.* p. 312.   [2] *The Atonement*, p. 144.

licitum? But it is going too far on the other hand to say, that the idea of a covenant does not in the smallest degree help to clear up the mysteriousness of Christ's sufferings in the room of the guilty. It renders this service at least, that it brings those sufferings within the scope of analogies, which help us to see that they are in harmony with the world in which we live. For it is a fact, that the closer men are connected by family, social, or political ties, the more they are dealt with, under divine Providence, as a joint-stock company both for good and for evil. Whether this be just or not according to our notions, it is, at all events, the sort of justice that is agoing. It is something to see this. It helps us to abstain from dogmatizing, and to submit to a mystery which we cannot understand. But we are not under the necessity of resigning ourselves, permanently, to the despairing attitude of men who regard divine justice as something simply inscrutable. On patient inquiry, we find that this perplexing sort of justice, which looks so very like injustice, has a good deal to say for itself. It is *less* than just, only because it is a great deal *more*. The constitution under which we live, in nature and in grace, departs from the strict rule of retributive justice which renders to each man according to his works, in the interest of that great principle of love for which alone, according to many, God has any regard. While inflicting on involuntary sufferers much suffering which they may gloomily regard as a dismal fate, it supplies to love, willing to suffer, a glorious opportunity, making it possible for one to do good to others by prayer, like Abraham; by character, like David; by holy obedience in life and death, like the great Captain of salvation.[1] Such a constitution is worthy

[1] The principle of vicariousness is involved in intercessory prayer not less than in the doctrine of atonement, and it admits of the same defence in the one case as in the other—viz. that its recognition by God affords opportunity and stimulus to love. On this aspect of the subject Dr. Price has some good observations in his *Dissertation on Prayer*. To the question of a supposed objector to intercessory prayer, What influence can our prayers have on the state of *others?* he replies by pointing out that it is not necessary to suppose that the treatment which beings shall receive depends in all cases solely on what they are in themselves; that though this is what the universal Governor *chiefly* regards, it is not all; and that while there are some benefits which no means can obtain for beings who have not certain qualifications, there are others which one being may obtain for another. He

of Him for whom are all things, and by whom are all things. It is a constitution based on grace, and pervaded by grace throughout. This holds true even with regard to the covenant of works, which we are accustomed to set in contrast to the covenant of grace. There was grace even in that earliest covenant in this respect among others, that it held the race to be represented by its first individual member as its head. That procedure was not according to the strict rule of retributive justice, which renders to each man, as an isolated unit, according to his individual desert; but it was a procedure subservient to the purposes of grace, for it caused sin and the curse to abound, that grace might superabound. And grace was not tardy in beginning its benign sway. It came into play from the moment Adam fell. The second Adam began His reign of grace the day sin entered the world, producing by His secret influence, long before He came in the flesh, effects which are undeniable as facts, but which are not always traced to their true cause. Bushnell and Ritschl both tell us that God's dealings with mankind in this life are not of a strictly judicial character, that mercy is largely mingled with judgment, and that wrath, in the absolute sense, is a thing to come. The latter of these writers even goes so far as to say, that the very idea of retributive justice is hardly to be found in Scripture, being traceable only in one or two texts in Paul's Epistles, where for the moment he accommodates himself to the Pharisaic standpoint of the unchristian Jews with whom he is arguing. Righteousness as an attribute of God, according to Scripture usage as interpreted by Ritschl, signifies the consistency with which God conducts His federally faithful people to their promised destiny, and is substantially the same thing as grace.[1] How differently different men read the Bible! Matthew Arnold sees in the Old Testament nothing but a Power making for

then goes on to say: "The whole scheme of nature seems to be contrived on purpose in such a manner as that beings might have it in their power in numberless ways to bless one another. ... One end of this constitution appears plainly to be, to give us room and scope for the exercise of beneficence."—*Four Dissertations*, p. 233, 2d edition.

[1] *Die christliche Lehre von der Rechtfertigung und Versöhnung*, ii. pp. 106, 110, conf. iii. 412.

righteousness, in the sense of tending to make character and lot correspond—that is, to render to men, individually and collectively, according to their works. Ritschl sees in the same Scriptures nothing but Grace, tending to conduct a chosen race to the attainment of an unmerited good. Each has seen but half the truth, though the theologian certainly comes nearer the truth than the *littérateur*, for the distinctive idea of revealed religion is God manifesting Himself as the God of grace. But passing from this, and reverting to the statement that God's dealings with the race in this world are not of a strictly or exclusively judicial character, I remark that such is the blessed fact. Though the fallen race is under the divine displeasure, it is also to a large extent under divine mercy: God is good to all, and His tender mercies are over all His works.[1] He is gracious, and full of compassion, slow to anger, and of great mercy,[2] to such an extent that His patience has often been a stumbling-block and an offence to the good; as to Job, who asked in wonder why God did not appoint periodic times of judgment, when, like a judge on circuit, He might try the wicked, and punish them for their iniquities;[3] and to Jonah, who deserted God's service, giving as a reason, "For I knew that Thou art a gracious God, and merciful, slow to anger, and of great kindness, and repentest Thee of the evil."[4] But, what is the *rationale* of this divine patience? God's patience with a sinful world, from the beginning had its *ground* in Christ; even as, after Christ's advent in the flesh, it received its *justification* through His sacrifice on Calvary. Hence the divine winking at heathen ignorance and idolatry;[5] hence the divine forbearance with the sin of pre-Christian times;[6] hence the divine patience with the chosen people, under the ever-accumulating load of unexpiated transgression, with which the inheritance was so heavily burdened as to be of little value to the heir;[7] hence the continued existence of the fallen race, banished from Paradise and under the curse, yet under a curse much and many ways modified, insomuch

---

[1] Ps. cxlv. 9. [2] Ps cxlv. 8. [3] Job xxiv. 1.
[4] Jonah iv. 2. [5] Acts xvii. 30. [6] Rom. iii. 25.
[7] Heb. ix. 15.

that Zuingli felt emboldened to say, that while original sin by itself would have made all men damnable, it does not in fact, because of the plan of redemption. The secret of all this marvellous forbearance with a dark, wicked world was the Son in the bosom of the Father, a mystery hid for many generations from men, so that it exercised little power over them as a subjective influence, except as the object of a dim starlight hope or presentiment; a mystery hid *in* God, but not hid *from* Him, but, on the contrary, determining His attitude towards, and influencing His dealings *with*, the world, as truly before as it has done since the Incarnation.[1] All this vast influence on the fortunes of the human race Christ exercised, as the Lamb slain, from the foundation of the world. As the Logos of God, He made the worlds; as the Son of God, He upheld all things by the word of His power; as the Lamb of God, He secured for a guilty race that it should have a history, and a history which, while bearing abundant traces of divine displeasure, should not less manifestly wear upon it a stamp of divine patience, goodness, and mercy. Hence, when the Lamb was actually slain in the fulness of time, the event was what the Apostle Paul calls a declaration of God's righteousness in His relation to the pre-Christian world.[2] It revealed the true ground of the divine procedure, and, if we may so say, redeemed the divine character from the charge of laxity, as if God had behaved Himself towards men like an absolute but benignant despot, dealing leniently with his slaves, partly in lofty contempt, partly in humane pity; by showing that in all His dealings with men, wherein He dealt not with them after their sins, He had regard to the perfect One who, in the end of the world, was to appear to atone for sin by the sacrifice of Himself. Be it observed, this is not to degrade Christ's sacrifice into a governmental display intended to act on men's fears, and prevent them from abusing divine goodness. An atonement after the fashion of a governmental display has no effect on God, and it has an effect on men only after the display has been made; and it affects them by making them believe that God is more severe than ex

[1] Eph. iii. 9.   [2] Rom. iii. 25, 26.

hypothesi He really is. The atonement made by Christ was a display of God's righteousness, in Paul's sense, as revealing the hidden ground of past forbearance on God's part towards men, clearing God's action of all appearance of laxity, and making manifest that He was in reality *more* severe than He *seemed*. And it accomplished all this, just because the Lamb of God, in His sacrifice, was the subject of judicial dealing, bearing on Him the sin of the world. God was justified in not dealing with men after their sins, by dealing with the sinless One as a sinner. Christ suffering under a penal-sanction discipline would not have served the purpose. This view makes Christ simply one factor in the world's moral education, coming in at the proper juncture and exercising a critical influence on the process, from that point onwards; contemplated by God from the first in that capacity, but exercising no influence whatever on the earlier stages of the process. In Paul's view, Christ is the mainspring of all human history, the hidden ground of the divine attitude and procedure towards the world from the first; not merely the power *of* God since His Incarnation, but a power *with* God, as the Lamb slain by foreordination, from the creation onwards through all the pre-Christian ages.

But supposing it to be conceded that Christ, as the sin-bearer in the eye of law, exercised a controlling influence on the whole history of God's relations to the world, an important question still remains, viz. how far is Christ's position as the sin-bearer reconcilable with His own personal relation to His heavenly Father, which, as exhibited in the gospel history, was one of perfect, unbroken mutual fellowship? Now, in proceeding to make some observations on this delicate topic, I remark at the outset, that the fact as to Christ's relationship to His Father is as stated, and that it must fare badly with any theory which cannot afford to make this admission. Throughout His life on earth Jesus loved His Father with His whole heart, and believed Himself to be so loved in turn by His Father. In this respect the relation between Father and Son continued as it was before the Incarnation. The only difference produced by that event was, that in the incarnate state the

Son had to maintain His fellowship of love with His Father through *faith*, and amid experiences by which His faith was more or less severely tried. The capacity of sin-bearer, in which He underwent those experiences, did not alter the relation; for if Christ was in fact legally the sin-bearer while on earth, He was the sin-bearer by destination before He came into the world; and if the purpose understood on both sides was compatible with perfect fellowship, while the Son was in the bosom of the Father, why should its execution in time interrupt the good understanding? We must here recall to mind the truth set forth in our eighth axiom, that Christ's state of humiliation was at the same time a state invested with moral dignity and glory, as one in which He had, by the favour of His Father, an opportunity of achieving a sublime task, in His high and honourable calling as the Captain of salvation. Christ Himself did not lose sight of this truth; it was ever present to His thoughts, carrying Him through the hardest experiences as the mere incidents of a congenial vocation. Hence, though a man of sorrow, He was even on earth anointed with the oil of gladness above His fellows. Does this seem strange? Why, even Apollo, unjustly banished from heaven, and cherishing a sense of injury done to him by Jove, in his state of exile, a neatherd in the service of Admetus, is represented by the poet as making the vale of Pheraea vocal with the sweet sounds of his lute, and gathering the wild beasts around him by the charms of celestial music.[1] Shall we wonder that there was divine gladness in the heart of Him who came into this world, not by constraint, but willingly; not with a burning sense of wrong, but with a grateful sense of high privilege; and that He had a blessed consciousness of fellowship with His Father, who sent Him, during the whole of His pilgrimage through this vale of tears? It is true, indeed, that the position assigned to Christ by the Catholic theory gives to His suffering experience an aspect which may *seem* incompatible with such fellowship; and therefore one who is determined to hold by the latter at all hazards may think it necessary to deny that Christ either did occupy such a position on earth, or

---

[1] Euripides, *Alcestis.*

that it was ever intended that He should occupy it. For if He suffered as the sin-bearer, then His sufferings were penal, and bore to His view the aspect of an expression of divine anger against sin. But the notion that such a way of viewing His sufferings could not be combined in the Saviour's consciousness with a fellowship of faith and love towards His Father, while not unnatural, is nevertheless mistaken, and based upon misunderstanding. For two things must be borne in mind if we would understand this matter aright. One is, that at no time was the Saviour the object of His Father's personal displeasure. This must be held to be a necessary corollary from Christ's *personal holiness*, and as such it has been accepted by all writers who have handled this topic with due discrimination; as, *e. g.*, notably by Calvin, who says: "We do not indeed insinuate that God was either ever opposed to or angry with Him. For how could He be angry with His beloved Son, in whom His mind rested? or how could Christ, by His intercession, propitiate for others a Father whom He had as an enemy to Himself?" The true relation of the Saviour to the divine anger is indicated by the same great theologian in the following sentence of the place from which I quote: "This we say, that He sustained the gravity of divine severity; since, being stricken and afflicted by the hand of God, *He experienced all the signs of an angry and punishing God.*"[1] The other thing most needful to be borne in mind is, that Christ was under the anger of God, in the sense explained so well in these words of Calvin, not only during His last sufferings, but during the whole time of His humiliation. It is true that the extreme and most striking signs of divine anger were concentrated in the brief crisis of the passion; the only signs which appear to have put a very severe strain upon the Saviour's faith, and in connection with which His consciousness of being under the divine anger against sin, found unmistakable expression in the confes-

---

[1] Calvini *Institutio*, lib. ii. cap. xvi. 11: Neque tamen innuimus Deum fuisse unquam illi vel adversarium vel iratum. Quomodo enim dilecto Filio, in quo animus ejus acquievit, irasceretur? aut quomodo Christus Patrem aliis sua intercessione placaret, quem infensum haberet ipse sibi? Sed hoc nos dicimus, divinae severitatis gravitatem eum sustinuisse: quoniam manu Dei percussus et afflictus, omnia irati et punientis Dei signa expertus est.

sion of weakness in Gethsemane, and in the complaints of desertion on the cross. But we are not to suppose that, in these final experiences, new not in kind but in degree, the Father entered into a new *relation* to His Son, which was the cause and explanation of these peculiar experiences, and of them alone. The relation was the same throughout, and was in the same sense cause and explanation of Christ's whole state of humiliation. Throughout that state the Son of God was under the divine anger against sin manifesting itself in one way at one time, in another way at another; sometimes from causes which we can understand, sometimes from causes which are unfathomable. This way of looking at the matter, I am aware, has not been very generally followed, theologians, for the most part, having treated Christ's experience of His Father's wrath as a special item in His humiliation, which He underwent in connection with the crucifixion. The other view, however, according to which the wrath of God embraces the whole state of humiliation, under a certain aspect, has not been left entirely out in the cold by theologians. It can quote in its own behalf at least two first-class authorities from the sixteenth century, the Heidelberg Catechism on the Reformed side, and Hutterus as representing the Lutherans; the former teaching that Christ, during the whole time of His life on earth, but especially at its close, sustained in His body and in His soul the anger of God against the sin of the whole human race;[1] the latter representing our Saviour as truly experiencing the sense of infernal pains, not for a moment, or some small space of time, but throughout the whole time of exinanition.[2] The same idea has been reproduced in modern times by at least two German theologians, Bodemeyer[3] and Hofmann; the former a hyperorthodox Lutheran; the latter occupying an independent

---

[1] See Lecture i. of this course, p. 37.
[2] Quoted by Schmid: *Die Dogmatik der evangelisch-lutherischen Kirche*, 5te Auf. p. 303. The words are: Quemadmodum sane Christus non ad momentum vel exiguum aliquod temporis spatium, sed per omne tempus exinanitionis, sensum dolorum istorum infernalium vere subiit, ita ut tandem exclamare necessum haberet, Deus meus, Deus meus, quare me dereliquisti?
[3] *Die Lehre von der Kenosis dargestellt*, Göttingen 1860. This author understands the kenosis in the old Lutheran sense of κρύψι.

theological view-point, and regarded by intelligent readers as making important approximations to orthodoxy; while he is universally admitted, by friends and foes alike, to be worthy of all honour for his ability, candour, and reverential regard for the authority of Scripture. Hofmann's remarks on this subject are so well fitted to convey a distinct idea of what is meant by saying that Christ was under the anger of God throughout His life, that I feel tempted to indulge in a somewhat lengthy quotation, all the more that the book from which I quote is not likely to become generally known in this country. Contrasting his own views with those of Thomasius, who limits Christ's experience of divine wrath to the passion, Hofmann says: "To me, that Christ assumed our nature, and that He came under the anger of God, are one and the same thing. Humanity being under God's anger, it is for me a matter of course that Christ's entrance into humanity is a self-subjection to this anger. As, now, the whole history of the Lord is the carrying out of that relation to His Father, in which He placed Himself by His Incarnation; so He experienced, from His conception to His death, the anger of the Father against humanity, according to the measure of the progress of His history; in one way before and during His unfolding to human self-conscious life, otherwise after the same; in one way as a man in general, otherwise as an Israelite in particular; in one way before the beginning of His public life, otherwise in the course of the same; in one way in the time of His work, otherwise in the hours of His passion and death. Is all evil in the world effect of the anger of God against sinful humanity?—then all experience of the former is experience of the latter. And is it God's anger against sinful humanity which brings about that Satan tempts and opposes us?—then Christ also experienced the same in all the temptations and assaults of Satan. God's anger against sin placed Israel under the law of commandments and prohibitions. Made under this law, Christ stands under the wrath, without which the law had not been. God's anger against Israel's transgression of the law brought that people into misery. This anger Jesus felt in sharing the misery of Israel and of the house of David. Finally, is it God's anger against sin which gives the righteous up to the unrighteous, that the latter may fill up the measure of his iniquity and be ripe for judgment?—even so, this same anger gives Christ up to His enemies; to Satan it delivers Him up as a victim, that the enmity against God, and what is God's, may fill up its cup of judgment. For in both shows itself the anger of God against sin; that it forgives not sin without Christ, and such a history of Christ: and that through the same Christ in whom God makes propitiation for sin for the benefit of the penitent, this very sin in the impenitent reaches the point at which, as completed enmity against God, it is given over to final judgment."[1] It appears to me that the way of viewing the present topic, here advocated by Hofmann,[2] has much to recommend it; and this not least, that it enables us to dispose easily of such a representation of the Catholic doctrine as is given by thoroughgoing opponents—by Martineau, *e.g.*, in the following horrible sentences, occurring in an account of the orthodox views of the crucifixion as understood by him: "The anguish He endures is not chiefly that which falls so poignantly on the eye and ear of the spectator; the injured human affections, the dreadful momentary doubt; the pulses of physical torture doubling on Him with full or broken wave, till driven back by the overwhelming power of love disinterested and divine. But He is judicially abandoned by the infinite Father, who expends on Him the immeasurable wrath due to an apostate race, gathers up into an hour the lightnings of eternity, and lets them loose upon that bended head. It is the moment of retributive justice, the expiation of all human guilt; that open brow hides beneath it the despair of millions of men, and to the intensity of agony there, no human wail could give expression. Meanwhile the future brightens on the elect; the tempests that hung over their horizon are spent. The

---

[1] *Schutzschriften*, Zweiter Stück, pp. 94, 95. The *Schriftbeweis* gave rise to considerable controversy in Germany, in the course of which Hofmann replied to his opponents, and gave important explanations on some points of his system. These replies were published, as a collection of pamphlets, under the title *Schutzschriften*.

[2] It is adopted also by Van Oosterzee, who quotes with approval the passage in which it is taught in the Heidelberg Catechism. Vid. *The Image of Christ*, p. 254.

vengeance of the Lawgiver having had its way, the sunshine of a Father's grace breaks forth, and lights up with hope and beauty the earth, which had been a desert of despair and sin."[1] Bear in mind the two axioms already enunciated, that Christ was at no time the object of His Father's personal displeasure, but suffered only the signs—the *effect*, not the *affection*—of divine anger; and that He suffered these signs in one form or another, not for an hour, but for a lifetime; and the force of the above passage, as a refutation, by mere statement, of the orthodox doctrine, is at once seen to be broken.

But does the orthodox doctrine not preclude us from adopting these axioms, especially the former of the two?— Does not the dogma of satisfaction imply that Christ suffered in sinners' stead the very thing that they should have suffered—that is to say, real positive, unqualified damnation, utter separation from God in spiritual death, nay, even eternal death itself? It suits the opponents of the dogma to say so. Thus Ritschl affirms that the assumption that Christ experienced, at least momentarily, eternal damnation, is the inevitable condition of the satisfactory value of His sufferings before the judgment of God;[2] and Socinus, to whose views on the whole subject of Christ's work those of Ritschl bear too close a resemblance, sought to involve the orthodox position in hopeless contradiction, by maintaining that while, on the one hand, the end for which the Saviour died—viz. the salvation of men—demanded that He should rise from the dead unto eternal life; the dogma of satisfaction, on the other hand, demanded that He should endure, not intensively merely, but extensively, eternal death.[3] The assumption on which both virtually proceed is, that the satisfaction required is of a pecuniary character, sin being conceived of as a debt which can be cancelled only by the endurance of suffering equal in amount to that due to sinners, or at least of the same quality and value. It must be acknowledged that the

---

[1] *Studies of Christianity*, p. 86.
[2] *Die christliche Lehre von der Rechtfertigung und Versöhnung*, iii. p. 416.
[3] *De Servatore*, pars tertia, c. iv.: Haec enim satisfactio, in eo, qui nos servaturus est, aeternam mortem; ista autem nos servandi ratio aeternam vitam requirit.

defenders of the dogma have too often weakened their position by virtually conceding this assumption to their opponents, and arguing as if they were under an obligation to make out not only a moral equivalence in respect of value, but so close a resemblance in the nature or quality of Christ's sufferings as amounts to a virtual identity. Thus, *e.g.*, Van Mastricht labours to prove that Christ endured death in all senses; not only death temporal, but death spiritual and eternal;[1] and indeed many dogmatists, both of the Lutheran and of the Reformed confessions, laid down the position that Christ experienced eternal death *intensive* though not *extensive;* though some, as *e.g.* Gerhard, shrank from the statement in this bald form, assigning as a reason why the Saviour could not endure eternal death, that He was personally the most innocent and most beloved Son of God. Sometimes the matter was put in this way, that our Lord suffered the essence, apart from the accidents, of eternal death; the accidents being remorse, despair, and the like.[2] In going into these lines of thought, the defenders of orthodoxy went off the right track; for, as Dr. Charles Hodge has pointed out, there is a more excellent way—that, viz., of emphasizing the distinction between the *nature* and the *design* of Christ's sufferings. It is a mistake to suppose that the doctrine of satisfaction requires these sufferings to be the same even in *kind*, not to speak of *degree*, as the sufferings of those whom Christ died to redeem. "The words 'penal' and 'penalty,'" to quote the well-weighed language of the American divine just referred to, "do not designate any particular kind or degree of suffering, but any kind or any degree which is judicially inflicted in satisfaction of justice. The word 'death,' as used in Scripture to designate the wages or reward of sin, includes all kinds and degrees of suffering inflicted as its punishment. By the words 'penal' and 'penalty,' therefore, we express nothing concerning the nature of the sufferings endured, but only the design of their infliction."[3] The same views are expressed with equal

---

[1] *Theoretico-practica Theologia*, lib. v. cap. xii. §§ vi.-ix.

[2] *Vid.* Appendix, Note C.

[3] *Systematic Theology*, vol. ii. p. 474.

point and clearness by another American theologian of the same name, Dr. Archibald Hodge: "He (Christ) did not render a pecuniary satisfaction, and therefore did not suffer the same degree nor duration, nor in all respects the same kind of sufferings, which the law would have inflicted on the sinner in person. ... The substitution of a divine for a human victim necessarily involved a change in the *quality*, though none whatever in the legal relations of the suffering."[1] Again: "We say that Christ suffered the very penalty of the law, not because He suffered in the least the same kind, much less the same degree, of suffering as was penally due those for whom He acted, because that is not at all necessary to the idea of penalty."[2] When this distinction between the design and the nature of our Lord's sufferings is grasped, it protects us from the temptation to which the older dogmaticians partly yielded, of reasoning deductively from the supposed requirements of a theory as to what these sufferings *must have been*, and leaves us free to inquire with unbiassed mind what the Scriptures represent them *actually to have been*. Instead of starting with the assumption, that the thing demanded was the exact pound of flesh, an eye for an eye, a tooth for a tooth, we are content to learn from the word of God wherein the satisfying virtue and value of the atonement consisted; remembering that the authoritative estimate of the virtue and the value lies, not with us, but with the unerring judgment of the all-wise God, and that while the divine estimate, as ascertained from Scripture, may approve itself to our minds and consciences afterhand, it may yet in some respects be different from what we should have conjectured beforehand, or from the *à priori* determinations of systematic theology. This attitude, it will be observed, is not to be confounded with that of those who, with Duns Scotus, make the acceptance of Christ's death by God, as a satisfaction for sin, a mere affair of arbitrary will or divine caprice. The theory of acceptilation, as it is called, recognises no standard by which the value of the atonement can be determined, and represents God as simply choosing

[1] *The Atonement*, by Rev. Archibald A. Hodge, D.D., p. 28.
[2] *Ibid.* p. 36.

to ascribe infinite worth to that which, in reality, had only a limited worth. The doctrine now contended for, on the contrary, is that the atonement rendered by Christ has the value of a sufficient satisfaction for the sin of the world, as determined by intelligible moral considerations, as opposed to mere caprice; only it makes the standard depend, not on man's judgment, in the first place, but on the infallible judgment of divine wisdom.

Looking, then, into the Scriptures with unbiassed mind, in order to find out the elements of value in our Lord's atoning work, as estimated by the wisdom of the omniscient Spirit, we observe that emphasis is laid on at least four things: *first*, the *dignity* of the Sufferer; *second*, His *obedience* to His Father's will; *third*, His *love* to sinners; and *fourth*, His *sufferings* themselves. The divine dignity of the Sufferer is pointed at as an important factor in the determination of the value of His atoning work in various places, as in the famous passage in Paul's Epistle to the Philippians, so often alluded to in these Lectures, where it is noted that He who was obedient unto death was One who had been in the form of God; and where Christ is spoken of as offering Himself unto God by the eternal Spirit;[1] and yet again, where the heinous nature of the sin of apostasy is indicated, by representing the apostate as trampling under foot the Son of God, and counting *His* blood, the blood of the new covenant, a common thing.[2] These passages imply that the divine dignity of Christ gives to His death infinite worth, eternal validity as a sacrifice, inexpressible sacredness. Socinus objected to this element being taking into account, as making God a respecter of persons.[3] The objection is utterly frivolous; for nothing is more evident to common sense, than that in a penal, as distinct from a pecuniary satisfaction, the person of the substitute comes into consideration as affecting the value of his performance. When a sum of money is due, it has to be paid in full, no matter by whom. When what is required is reparation of an injury done to the law by a moral offence, the imprisonment for a limited period of a

---

[1] Heb. ix. 14.   [2] Heb. x. 29.
[3] *De Servatore*, pars tertia, cap. iv.

prince may be equivalent to the incarceration of a plebeian for life. The other argument of Socinus, against taking the dignity of Christ into account—that if it were allowed, it would involve a charge of cruelty against God in subjecting His Son to more suffering than there was need for—is equally frivolous.[1] It does not follow, because the dignity is to be taken into account, that therefore the suffering may be reduced to a form, a mere bowing of the head, so to speak, by the way of obeisance to the law which governs the world. In that case there *might* be room for a charge of partiality. To exclude such a possibility, and to show that the law's claims were being earnestly dealt with, it was needful that the sin-bearer, though divine, should endure *all that it was possible for a holy Being to suffer in the way of penalty.*

That the holiness or obedience of Christ enters as an element into the estimate of value, is taught by clear implication in those words of the Apostle Peter, where he reminds his readers that they have been redeemed, not with corruptible things, such as silver and gold, but by the precious blood of Christ, *as of a lamb without blemish and without spot.*[2] The same truth is taught in the Epistle to the Hebrews, where the offering by Christ of His body in sacrifice is represented as the climax and consummation of His obedience to God's will.[3] In this text the passion of the Saviour is conceived of as having its value, in being an act of obedience which formed the crown of a life of obedience. Herein, according to the writer of the Epistle, lay the incomparable merit of Christ's sacrifice, as opposed to the legal sacrifices, wherein the blood-shedding of involuntary brute-victims had only a ritual and no ethical significance. What pleased God was not the mere fact that the blood of His Son was shed. To imagine such a thing were to fall back into Jewish ritualism, and to put the offering on Calvary on a level with the offering of bulls and goats. To quote the words of Turretine, " the satisfaction is not to be ascribed merely to the external oblation of blood, but specially to the internal act—that is, to the free and

---

[1] *De Servatore*, pars tertia, cap. iv.
[2] 1 Pet. i. 18, 19. [3] Heb. x. 4-10.

most stedfast will of Christ—by which we are said to be sanctified."[1]

Prominence is given to the element of love to the sinful, as entering into the divine estimate of the value of Christ's sacrifice, by the Apostle Paul in the familiar text: "Walk in love, as Christ also hath loved us, and hath given Himself for us an offering and a sacrifice to God for a sweet-smelling savour."[2] Here the beautiful thought is suggested, that the love to the sinful, manifested by Christ in dying for them, made His death well-pleasing to His Father, ascending up to heaven as a sweet savour, like the smoke of sacrificial victims from the altar of burnt-offering. This is poetry; but it is also sound theology, as Aquinas recognised when he spake of the passion of the Saviour as having value in God's sight, not only on account of the dignity of the Sufferer and the severity of His sufferings, but very specially on account of the greatness of the love which moved Him to suffer—*propter magnitudinem charitatis*.[3] And it is not unimportant to remark here, that when we regard "the magnitude of the charity" as an element of value, we see at once that the amount of suffering could not be other than great; for if we should be ready to accept as strictly true the sentiment on which the doctrine of *satisfactio superabundans* is based, that the smallest amount of suffering endured by such an august Being, even the shedding of a single drop of His blood, would have sufficed to satisfy divine justice, it is certain that it would not have sufficed to satisfy the Saviour's own love. For the gratification of its own yearning, as also to ensure a return of the greatest possible amount of grateful love for those

---

[1] *Institutio*, vol. ii. p. 394, locus decimus quartus, quaestio xiii. sec. xii.: Et satisfactio non externae tantum sanguinis oblationi adscribenda est, sed praecipue actui interno, nimirum spontaneae ejus et constantissimae voluntati, qua sanctificari dicimur.

[2] Eph. v. 2.

[3] *Summa*, pars tertia, q. xlviii. art. ii.: Christus autem ex charitate et obedientia patiendo majus aliquid Deo exhibuit quam exigeret recompensatio totius offensae humani generis: primo quidem propter magnitudinem charitatis ex quâ patiebatur. He gives as his second and third reasons: (2) Propter dignitatem vitae suae, quae erat vita Dei et hominis, (3) propter generalitatem passionis et magnitudinem doloris assumpti. On these grounds Aquinas based his doctrine of *satisfactio superabundans*.

receiving the benefit, that love would be content with nothing short of enduring all that it was barely possible for a sinless Being to experience in the way of suffering.[1]

Yet the statements of Scripture, in speaking of Christ's sufferings, are characterized by a dignified sobriety. Nowhere can we discover the slightest tendency to exaggeration or straining, either in support of a theory, or with a view to rhetorical effect. Sometimes the mere fact that Christ died is mentioned, as when Paul, summing up the gospel he had preached to the Corinthians, specifies as one item, "how that Christ died for our sins according to the Scriptures;" and as when, in the Epistle to the Hebrews, Jesus is spoken of as crowned with glory and honour, that He by the grace of God might *taste death* for every man;[2] and even where the connection of thought required the inspired writers to exhibit the sufferings of the Saviour in as intense a light as possible, their statements are not so strong as one accustomed to the dogmatic style of treatment might expect or desiderate. The writer of the Epistle to the Hebrews, when he would commend Jesus as the pattern of patience, says of Him simply, that He "endured the cross, despising the shame." Paul, when he would exhibit the humility of Christ in its utmost depth of self-abasement, indicates the limit of descent by the phrase, "obedient unto death, even the death of the cross." It did not occur to him to say, "even death spiritual," or "even death eternal," or "even the death of the damned." It may safely be concluded that such extreme phrases are not required for a correct statement of the true doctrine, and that it will suffice to say in general terms that Christ suffered in body and soul all that it was possible for a holy being to suffer. This general statement leaves the question open, whether the personal holiness of Christ did not fix a limit beyond which His experience of suffering could not go, even as it set bounds to His experience of temptation. That it did fix such a limit seems beyond question. To speak of the holy One of God as enduring spiritual and eternal death, is surely a gross and mischievous abuse of terms! Instead of following the example of Protestant

[1] *Vid.* Appendix, Note D.   [2] Heb. ii. 9.

scholastic theologians in the use of such expressions, we ought rather to regard such use as an instructive illustration of the danger to which the dogmatic spirit exposes us of wresting Scripture, and manufacturing facts in support of a preconceived theory. Happily all theologians have not yielded to the temptation in connection with the present topic, some having handled it with due care, caution, and discrimination: among whom the American divines already named deserve honourable mention,[1] but foremost of all, the great Transatlantic theologian of last century, President Edwards, whose statement on the question, in what sense Christ suffered the wrath of God, deserves and will repay the most attentive study of all who desire to think justly on the delicate theme.[2]

Summing up, then, the elements of value in our Lord's atoning death as inductively ascertained from Scripture, we get this formula, expressed in mathematical language, though the thing to be estimated is a moral quantity not admitting of mathematical measurement: The value of Christ's sacrifice was equal to His divine dignity, multiplied by His perfect obedience, multiplied by His infinite love, multiplied by suffering in body and soul carried to the uttermost limit of what a sinless being could experience. That is to say, in forming an estimate of the fitness of that sacrifice to satisfy justice, we must bear in mind from what a height the Priest who offered it descended, the spirit of filial obedience in which the self-emptied One fulfilled His ministry after He had assumed the form of a servant, the mind of lowly love to the sinful which brought Him down from heaven, and made Him willing to descend as near hell as was barely possible; and finally, the curriculum of suffering through which He passed in His state of humiliation, terminating in the cross, with its pain and shame, and gloom and desolation. All these things the First

---

[1] Vid. *Systematic Theology*, vol. ii. p. 614; and *The Atonement*, cap. v. Mr. Dale can hardly be reckoned among this class. He insists on taking Christ's complaint of desertion in the most literal sense, and represents the Redeemer as enduring that loss of fellowship with the divine blessedness, that exile from the joys of God's presence, which is the effect of the Divine wrath in the case of the impenitent.—*The Atonement*, p. 61, 7th edition.

[2] *Vid.* Appendix, Note E.

Cause and Last End of all took into account; and, taking them into account, He was well pleased with His Son's performance. All these things we, too, are to take into account, in endeavouring to say Amen to the divine judgment concerning the sacrifice offered on Calvary. And when we have duly weighed them all, we find the saying of a cordial Amen no hard matter. A mediaeval mystic gave utterance to the striking thought, that in order to the fulness of the satisfaction it was necessary that there should be as great humiliation in the expiation as there was presumption in the transgression.[1] That requirement is met by the Scripture doctrine, for it was One in the form of God who stooped to die. The other elements of value commend themselves equally to our minds. When we learn that Christ's obedience to God and His love to man enter into the worth of His sacrifice, we no longer rebel against the doctrine as one of immoral tendency, putting salvation within the reach of selfish men who simply regard Christ as their substituted victim; for we perceive that a spiritual appreciation of the ethical value of the atonement as a manifestation of the Redeemer's holiness and love is of the essence of faith in Him as the Saviour. Then, finally, the doctrine commends itself to our consciences in this, that while giving due prominence to these moral elements, it does not trifle with the penal aspect of the question, but represents the Saviour as undergoing suffering limited only by His inviolable holiness, limited in one direction only to be enhanced in others.

How different the moral effect of the scriptural formula, as above ascertained, from that produced by any formula intended to make out an atonement sufficient in respect of the mathematical quantum of suffering as the all-important matter, such an one, *e.g.*, as that proposed by Philippi!

[1] Richard of St. Victor, *De Verbo Incarnato*, cap. viii. Richard uses the thought as an argument for the divinity of Christ. His words are: Ad plenitudinem autem satisfactionis oportuit ut tanta esset humiliatio in expiatione quanta fuerat praesumptio in praevaricatione. Rationalis autem substantiae Deus tenet summum, homo vero imum. Quando ergo homo praesumpsit contra Deum, facta est elatio de imo ad summum. Oportuit ergo ut ad expiationis remedium fieret humiliatio de summo ad imum, sed hoc omnino non potuit nisi aliqua in Trinitate personarum.

Christ, according to this modern expounder of old Lutheran orthodoxy, suffered eternal death as fully and as really as the damned, the only difference being that He, as God, was able to suffer intensively, in a brief space of time, what the weak capacity of ordinary human nature requires to be extended, in the case of the damned, over an unending period of time. In this way the eternal death endured by Christ intensively was strictly equal to the eternal death endured *in extenso* by any one sinner. Then the impersonality of Christ's human nature is brought in as a factor, by which the eternal death of Christ is made equal to the sum of the eternal deaths, actual or possible, of all mankind. To the Socinian objection, that even if it be admitted that Christ could endure eternal death, yet at most He endured only one eternal death, while *ex hypothesi* there were as many eternal deaths to endure as there are single human individuals, this theologian reckons it a good reply to say, that Christ did not endure eternal death as a single common man, as one among many, but as the God-man, "who weighs more than all;" the point intended to be insisted on by the phrase within inverted commas being, not the dignity of the sufferer, but the impersonality of His humanity in virtue of which He is *Man*, not an individual man: manhood multiplied by Godhead was to make His humanity, not ethically, but metaphysically, equal to the sum of individuals bearing human nature. Thus the resulting formula is, divine capacity of suffering multiplied by the impersonality, multiplied by the intensively endured eternal death, equals the sum of the eternal deaths endurable *in extenso* of all the damned, and of all those liable to damnation.[1] A revolting equation, at once metaphysically inconceivable and morally offensive, degrading the sufferings of the Redeemer into a mere literal *quid pro quo*, and exhibiting His atoning death in the aspect least fitted to show forth the divine glory, to satisfy human consciences, or to become a moral power over human hearts. They are not the friends of a great truth, who present it in so repulsive a form. Even in the scholastic period of Protestant orthodoxy, Cotta, the learned editor of Gerhard's *Loci*,

[1] *Kirchliche Glaubenslehre*, Theil iv. 2te Hälfte, p. 32.

while claiming for himself the character of a sound Lutheran, yet found it necessary to explain that it must be taken with a grain of salt when theologians teach that Christ suffered in His soul infernal pains; and that the statement must be understood to refer, not to the very pains which the damned experience, but rather to the gravity of His pains, which can be compared with that of infernal torments.[1] Modern Lutherans of the Philippi type seem bent on serving up to their contemporaries a *réchauffé* of antiquated opinions, without the grain of salt deemed by Cotta necessary to make them palatable; with what result it is not difficult to foresee.

When the Redeemer breathed out His soul on the cross, His humiliation had reached its climax, if it did not then take end. The interval between death and the resurrection the Reformed confessions reckon to the state of exinanition; but they view it simply as a natural sequel to the death, and speak of it soberly as consisting in Christ's continuing under the power of death for a time. This sobriety has not been imitated by all theologians. What took place during the time when the Saviour's body rested in the tomb, has been the subject of an immense amount of curious and unprofitable speculation, based on a few obscure texts of Scripture. Into the ghostly questions relating to the *triduum* I have no space to enter, and, I must in honesty add, small inclination. To this dark region may be applied the word of prophecy concerning Babylon in ruins, "Owls shall dwell there." Instead, therefore, of flitting about like a theological night-bird in the territory of the dead, where nothing can be distinctly seen or known, I shall conclude this lecture with a brief summary of the theories concerning Christ's redeeming work, to which, in its course, I have had occasion to allude. One advantage which has come to us unsought from the study of that work from our chosen

---

[1] Cotta's words are: Atque ex his, quae modo diximur, satis patet, cum grano salis accipiendum esse quando theologi protestantes docent Christum in anima suâ dolores infernales passum esse. Neque enim hoc de iis ipsis doloribus quos damnati experiuntur, sed potius de gravitate dolorum, qui cum infernalibus comparari possunt, intelligendum est. (*Vid.* Dissertatio secunda. *De statibus et officio Christi mediatorio.*)

point of view, is the suggestion of a method of classifying theories of atonement or redemption. The value of a good method of classification in all departments of knowledge is universally acknowledged. When classification is wholly neglected, science degenerates into mere fact-knowledge, devoid of intellectual interest; when the classification is defective, facts are wrongly assorted, resemblances being overlooked, and differences unduly magnified, or *vice versâ*. These evils are not without exemplification in the present department of knowledge. The recent literature on the doctrine of atonement presents reviews of theories more or less elaborate, in many respects valuable, yet less instructive than they might have been, because the theories criticised are simply enumerated in an almost casual order, and opinions of certain writers are noticed as distinct theories, which are in reality simple varieties of one and the same theory[1]

The scheme of classification put into our hands as the spontaneous result of the inquiries in which we have been engaged in this lecture is as follows:—

1. Christ, we have seen, suffered as a prophet for righteousness' sake, and there is a theory which regards His sufferings solely from this point of view. On this theory, our Lord's sufferings, including His death, were simply incidental to His prophetic office, as exercised in this evil world; and their redemptive power lies in this, that they exhibit Christ as a fellow-combatant for truth and right, and show us that fellowship with God is independent of outward happiness, and so prevent our peace of mind from being disturbed by the mistaken notion that all suffering is on account of sin. This is substantially the view held in common by Socinus, Robertson, and Ritschl. It may be distinguished as the *prophetic theory*.

2. Christ, we have seen, as a priest acting for men before God, needed to have an experience fitted to develop and reveal sympathy, and so to gain the confidence of those whom He represents. There is a theory which looks on the sympathy of Christ manifested in a suffering, sorrow-

[1] This remark applies, to a certain extent, to the work of Professor Crawford.

ful experience, as the whole of His performance, and the source of all His redeeming power. In this theory suffering is not an *incident*, but a *chief end* of the Incarnation. Christ not only suffered inevitably by coming into contact with the evil of the world, but came into the world for the express purpose of revealing divine love through self-sacrifice carried to its utmost limit, in order to gain moral influence over men for their spiritual good. This view was first formally propounded by Abelard, and its most distinguished modern expounder is Bushnell. It may be named the *sympathetic theory*.

3. Christ, we have seen, as the priestly representative of men before God, performs acts which have validity for the whole community: the one sanctifying the whole. We have seen also that, under a certain aspect, Christ's priestly action may legitimately be regarded as including Himself. Now there is a theory which holds that Christ's priestly activity in its whole compass, and under all its aspects, is inclusive of Himself; that He does nothing for us which He does not do for Himself; that whatever He does for us, He does by first doing it for Himself; that He sanctifies the whole lump of humanity by sanctifying Himself as the first-fruits. On this theory, Christ's death is simply the crown of a life of obedience, in which He maintained an absolutely unbroken fellowship with His Father, and presented the ideal which all believers must strive to have realized in themselves. This view many of the Fathers entertained, without intending it as an exhaustive account of Christ's work; and in modern times it has been advocated as the true theory of redemption under various forms, by Schleiermacher, Irving, and Maurice. It may be called the theory of *redemption by sample*.

4. Christ, we have seen, was not only a priest, but a sacrificial victim; in the latter capacity acting not as a representative, but a substitute, bearing the world's sin imputed to Him, that sinners might be made the righteousness of God in Him. In connection with this branch of our subject we found it convenient to distinguish a twofold imputation—a *subjective* imputation of sin to Christ by Himself, and an *objective* imputation of sin to Him by the First

Cause and Last End of all. The former sort of imputation we found recognised by parties who deny the latter; their theory being, that Christ imputed to Himself, as a partaker of humanity, the world's sin, to the extent of making a sorrowful confession of it, which was accepted by God as a confession by humanity, and therefore as a ground of forgiveness. This theory assumes that it is not necessary, in order to pardon, that the *penalty* of sin be endured, adequate *confession* of sin being an alternative method of satisfying the claims of divine holiness. Its principal, we may almost say its sole, advocate is M'Leod Campbell. It may be distinguished as the theory of redemption by Christ's *self-imputation of sin*, or, by *perfect confession of sin*.

5. The fifth and last theory is the Catholic one of *redemption by substitute*, which, in addition to the subjective imputation of sin to Himself by Christ, and to the imputation of sin to Him by believers in their prayers and praises, *both* admitted by those who take exception to the received doctrine,[1] teaches, over and above, a corresponding *objective* imputation of sin to the Redeemer by the Supreme Ruler of the world, the ground at once of Christ's action in imputing human sin to Himself, of our action in imputing our sins to Him, and of God's action in imputing righteousness to us. This theory, like the rest, has assumed various forms in the hands of its advocates; some exaggerating the penalty endured by Christ as the sin-bearer, with a view to mathematical identity, supposed to be required by the principle on which the theory is based; others attenuating the penalty to a mere symbol or form; while others, again, have striven to steer a medium course between two extremes, laying emphasis not on the quantity or the quality of the Saviour's sufferings, but on their design; yet pointing out, in the interest both of divine justice and of divine love, that these sufferings went to the utmost limit of what it was possible for a holy being to endure.

While advocating the last-named theory, still entitled by comparison to be called the Catholic, I have not found it necessary to repudiate as utterly false all those preceding. I have been able to recognise each in succession as a

---

[1] See Bushnell, *The Vicarious Sacrifice*, p. 450 to the end.

fragment of the truth, one aspect of the many-sided wisdom of God revealed in the earthly ministry of His eternal Son. In this fact I find great comfort, with reference both to my own theological position on this great theme, and to that of many who occupy a different position. For, on the one hand, it is a presumption in favour of the Catholic doctrine, that it does not require to negative rival theories, except in so far as they are exclusive and antagonistic; and, on the other hand, one may hope that theories which have been a partial truth will bless their advocates by the truth that is in them, connecting them in some way with Him who is the fountain of life, and initiating a process of spiritual development which will carry them on to higher things. It is not impossible, it is not even uncommon, to grow to Catholic orthodoxy from the meagrest, even from Socinian, beginnings. Such was the way in which the apostles themselves, the first inspired authoritative teachers of the faith, attained to the elevated view-point from which they surveyed Christ's work on earth, when they had reached the position in the Church which their Lord designed them to occupy. Their first lesson in the doctrine of the cross did not rise above the watchword of the Socinian theory: " the righteous One suffering for righteousness' sake, and setting therein an example to all His disciples;" and not till long after, did they attain insight into the meaning of the baptismal name given by the Baptist to Jesus: "The Lamb of God, that taketh away the sin of the world." Let this fact ever be borne in mind by all to whom that name is fraught with peace and provocative of ardent love, and it will help them to maintain an attitude of patience, hope, and charity towards many who reject with determined unbelief, yea, with bitter scorn, truths dear to their own hearts.

APPENDIX.

LECTURE I.

NOTE A.—PAGE 15.

It is not my intention to attempt a complete history of the interpretation of this famous passage, which has occupied the thoughts of commentators and theologians in all ages. Those who desire full information on the history of opinion may consult, besides the leading commentaries, Tholuck's *Disputatio Christologica de loco Pauli Ep. ad Phil.* c. ii. 6-9, or Ernesti's monograph on the same passage in the *Theologische Studien und Kritiken* (1848, viertes Heft), in which the various methods of interpreting the passage are carefully classified, and an attempt made to explain it by the hypothesis of an allusion being intended by the apostle to the second and third chapters of Genesis. What I propose here is simply to jot down a few notes on particular expressions, and first on the phrase, ἐν μορφῇ Θεοῦ.

What is signified by μορφὴ Θεοῦ? The Fathers, as is stated in the text, generally took μορφή as equivalent to φύσις, their anxiety being to find in the passage an unequivocal testimony to the divinity of Christ. The only exception is Hilary, who vacillates on the point, as also on the question closely bound up therewith: whether the *forma Dei* was renounced or retained in the state of humiliation. In some places Hilary follows the ordinary patristic view, and in others he departs from it. A full list of the relative passages, and an instructive discussion of their import, will be found in Thomasius, *Christi Person und Werk*, ii. pp. 174-189. Thomasius thus states the fact as to Hilary's opinion: "Usually he distinguishes strictly between *forma servi* and *forma Dei*, as in ix. 14 (*De Trinitate*), and also between human nature and *forma servi*. *Forma Dei* is for him the glory-form of God, the form of appearance which belongs to the Son, in virtue of His likeness in essence to the Father. Forma et vultus et facies et imago non differunt, *De Trin.* viii. 44, 45. It is the stamp of the characteristic expression and impression (Aus- und Abdruck) of the Godhead of the Father: quod signatum in Dei forma est, hoc necesse est totum in se coimaginatum habere quod Dei est; on the other hand, *forma servi* is the *habitus humanus, forma hominis, humilitas;* not, however, so as if the appearing form were abstracted from the essence, but both go together in Hilary's view: the human nature in its earthly limited definiteness, the divine nature in the form of manifestation essential to it. Therefore speaks he thus at one time: The *evacuatio forma Dei* is not *evacuatio naturae, substantiae;* at another time: ut vero assumpsisse formam servi nihil aliud est, quam hominem natum esse, ita in forma Dei esse non aliud est, quam Deum esse; therefore he speaks now of a real renunciation of the *forma Dei* in the incarnation, the contrast to which is *interitus naturae;* and anon declares that the *forma Dei* preserved itself, to a certain extent, in the *evacuatio*, in which case the *forma* is identified with the essence" (p. 174). Among the principal passages bearing on Hilary's opinions on the two connected questions as to the meaning of *forma Dei*, and the retention or renunciation of the *forma Dei* in the state of exinanition, are the following. I place first those which imply a distinction between form and nature, and an exchange of divine form for human form in the state of humiliation. *De Trinitate*, ix. 51: Dei *forma* jam non erat, quia per ejus exinanitionem servi erat forma suscepta. Neque enim defecerat *natura*, ne esset; sed in se humilitatem terrenae nativitatis manens sibi Dei natura susceperat, generis sui potestatem in habitu assumptae humilitatis exercens. ix. 38: Exinaniens se igitur ex Dei *forma*, servi formam natus susceperat, sed hanc carnis assumptionem ea, cum quâ sibi naturalis unitas erat, Patris *natura*, non senserat. viii. 45: Exinanivit se ex Dei forma, id est ex eo quod aequalis Deo erat. On the other side, inclining to the ordinary patristic view, are the following passages:—

xi. 48: In formâ Dei *manens* formam servi assumpsit, non demutatus, sed se ipsum exinaniens, et intra se latens, et intra suam ipse vacuefactus potestatem. Form is here taken as equal to nature, therefore it *remains* in the servile state. xii. 6: Christus enim in formâ Dei manens formam servi accepit.... Esse autem in *forma* Dei non alia intelligentia est, quam in Dei manere *natura*. Passing on to modern times, we find that the tendency among all interpreters, and specially those who regard the kenosis as consisting in an exchange of the form of God for the form of a servant, is to identify μορφὴ Θεοῦ with the δόξα to which Jesus alluded in His intercessory prayer (John xvii. 5). Thus Thomasius: "That μορφή is equivalent neither to οὐσία, nor to φύσις, nor to *status*, but signifies its *forma*, the appearance with which anything shows itself, may be regarded as the common result of modern exegesis. Μορφὴ Θεοῦ is therefore, as Meyer expresses it, the condition-form corresponding to the essence and exhibiting the condition (die Zustandsform, dem Wesen entsprechend und den Zustand darstellend), or, more strictly, the glory-form answering to the essence of God (die dem Wesen Gottes entsprechende Herrlichkeitsgestalt), or, as Wiesinger puts it, the glory of the divine form of existence, distinguished from the δόξα (John xvii. 5), only thereby, that here the appearance of this glory before the world is conceived as included, as is evident from the contrast of μορφὴ δούλου" (vol. ii. p. 150). Ebrard, however dissents from this view, and contends that μορφή and δόξα are not to be identified. Δόξα, he says, "is not = μορφὴ Θεοῦ, (*a*) in respect of the sense of the words. Δόξα always denotes an outward glory answering to the inward essence, a concrete, never the immediate, existence-form of the essence itself. *Form* and *Herrlichkeit* are very different even in German. (*b*) If it is said that δόξα is not indeed equivalent to μορφή, but is equivalent to μορφὴ Θεοῦ; it signifies, not the abstract idea of existence-form, but that definite existence-form which the Son had before the Incarnation, it must be said in reply, that John xvii. 22 is against this view, where Christ denotes His inner glory which He had not laid aside in the Incarnation, and had given to the disciples by the term δόξα, and distinguishes it from the δόξα which He had laid aside, and is about to get back. Δόξα is therefore not = μορφὴ Θεοῦ, is not the name for this one definite existence-form, but is the name for every kind of glory. (*c*) Paul (Rom. viii. 17; Phil. ii. 9) denotes by the term δόξα the outer glory which forms the adequate appearance of an inner essence, *i.e.* the state of the glorification or transfiguration of the blessed at the resurrection, both of Christ and of believers. In John xvii. 5, 24, δόξα similarly denotes the outer glory which Christ possessed before the Incarnation, and should again receive after His resurrection, the worship of angels, recognition as Head and Lord of the world. But in ver. 22 δόξα is used to denote the *inner* glory which Christ never renounced. Nowhere is δόξα = existence-form." In accordance with this view, Erbrard assigns to μορφὴ Θεοῦ, as distinct from δόξα, the specific meaning: divine, that is, eternal form of existence. This Christ parted with at the Incarnation, not only for a time, but for ever. He exchanged once for all the eternal mode of existence for the time-form. He became and continues for ever man. See *Christliche Dogmatik*, vol. ii. 32–37. The view of Liebner is somewhat similar. He uses the expression μορφὴ δούλου as a clue to the meaning of the other contrasted phrase μορφὴ Θεοῦ: " The μορφὴ δούλου signifies the human existence-form as a condition of *dependence*, the existence-form of the creature-ly ethico-religious personality. What, then, is the necessary contrast which is expressed through the phrase μορφὴ Θεοῦ? Nothing else than the existence-form of absolute independence, freedom, absolute personality." That is, in the μορφὴ Θεοῦ the Son of God was not a *servant* of God, which He became when He assumed human nature, but an equal of God (vid. *Christologie*, p. 327). According to Nitzsch, the term μορφή is used in reference to God, mainly because it is used in the next clause in reference to humanity, to complete the parallelism of thought and language: " The direct occasion to use the word μορφή lay more on the human than on the divine side, as it belongs to the essence of man to be an incorporated, sense-endowed, apparent, shaped, visible personality. But the human form has the God form for its natural antithesis." " The important point," the author adds, "is this: Christ, who in the ground of His being is the Lord of glory, the Son of God, whose vocation it is to glorify the Father, and whom the Father purposes to glorify, in obedience to the Father, and in love to the Father, and to union with the human race, and to the glorifying of humanity and of the world along with Himself, emptied Himself of the brightness (*Klarheit*) which He had in Himself in entering into a Human state of servitude" (*System der Christlichen Lehre*, p. 260). In affinity with Nitzsch's opinion stands that of Ernesti. "If," he remarks, "we are to understand by μορφὴ Θεοῦ an outer appearance-form, shape, then arise these unanswerable questions: What is the specific form of God in which Christ found Himself in His pre-existence? and, What is the specific form of a servant? Is it that of men? Angels also can be God's servants. We can therefore, in the description of Christ by the phrase ἐν μορφῇ Θεοῦ ὑπάρχων, recognise only a pictorial expression (Phantasieausdruck) of the truth, that in His pre-existence He was more than a servant of God, as men are, υἱὸς τοῦ Θεοῦ in an eminent sense, the δεύτερος θεός of Philo, a pure light-reflection of God, εἰκὼν τοῦ Θεοῦ, and must give up the idea of making this pictorial expression conceptually clear, as also in Gen. iii. 2 the γέγονε ὡς εἷς ἡμῶν cannot be made conceptually clear. In short, Christ, being originally more than man made in God's image, might with more plausibility than Adam have entertained the thought of acting automatically; but He denied Himself, renounced this *moreness* (Mehrseyns), would only be what man ought to be, a servant of God. Therefore He remained in conscious dependence on God, and made Himself like men. The first is the οὐκ ἁρπαγμὸν ἡγήσατο τὸ εἶναι ἴσα Θεῷ; the second, the ἑαυτὸν ἐκένωσε" (*Studien und Kritiken*, 1848, pp. 912, 913). The parallelism between Christ's behaviour and Adam's, here hinted at and carried out in all particulars by Ernesti (Adam would be God, Christ renounces His Godlikeness; Adam suffered death as a doom, Jesus voluntarily; Adam incurred the divine curse, Jesus won the divine approval and a great reward, etc.), has not been approved by expositors, and seems far-fetched. His conception also of Christ's pre-existent state comes short of the standard of orthodoxy. But his view as to the meaning of μορφή, or rather as to the impossibility of fixing its meaning in precise theological thought, deserves serious consideration. If any theological fixation of its meaning be possible, it must be looked for in the direction pointed out by Ebrard and Liebner; for, as Ebrard has shown, the term δόξα hardly suffices to give the necessary definiteness. A similar remark may be made with reference to the expression πλούσιος ὤν in 2 Cor. viii. 9. The word πλούσιος suggests much, but specifies nothing; it points to a state very diverse from the impoverished condition of the Lord Jesus in His state of humiliation; but it gives us no inventory of the riches renounced, no indication of their nature. The term stimulates our imagination rather than informs our minds. We may put much meaning into it, according to our theological conception of what the Incarnation involved, but we cannot take much theology out of it by a reliable and legitimate process of exegesis. We may make the riches renounced, metaphysical, ethical, or eudamonistic, or all three together. The best clue to the nature of the riches renounced, the glory foregone, the form laid aside, is the μορφὴ δούλου, to which the μορφὴ Θεοῦ stands opposed. We have to consider what was involved in this servile state; and if we find that limitation of divine attributes, such as knowledge, exposure to temptation, liability to the curse pronounced on man for sin, hardships supplying severe tests of obedience, were all involved in it, and necessary to its completeness and thoroughness,—then we may infer that the μορφὴ Θεοῦ forms a contrast to the μορφὴ δούλου in all these respects: in respect to divine attributes (metaphysical), in respect to divine exemption from moral trial, and in respect to divine felicity; the kenosis, of course, extending to all, in whatever sense the kenosis is to be taken, whether as absolute or as relative.

2. Having discussed at length the expression μορφὴ Θεοῦ, it will not be necessary to enter into much additional detail on the correlate expression μορφὴ δούλου, having already anticipated much that relates thereto. In patristic literature μορφὴ δούλου signifies human nature, as μορφὴ Θεοῦ signifies divine nature. Modern interpreters, on the other

hand, are generally agreed that the form of a servant is not to be immediately identified with human nature, but points to some attribute of human nature, either accidental or essential. Ebrard understands by the phrase, not human nature in its ideal integrity, but human nature as it stands under the consequences of sin. According to this view, the servant-form is something accidental. Liebner gives to the phrase the meaning, the human existence-form, as one of dependence, according to which the attribute denoted is something essential to humanity; for it pertains to man, irrespective of sin, to be under law to God, to be God's servant. Meyer's interpretation is substantially the same. The servant-form signifies the position as a servant, not of one who serves in general (both God and man), or of one who serves others (as in Matt. xx. 28), or of one who is subject to the will of another (indefinitely), but specially of one who is the servant *of God*, this being manifestly implied in the contrast to ἐν μορφῇ Θεοῦ ὑπάρχων. As a matter of mere interpretation, Meyer and Liebner are right; but Ebrard's view is theologically correct. The form of a servant is, in point of fact, the state of humanity as it is on earth, subject to death in consequence of sin (vid. *Dogmatik*, ii. p. 203).

3. We come now, in the last place, to the puzzling clause, οὐκ ἁρπαγμὸν ἡγήσατο. The question here is, In what sense is ἁρπαγμός to be understood? this word being the key to the interpretation of the clause. Two quite different lines of interpretation have been followed by interpreters, one finding in the clause " the *assertion*," the other " the *surrender* of privileges," as Canon Lightfoot pithily puts it (*The Epistle of Paul to the Philippians*, 3d ed. p. 131). Ἁρπαγμός being taken actively to denote plundering, usurpation, robbery, the natural meaning of the clause is that given in our English version, following the Vulgate and the Latin Fathers, " thought it not robbery to be equal with God;" that is, was truly and by inherent right God's equal. This interpretation has the advantage, that it takes ἁρπαγμός in its most natural sense; for certainly the termination μος, as is generally conceded, suggests an active sense. But against it is the weighty consideration, that

the connection of thought requires another sense—viz. that borne by ἅρπαγμα, *praeda*, a piece of booty. What we expect to find the apostle saying is, that Christ, being in the form of God, did not regard equality in state with God as a robber regards his booty,—viz. as a thing to be clutched greedily and held fast at all hazards,—but emptied Himself. This accordingly was the view taken of the passage by many of the Greek Fathers, as Lightfoot in his *excursus* has shown; and this fact, by the way, may help us over the grammatical difficulty supposed to lie in the ending of the word ἁρπαγμός. If the Greek Fathers had no scruple in rendering the word as if it had been ἅρπαγμα, this may be held to prove that no hard and fast line separates the active from the passive form as to sense. Very many modern interpreters, accordingly, do render the word ἁρπαγμός as ἅρπαγμα, among whom may be mentioned Lightfoot, Ellicott, Alford, Tholuck, Liebner, Ebrard. The remarks of Ebrard on the passage are specially good. "To regard anything as booty," he says, "is an intensified double contrast to a voluntary renunciation of something which rightfully belongs to oneself. The disposition of self-seeking regards even foreign property as welcome booty, much more that which it can rightfully claim. The disposition of love does not even regard its own lawful property as the robber regards his *rapina*, but freely gives it away" (*Dogmatik*, ii. 34). Meyer, while practically agreeing with the interpretation given in the text and by the foregoing commentators, yet endeavours to retain for ἁρπαγμός its proper active signification. The word, he contends, signifies not *praeda*, *Geraubtes*, but actively *taking prey*, *Rauben*, *Beutemachen*. Therefore the clause must be interpreted thus: Not as a robbing regarded He the being equal with God, that is, not under the view-point of gaining booty did He place the same, as if in respect of His activity it amounted to this, that He appropriated that which did not belong to Him ("Demnach ist zu erklären: nicht als ein Rauben betrachtete er das gottgleiche Sein. d. h. nicht unter den Gesichtspunkt des Beutemachens stellte er dasselbe, als sollte es hinsichtlich seiner Thätigkeits-äusserung ihm darin bestehen, dass er ihm nicht Eignendes an sich raffete."—

An die Philipper, p. 72). On this interpretation of Meyer's, Tholuck remarks, comparing it with De Wette's: "Longe vere praestantior Meyeri interpretatio, ad quem si omnino ἁρπαγμός solam potestatem actus rapiendi habet, palma loci feliciter expediti deferenda videtur. Meyerus enim, postquam discrimen inter εἶναι ἴσα Θεῷ εἶναι ἐν μορφῇ Θεοῦ nullum esse demonstravit, hunc dicti Paulini sensum statuit; 'Demnach ist zu erklären, nicht für einen Raub hielt er das Gottgleichsein, d. h. nicht so sah er die Gottgleichheit welche er hatte, an, als wäre sie ein Verhältniss des Beutemachens, als bestehe sie im Ansichreissen fremden Besitzes.' Per se quidem, haec sententia Deum praedatum ire seque aliorum bonis locupletare noluisse admodum absona est, at ratione habita ad oppositum comma septimum non aliud nisi hoc declarat, tantum abfuisse ut aliorum copiis ditare voluerit Christus, ut in aliorum commodum divitiis suis se privaverit, ac ministrorum loco haberi voluerit" (*Disputatio Christologica*, p. 17). That is to say, Meyer's interpretation, in Tholuck's judgment, amounts to this, that Christ was so far from enriching Himself with the goods of others—equality with God being conceived of for the moment as the property of another to be got only by robbery—that He willingly parted with His own—this same equality with God—and became a servant. I confess that the turn given to the clause by Meyer seems to me too subtle, and even difficult to understand, and therefore I much prefer the rendering which has been adopted by many competent scholars: He did not deem equality with God a thing to be clutched and held fast at all hazards, as a robber holds his booty.

LECTURE II.

NOTE A.—PAGE 57.

I GIVE in this note all the extracts I have met with in Cyril's works bearing on the subject of Christ's knowledge, with a translation, in parallel columns.

The first extract is from *Adversus Anthropomorphitas*, cap. xiv., the subject of which is, " Of those who say that the Son knew not the last day, against the Agnoetes."

After arguing against the idea that the asserted ignorance was absolute, or referred to Christ as a divine Being, Cyril goes on to give his own opinion thus:

1. Πεφόρηκε μὲν ὁ μονογενὴς Λόγος τοῦ Θεοῦ μετὰ τῆς ἀνθρωπότητος καὶ πάντα τὰ αὐτῆς, δίχα μόνης τῆς ἁμαρτίας. Μέτροις δὲ ἀνθρωπότητος πρέπει ἂν εἰκότως, καὶ τὸ ἀγνοεῖν τὰ ἐσόμενα· οὐκοῦν καθ' ὃ μέν νοεῖται Θεός, οἶδε πάντα ὅσα καὶ Πατήρ· καθ' ὃ γε μὴν ἄνθρωπος ὁ αὐτός, οὐκ ἀποσείεται τὸ καὶ ἀγνοῆσαι δοκεῖν διὰ τὸ πρέπειν τῇ ἀνθρωπότητι. Ὥσπερ δὲ αὐτὸς ὢν ἡ ζωὴ πάντων καὶ δύναμις τροφὴν σωματικὴν ἐδέχετο, τὸ τῆς κενώσεως οὐκ ἀτιμάζων μέτρον, ἀναγέγραπται δὲ καὶ ὑπνῶν, καὶ κοπιάσας· οὕτω καὶ πάντα εἰδὼς τὴν πρέπουσαν τῇ ἀνθρωπότητι ἄγνοιαν οὐκ ἐρυθριᾷ προσνέμων ἑαυτῷ. Γέγονεν γὰρ αὐτοῦ πάντα τὰ τῆς ἀνθρωπότητος, δίχα μόνης τῆς ἁμαρτίας.

The only-begotten Word of God with humanity bore all that belonged to it, sin excepted. But to the measures of humanity it belongs to be ignorant of the future. Therefore, so far as He is God, He knows all things as doth the Father; but in so far as He is also man, He does not shake off the *appearance* of ignorance, because such ignorance is congruous to human nature. Even as He, being the life and power of all, received bodily food, not despising the measure of the kenosis (it is recorded also that He slept and was weary); so He who knew all was not ashamed to ascribe to Himself the ignorance pertaining to humanity. For all human properties became His,

Ἐπειδὴ δὲ τὰ ὑπὲρ ἑαυτοὺς οἱ μαθηταὶ μανθάνειν ἤθελον, σκήπτεται χρησίμως τὸ μὴ εἰδέναι καθ' ὃ ἄνθρωπος, καί φησι, μηδὲ αὐτοὺς εἰδέναι τοὺς κατ' οὐρανὸν ὄντας ἁγίους ἀγγέλους, ἵνα μὴ λυπῶνται ὡς μὴ θαρῥηθέντες τὸ μυστήριον.

saving sin. When, therefore, the disciples wished to learn things above them, He *usefully pretended not to know*, and said that not even the angels in heaven knew; that they might not be grieved because they were not admitted to the knowledge of the mystery.

The words in *italics* in English, and the corresponding words in Greek, show the kernel of Cyril's view.

II. The next passage is from the *Apologeticus pro XII. capitibus contra Orientales*, Anathematismus iv. Speaking of the text in which Jesus is said to have grown in wisdom as in stature, Cyril remarks, against the Orientals whom he charged with making Christ two persons, one of whom really did grow in wisdom:

Οὔτε γὰρ μερισμὸν τῶν ὑποστάσεων μετὰ τὴν ἕνωσιν δογματίζομεν, οὔτε τὴν τῆς Θεότητος φύσιν αὐξήσεώς τε καὶ προκοπῆς δεδεῆσθαί φαμεν· ἐκεῖνο δὲ μᾶλλον, ὅτι κατ' οἰκείωσιν οἰκονομικὴν ἑαυτοῦ πεποίηται τὰ ἴδια τῆς σαρκὸς, ὡς σὰρξ γεγονώς.

For we neither affirm as a dogma the division of the hypostases after the union, nor do we say that the nature of Deity needs increase and growth; but this rather we hold, that, by way of an *economical appropriation*, He made His own the properties of the flesh, as having become flesh.

What the *economical appropriation* means is more clearly and fully explained in the next quotation from *Quod unus sit Christus*, p. 1332 (Migne):

III. Ὁ γάρ τοι σοφὸς εὐαγγελιστὴς, σάρκα γεγονότα προεισενεγκὼν τὸν Λόγον, δείκνυσιν αὐτὸν οἰκονομικῶς ἐφέντα τῇ ἰδίᾳ σαρκὶ, διὰ τῶν τῆς ἰδίας φύσεως ἰέναι νόμων. Ἀνθρωπότητος δὲ τὸ προκόπτειν ἐστὶν ἡλικίᾳ τε καὶ σοφίᾳ, φαίην δ' ἂν ὅτι καὶ χάριτι, συναναπηδώσης τρόπον τινὰ τοῖς τοῦ σώματος μέτροις καὶ τῆς ἐν ἑκάστῳ συνέσεως. Ἑτέρα δὲ αὖ ἐν τοῖς ἤδη παισὶ, καὶ ὑπὲρ τοῦτο ἔτι. Ἦν μὲν γὰρ οὐκ ἀδύνατον ἤγουν

For the wise evangelist, introducing the Word as become flesh, shows Him economically submitting Himself to His own flesh and going through the laws of His own nature. But it belongs to humanity to increase in stature and in wisdom, and, I might add, in grace, intelligence keeping pace with the measures of the body, and differing according to age. For it was not impossible for the Word born of the Father to have

ἀνέφικτον, ὡς Θεῷ τῷ ἐκ Πατρὸς φύντι Λόγῳ, τὸ ἐνωθὲν αὐτῷ σῶμα, καὶ ἐξ αὐτῶν σπαργάνων αἴρειν τε ὑψοῦ, καὶ εἰς μέτρον ἡλικίας τῆς ἀρτιῶς ἐχούσης ἀνενεγκεῖν. Φαίην δ' ὅτι καὶ ἐν νηπίῳ σοφίαν ἐκφῆναι τεθαυμασμένην ῥᾴδιον τε καὶ εὐήλατον ἦν αὐτῷ· ἀλλ' ἦν τὸ χρῆμα τερατοποιίας οὐ μακρὰν, καὶ τοῖς τῆς οἰκονομίας λόγοις ἀνάρμοστον. Ἐτελεῖτο γὰρ ἀψοφητὶ τὸ μυστήριον. Ἱφίει δὴ οὖν οἰκονομικῶς τοῖς τῆς ἀνθρωπότητος μέτροις ἐφ' ἑαυτῷ τὸ κρατεῖν.

raised the body united to Himself to its full height from the very swaddling-clothes. I would say also, that in the babe a wonderful wisdom might easily have *appeared*. But that would have approached the thaumaturgical, and would have been incongruous to the laws of the economy. For the mystery was accomplished noiselessly. Therefore He economically allowed the measures of humanity to have power over Himself.

The accommodation to the laws of the economy, according to this passage, consisted in this: in stature, real growth; in wisdom, apparent growth. The wonderful wisdom was there from the first, but it was not allowed to appear (ἐκφῆναι), to avoid an aspect of monstrosity. That the growth in wisdom was simply graduated manifestation of an already present perfect knowledge, appears clearly in the next extract. It is from *Adversus Nestorium*, p. 154.

Alluding to the interpretation put by Nestorius on the text Luke ii. 52, viz. that a real growth in knowledge was meant, Cyril, after pointing out the absurdity of such an idea from the divine point of view, goes on to express his own opinion thus:

IV. Οὐκοῦν ἐδείχθη ἂν ἅπασιν ἀηθές τε χρῆμα καὶ ξένον, καὶ περιεργίας ἄξιον, εἰ βρέφος ὢν ἔτι, θεοπρεπῆ τῆς σοφίας ἐποιεῖτο τὴν ἔνδειξιν· κατὰ βραχὺ δὲ καὶ ἀναλόγως τῇ τοῦ σώματος ἡλικίᾳ κατευρύνων αὐτὴν, ἐμφανῆ τε ἅπασι καθιστῶν, προκόπτειν ἂν λέγοιτο, καὶ μάλα εἰκότως.

Therefore there would have been shown to all an unwonted and strange thing, if, being yet an infant, He had made a demonstration of His wisdom worthy of God; but expanding it gradually and in proportion to the age of the body, and (in this gradual manner) making it manifest to all, He might be said to increase (in wisdom) very appropriately.

The same idea is expressed with, if possible, still greater clearness in the next extract, which is taken from *Ad reginas de rectâ fide oratio altera*, cap. xvi.:

V. "Τὸ δὲ παιδίον ηὔξανε, καὶ ἐκραταιοῦτο πνεύματι, πληρούμενον σοφίας· καὶ χάρις Θεοῦ ἦν ἐπ' αὐτῷ." Καὶ πάλιν· "Ἰησοῦς προὔκοπτεν ἡλικίᾳ καὶ σοφίᾳ καὶ χάριτι Θεῷ καὶ ἀνθρώποις." Ἕνα λέγοντες τὸν Κύριον ἡμῶν Ἰησοῦν Χριστὸν, καὶ αὐτῷ προσνέμοντες τά τε ἀνθρώπινα καὶ θεοπρεπῆ, τοῖς μὲν τῆς κενώσεως μέτροις πρέπειν ἀληθῶς διαβεβαιούμεθα τό τε τὴν σωματικὴν αὔξησιν ἐπιδέχεσθαι, καὶ μὴν καὶ τὸ κραταιοῦσθαι, τῶν τοῦ σώματος ἀδρυνομένων μορίων κατὰ βραχύ· καὶ αὐτὸ δὲ τὸ δοκεῖν πληροῦσθαι σοφίας, διά γε τὸ οἱονεὶ πρὸς ἐπίδοσιν τῇ τοῦ σώματος ἡλικίᾳ πρεπωδεστάτην τῆς ἐνούσης αὐτῷ σοφίας ἀναφοιτᾶν τὴν ἔκφανσιν· καὶ ταυτὶ μὲν, ὡς ἔφην, τῇ μετὰ σαρκὸς οἰκονομίᾳ πρέποι ἄν, καὶ τοῖς τῆς ὑφέσεως μέτροις.

"But the boy increased and waxed strong in spirit, being filled with wisdom, and the grace of God was upon Him." And again: "Jesus increased in stature and wisdom, and in favour with God and men." In affirming our Lord Jesus Christ to be one, and assigning to Him both divine and human properties, we truly assert that it was congruous to the measures of the kenosis, on the one hand, that He should receive bodily increase and grow strong, the parts of the body gradually attaining their full development; and, on the other hand, that He should *seem* to be filled with wisdom, in so far as the *manifestation* of the wisdom dwelling within Him proceeded, as by addition, most congruously to the stature of the body; and this, as I said, agreed with the economy of the Incarnation, and the measures of the state of humiliation.

Here, again, observe that the growth in the body is real, the growth in the mind only apparent,—a growth in the sense of graduated manifestation made to correspond with the age of the body, so that no more wisdom might appear than suited the time of life, such correspondence being required by propriety or decency.

The next two quotations are from *Thesaurus*, Assertiones xxii. xxviii. I take the latter first, as referring to the same subject as the last, the growth of the child Jesus in wisdom. *Thesaurus*, p. 428:

VI. Φυσικός τις νόμος οὐκ ἐπιτρέπει τὸν ἄνθρωπον τῆς τοῦ σώματος ἡλικίας ὥσπερ μείζονα πολὺ τὴν φρόνησιν ἔχειν· ἀλλὰ συντρέχει πως καὶ ἡ ἐν ἡμῖν σύνεσις, καὶ συμβαδίζει τρόπον τινὰ ταῖς τοῦ σώματος προκοπαῖς. Ἦν οὖν

A certain physical law forbids man having more wisdom than corresponds to the stature of the body: our understanding runs and keeps pace *pari passu* with the growth of the corporeal frame. Now the Word became flesh, as

ὁ Λόγος ἐν σαρκὶ γενόμενος ἄνθρωπος καθὰ γέγραπται· καὶ ἦν τέλειος, σοφία τοῦ Πατρὸς καὶ δύναμις ὤν. Ἐπειδὴ δὲ τῷ τῆς φύσεως ἡμῶν ἔδει παραχωρεῖν πως ἐχρῆν, ἵνα μή τι ξένον παρὰ τοῖς ὁρῶσι νομισθῇ, ὡς ἄνθρωπος, κατὰ βραχὺ πρὸς αὔξην ἰόντος τοῦ σώματος, ἀπεκάλυπτεν ἑαυτὸν καὶ ὁσημέραι σοφώτερος παρὰ τοῖς ὁρῶσιν ἢ καὶ ἀκούουσιν ἐφαίνετο. . . . ὅτι παρὰ τοῖς ὁρῶσι σοφώτερος ἀεὶ καὶ χαριέστερος ἦν, προκόπτειν εἴρηται, ὡς ἐντεῦθεν ἤδη τὴν τῶν θαυμαζόντων προκόπτειν ἕξιν, ἢ τὴν αὑτοῦ.	it is written, and was perfect, being the wisdom and power of God. But seeing it was in a sense necessary that He should adapt Himself to the custom of our nature, lest He should be reckoned something strange as man by those who saw Him, while His body gradually advanced in growth He *concealed* Himself, and *appeared* daily wiser to those who saw and heard Him; . . . because He was ever wiser and more gracious in the esteem of beholders, He is said to have grown in wisdom and grace, so that His growth is to be referred rather to the habit of those who wondered at His wisdom than to Himself.

Here it is taught that Christ's growth in wisdom was simply a holding back, or concealment, of wisdom existing in perfection from the first, out of respect to the physical law, according to which, in ordinary men, body and mind keep pace in their growth.

The other passage in the *Thesaurus* (Assertio xxii. 220–224) is too long to quote in full, and after the foregoing it is not necessary to give it *in extenso*. The author's view will appear sufficiently from selected sentences. The subject of discussion is the profession of ignorance made by Jesus with reference to the day and hour:

VII. Οὐκ ἀγνοῶν ὁ λόγος οὐκ οἶδα φησίν, ἀλλὰ δεικνύων ἐν ἑαυτῷ καὶ τὸ ἀνθρώπινον, ᾧ μάλιστα πρέπει τὸ ἀγνοεῖν . . . Ἐπειδὴ γὰρ τὴν ἡμῶν περιεβάλετο σάρκα, διὰ τοῦτο καὶ τὴν ἡμῶν ἄγνοιαν ἔχειν ἐσχηματίζετο. . . . (P. 373.) Ἀγνοεῖν δὲ λέγων, καθὸ τῶν ἀγνοεῖν πεφυκότων, δηλονότι ἀνθρώπων, τὴν ὁμοίωσιν ἐνεδύσατο. (*Ibid.*)	Not as being ignorant the Word says I know not, but showing in Himself the human, to which ignorance is very specially congruous. For since He clothed Himself with our flesh, He *affected* to have (put on the fashion of) our ignorance. . . . In *saying* that He was ignorant, He put on the likeness of those whose nature it is to be ignorant, viz. men.

Appendix.—Lecture II.—Note A. 373

Ὥσπερ οὖν συγκεχώρηκεν ἑαυτὸν ὡς ἄνθρωπον γενόμενον μετὰ ἀνθρώπων καὶ πεινῆν καὶ διψῆν, καὶ τὰ ἄλλα πάσχειν ἅπερ εἴρηται περὶ αὐτοῦ, τὸν αὐτὸν δὴ τρόπον ἀκόλουθον μὴ σκανδαλίζεσθαι κἂν ὡς ἄνθρωπος λέγῃ, μετ' ἀνθρώπων ἀγνοεῖν, ὅτι τὴν αὐτὴν ἡμῖν ἐφόρεσε σάρκα. Οἶδε μὲν γὰρ ὡς σοφία καὶ Λόγος ὢν ἐν Πατρί· μὴ εἰδέναι δέ φησι δι' ἡμᾶς καὶ μεθ' ἡμῶν ὡς ἄνθρωπος. (P. 373).

As, then, He allowed Himself, as become man, to hunger and thirst with men, and to suffer the other things which are said concerning Him; in the same way it follows that we ought not to be scandalized, when, as man, He *says* that He is ignorant along with men, because He bore the same flesh with us. For as Wisdom and as the Logos in the Father He knew; but He *says* that He knew not on our account and along with us as man.

With reference to the question, "Whom do men say that I the Son of man am?" Cyril remarks (p. 376):

Οὐκοῦν οἰκονομεῖ τι πολλάκις τῆς ἀγνοίας τὸ σχῆμα.

Therefore He often puts on economically the fashion of (*i. e.* simulates) ignorance.

Further on, Cyril adduces the question put by Jesus to the disciples, "How many loaves have ye?" where ignorance was certainly only affected, to prove that σαφῶς οἰκονομικῶς ἔσθ' ὅτε τὴν ἄγνοιαν σχηματιζόμενος ὁ Σωτήρ.

that the Saviour manifestly sometimes economically puts on the fashion of ignorance.

A few sentences further on he says, with reference to the ignorance of the day and hour:

Οἰκονομεῖ γάρ τοι Χριστὸς μὴ εἰδέναι λέγων τὴν ὥραν ἐκείνην, καὶ οὐκ ἀληθῶς ἀγνοεῖ.

For Christ acts economically in saying that He does not know that hour, and is not really ignorant.

The last extract has reference to the same subject, Christ's profession of ignorance concerning the day and hour. It is from the *Apologeticus contra Theodoretum pro XII. capitibus* (Anathematismus iv. p. 416):

VIII. Καὶ εἴπερ ἐστὶν εἷς τε καὶ ὁ αὐτὸς διὰ τὸ τῆς ἀληθοῦς ἑνώσεως χρῆμα, καὶ οὐκ ἕτερος καὶ ἕτερος διῃρημένως τε καὶ ἀνὰ μέρος, αὐτοῦ πάντως ἔσται καὶ τὸ εἰδέναι καὶ μέν τοι καὶ τὸ μὴ εἰδέ-

And if He is one and the same in virtue of the true unity of natures, and is not one and another (two persons) disjunctively and partitively, to Him will belong both to know and to *seem* not to

ναι δοκεῖν. Οὐκοῦν οἶδε μὲν καὶ αὐτὸς θεϊκῶς ὡς σοφία τοῦ Πατρός. Ἐπειδὴ δὲ τὸ τῆς ἀγνοούσης ἀνθρωπότητος ὑπέδυ μέτρον, οἰκονομικῶς οἰκειοῦται καὶ τοῦτο μετὰ τῶν ἄλλων, καί τοι, καθάπερ ἔφην ἀρτίως, ἠγνοηκὼς οὐδέν, ἀλλ' εἰδὼς ἅπαντα μετὰ τοῦ Πατρός.	know. Therefore He knows on the divine side as the Wisdom of the Father. But since He subjected Himself to the measure of humanity, He economically appropriates this also with the rest, although, as I said a little ago, being ignorant of nothing, but knowing all things with the Father.

Neander, commenting on this passage, very justly remarks that Cyril expresses himself in words to which he could hardly attach any definite meaning. What Cyril does say, however, is not so utterly devoid of meaning as the words which are put into his mouth by the English translator of Neander (Bohn's edition), which are absolutely unintelligible, owing to a misrendering of the German original. The sentence beginning with Ἐπειδὴ δέ is thus rendered: "When Christ subjected Himself to the general *mass* of human nature, which is limited in its knowledge, He appropriated *this part of it* also by a special economy, although still He had no bounds to His knowledge, but was, with the Father, omniscient." It is evident that in using the word *mass* (printed in *italics* as here given), the translator has mistaken the German word *Mass*, measure (μέτρον), for *Masse*, mass (Neander's *Church History*, vol. iv. p. 151).

LECTURE III.

NOTE A.—PAGE 85.

IN tracing the origin of the Lutheran Christology to the controversy concerning the Supper, I am aware that the leading modern authorities of all schools, Dorner, Thomasius, Schneckenburger, Baur, agree in asserting that Luther's views of the person of Christ, in their main features, were fixed before the Sacramentarian dispute began. Dorner's opinions on the point are accessible to all, and need not be quoted (see *Doctrine of the Person of Christ*, div. ii. vol. ii. p. 53 ff.). Thomasius (*Christi Person und Werk*, ii. p. 13) says that the controversy with the Swiss only gave Luther the occasion for the construction of his Christology, the innermost motive lying, not in the doctrine of the Supper, but in the two great moments of his faith, living confidence in the historical fact of redemption, and actual communion with the living Christ, and, in Him, with God. Schneckenburger (*Vergleichende Darstellung*, ii. p. 193) says: "The dogma of the person of Christ became a subject of dispute in the first decade of the Reformation, through the difference on the subject of the Supper. But it must not therefore be imagined that the diverse conception of the person of Christ was simply a secondary, auxiliary theory, designed to justify that difference. The difference in reference to the Supper was rather only the occasion through which the, in some respects, more radical difference, in reference to Christ's person, became a matter of self-consciousness." Baur (*Die Lehre von der Dreieinigkeit*, iii. p. 399) expresses a similar opinion:

" It was Luther, as is well known, who through the dogma of the ubiquity of Christ's human nature (in connection with his doctrine of the Supper) gave occasion to the doctrine of Christ's person becoming a cause of division among the Protestants. That Luther connected the doctrine of ubiquity with that of the Supper, was the natural result of his way of viewing Christ's presence in the Supper; but the former doctrine in turn presupposes a view of the person of Christ which rested on the same mode of thinking with his view of the Supper, which was not first suggested, but only brought into clear consciousness, by the Sacramentarian controversy." I believe that the account thus given in common by such highly competent authorities, of Luther's opinions anterior to 1527, the date of his work, *Dass diese Worte " das ist mein Leib," noch feste stehen*, is substantially correct, and that the German reformer, previously to that publication, held a view of Christ's person which predisposed him to maintain the bodily presence in the Supper, when it was called in question. But it is open to doubt whether Luther previously held ubiquity to be a necessary consequence of the union of the natures, or whether he would ever have advocated that tenet, had it not been for the exigencies of the Sacramentarian controversy. Dorner, indeed, maintains that Luther changed his views on that point after the controversy with Zuingli arose, and claims Luther's authority in support of his own theory of a gradual Incarnation, which leaves room for a real human development, and does not prematurely overlay the humanity with divine attributes (*Person of Christ*, div. ii. vol. ii. p. 53 ff.). Thomasius, on the other hand, represents Luther as having always held a twofold aspect of Christ's humanity, a natural and a supernatural, a visible and an invisible (*Person und Werk*, vol. ii. p. 335).

NOTE B.—PAGE 107.

As the literature bearing on the Tübingen-Giessen dispute is all but inaccessible to students in this country, I have had to take my information from Thomasius, Baur, and the dissertation of Cotta on the states appended to the fourth

Locus of Gerhard's *Loci Theologici*. The following extract from the latter may give readers a sufficiently clear idea of the state of this controversy:—

Missa controversia hac leviori (as to whether the exinanition refers to both natures, or to one only) aliud jam nobis commemorandum est certamen theologicum, idque maxime infaustum, quod, ineunte seculo 17, inter ipsos ecclesiae nostrae doctores, ac speciatim Tubingenses atque Giessenses de idiomatum divinorum carni Christi communicatorum in *statu exinanitionis* usu, olim exarsit, ac per tempus bene longum fuit continuatum. Statuerunt *Giessenses*, Christum hominem in statu exinanitionis proprietatibus quidem divinis, verb. grat. omnipraesentia, omniscientia, omnipotentia, etc., fuisse gavisum, sed earum usu ordinario se penitus abdicasse, neque adeo acceptam majestatem divinam semper atque incessanter usurpasse, siquidem ejusdem usus ex divina magis voluntate, quam unione personali sit derivendus. In contrariam vero sententiam heic ivere theologi *Tubingenses*, asserentes, Christum hominem in ipso exinanitionis statu, vi unionis personalis, semper fuisse omnipraesentem, omniscium, nec omnipotentiae divinae usu sese abdicasse, nisi quoad *actum reflexum*, in munere suo *sacerdotali*, iisque quae operi redemptionis perficiendo obstare poterant; in officio autem regio, et quoad *actum directum* idiomata divina usurpasse, regimenque in ecclesiam omnesque creaturas, licet *latenter* (exceptis tamen miraculis atque operationibus extraordinariis, quae palam egit) semper exercuisse. Patet ex his, litem non fuisse de unione, quam vocant, personali, nec de idiomatum communicatione ac possessione, sed de eorum duntaxat usu. Quum vero controversia haec diversas ambitu suo complectatur quaestiones speciales, de quibus olim acriter fuit disceptatum, easdem sigillatim heic percensebimus. Quaestio *prima* erat de fundamento adaequato et formali omnipraesentiae, quin et reliquorum attributorum divinorum carni Christi communicatorum; an illud in sola unione personali, an vero in libera Christi voluntate ejusdemque sessione ad dextram patris sit collocandum? Prius statuebant *Tubingenses*, posterius *Giessenses*. *Altera* quaestio spectabat ad justam atque adaequatam omnipraesentiae divinae notionem. Docebant theologi Tubing.

omnipraes. consistere in adessentia vel propinquitate ad creaturas, Christumque vi unionis personalis, adeoque non actu naturae humanae sed personae in ipso exinanitionis statu, omnibus creaturis indistanter fuisse praesentem. Ast negabant hoc ex altera parte *Giessenses*, statuentes, ideam *operationis* ingredi definitionem omnipraesentiae, ejusdemque characterem constitutivum, quem vocant, partemque essentialem esse, nec Christum exinanitum, eo sensu, ut statuunt Tubingenses, praesentem se se exhibuisse. Accedebat *tertia* quaestio cum priori connexa, utrum Christo homini in statu exin. divina apud creaturas operatio eaque universalis sit tribuenda, ita ut cuncta in coelo et in terra, sapientia ac potentia secum communicata gubernarit, adeoque acceptam majestatem divinam semper et incessanter exercuerit. Adfirmantem sententiam amplexi sunt Tubing. atque docuerunt Christum exinanitum coelum atque terram gubernasse, eadem ratione, uti gubernationem hanc in statu exalt. ad dextram patris sedens, exerceat, hoc duntaxat observato discrimine, quod in st. exin. gubernationem istam texerit atque occultaverit sub forma servili, nunc autem conditione ista servili deposita, eandem gloriose ac majestatice declaret ac manifestet. Huic vero adserto contradixerunt Giess. atque negarunt Christum temp. exin. imperium in omnes creaturas exercuisse; hoc enim involvere plenarium div. majestatis usum, quem Christus, finito demum exin. statu sit consecutus, sec. oraculum Paulinum Phil. ii. 9, 10. Denique *quarto* disputatum quoque fuit, an exinanitio fuerit vera, realis atque omnimoda abstinentia ab usu tam *directo*, quam *reflexo* div. majest. in conjunctissima duarum naturarum unione acceptae? an vero tantum constiterit in *occultatione* maj. div. per formam servi assumptam? Priorem sententiam propugnarunt Giess. poster. Tubing., qui et hoc addebant, occultationem istam duntaxat locum habuisse in usu idiomatum divinorum *directo*, nec tamen semper, prout ex miraculis, palam a Christo perpetrato, quae divinitatis Christum inhabitantis fuerint radii, clare satis pateat. Quod vero ad proprietatum divinarum usum, quem vocant, *reflexum*, redemptionis operi obstiturum, attinet, Christum eodem sponte se se penitus abdicasse. Atque de hac ipsa evacuatione usus idiomatum divinorum *reflexi* exponenda esse verba gentium apostoli Phil. ii. 7 ἐκένωσε ἑαυτον. (*Dissertatio de Statibus et Officio Christi Mediatorio*, secs. v., vi.)

NOTE C.—PAGE 115.

Schneckenburger says: "When we review the Lutheran position, it is not difficult to discover the inner threads by which the speculative Christology is connected with and produced from it. The Reformed argues: That humanity of the Redeemer assumed into real personal unity, from the conception in *utero virginis*, existing illocally, and still after the exaltation at the right hand of God, on the one hand incorporated with the *collegium sanctae trinitatis*, on the other hand, on that account, almighty, omniscient, omnipresent in the world—is not the humanity of a particular man, but something exalted above all human individuals; so to speak, the idea of perfected humanity, and the idea of the Godhead as one with the essence of humanity, a perfect nonentity. And whereas in the Lutheran theory, from the moment of incarnation, or at least of exaltation, this divine-human personality has all authority over the world, this cannot be an absolutely new beginning for the divine Being, the unity of the divine with that general humanity cannot fall within time, what begins in time is simply the knowledge thereof by the individual man. God cannot have determined Himself in time to assume human nature; the assumption on God's part must be an eternal one, so that the assumed humanity is exempt from the limits of time as well as of space. This God-manhood, therefore, in its essence precedes individual human existence; and as, on the one hand, the individual man must have part therein to be truly man, and to correspond to his idea (*unio mystica*); so, on the other, must each human individual have the capacity to take part therein. All the functions ascribed to the God-man are in this way functions of humanity itself. Whence then have sprung the fantasies which Christendom has twined around a historical individual, but out of its own spirit, which, seeing in this person the proper essence of man, unconsciously gave objective existence to the ideal which lies hid in the depths of the race? What is the historical Christ but the occasional cause of this fantastic self-objectification? What is the κρύψις of the Idiom-communication, but the state of the finite spirit become unconscious in its concrete manner of existence, of what as absolute organizing world-reason it produced? And what, but a consequence of the doctrine that the *caro Christi* in *ipso statu exinanitionis tecte* ruled the world, is it, when to the human spirit the knowledge of nature and of her laws is ascribed, because all recollection has not died out in its mind of what as unconscious nature-spirit it created? And this its humiliation is the pole of its exaltation, in which as absolute spirit it returns to itself again. In this fashion does the speculative Christology in the hands of Strauss present itself as a phase in the development of the Lutheran type of the doctrine, and to this extreme the dogma was destined inevitably to come, as soon as the old system was delivered from the trammels of an extramundane God, and of sin." Similar remarks occur in the work on the two states (*Vom doppelten Stande Christi*, 38-40). [In German: Sehen wir nach der lutherischen Position hinüber, so fällt es auch hier nicht schwer, die inner Fäden zu entdecken, wodurch die speculative Christologie mit ihr zusammenhängt und von ihr hervorgetrieben wird. Der Reformirte argumentirt: jene Menschheit des Erlösers, als von der Conception in utero Virginis an real in die persönliche Einheit aufgenommen, illocal existirend und doch nach der Erhöhung zur Rechten Gottes, einerseits dem collegium sanctae trinitatis incorporirt, andererseits desshalb allmächtig, allwissend, allgegenwärtig in der Welt —das ist nimmermehr die Menschheit eines Menschen, sondern etwas über allen Menschen-Individuen Erhabenes, gleichsam die Idee der Menschheitsvollendung, und die Idee des Gottheit als Eins mit dem Wesen der Menschheit an sich, ein vollendetes non-ens. Wie lutherisch vom Momente der incarnatio, oder wenigstens der exaltatio an, diese gottmenschliche Persönlichkeit alles Regiment auf der Welt hat, so kann, so soll damit für das Göttliche an sich selbst doch nicht ein absolut Neues beginnen, das Einssein des Göttlichen mit jener allgemeinen Menschheit nicht eigentlich in die Zeit fallen, sondern was von ihm in die Zeit fällt und anfängt, ist bloss das Wissen des individuellen Menschen um dieselbe. Gott kann sich nicht erst in der Zeit zur Annahme der Menschennatur entschlossen haben, sondern diese Annahme muss von Seiten Gottes eine ewige sein, also jene den Schranken des Raums entrückte Menschheit auch den Schranken der Zeit entrückt sein. Diese Gottmenschheit geht also ihrem Wesen nach dem einzelnen Menschsein voraus; und so gewiss das Menschen-Individuum daran, um wahrhaft Mensch zu sein und seiner Idee zu entsprechen, Theil haben muss (unio mystica), so gewiss muss das einzelne Menschen-Individuum von Haus aus der Fähigkeit nach daran Theil haben. Alle jene dem Gottmenschen zugesprochenen Produkte und Funktionen sind so Funktionen des Menschheit selbst. Woher anders stammen also die Phantasieen, welche die Christenheit um ein historisches Individuum geschlungen hat, als aus dem eigenen Gemüthe, das in diesem Individuum, das eigen Wesen des Menschen anschauend, Alles bewusstloss objectivirte, was in der Tiefe der Gattung von Idealem verborgen liegt? Was ist der historische Christus anders als bloss der Veranlassungspunkt zu dieser phantastischen Selbstobjektivirung? Was ist die κρύψις der Idiomen-communication, wenn nicht der Zustand des endlichen Geistes, der sich in seiner concreter Existenzweise nicht mehr unmittelbar bewusst, was er als absolute organisirende Weltvernunft producirt hat? Was ist es, wenn nicht die Consequenz der Lehre dass die caro Christi in ipso statu exinanitionis tecte das Regiment der Welt ausübe. . . . wenn dem Menschen-geiste darum die Kenntniss der Natur und ihrer Gesetze zugeschrieben ist, weil ihm nicht durchaus alle Erinnerung dessen erloschen sei, was er als bewusstloser Naturgeist geschaffen? Und jene seine Erniedrigung ist der Pol seiner Erhöhung, in welcher er als absoluter Geist zu sich selbst zurückkehrt. In solcher Weise stellt sich die speculative Christologie wie sie namentlich bei Strauss auftritt, als eine Phase auf der Seite der christologischen Entwickelungen innerhalb des lutherischen Lehrtypus heraus, und es musste zu diesem Extrem fortgehen, so wie die dem alten Systeme anhaftende

Klammern des extramundanen Gottes, und der Sünde wegfielen (*Vergleichende Darstellung*, Zweiter Theil, pp. 218, 219).]

NOTE D.—PAGE 129.

Schweitzer says: "The Christology of the Reformed appears to rest on the following principles:—1. Christ fully belongs to our race, a man consisting of body and soul, named the *natura humana*, the *humanitas* of Christ. 2. Christ's humanity is by the highest fulness of gifts of grace as highly exalted as a human soul possibly can be; in particular, the proclivity called original sin is by this equipment so broken that soul and body can attain to a sinless course of life: *praestantia humanae Christi naturae*. 3. To this comparatively highest worth of Christ is joined a specifically unique one: the Logos life of God, the source of the prophetic illumination, dwells in Christ as the innermost animating principle of His personality, *divina Christi natura* or more strictly, the participation in God thereby, that this man is ἐνυπόστατος τῷ λόγῳ; He is the Son of God, and the Only-begotten. 4. The Being and Life emanating from God, or the Logos, is as such transcendent, infinite; but in the way in which He appears as the principle of the Personality of Christ, this divine Being and Life passed into human limitations without absorbing these: *idomata divina non communicantur humanae naturae, occultatio majestatis divinae*. 5. Precisely this theanthropically formed existence and activity is the redeeming work, and it appears as the completed religious life and religious moral activity: *opera redemtionis a persona secundum utramque naturam profisciscuntur*. 6. This economic Christology rests on the real Trinity in the economy of the divine Being: *non tres personae, non pater, non spiritus sanctus, non essentia tribus personis communis, sed filius, sive* ὁ λόγος, *incarnatus est qua* ὑπόστασις. The Christology resting on these foundations is not indeed carried fully out, because the old formulae exercised a disturbing influence. The disturbance, however, is not so great as appears. It is said, *e.g.*, starting from the formula, *duae naturae in unâ personâ:* in Christ is a humanly limited knowledge, *secundum hum. ejus naturam*, an absolute *secundum divinam;* the latter statement has reference to the divine nature only in the abstract. The concrete *Theanthropos* has emptied Himself of the absolute knowledge of God; for had He as a real possession the absolute and the limited beside each other, the personality would be cleft asunder; and had He the absolute knowledge really, the human finite knowledge would be absorbed. The intention, therefore, was to maintain the perfection of the religious life of Christ only in a humanly limited intelligence, and to derive His freedom from error from the divine elements. The reproach is unfounded that the Reformed shrank from the idea of the divine being realized in the temporal; all that they shrank from, and rightly, was the ignoring of the forms under which alone this process is conceivable, and can be accomplished; they aimed at a historic reality; they meant to teach that God really became man, became humanly determined; but they did not quite manage to put the matter rightly, to give the idea adequate expression." [In German: Es scheint die Christologie der Reformirten beruhe auf folgenden Grundlagen: 1. Christus ist völlig unserer Gattung angehörig, ein Mensch aus Leib und Seele bestehend, was man die *natura humana*, die *humanitas* Ch. nennt. 2. Christi Menschheit ist durch höchste Fülle von Gnadengaben so hoch gehoben, als eine menschliche Seele überhaupt gehoben werden kann, namentlich ist jener Erbsündenhang in Folge dieser Austattung so gebrochen, dass Seele und Leib eine sündlose Lebensführung erreichen: *praestantia humanae Ch. naturae*. 3. Zu dieser graduell höchsten Würde Christi kommt endlich eine specifisch einzige; das Logosleben Gottes, die Propheten erleuchtend, wohnt Christo ein als innerstes die Persönlichkeit beseelendes Princip, *divina Ch. natura*, oder genauer das Theilhaben an Gott dadurch, dass dieser Mensch ἐνυπόστατος τῷ λόγῳ ist; er ist der Sohn Gottes, und zwar der eingeborene. 4. Das emanirte göttliche Sein und Leben order der Logos ist als solcher transcendent, unendlich; in der Art aber, wie er als Kern der Persönlichkeit Christi zur Erscheinung kommt, ist dieses göttliche Sein und Leben in menschliche Bestimmtheit eingegangen, ohne diese zu absorbiren, *idomata divina non communicantur humanae naturae, occultatio majestatis divinae.* 5. Gerade diese theanthropisch gestaltete Existenz und Wirksamkeit ist die erlösende, und erscheint als das vollendete religiöse Leben und religiös sittliche Wirken—*opera redemtionis a persona secundum utramque naturam profisciscuntur.* 6. Diese ökonomische Christologie ruht auf der realen Trinität in der Oekonomie des göttlichen Wesens; *non tres personae, non pater, non spir. sanc. non essentia tribus personis communis, sed filius, sive ὁ λόγος, incarnatus est qua ὑπόστασις.* Die auf diesen Grundlagen ruhende Christologie ist freilich nicht rein durchgeführt worden, indem das Unbequeme der alten Formeln störend eingewirkt hat. Diese Störungen sind aber nicht so bedeutend als sie scheinen. Sagt man z. B., von der Formel ausgehend—*duae naturae in una persona,* in Christus sei ein menschlich beschränktes Wissen *secundum hum. ejus naturam*, ein absolutes *secundum divinam:* so gilt letzeres von der *div. natura in abstracto.* Der concrete Theanthropos aber hat sich dessen entäussert; denn hätte er als wirklichen Besitz das absolute und beschränkte neben einander, so würde allerdings die Persönlichkeit gespalten; hätte er das absolute wirklich, so wäre das menschlich endliche Wissen absorbirt. Man will also nur in menschlich bestimmter Intelligenz die Vollendung des Religiösen behaupten und hat diese Irrthumslosigkeit vom Göttlichen abgeleitet. Ungegründet ist der Vorwurf, man scheue sich reformirter Seits das Göttliche im Zeitlichen verwirklicht zu glauben; vielmehr scheut man sich nur, und mit Recht, die Formen zu ignoriren, unter denen allein dieser Process denkbar ist und vollzogen werden kann; man will gerade eine historische Realität, man will lehren, dass Gott wirklich Mensch werde, sich menschlich bestimme, aber man dringt noch nicht durch (*Die Glaubenslehre der evangelisch-reformirten Kirche*, Zweiter Band, pp. 336, 337).]

NOTE E.—PAGE 133.

The Reformed theologians were not altogether of one mind as to the relation of the humanity of Christ to the category of personality. The prevailing view, however, was that the human nature of our Lord, while ἀνυπόστατος in itself, was ἐνυπόστατος through the Logos. They did not hesitate to call Christ a man. Such phrases as these occur in the *Admonitio: iste homo Deus est; huic homini datam esse ipsam Deitatem.* Nevertheless, according to the same document, the human nature is so borne and preserved by the Logos, even in glory, that "*ne quidem persona sit per se; sed duntaxat natura, quae ne existeret quidem, nisi sic gestaretur a persona λόγου*" (*persona* is here used in the literal ancient sense of ὑπόστασις, what is placed under as a support, not in the modern sense of the Ego). To the same effect Zanchius, who starts the difficulty, If the Logos assumed a human body with a rational soul, does that not amount to assuming a person? and then disposes of the "*magna dubitatio*" by laying down the position, that the humanity was ἀνυπόστατος *in se*, because it never subsisted separately from the Logos (*De incarnatione*, lib. ii., theses ii. and iii.). He has no hesitation, however, in calling Christ a man; *e.g.*: aliud enim quum nominamus animam et carnem Christi, tunc enim de naturâ loquimur; et aliud quum eam nominamus hominem, Personam enim tunc indicamus quatenus in humana subsistat natura. Ideo damus Christum hominem esse ubique; negamus autem carnem vel animam ubique (lib. ii. thes. iii. p. 64). Again, p. 68: Haeresis est Nestoriana tam negare Deum Patrem esse hujus hominis quam negare Mariam matrem esse hujus Dei. The same view is given by Henry Alting: Non potest certe Natura Humana esse ὑπόστασις, Persona; verum necesse est ut in se ἀνυπόστατος, ἐνυπόστατος autem sit in λόγῳ qui accepit formam servi. Eo tamen nihil decessit Naturae Humanae *perfectioni;* quia mansit substantia, mansit partibus suis et proprietatibus integra, mansit etiam individualis. Imo tanto plus accesit, quanto majus est subsistere in Personâ Creatoris quam subsistentia creaturae (*Scriptorum Theologicorum*, vol. i. p. 149). The last thought reminds one of the sentiment of the Lutheran Hollaz, who enumerates ἀνυποστασία among the prerogatives of Christ's humanity, and speaks of the want of human personality as *Divina filii Dei hypostasi tanquam longe eminentiori com-*

pensata. Mastricht, on the other hand, denies personality in every sense to the humanity. He speaks of the human nature as id quidem omne habens, quod ad constitutionem nat. hum. est necessarium, eoque nobis quoad naturam, per omnia similis, solo excepto peccato, sed tamen personalitate, per quam incommunicabilis et completa fit natura, penitus destituta, *penitus* inquam, hoc est, non *propria* tantum et sibi peculiari quae duplicem inferat personalitatem, sed *participata* etiam per quam ἐνυπόστατος nonnullis dicitur, destituta; quod ea ratione, humana *natura* subsisteret personalitate *divina,* adeoque humana natura *persona* foret *divina* (*Theologia Theoret. Practica,* lib. v. c. iv. p. 538). Schneckenburger suggests, as a reason for the exclusion of *natural personality* from the human nature in the Reformed theory, that such personality was held. to come within the scope of the qualifying clause *peccato excepto,* on the ground that no self-consciousness is holy, except when absolutely surrendered to the guidance of the Holy Spirit. For this notion, however, he gives no citations. This author has some very subtle remarks on the *impersonalitas* in its bearing on the question of a double consciousness, which, as they may interest some minds, I here translate. He says (*Vergl. Darstell.* ii. p. 199): "The impersonality, strictly considered, is but the highest expression for what others call the absolute determination of the human nature by the Logos. They (the defenders of impersonality) say: Without the assumption of impersonality there would result a double personality, by which the unity of self-consciousness would be broken up, and the consequence would be no real Incarnation, therefore, after all, only one personality, that of the Logos. But do we now get, on the supposition of the impersonality, a certain double personality in the Logos? For as person of the Trinity, as *totus extra Jesum,* He is conscious of Himself after another fashion than He is as *occultatus natura humana.* This last divine-human self-consciousness is not the full comprehensive Logos-consciousness, though rooted therein; for in that case the world-embracing Logos-consciousness must have extinguished itself *pro tempore,* which (from the Reformed point of view) is impossible. If, therefore, such a temporary darkening of the divine self-consciousness be inadmissible, then the divine-human self-consciousness of the Logos *occultatus* must be only a shadowy time-image (abbildliche zeitliche Schattirung) of the eternal, absolute Trinitarian Logos-consciousness, resting thereon as its foundation: the latter must embrace the former as the *continens* of the *contentum*. Therefore the impersonality is not to be taken in the sense, that a human self-consciousness is not ascribed to Jesus. Quite opposed to this construction is the *scientia habitualis*, which, as a habitual knowledge in the objective sense, presupposes a focus of habitual self-consciousness, whereby alone the *verus et justus homo* can subsist. The *scientia personalis*, *i.e.* the omniscience of the second person of the Trinity, the God-man had only potentially (an sich), not as a knowledge really pervading and thereby annihilating the time-series of His inner life movement (seiner innern Lebensmomente), but the Logos self-consciousness was here only as the God-consciousness of the human self-consciousness, and so the being of God in Him was the light image of the eternal divine self-consciousness focusing itself in His human soul (der in seine menschliche Seele fallende abbildliche Strahl des ewigen göttlichen Selbstbewusstseins). The whole normal human soul of Jesus never had a self-consciousness, nay, not even a moment of unconscious vital feeling previous to the awakening of self-consciousness, in which the Logos had not an absolutely determining influence on the life-course, so that this person never stood outside the relation to the Logos as the determining power; that relation was for Him the living conscious First in His self-consciousness. Such is the *impersonalitas*."

LECTURE IV.

NOTE A.—PAGE 145.

To the Thomasian type of kenosis may be referred König, Delitzsch, and Kahnis. König anticipated Thomasius. The statement on page 139 is correct only in the sense that Thomasius was the first to present the kenotic theory in developed form. The idea had been propounded, previous to the appearance of his *Beiträge* in 1845, by König in *Die Menschwerdung Gottes als eine in Christus geschehene, und in der christlichen Kirche noch geschehende, dargestellt*, Mainz 1844. König, as may be gathered from the title of his book, teaches a double Incarnation, one of the Logos in Christ, and one of the Holy Spirit in the Church collectively. The former of the two Incarnations he regards from the kenotic point of view, and his mode of presenting the doctrine is substantially the same as that of Thomasius. The Logos empties Himself of omniscience and omnipotence in assuming human nature (in its integrity), and so becomes a divine-human personality. "The Scripture calls the transition of the Logos out of the infinitude of God into the finitude of human existence a κένωσις, self-emptying, or literally, self-void-making. . . . The self-emptying must, without doubt, be conceived in accordance with the words of Christ and of His apostle, as a true emptying of self; with the entering into humanity, and in its gradual development, and from its first beginnings, the λόγος freely subjected Himself, in the fulness of His infinite love, to the law of a human gradual development; He gave up the glory, brightness, and majesty which He had with the Father before the foundation of the world. . . . He renounced the majesty of His omniscience as such, and retained it only as a completely pure, untroubled conscience, or if one prefers the word, God-consciousness; the omnipotence as such He delivered over to the Father, and in passing into humanity He retained the decision for His Father and His will, and the impulse to do this will." ["Den Uebergang des Logos aus der Unendlichkeit des Gottes in die Endlichkeit des Menschendaseins bezeichnet die heilige Schrift als eine κένωσις; als Selbstentäusserung oder wörtlich Selbstleerung. . . . Die Selbstentäusserung muss aber ohne Zweifel als eine wahre Entäusserung oder Sich-Leermachung ganz dem Worte Christi und seines Apostels gemäss gefasst werden; mit dem Eintreten in die Menschheit und in deren allmählige Entwickelung, und zwar von ihren ersten Anfängen an, unterwarf sich der λόγος in der Fülle seiner unendlichen Liebe dem Gesetze menschlicher allmählige Entwickelung freiwillig, er gab die Herrlichkeit, Klarheit, und Majestät auf, die er hatte bei dem Vater vor Grundlegung der Welt. . . . auf die Majestät seiner Allwissenheit als solcher verzichtete er, und behielt sie als vollendet reines ungetrübtes Gewissen, oder wenn man lieber will, Gottesbewusstsein; die Allmacht als solcher überliess er dem Vater, und behielt, in die Menschheit übergehend, die Entschiedenheit für seinen Vater und dessen Willen, und den Trieb, diesen Willen zu thun" (pp. 296–298).] Again: "The kenosis is the great idea by which, apprehended in accordance with Scripture, the reality of a true Christology can come into existence. The kenosis contains the idea of self-limitation which the Logos in the exercise of His own will, in agreement with the will of His Father, has willed and carried into effect. . . . This limitation was possible only by God Himself in the Logos subjecting Himself to the process of mediation, out of love, yea, out of infinite love (to sinful humanity). He subjected Himself freely to the law of gradual development." ["Die κένωσις ist die grosse Idee durch deren offenbarung- und schriftgemässe Auffassung die Wirklichkeit einer wahren Christologie allein wird zu Stande kommen. Die kenosis enthält die Idee der Selbstverendlichung, Selbstbeschränkung die vom λόγος frei aus seinem eigenen dem väterlichen entsprechenden

Willen und Wesen gewollt und gesetzt wird. ... Diese Verendlichung war gar nicht anders möglich als dass Gott selbst im Logos dem Prozess der Vermittlung sich unterwarf; aus Liebe, ja aus unendliche Liebe (to sinful humanity) unterzog er frei sich dem Gezetze allmähliger Entwicklung" (p. 338).] To the objection that the kenosis violates the unchangeableness of God, König replies, that God the Logos, by submitting to the kenosis involved in Incarnation, showed the most unconditional love, and thereby asserted and maintained His inmost essence (p. 340). On the question to which nature the personality belongs, he remarks that it is inept, because "the God-man Jesus is the Logos in human form; when He thought and said 'I,' He embraced His whole divine-human Being, which became divine-human (or theanthropic) at His Incarnation. ... There never was a man Jesus apart from the Logos; but as the Logos, before He became in Jesus God-man, possessed personality, one can freely say that the personality of the God-man was the eternal element of the Logos, which, however, in the Incarnation became subject to the process and law of human development, gradual in time and space, and of course as personality of the Logos must cease from His supernatural form of existence in order to become the personality of the God-man, in a natural and historical form of existence" ["der Gottmensch Jesus ist der Logos in Menschengestalt; wenn er 'Ich' dachte und sagte, so fasste er seine ganzes gottmenschliches Wesen zusammen, welches als *Gottmenschliches* erst mit und in seiner Menschwerdung geworden oder entstanden. ... Einen Menschen Jesus ohne den Logos hat es niemals gegeben; da aber allerdings der Logos ehe er in Jesus Gottmensch wurde Persönlichkeit besass, so kann man freilich sagen dass die Persönlichkeit des Gottmenschen die ewige des Logos war, die aber eben mit der Menschwerdung dem Prozesse und Gesetze der menschlichen, als zeitlichen und räumlichen allmähligen Entwickelung sich unterwarf und natürlicherweise als Persönlichkeit des Logos, in seiner übernatürlichen Existenzform aufhören musste, um die Persönlichkeit des Gottmenschen in natürlicher und geschichtlicher Existenzform zu werden" (pp. 340, 341)].

König goes on to argue that if the personality of the Logos had not in free infinite love subjected Himself to a process of gradual human development, the kenosis would not have been real, the human and divine would simply have been parallel to each other. He regards the kenosis as an exchange of the divine for the human form of personality, and does not allow a double life of the Logos. I have thought it right to give this account of König's views, all the more that Thomasius, so far as I have observed, takes no notice of it, though he gives a list of other supporters of the kenotic theory (*Person und Werk*, ii. p. 196).

DELITZSCH gives his opinion on the kenotic theory in his *System der biblischen Psychologie*, pp. 326–333 (Zweite Auflage, 1861). He says that it is one of the greatest, holiest, and most worthy to be studied problems of modern theology, in accordance with the pervading impression of true humanity and undivided unity which the person of Christ makes as set forth in Scripture, to remove the self-contradictory dualism, above which the Church view of the God-man has not been able to raise itself, in such a way that, without relapse into long refuted errors, the substance of the Catholic dogma may remain intact. The right solution, he indicates, will be that which in the first place holds fast the *göttlich-menschliche Doppelwesen* of Christ, without assuming a transformation of the divine nature into the human, in contradiction to the eternal, unchangeable self-equality (*Selbstgleichheit*) of God; and, in the second place, which allows the thesis, that the Logos in Christ is the person-forming and the humanity the assumed, to remain in possession of its scriptural rights; and thirdly, which succeeds in showing how the Logos, without ceasing to be what He is eternally, could make Himself the subject of so truly human a being as meets us everywhere in the Christ of the Gospels. The main question is, according to Delitzsch, this: " How could the Logos so empty Himself, that He should give up His eternal glory, and yet more, His eternal mode of existence, and the properties flowing therefrom in relation to the world, the omnipotence, the omniscience, the omnipresence, without surrendering the identity of His eternal Being?"

["Wie konnte der Logos sich so entäussern dass er seine ewige Doxa und noch mehr; dass er seine ewige Seinsweise und die aus ihr der Welt gegenüber fliessenden Eigenschaften der Allmacht, der Allwissenheit, der Allgegenwart aufgab, ohne doch die Identität seines ewigen Seins aufzugeben" (p. 327).] The *fact*, he says, is indubitable. The incarnate Logos is not in possession of the eternal doxa, for He desires to regain it (John xvii. 5). He is not omniscient, for He knows not, as He Himself says, the day and hour of the end (Mark xiii. 32). He is not almighty, for power over all, as the risen One says, is *given* unto Him (Matt. xxviii. 18). He is not omnipresent, since He is ascended in order to fill all (Eph. iv. 10). To refer these expressions to the *humanity* alone, is to sever the unity of the person, and turn the reality of the human nature into a sham. The only question is, How is the fact to be accounted for? How could the Logos give up His eternal glory, and these attributes of His divine manner of being, without parting with His divine nature, whose effulgence that glory is, and whose energy those attributes are? The solution, according to our author, is to be found in this, that the essence of absolute personality consists in unlimited self-determination, and that the root of the divine Being is will, which is the *prius* of all actual self-consciousness. The Son of God could thus without renouncing His being " withdraw to this lowest basis, this root-power, this all-determining ground and origin of His Being, and so with the emptying of His unfolded Being make Himself the subject of a human personality, and become objective to Himself in a new up-springing self-consciousness, which, although it has His now double existence for contents, yet is no double consciousness, but a single one springing out of a single divine-human life ground" ["auf diese unterste Basis, diese wurtzelhafte Potenz, diesen alles beschliessenden Grund und Ursprung seines Wesens zurückziehen und so mit Entäusserung seiner Wesensentfaltung sich zum Subjecte einer menschlichen Persönlichkeit machen, und sich selbst in einem neu aufgehenden Selbstbewusstsein gegenständlich werden, welches, obgleich es sein nunmehriges Doppelwesen zum Inhalt hat, doch kein doppeltes, sondern ein aus einheitlichem gottmenschlichen Lebensgrunde aufgehendes einiges ist " (p. 328)]. Such self-reduction involves no interference with the immanent trinitarian process, because "the Son remained even in that withdrawal or systole of His unfolded Being in which the kenosis lay, the other divine will, in which the original will of the Father mirrors itself, and which has the fulness of the Father's Being for its contents " ["der Sohn blieb auch in jener Einzehung und, so zu sagen, Systole seiner Wesensentfaltung worin die Entäusserung besteht, der andere göttliche Wille, in welchem der urbildliche Wille des Vaters sich spiegelt, und welcher die Wesensfülle des Vaters zu seinem bewegenden Inhalt hat " (p. 329)]. Neither does it involve any suspension of the world-preserving and governing activity of the Trinity, because in "the self-emptying of the Son realizes itself the eternal will of love of the triune God, and therewith His own eternal will" ["in der Selbstentäusserung des Sohnes verwirklicht sich ja der ewige Liebeswille Gottes des dreieinigen, und somit sein eigener ewiger Will" (*ibid.*)]. Redemption is the centre of the upholding and governing of the world, therefore " so far from any blank entering into the world-sustaining, world-governing activity of the triune God, that activity rather concentrated itself centripetally in the self-emptying of the Son, and had therein its centre of gravity, without wholly resolving itself thereinto " ["Kam in die welterhaltende und weltregierende Thätigkeit des dreieinigen Gottes so wenig eine Lücke, dass sie sich viel mehr in dieser Selbstentäusserung des Sohnes, ohne darin aufzugehen, gleichsam centripetalkräftig zusammenfasste und daran ihren Schwerpunkt hatte " (*ibid.*)]; so that the $\varphi \acute{\epsilon} \rho \omega \nu$ $\tau \grave{\alpha} \pi \acute{\alpha} \nu \tau \alpha$ (Heb. i. 1) retained its truth, "even as the human spirit in the bonds of sleep, not less than in the full stir of waking hours, without interruption of its self-identical life, continues through the soul to be the life-power which dominates the body. The self-emptying of the Son, and His theanthropic suffering unto death connected therewith is, rightly viewed, the most strongly willed, most powerful, most intensive self-assertion; in this self-emptying culminates the free self-might of the everlasting Son, and concentrates itself in the eternal love which wills and carries through the completion of the world; its effects extend not only over the whole of humanity, but over heaven and earth" ["ähnlich wie der menschliche Geist in der Gebundenheit des Schlafes nicht minder, als in der vollen Regsamkeit des Wachens, ohne Abbruch seines selbstgleichen Lebens mittelst der Seele die den Leib durchwaltende Lebensmacht zu sein fortfährt. Die Selbstentäusserung des Sohnes und sein damit verbundenes gottmenschliches Leiden bis zum Tode ist ja, recht besehen, die willensstärkste thatkräftigste allerintensivste Selbstbethätigung; in dieser Selbstentäusserung gipfelt die freie Selbstmacht des ewigen Sohnes und concentrirt sich die der Welt Vollendung wollende und durchsetzende ewige Liebe: ihre Wirkungen erstrecken sich nicht allein auf die ganze Menschheit, sondern auf Himmel und Erde" (p. 330)]. The view here given of the continued participation by the self-emptied Logos in the government of the world, taught also by Hofmann (see next note), is quite compatible with the Thomasian theory of depotentiation. It is physical power replaced by moral; strength perfected in weakness. From the above it will be seen that Delitzsch does not hold that the Logos superseded the human soul; and he takes care, with express reference to Gess, to repudiate this view.

KAHNIS declares for the kenotic theory of Christ's person in *Die Lehre heiligen Geiste*, pp. 57, 58. He starts from the difficult question, How in Christ the relation of the divine consciousness to the human is to be conceived? On the Church doctrine of two natures in one person, the personality belonging to the divine nature, and the human nature being by consequence impersonal, he remarks, that as the essence of humanity lies in consciousness, Christ without a human Ego is not complete man; further, that human thought, will, and feeling are not conceivable without a human self-consciousness; and finally, that the certain fact of the gradual development of Jesus is reduced to seeming, if the Ego, which grows in wisdom, is at the same time wisdom itself; if the Ego, which grows in grace, is at the same time the source of grace. The human nature imperatively demands a human person. But as the divine Ego nevertheless stands fast, the only outlet seems two persons. This solution, however, has ever been rejected, and justly, for it reduces the whole life of Jesus to a lie, because in such a relation (a sort of possession) the Son of God is not man, nor is the man Son of God, and either person, in appropriating the properties of the other, is guilty of taking what does not belong to it. (Uebergriffe machte, die gottliche des Scheines, die menschliche des Raubes.) There must be but one person. This one person could unite the two natures only by being finite and infinite at the same time. The human self-consciousness, which is not an immoveable point, but in all life-relations is diversely shaped, sensuous, understanding, rational, religious, etc., consciousness (sinnliches, verständiges, vernunftiges, religiöses u. s. w. Bewusstsein), presents an analogy for the assumption in Christ of a self-consciousness which belongs at once to both natures. When Christ is tempted, weeps, trembles in the garden, feels Himself God-forsaken, His Ego enters wholly into human finitude; when He names Himself the resurrection and the life, is transfigured, when He desires the glory which He had with the Father, the divine consciousness dominates over all finite relations. The forthcoming of the one does not exclude the other, but it demands a retirement of it, yet without sin in the human (doch ohne Sünde beim menschlichen). John's word, "The Word became flesh," does not signify an assumption of, but a transition into, human nature (ein Annehmen oder Anziehen der menschlichen Natur, sondern ein Uebergehen in dieselbe); demands therefore that the Logos consciousness should become human (dass das unendliche Logosbewusstsein ein endlich menschliches geworden sei). The Logos consciousness therefore must be conceived of, during the infancy of Jesus, as latent in the human, and with the progressive human development out of the religious relation (aus dem religiösen Verhältnisse), growing into a consciousness of a peculiar childhood (als Bewusstsein einer besonderen Kindschaft), till in maturity Jesus assumed the divine life which the human Ego has as grace, as the nature of His Ego (das göttliche

Leben welches das menschliche Ich als Gnade hat, als Natur seines Ich aufnahm). Therefore, while the Church doctrine rightly derives the self-consciousness of Christ, not from the human nature, but from the Logos nature, it must take the additional step of assuming a becoming finite on the part of the Logos consciousness, in order to gain for the human nature a human consciousness ("eine Verendlichung des Logosbewusstsein anzunehmen, um für die menschliche Natur ein menschlich Bewusstsein zu gewinnen").

Kahnis proceeds to make some remarks on the assertion of the negative critics, that in the Christ of the synoptical Gospels the Divine is the Holy Ghost, while in John it is the Logos. He denies the accuracy of the statement, and maintains that the Logos in fact, though not in word, is recognised in the Synoptics, and that the influence of the Holy Ghost is recognised in John. The need for that influence is explained by the effect of the Incarnation on the Logos. In becoming flesh the Logos became subject to the laws of the flesh, therefore needed to be protected by the Spirit from taint in His human nature, so that He might be born free from sin. As a citizen of the divine kingdom, He needed the Spirit to consecrate Him to be Messiah. As perfect man, He required to have, not simply a finite Ego, but a life for the infinite in which all religion consists. This infinite life, for which the finite Ego exists, dwelt in Him from the conception as Holy Spirit. Out of the Holy Spirit, who pervaded the human nature more and more, the lost glory of the Logos came into consciousness, somewhat as Plato conceives of all spirit-life as a recollection. If we are to believe in an intimate mutual pervasion of the divine and human natures in Christ, the intermediate link must be found in the Holy Spirit, who condescends to finitude and weakness in order to form it into the divine image.

NOTE B.—PAGE 153.

To the Gessian type may be referred Gaupp, Hahn, Schmieder, Reuss, Godet, and (but with hesitation) Liebner and Hofmann, also Goodwin, an American theologian.

GAUPP (*Die Union*, Breslau 1847, pp. 112–117) finds the solution of the problem of the Incarnation, the union of the divine and human natures in one person, in the idea of the self-exinanition of the Logos, and the trichotomy of human nature into body, soul, and spirit; the Logos, by a voluntary kenosis, constituting Himself a human spirit, and assuming a soul and body, and thus subjecting Himself to a purely human development. " Happily the idea of the kenosis comes to our aid, and under the assumption of the biblical trichotomy of spirit, soul, and body, in the one human individual, makes a conception of the Incarnation of the Logos possible, according to which the Logos, by that act of infinite love, could constitute Himself into a human spirit, assume soul and body in His conception through the Holy Ghost in the virgin's womb, and so subject Himself to a purely human development." ["Da kommt uns glücklicherweise die Idee der Selbstentäusserung des Sohnes Gottes zu Hülfe, und macht, unter Voraussetzung der biblischen Trichotomie von Geist, Seele, und Leib, in dem einen Menschen-Individuum, eine Auffassung der Incarnation des Logos möglich; nach welcher dieser, mittelst jener unendlich liebreichen Entäusserungsthat, sich selbst zum Menschengeiste konstituiren, Seele und Leib bei seiner geheimnissvollen Empfängniss durch den heiligen Geist im Liebe der Jungfrau von aussen annehmen und hiermit einer rein menschlichen Entwickelung sich unterziehen konnte" (p. 113).] The kenosis Gaupp, like Gess, bases on a Subordinatian view of the Trinity. The Son has His eternal life from the Father, who alone is the original ground (*Urgrund*) of all being, and therefore can declare, not merely with reference to His humanity, but with reference to His divine nature, "The Father is greater than I." The Son, therefore, unlike the Father, is capable of self-exinanition; He can, so to speak, estrange Himself from His own divine nature, and divest Himself of His brightness and majesty, and all divine properties, depositing them, so to speak, with the Father, that He may be wholly man, and be subject to the law of growth as a child, knowing no more of Himself than other children, and attaining only gradually to His human self-consciousness, and meriting by a life of obedience the restitution of the glory He had voluntarily abnegated. To Christ, in the state of humiliation, Gaupp ascribes a moral likeness to God, due to the influence of the Holy Spirit communicating to Him gradually divine properties; the natural properties of Godhead, omnipotence, omniscience, and omnipresence he represents Christ as attaining only in the state of exaltation, and even then only in the relativity which the idea of human nature demands (in derjenigen Relativität die die Idee der Menschennatur erfordert, d. h. in den Ring der Menschheit gefasst, p. 116). To the glorified body of Christ, Gaupp ascribes circumscribedness; yet he thinks that from the humanity of the glorified Son a sphere of power rays forth pervading all space, after the analogy of the sensible atmosphere which some anthropologists, as he thinks rightly, ascribe even to men living on earth, in order thereby to solve certain riddles of human nature.

HAHN (*Die Theologie des Neuen Testaments*, Leipzig 1854, Erster Band, pp. 195-210) takes a similar view of the constitution of Christ's person, the Logos taking therein, according to him, the place of the human spirit. The change of condition which the Son of God underwent in becoming man had a positive and a negative side; He assumed something, and He gave away something. What He assumed was the σάρξ, that is, the material, human corporeality, and the condition which goes along therewith ("die *materielle menschliche Leiblichkeit* und der mit dieser verbundene Zustand"). What He gave up was the condition of His premundane absoluteness (seiner vorweltlichen Absolutheit). The son of God entered into the flesh emptied of all His divine prerogatives, in a state of limitation corresponding to the human σάρξ, retaining, indeed, the essence of Godhead, but reduced to a potence, in which the divine majesty lay only as a germ. ["Das absolute πνεῦμα ist zum beschränkten πνεῦμα eines sinnlichen Menschen geworden, es hat sich bis zu dem Grade der Keimartigkeit, beschränkt, dass es gleich geworden ist dem noch unentwickelten πνεῦμα jedes Menschen im Momente seiner Entstehung, so dass alles göttliche Bewusstsein und alle göttliche Kräfte in ihm völlig gebunden waren, und erst der Entwickelung bedurften, wenn er sich als Sohn Gottes manifestiren sollte, und als solches beschränktes πνεῦμα ist er in die σάρξ eingegangen" (p. 199).] This truth is most plainly expressed in the words ὁ γυλος σάρξ ἐγένετο, which mean, not merely that the Logos appeared in the flesh (ἐφανερώθη ἐν σαρκί, 1 Tim. iii. 16), but that in His consciousness and spiritual power He entered into the limits of a sensuous existence (" dass er ganz und gar zu einem fleischlichen d. h. sinnlichen Wesen geworden sei ") (p. 200). In thus limiting Himself to the dimensions of a human spirit, and uniting Himself as a human spirit to human flesh, the Son of God became a full and true man, for human nature consists of two parts, σάρξ and πνεῦμα. Yet three things distinguished Christ from all other men: 1. His supernatural birth; 2. His spirit, while human, was yet not of temporal origin, like that of other men, except indeed as to form of being, but in its essence was eternal αἰώνιον; and, moreover, it was a πνεῦμα in which dwelt in germ the fulness of Godhead. The former attribute of Christ's spirit the author finds attested in such passages as Heb. ix. 14 (διὰ Πνεύματος αἰωνίου), 1 Tim. iii. 16 (ἐφανερώθη ἐν σαρκί), 1 John iv. 2 (ἐν σαρκὶ ἐγηλυθότα), Heb. ii. 14 (κεκοινώνηκεν αἵματος καὶ σαρκός); the expressions quoted showing that, according to the view of the N. T., the Incarnation of the Son of God did not consist in His *assuming* an entire human nature consisting of body and soul, but in this, that He assumed a human body [" dass der schon vorhandene (präexistirende) Geiste Christi (natürlich in einem Züstande der Beschränkung) in einen menschlichen Leib eingegangen sei" (p. 206)]. The third distinctive feature of Christ's humanity is its *sinlessness*, which is explained by the fact that His spirit was not derived from sinful humanity, was therefore pure and strong, and could keep the σάρξ in its own place, though from its nature the latter supplied material for temptation, especially as it was reinforced by the power emanating from the close connection in which He stood to His heavenly Father. [" Ein Princip (die σάρξ) von dem zwar Vesuchungen ausgingen, die aber Jesus, vermöge des Lebens seines πνεῦμα, und vermöge der unmittelbaren Verbindung, in welcher er mit seinem himmlischen Vater stand, und der von diesem ausgehenden Kräftigung stark genug war, in jedem Momente zu überwinden " (p. 210).]

SCHMIEDER (*Das hohepriesterliche Gebet unsers Herrn Jesu Christi*, Hamburg 1848) expresses his view in these terms (pp. 36-42): " The Son of God became man; that is, He renounced His self-conscious divine personal being and took the form of a spiritual potence, which self-forgotten, as unconscious formative power worked in the womb of Mary, and formed a body which was fitted so to serve the development of this spiritual potence that it could use it as its own property and become conscious, could develop itself therein, and by means thereof put forth its energy The spiritual power works in the beginnings of the formation of the body simply on nature, as unconscious force, later in the body as spiritual nature, as soul, which becomes conscious of its sensations and conceptions, and self-active, but does not yet with full self-consciousness react against it; lastly, in the soul or spirit as self-conscious, self-determining, self-activity. The spirit is the first and the last; it forms the body, it moves the soul, but it can be named spirit properly only when it has come to itself, when it knows its power, and fully wields it." [" Der Sohn Gottes ward Mensch: das heisst, er begab sich seines selbstbewussten göttlichen Personseyns und nahm die Gestalt eines geistigen Vermögens an, das selbstvergessen als bewusstlose bildende Kraft im Eingeweide der Maria wirkt und aus den belebten Säften einer menschlichen Mutter einen Leib bildet, der geeignet ist, der Entwickelung dieses bestimmten geistigen Vermögens so zu dienen, dass dasselbe sich dessen als seines zugehörigen Eigenthums bedienen und bewusst werden, sich selbst darin und mittelst desselben selbstthätig entwickeln kann. Das geistige Vermögen wirkt in den Anfängen der Leibbildung bloss als Natur, als bewusstloses Vermögen, später in dem Leibe als geistige Natur, als Seele, die sich ihrer Empfindungen und Vorstellungen bewusst wird und selbstthätig, aber noch nicht völlig selbstbewusst dagegen zurückwirkt, endlich in der Seele als Geist, als selbstbewusst sich selbst bestimmende Selbstthätigkeit. Der Geist ist das Erste und das Letste;

er bildet den Leib, er bewegt die Seele; aber Geist verdient er erst genannt zu werden, wenn er zu sich selbst gekommen ist, wenn er sein Vermögen erkennt und frei darüber schaltet" (p. 38).] The Logos becomes an unconscious power, producing a body in the Virgin, working first as nature, then in the formed body as soul, then in the soul as spirit self-conscious and self-determining. Jesus on earth was, according to this author, the divine genius of the human race, knowing Himself to be the same person as before the kenosis, but taking up into His self-consciousness the body with its sensitive soul (empfindende Seele), and using this animated body as the servant of His divine spirit, till, in the state of exaltation, body and soul become spiritualized ($\pi\nu\epsilon\nu\mu\alpha\tau\iota\kappa\acute{o}\nu$), when Christ is no longer simply a divine genius, but the God of humanity in constant fellowship with the Father.

REUSS (*Histoire de la Théologie Chrétienne au Siècle Apostolique*, 1864), speaking of the Pauline view of Christ's person, indicates briefly his opinion as to the meaning of the passage in Phil. ii., in these terms: "Il est dit expressément que l'élément divin est l'essentiel; l'élément humain, quelque chose d'adopté, d'ajouté, d'extérieur. Cela implique l'idée d'un abaissement, d'une espèce de privation, d'un dépouillement, et nous conduit directement à nous représenter l'union des deux natures comme l'alliance d'un esprit divin avec un corps humain, explication qui se recommande par sa simplicité même; mais qui n'a jamais été du goût des théologiens. Il est vrai qu'elle n'est pas ainsi formulée dans les textes, mais ceux-ci ne contiennent pas un mot qui lui soit contraire" (vol. ii. p. 71). That is to say, the most natural construction of the apostle's statement is to find in it Gess's theory of the kenosis, the Logos, as a human soul, assuming a human body. On the other hand, Reuss finds no trace of a *status exinanitionis* in John's writings. The Incarnation for John is not a humiliation, but a glorification—even in His death the Son of man is glorified; and this idea is held to be quite incompatible with the scholastic view, according to which Christ's death was the lowest degree of abasement. This is very superficial theology (see tome ii. p. 455).

GODET (*Commentaire sur l'Evangile de Saint Jean*, Paris 1864) expresses the opinion that the Church doctrine of the two natures does not perfectly set forth the sense of the Scriptures, and that both Reformed and Lutheran theories fail to solve the problem of reconciling the real humanity with the pre-existence, and says that the Scriptures do not teach the presence of the divine nature with its divine attributes in Jesus on earth. The expression in John i. 14 conveys the idea of a divine subject reduced to a human state, but not of two states, divine and human, co-existing. Paul teaches the same idea in Phil. ii. 6. The words of the apostle (ἐκένωσε, etc.) can only mean, " qu'il a déposé son état divin pour prendre l'état humain; il ne les a donc pas combinés en s'incarnant, mais il a échangé celui-là pour celui-ci." The glory referred to in John xvii. is "l'état divin avec tous ses attributs, sa *forme de Dieu*, selon l'expression de Saint Paul, dont il s'était dépouillé en se faisant homme." This self-exinanition implies, to begin with, the loss of self-consciousness. "Il faut ensuite que le sujet divin consente à perdre pour un temps la conscience de lui-même, comme tel. La conscience d'une relation si particulière avec Dieu et le souvenir d'une vie antérieure à cette existence terrestre seraient incompatibles avec l'état d'une véritable enfant et avec un développement réellement humain." But at His baptism Jesus at length attained to the consciousness of His being the Logos. His ministry required this, because " pour témoigner de lui même, il doit se connaître." This self-consciousness, however, did not restore the divine state, the form of God. He had the use of the treasures of wisdom and power which are in God. But He possessed nothing. He could therefore say: " Père rends-moi ma gloire." After the ascension He regained His divine *state*. "Dès ce moment il est mis en possession, et cela comme Fils de l'homme, de tous les attributs divins, de l'état de Fils de Dieu, tel qu'il le possédait avant son Incarnation: *Toute la plénitude de la divinité habite* CORPORELLEMENT *en lui*" (Col. ii. 9). Godet refers to Gess, and expresses his general agreement with the view presented by the latter: "dans son bel ouvrage (*Lehre von der Person Christi*, 1856) dont (he adds) j'ai eu l'honneur de rendre compte a l'époque de son apparition," *Revue Chrétienne*, 1857-58. (See *Commentaire*, tome premier, 247-265.)

LIEBNER (*Christologie oder die christologische Einheit des dogmatischen Systems dargestellt*, Erste Abtheilung [all that has appeared], Göttingen 1849) may be classed under the Gessian type, because, so far as appears, he does not recognise any human soul in Christ distinct from the Logos, and because he teaches a Subordinatian view of the Trinity as the foundation of an absolute kenosis of the Son, whereby He empties Himself of divine contents, and becomes, as it were, a mere form or empty vessel to be re-filled by a process of human development. Liebner's speculations, Trinitarian and Christological, while extremely interesting and suggestive, are rather abstruse; but the following sketch, it is hoped, may afford a clear and sufficient outline of his system. The doctrine of the Trinity is based on the idea of personality, which is not a solitary, but a social thing. Not merely self-assertion over against another, as conceived by Strauss and Fichte and many modern philosophers, but—and this is the positive moment—it is reaching beyond self, including another, and allowing itself to be included, in a word, love (not mere "Selbstheit gegen Anderes, Fürsichsein gegen Anderes, Anderes von sich Ausschliessen," but "das über sich Uebergreifende, das Andere Einschliessende, und sich Einschliessenlassende, und das ist die Liebe," p. 115). The Trinitarian process turns upon the nature of love as self-communication. God wills to realize Himself as absolute love, or, what is the same thing, to be real absolute personality; hence the tendency to transpose Himself, as it were to lose Himself in His own Other—God the Son. But this second, in order to realize Himself in turn as love, tends to lose Himself again in the first as His absolute object. Thus, on the one side, God the Father goes forth from Himself, and posits the Son, transposes Himself into the latter, makes Himself, after the nature of love, dependent with respect to the Son, empties Himself into the Son. On the other, side the Son, moved by the same impulse, makes Himself in turn dependent on the Father, empties Himself into the Father. But as this process of love makes Father and Son mutually dependent on each other, and so tends to repeat itself *ad infinitum*, a necessity arises for a third hypostasis, who preserves the distinction in unity, and *vice versâ*, and brings the process of the absolute life and love to rest, and completes it. Without the third person the mutual love of Father and Son would resolve itself into an everlasting seesaw, an eternal unrest—each in turn losing Himself in the other. In order that the two first persons in their mutual self-communication should be at the same time eternally independent, there is needed a third object-subject of their love, whom they love in common, and by whom they are both beloved, as the principle of absolute equipoise, of true union in distinction (p. 127). In this trinitarian process the initiative lies with the Father, and in this respect there is a certain element of subordination in the relation of the Son to the Father. This element may be called an eternal kenosis, which is at the same time posited and cancelled, but is still there as a cancelled moment (die Subordination des Sohnes als Sohnes nach seinem *character hypostaticus* ist ewig trinitarisch gesetzt und aufgehoben, überwunden: doch ist sie eben an sich da, nämlich als aufgehobene, als überwundenes Moment, p. 150). This eternal element of kenosis is the eternal possibility of Incarnation (p. 150). In the Incarnation that eternal kenosis becomes temporal. The self-emptying of the Son, and His being re-filled from the fulness of the Father, which are simultaneous in the trinitarian life, in the incarnate state are unfolded into a succession of moments, first the self-emptying, then the being re-filled. This temporal kenosis, in abstract language, may be defined as the Son of God entering into Becoming (*Werden*), becoming a mere form to be gradually filled with divine contents. This entering into *Werden*, according to Liebner, cannot take place in any other way than by Incarnation; God cannot enter into the creation except as man. The entrance of the Logos into *Werden* is *eo ipso* Menschwerden. Hence the problem of Christology is to exhibit the process by which the Logos, reduced to a form by becoming flesh, becomes as a man progressively filled with divine contents. The interest in this process turns mainly on the moral and the intellectual growth of Christ. As to the former, Liebner, as his theory requires, recognises the distinction in reference to Christ between formal and real freedom—the former consisting in liberty of choice, and involving the possibility of a wrong choice; the latter, in the free yet necessary doing of the good, excluding the possibility of sin. By the kenosis, the will of Christ became a *form* to be filled by a process of ethical development, involving temptation, with ethical contents, perfect holiness. But Liebner differs from Gess in treating the possibility of sinning involved in formal freedom as a mere abstraction in the case of Christ. He could be tempted, but He could not sin. The personal peculiarity of Christ consists in the marvellous identity of the *posse non peccare*, the *posse peccare*, and the *non posse peccare* (p. 295). In answer to the objection, that on this view Christ is after all not truly human, Liebner remarks that He is *divine-human*—that is His peculiarity; and asks, "Is it not the highest possible form of humanity—*das gottmenschliche Urbild der Menschheit*—this complete ethical infallibility?" (p. 298). To justify the ascription of the *non posse peccare* to Christ, he lays stress on the consideration, that in His case an ethical existence preceded His entrance into time, whereas in the case of man (Adam) only an ethical idea preceded his existence (Seinem Werden geht ein (ethisches) Sein voraus; unserm Werden nur die Idee, die ideelle Bestimmung, p. 303). With regard to the intellectual development of Christ, Liebner thinks that his theory enables him to resolve the difficulties very simply. The doctrine of the Logos entered into *Werden*, as to self-consciousness, takes the following shape: In infancy the Logos had no actual self-consciousness, only the divine-human Potenz. He had His consciousness in the Father, He was lost in the Father, and came only in the course of development through the mediation of the Spirit to self-consciousness, which from the very first was *divine-human*. It took the form of presentment in the boy of twelve. The baptism was a critical point in the self-consciousness of Jesus, at which He became fully acquainted with Himself (p. 311). Liebner further discusses the development of Christ on what he calls the nature-side. He says, Christ as the Head is the sum of human nature, of the whole organic system of the natural gifts of humanity, an individual and yet a universal man. Not, however, as if in Christ all human gifts attained to actual development. His vocation as Redeemer demanded the actualization only of the highest moments. Nevertheless in these, in His holiness, all possible human gifts were sanctified. In Christ lay the principle of the true artist, statesman, etc.; though He was neither *actu*, because He did not need to be. This doctrine of a pleromatic humanity is connected in Liebner's case, as in the case of many other German theologians (*e.g.* Ebrard), with the theory that the Incarnation was destined to take place irrespective of sin. Sin affected the accidental conditions, but not the fact of Incarnation. The Christological theory of Liebner is summed up by himself in these terms: "Christ was the Logos entering into *Werden*, which *eo ipso* is to become man. Hereby a theanthropic personality is formed with the to it adequate universal nature, as condition of its realization in the world, which personality, at first pure Potence, in successive developments under the form of human knowledge and will (reason and freedom), at each stage of human life, as it came in natural course, infallibly, and yet in a truly human ethical process, identified itself with the divine element. This is the notion which alone helps to solve the problem of the union of the two moments, which irresistibly press themselves upon our view as we survey the Christological contents of Scripture; on the one hand, that Christ receives all in truly human ethical activity from the Father, and yet, at the same time, on the other hand, is conscious of all as originally and essentially His own." ["Christus war der Logos ins Werden eingegangen, was *eo ipso* Menschwerden ist. Hiemit ist eine gottmenschliche Persönlichkeit gesetzt mit der ihr adäquaten universalen Natur als Bedingung ihrer Realisirung in der Welt; welche Persönlichkeit, zunächst reine Potenz, in successiver Entwickelung unter der Form des menschlichen Wissens und Wollens (Vernunft und Freiheit) auf jeder menschlichen Lebensstufe, wie sie mit der natürlichen Entwickelung gegeben war, unfehlbar und doch in einem wahrhaft menschlich ethischen Process sich mit dem göttlichen Inhalt wieder zusammenschloss. Dieses ist der allein lösende Begriff für die Verbindung der beiden Momente, die aus dem Totaleindruck des christologischen Schriftinhalts sich unwiderstehlich aufdrängen: das Christus Alles in wahrer menschlicher ethischer Arbeit von seinem himmlischen Vater empfängt und doch zugleich Alles ursprünglich und wesentlich sich zugehörig weiss" (p. 345).] Liebner repels the charge of Apollinarism which, he imagines, many may be ready to bring against his theory, by pointing out that in the Apollinarian theory the sinlessness of Christ is guaranteed by the exclusion of freedom: Christ's holiness is a physical thing, there is no ethical development. He also remarks, that the idea of the Head of humanity, by which the doctrine of God-manhood is completed, is strange to the Apollinarian system. At the same time, he attaches high value to Apollinaris in the history of Christology, and says that the great questions he raised were not answered in his age by the Church, and have not even yet been truly answered (p. 372). Having ranged Liebner under the Gessian type, it is necessary in justice to him to add, that he condemns the Zinzendorfian metamorphic kenosis as exaggerated, unscriptural, monstrous, and beset with the greatest difficulties. The Christological image in Scripture, he thinks, shows, along with true humanity, a surplus of the superhuman, superadamitic, which cannot be reconciled with the fiction of the transformation of the Logos into a man (pp. 338-340).

HOFMANN discusses the Incarnation in the second volume of his work, *Der Schriftbeweis, ein theologischer Versuch* (pp. 1-43, Zweite Auflage). His Christology is of the kenotic type, but it is not easy to fix his precise whereabouts, as on some points he does not explain himself clearly. This is especially the case in reference to the question whether Christ had a rational soul distinct from the depotentiated Logos. In reply to Dorner, who classed him among those who supported that view of the kenosis, according to which the Logos became a human soul, he says: " What good can it do to bring together texts in which, in an accidental way, mention is made of the body, soul, and spirit of Jesus? After it has once been said that He became man, it is self-evident that to Him all that belongs whereby a man is a man. And I think I may leave the matter thus, after Dorner has made the discovery, that I evidently, not altogether without design, avoid expressing myself concerning the soul of Christ, on which account he forthwith reckons me among those who patronize the form of the kenosis, according to which the Logos became a human soul. All that he says on that score does not affect me in the least, and only in the one point is he right, when he says: the thesis that God in reducing His actuality to a Potence thereby becomes man, or inversely that man is God potentially, God standing in need of development, lies outside of my range of vision. But the question which lately *Gess* has propounded in order to answer it in the negative, whether there was in Jesus, beside the Logos, a soul derived from Mary, has not for me any sense at all, as every one will understand who from this book knows what the soul and what the Incarnation means for me. The case stands for Christ's soul-life not otherwise than with that of every one born of woman." ["Was kann es nützen, solche Schriftstellen zusammen-zutragen, in welchen zufälliger Weise von Jesu Leib oder Seele oder Geist die Rede ist? Nachdem einmal gesagt ist, dass er Mensch geworden, versteht sich von selbst, dass ihm alles das geeignet hat, was dazu gehört damit ein Mensch Mensch sei. Und hiebei, meine ich, kann ich es auch jetzt lassen, nachdem Dorner die Entdeckung gemacht hat, dass ich über Christi Seele mich auszusprechen offenbar nicht ganz absichtslos vermeide, weshalb er mich sofort denen beizählt, welche diejenige Wendung der Kenosis vertreten, wornach durch sie der Logos menschliche Seele geworden. Alles das, was er dort ausführt, geht mich auch nicht das Mindeste an, und nur in dem Einem hat er das Rechte getroffen, dass er sagt, der Satz, dass der seine Actualität zur Potenz herabsetzende Gott eben damit an ihm selbst Mensch, oder umgekehrt, der Mensch potenzieller, entwikelungsbedürftiger Gott sei, liege ausserhalb meines Gesichtskreises. Die Frage aber welche sich neuerlich *Gess* gestellt hat, um sie zu verneinen, ob in Jesu neben dem Logos eine aus

Maria stammende Seele gewesen, hat für mich gar keinen Sinn, wie Jeder begreifen wird, der aus diesem Buche kennt, was mir die Seele und was mir Christi Menschwerdung ist. Es verhält sich mit Christi seelischem Leben nicht anders, als mit dem eines jeden vom Weibe Geborenen" (p. 43).]
. Instead of distinctly answering the question whether the Logos and the human soul of Christ were the same or distinct, Hofmann here tells us it has no meaning for him, and for the rest refers us to his representation of the Incarnation. Turning to that, we find him interpreting Phil. ii. 6 f. as teaching an exchange of the form of God for the form of a servant, and extracting from John i. 14 the idea that the Word exchanged His previous form of being for another which is its opposite (Widerspiel), giving up His Godhead and assuming our nature. "We are flesh, He became it." [" Wir sind σάρξ, er ist es geworden" (p. 26).] In accordance with this view, we are told that all the *formulae* must be given up which are derived from a conception of the incarnation as a union of the divine and human natures (p. 22). Yet we are not to suppose that the incarnate Logos has ceased to be God. "He remains *who* He was, though He has ceased to be *what* He was:" [" Allerdings aber ist er der geblieben, der er war (oder besser gesagt, der er ewiger Weise ist). Dies liegt schon darin, dass er, derselbe, welcher Gott bei Gott gewesen, Fleisch geworden, hiezu in die Welt gekommen ist. Nur das, was er war (nämlich geschichtlicher Weise war), hat er aufgehört zu sein, um etwas Anderes zu werden" (p. 26)]. The two clauses put within brackets in the above extract (by me, not by the author) contain hints of the view taken by Hofmann of the bearing of the Incarnation on the doctrine of the Trinity. The Logos remains in an eternal manner (*ewiger Weise*) God after He has become man. That does not mean, however, that the incarnate Logos has a double historical existence, one in the flesh, the other as world-governing Logos. The one form of existence has been exchanged for the other (p. 23). It is true, indeed, that even on earth, even in His mother's womb, as a child growing in wisdom and stature, sleeping and waking, working and suffering, the Son of God took part in the government of the

world, because in all these He was fulfilling the eternal purpose of God for the salvation of men, in which the divine government of the world has its unity. But the incarnate Logos in His state of exinanition takes part in the government of the world, not as a Lord, but as a servant (pp. 26, 27). In this part of his scheme of thought, Hofmann *substantially* agrees with Gess, who makes Christ cease from the government of the world during His life on earth; only he does not agree to call the fact a *cessation* from such government, because he holds that even in serving, Christ was, in a new way, ruling (p. 27, where Gess's view is referred to). Hofmann declines Ebrard's way of stating the case, that the *eternal* form of existence was exchanged for the temporal. He maintains that the right way to put the matter is to say that the Logos, retaining throughout the eternal form of existence, exchanges one form of *historical* existence for another. For he holds that the Logos was a historical person before He became man. Previous to the Incarnation, He occupied the historical position of a supramundane, omnipotent, world-governing Power and Will. In the Incarnation He entered into an intramundane state of being, —into the human finitude of existence, knowledge, and power. [" Aber so ist es nicht, dass er die Ewigkeitsform mit der Zeitlichkeitsform vertauscht hat, sondern aus seinem geschichtlichen Stände der Ueberweltlichkeit, des weltbeherrschenden Könnens und Wollens und Gegenwärtigseins, ist er, der hier und dort gleich Ewige, in die Innerweltlichkeit, in die menschliche Umschränktheit des Daseins und Wissens, und Könnens eingegangen, die eine geschichtliche Bethätigung seines ewigen Wesens mit der andern vertauschend " (p. 24).] The import of this view, in its bearing on the doctrine of the Trinity, is, that the Incarnation affected not the essential, but only the economical Trinity. Hofmann's doctrine with reference to the Trinity is as follows:—The names Father, Son, and Spirit express an interdivine relation,—that is to say, there is such a thing as an essential Trinity, but the essential Trinity is only the presupposition of God's historical self-manifestation. As it is of this self-manifestation alone that the Scriptures directly speak, the interdivine relations are always represented as involving inequality. Christ is God's, and God is the Head of Christ, and the Spirit is spoken of in the neuter gender (vol. i. p. 200). The interdivine relation is one of equality: all three persons are equal in power and glory; but the relation becomes one of inequality as soon as it enters on a process of self-fulfilment (i. 268). This process began with the creation, and was completed by the Incarnation. In the creation the interdivine relation entered into its lowest degree of inequality, the three persons of the Godhead becoming respectively the Father, the supramundane Creator; the Son, the original world-aim, "urbildliches Weltziel" (i. 270); and the Holy Spirit, the intramundane active Life-ground, "der inweltliche wirksame Lebensgrund" (i. 190). In the Incarnation the interdivine relation between Father and Son entered into its highest degree of inequality, becoming as great, in fact, as it could, without involving a self-negation of God [Da ward die Ungleichheit des innergöttlichen Verhältnisses in seiner geschichtlichen Gestaltung so gross, als sie ohne Selbstverneinung Gottes werden konnte, ii. 24]. But even in this extreme inequality the relation remained essentially the same. Though Christ, not partially only, but completely, unreservedly, renounced all supramundane self-manifestation, yet He did not cease to be God, ewiger Weise. He entered into human finitude, but He did not become a finite creature [Nicht theilweise, sondern völlig und ohne Vorbehalt hat sich Christus in seiner Menschwerdung aller überweltlichen Selbsterweisung begeben, ohne dass er darum aufhörte, was ja nicht aufhören kann, weil es auch nicht angefangen hat, ewiger Weise Gott zu sein. Er hat sich in die menschliche Umschränktheit dahingegeben, ohne dadurch ein endliches Geschöpf zu werden. Die Art und Weise seiner Selbsterzeigung ist eine andere geworden, aber was er erzeigt, ist nachher wie vorher seine nicht zum blossen Sein der Potenz reducirte, sondern ewige, also ihrer selbst und damit der Welt mächtige Gottheit, ii. 24]. Hofmann characterizes Gess' Subordinatian view of the Trinity as an error, and ascribes Gess' mistake to a neglect of the distinction on which he (Hofmann) insists between the historical inequality and the eternal equality of the interdivine relation (i. p. 271). On another point this instructive writer differs from Gess, viz. in reference to the moral development of Christ. He says, with reference specially to Ebrard's view, that it is false to say of Jesus in His earthly life only *potuit non peccare*, reserving the *non potest peccare* for the glorified state. The true distinction between the two states is, that in the *status exinanitionis* Christ could be tempted, while in the glorified state He cannot be tempted (ii. 65). Hofmann holds that the sinlessness of Christ's human nature is a matter of course (ii. 31), and that it was impossible for the man Jesus to sin, because the everlasting God, become man, could not deny Himself. His human historical will could not enter into contradiction with His eternal divine will, which dwelt within the former, and the eternal God became man just because that was the sure way to victory over sin. [Der menschgewordene ewige Gott konnte nicht sich selbst verneinen, der Mensch Jesus also konnte nicht sündigen, sein menschlich geschichtliches Wollen nicht in Widerspruch treten mit seinem demselben innewohnenden ewig göttlichen Wollen, und der ewige Gott ist eben deswegen Mensch geworden, weil dies der gewisse Sieg über die Sünde war. Es ist also falsch von Jesu in seinem Fleischesleben nur zu sagen, *potuit non peccare*, und erst von dem Verklärten, *non potest peccare*. Der Unterschied allein ist zu setzen, dass er dort hat versucht werden können, hier aber unversuchbar ist, ii. p. 65.] It remains to add that Hofmann is substantially at one with Liebner in regard to the sense in which the exchange of forms implied in the kenosis is to be understood. Liebner makes the μορφὴ δούλου signify the human existence-form as one of dependence and subjection to God, the existence-form of the creaturely ethico-religious personality. The μορφὴ Θεοῦ, on the other hand, signifies the existence-form of absolute independence, freedom, absolute personality (p. 327). Hofmann says the apostle's meaning is, that Christ deprived Himself of the appearance in divine self-glorious might, in which He existed over against the world, in order to assume the appearance of intramundane servitude and dependence; not, indeed, of servitude to men, but of creaturely dependence on God; and in this exchange of the one μορφή for the other did the kenosis consist (i. p. 140).

GOODWIN (*Christ and Humanity*. London: Hodder & Stoughton, 1875) gives a lengthened sketch of the history of the doctrine of Christ's person, with a view to show the unsatisfactoriness of the Church Christology in all its forms, and then proceeds to state and vindicate his own view, which is essentially the same as those of the German writers above referred to, especially Gess and Liebner. This author is familiar with the German kenotic literature, but he arrived at his opinions independently, and previous to his acquaintance with European advocates of them. The Incarnation, according to him, was the human element (the Logos), eternally in God, becoming man by taking flesh, and occupying the place of a soul. He founds his theory on the basis of the essential unity of the divine and human.

NOTE C.—PAGE 153.

Das Dogma vom heiligen Abendmahl und seine Geschichte, Frankfurt-a-M. 1845; and *Christliche Dogmatik*, Königsberg 1851. The prefaces to these works contain interesting particulars, affording a glimpse into the circumstances and feelings out of which they arose. The preface to the earlier work especially reveals the state of the writer's mind, as that of one full of high hopes with regard to the union of the two branches of the German Church, and burning with desire to serve that sacred cause. The author dedicates his work to four friends who were in one way or another associated with the formation of its plan or the execution. Two of the friends he reminds of the many never-to-be-forgotten Sunday evening conversations in which they discussed together the questions at issue between the two confessions, he representing the Reformed, they the Lutheran, but all being one in heart, and cherishing the hope of being one day one in outward church fellowship. It was amidst these conversations that the purpose was formed to make an attempt at a solution of the weightiest doctrinal differences. Another of the friends he reminds of the evening of 1st September 1840, when, refreshed by a delightful walk among the hills, and inspired by the harvest sunshine and the fragrance of the shrubbery, they sat by the murmuring spring, and, amid deepening shadows of the advancing day, talked of the unity of their faith and love and hope,—and were glad because they were at one in their views on the Holy Supper of the Lord. The fourth friend he thanks for valuable aid in procuring out of the chaos of the Erlangen library the literary material necessary for the execution of a ten years' task. In His preface to the *Christliche Dogmatik*, the author mentions a fact which illustrates to what an extent the works of the older dogmaticians have been studied in Germany in recent times, viz. that his citations are taken from forty-six volumes of Reformed authors, belonging to the sixteenth, seventeenth, and eighteenth centuries. Such particulars may savour somewhat of egotism, but they bring before us in an interesting way the laudable habit, characteristic of German students, of combining exact and extensive historical research with original and independent thought. German theologians are not the slaves of their old writers, but they know them and value them.

NOTE D.—PAGE 159.

For the satisfacion of such as may wish fuller information respecting Ebrard's method of dealing with the speculative problems of Christology, I give here, in condensed form, his views on the two questions: How can divine and human properties be united in the same subject? and how can the eternal and the incarnate Logos have an identical consciousness? The original passages on which this statement is based will be found in *Abendmahl*, i. 186-202; *Dogmatik*, ii. 144-148. The two questions (above stated) cannot be answered so long as time and eternity are regarded as two mutually exclusive forms, and it is not understood that it is an everlasting determination of God to reveal His essence in the form of a temporal development, as werdender Gott, as entwickelender Gottmensch. Everything turns on regarding the wall of partition between eternity and time, not as absolute, but only as requiring mediation. Eternity as the form of extra temporality (Auserzeitlichkeit), having time standing over against it as the Other, non-eternal, is not the highest, but the time-form filled with eternal essence is the highest goal. Eternity as form of the extra-temporal is the form of the Trinity as the world-governing; but God wills to glorify His Essence in the world, and in order to this He must give up the Ewigkeitsform and assume the time-form. God, indeed, as *causa sui*, cannot enter into time; but as objective to Himself, as eternal personal Logos, He can, and He has, Scripture being witness (Phil. ii. 6 ff.), and in so doing He has exchanged the Ewigkeitsform for the time-form. In the incarnate Logos we can have no difficulty in finding all divine properties, if only one do not conceive these in a stiff, external way, but separate between the Ewigkeitsform appropriate to the world-governing God, and the eternal Essence appearing in the incarnate God. Omnipotence is not to be thought of as meaning that God can do all that is possible, "alles Mögliche kann," as if there were a sphere of *possibilia* outside and independent of God; but as signifying that the sphere of the actual (geschehenes) has its principle and *prius* in the divine will. In the world-governing God this omnipotence appears as a willing and positing of the whole world in all times and places; in the incarnate God it appears in time-form as a will having dominion over particular powers of nature coming in its way (Wunderkraft), which is just the individual expression of the dominion of the spirit over nature to which man is destined. In like manner omnipresence does not mean that God is in all places "an allen Orten wäre," as if there were a space outside and independent of God; but that space is in God, and everything in time and space has its *prius* in the being of God. In the world-governing God omnipresence is all-space embracing being; in the incarnate God it signifies that Jesus finds in this or that space no limit of His corporeal being, is not ruled by space, but rules it, and is where He will,—a dominion to which man is destined. Omniscience does not mean that God knows all real and possible things, but that His will and vision are the principle and *prius* of all that is for us knowable of the whole world. In the world Governor it is a real overlooking (Ueberschauen) of all spaces and times; in the Incarnate it amounts to this, that the knowable is no limit for the knowledge of Jesus, but He sees through (durchschaut) single objects, coming in His way in time, unerringly in the light of the Truth which He brings with Him as His essence,—a dominion of spirit over the objects of knowledge to which man is destined. With these explanations the first of the two problems, the combination of divine and human properties in Christ, appears no longer insoluble. As for the second, three considerations go far towards its solution: (1) The existence and manner of existence (Daseyn und Soseyn) of the world—human freedom, and its results included—are grounded in an eternal free necessary act of God. The love of God, which calls forth and mediates the contrast I and thou in God Himself, also calls forth the existence of a time-sphere (Welt), whose special manner of being is determined by the purpose that God's essence should be glorified therein. This sphere is first nature,—with man it becomes ethical, spiritual. Nature is for man's sake. Man is nature's crown, yea, its centre or principle, last in creation, but spiritually the *prius*. But humanity itself is an organism; and as nature seeks man, so humanity seeks to gather up its multitude into a last highest unfolding, in a king, a perfect man, in whom the unity of man with God, the glorification of the Divine Essence in time, will be completed. (2) Now the Logos knows Himself as the world-creating, organizing Word of the Father, as the Wisdom of the Father appearing in the world. The world is objective to the Logos, and He sees Himself therein. But not in it, so far as it forms an abstract time-line (Zietlinie), or so far as it is corrupted by abuse of human freedom, but only so far as it is an organism ordered by God's essence and sanctified by God's grace. The eternal intuition by which the Logos sees the world must not be regarded, after the analogy of human vision, as an abstract overlooking (Uberschauen) of the time-line, but as a through-looking (Durchschauen) of the organism of humanity. Time and the world, humanity in its historical course, are for the eye of the Logos not a line, but a body with a centre. That centre is the God-man. Jesus of Nazareth is the middle point of history, blossom of the old, principle of the new time; the King, to whose kingdom we are all called, the last, highest crown of all development. So He appears to the view of the Logos. Not as the particular individual who lived under Augustus, but as the centre of the world and of humanity: He beholds the world as the appearance of His own eternal being; He beholds it in the microkosm of the person Jesus Christ as in Himself; He knows Himself from eternity, as Jesus the Christ who is end and centre of the rational universe (des logischen Wesens). (3) Jesus Christ underwent development as a man, but His development was *normal* and *all-sided*. Normal: That inborn feeling of every man, that he is created to be one in life with God, which is repressed in the sinful, was present in Jesus the sinless, first as feeling, in all its force. He felt God to be His Father. When reflection came, His knowledge of objects and relations, of His own being and of God, was unerring. He knew Himself as holy, as the only Holy One; out of the prophets He knew the desire of humanity for salvation, and His own vocation as Redeemer; He knew, from the relations in which He was placed, the necessity that He, the sinless, should experience in vicarious suffering the culmination of sin. His baptism was probably the point at which He made the transaction from mere presentiment to clear knowledge of His calling. But if He knew Himself as the Redeemer, He could not fail to know Himself also as the centre of the world's history, as the Son of man, the δεύτερος Ἀδάμ, in whom was to be found the πλήρωμα of human powers, the exaltation of humanity to God, the *absolute* communication of God to humanity. That is, He knew Himself as the God-man, as the Logos of the Father (the eternal hypostatic thought of the Father concerning the world) come to manifestation, as the incarnate Logos who before Abraham—is. In short, the eternal Logos knows Himself as the Logos appearing in time, the incarnate Logos knows Himself as the incarnate eternal Logos. The consciousness of both is perfectly coincident. It is the consciousness of the eternal Essence destined to appearance in time, the consciousness of the time-form filled with the eternal Essence; in a word, the neither extra-temporal eternal, nor the relative temporal consciousness, but the consciousness of the perfect interpenetration of time and eternity, the festive consciousness of the marriage of time and eternity.

NOTE E.—PAGE 164.

Under the Martensen type of kenosis may be reckoned Schöberlein (*Die Grundlehren des Heils entwickelt aus dem Princip der Liebe, von Ludwig Schöberlein*, Berlin 1851) and Mr Hutton (*Essays Theological and Literary*).

Schöberlein represents Christ as becoming, in the Incarnation, a single human personality. The Ego of this human being is not a new one, having a beginning as a creature, above which His own eternal Ego hovers as a higher, or with which the latter was united as the Spirit of God with our soul, but is His own eternal Ego in full reality. In time He is wholly Himself, the Ego of the Son of God remains. But, nevertheless, in virtue of the human individual nature received from the Virgin, He lives here below wholly as man, and only as man, as *pneumatico-corporeal* (geistig-leibliche) human soul; that is, He has at once natural human feelings and impulses, and human self-consciousness and will, in a word, complete human personality. The Son of God is become completely like us, truly emptied of His δόξα, His μορφὴ Θεοῦ, though not of His θεότης. In respect of this pure human existence in time, He is distinguished from us only by this, that He is not, as we are, simply a single man among others, but— seeing that in Him from eternity the whole of humanity is fore-ordained by love to its holy destiny—although living as single personality, yet bears in Himself the fulness of the whole human race, is the second Adam, made for the spiritual life, as the first was for the natural—is the personal centre, the blossom of humanity, the man καθ' ἐξοχήν. As the Son of God became a truly human personality, Christ had a truly human development. There is nothing in His life which exceeds the limits of human nature, and which we through Him cannot attain to. Yet while emptied of His divine δόξα (seiner göttlichen δόξα ganz und gar entäussert) with purely human consciousness and will, perfectly like us, His divine, trinitarian being and government suffered no interruption. " The love remains in all its humility exalted: really sharing the life of the Beloved, it preserves the specific peculiarity of its being. Such a peculiarity in the Son of God is His trinitarian Being and Rule. Action and Being in God, who is Spirit καθ' ἐξοχήν, the essence of which is energy, are inseparable." [" Die Liebe bleibt in all ihrer Demuth erhaben: das Leben des Geliebten wirklich theilend, bewahrt sie die spezifische Eigenthümlichkeit ihres Wesens. Eine solche ist aber beim Sohne Gottes sein trinitarisches Seyn und Walten. Wirken, und Seyn lässt sich bei Gott, dem Geiste καθ' ἐξοχήν dessen Wesen ἐνέργεια ist, nicht trennen " (p. 65).] In the Son, therefore, there is a union of two ways of being and existence. He wills and knows Himself double. " He, the same Ego, who is from eternity to eternity, is also in time, there eternal, here temporal, there without beginning and end, here during the span of a human life, there as the unlimited, here as the emptied, there with eternal consciousness and divine will, here with temporal consciousness and human will, but so that He, existing in the one, knows Himself one with the other, and *vice versâ*." [" Er, dasselbe Ich, das von Ewigkeit ist und bis in Ewigkeit, ist auch in der Zeit, dort ewig, hier zeitlich, dort ohne Anfang und Ende, hier während der Spanne eines Menschenlebens, dort als der Unumschränkte, hier als der Entäusserte, dort mit ewigem Bewusstsein und göttlichem Willen, hier mit zeitlichem Bewusstsein und menschlichem Willen, so aber, dass er, in jenem seyend, sich Eins mit diesem weiss und umgekehrt."] The author admits that this *double life* wears an appearance of a double personality. This appearance disappears, however, " as soon as we consider more closely the relation of eternity and time, of heaven and earth, into which the life of the Son of God appears divided. We must not combine therewith the representation as if the Son of God, during the time of His earthly sojourn, had a life in eternity parallel to that in time, a life of temporal succession during some thirty odd years, and within the same space of time in which He here walks after the flesh, there governs the world, or as if He existed in part here on earth, in part in heaven, spatially separated from the earth. Eternity stands not to time in a temporal, nor heaven to earth in a spatial relation; but the relation between them is causal. Eternity is the cause of time, the enduring life-ground out of which all time proceeds, and to which it returns. Doubtless it also has its process of development or unfolding, but not as time, and therefore not temporally parallel with time. It is the existence-form of the idea, of the complete life, which as life is as far as possible from being stagnant; whilst time is the form in which development runs through the *momenta* of incompleteness (in a succession of stages mutually exclusive). Time is only a special mode of appearing, characteristic of creaturely being, which breaks forth out of the eternity of the idea, and enters into it again without causing therein a temporal interruption. One may therefore not properly say that eternity is before time or after time, as little as during time, understanding during in a temporal sense. Time is for eternity and for the eternal consciousness a moment, and that again not a temporally measurable, although it unfolds itself in time and for the temporal consciousness as an unending succession" [" sobald wir das Verhältniss von Ewigkeit und Zeit, von Himmel und Erde, in welche das Leben des Sohnes Gottes getheilt erscheint, näher betrachten. Man darf nicht die Vorstellung damit verbinden, als ob der Sohn Gottes die Zeit seines irdischen Aufenthaltes auch in der Ewigkeit, parallel mit jenem, als ein gleiches Nacheinander von etlichen und dreissig Jahren durchlebe, und innerhalb desselben Zeitraums, in welchem er hier nach dem Fleische einhergeht, dort die Welt regiere, als ob er zum Theil hier unten auf der Erde, zum Theil oben im Himmel räumlich getrennt von der Erde existire. Die Ewigkeit steht zur Zeit nicht in einem zeitlichen, noch der Himmel zur Erde in einem räumlichen Verhältniss, sondern das Verhältniss zwischen ihnen ist ein causales. Die Ewigkeit ist die *causa* der Zeit, der währende Lebensgrund, aus welchem alle Zeit aus- und eingeht. Wohl hat auch sie einen Entwickelungs oder vielmehr Entfaltungsprozess, aber nicht wie die Zeit, und darum nicht irgend zeitlich-parallel mit der Zeit. Sie ist die Existenzform der Idee, des vollkommenen Lebens, das als Leben eben nichts weniger denn stagnirt, während die Zeit die Form ist in welcher die Entwicklung durch die Momente der Unvollkommenheit (in einem auschliessenden Nacheinander) verlaüft. Die Zeit ist nur eine besondere Erscheinugsweise des creatürlichen Seyns, welche aus der Ewigkeit der Idee hervorbricht und in sie wieder eingeht, ohne in ihr selbst eine zeitliche Unterbrechung zu verursachen. Man kann desshalb im Grunde auch nicht sagen, dass die Ewigkeit vor der Zeit oder nach der Zeit sei, ebenso wenig als während, nemlich zeitlich-während der Zeit. Die Zeit ist für die Ewigkeit und für das ewige Bewusstsein ein Moment, und zwar wiederum nicht ein zeitlich messbarer, wiewohl er sich in der Zeit und für das zeitliche Bewusstseyn als eine unübersehbare Folge auseinanderlegt" (p. 67)]. Having further elaborated this doctrine of the relation of eternity to time and of heaven to earth, Schöberlein goes on to apply the doctrine to Christ, thus: " Transferring this now to the Son of God, who as Son of man lives here below, we understand how His divine Being existed neither temporally nor spatially outside His earthly personality, but His eternal glory and His temporal self-exinanition, His dwelling in heaven and conversation on earth, His eternal and His temporally unfolding love were equally included in it. But this eternal heavenly being and activity never entered into His experience in so far as He entered into the world with temporal human consciousness, not to mention that He never *used* it for Himself or for His redemption work. But even as, to our mind, the eternal life appears as a life purely beyond, although we through faith bear it within us here below, so was it with Him; only with the difference that it represented itself to Him not simply as future, but as past, because He had already had a place as an Ego in the Trinity before the Incarnation. Therefore when He spoke out of His own immediate consciousness, He spoke of a glory which He had with the Father, and which the Father will give Him again; and yet at other times He referred very distinctly to a presence and immanence of this heavenly being and rule in His person, when He spoke as a teacher, and not out of immediate experience, so that we must maintain a real κένωσις, and yet at the same time the κτῆσις, yea χρῆσις, without κρύψις of the divine δόξα on the part of the incarnate Son of God." ["Tragen wir diess, nun auf den Sohn Gottes über, der als Menschensohn hienieden wandelt, so verstehen wir, wie sein göttliches Wesen weder zeitlich noch räumlich ausser seiner irdischen Persönlichkeit bestanden, sondern wie seine ewige Herrlichkeit und seine zeitliche Entäusserung, sein Wohnen im Himmel und sein Wandel auf Erden, seine ewig unendliche und seine zeitlich sich entfaltende Liebe gleicherweise in ihr geschlossen gewesen. Aber diess ewig himmlische Wesen und Wirken war ihm, insofern er in diese Welt mit zeitlich menschlichen Bewusstsein, hereingetreten war, niemals zur Erfahrung gekommen, geschweige dass er sich desselben je für sich oder sein Erlösungswerk bedient hätte. Sondern ebenso wie unsrer Vorstellung das ewige Leben als ein rein jenseitiges erscheint, obwohl wir durch den Glauben es hienieden schon in uns tragen, so war's auch bei ihm, nur mit dem Unterschiede dass sich ihm dasselbe nicht bloss zukünftig, sondern zugleich vergangen darstellte, weil er bereits vor der Menschwerdung als Ich in der Trinität bestanden hätte. Er sprach desshalb, wo er aus seinem unmittelbaren Bewusstsein heraus redete, von einer Herrlichkeit, die er bei dem Vater hatte, und die der Vater ihm wieder geben wird; und doch wies er andrerseits selbst wiederum sehr bestimmt auf eine Gegenwart und Immanenz dieses seines himmlischen Seyns und Waltens in seiner Person hin, wo er lehrend und nicht aus unmittelbarer Erfahrung heraus redete, so dass wir eine wirkliche κένωσις, und doch zugleich die κτῆσις, ja χρῆσις, ohne κρύψις, von der göttlichen δόξα des menschgewordenen Gottessohnes behaupten müssen" (pp. 69, 70).]

The English Essayist keeps clear of the metaphysics by which the German theologian endeavours to justify the theory of a *double life*—that is, a *real* yet *relative* kenosis. He simply asserts its possibility in the following terms: "And this brings me to the supposed metaphysical contradiction in the fact of Incarnation, which I used to think fatal. That difficulty was, that an infinite being *could* not become finite, or take up a human form, except as a mere simulated appearance. To me it would be far more painful to believe in the unreality of Christ's finite nature and human condition, than to give up Christianity altogether; in fact, it would involve giving up Christ to believe it for a moment. But this metaphysical contradiction, which once seemed so formidable, does not now exist for me at all. That the Son of God, even though eternal, co-eternal with the Father, may pass through any changes through which any derived being may pass, seems undeniable. When we note how little the powers which we ourselves possess, and which seem to belong to us, are identified with our personality,—how, by a stroke of paralysis, for example, a man of genius is stripped of all his richest qualities of mind, and reduced to a poor solitary *Ego*,—or, if that be not so, how he lives in two worlds, in one of which he is feeble, helpless, isolated will, and in the other (if there be another in which he is still his old self) a man of genius still,—when we note this, it seems to me to be simply the most presumptuous of all presumptuous assumptions to deny that the Son of God might have really become what He seemed to be, a finite being, a Jew of Jewish thought and prepossessions, and liable to all the intellectual errors which distinguished the world in which He lived. If there is an indestructible moral individuality which constitutes *self*, which is the same when wielding the largest powers and when it sits alone at the dark centre, which, for anything I know, may even live under a double set of conditions at the same time, I can see no metaphysical contradiction in the Incarnation" (pp. 259, 260). Mr. Hutton, in speaking of Christ's temptation, represents His superiority to all temptations as arising out of the predominant *passion* of His will, which " prevented the slightest trembling in the balance " (p. 261). It will be observed that the author goes a considerable length in the assertion of Christ's ignorance, making Him share the prejudices of a Jew and the intellectual errors of His time. The statement of opinion here does not seem sufficiently guarded.

Does not the all-important limit *without sin* exclude prejudices into which a moral element enters, and all errors, even intellectual ones, which would influence conduct?

NOTE F.—PAGE 166.

I am acquainted with the theological views of Zinzendorf only through J. A. Bengel's *Abriss der sogenannten Brüdergemeine*, and the recently published work of Plitt, *Zinzendorf's Theologie dargestellt von D. Hermann Plitt*, Gotha 1869-74. In the first volume of the last-named work the author gives an account of the original sound doctrine of Zinzendorf, as taught by him during the period 1723-1742; in the second he gives the history of the time of morbid malformations in Zinzendorf's doctrinal system (1743-1750); and in the third he exhibits that system in its restored final form, as set forth in works published between 1750 and 1760. Plitt disputes the accuracy of the representation given by Schneckenburger and others of the Zinzendorfian Christology, as of a purely metamorphic character. He admits, of course, that the Christ of Zinzendorf, especially during the second period, is to all intents and purposes a man whose Godhead, far from being apparent to others, was for the most part hidden from Himself. But he denies that the Zinzendorfian Christ is one who has ceased to be God, and quotes passages to show that Zinzendorf conceived of the Incarnation as the assumption of a human soul with a body, and taught an indissoluble hypostatic union of the humanity so assumed and the Godhead. He thinks that the idea present to Zinzendorf's mind was, that in the Incarnation an intimate union was freely formed by the divine Ego with a human soul, and through it with a body, in virtue of which the God-man in the ground of His being continued to be God, but completed His collective outward and inward life in human form. Therein was involved not an essential and central, but a modal peripheral alteration of His Godhead. [In Zinzendorf's own words: "Der Heiland hat von seinen Schätzen und Herrlichkeiten, die er als Sohn und rechtmässiger Besitzer τοῦ πᾶν hatte, schon disponirt, da er seine Gottheit verlassen hat bei der κένωσις, beim Hingang in die Zeit, in der Mutter Leib als das erste Grab. Sie blieben ein depositum in der Hand des Vater, sowie er hernach am Kreutze seine Seele auch deponirte bis zur Wiedervereinigung mit der menschlichen Hülle" (ii. p. 166).] The kenosis is here asserted in strong terms; yet Zinzendorf guards himself against a view of the kenosis which excludes the *Unio hypostatica*, as when he says: "In the kenosis the reference is not to the inhesive divinity, τῷ θείῳ: He was God throughout. One cannot conceive of a finger, hair, or morsel of skin which stood not in a *unione hypostaticâ* with His Godhead." ["Die Rede ist bei der Kenosis nicht von seiner inhäsiven Göttlichkeit, τῷ θείῳ: er ist Gott gewesen alle Augenblicke. Man kann sich keinen Finger, kein Härlein, kein Häutlein vom Heilande concipiren, das nicht in einer *unione hypostaticâ* mit seiner Gottheit stünde" (ii. p. 166).] Plitt cites one passage in which Zinzendorf seems inclined even to entertain the idea of a double life of the Logos, one of passivity of quiescence in the man Jesus, and one of full activity in relation to the world. [The words are: "Es wäre für den Schöpfer der Welt nicht zu viel wenn er zugleich die ganze Welt regiert hätte und wäre zugleich Zimmermann in Nazaret gewesen. Denn es ist bekannt, dass es Leute gibt, die zugleich schreiben und dictiren und zugleich hören können " (ii. p. 174).] The truth appears to be, that Zinzendorf had no carefully thought out consistent theory of Christ's person, but expressed himself in strong unqualified language on whatever aspects of the subject were congenial to his religious feelings, and so gave utterance to views not easily reconcilable with each other, and referable to different types of the kenotic theory. Plitt remarks: "Ontologically and psychologically considered, Zinzendorf is not the adequate representative of his own fundamental views (Grundanschauung). But we know that properly speculative questions are not his affair, and that escapade (Auschreitung, *i.e.* the double life of the Logos), in a psychological respect, is only a hasty thought thrown out hypothetically as a metaphysical possibility which he has no wish to make his own " (ii. p. 174). The kenosis seems to have been conceived by Zinzendorf habitually as *absolute*, not *relative*, as in the following passage: "*ἐκένωσεν ἑαυτόν*; with His whole heart He disengaged Himself from the work and activity of His proper Godhead, when He had to enter, and wished to enter, into time. He delivered over to His Father the government of the world so heartily, so directly, so *plenarie*, that all things whereof He was the sole Lord and Master appeared to Him when on earth not otherwise than as His Father's business . . . and He had received all out of His Father's hand, into which He had Himself previously placed all" ["*ἐκένωσεν ἑαυτόν*; er hat sich von ganzen Herzen, da er in die Zeit gehen sollte und gehen wollte, von der Wirkung und Activität seiner eigenen Gottheit losgesagt. Er hatte seinem Vater das Regiment über die Welt so herzlich, so gerade, so *plenarie* übertragen, dass alle Dinge, davon er doch allein der Herr und Meister war, zu der Zeit, da er auf Erden wandelte, ihm nicht anders vorgekommen sind, als seines Vaters Geschäfte. . . und er Alles aus seines Vaters Hand genommen hat, in die er zuvor Alles erst selbst gestellet hat" (ii. p. 172).] How complete the kenosis was in Zinzendorf's view may be gathered from such a statement as this, that as the man Jesus Christ was ignorant of all sorts of things, He, at least at times, did not know, or had it not present to His thoughts, that He was God (ii. p. 172). Also from the graphic descriptions given of the psychological life and human development of Jesus as a boy, a youth, and a man; and in His various relations to the Jewish hierarchy, the political authorities, and society; and in His work as Redeemer. As a child, Jesus was a diligent scholar, and got His head filled with Bible texts, but also with much Rabbinical rubbish; for He was no *spiritus particularis*, He had a *spiritus universalis catholicus;* He was a man who from earliest childhood practised obedience, and whose work was not to inquire whether His parents or the Rabbis in Nazareth were right or wrong. ["Er war von einer viel zu simplen Art und ordinairem Naturell, als dass er sich sollte die Mühe gegeben haben, in seiner Vorfahren Anordnung zu stören, zu raffiniren, und zu scrupuliren, oder *objectiones* gegen seine Anführer zu machen; sondern ich glaube von Herzen, was sie ihm vorgelegt haben zu lernen das hat er gelernt."] But the

Holy Spirit helped Him, expounding the true to Him, making Him forget the superfluous, gathering for Him the quintessence, *aurum ex stercore*, and writing it on His heart (ii. pp. 175, 176). The description of the Temptation is very graphic. Jesus had been weakened in body and mind by forty days' fasting, so that "when Satan came upon Him with all his angelic power and panurgy, the Saviour was directly, as we say, a man without head, did not know where His head stood, and the Holy Spirit, whose fosterchild and Jesulein (little Jesus) He was, had to suggest to Him at the moment three little words, which might meet the exigencies of the hour." ["Da der Satan ihm mit aller seiner Engelskraft und Panurgie auf den Hals trat, der Heiland gerade, wie man redt, ein Mensch ohne Kopf sein, nicht mehr hat wissen sollen, wo ihm der Kopf steht, und der heilige Geist, dessen Pflegekind und Jesulein er war, ihm zu der Stunde hat müssen drei Sprüchelchen einfallen lassen, die da haben ausrichten können, was zu der Stunde auszurichten war " (ii. p. 183).] Even in working miracles —as in raising Lazarus—the human weakness of Jesus appears. The rising of Lazarus was, according to Zinzendorf, the only instance of bringing a *dead* person back to life. Therefore, when Jesus learned that Lazarus was dead and *buried*—therefore *really* dead,—He was troubled in spirit (lest He should not be able to raise him). Arrived at the grave, He prayed, "as a child can pray now, a prayer which sounded like the answers which He had given in the desert and on the pinnacle of the temple. All ordinary authority, all His cheerful manner ceased; He behaved quite humanly, and as one quite disheartened. He might also mark that that was His last miracle, and that the wickedness of the people would become so great over the present miracle that it would certainly cost Him His life. The full *status exinanitionis* was therefore there. And when the deed was done, and the dead man raised, and God had heard Him, He went away at length to His own predestined death, with passion- and death-fear." [" Wie ein Kind beten kann heutzutage, ein Gebet, das natürlich klang, wie die Antworten, die er in der Wüsten und auf der Zinne des Tempels gegeben. Alle gewöhnliche Autorität, alle seine muntere Art cessirte, es ging ganz menschlich zu, ganz kleinlaut. Er mochte auch merken, dass das sein letztes Wunder sein und die Bosheit der Leute so gross werden würde über dem itzigen Wunder, dass es ihm nun gewiss sein Leben kosten würde. Es war also der volle *status exinanitonis* da. Und da es nun geschehen war, und er den Todten auferweckt, und Gott ihn erhört hatte, so ging er endlich an seinen bestimmten Tod mit Liedens- und Todesfurcht " (ii. p. 184).]

NOTE G.—PAGE 169.

Cyril refers to the metamorphic theory of the Incarnation in his work *Adversus Nestorium*, lib. i. cap. i., where he expresses the opinion, to put it briefly, that kenosis in the metamorphic sense, or in the sense of dopotentiation, is excluded by the skenosis. Having quoted John i. 14, he says: " The Word became flesh, manifesting the power of the true union, that, of course, which is conceived καθ' ὑπόστασιν; but because He also says that He sojourned among us, He does not allow us to think of the Logos, by nature from God, as passing over into earth-born flesh. I fancy an ill-instructed person might think that the divine uncreated nature was susceptible of change, and could part with its essential properties and be transformed into something different from what it is, and by alterations be subjected to the measures of the creature." [" Σάρκα μὲν ἔφη τὸν λόγον, τῆς ἀληθοῦς ἑνώσεως, δῆλον δὲ ὅτι τῆς καθ' ὑπόστασιν νοουμένης, ἐμφανίζων τὴν δύναμιν· διὰ δὲ τοῦ καὶ ἐν ἡμῖν αὐτὸν σκηνῶσαι λέγειν, οὐκ ἐφήσει νοεῖν εἰς σάρκα τὴν ἀπὸ γῆς τὸν ἐκ Θεοῦ κατὰ φύσιν μεταχωρῆσαι λόγον. Ὤήθη μὲν ἂν οἶμαι, τίς τῶν οὐ λίαν γεμριβωκότων ὅ τί ποτέ ἐστιν ἡ θεία τε καὶ γεννητοῦ παντὸς ἐπέκεινα φύσις, τάχα που καὶ τροπῆς εἶναι δεκτικὴν αὐτὴν, καὶ καταρραθυμῆσαι μὲν δύνασθαι τῶν ἰδίων, καὶ οὐσιωδῶς αὐτῇ προσπεφυκότων ἀγαθῶν, μεταφῦναι δὲ ὥσπερ εἰς ἕτερόν τι, παρ' ὅπερ ἐστι, καὶ τοῖς τῆς κτίσεως ἐγκαθικέσθαι μέτροις, ἀλλοιώσεσι, καὶ μεταβολαῖς ἀδοκήτως ὑπενηνεγμένην."] But this is impossible, the evangelist testifies when he says: " The Logos tabernacled among us, although become flesh." [ἐσκήνωσεν ἐν ἡμῖν· καίτοι σάρξ γεγονὼς ὁ λόγος.] Cyril discusses the same question at

Appendix.—Lecture IV.—Note G.

greater length in his tract *Adv. Anthropomorphitas*. The views against which he argues in that work are similar to those of Gess, that the Logos took only flesh and was Himself in place of a human soul (c. xv.); that He emptied the heavens of His divinity when He became man (κενοὺς τῆς ἑαυτοῦ θεότητος ἀφῆκε τοὺς οὐρανούς, c. xix.); that Christ could sin, because He was made in the likeness of men, c. xxiii. In c. xviii. of this treatise, Cyril discusses at some length another form of the kenotic theory, viz. that the Son, as to the dignity of His divinity, was still with the Father when He became man and was on the earth; but that, as to His hypostasis, He was not [Κεκένωτο γὰρ πᾶσα, ὥς αὐτοί φασι, καὶ υἱοτικὴ ὑπόστασις ἔκ τε τῶν οὐρανῶν, καὶ αὐτῶν τῶν πατρικῶν κόλπων]. In the former form of the theory the kenosis affects both nature and person of the Logos; in the latter, the person only.

LECTURE VI.

NOTE A.—PAGE 263.

THE question has been discussed by writers on Christology, whether Christ had any particular temperament. The advocates of the ideality of Christ's humanity, whether those who believe Christ to be more than man, or only man, agree in answering the question in the negative. Thus Ebrard maintains that the pleromatic man was, on the one hand, endowed with all natural as well as spiritual gifts, though these gifts might not be all developed, His vocation not requiring it; and on the other, was free from all one-sidedness of endowment, and also of temperament (*Dogmatik*, ii. 23). Martensen, to the same effect, remarks: "As every man has in his temperament for his development not only a supporting foundation, but a confining limit, it belongs to the sinlessness of the second Adam that He is not bound in the sinful one-sidedness of temperament, as it belongs to His ideal perfection that no single temperament can be regarded as predominating in Him. We find in the new Adam, as well the careless light mind, which lets every day have its own trouble, who is unconcerned as the lily in the field and the bird under the heaven, as also the deep pain-fraught sensibility, out of whose inmost heart, in a much wider sense than out of the old prophet, the complaint resounds: 'Where is there a sorrow like my sorrow?' We find in Him, as well the quiet spirit unmoved by the world, as the powerfully-stirred, vehement, and zealous spirit, while none of these contrasts is perverted into one-sidedness" (*Dogmatik*, p. 259). Liebner takes a similar view (*Christologie*, p. 315). On the other hand, Keim finds in the gospel records clear traces of individual idiosyncrasy. He ascribes to Jesus a combination of the choleric, sanguine, and melancholic temperaments, and regards Him in this combination as a genuine Jew, a Jew of the strongest southern melancholy type. ["In der Wahrnehmungslust ein Sanguiniker, im Feuereifer ein Choleriker, in Beidem ein ächter Galiläer, ist er durch seinen Frömmigkeitszug, wie er ihn durch Erziehung anlernte und von Natur immer schon im Vollmass besass, ein ächtester Jude schlechthin, ja ein Jude vom kräftigsten südlichen melancholischen Typus gewesen"] (*Geschichte Jesu*, Dritte Bearbeitung, 1873, pp. 111, 112). Of the melancholy religious disposition, Keim finds proof in the love of solitude and of religious devotion. He discovers no trace of the phlegmatic temperament (vid. *Jesu von Nazara*, i. 442). It is probably not advisable to enter into minute discussions on such a question; but I confess I see no evidence in the gospel of that generalized humanity which the advocates of the Ideal Man theory are so fond of ascribing to Jesus. I see in Him traces of a strongly marked, though not one-sided, individuality—poetry, passion, intensity, vehemence, all that gives pathos, power, and human interest to character, even humour not excepted. Generally speaking, the reality, not the ideality, of the humanity is the thing that lies on the surface; although the latter is not to be denied, nor the many-sidedness which is adduced in proof of it by Martensen and others.

NOTE B.—PAGE 268.

In the text I have made no reference to the views entertained on the subject of the flesh by those whose theological opinions are controlled by a naturalistic philosophy. I propose to give a brief account and criticism of these in this note. Theologians of this school, then, bluntly deny the possibility of a real, thoroughgoing experience of temptation without the presence in the flesh of sinful proclivity. They maintain that such sinful proclivity did exist in Christ's flesh, and that to teach anything else is to give a doketic view of His humanity, in this agreeing with the Adoptianists, Menken and Irving. They maintain further, and in this they go beyond the theologians just referred to, that sinful proclivity is inseparable from the flesh, is no mere accident of the *fall*, but an essential characteristic of the σάρξ. In fact, they do not believe in a fall at all, or in any change in the physical constitution of human nature. They regard the "fall" as a fiction of church theology, arrived at by an illegitimate combination of Paul's doctrine concerning the σάρξ in the 7th chapter of Romans with his doctrine of sin coming into the world through Adam in the 5th. The true origin of sin is the proclivity to sin inherent in the flesh; it was this that gave rise to sin in Adam, it is this which gives rise to sin in all men. When it said that sin came into the world through Adam, it is merely meant that he was the first person in whom the sinful propensity of the σάρξ manifested itself. This doctrine of the inherent sinful proclivity of the σάρξ it is maintained, is the doctrine taught in the New Testament, and especially in the Epistles of Paul. In this opinion Baur, Pfleiderer, and Holsten concur. In proof, Baur points to the peculiar phrase employed by Paul to describe our Lord's humanity in Rom. viii. 3: "God sending His Son *in the likeness of sinful flesh*" (ἐν ὁμοιώματι σαρκὸς ἁμαρτίας), which he says is an attempt to cover an antinomy between the sinlessness of Christ's character and the sinfulness inseparable from corporeal life. Even Christ's flesh was sinful, but reverence would not permit Paul to say so; therefore, instead of saying in the flesh of sin, he adopts the milder phrase: "in the likeness of the flesh of sin;" so saving Christ's personal holiness by the adoption of a virtually doketic view of His humanity (*Vorlesungen über neutestamentliche Theologie*, p. 189). Pfleiderer seeks to prove the same position by laying stress on the epithet σάρκινος in Rom. vii. 14. Assuming that adjectives in ινος always denote the material out of which anything is made, he interprets the passage thus: I am made of flesh, I have a material body, therefore I am sold under sin. That is, man is σαρκικός, opposed to good in his life tendency, because he is σάρκινος; that is, "because he has flesh-matter for His substance, in the fact of his being physically flesh lies the inevitable ground of his moral fleshliness" (*Paulinismus*, p. 56). Pfleiderer agrees with Baur in the interpretation of the phrase already quoted from Rom. viii., finding in it traces of one of the antinomies with which Paulinism abounds. And along with this, it is interesting to note, goes a construction put by him and others of the same school on the death of Christ, similar to that given by the Adoptianists and Irving. Christ's death was the crucifixion of His own sinful flesh, and by way of type and first-fruits, of the sinful flesh of His people. The condemnation of sin in the flesh, spoken of in Rom. viii. 3, signifies the judicial execution of sin as centred in Christ's own flesh. Holsten expresses similar views in his work, *Zum Evangelium des Petrus und des Paulus*.

Now there are several facts which raise a strong presumption against the truth of this Manichaean interpretation of Paul's teaching on the subject of the flesh. In the first place, it is decidedly *un-Hebrew*. Secondly, according to this theory the flesh must be regarded as unsanctifiable, whereas in Paul's Epistles it is not so regarded. Sometimes, indeed, it might seem as if the apostle did regard the flesh as hopelessly evil, as when he speaks of killing the deeds of the body, and in the phrase: "this body of death." But in other places the body is represented as the subject of sanctification not less than the soul or spirit, as in 1 Cor. vi., where the body is called the temple of the Holy Ghost, and it is set forth as a duty arising directly out of the consciousness of redemption to glorify God in the body; and in 2 Cor. vii. 1, in which it is set forth as a Christian duty to cleanse ourselves from all filthiness of the *flesh* and *spirit*—the same need and the same possibility of sanctification being implied in both cases. In proof that this text bears against the theory of the essential sinfulness of the flesh being Pauline, it may be mentioned that Holsten disputes its genuineness, the whole passage from vi. 14 to vii. 1 being, he thinks, foreign to the Pauline mode of thought (*Zum Evangel.* p. 387). Yet, again, against this Manichaean interpretation is the consideration that such a doctrine, teaching a dualistic opposition between flesh and spirit, and implying that the flesh, as distinct from the spirit, is essentially evil, ought to be accompanied by a *pagan Eschatology*, that is, by the doctrine that the life after death will be a purely spiritual disembodied one. Such, however, was not the view of Paul; the object of his hope being not the immortality of the naked soul, but the immortality of man, body and soul, implying a resurrection of the dead,—a noteworthy fact, whatever difficulties may beset the distinction taken by Paul between the *natural* body and the *spiritual* body.

The exegetical argument in support of the interpretation in question is by no means unassailable. Granting that σάρκινος in Rom. vii. 14 means fleshy, " of flesh," not carnal in the ethical sense, the text does not necessarily mean every man who possesses a material organism is inevitably a slave to sin. We can assign a definite meaning to σάρκινος without going that length, and that whether we take the sentence as containing a personal statement about Paul himself, or as a statement about humanity at large, personal in form, universal in scope. Take it as a personal statement, we can easily see why Paul should here prefer σάρκινος to σαρκικός. The latter epithet conveys the idea of a man whose whole character and conduct are under the dominion of the fleshly mind. But he could not consistently characterize himself thus, and at the same time represent himself as he does immediately after as with his mind serving the law of God. He must divide himself into two parts, νοῦς and σάρξ, and indicate distinctly the side of his double self on which he is open to the influence of evil. This he does by the use of σάρκινος. It is as if he had said: I am νοῦς νοητικός, and so far I am on the side of good; but I am also σάρξ, σάρκινος, and on that side of my nature I am on the side of evil. The statement certainly implies that for some reason or other the σάρξ has an evil bias, but it conveys no hint as to the cause of this bias. It is a fact of consciousness, not a philosophico-anthropological doctrine that is enunciated. Take the statement, again, as a universal one, the I who speaks being not the individual ego of Paul, but the ego of the race: in this case also we can see the appropriateness of the term σάρκινος as serving to give universality to the proposition. It may be or it may not be true of every man that he is σαρκικός, carnally-*minded*— that is a proposition to be proved, not assumed; but it is certainly true of every man that he is σάρκινος. And this being certain, it is further certain that every man is more or less in bondage to sin. That seems to be what Paul means to convey in this verse. It is in effect a syllogism. Wherever there is flesh there is sin; I am partaker of flesh, therefore I am under law to sin. But does this syllogism imply a metaphysical doctrine, to the effect that flesh, organized matter, from its own inherent nature involves for all associated with it enslavement to sin? No; it implies that sinful bias is universal in the human race, but not that it is absolutely necessary. The categories of universality and necessity are not co-extensive. After it has been ascertained that as a matter of fact sinful bias inheres in human nature viewed as ensouled flesh, all the world over, it remains to be determined whence comes this universal bias. It may arise from the nature of matter, or it may be an accident, a vice of nature, introduced at a given time, and transmitted by inheritance. Both of these explanations have been given, and we are not entitled to assume that either of them is, as a matter of course, the correct one.

Passing now to the other text, Rom. viii. 3. With reference to the phrase: ἐν ὁμοιώμ. σ. ἁ., there are two questions —(1) Is the emphasis to be laid on the likeness or on the implied unlikeness? (2) Do the words σάρξ ἁμαρτίας constitute a single idea, implying that sin is an essential attribute of the flesh, or are they separable, so that ἁμαρτίας points at an accidental, though it may be universal, property of the σάρξ? As to the former, the implied unlikeness is regarded as the thing to be emphasized by Baur, Zeller, and Hilgenfeld, and the interpretation they put on the clause is, that Paul regarded sin as an essential property of flesh (thus making σάρξ ἁμαρτίας a single idea); but he hesitated to ascribe to Christ sinful flesh, and therefore said not that Christ was made sinful flesh, but that He was made in the likeness of sinful flesh, implying likeness in all respects, sin excepted. Others, among whom may be specially mentioned Lüdemann (Die Anthropologie des Ap. Paulus), agreeing with the fore-mentioned writers in taking σάρξ ἁμαρτίας as one idea, differ from them in regard to ὁμοιώμ., emphasizing not the unlikeness, but the likeness, and holding that it is Paul's purpose boldly to teach that God furnished His Son with a flesh made exactly like ours, in this special respect that it, too, was a flesh of sin. Not that Lüdemann means to say that Paul did not believe in the sinlessness of Christ. He contends that this does not follow, and that there is no antinomy involved, such as Pfleiderer asserts. For though ἁμαρτία was immanent in the flesh of Christ, as in that of other men, it was only objective sin, not subjective—it never came to παράβασις; it was prevented from doing so by the ἅγιον πνεῦμα, who guided all Christ's conduct, and kept the flesh in perfect subjection. A third class of interpreters, such as Weiss and Hofmann, follow the old orthodox view, which treats σάρξ and ἁμαρτία as expressive of separable ideas, and take ὁμοίωμα as implying a limitation of likeness in respect of the sinfulness of ordinary human nature. Now, none of these three interpretations is exegetically self-evident. They are all exegetically admissible, and our decision must turn upon other considerations. I may observe that, assuming Baur's view of ἐν ὁμοιώμ. to be correct, it is an argument in favour of the separability of σάρξ and ἁμαρτία. For why should it be assumed that the motive of the limitation is mere shrinking in reverence from applying a principle to Christ which is firmly held by the writer as a necessary truth? If Paul believed that where σάρξ is there must be sin, ἁμαρτία at least, if not παράβασις, would he, whose general habit of thinking was so bold, have hesitated to ascribe it to Christ also; would he not rather have done what Lüdemann says he has done, viz. ascribed to Christ's flesh ἁμαρτία, and then sought to guard His personal sinlessness by emphasizing the indwelling of the Divine Spirit as the means of preventing ἁμαρτία, sin objective, from breaking out into παράβασις, sin subjective? Surely he was more likely to do this than to adopt the weak expedient of covering over a difficulty with a word.

But this view of Lüdemann's has its own peculiar weaknesses, which appear most clearly in connection with the doctrine of the Atonement, which naturally goes along with it—that already referred to in connection with the name of Pfleiderer, the theory of *Redemption by sample*.

It is a theory very open to criticism. First, if the ἁμαρτία in Christ's flesh was a thing which could be completely kept under by the holy will of Christ, was it not morally insignificant, therefore not calling for judicial condemnation? Is there not something theatrical in this pouring out of divine wrath on the flesh of Christ for the objective ἁμαρτία latent therein? Then, how is this judicial condemnation of ἁμαρτία in Christ's flesh to be made available for us, in the way of keeping the vicious bias of our flesh from breaking out into παράβασις? The communication of that Holy Spirit which helped Christ to be sinless would give us real assistance, but is it not apparent how that judicial execution of the Redeemer's sinful σάρξ will. We may say to ourselves: in that death my flesh was crucified, but this mystic faith will not help us here. The faith-mysticism acts on the imagination and the heart powerfully, but hardly on the σάρξ. It remains as obstinately opposed as ever to all good, for anything that the condemnation on Calvary effected. Instead of faith-mysticism we must have recourse to *sacramental magic*, and say that in the Lord's Supper the Lord's resurrection-body, purged from ἁμαρτία by the fire of the Cross, passes into our bodies, and becomes there a transforming influence. That seems the only way open, and it was the way which Irving's adventurous spirit took in carrying out his pet theory. On the biblical meaning of the term σάρξ, the reader may consult Laidlaw on the *Bible Doctrine of Man*, Cunningham Lectures, 7th series.

Note C.—Page 282.

Faustus Socinus expresses his views on this point in his famous *Disputatio De Jesu Christo Servatore*, pars ii. caput xxiii. The heading of the chapter is as follows: Ostenditur, Christum revera sacerdotem non fuisse ante suum in coelum ingressum, hacque in re legali pontifici esse dissimilem, etc. In proof of this position, he remarks: Quod ante mortem sacerdos seu pontifex noster non esset probatur per verba illa ad finem 2 cap. illius Epist. (ad Hebraeos), *unde debuit per omnia fratribus similari; ut misericors fieret (sive esset) et fidelis Pontifex*, etc. Ex quibus satis constare potest,

Christum, antequam omnes infirmitates nostras, inter quas mors praecipua est, expertus esset, pontificem revera factum non fuisse. Neque enim credendum est, eum pontificem revera fuisse constitutum prius, quam vere fidelis et misericors esse posset. Idem manifestum facere videntur ea verba, cap. v. 5: *Sic et Christus non semetipsum clarificavit ut Pontifex fieret, sed qui locutus est ad eum, Filius meus es tu; ego hodie genui te.* Hinc enim apparet non prius creatum vere pontificem a Deo Christum fuisse, quam ei diceretur: *Filius meus es tu*, etc. Sed id ante resurrectionem ei dictum non fuit, teste Paulo, Act. xiii. 33. Ergo ante resurrectionem, et sic antequam pateretur, Christus sacerdos inauguratus vere non fuit.

Quod autem etiam post mortem, antequam coelos conscenderet, pontifex consecratus non fuerit, probant verba illa ad finem 7 cap., *Talis enim decebat*, etc. Ubi liquido perspicitur, consentaneum fuisse, ut is, qui pontifex noster futurus esset, sublimior coelis fieret. Quoad igitur sublimior coelis non est factus, nostrum pontificem eum esse non decuit; nec porro fuit. Probat idem id, quod cap. viii. 4, scriptum est: *Si enim esset super terram, nec esset sacerdos.* Ex quo intelligitur, ad sacerdotium Christi perficiendum mansionem in coelis requiri, et extra coelum eum sacerdotem esse non posse. Multa alia ex eadem epistola afferri possent, quae idem comprobarent. Sed haec satis fuerint.

Ex hac autem Christi, et antiqui sacerdotis dissimilitudine, id verum esse, vehementer confirmatur, quod etiam citra eam a me ex ipsorum collatione jam demonstratum fuit; non expiasse videlicet Christum peccata nostra, antequam in coelum ingrederetur. Nam si legalis pontifex qui vere, et perfecte sacerdos jam erat, non ante expiasse peccata populi dici poterat, quam in Sanctuarium ingressus esset, quanto magis id de Christo ante suum in coelum ingressum (coelum enim hac in re Sanctuario illi respondere, antea demonstratum fuit) dicendum est, cum ante ingressum istum sacerdos nondum esset consecratus? Coepit quidem quodammodo hic in terris Christi sacerdotium, sicut et oblatio coepit. Sed utrumque in coelis absolutum fuit, que pro nobis praecursor ingressus Jesus secundum ordinem Melchisedec in aeternum pontifex est factus, Heb. vi. 20.

LECTURE VII.

NOTE A.—PAGE 316.

HAVING referred in the text to the views of the Atonement set forth in two texts from one of Paul's Epistles, I may here add some further observations on the Pauline doctrine on that great theme. That Paul held the doctrine of an imputed or objective righteousness ascribed to him, there can be no reasonable doubt. Pfleiderer, in his able delineation of Paulinism, finds in Paul's Epistles the two correlative ideas of an objective sin and an objective righteousness treated as transferable quantities, in this confirming the Reformed interpretation of Paulinism by his exegesis, while dissipating all the great theological ideas of Paulinism by his philosophy. As to the text, 2 Cor. v. 21, the word ἁμαρτίαν applied to Christ does not mean sin-offering. Paul is not thinking in this place of the sacrificial system, but of the general principle of God's dealings with Christ, and those who join themselves to Him. On the one hand, Christ is treated as a sinner, though personally sinless, as far as that is possible for one who is personally holy. The main fact covered by the term is Christ's experience of death, the common lot of sinful mortals. That alone, without any additional particulars, in Paul's view sufficed to constitute Christ's sin, to bring Him under the category of sin. He reasoned thus: death is the wages of sin; Christ died, therefore Christ was for the Providence of God as a sinner. But as He was sinless, He must have been treated as a sinner for our sakes, who are real sinners. The truth therefore is, that He was made sin that we might become righteous, and so escape the penalty of sin. The idea of substitution is thus involved. But it is important to remark, that even in this text the principle of representation or solidarity underlies that of substitution. For Paul, as for the writer of the Epistle to the Hebrews, it is a great principle that Sanctifier and sanctified are all of one. He would apply it to all parts of Christ's work. Whatever belongs to the state of those to be saved, the Saviour must experience; the saved, on the other hand, receiving from Him a blessing answering to that feature in their natural condition which Christ becomes subject to, and thereby removes. Thus: Are the Jews under the law? then Christ must become under the law, and so redeem them which were under it, that they may receive sonship. Or, again: Are men subject to the curse of the law, or all who fail to comply with its behests? then Christ must become subject to that curse, as He did in its most repulsive form. So here, in 2 Cor. v. 21: Because we are sinners, Christ must become sin; and the result is, we become partakers of righteousness. The Epistle to the Hebrews extends the application of the principle to Christ's participation in human nature, to the fear of death, to death itself, and to the experience of temptation. The principle essentially signifies moral identity between Saviour and saved,—community of interest, of experience, and of privilege. It brings the two parties closer together than the vicarious principle implied in the sacrificial view presented in Rom. iii. 25, where Christ is called a ἱλαστήριον, that is, a propitiatory sacrifice. There Christ appears merely as a substitute, here He is more—a representative, a central person in whom the race of Adam is gathered up into a moral unity, having one responsibility and one interest, all things, even moral characteristics, being as far as possible common; even sin and righteousness, which one would think inseparable from persons being treated as separable entities, passing freely from the one side to the other—sin to the Sinless One, righteousness to the unrighteous. This doctrine of the moral solidarity of Christ and believers is a very vital element in Paul's system. Paul's aim was ever to represent the relation between Christ and believers as of the closest possible character. Hence the idea of mere substitution could not content him; he must add to that the idea of an *objective identity*, valid for God, acknowledged in the divine government. And even that could not quite satisfy the craving of his heart. Therefore he added still another idea, that, viz., of "mystic union," or what we may call *subjective identity*, according to which Christ is one, not only by divine appointment and by outward lot, but in conscious sympathy with men; and, on the other hand, men are one with Him in the same manner, making His experience in death and resurrection their own. The former aspect of this subjective identity, that of Christ with sinners, is indeed not at all so prominent in Paul's Epistles as in the Epistle to the Hebrews, in which the sympathy of Christ is one of the great outstanding ideas. Hints, however, are not wanting, as in Rom. xv. 3, 4: "Even the Christ pleased not Himself, but, as it is written, The reproaches of them that reproached thee fell upon me;" and in Gal. vi. 2: "Bear ye one another's burdens, and so fulfil the law of Christ." The other aspect of the subjective identity between the Saviour and the saved, the sympathy of believers with Christ, occupies a position of much greater prominence. It is a favourite thought with Paul, that in believing in Jesus men die along with Him, nay, not only die, but rise and ascend to heaven. We find it in the earliest of the four great Epistles, Gal. ii. 20: Χριστῷ συνεσταύρωμαι, and it recurs in 2 Cor. v. 14; the one text containing the idea of co-dying, the other not only that, but also the correlate idea of a co-resurrection. It thus appears that, to express all that Christ crucified was to Paul's faith, we would require to use three words. In that faith Christ the *Vicar*, Christ the *Representative* (before God), and Christ the *Brother* were blended together in indissoluble unity. In this blending lies the peculiarity of Paul's doctrine, the *Glaubensmystik* (faith-mysticism), which it is one of the chief merits of Pfleiderer's work to have duly signalized. On the bearings of the doctrine of Christ's intimate relation to men, on the theory of the Atonement, the reader may consult Dale's *Lectures on the Atonement*, delivered in 1875. The amount of light thrown on the subject is not considerable, but the discussion is genial.

NOTE B.—PAGE 320.

THE passage referred to is in his *Commentarium in Joannem*, lib. ii. 107 (Ruperti Titiensis, *Opera*, vol. iii. p. 244, Migne's edition). Speaking of the meaning of John's baptism in general, and of Christ's baptism by him in particular, Rupert says: Igitur ad agendum pro cuncto mundo poenitentiam qua peccata cunctorum expiaret, Dominum nostrum venisse dubium non est . . . Igitur causa, cur Joannes venit in aqua baptizare et praedicare baptismum poenitentiae, non est alia quam haec, ut ille Sanctus sanctorum, qui solus erat idoneus ferre poenitentiam, pro peccatis omnium electorum, adventum ejus ab origine mundi expectantium, hac voce publica vocatus, accederet palam ad coeleste sanctuarium, in conspectu Dei Patris et sanctorum angelorum, ubi eodem spiritu in columbae specie super se descendente designaretur Pontifex, quo dudum in Mariam superveniente, idem sanctus et immaculatus homo conceptus est, non aliam habiturus quam offerret hostiam nisi carnem propriam, quam statim quadraginta dierum et quadraginta noctium jejunio, deinde omnibus poenitentiae modis afflictam, tandem pro peccatis nostris oblaturur erat Deo Patri, "hostiam in odorem suavitatis" acceptam. Rupert, in another place, gives as one reason of Christ's baptism: Ut pro omnibus poenitentiam ipse agendam susciperet, quod et fecit continuo ut baptizatus est, jejunavit enim quadraginta diebus et quadraginta noctibus, et deinde incessanter afflictus est tentationibus, persecutionibus, contumeliis, opprobriis, flagellis, et tormento ultimae mortis (*In quatuor Evang.* cap. xiii. 4, vol. i. p. 1546, Migne). Rupert, however, repudiated the idea of the Adoptianists, that Christ, in being baptized, underwent regeneration (*De Divinis Officiis*, lib. iii. c. xxiv., nec quaerens remedium renascendi sic voluit baptizari). He does, indeed, speak of Jesus as, like Joshua, clothed with filthy garments, and as being washed from pollution in the baptism of His passion; but the filthy garments are merely mortalitatem nostram et passibilitatem propter quam sordidus, et contemptibilis apparebat hominibus (*In Joannem*, lib. xiii. vol. iii. p. 795, Migne).

Note C.—Page 340.

The doctrine that Christ suffered spiritual and eternal death in essence, if not in accidents, was held both by the Lutheran and by the Reformed dogmatists. It was a doctrine little known before the Reformation. Anselm, for example, laid no stress upon the mental sufferings of Christ, but simply on the fact that He died, gave His infinitely precious life freely for man's redemption. There is not much in patristic literature bearing on the subject, and what there is, is different in tone from the statements to be found in Protestant dogmatic literature. Cyril has one important passage on Christ's exclamation on the cross, " My God, my God, why hast Thou forsaken me ! " which may be taken as a sample of the way in which the subject struck the patristic mind. The passage occurs in *Quod unus sit Christus*, p. 1325. Cyril teaches that Christ, in uttering these words, spoke in the name of humanity. He was entitled to exclaim, " Why hast Thou forsaken me ! " because He was *holy;* and in uttering the cry of desertion He was, as it were, entreating God to regard men as holy in Him, and to remove from *them* His anger. Ἐκάλει γὰρ οὐκ ἐφ' ἑαυτὸν μᾶλλον, ἀλλ' ἐφ' ἡμᾶς αὐτούς, τὴν παρὰ πατρὸς εὐμένειαν. John of Damascus makes Christ partake of the curse σχετικῶς, as being ranked with us; not really in the sense in which He took human nature, but only *quasi.* He distinguishes between two kinds of appropriation (οἰκειώσεις), one physical and substantial (φυσικὴ καὶ οὐσιώδης), and one personal and relative (προσωπικὴ καὶ σχετική). The curse was appropriated in the latter way: τήν τε κατάραν καὶ τὴν ἐγκατάλειψιν ἡμῶν, καὶ τὰ τοιαῦτα οὐκ ὄντα φυσικά, οὐκ αὐτὸς ταῦτα ὢν ἢ γενόμενος ᾠκειώσατο, ἀλλὰ τὸ ἡμέτερον ἀναδεχόμενος πρόσωπον, καὶ μεθ' ἡμῶν ταςςόμενος. Τοιοῦτον δέ ἐστι, καὶ τὸ γενόμενος ὑπὲρ ἡμῶν κατάρα (*De Fide Orthodoxa*, lib. iii. cap. 25). The doctrine in question may thus be regarded as a Protestant elaboration—the theory of substitution carried out to its last consequence, and one is almost inclined to add, *ad absurdum.* Statements of this doctrine equally strong may be found both in Lutheran and in Reformed theologians. The following are samples:—

HEIDEGGER, a Reformed divine (in loc. 18, *De statu Christi*), teaches that Christ suffered " cruciatus graviores, imo *infernales*, utpote peccato debitos, et sine quibus exantlatis liberatio nostra a potestate Diaboli et inferni non constetisset " (cap. 34). The principle is stated in cap. 35, that the Sponsor puts Himself in place of the guilty, and must be taken as guilty, which He cannot be, "si non obnoxius sit eidem cum reo damnationi."

II. ALTING (*Problemata Theolog.* pars i. p. 179) says: Dolores infernales, quales, impii omnes in aeternum patientur animâ est perpessus (Christus). He is discussing the meaning of the words of the Creed, " He descended into hell," and he interprets them, as Calvin, Beza, etc., as referring to the endurance of hell pains on the cross, saying that it is not credible that the authors of the Creed would have omitted the *mental* sufferings of Christ ! This is an assertion similar to that of Calvin, that Elisha would doubtless instruct Naaman the Syrian in the truth of the gospel, it being assumed that no man could be among the saved (as Naaman was believed to be), unless he possessed a certain amount of doctrinal knowledge of the way of salvation. (On this point, consult Dr. Rainy, *Cunningham Lectures*, Lect. II.) In another place, Alting states the same view in connection with the doctrine that Christ offered a perfect satisfaction for sins. He specifies three things as entering into a perfect satisfaction: 1. The dignity of the Person; 2. The gravity of the passion, in connection with which it is taught that Christ suffered *mors aeterna* and *ex judicio*, is taken as equivalent to *aeterna damnatione*, and the curse as including both temporal and eternal death; 3. The approbation of God. (*Loci communes*, vol. i. 164-167).

WENDELINE expresses himself in a qualified manner. To the question, An Deus revera Christum deseruerit ? he replies: Distinguenda desertio perpetua et totalis, qualis est reproborum,—et temporalis, eaque non totalis sed partialis tantum, et secundum quid. Fuit haec desertio non paterni animi a dilecto filio, vel ad momentum alienatio, sed gratiosae praesentiae occultatio et auxilii et liberationis ex angustiis, quibus abjecti et derelicti a Deo solent urgeri, dilatio (quoted by Schweitzer, *Die Glaubenslehre der evan-*

Appendix.—Lecture VII.—Note C.

gelisch-reformirten Kirche, vol. ii. p. 330). To the same effect in *Christiana Theologia*, Wendeline says: Spiritualis passionis inchoatio fuit amissio gaudii, quod fruitio et gratiae plenitudo ei solebat adferre: accessit animae tristitia, pavor et horror in ἀγωνίᾳ, Matt. xxvi. 37–39. Consummatio fuit in illa patris derelictione, qua omnem consolationis sensum amisit ad tempus, Matt. xxvii. 46. De hac passione nostri accipiunt *descensum ad inferos* (lib. i. cap. xviii. p. 300). He held, nevertheless, that Christ suffered eternal death as to intensity, though not as to duration: Etiamsi non sensit mortem aeternam quoad durationem, tamen quoad intensionem (quoted by Heppe, *Die Dogmatik der evangelisch-reformirten Kirche*, p. 340). To the same effect Heppe quotes Burmann. Turretine expresses himself in much the same way as Wendeline.

The Lutheran theologians went even beyond the Reformed in the strong way in which they asserted the doctrine.

HOLLAZ calls Christ, in the agony and passion, a speculum irae, gratiae, virtutis, and decides that He sustained infernal pains *qua substantiam non qua accidentia*, and of intensity equal to the pains of hell, not in the place of the damned, but on Mount Olivet. Christus (he says in one place) sustinuit poenam equipollentem aeternae poenae, subivit quippe poenas infernales *intensive* quoad earum vim, pondus ac substantiam, licet non extensive, quoad durationem ac subjectorum patientium accidentia. Sustinuit cruciatuum extremitatem non aeternitatem (*Examen theologicum*, p. 742, conf. p. 769).

QUENSTEDT goes so far as to speak of Christ being the object of God's extreme hatred: Non quidem Deus Pater filio suo ratione personae suae irascebatur; sed quia peccata totius mundi in se susceperat, non potuit non vi justitiae suae vindicatricis eum *extreme odisse*, tanquam peccatorem omnium quos sol unquam vidit, maximum (*Excursus de derelictione Christi theol. did. pol.* t. iii. p. 358; conf. Steinmeyer, *Die Leidensgeschichte des Herrn*, p. 205). In another place he represents Christ as suffering exactly what sinners had to suffer: Neque enim acceptavit Deus aliquid in hac satisfactione ex liberalitate, quod in se tale non esset, nec de jure suo in exactione poenae nobis debitae et a sponsore praestitae aliquid remisit, sed quod justitiae ejus rigor postulabat, id etiam omne Christus in satisfactione sustinuit; adeo ut ipsas etiam infernales poenas senserit, licet non in inferno et in aeternum (iii. p. 246, quoted by Schmid, *Die Dogmatik der evangelisch-lutherischen Kirche*, p. 302).

HUTTERUS speaks not less explicitly: Neque enim ideo meritum Christi non est infiniti pretii quia Christus non aeternam mortem subiit: quemadmodum enim inobedientiae nostrae peccata sunt actu finita, reatu vero infinita: siquidem impingunt in infinitam Dei justitiam: sic obedientia et mors Christi fuit quidem actu finita quatenus certi temporis periodo, diebus nimirum exinanitionis fuit circumscripta; meriti vero ratione est infinita, siquidem ab infinita persona profisciscitur, ipso nimirum unigenito filio Dei. Deinde neque illud simpliciter verum est, quod execratio legis tantum definienda sit per mortem aeternam. Hoc enim verum si esset, perquam incommode apostolus execrationem illam legis definivisset per illud Mosaicum (Deut. xxi. 23): "Execrabilis omnis, qui pendet in ligno." Tum mors aeterna non modo definitur perpetua continuatione sive perpessione cruciatuum infernalium: sed et sensu dolorum infernalium, cum abjectione sive desertione a Deo conjuncto; ita ut qui vel ad momentum saltem hujusmodi dolores sustinet, is aeternam mortem sensisse dici queat. Quemadmodum sane Christus non ad momentum vel exiguum aliquod temporis spatium, sed per omne tempus exinanitionis, sensum dolorum istorum infernalium vere subiit, ita ut tandem exclamare necessum haberet; Deus meus, Deus meus, quare me dereliquisti? Quod vero posteriore modo aeternam mortem non subiit, in causâ fuit, quod ipse innocens moriendo legi satisfecerat (*Loci communes*, p. 427, quoted by Schmid, p. 303).

The subject to which the foregoing extracts relate formed the subject of a bitter controversy in England, in which Bishop Bilson took a prominent part, and to which he gave rise by certain sermons which he preached at St. Paul's Cross, on the redemption of sinners by Christ's blood (*The effect of certain Sermons preached at St. Paul's Cross, concerning the full Redemption of Mankind by the Death and*

Blood of Christ Jesus). The Bishop, in these sermons, promulgated the idea that Christ did not endure spiritual and eternal death, and insisted on the fact that such a view was unknown to Scripture or the Fathers. Christ, he held, suffered all that a holy Being could suffer, but no more; and among the things which He could not suffer, were the death of the soul, in the sense of a real separation from God, and eternal death. These views met with animated contradiction, which led Bilson to publish another work, entitled *The Survey of Christ's Sufferings for Man's Redemption;* the latter work was published in 1603, the former work being published in 1599. The controversy which then raged made a great noise and gave rise to a considerable literature, which is now almost entirely unknown, and probably not worth reading, though Bilson's books have an interest of their own. The echo of the controversy seems to have reached Germany, for Cotta in his Second Dissertatio, *de Statibus et Officio Christi*, quoted at p. 351, refers to Bilson's book, *De descensu Christi ad inferos*, published at London 1604.

Note D.—Page 345.

Philippi quotes from Dannhauer, *Catechismusmilch*, the following passage in which the exacting nature of Christ's *love* is recognised: " Ein einiges Tröpflein seines vergossenen Blutes wäre genugsam den unendlichen Zorn des himmlischen Vaters zu stillen, wo er nicht aus überfliessender Liebe alle sein Blut zumal vergeissen wollte " (*Kirchliche Glaubenslehre*, Band iv. 2 Hälfte, p. 96, note) [" a single drop of His shed blood were enough to still the infinite anger of the heavenly Father, if it were not His will in infinite love to shed all His blood at once"]. He also quotes from Bernard's *Sermons on the Canticles*, a passage in which is set forth, as a reason for the greatness of Christ's sufferings, His desire to ensure gratitude by a signal display of love. The words are: " Suffecisset ad redemptionem orbis una pretiosissimi sanguinis gutta, sed data est copia, ut in beneficii recordationem virtus nos diligentis claresceret." This passage I have not been able to find; but the following, containing the same thought, is from *Sermo* xi. 7. The subject of the extract is " The Exinanition of the Son of God in the Work of Redemption." Bernard says: "Non simplex aut modica illa exinanitio fuit: sed semetipsum exinanivit usque ad carnem, ad mortem, ad crucem. Quis digne pensit, quantae fuerit humilitatis, mansuetudinis dignationis, dominum majestatis carne indui, mulctari morte, turpari cruce ? Sed dicit aliquis: non valuit opus suum reparare Creator absque ista difficultate ? Valuit, sed maluit cum injuria sui, ne pessimum atque odiosissimum vitium ingratitudinis occasionem ultra reperiret in homine. Sane multum fatigationis assumpsit, quo multae dilectionis hominem debitorem teneret: commoneretque gratiarum actionis difficultas redemptionis, quem minus esse devotum fecerat conditionis facilitas. Quid enim dicebat homo creatus et ingratus ? Gratis quidem conditus sum, sed nullo auctoris gravamine vel labore. Siquidem dixit, et factus sum, quemadmodum et universa. Quid magnum est, quamlibet magna in verbi facilitate donaveris ? Sic beneficium creationis attenuans humana impietas ingratitudinis materiam inde sumebat, unde amoris causam habere debuerat, idque ad excusationes in peccatis. Sed obstructum est os loquentium iniqua. Luce clarius patet quantum modo pro te, O homo, dispendium fecit: de Domino servus, de divite pauper, Caro de Verbo, et de Dei Filio hominis filius fieri non despexit. Memento jam te, etsi de nihilo factum, non tamen de nihilo redemptum. Sex diebus condidit omnia, et te inter omnia. At vero per totos triginta annos operatus est salutem tuam in medio terrae. O quantum laboravit sustinens! Carnis necessitates, hostis tentationes, nonne sibi crucis aggravavit ignominia, mortis cumulavit horrore ? Necessarie quidem. Sic, sic homines et jumenta salvasti, Domine, quemadmodum multiplicasti misericordiam tuam Deus."

NOTE E.—PAGE 346.

In his miscellaneous remarks (chap. v., on "Satisfaction for Sin." *Works*, ii. p. 574), Edwards thus deals with the question, in what sense Christ suffered the wrath of God: "Christ suffered the wrath of God for men's sins in such a way as He was capable of, being an infinitely holy person, who knew that God was not angry with Him personally, knew that God did not hate Him, but infinitely loved Him. The wicked in hell will suffer the wrath of God, as they will have the sense, and knowledge, and sight of God's infinite displeasure towards them, and hatred of them. But this was impossible in Jesus Christ. Christ, therefore, could bear the wrath of God in no other but these two ways.

"1. In having a great and clear sight of the infinite wrath of God against the sins of men, and the punishment they had deserved. This it was most fit that He should have at the time when He was suffering in their stead, and paying their ransom to deliver them from that wrath and punishment. That He might know what He did, that He might act with full understanding at the time when He made expiation, and paid a ransom for sinners to redeem them from hell, *first*, it was requisite that at that time He should have a clear sight of two things—viz. of the dreadful evil and odiousness of that sin that He suffered for, that He might know how much it deserved punishment; that it might be real and actual grace in Him, that He undertook and suffered such things for those that were so unworthy and so hateful, which it could not be, if He did not know how unworthy they were. *Secondly*, it was requisite He should have a clear sight of the dreadfulness of the punishment that He suffered to deliver them from, otherwise He would not know how great a benefit He vouchsafed them in redeeming them from this punishment, and so it could not be actual grace in Him to bestow so great a benefit upon them; as, in the time that He bestowed, He would not have known how much He bestowed; He would have acted blindfold in giving so much." After showing that all the circumstances of the passion tended to produce such a clear view of both these things in Christ's mind, Edwards goes on to remark that Christ suffered that which the damned do not suffer, inasmuch as they have no clear idea of the hateful nature of sin, such as a holy being has; and to point out that Christ's *love* to the sinful was a source of mental suffering through sympathy, another ingredient different from the suffering of the lost; and then he arrives at the second way in which Christ could endure the wrath of God—viz. by enduring the *effects* of that wrath. "All that He suffered was by the special ordering of God. There was a very visible hand of God in letting men and devils loose upon Him at such a rate, and in separating Him from His own disciples. Thus it pleased the Father to bruise Him and put Him to grief; God dealt with Him as if He had been exceedingly angry with Him, and as though He had been the object of His dreadful wrath. This made all the sufferings of Christ the more terrible to Him, because they were from the hand of His Father, whom He infinitely loved, and whose infinite love He had had eternal experience of. Besides, it was an effect of God's wrath that He forsook Christ. . . . This was infinitely terrible to Christ. Christ's knowledge of the glory of the Father, and His love to the Father, and the sense and experience He had had of the worth of the Father's love to Him, made the withholding the pleasant ideas and manifestations of His Father's love as terrible to Him as the sense and knowledge of His hatred is to the damned, that have no knowledge of God's excellency, no love to Him, nor any experience of the infinite fulness of His love." Yet another element Edwards reckons to have entered into the cup of wrath put into Christ's hand by His Father: "It was a special fruit of the wrath of God against our sins, that He let loose upon Christ the devil, who has the power of death, is God's executioner, and the roaring lion that devours the damned in hell. Christ was given up to the devil as his captive for a season. . . . He was let loose to torment the soul of Christ with gloomy and dismal ideas. He probably did his utmost to contribute to raise His ideas of the torments of hell." One thing needs to be added to give a complete view of Edwards' opinion—viz. that he thinks it probable that as God ordained external circumstances to produce the vivid ideas of the end of sin and the horrible nature of its punishment spoken of under the first head, so "His own influences were agreeable hereto, His spirit acting with His providence to give Him a full view of these things." In this statement Edwards does not profess to give express Scripture proof. He merely says, "there is all reason to think."

INDEX.

ABBOTT, Dr., on Christ's miracles, 209; on Christ's resurrection, 215.

Admonitio Neostadtiensis, or Christiana: on Lutheran distinction between various sorts of presence, 109; on the figure of the heated mass of iron, 110; when published, 118; title of, 118; written by Ursinus, 118; summary of its Christological statement, 118–121, *gemina mens*, 121; on the *impersonalitas*, 385.

Adoptianism, 67, 68; Adoptianist doctrine concerning Christ's human nature as fallen, 249.

Agnoetes, 69; Baur and Dorner on, 70.

Alcuin on voluntariness of Christ's sufferings, 244.

Alford on Phil. ii. 5–9, 18.

Alting, Henry, on the physical infirmities of Christ, 264; on Christ's endurance of hell pains, 444.

Ambrose, of Milan, on the kenosis, 168.

Anselm: Christ's sufferings not penal, 319; laid no stress on Christ's mental sufferings, 443.

Antioch, theological school of, 49; Theodore of Mopsuestia; Nestorius of Constantinople, Theodoret of Cyrus, members of, 49, views of, on Christology, 49; on the title Θεοτόκος, 49; held Christ's growth in knowledge, ignorance, and experience of temptation to be real, 57; on priesthood of Christ, 281, 283; affirmed moral development of Christ, 281, 285.

Aphthartodoketism, 68; Aphthartodoketic doctrine as to Christ's human nature, 258.

Apollinaris, character of, 40; his theory of Christ's person, 40–45; theory criticised, 45–48; death of, 48; Liebner on Apollinarism, 406.

Aquinas, Thomas, three new ideas in his *Summa* relating to Christology, 75; the Word incarnate *in persona*, not *in natura*, 75; Christ a recipient of *grace*, 78; Christ the Head of the Church, 80; Christ's body perfect from the moment of conception, 81; Christ had not the graces of faith and hope, 82; a *comprehensor* as well as a *viator*, 82; His soul possessed vision of all things in God, 82; on the elements of value in Christ's passion, 346; *satisfactio superabundans*, 346.

Arnold, Matthew, idea of God, 11; ridicule of dogmas, 13; on moral Therapeutics, 214; leading idea of the Bible, a Power making for righteousness, 333; his view compared with Ritschl's, 333.

Athanasius, on Apollinarian theory, 42; on Apollinarian doctrine of redemption, 47.

Axioms, Christological, 22, 23; additional axioms, 36.

BAUER, on Quenstedt's idea of God, 13; on the Epistle to the Philippians, 24; on Apollinarian theory, 44; on Agnoetism, 70; Thomas Aquinas' idea of the Incarnation, 77; on Aquinas' doctrine of Christ's headship, 80; on Christ's claim to be Judge, 202, 203; three types of Christology in the New Testament, 224; on Schleiermacher's theory of redemption, 317; on Luther's Christological views in connection with Supper controversy, 375; the Pauline doctrine of the σάρξ, 432, 436.

Bernard, St.: Christ's sufferings a maximum to increase gratitude, 448.

Beyschlag: the use of the name Christ for the pre-existent Logos, 17; advocate of the Ideal Man theory, 223 ff.; on the titles Son of man and Son of God, 225–234; the pre-existence, 234.

Bilson, Bishop: controversy concerning the nature of Christ's sufferings, 447.

Bodemeyer: Christ under wrath of God during whole state of humiliation, 338.

Brentz, John, 86; his Christology, 86; to be *in loco* not an essential property of body, 88; heaven not a place, 89; Christ's glorified body without form, 90; ubiquity illocal, 92; local and personal ubiquity distinguished, 92; the humanity of Christ on earth possessed divine majesty, 93; incarnation and exaltation identical—a twofold humanity in Christ, 94; appearances of Christ after resurrection economical, 94; dissembled majesty, 95; Brentian and Chemnitzian schools contrasted as to exinanition, 102.

Bushnell, Horace, love a vicarious principle, 305; advocate of sympathy theory of redemption, 307; latest views of, 322; God's present dealings with mankind not judicial, 324.

CALVIN, on sense in which Christ suffered divine wrath, 337.

Campbell, M'Leod, theory of atonement, 319; Professor Park on, 320.

Chalcedon, Council of, 39; decree of, concerning Christ's person, 39; condemned Eutychianism, 62; policy of the Council, 62.

Chemnitz, Martin, 86; author of *De duabus naturis in Christo*, 96; his Christological views expounded, 97; his idea of the περιχώρησις, 98; classification of idiomatic propositions, 98; potential omnipresence, 100; *praesentia intima* and *praesentia extima*, 101; view of exinanition, 102; adopted Ambrosian idea of a *retractio* of the Logos, 103; did he hold the principle, *Logos non extra carnem?* 104; helped to prepare the *Formula Concordiae*, 105; Chemnitzian and Brentian schools contrasted in reference to exinanition, 112.

Christology, Lutheran, 83; characterized, 84; two types of, Brentian and Chemnitzian, 85; criticism of, 107–115; applies its principle arbitrarily, 107; threatens the reality of Christ's humanity, 108; leaves no room for exinanition, 110; exinanition an effect without a cause, 113; robs us of the Incarnation, 114; relation to modern speculative Christology, 115; contrasted with Reformed Christology, 115; relation to kenosis, 169; connection of, with Supper controversy, 375; affinity with modern speculation—Schneckenburger on, 380.

Christology, Reformed, 115; contrasted with Lutheran, 116; a consistent scheme in which all Reformed agreed, 117; criticism of, 120; its idea of the union, 121; communication of *charisms*, 122; the divine nature participant in suffering, 123; wisdom and virtue wrought in Christ's human nature *by the Logos through His own Spirit*, 125, 271; doctrine of exinanition, 126; affected the divine nature as occultation, 126; import of the *gemina mens*—Schneckenburger on, 127; a *double life*, 127; does the *gemina mens* imply a double series of parallel states of consciousness? 128; antidoketic realism of Reformed Christology—Schneckenburger on, 131; relation to kenosis, 170; Schweitzer on, 382; Reformed view of *impersonalitas*, 385.

Cotta (editor of Gerhard's *Loci*), on the doctrine that Christ suffered infernal pains, 351; refers to Bishop Bilson's works, 447.

Crawford, Professor, D.D., on Archbishop M'Gee's views concerning the nature of Christ's sufferings, 319; inductive method of inquiry in *The Atonement*, 328; idea of a covenant, value of, in solving difficulties, 331; his classification of theories, 352.

Cyril, of Alexandria, on Apollinarian doctrine of redemption, 47, 311; on opinion of Nestorius on the title Θεοτόκος, 50; on the kenosis, 51, 169; reign of physical law in Christ's humanity, 54; Christ's intellectual and moral growth only apparent, 55; Cyrillian Christology monophysitic in tendency, 58; affinity of, with Lutheran Christology, 59; his view of the kenosis compared with Bishop Leo's, 66; Christ's death voluntary, 245; on priesthood of Christ, 281, 282; denied moral development of Christ, 286; on the ignorance of Christ (extracts from works), 368–374; opposition to metamorphic views of the Incarnation, 428; on the desertion on the cross, 439.

DALE, on Christ suffering the wrath of God, 347; on Christ's intimate relation to men, 412.

Dannhauer: extent of Christ's sufferings enhanced by His love, 447.

Death, eternal, did Christ suffer it? 342; opinions of Ritschl, Socinus, Van Mas-

tricht, and Gerhard on the point, 342, 343; Hodge (Dr. Charles) on, 343.
Delitzsch, his theory of Christ's person (kenotic, Thomasian type), 381.
Development, moral, implied in temptation, 273; places in which perfecting predicated of Christ in the Epistle to Hebrews, 274; in what senses used, 276; compatible with sinlessness, 285; conceived by analogy, 286; intellectual development of Christ complete before ministry began, 288; moral development went on, 290.
Dods (M., the elder), on voluntariness of Christ's death, 261; sermon by M'Lagan on sympathy of Christ, 270.
Dorner, on rationalism, 6; on Apollinarian theory, 43; on Cyril's Christology, 58; on Leo's letter to Flavian, 66; on the patristic idea of personality, 67; on Agnoetism, 70; on the Christology of John of Damascus, 70; Christological transubstantiation, 71; Thomas Aquinas' idea of the Incarnation, 77; Lutheran Christology, 96; Danaeus on Chemnitz, 99; on Lutheran Christology, 114; gradual Incarnation, 137, 170; on kenotic theories, 167, 172, 176, 178, 179; on the title Son of man, 231.
Double life of the Logos, 20; double aspect of, held by Apollinaris, 46; theory of a double life not held by Aquinas, 77; a double life involved in Reformed theory according to Schneckenburger, 127; theory of, held by Mr. Hutton (R. H.), 129; rejected by Gess, 151; asserted by Martensen, 163; bearing of this idea on Phil. ii. 7, 189; use of this and other hypotheses, 192; held by Schöberlein, 418.
Duns Scotus: held acceptilation theory of atonement, 343.

EBRARD, on Heb. ii. 9 (χωρὶς Θεοῦ preferred to χάριτι Θεοῦ), 33; Reformed doctrine as to relation of incarnation and exinanition, 116; his theory of kenosis, 153-160; criticism of, 182-187; status humilis, in relation to the fall, 261-264; views on μορφὴ Θεοῦ, 361; μορφῇ δούλου, 365; on οὐκ ἁρπαγμὸν ἡλήσατο, 366; extracts from prefaces to his works, 414, 415; solution of speculative problems in Christology, 415; on Christ's temperament, 430.
Edwards, President: a perfect confession of sin an alternative method of satisfying for sin, 319, 320; in what sense Christ suffered the wrath of God, 349; 449.
Epiphanius, account of Apollinaris, 40; on Apollinarian theory, 43.
Ernesti, on Phil. ii. 6-9, 359, 363.
Euripides, *Alcestis* quoted (Apollo banished from heaven), 336.
Eutyches, opinions of, 61; relation of Eutychianism to Cyril's views, 61; description of, in Eranistes, 61; under consideration of three Synods, 62; condemned as a heresy at Council of Chalcedon, 62.
Ewald: belongs to the school of sentimental naturalism, 209; his mode of dealing with the resurrection of Christ, 212, 213.

FELIX, of Urgelles, his views (Adoptianism) opposed by Alcuin, 244; held Christ's human nature to be "fallen," 249-251.
Formula Concordiae, 105; a compromise, 106; failed to produce peace, 107; the Kryptic controversy between Giessen and Tübingen theologians arose out of it, 107.

GAUPP: theory of Christ's person (kenotic, Gessian type), 397.
Gerhard, "De Statu exinanitionis et exaltationis," 3; on Phil. ii. 5-9, 16; on reciprocal *communicatio idiomatum*, 107; *exinanitio* and *incarnatio* distinct, 107; on Christ's omniscience, 111; Christ did not suffer eternal death, 342.
Gess, his theory of kenosis, 145-153; criticism of, 179; on sinlessness of Christ, 149, 273; Godet on, 402.
Giessen-Tübingen controversy, 84, 104; dispute about *praesentia intima* and *praesentia extima*, 101; krypsis and kenosis, the respective war-cries, 107: Giessen and Tübingen theologians neutralized each other, 113; account of controversy, by Cotta, 377-380.
Godet, on John i. 17, 294; Christological views (kenotic, Gessian type), 402.
Goodwin: advocates kenotic theory (Gessian), 413.
Gregory, of Nazianzum, on Apollinarian theory, 46.
Gregory, of Nyssa, *Adv. Apollinarem*, 43-46; on the drift of Apollinaris' treatise on the Incarnation, 44.

HAHN, theory of Christ's person (kenotic, Gessian type), 398.
Haweis: his views of Christ, 195; expounded and criticised, 218-223.

Hebrews, Epistle to the, doctrine of humiliation, 25; view of salvation, 29; disputed reading in chap. ii. 9, 32; places in which Christ is spoken of as perfected, 274; that Christ not ambitious to be a priest, taught, chap. v. 7, 278; doctrine of Christ's priesthood, 283; principle of redemption enunciated, chap. ii. 11, 301; a priest must be able μετριοπαθεῖν, 303.

Heidegger, on the states, 2; distinguished between incarnation and exinanition, 116; on the kenosis as *occultatio*, 128; on Christ's endurance of hell pain, 444.

Heidelberg Catechism: Christ suffered the wrath of God throughout the whole state of humiliation, 37.

Hilary, 2; view of kenosis, 168; denied that Christ was subject to physical infirmity, 240; apology for his views by theologians, 242; voluntariness of Christ's experience of infirmity, how understood by, 246; mislead by opposition to Arianism, 247; view of μορφῇ Θεοῦ, 359.

Hodge, Dr. Archibald, on nature of Christ's sufferings, 343, 347.

Hodge, Dr. Charles, on kenotic theories, 182; on Ebrard's theory, 190; on nature of Christ's sufferings, 343, 348.

Hofmann, on Heb. ii. 11, 27; on διὰ τὸ πάθημα τοῦ θανάτον (Heb. ii. 9), 30; belongs to kenotic school, 165; on title Son of man, 230; on sinlessness of Christ, 273; Christ under divine wrath during whole state of humiliation, 340; his Christological views (kenotic), 407.

Hollaz, on the *impersonalitas*, 385; on Christ's endurance of hell pains, 445.

Holsten, on Pauline doctrine of the σάρξ, 432, 433.

Homoüsia, defined, 3; inferred from Phil. ii. 5-9, 25; taught in Epistle to the Hebrews, 27; Aquinas taught views favourable to, 80; highly valued in Reformed Christology, 129; emphasized by Adoptianists, 250.

Hulsius, on Christ's ignorance, etc., 132; quoted by Schneckenburger, 132; Ritschl's comments on the views of Hulsius, as reported by Schneckenburger, 132.

Hutterus: Christ under the wrath of God during whole state of humiliation, 338; on Christ's endurance of hell pains, 446.

Hutton, R. H., believes in possibility of a double life of Logos, 129, 422; on sinlessness of Christ, 273, 423.

IMPERSONALITY of Christ's humanity, opinions of Reformed theologians on, 384, Schneckenburger's view, 386.

Incarnation, an exchange of divine form for human form of existence (Phil. ii. 5-7), 20; an incarnation independent of fall taught by Ebrard, 184, 262, 416; by Liebner, 405.

Infirmities, sinless, of Christ, a source of temptation, 237; Damascenus on, 238.

Irving, Edward, taught that Christ's human nature was "fallen," 254; Irvingism criticised, 255–258.

JOHN, of Damascus, 70; on the monothelite controversy, 71; Christ's humanity possessed personality, 71; makes Christ's humanity lifeless, 71; and Christ's temptations unreal, 72, 270; doctrine of περιχώρησις, 73; his Christology resembles Cyril's and the Lutheran, 73, 74; Christ not a servant, 74; Logos in the humanity like sunbeams in an oak, 74; senses of the word *nature*, 186; on the physical infirmities of Christ, 238; voluntariness of, 245.

KAHNIS, theory of Christ's person (kenotic, Thomasian type), 394.

Keim, on Christ's sinlessness, 198; belongs to school of sentimental naturalism, 209; Strauss on, 211; his History of Christ characterized, 211; on the miracles of healing, 213; on the resurrection of Jesus, 215, on Christ's person (Matt. xi. 27), 216; on the title Son of man, 230; on Christ's temperament, 430.

Kenosis, 4; kenosis and skenosis, 8; negative aspect of, 16; positive aspect, 20; *vide* Cyril, Lutheran, and Reformed Christologies, and Modern Kenotic Theories, in this table; modern idea of, due to Zinzendorf, 137.

Kenotic theories (modern), 134; connection with union movement in Germany, 134, 135; relation to old Lutheran and Reformed Christologies, 135; humanistic tendency of modern Christology in general, and of kenotic school in particular, 136; common idea of, 137; four leading types, 139; *vide* Thomasius, Gess, Ebrard, Martensen; religious and scientific aims of, 165; criticism of, 165; Dorner on religious tendency of, 167; kenotic and Socinian theories compared, 168; Ritschl on, 168; literature of various types, 386–426.

König, his theory of kenosis, 388; anticipated Thomasius, 388.

Le Blanc, characterized dispute about ubiquity as a logomachy, 109; his *theses theologicae* quoted to this effect, 109; on Zanchius' view of Christ's knowledge, 130.
Leo, Bishop of Rome, 63; pilot of the church in the Nestorian and Eutychian controversies, 63; his letter to Flavian analysed, 63; criticism of, 64-67.
Liebner, his *Christologie* characterized, 7; on the ethical idea of God, 7; on Pantheism and modern Theism, 11; on the impeccability of Christ, 181, 272; views on $\mu o \rho \phi \dot{\eta}\ \Theta \varepsilon o \tilde{v}$, 362; on $\mu o \rho \phi \dot{\eta}\ \delta o \dot{v} \lambda o v$, 364; his Christological views (Gessian type), 403; Incarnation irrespective of sin. 405; on Apollinarism, 407; on Christ's temperament, 430.
Lightfoot, on $o \dot{v} \chi\ \dot{\alpha} \rho \pi \alpha \gamma \mu \dot{o} v\ \dot{\eta} \gamma \dot{\eta} \sigma \alpha \tau o$, 365.
Lüdemann, on the Pauline doctrine of the $\sigma \dot{\alpha} \rho \xi$, 436, 437.
Luther, on the different modes in which a thing can be in place, 92; his Christological views before sacramentarian controversy arose, 375.

MacDonnel: Christ's sufferings improperly called penal, 319.
MacGee, Archbishop: Christ's sufferings not penal, 318.
M'Lagan (Professor), on sympathy of Christ, quoted, 270.
Mansel: idea of God, 12.
Martensen, on Schleiermacher's Christology, 14; theory of a double life of the Logos, 20; a glory in Christ's humiliation, 35; his theory of kenosis, 160-164; holds a double life of the Logos, 163; his theory criticised, 188; on sinlessness of Christ, 274; on Christ's temperament, 430.
Martineau, James, on Christ's suffering of divine wrath, 340, 341.
Maurice, on Mansel's apology for Christianity, 13; his theory of Atonement, 312.
Menken, Gottfried, of Bremen: Christ's human nature "fallen," 251.
Meyer, on Phil. ii. 6-9, 365, 366; on title Son of man, 367.
Monophysitism, 66, 67; internal disputes about Christ's human nature, 257.
Monothelitism, 67, 68.
Müller, on sinless development of Christ, 288.

Neander, on Cyril's view as to Christ's ignorance, 374.
Nestorius, patriarch of Constantinople, belonged to Antioch school, 48; Nestorian controversy, 48; Nestorian theory of Christ's person, 48, 49; does the theory involve a duality of persons? 50; Christ underwent moral development, 281.
Nitzsch, on kenotic theories, 192; his view of redemption, 317; view of $\mu o \rho \phi \dot{\eta}\ \Theta \varepsilon o \tilde{v}$, 362.
Nösgen, on Ebrard's conception of the person of Christ, 182.

Offices of Christ, priestly office when begun, 280; double aspect of, 282; Melchisedec priesthood, 283; apostolic or prophetic office described, 294; humiliations connected with, 301 sqq.; priestly office, 301; Christ's sufferings both a qualification for office and endured in performance of priestly duty, 303; Christ as a priest, representative; as a victim, substitute, 310.
Origen, on Heb. ii. 9 (Christ died for every being, God excepted, $\chi \omega \rho \dot{\imath} \varsigma\ \Theta \varepsilon o \tilde{v}$), 33.

Paulinus, of Aquileia: Christ's soul-trouble voluntary, how? 246.
Pecaut, on the sinlessness of Christ, 197, 198.
Peter the Lombard, his view of the Incarnation, 75.
Pfleiderer, on Pauline doctrine of the $\sigma \dot{\alpha} \rho \xi$, 432 ff.; Pauline doctrine of righteousness, 439; faith mysticism, 441.
Philippi, his satisfaction equation, 350; quotations in, from Dannhauer and Bernard on the *satisfactio superabundans*, 448.
Plato, description of Eros, 263.
Price, Dr., *rationale* of intercessory prayer, 331.
Priesthood of Christ. *See* Offices of Christ.
Prophetic office of Christ. *See* Offices of Christ.

Quenstedt: idea of God, 12; Christ, the object of God's extreme hatred, 445.

Rainy, Principal, on limit of theological knowledge, 193.
Redemption, by *sample*, 47; the patristic view of redemption so named, 47, 253; taught by Menken and Irving, 254; Socinian theory of redemption,

298; sympathy, theory of, 305; theory of redemption by sample or mystic theory, advocated by Schleiermacher, Menken, Irving, Maurice, and Ritschl, 311-313; Hilary and Cyril on same theory, 311; M·Leod Campbell's theory, 319; Bushnell's latest theory, 322; wisdom of God in redemption, 326; governmental theory, 334; acceptilation theory, 343; elements on which value of atonement depends, 344; theories of redemption classified, 352-355.

Reuss: no doctrine of humiliation in the Gospel of John, 35; kenotic in Christology after Gessian type, 401.

Richard of St. Victor, the humiliation of Christ as great as Adam's presumption, 349.

Riehm, on Christ's humanity in relation to the fall, 259; limitation of Christ's experience of temptation, 264; when did Christ's priesthood begin, history of question, 284, 285.

Ritschl, on the views of Hulsius on Justification, 132; the person of Christ an insoluble problem, 133; on kenotic theory, 168; Christianity an ellipse with two foci, 292; his theory of redemption, 313; orthodox theory of redemption makes God a Pharisee, 329; views on imputation, 330; God's dealings with mankind not judicial, 330; idea of retributive justice not in Bible, 332; Christ, according to orthodox theory, must suffer eternal death, 340.

Rothe: theory of Christ's person, 223; on sinlessness of Christ, 272.

Rupert of Duytz: Christ doing penance, 320, 321, 442.

SADEEL, on the illustration of heated iron, 110; author of *De veritate hum. nat. Christi*, 261; Christ's human nature patible, 261.

Schleiermacher, on Phil. ii. 5-9, 15; his Christology, 207; a failure as a compromise, 209; on sinlessness of Christ, 272; his theory of redemption (mystical = redemption by sample), 311, 330; on the title Son of man, 226.

Schmieder, theory of Christ's person (kenotic, Gessian type), 400.

Schneckenburger, 4; his Christological works, 5; on Thomasius, 5; on Lutheran Christology, 114; connection between Luth. Christology and modern speculative Christology, 115; Reformed idea of the union as a morally mediated one, 126; import of the *gemina mens* in the Reformed Christology, 127; antidoketic realism of Reformed Christology, 130; on the views of Hulsius concerning the ignorance of Christ, 132; kenotic theory destructive of the Trinity, 165; re-statement of the Reformed theory, 170; on Thomasian theory, 174; Reinhard's view of kenosis, 177; on Luther's Christological views in their relation to Supper controversy, 376; on relation of Lutheran Christology to modern speculation, 380; on Reformed doctrine of *impersonalitas*, 386.

Schöberlein, his Christological views (kenotic), 418; holds a *double life*, 418.

Schweitzer, on the meaning of the *gemina mens* in Reformed Christology, 129, 382.

Shorter Catechism: the wrath of God a particular item in Christ's humiliation, 37.

Sinlessness of Christ, how secured, 269; *potuit non peccare* and *non potuit peccare*, 269; various theories as to sinlessness, 272; compatible with moral development, 285; integrity and perfection distinct, 286.

Smyth (Newman, American), derives theory of atonement from the idea of love, 328.

Socinus Faustus, on priesthood of Christ, 281, 282, 434, 437, 438; his theory of salvation, 298; according to orthodox theory of atonement, Christ must suffer eternal death, 341; dignity of sufferer not to be taken into account, 344.

Son of man, meaning of the title as used by Christ, 226-231.

Spencer, Herbert, unknowableness of God, 12.

Status humilis, Ebrard on, 262.

Strauss, on the Lutheran doctrine of the states, 2; on the idea of God, 11; on Phil. ii. 5-10, 15; on classification of idiomatic propositions, 99; the Absolute cannot perform special acts, 172.

TEMPERAMENT: had Christ a particular one? 430.

Theodore, of Mopsuestia, on Heb. ii. 9 (the reading χωρις θεου preferred), 33; Christological views of, 48 ff.

Theodoret, of Cyrus, opposed to a physical union of the natures, 48; view of the kenosis in opposition to Cyril, 54.

Tholuck, on Phil. ii. 6-9, 359 ff.

Thomasius, founder of modern kenotic school, 5; Christological presuppositions, 10; on Heppe's view of the Brentian doctrine of ubiquity, 91; account of Lutheran Christology, 96; on Chemnitz' classification of idiomatic propositions, 99; on *genus tapeinoticum*, taught by Tübingen theologians, 108; on their doctrine of omnipresence, 112; his kenotic theory expounded, 139-145; criticised, 178; on sinlessness of Christ, 273; account of Hilary's views on $\mu o \rho \varphi \eta$ $\Theta \varepsilon o \tilde{v}$, 359; his own view, 360; on Luther's Christological views, 375.

Triduum: belongs to the state of exinanition, 351.

Tübingen school, *see* Giessen: declared abstinence from use of omniscience to be impossible, 104; taught a *genus tapeinoticum*, 108; later Tübingen theory of exinanition, 113.

Turretine, on the states, 2; wherein lay the value of Christ's atonement, 344; on Christ's endurance of hell pains, 445.

ULLMANN, distinction between *Unsündlichkeit* and *Sündlosigkeit*, 252; his opinion of the advocates of the doctrine that Christ's human nature was fallen, 256.

VAN MASTRICHT, on Phil. ii. 5-9, 24; idea of the hypostatic union, 122; Christ suffered death in all senses, temporal, spiritual, eternal, 342; on the *impersonalitas*, 383.

WEIZSÄCKER: belongs to school of sentimental naturalism, 209.

Wendeline, quoted by Ebrard, 186; on Christ's experience of divine wrath, 444

Wrath of God, endured by Christ during whole state of humiliation, 37, 337; Heidelberg and Westminster Catechisms on, 37; Hutterus, Bodemeyer, Hofmann, Van Oosterzee, hold views of Heidelberg Catechism on, 339 ff.; Martineau's representation of Christ under divine anger, 340; Calvin on, 337; views of Cyril and Anselm on, 443; views of Reformed and Lutheran theologians on, 444 ff.

ZANCHIUS, *de Incarnatione*, 3; on the word $\dot{\alpha}\lambda\lambda\dot{\alpha}$ (Phil. ii. 7), 18; on the kenosis as occultation of the divine glory, 128; followed Aquinas in reference to Christ's knowledge, 130; on the kenosis, 187; on the *impersonalitas*, 385.

Zinzendorf, father of modern kenosis, 137; his view of the Incarnation, 166; Bengel on, 166; Liebner on his Christology, 407; Plitt's account of his Christology, 424.

Zuingli, effect of original sin, 334.

STANDARD RELIGIOUS WORKS.

IS THERE SALVATION AFTER DEATH?
A Treatise on the Gospel in the Intermediate State.

By E. D. MORRIS, D.D., LL.D., Professor in Lane Theological Seminary, Cincinnati. Crown 8vo, cloth, $1.25. *2d Edition.*

N. Y. Observer says: "The various views are stated with fairness and precision, the specific passages of Scripture, bearing upon the subject, are carefully considered, as well as the general testimony of Scripture in relation to it. We commend the volume to ministers and teachers."

N. Y. Evangelist: "*Clear in method and cogent in argument, it is saturated throughout with the large literature of its subject, is free from all acerbity and unfairness, and is loyal to God's Word as the final test of Christian truth. It will settl doubt and confirm faith.*"

THE HUMILIATION OF CHRIST
In its Physical, Ethical, and Official Aspects.

(Being the Sixth of the Cunningham Lectures.) By Rev. A. B. BRUCE, D.D. Octavo, cloth, gilt top, $2.50. Uniform with the same author's "*Parabolic Teaching of Christ,*" and "*Miraculous Element in the Gospels.*"

"*These lectures are well worthy of the name they bear, and of their precursors in the series; and the book in which they are published, with ample notes and references, will be valuable to theologians, supplying a want in the literature of the subject, and containing many fruitful germs of thought. Dr. Bruce's style is uniformly clear and vigorous, and this book has the rare advantage of being at once stimulating and satisfying to the mind in a high degree. He has given us a book that will really advance the theological understanding of the great truth that forms its subject.*"—BRITISH AND FOREIGN EVANGELICAL REVIEW.

The English Churchman says: "The title of the book gives but a faint conception of the value and wealth of its contents. . . . . Dr. Bruce's work is really one of exceptional value; and no one can read it without perceptible gain in theological knowledge."

BY REV. DR. A. B. BRUCE.

THE TRAINING OF THE TWELVE,
Or, PASSAGES OUT OF THE GOSPELS.

Exhibiting the twelve Disciples of Jesus under Discipline for the Apostleship. Uniform with same Author's "*The Humiliation of Christ,*" &c. Octavo, nearly 600 pages, cloth, gilt top, $2.50.

"A really great book on an important, large, and attractive subject—a book full of loving, wholesome, profound thoughts about the fundamentals of Christian faith and practice."—*British and Foreign Evangelical Review.*

"Full of suggestion and savour. It should be the companion of the minister, for the theme is particularly related to himself, and he would find it a very pleasant and profitable companion."—*Spurgeon's Sword and Trowel.*

"A more wise, scholarly, and more helpful work has not been published for many years past."—*Wesleyan Magazine.*

Copies sent by mail, post-paid, on receipt of price, by

A. C. ARMSTRONG & SON, 714 Broadway, New York.

REV. DR. ALEXANDER BRUCE'S WORKS.

THE MIRACULOUS ELEMENT IN THE GOSPELS.

By ALEXANDER BALMAIN BRUCE, D.D., Author of "The Parabolic Teaching of Christ." 8vo, cloth. $2.50.

This work, though constructed on a different method, may be regarded as a companion to my work on THE PARABOLIC TEACHING OF CHRIST, published a few years ago. In the Fifth and Sixth Lectures I have considered from my point of view, at considerable length, a large number of the miraculous narratives, and made observations on nearly the whole of the narratives of this character contained in the Gospels. My object in these portions of the work is not to expound homiletically the whole narrative in which a miracle is recorded, but to inquire whether the event recorded be indeed a miracle.

"*It will take rank at once among the standard treatises upon its always important and engrossing theme. It is an elaborate study—the fruit of wide-reaching and profound research and patient reflection. The result of these studies is that the volume is a powerful defense of the miracles as an essential feature of the religion of Christ. It is a cause of congratulation to the whole Christian public that so valuable a course of lectures has been given to the whole world in so available shape,*"—BOSTON CONGREGATIONALIST.

"An exhaustive discussion of the New Testament Miracles. The topics are candidly, lucidly, and very ably considered. The volume is a rich addition to our apologetic literature, which every Biblical student will desire to add to his library."—*Zion's Herald.*

The Parabolic Teaching of Christ.

A Systematic and Critical Study of the Parables of our Lord. By Rev. Prof. A. B. BRUCE, D.D. 1 vol., 8vo, cloth, 527 pp. Price, $2.50.

"A work which will at once take its place as a classic on the Parables of our Saviour. No minister should think of doing without it."—*American Presbyterian Review.*

American Literary Churchman says: "We recommend this book with the most confident earnestness. It is a book to be bought and kept; it has both depth and breadth and minute accuracy; it has a living sympathy with the teaching of the Parables and with the spirit of the Master."

ENGLISH NOTICES.

"Prof. Bruce brings to his task the learning and the liberal and finely sympathetic spirit which are the best gifts of an expositor of Scripture. His treatment of his subject is vigorous and original, and he avoids the capital mistake of overlaying his exegesis with a mass of other men's views."—*Spectator.*

"The studies of the Parables are thorough, scholarly, suggestive and practical. Fullness of discussion, reverence of treatment, and sobriety of judgment, mainly characterize this work."—*Christian World.*

"Each Parable is most thoughtfully worked out, and much new light is thus thrown on the difficulties which surround many of these beautiful and suggestive examples of Divine teaching."—*Clergymen's Magazine.*

"This volume has only to be known to be welcomed, not by students alone, but by all earnest students of Christ's oracles. On no subject has Dr. Bruce spoken more wisely than on the question why Jesus spoke in parables. The one end the author sets before himself is, to find out what our Lord really meant. And this he does with a clearness and fullness worthy of all praise. **Familiar as we are with some of the best and most popular works on the Parables**, we do not know any to which we could look for so much aid in our search after the very meaning which Christ would have us find in His words."—*Nonconformist.*

Copies sent by mail, postpaid, on receipt of price.

A. C. ARMSTRONG & SON, 714 Broadway, New York.

A DICTIONARY OF RELIGIOUS SUBJECTS.

CLASSIFIED GEMS OF THOUGHT
FROM THE GREAT WRITERS AND PREACHERS OF ALL AGES.

In convenient form for use as a DICTIONARY OF READY REFERENCE ON RELIGIOUS SUBJECTS. Edited by Rev. F. B. PROCTOR, supervised in proof by Principal HENRY WACE, D.D., both of King's College, London. Royal octavo volume, 850 pages, including a full index of 32 pages. Strongly bound in cloth, $5.50; in half morocco, $6.50.

> A Ready Means of Comparing Views (Critical and Suggestive) with the Great Writers of All Ages. Treating Upward of 3,000 Subjects.

OCCUPYING A FIELD COVERED BY NO OTHER PUBLICATION.

A thoroughly critical and suggestive classification of the best religious thought—ancient and modern—including also, as a special feature, passages remarkable for lucidity in the treatment of difficult themes.

As a ready means of comparing views with eminent writers and preachers on a wide range of subjects, it occupies a field entirely its own. Upward of 3,000 *subjects (in alphabetical order) appear in the list of titles, and among the large number of authorities quoted are many not readily accessible in other forms.*

The plan adopted in the preparation of the work adds much to its utility in securing just the ends desired. Each important subject receives careful analysis at the hands of the author, and the citations are so placed as to develop each phase of the subject separately. In this way the best thought of many writers is applied directly to the elucidation of the great problems of the day, and in a form to be available for immediate use.

ENGLISH NOTICES OF THIS WORK.

"Incomparably one of the most useful books of the kind recently published."—*Nonconformist.*

"One of the best of the many collections of choice literary extracts now in circulation. It is not a book of anecdotes, but a casket filled with gems of thought."—*Primitive Methodist.*

"It contains innumerable quotations from authors and divines of all ages.... To preachers whose libraries are limited, or who are too much occupied for extensive reading, these 'Gems' will prove invaluable."—*Christian World Pulpit.*

"This book of thoughts and pregnant sayings asks for a place as a book of reference, which may be opened anywhere and at any time, that it may furnish a train of thought, and help to elucidate and interpret that Word which is able to make us wise unto salvation. We think it will not ask in vain."—*The Rock.*

"No one supplied with 'Gems of Thought' should be guilty of a dry sermon."—*Ecclesiastical Gazette.*

"Ministers are sure to value it, and find it of great service in their work."—*The Freeman.*

"Entitled to very high praise.... The selections are for the most part admirable.... It is likely to prove one of the most useful volumes that has been issued from the press for some time."—*The Commonwealth.*

Copies sent by mail, postpaid, on receipt of price.

CHOICE STANDARD WORKS.

A NEW AND HANDSOME LIBRARY EDITION
OF
MILMAN'S COMPLETE WORKS,
With Table of Contents and Full Indexes.

IN 8 VOLS., CROWN 8VO, CLOTH.

PRICE, $12.00 PER SET. (Reduced from $24.50.

(Bound in Half Calf extra, $25.00 per set.)

THIS EDITION OF MILMAN'S WORKS, THOROUGHLY
REVISED AND CORRECTED, COMPRISES

The History of the Jews, 2 Vols.
The History of Christianity, 2 Vols.
History of Latin Christianity, 4 Vols.

DR. MILMAN has won lasting popularity as a historian by his three great works, HISTORY OF THE JEWS, HISTORY OF CHRISTIANITY, and HISTORY OF LATIN CHRISTIANITY. These works link on to each other, and bring the narrative down from the beginning of all history to the middle period of the modern era. They are the work of the scholar, a conscientious student, and a Christian philosopher. DR. MILMAN prepared this new edition so as to give it the benefit of the results of more recent research. In the notes, and in detached appendices to the chapters, a variety of very important questions are critically discussed.

The author is noted for his calm and rigid impartiality, his fearless exposure of the bad and appreciation of the good, both in institutions and men, and his aim throughout, to utter the truth always in charity. The best authorities on all events narrated have been studiously sifted and their results given in a style remarkable for its clearness, force and animation.

MILMAN'S WORKS HAVE TAKEN THEIR PLACE AMONG THE APPROVED CLASSICS OF THE ENGLISH LANGUAGE. The general accuracy of his statements, the candor of his criticisms and the breadth of his charity are everywhere apparent in his writings. His search at all times seems to have been for truth, and that which he finds he states with simple clearness and with fearless honesty. HIS WORKS ARE IN THEIR DEPARTMENT OF HISTORY AS VALUABLE AS THE VOLUMES OF GIBBON ARE IN SECULAR HISTORY. THEY DESERVE A PLACE IN EVERY LIBRARY IN THE LAND. THIS NEW EDITION, in 8 vols., contains AN AVERAGE OF OVER 900 PAGES per volume. PRICE, $12.00 PER SET. (Formerly published in 14 vols. at $24.50.)

Sent on receipt of price, charges prepaid, by
A. C. ARMSTRONG & SON, 714 Broadway, New York.

NEW AND IMPORTANT HOMILETIC WORK.

Now ready 2 Vols.—Genesis to 2d Samuel, Volume I.,
and Kings to Psalm LXXVI, Volume II.

THE SERMON BIBLE.

EMBRACING THE WHOLE OF THE SACRED SCRIPTURES.

This Series of Volumes will give in convenient form the essence of the best homiletic literature of this generation. As yet, the preacher desirous of knowing the best that has been said on a text has had nothing to turn to but a very meagre and inadequate Homiletical Index. In this he is often referred to obsolete or second-rate works, while he misses references to the best sources. The new Sermon Bible will take account of the best and greatest preachers, and will be compiled from manuscript reports and fugitive periodical sources as well as from books. Many of the best sermons preached by eminent men are never printed in book form. It will thus contain much that will be new to its readers.

UNDER EVERY TEXT WILL BE GIVEN:—

1. *Outlines of important sermons by eminent preachers existing only in manuscript or periodicals, and thus inaccessible.*
2. *Less full outlines of sermons which have appeared in volumes which are not well known or easily obtained.*
3. *References to or very brief outlines of sermons which appear in popular volumes such as are likely to be in a preacher's library.*
4. *Full references to theological treatises, commentaries, etc., where any help is given to the elucidation of the text.*

Thus the preacher, having chosen his text, has only to refer to the Sermon Bible, to find some of the best outlines and suggestions on it and full references to all the helps available.

The range of books consulted will be far wider than in any Homiletical Index—we cannot say than in any work of the kind, because no work of the kind is in existence.

The Series will be under the general supervision of the Editor of the "Clerical Library," who will be assisted by specialists in each department.

It will extend to 12 vols., of about 500 pages, *with 24 blank pages for memorandum notes at end of each vol.* Price $1.50 each, and will be published at the rate of at least two vols. a year.

Great care will be taken to observe due proportion in the volumes—the space given to each book of the Bible depending on the number of sermons that have been preached from it.

As the volumes will be INDISPENSABLE TO EVERY PREACHER, and as they will be in constant use, they will be issued well bound, and at an exceedingly moderate price when the amount of matter is considered.

Copies sent, postpaid, on receipt of price, by

A. C. ARMSTRONG & SON, 714 Broadway, N. Y.

THE EXPOSITOR'S BIBLE.

Edited by Rev. W. R. NICOLL, Editor *London Expositor*.

THIS series consists of Expository Lectures on **ALL THE BOOKS OF THE BIBLE** by the foremost Preachers and Theologians of the day. While regard is had up to the latest results of Scholarship, the volumes will be essentially popular, and *adapted to general readers* quite as much as to the clergy. Six volumes published a year, in large crown 8vo volumes of about 450 pages each, strongly bound. Price per vol. $1.50.

Six Volumes for 1889.

THE PASTORAL EPISTLES. By Rev. ALEXANDER PLUMMER, D. D.

THE BOOK OF ISAIAH. Vol. 1 (chapters 1-39). By Rev. GEORGE ADAM SMITH.

THE EPISTLE TO THE GALATIANS. By Rev. Prof. G. G. FINDLAY.

THE EPISTLES OF ST. JOHN. By Rt. Rev. W. ALEXANDER, D. D.

THE BOOK OF REVELATION. By Rev. Prof. WILLIAM MILLIGAN.

THE FIRST EPISTLE TO THE CORINTHIANS. By Rev. MARCUS DODS, D. D.

Six Volumes Published in 1888.

COLOSSIANS AND PHILEMON. By Rev. ALEX. MACLAREN, D.D.
ST. MARK. By Rev. G. A CHADWICK, D. D.
GENESIS. By Rev. MARCUS DODS, D. D.
I. AND II. SAMUEL. By Rev. Prof. W. G. BLAIKIE, D. D. 2 vols.
EPISTLE TO THE HEBREWS. By Rev. Principal T. C. EDWARDS, D. D.

A complete descriptive circular (*sent on application*) of this series, with critical notices of the first six volumes published, and names of the Expositors engaged on the other Books of the Bible, viz.: Rev. Prof. B. B. WARFIELD, of Princeton Theological Seminary; Rev. Dr. J. MUNRO GIBSON (formerly of Chicago); Rev. Prof. T. K. CHEYNE; Rev. Prof .J. M. FULLER, Editor of *Speakers' Commentary;* Rt Rev. Dr. A. BARRY; Rev. C. G. MOULE, of Cambridge; Rev. Principal RAINY, D. D.; Rev. ALEX. MACLAREN, D. D., etc., etc.

Copies sent by mail, post-paid, on receipt of price.

A. C. ARMSTRONG & SON, 714 Broadway, New York.

www.ingramcontent.com/pod-product-compliance
Lightning Source LLC
Chambersburg PA
CBHW022101300426
44117CB00007B/539